Lecture Notes in Computer Scien

Norbert Fuhr Mounia Lalmas
Saadia Malik Zoltán Szlávik (Eds.)

Advances in XML Information Retrieval

Third International Workshop of the Initiative for the Evaluation of XML Retrieval, INEX 2004
Dagstuhl Castle, Germany, December 6-8, 2004
Revised Selected Papers

Volume Editors

Norbert Fuhr
University of Duisburg-Essen
Faculty of Engineering Sciences, Information Systems
47048 Duisburg, Germany
E-mail: fuhr@uni-duisburg.de

Mounia Lalmas
Queen Mary University of London, Department of Computer Science
London E1 4NS, England, United Kingdom
E-mail: mounia@dcs.qmul.ac.uk

Saadia Malik
University of Duisburg-Essen
Faculty of Engineering Sciences, Information Systems
47048 Duisburg, Germany
E-mail: malik@is.informatik.uni-duisburg.de

Zoltán Szlávik
Queen Mary University of London, Department of Computer Science
London E1 4NS, England, United Kingdom
E-mail: zolley@dcs.qmul.ac.uk

Library of Congress Control Number: 2005926830

CR Subject Classification (1998): H.3, H.4, H.2

ISSN 0302-9743
ISBN-10 3-540-26166-4 Springer Berlin Heidelberg New York
ISBN-13 978-3-540-26166-7 Springer Berlin Heidelberg New York

Springer is a part of Springer Science+Business Media

springeronline.com

Printed in Germany

Typesetting: Camera-ready by author, data conversion by Scientific Publishing Services, Chennai, India
Printed on acid-free paper SPIN: 11424550 06/3142 5 4 3 2 1 0

Preface

The ultimate goal of many information access systems (e.g., digital libraries, the Web, intranets) is to provide the right content to their end-users. This content is increasingly a mixture of text, multimedia, and metadata, and is formatted according to the adopted –W3C standard for information repositories, the so-called eXtensible Markup Language (XML). Whereas many of today's information access systems still treat documents as single large (text) blocks, XML offers the opportunity to exploit the internal structure of documents in order to allow for more precise access thus providing more specific answers to user requests. Providing effective access to XML-based content is therefore a key issue for the success of these systems.

The aim of the INEX campaign (Initiative for the Evaluation of XML Retrieval), which was set up at the beginning of 2002, is to establish infrastructures, XML test suites, and appropriate measurements for evaluating the performance of information retrieval systems that aim at giving effective access to XML content. More precisely, the goal of the INEX initiative is to provide means, in the form of a large XML test collection and appropriate scoring methods, for the evaluation of content-oriented XML retrieval systems.

INEX 2004 was responsible for a range of evaluation activities in the field of XML information retrieval, with five tracks: (1) *Ad Hoc Retrieval Track*, the main track, which can be regarded as a simulation of how a digital library might be used, where a static set of XML documents and their components is searched using a new set of queries (topics) containing both content and structural conditions; (2) *Interactive Track*, which aimed to investigate the behavior of users when interacting with components of XML documents; (3) *Heterogeneous Collection Track*, where retrieval is based on a collection comprising various XML subcollections from different digital libraries, as well as material from other resources; (4) *Relevance Feedback Track*, dealing with relevance feedback methods for XML; and (5) *Natural Language Track*, where natural language formulations of structural conditions of queries have to be answered.

The INEX 2004 workshop, held at Schloss Dagstuhl (Germany), 6–8 December 2004, brought together researchers in the field of XML retrieval who participated in the INEX 2004 evaluation campaign. Participants were able to present and discuss their approaches to XML retrieval. These proceedings contain revised papers describing work carried out during INEX 2004 in the various tracks by the participants.

INEX is partly funded by the DELOS Network of Excellence on Digital Libraries, to which we are very thankful. We would also like to thank the IEEE Computer Society for providing us the XML document collection. Special thanks go to Shlomo Geva for setting up the WIKI server and Gabriella Kazai for helping with the various documentation. We gratefully acknowledge the involvement of Börkur Sigurbjörnsson and Andrew Trotman (topic format specification), Benjamin Piwowarski (online assessment tool), and Gabriella Kazai and Arjen de Vries (metrics). The organizers of the various tracks did a great job and their work is greatly appreciated: Anastasios Tombros, Birger Larsen, Thomas Rölleke, Carolyn Crouch, Shlomo Geva and Tony Sahama. Finally, we would like to thank the participating organizations and people for their participation in INEX 2004.

March 2005

Norbert Fuhr
Mounia Lalmas
Saadia Malik
Zoltán Szlávik

Organizers

Organizers

Project Leaders

Norbert Fuhr, University of Duisburg-Essen
Mounia Lalmas, Queen Mary University of London

Contact Person

Saadia Malik, University of Duisburg-Essen

Topic Format Specification

Börkur Sigurbjörnsson, University of Amsterdam
Andrew Trotman, University of Otago

Online Relevance Assessment Tool

Benjamin Piwowarski, University of Chile

Metrics

Gabriella Kazai, Queen Mary University of London
Arjen P. de Vries, Centre for Mathematics and Computer Science

Interactive Track

Birger Larsen, Royal School of Library and Information Science
Saadia Malik, University of Duisburg-Essen
Anastasios Tombros, Queen Mary University of London

Relevance Feedback Track

Carolyn Crouch, University of Minnesota-Duluth
Mounia Lalmas, Queen Mary University of London

Heterogeneous Collection Track

Thomas Rölleke, Queen Mary University of London
Zoltán Szlávik, Queen Mary University of London

Natural Language Processing

Shlomo Geva, Queensland University of Technology
Tony Sahama, Queensland University of Technology

Table of Contents

Ad Hoc Retrieval and Heterogeneous Document Collection

Heterogeneous Document Collection

Natural Language Processing of Topics

Interactive Studies

Overview of INEX 2004

Saadia Malik[1], Mounia Lalmas[2], and Norbert Fuhr[3]

[1] Information Systems, University of Duisburg-Essen, Duisburg, Germany
malik@is.informatik.uni-duisburg.de
[2] Department of Computer Science, Queen Mary University of London, London, UK
mounia@dcs.qmul.ac.uk
[3] Information Systems, University of Duisburg-Essen, Duisburg, Germany
fuhr@uni-duisburg.de

1 Introduction

The widespread use of the eXtensible Markup Language (XML) in scientific data repositories, digital libraries and on the web, brought about an explosion in the development of XML retrieval systems. These systems exploit the logical structure of documents, which is explicitly represented by the XML markup: instead of whole documents, only components thereof (the so-called XML elements) are retrieved in response to a user query. This means that an XML retrieval system needs not only to find relevant information in the XML documents, but also determine the appropriate level of granularity to return to the user, and this with respect to both content and structural conditions.

Evaluating the effectiveness of XML retrieval systems requires a test collection (XML documents, tasks/topics, and relevance judgements) where the relevance assessments are provided according to a relevance criterion that takes into account the imposed structural aspects. A test collection as such has been built as a result of three rounds of the Initiative for the Evaluation of XML Retrieval[1] (INEX 2002, INEX 2003 and INEX 2004). The aim of this initiative is to provide means, in the form of large testbeds and appropriate scoring methods, for the evaluation of content-oriented retrieval of XML documents.

This paper presents an overview of INEX 2004. In section 2, we give a brief summary of the participants. Section 3 provides an overview of the test collection along with the description of how the collection was constructed. Section 4 outlines the retrieval tasks in the main track, which is concerned with the ad hoc retrieval of XML documents. Section 5 briefly reports on the submission runs for the retrieval tasks, and Section 6 describes the relevance assessment phase. The different metrics used are discussed in Section 7, followed by a summary of the evaluation results in Section 8. Section 9 presents a short description of four new tracks that started in INEX 2004, namely the heterogenous collection track, the relevance feedback track, the natural language processing track and the interactive track. The paper finishes with some conclusions and an outlook for INEX 2005.

[1] http://inex.is.informatik.uni-duisburg.de/

N. Fuhr et al. (Eds.): INEX 2004, LNCS 3493, pp. 1–15, 2005.

2 Participating Organisations

In response to the call for participation issued in March 2004, around 55 organisations registered from 20 different countries within six weeks. Throughout the year, the number of participants decreased due to insufficient contribution while a number of new groups joined later at the assessment phase. The active participants are listed in Table 1.

3 The Test Collection

The INEX test collection, as for any IR test collection aiming at evaluating retrieval effectiveness, is composed of three parts: the set of documents, the set of topics, and the relevance assessments (these are described in Section 6).

3.1 Documents

The document collection was donated by the IEEE Computer Society. It consists of the full-text of 12,107 articles, marked up in XML, from 12 magazines and 6 transactions of the IEEE Computer Society's publications, covering the period of 1995-2002, and totalling 494 MB in size, and 8 millions in number of elements. The collection contains scientific articles of varying length. On average, an article contains 1,532 XML nodes, where the average depth of the node is 6.9. More details can be found in [3].

3.2 Topics

As in previous years, in INEX 2004 we distinguish two types of topics, reflecting two user profiles, where the users differ in the amount of knowledge they have about the structure of the collection:

- **Content-only (CO) topics** are requests that ignore the document structure and contain only content related conditions, e.g. only specify what a document/component should be about (without specifying what that component is). The CO topics simulate users who do not (want to) know, or do not want to use, the actual structure of the XML documents. This profile is likely to fit most users searching XML digital libraries.
- **Content-and-structure (CAS) topics** are topic statements that contain explicit references to the XML structure, and explicitly specify the contexts of the user's interest (e.g. target elements) and/or the contexts of certain search concepts (e.g. containment conditions). The CAS topics simulate users that have some knowledge of the structure of the XML. Those users might want to use this knowledge to try to make their topics more concrete, by adding structural constraints. This user profile could fit librarians that have some knowledge of the collection structure.

The topic format and guidelines were based on TREC guidelines, but were modified to accommodate the two types of topics used in INEX. Both CO and CAS topics are made up of four parts. The parts explain the same information need, but for different purposes.

Table 1. List of active INEX 2004 participants

Organisations	Assessed topics	no of runs submitted
University of Amsterdam	2	6
University of California, Berkeley	2	5
VSB-Technical University of Ostrava	2	0
RMIT University	1	6
University of Otago	2	1
IBM Haifa Research Lab	2	6
University of Illinois at Urbana-Champaign	2	0
Nara Institute of Science and Technology	2	4
University of Wollongong in Dubai	2	0
Fondazione Ugo Bordoni	2	3
IRIT	2	6
Ecoles des Mines de Saint-Etienne, France	1	2
University of Munich (LMU)	2	5
Queen Mary University of London	2	0
Royal School of LIS	1	3
LIP6	1	6
University of Tampere	2	6
University of Helsinki	2	3
Carnegie Mellon University	1	6
Cirquid project (CWI and University of Twente)	2	6
The Selim and Rachel Benin School of Engineering and Computer Science	2	0
University of Minnesota Duluth	1	2
Bamberg University	2	0
UCLA	2	6
Max-Planck-Institut fuer Informatik	4	4
Kyungpook National University	2	4
Utrecht University	1	6
The Robert Gordon University	0	2
University of Milano	2	0
Oslo University College	2	6
Cornell University	2	0
Universität Rostock	2	0
Universidade Estadual de Montos Claros	2	6
INRIA	2	0
LIMSI/CNRS	2	0
University of Waterloo	2	3
Queensland University of Technology	2	6
Indiana University	2	2
University of Granada	2	0
University of Kaiserslautern	2	0
The University of Iowa	2	0
Rutgers University	2	0
IIT Information Retrieval Lab	2	0

- **Title:** a short explanation of the information need. It serves as a summary of both the content and, in the case of CAS topics, also the structural requirements of the user's information need. For the expression of these constraints the Narrowed Extended XPath I (NEXI) query syntax is used [8].
- **Description:** a one or two sentence natural language definition of the information need.
- **Narrative:** a detailed explanation of the information need and the description of what makes a document/component relevant or not. The narrative was there to explain not only what information is being sought for, but also the context and motivation of the information need, i.e., why the information is being sought and what work task it might help to solve. The latter was required for the interactive track (see Section 9.4).
- **Keywords:** a set of comma-separated scan terms that were used in the collection exploration phase of the topic development process (see later) to retrieve relevant documents/ components. Scan terms may be single words or phrases and may include synonyms, and terms that are broader or narrower terms than those listed in the topic description or title.

The title and the description must be interchangeable, which was required for the natural language processing track (see Section 9.3). The DTD of the topics is shown in Figure 1.

```
<!ELEMENT inex_topic  (title,description,narrative,keywords)>
<!ATTLIST inex_topic
  topic_id    CDATA  #REQUIRED
  query_type CDATA  #REQUIRED
  ct_no       CDATA  #REQUIRED
>
<!ELEMENT title (#PCDATA)>
<!ELEMENT description    (#PCDATA)>
<!ELEMENT narrative      (#PCDATA)>
<!ELEMENT keywords       (#PCDATA)>
```

Fig. 1. Topic DTD

The attributes of the topic are: topic_id (which ranges from 127 to 201), query_type (with value CAS or CO) and ct_no, which refers to the candidate topic number (which ranges from 1 to 198). Examples of both types of topics can be seen in Figure 2 and Figure 3.

The topics were created by participating groups. Each participant was asked to submit up to 6 candidate topics (3 CO and 3 CAS). A detailed guideline was provided to the participants for the topic creation. Four steps were identified for this process: 1) Initial Topic Statement creation 2) Collection Exploration 3) Topic Refinement and 4) Topic Selection. The first three steps were performed by the participants themselves while the selection of topics was decided by the organisers.

During the first step, participants created their initial topic statement. These were treated as a user's description of his/her information need and were formed without

```
<inex_topic topic_id="127" query_type="CAS" ct_no="13">
<title>//sec//(p| fgc)[about( ., Godel Lukasiewicz and other
fuzzy implication definitions)]</title>
<description>Find paragraphs or figure-captions containing the
definition of Godel, Lukasiewicz or other fuzzy-logic
implications</description>
<narrative>Any relevant element of a section must contain the
definition of a fuzzy-logic implication operator or a pointer to
the element of the same article where the definition can be
found. Elements containing criteria for identifying or comparing
fuzzy implications are also of interest. Elements which discuss
or introduce non-implication fuzzy operators are not relevant.
</narrative>
<keywords>Godel implication, Lukasiewicz implication, fuzzy
implications, fuzzy-logic implication </keywords>
</inex_topic>
```

Fig. 2. A CAS topic from the INEX 2004 test collection

```
<inex_topic topic_id="162" query_type="CO" ct_no="1">
<title> Text and Index Compression Algorithms </title>
<description>Any type of coding algorithm for text and index
compression</description>
<narrative>We have developed an information retrieval system
implementing compression techniques for indexing documents. We
are interested in improving the compression rate of the system
preserving a fast access and decoding of the data. A relevant
document/component should introduce new algorithms or compares
the performance of existing text-coding techniques for text and
index compression. A document/component discussing the cost of
text compression for text coding and decoding is highly relevant.
Strategies for dictionary compression are not
relevant.</narrative>
<keywords>text compression, text coding, index compression
algorithm</keywords>
</inex_topic>
```

Fig. 3. A CO topic from the INEX 2004 test collection

regard to system capabilities or collection peculiarities to avoid artificial or collection biased queries. During the collection exploration phase, participants estimated the number of relevant documents/components to their candidate topics. The HyREX retrieval system [1] was provided to participants to perform this task. Participants had to judge the top retrieved results and were asked to record the relevant document/component (XPath) paths in the top 25 retrieved components/documents. Those topics having at least 2 relevant documents/components and less than 20 documents/components in the top 25 retrieved elements could be submitted as candidate topics. In the topic refinement stage, the topics were finalised ensuring coherency and that each part of the topic could be used in stand-alone fashion.

Table 2. Statistics on CAS and CO topics on the INEX test collection

	CAS	CO
no of topics	34	39
avg no of words in title	11	5
no of times +/- used	12	52
avg no of words in topic description	20	23
avg no of words in keywords component	6	7
avg no of words in narrative component	67	98

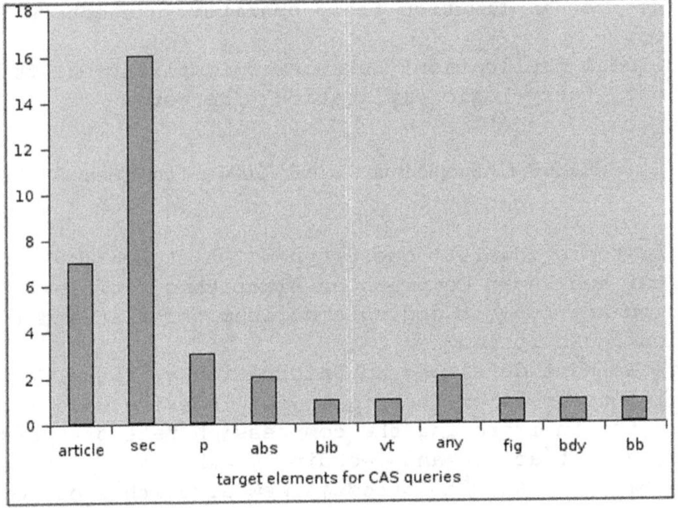

Fig. 4. Target elements in CAS topics

After the completion of the first three stages, topics were submitted to INEX. A total of 198 candidate topics were received, of which 73 topics (39 CO and 34 CAS) were selected. The topic selection was based on the basis of a combination of criteria such as 1) balancing the number of topics across all participants, 2) eliminating topics that were considered too ambiguous or too difficult to judge and 3) uniqueness of topics, and 4) considering their suitability to the different tracks. Table 2 shows some statistics on the INEX 2004 topics[2]. Figure 4 shows the distribution of target elements in the CAS topics.

4 The Retrieval Tasks

The retrieval task to be performed by the participating groups at INEX 2004 was defined as the ad hoc retrieval of XML documents. In information retrieval (IR) literature, ad

[2] A word in the title component of the topic can have either the prefix + or −, where + is used to emphasize an important concept, and − is used to denote an unwanted concept.

hoc retrieval is described as a simulation of how a library might be used, and it involves the searching of a static set of documents using a new set of topics. While the principle is the same, the difference for INEX is that the library consists of XML documents, the queries may contain both content and structural conditions and, in response to a query, arbitrary XML elements may be retrieved from the library. Within the ad hoc retrieval task, INEX 2004 defined the following two sub-tasks: CO and VCAS.

The **CO task** stands for content-oriented XML retrieval using CO queries. The elements to retrieve are components that are most specific and most exhaustive with respect to the topic of request. Most specific here means that the component is highly focused on the topic, while exhaustive reflects that the topic is exhaustively discussed within the component.

The **VCAS task** stands for content-oriented XML retrieval based on CAS queries, where the structural constraints of a query can be treated as vague conditions. The idea behind the VCAS sub-task was to allow the evaluation of XML retrieval systems that aim to implement approaches, where not only the content conditions within a user query are treated with uncertainty but also the expressed structural conditions. The structural conditions were to be considered hints as to where to look.

5 Submissions

Participants processed the final set of topics with their retrieval systems and produced ranked lists of 1500 result elements in a specified format. Participants could submit up to 3 runs per sub-task, CO and VCAS. In total 121 runs were submitted by 26 participating organisations. Out of the 121 submissions, 70 contained results for the CO topics, and 51 contained results for the CAS topics. For each topic, around 500 articles along with their components were pooled from all the submissions in round robin way for assessment. Table 3 shows the pooling effect on the CAS and CO topics.

Table 3. Pooling effect for CAS and CO topics

	CAS topics	CO topics
no of documents submitted	160264	200988
no of documents in pools	17092	19640
no of components submitted	677022	858724
no of components in pools	45244	45280

6 Assessments

The assessment pools were assigned then to participants; either to the original authors of the topic when this was possible, or on a voluntary basis, to groups with expertise in the topic's subject area. Each group was responsible for about two topics. In order to obtain some duplicate assessments, 12 topics were assigned to two participants, thus resulting in two sets of relevance assessments, referred to as Ass. I and Ass. II here.

Since 2003, relevance in INEX is defined according to the following two dimensions:

- **Exhaustivity (e)**, which describes the extent to which the document component discusses the topic of request.
- **Specificity (s)**, which describes the extent to which the document component focuses on the topic of request.

Table 4. Assessments at article and component levels with Assessment (Ass.) set 1 and Assessment set II

e+s	VCAS Ass. I		VCAS Ass. II		CO Ass. I		CO Ass. II	
	article level	non-article	article	non-article	article	non-article	article	non-article
e3s3	0.87%	0.85%	0.91%	0.82%	0.98%	0.61%	1.10%	0.63%
e3s2	0.74%	0.16%	0.95%	0.16%	0.89%	0.49%	0.98%	0.51%
e3s1	7.88%	0.24%	8.29%	0.25%	1.61%	0.12%	1.64%	0.13%
e2s3	0.26%	0.34%	0.39%	0.38%	0.41%	0.66%	0.41%	0.72%
e2s2	0.73%	0.26%	1.02%	0.30%	0.49%	0.86%	0.63%	0.92%
e2s1	2.76%	0.18%	3.04%	0.19%	2.07%	0.30%	2.23%	0.31%
e1s3	0.19%	1.62%	0.25%	1.97%	0.47%	0.92%	0.45%	1.23%
e1s2	0.84%	0.46%	1.11%	0.61%	0.34%	0.57%	0.35%	0.67%
e1s1	8.36%	1.46%	9.42%	1.48%	5.20%	1.28%	6.10%	1.47%
e0s0	77.36%	94.42%	74.63%	93.84%	87.55%	94.20%	86.10%	93.41%
All	100.00%	100.00%	100.00%	100.00%	100.00%	100.00%	100.00%	100.00%

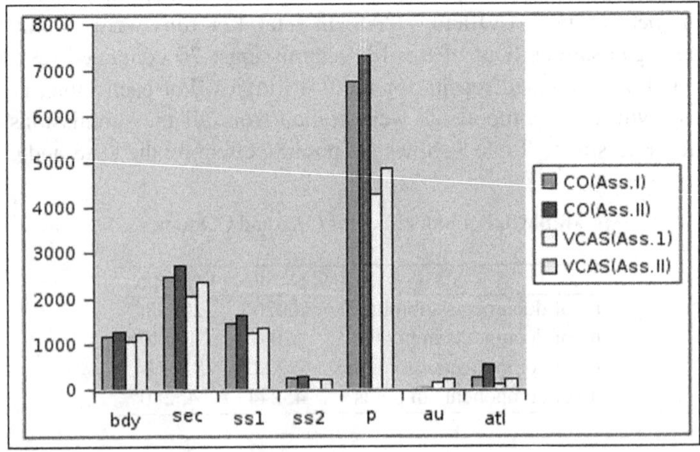

Fig. 5. Distribution of relevant elements

Exhaustivity was measured on the following 4-point scale: Not exhaustive (e0): the document component does not discuss the topic of request at all; Marginally exhaustive (e1): the document component discusses only few aspects of the topic of request; Fairly exhaustive (e2): the document component discusses many aspects of the topic of request; and Highly exhaustive (e3): the document component discusses most or all aspects of the topic of request.

Specificity was assessed on the following 4-point scale: Not specific (s0): the topic of request is not a theme of the document component; Marginally specific (s1): the topic of request is a minor theme of the document component (i.e. the component focuses on other, non-relevant topic(s), but contains some relevant information); Fairly specific (s2): the topic of request is a major theme of the document component (i.e. the component contains mostly relevant content and only some irrelevant content); and Highly specific (s3): the topic of request is the only theme of the document component.

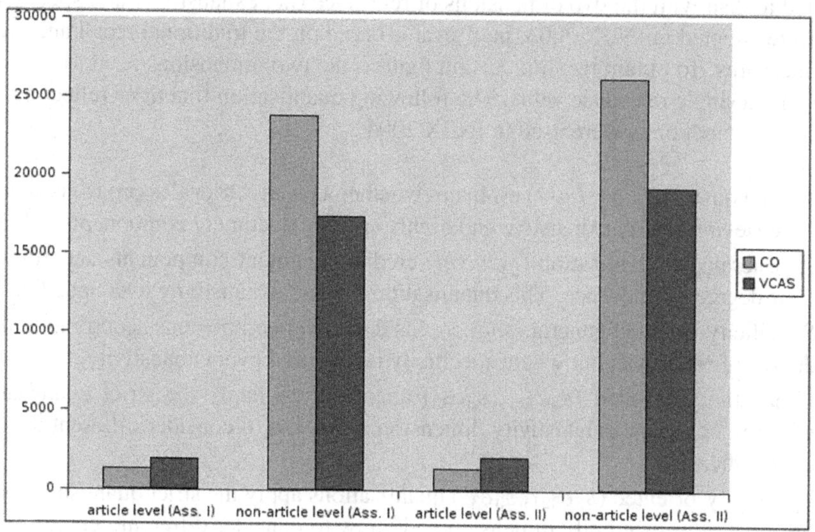

Fig. 6. Distribution of relevant article and non-article elements (e > 0 and s > 0)

Although the two dimensions are largely independent of each other, a not-exhaustive (e0) component can only be not specific (s0) and vice versa. Other than this rule, a component may be assigned any other combination of exhaustivity and specificity, i.e. e3S3, e3s2, e3s1, e2s3, e2s2, e2S1, e1s3, e1s2, and e1s1. For example, a component assessed as e1s1 is one that contains only marginally exhaustive relevant information (e1) where this relevant content is only a minor theme of the component, i.e. most of the content is irrelevant to the topic of request (s1).

A relevance assessment guideline explaining the relevance dimensions and how and what to assess was distributed to the participants. This guide also contained the manual to the online assessment tool developed by LIP6 to perform the assessments of the XML documents/components. Features of the tool include user friendliness, implicit assessment rules whenever possible, keyword highlighting, consistency checking and completeness enforcement. Table 4 shows a statistics of the relevance assessments. Figures 5 and 6 show the distribution of relevance for (some of) the elements.

Initial investigations show that agreements on the relevance assessments is significantly lower than in other evaluation initiatives. However, this outcome is affected by two unique features of INEX, the multivalued relevance scale, and the nesting of result elements in non-atomic documents. Further analysis is needed in order to quantify the effect of these factors, and their impact on the overall retrieval quality.

7 Evaluation Metrics

For evaluation the inex_eval (also referred to as inex-2002) metric is used with a number of quantization functions. This metric was developed during INEX 2002, and was adapted to deal with the two dimensions of relevance (i.e. exhaustivity and specificity) that were adopted in INEX 2003. inex_eval is based on the traditional recall and precision measures. To obtain recall/precision figures, the two dimensions need to be quantised onto a single relevance value. The following quantisation functions reflecting different user standpoints were used in INEX 2004:

- A strict quantisation (*strict*) evaluates whether a given retrieval approach is capable of retrieving highly exhaustive and highly specific document components (e3s3).
- A generalised quantisation (*general*) credits document components according to their degree of relevance. This quantisation favours exhaustivity over specificity.
- Specificity-oriented general (*sog*) credits document components according to their degree of relevance, but where specificity is favoured over exhaustivity.
- Exhaustivity-oriented (s_3e_{321}, s_3e_{32}) quantisations apply the strict quantisation with respect to the exhaustivity dimension and allow to consider different degrees of specificity.
- Specificity-oriented (s_3e_{321}, s_3e_{32}) quantisations apply the strict quantisation with respect to the specificity dimension and allow to consider different degrees of exhaustivity.

Based on the quantised relevance values, procedures that calculate recall/precision curves for standard document retrieval were directly applied to the results of the quantisation functions. The method of *precall* described by [5] was used to obtain the precision values at standard recall values. Further details are available in [4].

8 Summary of Evaluation Results

As mentioned in Section 5, out of the 121 submissions, 70 contained results for the CO task, and 51 contained results for the VCAS task. A summary of the results obtained with the evaluation metric (inex_eval) is given here[3]. The submissions have been ranked according to the average precision over all the quantisations (arithmetic mean). The top ten submissions for each task and with both assessment sets are listed in Table 5 and Table 6. Furthermore, an overlap indicator characterising a run by the percentage of overlapping items in the submission was also calculated.

[3] All evaluation results have been compiled using the assessment package version 3.0 and evaluation package version 2004.003.

Table 5. Ranking of submissions for CO task; average precision over all quantisations and overlap indicator

rank	organisation(run ID)	avg precision	overlap(%)
1.	IBM Haifa Research Lab(CO-0.5-LAREFIENMENT)	0.1437	80.89
2.	IBM Haifa Research Lab(CO-0.5)	0.1340	81.46
3.	University of Waterloo(Waterloo-Baseline)	0.1267	76.32
4.	University of Amsterdam(UAms-CO-T-FBack)	0.1174	81.85
5.	University of Waterloo(Waterloo-Expanded)	0.1173	75.62
6.	Queensland University of Technology(CO_PS_Stop50K_099_049)	0.1073	75.89
7.	Queensland University of Technology(CO_PS_099_049)	0.1072	76.81
8.	IBM Haifa Research Lab(CO-0.5-Clustering)	0.1043	81.10
9.	University of Amsterdam(UAms-CO-T)	0.1030	71.96
10.	LIP6(simple)	0.0921	64.29

a) Ranking based on assessment set I

rank	organisation(run ID)	avg precision	overlap(%)
1.	IBM Haifa Research Lab(CO-0.5-LAREFIENMENT)	0.1385	80.89
2.	IBM Haifa Research Lab(CO-0.5)	0.1285	81.46
3.	University of Amsterdam(UAms-CO-T-FBack)	0.1212	81.85
4.	University of Waterloo(Waterloo-Baseline)	0.1195	76.32
5.	University of Waterloo(Waterloo-Expanded)	0.1113	75.62
6.	Queensland University of Technology(CO_PS_Stop50K_099_049)	0.1084	75.89
7.	Queensland University of Technology(CO_PS_099_049)	0.1064	76.81
8.	University of Amsterdam(UAms-CO-T)	0.1047	71.96
9.	IBM Haifa Research Lab(CO-0.5-Clustering)	0.1016	81.10
10.	LIP6(simple)	0.0967	64.29

b) Ranking based on assessment set II

9 INEX 2004 Tracks

INEX 2004 had four new tracks, which are briefly described in this Section.

9.1 Relevance Feedback Track

The aim of this track is to investigate relevance feedback in the context of XML retrieval. In standard full text search engines, relevance feedback (RF) has been translated into detecting a "bag of words" that are good (or bad) at retrieving relevant information. These terms are then added to (or removed from) the query and weighted according to their power in retrieving relevant information. With XML documents, a more sophisticated approach - one that can exploit the characteristics of XML - is necessary. The approach should ideally consider not only content but also the structural features of XML documents. The query reformulation process must therefore infer which content and structural elements are important for effectively retrieving relevant data.

For the first year of the RF track, the focus was on CO topics. The participant's CO runs served as the baselines, upon which RF was performed - based on the relevance assessments - from the top-ranked 20 elements retrieved in the original CO run. There

Table 6. Ranking of submissions for VCAS task; average precision over all quantisations and overlap indicator

rank organisation(run ID)	avg precision	overlap(%)
1. Queensland University of Technology(VCAS_PS_stop50K_099_049)	0.1260	82.46
2. Queensland University of Technology(VCAS_PS_099_049)	0.1244	82.89
3. Queensland University of Technology(VCAS_PS_stop50K_049025)	0.1171	78.64
4. University of Amsterdam(UAms-CAS-T-FBack)	0.1065	77.76
5. IRIT(VTCAS2004TC35xp200sC-515PP1)	0.0784	76.33
6. Carnegie Mellon U.(Lemur_CAS_as_CO_NoStem_Mix02_Shrink01)	0.0759	74.00
7. Cirquid Project (CWI and U. of Twente)(LMM-VCAS-Relax-0.35)	0.0694	24.31
8. IBM Haifa Research Lab(CAS-0.5)	0.0685	38.76
9. Cirquid Project (CWI and U. of Twente)(LMM-VCAS-Strict-0.35)	0.0624	22.78
10. University of Amsterdam(UAms-CAS-T-XPath)	0.0619	18.78

a) Ranking based on assessment set I

rank organisation(run ID)	avg precision	overlap(%)
1. Queensland University of Technology(VCAS_PS_099_049)	0.1245	82.89
2. Queensland University of Technology(VCAS_PS_stop50K_049025)	0.1168	78.64
3. Queensland University of Technology(VCAS_PS_stop50K_099_049)	0.1159	82.46
4. University of Amsterdam(UAms-CAS-T-FBack)	0.1097	77.76
5. Carnegie Mellon U.(Lemur_CAS_as_CO_NoStem_Mix02_Shrink01)	0.0788	74.00
6. IBM Haifa Research Lab(CAS-0.9-LAREFIENMENT)	0.0781	43.52
7. IBM Haifa Research Lab(CAS-0.5)	0.0750	38.76
8. IRIT(VTCAS2004TC35xp200sC-515PP1)	0.0737	76.33
9. Cirquid Project (CWI and U. of Twente)(LMM-VCAS-Relax-0.35)	0.0700	24.31
10. University of Amsterdam(UAms-CAS-T-XPath)	0.0642	18.78

b) Ranking based on assessment set II

were no restrictions on the number of iterations of relevance feedback for a given query. Participants were allowed to submit at most three RF runs per initial ad hoc run. Three groups submitted 15 RF runs, where the best performing run was CO-0.5-ROCCHIO by IBM Haifa Research Lab.

One major issue was the evaluation methodology itself. Given that RF attempts to improve performance by using information in marked relevant documents (in the case of INEX the top 20 elements), it is usually the case that one of the main effects of the RF process is to push the known relevant documents to the top of the document ranking. This ranking effect, will artificially improve performance figures for the new document ranking simply by re-ranking the known relevant documents. What is not directly tested is how good the RF technique is at improving retrieval of unseen relevant documents - the feedback effect. There are two main alternatives to measure the effect of feedback on the unseen documents.

In the residual ranking methodology, the documents which are used in RF are removed from the collection before evaluation. This will include the relevant and some non-relevant documents (in our case the top 20 elements). After RF, the performance figures are calculated on the remaining (residual) collection. The problem with this approach is that the feedback results are not comparable with the original ranking. This is because the residual collection has fewer documents, and fewer relevant documents, than the original collection. A further difficulty is that, at each successive iteration of feedback, performance figures may be based on different numbers of queries because some queries may not have any relevant documents in the residual collection, and hence are removed. This implies that RF runs are not comparable across participants.

In the freezing methodology, the rank positions of the top n documents (our top 20 elements), the ones used to modify the query, are frozen. The remaining documents are re-ranked and performance figures are calculated over the whole ranking. As the only documents to change rank position are those below n (the ones used for RF) any change in performance happens as a result of the change of rank position of the unseen relevant documents. The freezing method was adopted in INEX 2004.

9.2 Heterogeneous Collection Track

The current INEX collection is based on a single DTD. In practical environments, such a restriction will hold in rare cases only. Instead, most XML collections will comprise documents from different sources, and thus with different DTDs. Also, there will be distributed systems (federations or peer-to-peer systems), where each node manages a different type of collection. The heterogeneous document collection track aims at investigating these issues, and in particular the following challenges:

- For content-only queries, most current approaches use the DTD for defining elements that would form reasonable answers. In heterogeneous collections, DTD-independent methods should be developed.
- For CAS queries, there is the problem of mapping structural conditions from one DTD onto other (possibly unknown) DTDs. Methods from federated databases could be applied here, where schema mappings between the different DTDs are defined manually. However, for a larger number of DTDs, automatic methods must be developed.

In the first year, the track was mainly explorative. The focus was on the construction of an appropriate test collection and the elaboration of the research issues and challenges. A collection comprised of several sub-collections was built. Twenty ad hoc topics (CO and CAS) were reused and four new topics were created. Three participants submitted 19 runs. The pooling, assessment, evaluation and browsing of the collection were shown to pose new challenges. Full details can be found in [6].

9.3 Natural Language Processing Track

The natural language processing track at INEX 2004 focused on whether it is possible to express topics in natural language, to be then used as basis for retrieval. During the topic creation stage, it was ensured that the description component of the topics were equivalent in meanings to their corresponding NEXI title, so it was possible to re-use the same topics, relevance assessments and evaluation procedures as in the ad hoc track. The descriptions were used as input to natural language processing tools, which would process them into representations suitable for XML search engines.

Four groups submitted 7 runs (4 CO and 3 VCAS). The best performing run for the CO task was CO-FRAGMENT-RANKING-NLP-0.5 by IBM Haifa Research Lab; and for the VCAS task, it was NLP_CAS_099_049_PS_100K by Queensland University of Technology.

9.4 Interactive Track

The main motivation for the track was twofold. First, to investigate the behaviour of users when interacting with components of XML documents, and secondly to investigate and develop approaches for XML retrieval which are effective in user-based environments.

In INEX 2004, only the first issue was addressed: to investigate the behaviour of searchers when presented with components of XML documents that have a high probability of being relevant (as estimated by an XML-based IR system). Presently, all metrics that are in use for the evaluation of system effectiveness in INEX are based on certain assumptions of user behaviour which are not empirically validated. The track also aimed to investigate those assumptions.

Four topics from the ad hoc CO topic set were reused and classified into two topic types: background and comparison. Experiments were designed to isolate the effect of topic and searcher from that of search system so that to investigate searcher behaviours. The narratives, which included a work task scenario, provided searchers (users) with background information needs. An online baseline system was provided to the participants. Ten institutions participated with the fulfilment of a minimum requirement of 8 searchers participating in the experiments. Data gathering sources were questionnaires, informal interviews and log files. Initial analysis and findings are presented in [7].

10 Conclusion and Outlook

INEX 2004 was a success and showed that XML retrieval is a challenging field within IR and related research. In addition to learning more about XML retrieval approaches, INEX 2004 has also made further steps in the evaluation methodology for XML retrieval.

INEX 2005 will start in April of this year, and in addition to its current five tracks, will have two new tracks: XML multimedia track and document mining track. The former will look at issues regarding the access to multimedia content embedded in XML document; and the latter is concerned with clustering and categorising tasks in the context of XML documents.

References

1. N. Fuhr, N. Gövert, and K. Großjohann. HyREX: Hypermedia retrieval engine for XML. In *Proceedings of the 25th Annual International Conference on Research and Development in Information Retrieval*, page 449, 2002. Demonstration.
2. N. Fuhr, N. Gövert, G. Kazai, and M. Lalmas, editors. *INitiative for the Evaluation of XML Retrieval (INEX). Proceedings of the First INEX Workshop. Dagstuhl, Germany, December 8–11, 2002*, ERCIM Workshop Proceedings, March 2003. http://www.ercim.org/publication/ws-proceedings/INEX2002.pdf.

3. N. Gövert and G. Kazai. Overview of the INitiative for the Evaluation of XML retrieval (INEX) 2002. In Fuhr et al. [2], pages 1–17. http://www.ercim.org/publication/ws-proceedings/INEX2002.pdf.
4. N. Gövert, G. Kazai, N. Fuhr, and M. Lalmas. Evaluating the effectiveness of content-oriented XML retrieval. Technical report, University of Dortmund, Computer Science 6, 2003. http://www.is.informatik.uni-duisburg.de/bib/pdf/ir/Goevert_etal:03a.pdf.
5. V. V. Raghavan, P. Bollmann, and G. S. Jung. Retrieval system evaluation using recall and precision: Problems and answers. In *Proceedings of the Twelfth Annual International ACM SIGIR Conference on Research and Development in Information Retrieval*, pages 59–68, 1989.
6. Z. Szlávik, and T. Rölleke. Building and Experimenting with a Heterogeneous Collection. In this volume, 2005.
7. A. Tombros, B. Larsen, and S. Malik. The Interactive Track at INEX 2004 In this volume, 2005.
8. A. Trotman, and B Sigurbjörnsson. Narrowed Extended XPath I (NEXI). In this volume, 2005.

Narrowed Extended XPath I (NEXI)

Andrew Trotman[1] and Börkur Sigurbjörnsson[2]

[1] Department of Computer Science, University of Otago, Dunedin, New Zealand
andrew@cs.otago.ac.nz

[2] Informatics Institute, University of Amsterdam, Amsterdam, The Netherlands
borkur@science.uva.nl

Abstract. INEX has through the years provided two types of queries: Content-Only queries (CO) and Content-And-Structure queries (CAS). The CO language has not changed much, but the CAS language has been more problematic. For the CAS queries, the INEX 02 query language proved insufficient for specifying problems for INEX 03. This was addressed by using an extended version of XPath, which, in turn, proved too complex to use correctly. Recently, an INEX working group identified the minimal set of requirements for a suitable query language for future workshops. From this analysis a new IR query language NEXI is introduced for upcoming workshops.

1 Introduction

The INEX [4] query working-group recently identified the query language requirements for future workshops. While no changes were suggested for the CO queries, several amendments were suggested for the CAS queries. The most overriding requirement was a language continuing to look like XPath [2], but not XPath. An alternative syntax was proposed at the workshop [6].

The working group identified many aspects of XPath to be dropped (e.g. functions), aspects to be severely limited (e.g. the only operator to be allowed in a tag path is the descendant operator). New features were also added (e.g. the about() filter). The shape of XPath was considered appropriate while the verbosity was considered inappropriate. The complete list of changes is outlined in the working group report [8]. Amendments were considered sufficient to warrant an XPath derivative language. NEXI is now introduced as that language. Extra to the working group list, the use of wildcards in search terms has been dropped.

The most significant diversion from XPath is semantics. Whereas in XPath the semantics are defined, in NEXI the retrieval engine must deduce the semantics from the query. This is the information retrieval problem - and to do otherwise is to make it a database language. For clarity, strict and loose interpretations of the syntax are included herein, however these should not be considered the only interpretations of the language.

A NEXI parser has been implemented in Flex [7] and Bison [3] (the GNU tools compatible with LEX and YACC). The parser is made available for public

N. Fuhr et al. (Eds.): INEX 2004, LNCS 3493, pp. 16–40, 2005.

use (and is included in the appendices).The existing INEX queries (queries 1-126) have been translated into NEXI (where possible) and are also included.

2 Query Types

There are currently two query types in INEX, the content only (CO) query and the content and structure (CAS) query [5].

2.1 The Content Only (CO) Query

This is the traditional information retrieval query containing words and phrases. No XML [1] element restrictions are allowed, and no target element is specified. This kind of query occurs when a user is unfamiliar with the tagging structure of the document collection, or does not know where the result will be found. To answer a CO query a retrieval engine must deduce the information need from the query, identify relevant elements (of relevant documents) in the corpus, and return those sorted most to least relevant.

Deduction of the information need from the query is to determine semantics from syntax. This is the information retrieval problem, the problem being examined at INEX. As such, the queries must be considered as "hints" as to how to find relevant documents. Some relevant documents may not satisfy a strict interpretation of the query. Equally, some documents that do satisfy a strict interpretation of the query may not be relevant.

2.2 The Content and Structure (CAS) Query

Content and structure queries may contain either explicit or implicit structural requirements. Such a query might arise if a user is aware of the document structure. To answer a CAS query a retrieval engine must deduce the information need from the query, identify elements that match structural requirements, and return those sorted most to least relevant. CAS queries can be interpreted in two ways, either strictly (SCAS) or loosely (VCAS).

The SCAS Interpretation
The target structure of the information need can be deduced exactly from the query. All target-path constraints must be upheld for a result to be relevant. If a user asks for <sec> tags to be returned, these must be returned. All other aspects of the query are interpreted from the IR perspective, i.e. loosely.

The VCAS Interpretation
Specifying an information need is not an easy task, in particular for semi-structured data with a wide variety of tag-names. Although the user may think they have a clear idea of the structural properties of the collection, there are likely to be aspects to which they are unaware. Thus we introduce a vague interpretation where target-path requirements need not be fulfilled. Relevance of

a result will be based on whether or not it satisfies the information need. It will not be judged based on strict conformance to the target-path of the query.

3 The INEX Topic Format

This discussion of the INEX topic format is included for context. As the topic format is likely to change from year to year readers are advised to consult the latest edition of the guidelines for topic development for complete details.

3.1 Restrictions on Queries

For an individual query to be useful for evaluation purposes it must satisfy several requirements (the details of which are explained below):

- It must be interpretable loosely. To satisfy this requirement, every query must contain at least one about() clause requiring an IR interpretation (i.e. non-numerical). That clause must occur in the final filter. In //A[B] queries, this is B. In //A[B]//C[D], this is D.
- It must not be a simple mechanical process to resolve the path. To satisfy this requirement, every query must be in the form //A[B] or //A[B]//C[D]. The form //A[B]//C is not allowed at INEX as the resolution of //C from //A[B] is a simple mechanical process.

Additionally, when developing a topic for INEX:

- It must have more than 5 known results. If this cannot be satisfied, abandon the query and choose another.
- It must be "middle" complex. Perform the search and examine the top 25 results. If there are less than 2 or more than 20 relevant results, the query is not middle-complex.
- Queries should reflect a real information need. Contrived queries are unlikely to be accepted.
- Queries should be diverse. If submitting more than one query, please make each different.

3.2 Equivalence Tags

In the current INEX collection there are several tags used interchangeable (for historical paper-publishing reasons). Tags belonging to the following groups are considered equivalent and interchangeable in a query:

Paragraphs:

`ilrj, ip1, ip2, ip3, ip4, ip5, item-none, p, p1, p2, p3`

Sections:

`sec, ss1, ss2, ss3`

Lists:

`dl, l1, l2, l3, l4, l5, l6, l7, l8, l9, la, lb, lc, ld, le, list, numeric-list, numeric-rbrace, bullet-list`

Headings:

`h, h1, h1a, h2, h2a, h3, h4`

Example
Due to tag equivalence, the query

`//article//sec[about(.//p, Computer)]`

and

`//article//ss2[about(.//item-none, Computer)]`

are identical.

3.3 Submission Format

Topics are submitted in the INEX topic format detailed each year in the annual guidelines for topic development [5]. Detailed here is the 2003 format, which to date has not changed for subsequent workshops.

```
<?xml version="1.0" encoding="ISO-8859-1" ?>

<!ELEMENT inex_topic (title, description, narrative, keywords)>

<!ELEMENT title (#PCDATA)>

<!ELEMENT description (#PCDATA)>

<!ELEMENT narrative (#PCDATA)>

<!ELEMENT keywords (#PCDATA)>

<!ATTLIST inex_topic
    topic_id CDATA #REQUIRED
    query_type CDATA #REQUIRED>
```

<inex_topic topic_id=“”> - Supplied by INEX once all topics have been collected. This and other attributes may be present in the final topics selected by INEX.

<inex_topic query_type=“”> - either “CO” or “CAS”. This attribute determines whether the topic is a content only (CO) or content and structure (CAS) topic. It consequently determines the query type used in the <title> tag.

<title> - a NEXI query (either CO or CAS, depending in the query_type attribute of the inex_topic tag). It should be noted the usual XML character encoding will be necessary, this includes substituting '<' with '<'. See sections 4 and 5 for details.

<description> - a short (one or two sentence) natural language translation of the title. Although this can be used by any track, it is also used by the Natural Language track as the query specification.

<narrative> - a detailed explanation of the information need including a description of what makes a result relevant. It should be possible for someone other than the author to read the narrative and a result and determine unambiguously if the result is relevant or not.

<keywords> - a comma separated list of terms and phrases used during the topic formulation.

It is important that the title, description, and narrative all describe the same information need.

3.4 Example of an INEX Topic

```
<inex_topic query_type="CAS">
<title>
    //article[.//yr = 2001 or .//yr = 2002]//sec[
        about(.,summer holidays)]
</title>
<description>
    Summer holidays either of 2001 or of 2002.
</description>
<narrative>
    Return section elements, which are about summer holidays,
    where the sections is descendent of article element, and
    the article is from 2001 or 2002.
</narrative>
<keywords>
    summer, holiday, 2001, 2002
</keywords>
</inex_topic>
```

3.5 Topic Titles

The topic title contains the information retrieval query expressed in NEXI. The syntax of such queries is precisely defined below and a parser written in FLEX and BISON is included in the appendices. It is the information retrieval problem to deduce the semantics from the information need, however no meaningful language can exist without semantics. This duality can only be resolved by strictly defining the semantics to be loose.

4 The Content Only (CO) Query

4.1 Searching for Words and Numbers

The smallest searchable unit in a CO query is the word:

```
word: NUMBER | ALPHANUMERIC

ALPHANUMERIC: {LETTER}{LETTERDIGITEXTRAS}*

NUMBER: "-"?{DIGIT}+

LETTER: [a-zA-Z]

DIGIT: [0-9]

LETTERDIGIT: [a-zA-Z0-9]

LETTERDIGITEXTRAS [a-zA-Z0-9'-]
```

Positive numbers, negative numbers and sequences of alphanumerics proceeded by an alphabetic character are all valid search words. Alphanumerics have already been used in query 41 so must be included. Hyphens are allowed after the first character of an alphanumeric (to avoid confusion with term restrictions, see section 4.3). The apostrophe can only occur after the first character of an alphanumeric.

Example: To search for the single word Apple, the CO query is

```
Apple
```

Loose interpretation: It is anticipated that using the word Apple will help locate relevant documents. I won't tell you if I mean "Macintosh Computer", "Granny Smith", or "Mr Apple" but find what I want anyway.

4.2 Searching for Phrases

A phrase is a double quoted sequence of words:

```
phrase: '"' word_list '"'

word_list: word word | word_list word
```

A phrase must contain two or more words. A phrase containing only one word is erroneous and the quotes should be removed to make a single word query.

Example: To search for Charles Babbage, the CO query will be

```
"Charles Babbage"
```

Loose interpretation: Relevant documents are anticipated to contain these two words adjacent to each other, but need not. They may contain both words non-adjacent. For that matter they might not contain both words. A relevant document might not even contain either word.

4.3 Term Restrictions

Terms can be preceded by either a plus (+) or minus (-) sign

```
term: term_restriction unrestricted_term

term_restriction: EMPTY | '+' | '-'

unrestricted_term: word | phrase
```

Loose interpretation: The '+' signifies the user expects the word will appear in a relevant element. The user will be surprised if a '-' word is found, but this will not prevent the document from being relevant. Words without a sign are specified because the user anticipates such terms will help the search engine to find relevant elements. As restrictions are only hints, it is entirely possible for the most relevant element to contain none of the query terms, or for that matter only the '-' terms.

4.4 CO Queries

A CO query is a sequence of one or more searchable terms.

```
co : term | co term
```

Example:

```
+"face recognition" approach
```

Loose interpretation: "I expect the phrase 'face recognition' will appear in a relevant document, I also anticipate the word 'approach' will help you find the documents I want".

4.5 Bag of Words

Term ordering in IR queries is often assumed to be irrelevant. In the "bag of words" interpretation, a query is an unordered set of search terms (and phrases). The assumption does not hold true for some queries. For example,

```
computer history
```

and

```
history computer
```

express different information needs even though the "bag of words" is identical.

Additionally, if a term occurs multiple times, the occurrence count is lost when the term is added to the "bag of words". For some queries, multiple term occurrences are needed to adequately specify the information need. For example, the query

```
The The
```

should search for documents about the well known rock band of the same name, and cannot be specified without the use of the multiple occurring term. Further, some search engines "stop" common words not considered useful for searching (such as the, and, of, etc). This query requires the use of such a term.

Loose interpretation: There may or may not be an implied order to the terms in a query. If a term occurs multiple times this may or may not imply meaning. Stopping common words may or may not alter the meaning of the query.

4.6 The Pitfalls of Queries

The minus sign (-) maintains two meanings; it is used for both exclusionary terms and negative numbers. For the purpose of clarity, 12 and -12 are numbers. By inserting a space (represented as '␣' in this paragraph) between the - and the 12 (-␣12), the meaning is changed to exclusionary. "Don't search for the number -12" can be expressed as --12 or -␣-12. Equally, --␣12 is an error.

5 The Content and Structure (CAS) Query

CAS queries can take three possible forms:

//A[B]	Return A tags about B
//A[B]//C	Return C descendants of A where A is about B (used in INEX'02)
//A[B]//C[D]	Return C descendants of A where A is about B and C is about D

A and C are paths whereas B and D are filters. The syntax is defined as:

```
cas: path cas_filter
    | path cas_filter path
    | path cas_filter path cas_filter

cas_filter: '[' filtered_clause ']'
```

Use of the form //A[B]//C is not useful for information retrieval evaluation purposes. Once the result of //A[B] has been determined, it is a mechanical process to extract the //C descendants. Use of this form was deprecated in INEX'03.

5.1 Path Specification

Tag and attribute names follow the XML 1.1 [1] specification

```
XMLTAG: {XML_NAME}{XML_NAMECHAR}*

XML_NAMECHAR: [-_.:a-zA-Z0-9]

XML_NAME: [_:a-zA-Z]
```

Element nodes in the XML tree are identified as "//tag" and attribute nodes as "//@attribute". The wildcard "//*" is included to identify first or subsequent descendant (tag or attribute). Convoluted use of attributes and wildcards is discouraged.

```
node: named_node | any_node | tag_list_node

NODE_QUALIFIER: "//"

named_node: NODE_QUALIFIER tag

attribute_node: NODE_QUALIFIER '@' tag

any_node: NODE_QUALIFIER '*'
```

In cases where either tag A or tag B is required, it is written "//(A|B)".

```
tag_list: tag '|' tag | tag_list '|' tag

tag_list_node: NODE_QUALIFIER '(' tag_list ')'
```

A path through the XML tree is specified as a sequence of nodes. The only relationship between nodes in a path is descendant. There is no way to specify the child relationship or other XPath axes. Attributes cannot have descendant nodes so may only be specified at the end of a path.

```
path: node_sequence | node_sequence attribute_node

node_sequence: node | node_sequence node
```

Strict interpretation: "//A" is any A tag in the tree. "//A//B", any B descendant of an A tag in the tree. "//@C" is the C attribute of any tag. "//A//@C" is any C attribute anywhere in the tree beneath an A tag in the tree.

For any descendant of A use "//A//*". Any descendant of the root, "//*", is also any tag in the tree. "//*//*//*" is any tag at least three levels deep in the tree. "//*//A" is an A that is not the root of the tree, while "//*//A//*" means any descendant of A so long as A is not the root.

The path "//(A|B)" means any A tag in the tree or any B tag in the tree. "//(A|B)//(C|D)" is any C or D descendant of either an A or B tag. This includes "//A//C", "//A//D", "//B//C" and "//B//D". Convoluted use of this syntax is discouraged.

The path $//T_1 \ldots //T_n$ is an ordered sequence of nodes in the tree starting with T_1 and terminating at T_n such that for all $p \in n$, T_{p+1} is a descendant of T_p.

Loose interpretation: There is likely to be relevant information in the document in places not specified in a user query. The path specifications should therefore be considered hints as to where to look.

A Note on Attributes

No real query using attributes on the INEX collection is believed to exist. Query authors are discouraged from using attributes simply because they can.

5.2 Path Filters

At present paths can be filtered either with search strings, or numerically. In future versions, filtering based on proper nouns (e.g. Author Names), and other data types is anticipated.

String Filtering

Documents can be filtered to only those that satisfy a given textural (CO) query in the given path (or relative to the given path).

```
about_clause : ABOUT '(' relative_path ',' co ')'

relative_path: '.' | '.' path

ABOUT: "about"
```

Relative paths are specified relative to a context path. At B in //A[B] the context path is //A. At B in //A[B]//C[D] the context path is //A. At D in //A[B]//C[D] the context path is //A//C. The relative path "." is interpreted as "the context path". The relative path ".//p" is interpreted as "a p descendant of the context path".

Example:

```
//article[about(.//p, "information retrieval")]
```

Strict interpretation: "What ever you do, you must return article tags. Now, as a suggestion, look for //article//p elements about information retrieval."

Loose interpretation: "What I want is most likely a whole article that mentions information retrieval in a p tag. Relevant results are not limited to this, but I'm pretty sure it'll help you find what I want."

Arithmetic Filtering
Documents can also be filtered to only those that satisfy a numeric query. As with string filtering, this is specified with a relative path.

```
arithmetic_clause: relative_path arithmetic_operator NUMBER
arithmetic_operator: '>' | '<' | '=' | '>=' | '<='
```

Example:

```
//article[.//pdt//yr = 2003]
```

Strict interpretation: Retrieve article elements from documents that loosely "contain the value 2003 in an //article//pdt//yr element".

Loose interpretation: A loose interpretation could be to look at a year range (2002, 2003, and 2004). This might be useful if, for example, a workshop held in December 2003, published the formal proceedings in 2004. Alternatively, a paper published electronically in December 2002 might finally appear in print in January 2004 leading to confusion over the publication date.

The above example could also be described using string filtering

```
//article[about(.//pdt//yr, 2003)]
```

however, the arithmetic syntax is preferred.

Both positive and negative numbers are supported by CO and CAS queries. The ambiguity arising from the multiple meaning of the minus (-) was discussed in section 4.6.

Boolean Operators
Path filters can be joined with Boolean operators AND and OR. They can also be bracketed.

```
filter: about_clause | arithmetic_clause

filtered_clause: filter
    | filtered_clause AND filtered_clause
    | filtered_clause OR filtered_clause
    | '(' filtered_clause ')'

AND: "AND" | "and"

OR: "OR" | "or"
```

Examples:

```
//article[about(., apple) and about(., computer)]

//article[about(., apple) or about(., computer)]
```

Strict interpretation: The first example will return article elements from documents about apple and about computer, the second about apple or about computer (remember: these are only hints). This introduces a subtle difference in query meaning between the two queries:

```
//article[about(.//sec, apple computer)]
```

and

```
//article[about(.//sec, apple) and about(.//sec, computer)]
```

The first query asks for articles that have a section discussing 'apple computer'. The second asks for articles that have a section discussing 'apple' and a section discussing 'computer' (even if they are not the same section). In the first query, the topics must co-occur. In the second they may co-occur.

Loose interpretation: AND is interpreted as ANDish, OR as ORish. The query contains the Boolean operators strictly as hints on how to resolve the information need. CO, SCAS and VCAS all interpret Boolean operators loosely.

Examples
Examples of some CAS queries are given here along with strict interpretations. Loose interpretation of each is the same "I'm sure this'll help find what I want".

```
//sec[about(., mobile electronic payment system)]
```

Return sec tags where the sec tag mentions mobile electronic payment systems.

```
//*[about(., singular value decomposition)]
```

Return elements about singular value decomposition. The retrieval engine must deduce the most appropriate element to return.

```
//article[.//fm//yr >= 1998]//sec[about(.//p, "virtual reality")]
```

Return sec tags of documents about virtual reality and published on or after 1998.

```
//article[(.//fm//yr = 2000 OR .//fm//yr = 1999) AND
    about(., "intelligent transportation system")]
    //sec[about(., automation +vehicle)]
```

Return sec elements about vehicle automation from documents published in 1999 or 2000 that are about intelligent transportation systems.

6 Conclusions

The INEX query working-group at the INEX workshop outlined a set of requirements necessary for a query language to be used for future workshops. The language was to be similar in form to XPath, while at the same time being both severely reduced, and expanded. The language, NEXI, is defined herein and satisfies these needs.

A parser written in Flex and Bison is included. The existing INEX topics have been translated into NEXI and checked against the parser. Only those queries using features deprecated by the working-group could not be translated - in these cases a near translation is included.

7 Addendum

NEXI was developed to satisfy the needs of INEX however it should not be considered inextricably tied to the workshop. As a formally defined query language it could be used in other situations in which content and structure (or content only) querying of XML collections is needed.

Acknowledgements

Richard A. O'Keefe read several drafts and commented on many aspects of this language.

References

1. Bray, T., Paoli, J., Sperberg-McQueen, C. M., Maler, E., Yergeau, F., and Cowan, J. (2003). Extensible markup language (XML) 1.1 W3C proposed recommendation. The World Wide Web Consortium. Available:http://www.w3.org/TR/2003/PR-xml11-20031105/
2. Clark, J., and DeRose, S. (1999). XML path language (XPath) 1.0, W3C recommendation. The World Wide Web Consortium. Available:http://www.w3.org/TR/xpath
3. Donnelly, C., and Stallman, R. (1995). Bison - the yacc-compatible parser generator. Available: http://www.gnu.org/directory/bison.html
4. Fuhr, N., Gövert, N., Kazai, G., and Lalmas, M. (2002). INEX:Initiative for the evaluation of XML retrieval. In *Proceedings of the ACM SIGIR 2000 Workshop on XML and Information Retrieval.*
5. Kazai, G., Lalmas, M., and Malik, S. (2003). INEX'03 guidelines for topic development.
6. O'Keefe, R. A., and Trotman, A. (2003). The simplest query language that could possibly work. In *Proceedings of the 2nd workshop of the initiative for the evaluation of XML retrieval (INEX).*
7. Paxson, V. (1995). Flex, version 2.5, a fast scanner generator. Available: http://www.gnu.org/directory/flex.html
8. Sigurbjörnsson, B., and Trotman, A. (2003). Queries: INEX 2003 working group report. In *Proceedings of the 2nd workshop of the initiative for the evaluation of XML retrieval (INEX).*

A Appendices

A.1 Makefile

```
#
#     Makefile
#     --------
#     Andrew Trotman
#     University of Otago 2004
#
#     Script to build the NEXI parser
#
tokenizer : parser.tab.c lex.yy.c
    gcc lex.yy.c parser.tab.c -lm -o tokenizer

lex.yy.c : tokenizer.l parser.tab.h
    flex tokenizer.l

parser.tab.c : parser.y
    bison parser.y -d

clean :
    rm tokenizer parser.tab.h parser.tab.c lex.yy.c
```

A.2 FLEX Script

```
%{
/*
    TOKENIZER.L
    -----------
    Andrew Trotman
    University of Otago 2004

FLEX script to tokenize INEX NEXI queries and check for syntax errors
*/
#include <stdio.h>
#include "parser.tab.h"
int c;
extern int yylval;
extern int line_number;
extern int char_number;

%}

LETTER [a-zA-Z]
DIGIT [0-9]
LETTERDIGIT [a-zA-Z0-9]
```

```
LETTERDIGITEXTRAS [a-zA-Z0-9'\-]
XML_NAMECHAR [a-zA-Z0-9_:.\-]
XML_NAME [a-zA-Z:_]

%%

" " { char_number++; }

"\r" { char_number++; }

"\n"    {
    line_number++;
    char_number = 1;
    return yytext[0];
    }

"about"    {
    char_number += 5;
    yylval = yytext[0];
    return ABOUT;
    }

"AND"    {
    char_number += 3;
    yylval = yytext[0];
    return AND;
    }

"and"    {
    char_number += 3;
    yylval = yytext[0];
    return AND;
    }

"OR"    {
    char_number += 2;
    yylval = yytext[0];
    return OR;
    }

"or"    {
    char_number += 2;
    yylval = yytext[0];
    return OR;
    }
```

```
">" {
    char_number++;
    yylval = yytext[0];
    return GREATER;
    }

"<" {
    char_number++;
    yylval = yytext[0];
    return LESS;
    }

"=" {
    char_number++;
    yylval = yytext[0];
    return EQUAL;
    }

{LETTER}{LETTERDIGITEXTRAS}* {
    char_number += strlen(yytext);
    yylval = yytext[0];
    return ALPHANUMERIC;
    }

"-"?{DIGIT}+    {
    char_number += strlen(yytext);
    yylval = yytext[0];
    return NUMBER;
    }

"//"    {
    char_number += 2;
    yylval = yytext[0];
    return NODE_QUALIFIER;
    }

{XML_NAME}{XML_NAMECHAR}*    {
    char_number += strlen(yytext);
    yylval = yytext[0];
    return XMLTAG;
    }

.    {
    char_number++;
```

```
    return yytext[0];
    }

%%

/*
    YYWRAP()
    --------
*/
int yywrap(void)
{
return 1;
}
```

A.3 BISON Script

```
%{
/*
    PARSER.Y
    --------
    Andrew Trotman
    University of Otago 2004

BISON script to tokenize INEX NEXI queries and check for syntax errors
*/

#define YYDEBUG 1
#include <math.h>
#include <stdio.h>
#include <ctype.h>

int line_number = 1;
int char_number = 1;
extern char *yytext;

void yyerror(char *err) /* Called by yyparse on error */
{
printf ("Line %d (char %d): %s at '%s'\n", line_number, char_number, err, yytext);
}

/*
    NOTES:
INEX topics 10, 14, 19, 20 are not strict translations as they cannot be
expressed (multiple specified target elements)
INEX topic 13 is not a strict translation due to instance (au[1]) usage
*/
```

```
%}

%token NUMBER ALPHANUMERIC XMLTAG
%token ABOUT NODE_QUALIFIER
%token AND OR
%token GREATER LESS EQUAL

%left AND OR

%%/* Grammar rules and actions follow */
input: /* empty */ | input line;

line: '\n'
    | co '\n'  { printf("CO Passed\n"); }
    | cas '\n' { printf("CAS Passed\n"); };

/*
    in a CAS query:
the initial can be the terminal "//*" to specify "a descendant of"
the final part can be an unrestricted target path (for compatibility with INEX 2
*/
cas: path cas_filter | path cas_filter path | path cas_filter path cas_filter;

cas_filter: '[' filtered_clause ']';

filtered_clause : filter
        | filtered_clause AND filtered_clause
        | filtered_clause OR filtered_clause
        | '(' filtered_clause ')';

filter: about_clause | arithmetic_clause;

about_clause : ABOUT '(' relative_path ',' co ')';

arithmetic_clause: relative_path arithmetic_operator NUMBER;

arithmetic_operator: GREATER | LESS | EQUAL | greater_equal | less_equal;

greater_equal: GREATER EQUAL;

less_equal: LESS EQUAL;

/*
child has been eliminated and replaced with descendant.  In the unlikley event
```

```
child is ever needed, it can (most likley) be specified as those descendants enough
    to make the specification unambigious.

now, a PATH is either:
    "//" for root
    "//A" for tag A
    "//A//B" for tag B within tag A
    "//*" for any tag
    "//A//*" for any descendant of A
    "//@A" for attribute A
    "//A//@B" for attribute B descendant of node A
*/
path: node_sequence | node_sequence attribute_node;

relative_path: '.' | '.' path;

node_sequence: node | node_sequence node;

any_node: NODE_QUALIFIER '*';

attribute_node: NODE_QUALIFIER '@' tag;

named_node: NODE_QUALIFIER tag;

tag_list: tag '|' tag | tag_list '|' tag;

tag_list_node: NODE_QUALIFIER '(' tag_list ')';

node: named_node | any_node | tag_list_node;

tag: alphanumeric | XMLTAG;

/*
CO topics are sequences of numbers, terms and phrases with optional specifiers
    mandatory (+) and unwanted (-)
note:
    "12" is a number
    "-12" is number
    "- 12" is don't search for number 12
    "--12" | "- -12" is don't search for number -12
    "-- 12" is an error
    "content-based" is an error
*/
co : term | co term;
```

```
term: term_restriction unrestricted_term;

term_restriction: /* empty */ | '+' | '-';

unrestricted_term: word | phrase;

/*
A phrase is a sequence of two or more words surounded by double quotes
*/
phrase: '"' word_list '"';

word_list: word word | word_list word;

/*
a word is a sequence:
of alphabetics
of digits
of digits preceeded by a negative (-) sign (a negative number)
alphanumerics starting with an alpha (for both ip1 tags and Y2K queries)
As the operators are also valid search terms, a word is
operator or a sequence of alphabetic characters
*/

word: NUMBER | alphanumeric;

alphanumeric : ALPHANUMERIC | ABOUT | AND | OR;

%%

/*
    MAIN ()
    -------
*/
int main(void)
{
//yydebug = 1;
yyparse();

return 0;
}
```

A.4 INEX Queries 1-126

The pre-existing INEX queries have all been converted and checked against the parser. Topics 10, 14, 19 and 20 originally specified a set of target elements. This practice was banned for INEX'03 and is not supported here either. Topic

13 specifies a particular instance of an element as the target, again outlawed for INEX'03 and not supported here. Topic 44 used wildcards. As such, these 6 queries are not accurately translated.

1. `//article[about(.//(abs|kwd), description logics)]//fm//au`
2. `//ack[about(., research funded america)]`
3. `//*[about(.//kwd, information data visualization) and about(., large information hierarchies spaces multidimensional data databases)]`
4. `//*[about(.//(atl|abs|st), experience results problems) and about(., extreme programming)]`
5. `//article[about(.//bibl, QBIC) and about(., image retrieval)]//tig`
6. `//article[about(., Survey on Software Engineering) and about(.//sec, programming languages)]//tig[about(., software engineering survey programming survey programming tutorial software engineering tutorial)]`
7. `//article[about(., Content-based retrieval of video databases)]//sec`
8. `//article[about(.//fm//aff, ibm) and about(.//bdy//sec, certificates)]`
9. `//article[about(.//bdy//sec, nonmonotonic reasoning) and (.//hdr//yr = 1999 or .//hdr//yr = 2000) and about(.//tig//atl, -calendar) and about(., belief revision)]`
10. `//*[about(.//(atl|st|title), book review) and about(.//(st|p), machine learning adaptative algorithm probabilistic model neural network support vector machine kernel methods numerical computation)]`
11. `//*[about(.//p, wireless) and about(.//(abs|kwd), security) and about(., security applications)]`
12. `//article[.//pdt//yr = 2001 or .//pdt//yr = 2002]//bdy//sec[about(., internet search engine)]`
13. `//article[about(.//fm//au//@sequence, additional) and about(.//fm//abs, review) and about(., AR VR virtual augmented reality system)]//fm//au`
14. `//*[about(.//fgc, Corba architecture) and about(.//p, Figure Corba Architecture)]`
15. `//article[.//fm//hdr//hdr2//pdt = 1996 or .//fm//hdr//hdr2//pdt = 1997]//bm//bib//bibl //bb[about(., hypercube mesh torus toroidal non-numerical database)]`
16. `//article[about(.//bm//bib//bibl//bb//atl, concurrency control)]//fm//tig//atl`
17. `//article[about(.//fm//au, -W -Bruce -Croft)]//bb[about(.//au, W Bruce Croft)]`
18. `//article[about(., Hypertext Information Retrieval) and about(.//bib//bibl//bb//atl, Hypertext Information Retrieval)]`

19. //*[about(., singular value decomposition svd formula)]
20. //article[about(.//atl, Concurrency Control) and about(.//fm//hdr//hdr1//ti, data)
    and about(., Concurrency Control in real-time databases)]//sec
21. //*[about(.//(p|st|it|bb), recommender system recommender agent)]
22. //article[about(.//bb//au//snm, Mannila) and (about(.//bb//au//fnm, Heikki)
    or about(.//bb//au//fnm, H)) and about(., Mannila)]//fm//au
23. //article[(.//yr = 1995 or .//yr = 1996 or .//yr= 1997 or .//yr = 1998
    or .//yr = 1999) and about(.//bdy, XML electronic commerce)]
24. //article[about(.//au, Smith Jones) and about(.//bdy, software engineering and
    process improvement)]
25. //article[about(.//fm//hdr//hdr1//ti, IEEE MultiMedia) and about(., QoS Quality of
    Service)]
26. //article[about(.//st, XML) and about(., data processing system)]//fm//tig//atl
27. //article[about(.//atl, 1999 Reviewers List) and about(.//ti, IEEE Transactions
    Visualization and Computer Graphics) and .//yr = 2000]//reviewer//name
28. //article[about(.//sec1//title, Special Feature) and about(.//ti, IEEE Micro)]//atl
29. //*[about(.//atl, image retrieval) and about(., image retrieval colour shape texture)]
30. //article[.//yr >= 1996 and about(., parallelism)]//au
31. computational biology
32. semantic web
33. software patents
34. Efficient database search structures and techniques
35. Parallel query optimization
36. Heat dissipation of microcomputer chips
37. Temporal database queries and query processing
38. multidimensional indices
39. Video on demand
40. Content-based retrieval
41. Y2K spending
42. Decryption of the Enigma code
43. approximate string matching algorithm
44. internet society communication netizen social sociology web usenet mail network culture
45. augmented reality and medicine
46. Firewalls in internet security
47. concurrency control semantic transaction management application performance benefit
48. active database rule specification

49. Query relaxation approximate and intelligent query answering
50. XML editors or parsers
51. Text Data Mining
52. History of Computing of USSR
53. information retrieval xml
54. knowledge building acquisition and sharing
55. Digital Divide city planning neighbourhood planning
56. open hypermedia systems and agents
57. public key cryptography RSA EC DSA algebraic number field
58. Location management scheme
59. schema integration methods
60. Internet speed
61. //article[about(.,clustering +distributed) and about(.//sec,java)]
62. //article[about(.,security +biometrics) AND about(.//sec,"facial recognition")]
63. //article[about(.,"digital library") AND about(.//p, +authorization +"access control" +security)]
64. //article[about(., hollerith)]//sec[about(., DEHOMAG)]
65. //article[.//fm//yr > 1998 AND about(., "image retrieval")]
66. //article[.//fm//yr < 2000]//sec[about(.,"search engines")]
67. //article//fm[about(.//(tig|abs), +software +architecture) and about(., -distributed -Web)]
68. //article[about(., +Smalltalk) or about(., +Lisp) or about(.,+Erlang) or about(., +Java)]//bdy//sec[about(., +"garbage collection" +algorithm)]
69. //article//bdy//sec[about(.//st,"information retrieval")]
70. //article[about(.//fm//abs, "information retrieval" "digital libraries")]
71. //article[about(.,formal methods verify correctness aviation systems)] //bdy//*[about(.,case study application model checking theorem proving)]
72. //article[about(.//fm//au//aff,United States of America)]//bdy//*[about(.,weather forecasting systems)]
73. //article[about(.//st,+comparison) and about(.//bib,"machine learning")]
74. //article[about(., video streaming applications)]//sec[about(., media stream synchronization) OR about(., stream delivery protocol)]
75. //article[about(., Petri net) AND about(.//sec, formal definition) AND about(.//sec, algorithm efficiency computation approximation)]
76. //article[(.//fm//yr = 2000 OR .//fm//yr = 1999) AND about(., "intelligent transportation system")]//sec[about(.,automation +vehicle)]
77. //article[about(.//sec,"reverse engineering")]//sec[about(., legal) OR about(.,legislation)]
78. //vt[about(.,"Information Retrieval" student)]
79. //article[about(.,XML) AND about(.,database)]

80. //article//bdy//sec[about(.,"clock synchronization" "distributed systems")]
81. //article[about(.//p,"multi concurrency control") AND about(.//p, algorithm)
AND about(.//fm//atl, databases)]
82. //article[about(.,handwriting recognition) AND about(.//fm//au,kim)]
83. //article//fm//abs[about(., "data mining" "frequent itemset")]
84. //p[about(.,overview "distributed query processing" join)]
85. //article[.//fm//yr >= 1998 and .//fig//no > 9]//sec[about(.//p,VR "virtual reality" "virtual environment" cyberspace "augmented reality")]
86. //sec[about(.,mobile electronic payment system)]
87. //article[(.//fm//yr = 1998 OR .//fm//yr = 1999 OR .//fm//yr = 2000 OR .//fm//yr = 2001 OR .//fm//yr = 2002) AND about(., "support vector machines")]
88. //article[(.//fm//yr = 1998 OR .//fm//yr = 1999 OR .//fm//yr = 2000 OR .//fm//yr = 2001) AND about(., "web crawler")]
89. //article[about(.//bdy,clustering "vector quantization" +fuzzy +k-means +c-means -SOFM -SOM)]//bm//bb[about(.,"vector quantization" +fuzzy clustering
+k-means +c-means) AND about(.//pdt,1999) AND about(.//au//snm, -kohonen)]
90. //article[about(.//sec,+trust authentication "electronic commerce" e-commerce
e-business marketplace)]//abs[about(., trust authentication)]
91. Internet traffic
92. "query tightening" "narrow the search" "incremental query answering"
93. "Charles Babbage" -institute -inst
94. "hyperlink analysis" +"topic distillation"
95. +"face recognition" approach
96. +"software cost estimation"
97. Converting Fortran source code
98. "Information Exchange" +XML "Information Integration"
99. perl features
100. +association +mining +rule +medical
101. +"t test" +information
102. distributed storage systems for grid computing
103. UML formal logic
104. Toy Story
105. +categorization "textual document" learning evaluation
106. Content protection schemes
107. "artificial intelligence" AI practical application industry "real world"
108. ontology ontologies overview "how to" practical example
109. "CPU cooling" "cooling fan design" "heatsink design" "heat dissipation" airflow casing

110. "stream delivery" "stream synchronization" audio video streaming applications
111. "natural language processing" -"programming language" -"modeling language"
 +"human language"
112. +"Cascading Style Sheets" -"Content Scrambling System"
113. "Markov models" "user behaviour"
114. +women "history of computing"
115. +"IP telephony" +challenges
116. "computer assisted art" "computer generated art"
117. Patricia Tries
118. "shared nothing" database
119. Optimizing joins in relational databases
120. information retrieval models
121. Real Time Operating Systems
122. Lossy Compression Algorithm
123. multidimensional index "nearest neighbour search"
124. application algorithm +clustering +k-means +c-means "vector quantization" "speech
 compression" "image compression" "video compression"
125. +wearable ubiquitous mobile computing devices
126. Open standards for digital video in distance learning

NEXI, Now and Next

Andrew Trotman[1] and Börkur Sigurbjörnsson[2]

[1] Department of Computer Science, University of Otago, Dunedin, New Zealand
andrew@cs.otago.ac.nz
[2] Informatics Institute, University of Amsterdam, Amsterdam, The Netherlands
borkur@science.uva.nl

Abstract. NEXI was introduced in INEX 2004 as a query language for specifying structured and unstructured queries on XML documents. A language expressive enough for INEX yet simple enough for users to get right. These goals have been achieved. In particular, the error rate in CAS queries has dropped from 63% in 2003 to 12% in 2004. This drop is shown to be a consequence of not only the language, but the tools introduced with it: the source code for a parser was downloaded by 13 IP addresses, while a web implementation was accessed 635 times from 71 addresses.

Although NEXI is suitable for the *ad hoc* track, it is not sufficiently expressive enough for the heterogeneous track, or for question answering. The syntax necessary to extend to these purposes is proposed. This includes weighted terms and weighted paths. The new syntax is strictly an extension so does not invalidate any existing queries.

1 Introduction

Each of the first three INEX [4] workshops used a different query language. At the first workshop queries were specified in XML [6], at the second in XPath [7], and at the third in NEXI [14]. This succession of languages occurred because, as a consequence of each workshop, new and different query types, and how to specify them, have become clear.

The first INEX workshop was modeled on TREC, and consequently a TREC-like topic format was chosen. Topics were broken into four parts, title, description, narrative and keywords. Of these, the title contained the IR query, and is consequently of focus. For Content Only (CO) queries, the title was a two or three word description of the topic. For Content And Structure (CAS) queries, the title was further marked up in XML. The optional <te> tag was used to specify target elements for the search, while <cw> was used to identify content words that were optionally associated with a container element, <ce>.

An example query, the title element from INEX topic 05 is given in Figure 1. In this example, the user is searching for documents that contain the phrase "image retrieval", contain the word QBIC in a <bibl> element, and asking for <tig> elements to be retrieved.

N. Fuhr et al. (Eds.): INEX 2004, LNCS 3493, pp. 41–53, 2005.

```
<Title>
  <te>tig</te>
  <cw>QBIC</cw><ce>bibl</ce>
  <cw>image retrieval</cw>
</Title>
```

Fig. 1. An INEX 2002 query fragment (INEX topic 05)

It was quickly established that this query language was insufficient for the need [11].

First, the XML format allowed the user to specify queries that were simple mechanical processes. In the above example, once relevant documents have been identified, the process of extracting the <tig> (or title group) is mechanical. There is one, and only one, <tig> element in each document. Identifying and extracting it can be done with a simple text search.

Second, the language was not expressive enough. The target element was specified irrespective of the context of the query. It was not possible to specify a query of the nature "find sections about sunny New Zealand"; the nearest such query was "find sections from documents about sunny New Zealand" - two quite different queries.

For the second workshop XPath [1] was adopted in the hope it would alleviate these problems, and it did. With the addition of a function for ranked information retrieval (*about*), and the elimination of non-IR functions (e.g. *contains*) XPath proved sufficiently expressive.

XPath introduced new problems! O'Keefe and Trotman [10] provide an analysis of the failure of XPath as a query language for INEX. Perhaps the most damming evidence is the error rate in the official topics. Of the 30 CAS topics, 19 contained errors; that is a 63% error rate in queries written by IR experts.

Subsequently, the INEX 2003 Queries Working Group identified the requirements for a query language suitable for INEX [13]. In brief, it had to look like XPath, be easier to use, and oriented to IR.

Considerable effort was spent defining the query language NEXI [14], used at the 2004 workshop. Designed with the sole purpose of satisfying the requirements of INEX (and the Queries Working Group), this language is a simplified XPath containing only the descendant axis; while at the same time an extended XPath containing the *about* function. NEXI is in use at the current (2004) workshop.

The use of NEXI within and without INEX is examined. From this, the conclusion is drawn that it has successfully proven to be a suitable language for XML retrieval. Future requirements are examined, and extensions are proposed. Adoption of these extensions is recommended.

2 Current State of Play

The *ad hoc* track at INEX consists of two tasks, the Content Only (CO) and Content and Structure (CAS) tasks.

In the CO task, it is the task of the search engine to identify relevant document elements that satisfy a user query. By definition, the query does not specify where to look, or what elements to retrieve. A CO query is a sequence of terms, and example of which is INEX Topic 37: "temporal database queries and query processing". For this query, the search engine is expected to identify and return a relevance ranked list of document elements about temporal database queries and query processing.

There are two variants of the CAS task, the Strict CAS (SCAS)[1] and the Vague CAS (VCAS). The queries for both are the same; it is only the interpretation that differs - the reader is referred to Fuhr, Malik, and Lalmas [3] for details. In a CAS query, structural elements are included in the query. If a user wishes to find document abstracts that discuss INEX, it is necessary to specify <abstract> as the target element. If a user is searching for smith, but knows they want Dr. Smith and not an ironmonger, they may specify that Smith is an author.

The Queries Working Group at INEX 2003 [13] identified the requirements of a query language necessary to satisfy CAS queries within the context of INEX. In brief, that language must:

- Be a subset of XPath, so as to be familiar to the XML community. Tag instancing was removed, axes were limited to only the descendant axis, filters remained but the not-equals operator was not permitted with string types.
- Support multiple data types. String and numeric types were specified. XPath filters remained, but a restricted set of operators was included.
- Be vaguely interpretable. It must be an IR language. To this end, the AND operator and OR operator were specified as ANDish and ORish.
- Specify one and only one target element (shown below to have been violated).

Additionally, this language allowed the specification of CO queries. It was also specified as extensible.

Trotman and Sigurbjörnsson [14] proposed NEXI, an IR query language for XML that satisfied the requirements of the Working Group and was subsequently adopted for the 2004 INEX. They also provided the source code to a parser, and for INEX 2004 an on-line parser.

2.1 Query Errors at INEX 2004

Examining the first release of the topics for 2004 (version 2004-01), 4 of the 34 CAS queries contain errors (12%). In the CO queries 6 of 39 contain errors (15%). The error rate in CAS is now lower than that in CO.

Examining CAS Errors

Topics 137 and 158 were missing a close bracket at the end of the query. There are corrected by appending ']'.

[1] At INEX 2004, SCAS was deprecated.

Topic 138 contained the incorrect expression "about(.,//sec,thread implementation)" which is incorrect in the first comma. This is corrected by removing the erroneous comma.

Topic 161 contained the incorrect expression "about(./atl, database access methods)" which is incorrect in so far as it uses the child axis. This is corrected by replacing "/" with "//".

Examining CO Errors

Topics 176, 177, and 196 contained illegal punctuation. This is corrected by removing the punctuation.

Topic 190 contained the quoted expression ""e-commerce"" which, as the hyphen makes e-commerce a single word, is a single word phrase. Phrases consist of strictly more than one word so this is erroneous. This is corrected by removing the quotes.

Topics 178 and 179 contain phrases delimited with question mark characters "?". This is corrected by replacing those characters with quotes.

2.2 Online Parser

In 2004 an online query syntax checker was introduced. Use was logged, with accesses from the University of Otago stripped (to avoid skewing by the developers). Logs were analyzed for the period April 12th through to October 26th; between the date when the parser went online, and when analysis began. Table 1 shows the number of times the parser was accessed each month.

Table 1. Parse requests to the online NEXI parser

Month	Requests
April	167
May	447
June	4
July	3
August	5
September	9

There was a total of 635 requests on 37 distinct dates from 71 internet addresses. Most of the requests occurred during April and May. The topic submission date was May 7th. In Figure 2, the cumulative number of requests on each day of activity is shown. There is a clear burst of activity around the submission date, and finishing on 11th May. Activity immediately after submission date may be caused by late submissions.

After the submission date, but before the first release of the topic set, there was a clear burst of activity (18th through 28th May), this is likely to be the period in which topics were corrected. There was very little activity during the period in which the topic set was under revision, with only 3 requests between the first release (version 2004-001) and the final release (version 2004-07).

It is hard to account for activity in August and September. The requests were valid and the authors are using the parser for the purpose in which it was designed (users are not hacking the parser).

The parser was in the New Zealand time zone, whereas a time-zone for the due and release dates was not given. Requests from the University of Otago were removed from the logs before analysis.

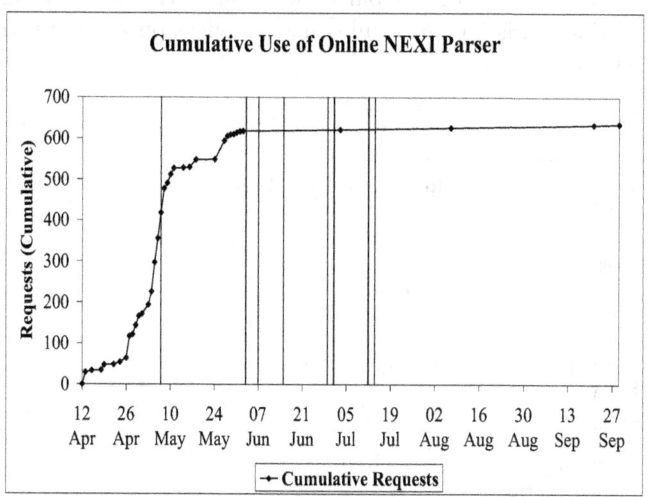

Fig. 2. Cumulative use of the online NEXI parser shows considerable use between April 27th and May 11th. The topic submission date was May 7th. Vertical lines are shown for the topic submission date, and each revision date

Figure 3 shows the number of requests for each accessing IP address. The number of requests ranged from 94 to 1. The 94 accesses appears to be an outlying point; with the next highest accesses being 36 and then 27 requests. The mean number of requests per address was 8.9, the median being 5.

No effort has been spent trying to resolve IP addresses to institutions; doing so is likely to decrease the number of addresses and increase the mean and median.

2.3 Was NEXI Successful?

The initial error rate in queries has dropped from 63% in 2003 to 12% in 2004. The error rate for CAS topics is now about the same as that in CO topics. The number of topic revisions has halved. From this is would be reasonable to conclude changes made between 2003 and 2004 had a marked effect on syntactic correctness of queries. Those changes were not, however, limited to query language changes.

First, the queries submitted to INEX were checked for syntax errors as part of the selection process. This bias, although present, is not a major contributing factor. Of the originally submitted 84 CAS queries, 18 (21%) contained errors, whereas of the 107 CO topics, 19 (18%) contained errors. These two error rates are about equal. The error rate in the original submissions in 2003 is not known.

Second, having written XPath parsers for 2003, the participants themselves should have been familiar with the language, and therefore more able to write syntactically correct queries than before.

Third, web access to an online parser was made available during the topic development period. This has, no doubt, had an effect on the correctness of the submitted queries.

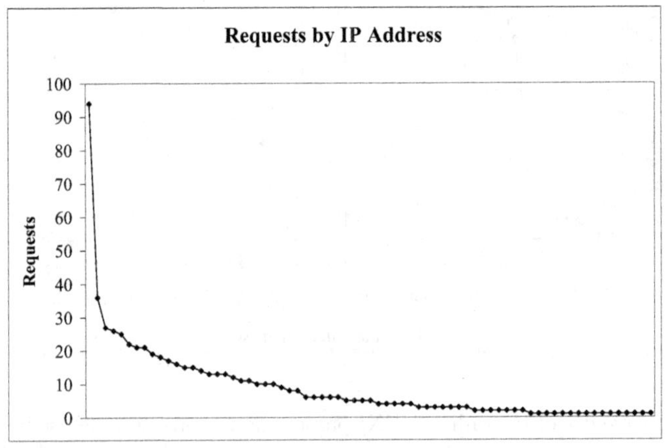

Fig. 3. Number of requests from each IP address in decreasing order

Fourth, the source for a command line version of the parser was attached to the language specification; and downloadable from the web site. It was downloaded by 13 IP addresses; discussion with some INEX participants suggests it was also used.

The decrease of errors in CAS topics is considered a sign of NEXI success; however, there are still areas that need addressing. During 2003, the topics underwent 12 revisions over a period of 38 days. In 2004, it took only 7 revisions, but 41 days. One can but hope that in future years topics are submitted correctly and on time.

3 The Future

NEXI was, by design, the simplest query language that could possibly work. The subset of XPath was chosen in order to ensure nothing unnecessary was included. To this end, NEXI has proven a success for *ad hoc* searching, but only for *ad hoc* searching - it has proven unsuitable for other types of search. This shortfall is now addressed with additions for question answering, heterogeneous searching, and a new wildcard.

There are many ways in which the language could be extended to address the shortfalls. Below the issues are outlined, previous proposals are examined, and possible extensions are proposed. Although these extensions are inline with each other and other pre-existing language constructs, these extensions remain untested. The added complexity introduced could result in an increased query error rate (a reversal of the effect shown above). To this end, the extensions should be considered a proposal to extend the language, not pre-accepted additions.

3.1 Wildcards

The NEXI path wildcard operator, *, is defined as meaning "first or subsequent descendant" [14]. A new "here or below" wildcard, +, is introduced, but it is of limited use.

As //article//+ means "article or below", //+ must mean "nothing or below". This nothingness is meaningless, as there must be at least one element present. Specifying the existence of one or more elements is done with //*. Use of //+ is therefore prohibited.

Use of two or more adjacent //+ operators is meaningless; //article//+ and //article//+//+ are semantically equivalent. The two forms //article//+//bm and //article//bm are also equivalent. Use of the + inside a path is meaningless as it simply specifies there might be a node, which is implicit in the descendant operator.

There exists only one place this new operator can be used; the end of a path specification. The form //*//+ is redundant, and equivalent to //*, further restricting the use of +.

The new addition to the path syntax is:

```
zero_any_node: NODE_QUALIFIER '+'
```

which requires the following changes:

```
path: any_node
    | node_sequence
    | node_sequence any_node
    | node_sequence attribute_node
    | node_sequence any_node attribute_node
    | node_sequence zero_any_node

node_sequence: node
    | node_sequence node
    | node_sequence any_node node
    | node_sequence any_node any_node

node: named_node | tag_list_node
```

It is unfortunate that the late addition of the + wildcard operator results in * meaning one or more and + meaning zero or more because these two operators have each other's definition in regular expressions.

Strict interpretation: "//A//+" means at or below the "//A" element.

Loose interpretation: "As paths are only hints, feel free to ignore this".

3.2 Multiple Target Elements

The tag list syntax, "//(A|B)" means "either the A or the B element". As this syntax is not forbidden as the target element, it might be exploited by a topic author to identify multiple target elements. This use, although valid, is discouraged.

3.3 NEXI for Question Answering

There is currently no question answering (QA) track at INEX, however the authors anticipate there being so. Ogilvie [9] has already discussed the inadequacies of NEXI to fulfill this role. We concede, it was not designed for this purpose and does not fulfill the role. Ogilvie does, however, propose syntax for the purpose.

In place of an *about* function, Ogilvie suggests a *weight* function; which he gives by example:

```
//sentence[.//event//VBD[weight(0.4 kill 0.3 assassinate 0.2
murder 0.1 shoot)] AND .//patient//person[weight(0.4 'Abraham
Lincoln' 0.4 'President Lincoln' 0.1 'honest Abe' 0.1 Lincoln)]]
//agent//person
```

weight differs from *about* in three ways. First, phrases are specified using single quotes in place of double quotes. Second, the path occurs outside the clause rather than inside it. Third, weights for each term are given. Altering *weight* to resemble *about* results in:

Example:

```
//sentence[weight(.//event//VBD, 0.4 kill 0.3 assassinate 0.2
murder 0.1 shoot) AND weight(.//patient//person, 0.4 "Abraham
Lincoln" 0.4 "President Lincoln" 0.1 "honest Abe" 0.1 Lincoln)]
//agent//person
```

the formal syntax of which is:

```
decimal: NUMBER | NUMBER '.' NUMBER

WEIGHT: "weight"

weighted_co: decimal term | weighted_co decimal term

weight_clause: WEIGHT '(' relative_path ',' weighted_co ')'
```

additionally, the definition of filter is altered to:

```
filter: about_clause
    | weight_clause
    | arithmetic_clause
```

Strict interpretation: "In the example, only a //sentence//agent//person element is correct, that said, it will most likely tell me who killed honest Abe".

Loose interpretation: "What I want is likely a //sentence//agent//person element that will tell me who assassinated honest Abe. I know several ways of saying assassinate, and honest Abe, here are some and how likely I think you are to see them - but I might be wrong about this".

QA Paths. Ogilvie notes that path semantics may require relaxation for Question Answering. The paths may, instead, refer to a structural annotation of the document content. In no way should NEXI be interpreted as prohibiting any such interpretation of paths - this is the loose interpretation embraced.

3.4 NEXI for Heterogeneous Searching

The heterogeneous track chose a subset of topics from the *ad hoc* track, and added to them some special purpose topics. Of the chosen topics, 161 and 196 contained errors (discussed above). In version 2 of the heterogeneous topics there are 4 added topics, one of which contains spurious punctuation (topic 4). Topics should be checked for syntax errors before inclusion in any topic list.

The heterogeneous track has four types of queries, Content Only (CO), Basic CAS (BCAS), Complex CAS (CCAS) and Extended CCAS (ECCAS).

This year CO topics from the *ad hoc* track were used for the heterogeneous track. As the IEEE collection is part of the heterogeneous collection, this decision avoids any additional relevance assessing on that collection. Consequently, all CO topics in the heterogeneous track are already in NEXI.

Basic CAS topics contain one structural constraint and one content constraint. They can all be specified in the form

```
//structure[about(., content)]
```

where structure and content are single terms. This is a subset of NEXI which was, consequently, chosen for specifying BCAS topics.

Compex CAS topics are the heterogeneous equivalent of *ad hoc* CAS topics. They are in the form //A[B] or //A[B]//C[D]. CCAS topics are specified in NEXI.

Extended Complex Content and Structure (ECCAS) topics allow the query author to specify a belief in the correctness of a structural constraint. The example given in the track guidelines [2] is:

```
//author(0.8)[about(title(0.5), 'Information Retrieval')],
```

in which the user has an 80% certainty the answer is an author element, thinks the article will be about information retrieval, but has only a 50% certain that this will be discussed in the title. There were no ECCAS topics submitted and NEXI did not support syntax for them.

ECCAS topics are expected in future years. To this end, syntax supporting user certainty in tag specification is needed. Extending NEXI would require only small changes from the syntax proposed in the heterogeneous track guidelines.

First, in NEXI phrases are specified using double quotes, phrases in ECCAS should be specified in the same way. Second, paths in a NEXI *about* function are relative to the context path (the path being filtered) but in the example given in the heterogeneous track guidelines [2], the path is an absolute path. The change to absolute paths prevents the specification of queries that can be resolved through a mechanical process, however it also restricts the expressiveness of the query - these kinds of queries can't be written. This tradeoff is considered acceptable.

The syntax requires only small changes:

```
weight: '(' decimal ')'

tag: XMLTAG | XMLTAG weight
```

Strict interpretation: "//A(0.5)" is a 0.5 certainty in the correctness of "//A" for the purpose in which it is being used. "//A(0.5)//B(0.3)" is a 0.3 certainty of "//A//B" for its purpose and a 0.5 certainty in "//A" for its purpose. In the expression "//(A(0.2)|B(0.5))", the certainty of being "//A" is given along with the certainty of "//B". The certainty values are only hits, and are open to interpretation.

Loose interpretation: "I'm not sure where to look, these places might be good."

3.5 Uncertain NEXI

The heterogeneous additions combined with the question answering additions provide the syntax necessary for certainty of path and certainty of search term combinations. A query of this nature can be considered super-loose or utterly uncertain; the user is uncertain of everything (a THISish search?).
Example:

```
//bb(0.3)[weight(., 0.2 "Information Retrieval")]
```

Strict interpretation: There is no strict interpretation.

Loose interpretation: "The answer is probably a <bb> element, and it probably says something about Information Retrieval, but I'm not certain about this".

3.6 Relevance Feedback NEXI

In relevance feedback it is not uncommon to add additional search terms or to weight search terms. The natural analogue for structured searching is adding paths and weighting paths. Syntax for both weighting terms and paths is suggested above. Here the applicability to relevance feedback is identified.

3.7 Weighted CAS

The certainty of the structural constraint in a CAS query could be stated using the syntax proposed above for ECCAS. Doing so would remove the distinction between SCAS and VCAS, instead creating a continuum of CAS - a query author stating constraint certainty as part of the query itself.

4 Other NEXI Related Work

Kamps *et al.* [5] suggest adding the ancestor axis to NEXI. They call this superset Positive Temporal XPath. Although this syntax is not more expressive (all queries specifiable in Positive Temporal XPath can be expressed in NEXI), they suggest specifying a path from child to parent is more natural to some users than *vice versa*. They conjecture that paths specified using both ancestor and descendant may be more succinct than using just one or the other.

It is unfortunate that some users prefer parent to child, while others prefer child to parent; using one or the other is simpler than using either or both. In an effort to remain simple, the introduction of an ancestor axis to NEXI is left as future work.

Mihajlovic *et al.* [8] choose to store the INEX collection in a relational database. Between the relational database and NEXI they introduce an algebra. With this approach it is possible to change (and experiment with) the underlying relational structure independent of the algebraic optimization of query expressions. It also allows the introduction and optimization of XML IR operators such as *about*. They choose the range approach for searching structured documents and consequently their introduced algebra is an algebra of regions. Piwowarski and Gallinari [12] prefer a probabilistic implementation and introduce a probabilistic algebra for a subset of XPath which is a superset of NEXI.

5 Conclusions

NEXI has proven to be successful for INEX. This success is due to a combination of the simple XPath like syntax, the online parser, and the command-line parser. The online parser was used a total of 635 times from 71 IP addresses, the command line parser was downloaded from 13 IP addresses. As a consequence of this use the error rate in CAS queries dropped from 63% in 2003 to 12% in 2004.

Although NEXI has proven suitable for *ad hoc* retrieval, it has also proven inadequate for question answering and heterogeneous searching. New syntax is added for these purposes. In essence, this new syntax adds weighted paths and weighted search terms. These extensions might also be used for relevance feedback.

Wildcards in paths are extended to include a zero or more descendants wildcard, +. The new wildcard is meaningless except at the end of a path.

The adoption of the extensions proposed herein will allow tracks in addition to *ad hoc* to use NEXI. This use, and continued use in the *ad hoc* track, is recommended.

References

1. Clark, J., and DeRose, S. (1999). XML path language (XPath) 1.0, W3C recommendation. The World Wide Web Consortium.
   Available: http://www.w3.org/TR/xpath.
2. Dignum, V., and van Zwol, R. (2004). Guidelines for topic development in heterogeneous collections.
   Available: http://inex.is.informatik.uni-duisburg.de:2004/internal/hettrack/downloads/hettopics.pdf.
3. Fuhr, N., Malik, S., and Lalmas, M. (2003). Overview of the initiative for the evaluation of XML retrieval (INEX) 2003. In *Proceedings of the INEX 2003 Workshop*, (pp. 1-11).
4. Gövert, N., and Kazai, G. (2002). Overview of the initiative for the evaluation of XML retrieval (INEX) 2002. In *Proceedings of the 1st Workshop of the INitiative for the Evaluation of XML Retrieval (INEX)*, (pp. 1-17).
5. Kamps, J., Marx, M., de Rijke, M., and Sigurbjörnsson, B. (2004). Best-match querying for document-centric XML. In *Proceedings of the 7th International Workshop on the Web and Databases (WebDB 2004)*, (pp. 55-60).
6. Kazai, G., Lalmas, M., and Malik, S. (2002). INEX guidelines for topic development. In *Proceedings of the 1st workshop of the initiative for the evaluation of XML retrieval (INEX)*, (pp. 178-181).
7. Kazai, G., Lalmas, M., and Malik, S. (2003). INEX '03 guidelines for topic development. In *Proceedings of the 2nd workshop of the initiative for the evaluation of XML retrieval (INEX)*.
8. Mihajlovic, V., Hiemstra, D., Blok, H. E., and Apers, P. M. G. (2004). An XML-IR-db-sandwich: Is it better with an algebra in between? In *Proceedings of the SIGIR workshop on Information Retrieval and Databases (WIRD'04)*.
9. Ogilvie, P. (2004). Retrieval using structure for question answering. In *Proceedings of the 1st Twente Data Management Workshop - XML Databases and Information Retrieval*, (pp. 15-23).
10. O'Keefe, R. A., and Trotman, A. (2003). The simplest query language that could possibly work. In *Proceedings of the 2nd workshop of the initiative for the evaluation of XML retrieval (INEX)*.
11. Pehcevski, J., Thom, J., and Vercoustre, A.-M. (2003). XML-search query language: Needs and requirements. In *Proceedings of the AusWeb 03: Changing the Way We Work.*
12. Piwowarski, B., and Gallinari, P. (2004). An algebra for probabilistic XML retrieval. In *Proceedings of the 1st Twente Data Management Workshop - XML Databases and Information Retrieval.*

13. Sigurbjörnsson, B., and Trotman, A. (2003). Queries: INEX 2003 working group report. In *Proceedings of the 2nd workshop of the initiative for the evaluation of XML retrieval (INEX).*
14. Trotman, A., and Sigurbjörnsson, B. (2004). Narrowed Extended XPath I (NEXI). In *Proceedings of the 3rd workshop of the initiative for the evaluation of XML retrieval (INEX).*

If INEX Is the Answer, What Is the Question?

Richard A. O'Keefe

CS Dept, University of Otago

Abstract. The INEX query languages allow the extraction of fragments from selected documents. This power is not much used in INEX queries. The paper suggests reasons why, and considers which kind of document collection this feature might be useful for.

1 What Is the INEX Answer?

INEX [1,2,3] is all about extracting information from XML document collections.

We can distinguish four kinds of IR-like query for semi-structured data:

CO (Content Only)—a classical information retrieval query to select a document from a collection of documents based on the occurrence of terms and phrases anywhere within it. Example: "find all documents mentioning 'Malacostraca' and 'Edgar Allen Poe'."

CC (Content-in-Context)—a combination of contexts (paths) and CO queries to apply in those contexts, used to select documents from a collection of documents. Queries like this have been around almost as there have been SGML collections to search in. Example: "find all documents where author mentions 'Edgar Allen Poe' and body mentions 'Malacostraca'."

EC (Element-in-Context)—a CC-like query is used to select elements from documents in a collection, with each element being treated as if it were a document and reported separately. These are NEXI [4,5] "Basic CAS" queries. You can see CC queries as BCAS queries that just happen to select `article` elements, but the distinction between CC and EC is useful. Example: "find ⟨bibitem⟩s mentioning 'INEX'."

2S (Two-Stage)—An EC query is used to select elements, and then a further EC query is used to select portions of those elements. This is not used for highlighting within documents; the elements selected in the second stage are reported separately. Example: "find ⟨back-matter⟩ where any ⟨author-bio⟩ mentions 'Edinburgh' then report contained ⟨bibitems⟩ mentioning 'DAI'."

The INEX Answer is "EC and 2S queries", or "element extraction".

Because an XPath query that is purportedly about some element can examine remote descendants of ancestors of that element, it can be difficult to tell the difference between EC and 2S queries. I regard a query that examines an element and its descendants and at most the attributes of its ancestors as an EC query, others as disguised 2S queries. This classification is sensitive to whether publication date, for example, is an attribute or an element, which is why both EC and 2S queries must be allowed.

N. Fuhr et al. (Eds.): INEX 2004, LNCS 3493, pp. 54–59, 2005.

2 What Is Problematic About the INEX Answer?

It turns out that INEX participants have found it very hard to formulate non-trivial EC and 2S queries, and even harder to evaluate them. The INEX'03 [2] topics included thirty Content and Structure queries:

That is, nearly half of the queries did not exploit the INEX Answer. One reason for this is simply that there is not a lot of structure that one can usefully exploit in the INEX collection. Basically, there are front matter, including authors, title, and abstracts, body with a whole bunch of variously tagged sections and subsections, and back matter with bibliography and author biographies.

count	type	tag returned	what that tag means
14	CC	`article`	whole articles
3	EC	`sec`	sections
1	EC	`abs`	abstracts
1	EC	`p`	paragraphs
1	EC	`vt`	*curricula vitæ*
6	2S	`sec`	sections
2	2S	`abs`	abstracts
1	2S	`bb`	bibliography items
2	2S	`*`	IR engine's choice

Things changed in INEX'04 [3], but not much. There were 35 CAS topics.

A little over three quarters of the INEX'04 CAS queries did exploit the INEX Answer, but how usefully?

count	type	tag returned	what that tag means
8	CC	`article`	whole articles
2	EC	`sec`	sections
1	EC	`abs`	abstracts
1	EC	`p`	paragraphs
1	EC	`vt`	*curricula vitæ*
1	EC	`bib`	entire bibliographies
1	EC	`(p|fgc)`	paragraphs or figure captions
8	2S	`sec`	sections
1	2S	`abs`	abstracts
1	2S	`bb`	bibliography items
1	2S	`p`	paragraphs
1	2S	`fig`	figures
1	2S	`bdy`	whole bodies
2	2S	`*`	IR engine's choice

Some of these queries are thought-provoking.

- In query 161, the containing `article` must be about access methods for spatial data and text, while the selected `bb` elements need not be about either. They could be about access methods for time series, for example.

- In query 158, the containing `article` must be about the Turing test, while the selected `bdy` element must be about the "turning" test. Nor is it clear why it is useful to see an article without its title, authors, or abstract.
- Query 158 also makes one wonder how a query of the form `about(.//fm,` x`)` `or about(.//abs,` x`)` differs from a simple `about(.//fm,` x`)`, since `abs` only occurs inside `fm`.
- Query 127 with its `(p|fgc)` reminds us that while the average `p` in the INEX collection has about 300 characters of text, the average `fgc` has about 150 characters. So perhaps more (all?) queries that accept `p` elements should also accept `fgc` elements.
- Query 136, selecting entire bibliographies on the basis of "text" and "categorisation" appearing somewhere, and "SVM" and "Support Vector Machines" appearing somewhere else, reminds us that titles are not a reliable guide to relevance. Who would dream from the title alone that *Bananas in Space* was about "functional programming" using the "Bird-Meertens" formalism?
- Query 142, of the form `//abs[about(...)]`, makes one wonder why it is useful to find an interesting abstract if you cannot tell which article it is an abstract *of*.

Queries must not only be formulated, they must be evaluated. And to evaluate the relevance of an element, you may need a greater or lesser amount of context. As IR researchers well know, words are ambiguous. If you see "Algol is very old", is that talking about the star or the programming language (and if so, which)? If you see "The tables were too crowded", is this a complaint about a paper or a dining hall?

This points out a serious methodological problem in the INEX evaluation procedure. Judges rate elements within the scope of complete articles (which they can and do look at), while users would presumably just see the elements. That is, for CO and CC queries, the judge and the user have the same information available to them, while for EC and 2S queries, the judge has far more information at his or her disposal in making relevance judgements than someone just receiving the paragraphs or sections in question would. For abstracts and sections, this may not be too much of a problem, but paragraph, title, and bibliography item it is almost certainly a distortion. Even for sections, I know that I found myself either able to dismiss an entire article quickly (having looked at a portion that was not part of the selected response) or else having to read the entire article with care to decide what the flagged elements actually *meant* before I could decide how relevant they were. Does it even make sense to talk about a small element *having* any relevance without its context?

3 What Might the Question Be?

What should our collection be like for the INEX Answer (element extraction) to be useful?

3.1 Strong Semantics for Markup

Some markup in the INEX collection has strong semantics. An `ead` element should be an e-mail address, nothing else. The `mo`, `day`, and `yr` elements are parts of dates. A `bb` element is always a bibliographic reference. The `abs`, `bb`, and `vt` elements are clearly useful in queries.

Some markup in the INEX collection has presentation semantics. The `it` and `rm` elements select italic and roman faces, but say nothing about why. It is not accidental that none of the queries mention these elements, and it is only regrettable that the evaluation system requires people to judge these elements.

Some markup is structural, without having much semantics. There is nothing to mark the rhetorical structure of a document or the rhetorical force of any element. There is, for example, no distinction between "quoted in support" and "quoted for rebuttal". Structural elements are surprisingly popular in queries, principally `sec` with some `p`. One feels that this may be an artefact of the INEX setup: people are under pressure to select *something* to show that the INEX Answer is useful, and `sec` is the smallest nearly-self-contained element. It is difficult to imagine any queries where `ss1` or `ss2` would be meaningful choices.

An INEX Question really needs a wider range of elements with strong semantics: `exercise`, `example`, `poetry` (in the INEX DTD, but apparently not used anywhere), `warning`, `listing`, `scene`, `design.pattern`, that kind of thing.

3.2 Memorable Markup

You cannot ask about tags that you cannot remember. A DTD or Schema may contain more tags than people can recall; the present 192 is almost certainly too many. Tag names may be difficult to recall. The present DTD uses names that have been heavily abbreviated, like ⟨ilrj⟩. Users may not be provided with enough information about the meaning of tags; how is an ⟨ilrj⟩ different from other paragraphs?

This suggests that the markup assumed in queries should contain not too many tags, which should not be too heavily abbreviated, and should be clearly explained to query users.

The "query DTD" need not be the actual DTD used for markup. This is already the case in INEX, where several kinds of paragraph are mapped to ⟨p⟩. Architectural form processing (a major concept in SGML) means that a small "authoring" DTD can be mapped to a rich one and that a rich DTD can be mapped to a small "querying" DTD.

3.3 Low Coupling

What really matters is not how big the fragments are but how tightly they are coupled to their context. The Wall Street Journal documents from TREC are smaller than most of the IEEE `sec` elements, but they were written to be free-standing. The `bb` and `vt` elements make good sense as fragments in the existing INEX collection because they depend hardly at all on their context. Abstracts are crafted to be fairly self-contained. In contrast, `p` elements are so tightly linked to their context as to be difficult to judge, even though they are bigger than most `bb` elements. The very smallest body extracts that work are `sec`, and even they depend too much on context for comfort.

We need a collection of documents which have pieces whose relevance can be judged on their own.

3.4 Some Coupling

If the fragments we want are not coupled to their containing document at all, why are they not stored as free-standing documents in the first place? There has to be enough coupling so that the first EC filter usefully limits the scope of the second EC filter.

3.5 Sizeable Fragments

If you find a relevant `sec`, do you not want to know what article it came from in case there is more good stuff there, or to find the author's address to write for more information? One reason you might not want to do this is if the "documents" are too big to examine or or too unlikely to contain other relevant material.

3.6 Examples

2S From the Otago Daily Times, issues in 2003, find stories about Don Brash. Newspapers contain many stories with low or no coupling. This is almost a WSJ query. The trick is to find queries with more constraints on the container (issue).

2S From the Otago Daily Times, issues since 2000 having editorials about the foreshore or race relations, find stories about Don Brash and the foreshore or race relations.

This is almost the same as the previous query, but basically uses the newspaper editor as a relevance filter. It feels contrived; basically these two examples fail the "some coupling" requirement.

2S From movies in the detective story genre set in San Francisco, select scenes where Nicole Kidman speaks.

This satisfies the "sizeable fragment" requirement.

EC From CDs that contain Irish music, select planxties.

This satisfies "low coupling", "sizeable fragment", and "some coupling".

2S From movies whose sound track was composed or arranged by John Williams, select producer and director.

This shows that a meaningful query need not satisfy "sizeable fragment", but it is not an IR query, let alone an INEX one.

2S From books about anatomy, select sections about the articulation of the jaw.

This is a real query I had while I was writing the paper. The answers I found satisfied "low coupling" and "sizeable fragment".

2S From books about Bioinformatics published after 1994, select portions about Dynamic Time Warps.

Publication date is a property of the books as wholes, not of sections. Dynamic Time Warps have many applications other than Bioinformatics. So this satisfies "some coupling" as well as "sizeable fragments".

EC From books by Terry Pratchett, select chapters that mention a "Soul Cake" day. This illustrates the query-relative nature of coupling. Chapters are coupled to their contexts, but if all you want to know is which day of the week Soul Cake day is on, that does not matter. This is a small example of an information extraction query, suggesting that we should look to information extraction problems and collections for models.

EC From all Koine Greek documents in a collection of ancient documents, select paragraphs containing the word "$\pi\alpha\iota\sigma$". This is a real question I'd like to ask. It is a typical word study where the question is "how is this word used". The language, period, genre, even author of the documents could be relevant to the scope of the study. The fragments are, from a general point of view, tightly coupled to their context, but for the purposes of this kind of query, that semantic coupling is not relevant. Because it is concerned with a specific word rather than the meaning of the word, it is not really an IR or INEX query, so "low coupling" remains a desideratum for the INEX Question.

2S From R packages that are about trees, select function descriptions that are about pruning trees.

There are over 1200 pages of function documentation for core R; the contributed packages add about as much more. The function descriptions are similar to UNIX manual pages, only bigger. This satisfies "some coupling" and "sizeable fragments".

EC From volumes of Otago examination papers dated 2000 or later, find questions in COSC papers that mention Pascal. I have a DTD for this, and have personally marked up many COSC exam papers. I do not, however, have complete volumes, otherwise this would be a real question.

This satisfies "strong semantics", "low coupling", "some coupling", and "sizeable fragments", in that questions are a paragraph to half a page in size.

References

1. Proceedings of the First Workshop of the Initiative for the Evaluation of XML Retrieval (INEX); December 9–11, 2002; Schloss Dagstuhl; `http://www.ecrim.org/publication/ws-proceedings/INEX2002.pdf`
2. INEX 2003 Workshop Proceedings (2003); December 15–17, 2003; Schloss Dagstuhl; `http://citeseer.ist.pesu.edu/649846.html`
3. INEX 2004 Workshop Proceedings (2004), this volume.
4. Narrowed Extended XPath I; Trotman, A., & Sigbjörnsson, B., (2004); in [3].
5. NEXI, Now and Next; Trotman, A., & Sigbjörnsson, B., (2004); in [3].

Reliability Tests for the XCG and inex-2002 Metrics

Gabriella Kazai[1], Mounia Lalmas[1], and Arjen de Vries[2]

[1] Dept. of Computer Science, Queen Mary University of London, London, UK
{gabs, mounia}@dcs.qmul.ac.uk
[2] CWI, Amsterdam, The Netherlands
arjen@acm.org

Abstract. In this paper we compare the effectiveness scores and system rankings obtained with the inex-2002 metric, the official measure of INEX 2004, and the XCG metrics proposed in [4] and further developed here. For the comparisons, we use simulated runs as we can easily derive the desired system rankings that a reliable measure should produce based on a predefined set of user preferences. The results indicate that the XCG metrics are better suited for comparing systems for the INEX content-only (CO) task, where systems aim to return the highest scoring elements according to the user preferences reflected in a quantisation function, while also aiming to avoid returning overlapping components.

1 Introduction

The official metric of INEX 2004 is inex_eval or, as referred here, the inex-2002 metric. This metric has been chosen by INEX as the official measure partly because at the time it was still not clear how much its known weaknesses would effect the overall system rankings and partly because alternative measures were not yet ready to take this role. Some of the known weaknesses were reported in [4, 5]. One such issue is that the metric does not take into account the overlap between result elements and hence produces better effectiveness scores for systems that return multiple nested components, e.g. a paragraph and its container section and article. At the INEX 2003 workshop, it was agreed that such a system behaviour should not be rewarded, but in fact should be penalised [4]. Furthermore, comments collected as part of the user studies run by the interactive track at INEX 2004 confirm that "searchers generally recognised overlapping components, and found them an undesirable 'feature' of the system" [9]. Another issue with the inex-2002 metric is that it calculates recall based on the full recall-base, which also contains large amounts of overlapping components. This means that 100% recall can only be reached by systems that return all elements of the full recall-base including all overlapping components. An affect of the latter issue is that the precision scores of systems, that aim to avoid inundating users with overlapping, and hence redundant, elements, are plotted against lower recall values than merited [5].

An argument for the inex-2002 metric is that it can produce reliable rankings of systems provided none of the systems retrieve overlapping result elements. Although the effectiveness scores would still reflect a pessimistic estimate of performance (due to the overlap amongst the reference elements in the full recall-base), the relative ranking of systems may provide a suitable reflection of performance.

N. Fuhr et al. (Eds.): INEX 2004, LNCS 3493, pp. 60–72, 2005.

However, most of the current systems at INEX output result lists, where high overlap ratios in the region of 70-80% are not uncommon. This then raises the question whether we can trust the scores obtained by the inex-2002 metric.

In this paper, we investigate this question by means of a basic reliability test. We refer to the reliability test of this study as basic, as we do not provide here a comprehensive survey of acceptable error rates, levels of significant differences in effectiveness scores and so on, but we concentrate only on evaluating "the metrics' ability to rank a better system ahead of a worse system" [10]. We test the inex-2002 metric [2] and the XCG metrics proposed in [5] and further developed in this paper. For the comparisons, we use simulated runs instead of the actual INEX runs submitted by participants. The reason for this is that by controlling which elements and in what order should make up a run, we can get clearer conclusions regarding the behaviours of the metrics under evaluation.

In the following, we first give a quick overview of the two metrics (Section 2) and then describe the setup and results of our metric reliability test (Section 3). As an indication of the effect of overlap on the rankings of the official INEX 2004 runs, in Section 3.5 we give the ten highest scoring runs obtained for the two metrics. We close with conclusions in Section 4.

2 The Metrics

This section gives a brief summary of the inex-2002 (aka. inex_eval) [2] and the XCG metrics introduced in [5] and extended here.

2.1 The inex-2002 Metric

The inex-2002 metric applies the measure of *precall* [8] to document components and computes the probability $P(rel|retr)$ that a component viewed by the user is relevant:

$$P(rel|retr)(x) := \frac{x \cdot n}{x \cdot n + esl_{x \cdot n}} \tag{1}$$

where $esl_{x \cdot n}$ denotes the *expected search length* [1], i.e. the expected number of non-relevant elements retrieved until an arbitrary recall point x is reached, and n is the total number of relevant components with respect to a given topic.

To apply the above metric, the two relevance dimensions are first mapped to a single relevance scale by employing a quantisation function, $\mathbf{f}_{quant}(e, s) \colon ES \to [0, 1]$, where ES denotes the set of possible assessment pairs (e, s):

$$ES = \{(0,0), (1,1), (1,2), (1,3), (2,1), (2,2), (2,3), (3,1), (3,2), (3,3)\}$$

There are a number of quantisation functions currently in use in INEX, e.g. strict or generalised (see Equations 2 and 3 in [4]), each representing a different set of user preferences. In this paper we concentrate on the "specificity-oriented generalised" (*sog*) quantisation function proposed in [5]:

$$\mathbf{f}_{sog}(e,s) := \begin{cases} 1 & \text{if} \quad (e,s) = (3,3) \\ 0.9 & \text{if} \quad (e,s) = (2,3) \\ 0.75 & \text{if} \quad (e,s) \in \{(1,3),(3,2)\} \\ 0.5 & \text{if} \quad (e,s) = (2,2) \\ 0.25 & \text{if} \quad (e,s) \in \{(1,2),(3,1)\} \\ 0.1 & \text{if} \quad (e,s) \in \{(2,1),(1,1)\} \\ 0 & \text{if} \quad (e,s) = (0,0) \end{cases} \tag{2}$$

The argument in [5] is that the relative ranking of assessment value pairs in the above formula better reflects the evaluation criterion for XML retrieval as defined within the CO task. According to this, specificity plays a more dominant role than exhaustivity. This is not the case for the generalised quantisation function, which shows slight preference towards exhaustivity, assigning high scores to exhaustive, but not necessarily specific components. Due to the propagation effect and the cumulative property of exhaustivity, such components are generally large, e.g. `bdy` or `article`, elements [6]. This means that relatively high effectiveness scores could be achieved with simple article runs, which contradicts the goal of the retrieval task. The *sog* mapping aims to overcome this bias.

Like all quantisation functions, the *sog* quantisation captures a relative ranking of exhaustivity-specificity value pairs reflecting user preferences, such that, e.g., $(e, s) = (3, 3)$ nodes are preferred to $(e, s) = (2, 3)$ nodes, which in turn are better than $(e, s) \in \{(1, 3), (3, 2)\}$ nodes and so on.

2.2 Cumulated Gain Based Metrics

The XCG metrics described in the next Section are extensions of the cumulated gain (CG) based metrics proposed by Järvelin and Kekäläinen in [3]. The motivation for the CG metrics was to develop a measure for multi-grade relevance values, i.e. to credit IR systems according to the retrieved documents' degree of relevance. The CG 'metrics-family' includes four measures: the Cumulated Gain (CG) measure, the Discounted Cumulated Gain (DCG) measure and their normalised versions, the normalised Cumulated Gain (nCG) and the normalised Discounted Cumulated Gain (nCG) measures. Here we only cover the CG and the nCG metrics as the discounting method can be implemented directly within our extensions rather than defining a separate measure.

The Cumulated Gain (CG) measure, accumulates the relevance scores of retrieved documents along the ranked list G, where the document IDs are replaced with their relevance scores. The cumulated gain at rank i, $CG[i]$, is then computed as the sum of the relevance scores up to that rank:

$$\mathbf{CG[i]} := \sum_{j=1}^{i} G[j] \tag{3}$$

For example, based on a four-point relevance scale with relevance degrees of $\{0, 1, 2, 3\}$, the ranking $G = <3, 2, 3, 0, 1, 2>$ produces the cumulated gain vector of $CG = <3, 5, 8, 8, 9, 11>$.

For each query, an ideal gain vector, I, can be derived by filling the rank positions with the relevance scores of all documents in the recall-base in decreasing order of their degree of relevance.

A retrieval run's CG vector can be compared to the ideal ranking by plotting the gain value of both the actual and ideal CG functions against the rank position. We obtain two monotonically increasing curves, levelling after no more relevant documents can be found.

By dividing the CG vectors of the retrieval runs by their corresponding ideal CG vectors, we obtain the normalised CG (nCG) measure. Here, for any rank the normalised value of 1 represents ideal performance. The area between the normalised actual and ideal curves represents the quality of a retrieval approach.

2.3 The XCG Metrics: Cumulated Gain Based Metrics for XML Retrieval

The XCG metrics include extensions of both the CG and nCG measures: XCG and nXCG, respectively. The motivation for the XCG metrics was to extend the CG measures in such a way that the problem of overlapping result and reference elements can be addressed within the evaluation framework. The extension of the CG metrics to XML documents, and in particular to INEX, lies partly in the way the relevance score for a given document - or in this case document component - is calculated via the definition of so-called relevance value (RV) functions, and partly in the definition of ideal recall-bases, while the actual formula of calculating cumulated gain (Equation 3) is unchanged.

An ideal recall-base is a set of ideal result nodes selected from the full recall-base based on a given quantisation function and the following methodology. Given any two components on a relevant path[1], the component with the higher quantised score (as per chosen quantisation function) is selected. In case two components' scores are equal, the one deeper in the tree is chosen[2]. The procedure is applied recursively to all overlapping pairs of components along the relevant path until one element remains. After all relevant paths have been processed, a final filtering is applied to eliminate any possible overlap among the selected ideal components, keeping from two overlapping ideal paths the shortest one.

Consider Figure 1 as an example. The figure shows the elements and their structural relationships within an article file (co/2001/r7022.xml) of the INEX test collection, where only the nodes that have been assessed as relevant (for topic 163) are included. For each node, the node name, the assigned assessment value pair (in the form of (es)), the size of the element in number of characters contained, and the size ratio of the node to its parent node is shown. According to the algorithm above, in the first step one ideal node is selected from each relevant path. For example, from the relevant path {`article1`, `bdy1`, `sec4`, `sec4/p2`}, `sec4` is selected as ideal as it obtains the highest score of 0.5 based on the *sog* quantisation function, with all other nodes on the path each scoring 0.25. From the relevant path {`article1`, `bdy1`, `sec4`, `sec4/p1`}, `sec4/p1` is selected as the ideal node with a score of 0.9. Once all relevant paths have

[1] A relevant path is defined as a path in the XML tree of a document, such as an article file in the INEX collection, whose root node is the `article` element and whose leaf node is a relevant component (i.e. $(e > 0, s > 0)$) that has no or only irrelevant descendants. E.g. in Figure 1 there are 6 relevant paths.

[2] We are also experimenting with the alternative option, i.e. selecting the node higher in the tree.

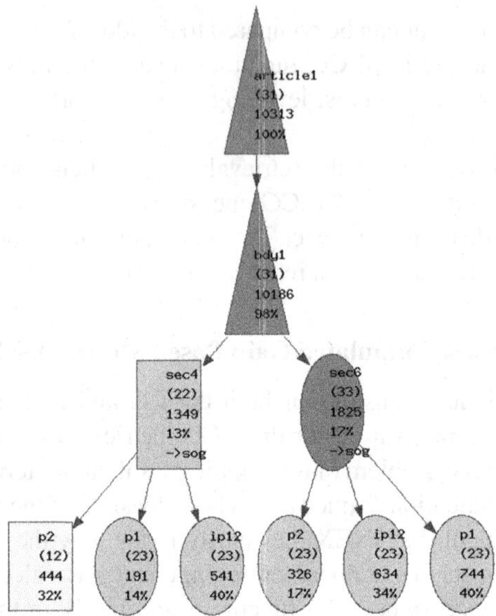

Fig. 1. Sample assessments showing only relevant nodes (i.e. $e>0$ and $s>0$) for topic 163 in the article file co/2001/r7022.xml. For each node, the node name, the assessment value pair (es), the size in characters and the size ratio to its parent node is shown

been processed, in the final step any remaining overlap is removed. For example, from the overlapping ideal nodes `sec4` and its descendant `sec4/p1` only the former is kept.

The resulting ideal recall-base contains the best elements to return to a user based on the assumptions that overlap between result nodes should be avoided and that the user's preferences are reflected within the employed quantisation function. The derived ideal recall-bases then form the basis for the ideal gain vectors for each topic.

While I is derived from the ideal recall-base, the gain vectors, G, for the runs under evaluation are based on the full recall-base in order to enable the scoring of near-miss components[3].

In order to obtain a given component's relevance score (both for I or G) at a given rank position, XCG defines the following result-list dependent relevance value (RV) function:

$$rv(c_i) = f(quant(assess(c_i))) \tag{4}$$

where $assess(c_i)$ is a function that returns the assessment value pair for the component c_i if given within the recall-base and $(e, s) = (0, 0)$ otherwise. The $rv(c_i)$ function then returns, for a not-yet-seen component c_i the quantised assessment value pair $quant(assess(c_i))$, where quant is a chosen quantisation functions, e.g. *sog*. In this case $f(x) = x$. For a component, which has been previously fully seen by the user, we have $rv(c_i) = (1 - \alpha) \cdot quant(assess(c_i))$, i.e. $f(x) = (1 - \alpha) \cdot x$. With α set to

[3] All relevant components of the full recall-base that are not included in the ideal recall-base are considered as near-misses.

1, the RV function returns 0 for a fully seen, hence redundant, component, reflecting that it represents no value to the user any more. Finally, if c_i has been seen only in part before (i.e. some descendant nodes have already been retrieved earlier in the ranking), then $rv(c_i)$ is calculated as:

$$rv(c_i) = \alpha \cdot \frac{\sum_{j=1}^{m} (rv(c_j) \cdot |c_j|)}{|c_i|} + (1 - \alpha) \cdot quant(assess(c_i)) \quad (5)$$

where m is the number of c_i's relevant child nodes.

In addition to the above, the final RV score is obtained by applying a normalisation function, which ensures that the total score for any group of descendant nodes of an ideal result element cannot exceed the score achievable if retrieving the ideal node itself. For example, in Figure 1 the two ideal result nodes within the ideal recall-base for the quantisation function *sog* are `sec4` and `sec6`. Since these results represent the best nodes for the user, a system returning these should be ranked above others. However, if another system retrieved all the leaf nodes, it may achieve a better overall score if the total RV score for these nodes exceeds that of the ideal nodes. For example, in Figure 1, the ideal node `sec4` has a score of 0.5, but the total score of its three child nodes is 2.05. The following normalisation function safeguards against this by ensuring that for any $c_j \in S$:

$$\sum_{c \in S} rv(c) \leq rv(c_{ideal}) \quad (6)$$

where S is the set of retrieved descendant nodes of the ideal node and where c_{ideal} is the ideal node that is on the same relevant path as c_j.

3 Evaluation Setup

3.1 What to Evaluate?

The evaluation of a metric requires a number of tests. Voorhees in [10] identifies two aspects to qualify an evaluation: fidelity and reliability. Fidelity reflects the extent to which an evaluation metric measures what it is intended to measure, while reliability is the extent to which the evaluation results can be trusted. In this paper we concentrate on the latter test. We take the viewpoint of [10] that in a comparative evaluation setting, reliability reflects "a metric's ability to rank a better system ahead of a worse system". This is, of course, highly dependent on a definition on what makes a system better or worse than another. The basis for such a decision lies within the user satisfaction criterion defined within the given retrieval task.

This criterion in the INEX CO track is (largely) defined by the task definition. According to this, within the CO task, the aim of an XML retrieval system is to point users to the specific relevant portions of documents, where the user's query contains no structural hints regarding what the most appropriate granularity of relevant XML elements may be. The evaluation of a system's effectiveness should hence provide a measure with respect to the system's ability in retrieving such components.

But what exactly are these "most appropriate" components? At the moment, we don't actually have an exact answer to this in INEX. Intuition dictates that users would prefer elements that contain as much relevant information and as little irrelevant information as possible. Therefore, given a set of possible retrievable components in an arbitrary document (such as an article in INEX), the best elements to return to the user should be those that are "most" exhaustive and "most" specific to the user's request[4]. However, given two relevant components, one highly exhaustive but only fairly specific ($(e, s) = (3, 2)$) and another which is only fairly exhaustive but highly specific ($(e, s) = (2, 3)$), which one should be regarded as better? The quantisation functions provide a flexible means for addressing this issue by allowing to model various sets of possible preferences, which can be adjusted according a given user model. Based on these preferences, it is then possible to identify the "best" components as those elements that score highest. For example, a user whose preferences are described by the *sog* quantisation function would prefer a $(e, s) = (2, 3)$ component to a $(e, s) = (3, 2)$.

Overall, systems should then rank these "best" components in decreasing order of their quantised scores, i.e. highest scoring elements should be ranked first. In addition, we reason that users do not want to be returned overlapping redundant elements, so systems should be either penalised or at least not rewarded for such redundancy.

Given a user satisfaction criterion, a simple method to evaluate a metric's reliability is to construct appropriate test data for which we can derive expectations as to what the metric's outcome should be and check if the expected output is indeed obtained. The expected output is in the form of rankings of systems that meets user expectations. A system ranking is simply an ordered list of runs sorted by decreasing value of effectiveness. For example, according to the user preference that non-overlapping results are preferred to overlapping ones, we would expect that from two systems producing respective result rankings, the former would be regarded as the better system by a reliable evaluation metric.

For our test data, we constructed a number of simulated runs, which are described next.

3.2 Simulated Runs

Each simulated run is populated with components derived from the full recall-base[5] of all INEX 2004 CO topics, where the selection and ordering of the result components in a run is according to the assumed set of user preferences as defined by the *sog* quantisation function (Equation 2). We constructed the following simulated runs:

***irb*:** a ranked result list derived from the ideal recall-base containing only ideal results selected according to the quantisation function *sog*, where the ordering of the components within the ranking is also according to *sog*. The selection of the ideal results follows the procedure described in Section 2.3. For example, if the relevant nodes in

[4] Note that most exhaustive and specific here **does not** equate to $(e, s) = (3, 3)$ nodes, but refers to the nodes with the highest available exhaustivity and specificity score. For example, it may be that amongst all the possible retrievable components in an article, the most exhaustive node is $e = 1$, or the most specific node is $s = 2$.

[5] We used v3.0 of the assessments file for INEX 2004: assessments-3.0.tar.gz.

Figure 1 would form our imaginary full recall-base, then we obtain the following result ranking for our *irb* run: {`sec6`, `sec4`}.

***frb*:** a run that contains all relevant components of the full recall-base, where the components are ordered by decreasing quantised value according to the quantisation function *sog*. E.g. for Figure 1, all shown nodes will be included as follows: {`sec6`, `sec6/p1`, `sec6/p2`, `sec6/ip12`, `sec4/p1`, `sec4/ip12`, `sec4`, `sec4/p2`, `bdy1`, `article1`}.

***ia*:** contains all ideal results and all their relevant ascendant nodes ordered by *sog*. E.g. from Figure 1, we obtain: {`sec6`, `sec4`, `bdy1`, `article1`}.

***id*:** contains all ideal results and all their relevant descendant nodes ordered by *sog*. E.g. from Figure 1, we get: {`sec6`, `sec6/p1`, `sec6/p2`, `sec6/ip12`, `sec4/p1`, `sec4/ip12`, `sec4`, `sec4/p2`}.

***lo*:** contains all relevant leaf nodes ordered by *sog*. E.g. from Figure 1, we get: {`sec6/p1`, `sec6/p2`, `sec6/ip12`, `sec4/p1`, `sec4/ip12`, `sec4/p2`}. Note that a leaf node here refers to leaf nodes on the relevant paths within an article, which may be non-leaf nodes within the article file itself (e.g. `sec[6]/p[2]` may have a number of irrelevant descendant nodes).

***ao*:** contains only relevant article nodes ordered by *sog*. E.g. from Figure 1, we get: {`article1`}.

3.3 Expected System Rankings

Based on the user preferences captured by the *sog* quantisation function, systems that return the best components (i.e. highest quantised-scoring elements) should be ranked above others. In addition, based on the intuition that users do not want to be inundated with multiple redundant, nested components, systems that return minimum amount of overlapping results would be preferred.

From these two assumptions, we can derive a relative ranking of simulated runs that should then be matched by a metric if it is to be proved reliable. From the latter assumption, we can reason that the runs should be ranked as follows:

$$irb\ (0\%) \succeq lo\ (0\%) \succeq ao\ (0\%) \succ id\ (57.9\%) \succ ia\ (70.7\%) \succ frb\ (77.5\%)$$

where the percentage values show the overlap ratio among result elements contained in a run and where $a \succ b$ signals that 'run a performs better than run b'.

Based on the quantisation function, a metric should rank those systems first that are able to return the best components. Since, the best components are defined by the quantised score of the quantisation function, without looking at the document collection and the actual relevance assessments we cannot safely predict much more than:

$$irb \succeq r$$

where $r \in \{lo, ao, id, ia, frb\}$. This is because the best scoring elements could be, e.g., the leaf or article nodes within a collection (depending entirely on the judgements of the assessor) in which case these runs (*lo*, *ao*) could achieve the same performance as *irb*.

With respect to the runs *id*, *ia*, *frb*, since *irb* is a subset of all these runs, the expectation is that they could possibly produce as good results as the ideal run, but never better.

The combination of the two user satisfaction criteria, if producing conflicting rankings, is currently an open question. It may be solved by defining the relative importance of the two aspects, which may be a parameter of a given user's model for XML retrieval. Within the XCG metrics, this issue is addressed by considering the overlap of result elements directly within the way the relevance scores are calculated (RV function) for a run.

3.4 Metric Reliability Tests

We evaluated each of the simulated runs using the two metrics[6]. The resulting graphs are shown in Figures 2 and 3.

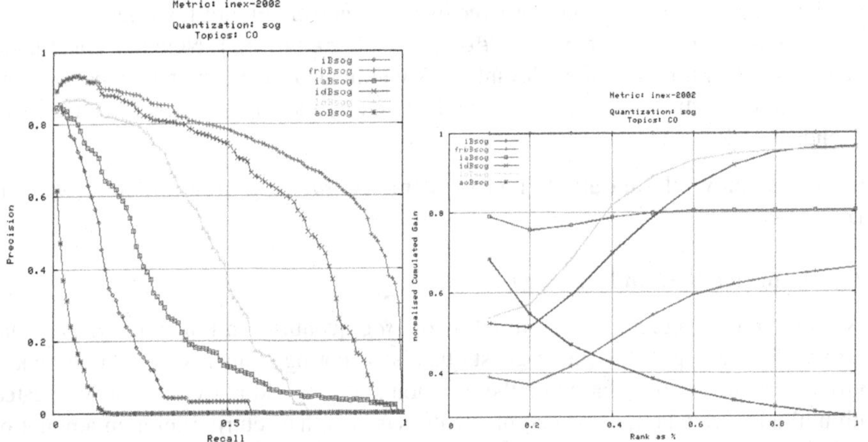

Fig. 2. Results of the inex-2002 metric

Fig. 3. Results of the nXCG metric

In order to obtain an overall ranking, we use the MAP measure for the inex-2002 metric and the mean average of the normalised cumulated gain values for nXCG (averaged over 10 rank % points). Table 1 summarises the results. The numbers in brackets show the achieved system (run) ranks.

For the inex-2002 metric, both the graph and the MAP results clearly illustrate that better effectiveness is achieved by systems that return not only the most desired components, but also their ascendant (*ia*) or descendant (*id*) elements, hence inundating users with redundant components. In fact, according this measure only the article-only run (*ao*) has worse performance than the ideal run (*irb*). Best performance is achieved by the run that returns the full recall-base (*frb*).

Looking at the results for the nXCG metric, we can see that best performance is achieved by the ideal run (*irb*), which is registered at a constant 1 normalised cumulated

---

[6] Throughout the paper, we used $\alpha = 1$ within the XCG metrics.

gain value (Figure 3). The worse performer is the article-only run (*ao*), followed by the full recall-base run (*frb*). The performance of the remaining runs (*ia*, *id* and *lo*) is evaluated as worse than the ideal, but better than the full recall-base run. Their relative performance to each other will vary depending on the collection and the recall-base.

Table 1. System Rankings produced by inex-2002 and nXCG, based on performance over all INEX 2004 CO topics. For inex-2002 the MAP is shown, for nXCG the mean average normalised cumulated gain (averaged over 10 rank % points) is shown. The numbers in brackets indicate the achieved rank

	inex-2002	nXCG
irb	0.1430 (5)	1.0000 (1)
frb	0.7437 (1)	0.5369 (5)
ia	0.2567 (4)	0.7936 (3)
id	0.6195 (2)	0.7790 (4)
lo	0.3944 (3)	0.8269 (2)
ao	0.0296 (6)	0.4096 (6)

What is clear from the above is that the inex-2002 metric cannot reflect true performance differences when systems return overlapping elements as these can artificially raise the performance indicator. The nXCG metric's ranking of systems, on the other hand, corresponds to the user satisfaction criterion: the retrieval of ideal nodes representing the best nodes for the user (in accordance with a given set of user preferences expressed within a chosen quantisation function) is rewarded, while the retrieval of near-misses is also considered. Systems that retrieve such near-misses can achieve good performances, but cannot surpass an ideal system's score.

In both graphs, the comparison of the article-only (*ao*), the leaf-only (*lo*) and the ideal (*irb*) runs gives an indication of the metrics' capabilities for ranking systems whose output contains no overlapping results. The article-only run achieves worst performance in both cases. With the inex-2002 metric, the ideal run is scored lower than the leaf-only run, while with the nXCG metric, although the leaf-only run's performance is the second best, it never beats the ideal run's effectiveness. This suggests that the inex-2002 metric is able to rank systems when no overlapping results are returned. However, the fact that the leaf-only run seems to perform better than the ideal run points to the need that a similar score-normalisation function to that described in Section 2.3 would be required.

3.5 Top Ten INEX CO Runs

In this section, we list the top ten INEX 2004 runs for both metrics as an indication of how the rankings are effected, see Tables 2 and 3. As it can be seen, amongst the top ten only the run by Carnegie Mellon University appears in both tables, although the University of Amsterdam and the University of Waterloo also appear in both, but with different runs (and one run by Queensland University of Technology is actually ranked 11th by nXCG).

It can be observed that runs with less overlap score better in nXCG, but overlap-free runs are not a sufficient condition for obtaining high values, but relevant nodes still need to be found. In fact, from the submitted 69 runs, a total of 18 runs have 0% overlap (while several other runs also have minimal overlap, e.g. 1% or less), but their average rank is only 41. There are a couple of runs, which nicely reflect the effect of overlap on the nXCG scores: e.g. the University of Amsterdam submitted these runs:

Table 2. Top ten INEX 2004 runs according to the inex-2002 metric, quant: sog, task: CO. The rank numbers in brackets indicate the rank obtained based on the nXCG metric

rank	Run	MAP	overlap %
1(27)	IBM Haifa Research Lab (CO-0.5-LAREFIENMENT)	0.1327	80.89
2(21)	IBM Haifa Research Lab (CO-0.5)	0.1274	81.46
3(18)	University of Amsterdam (UAms-CO-T-FBack)	0.1060	81.85
4(10)	LTI, Carnegie Mellon University (Lemur_CO_KStem_Mix02_Shrink01)	0.0941	73.02
5(28)	IBM Haifa Research Lab (CO-0.5-Clustering)	0.0923	81.10
6(26)	LTI, Carnegie Mellon University (Lemur_CO_NoStem_Mix02_Shrink01)	0.0879	74.82
7(11)	Queensland University of Technology (CO_PS_Stop50K_049_025)	0.0839	71.06
8(31)	Queensland University of Technology (CO_PS_099_049)	0.0803	76.81
9(29)	Queensland University of Technology (CO_PS_Stop50K_099_049)	0.0784	75.89
10(25)	University of Waterloo (Waterloo-Baseline)	0.0781	76.32

Table 3. Top ten INEX 2004 runs according to the nXCG metric, quant: sog, task: CO The rank numbers in brackets indicate the rank obtained based on the inex-2002 metric

rank	Run	MAnCG	overlap %
1(40)	University of Tampere (UTampere_CO_average)	0.3725	0
2(42)	University of Tampere (UTampere_CO_fuzzy)	0.3699	0
3(41)	University of Amsterdam (UAms-CO-T-FBack-NoOverl)	0.3519	0
4(34)	Oslo University College (4-par-co)	0.3418	0.07
5(25)	University of Tampere (UTampere_CO_overlap)	0.3328	39.58
6(27)	LIP6 (bn-m1-eqt-porder-eul-o.df.t-parameters-00700)	0.3247	74.31
7(23)	University of California, Berkeley (Berkeley_CO_FUS_T_CMBZ_FDBK)	0.3182	50.22
8(43)	University of Waterloo (Waterloo-Filtered)	0.3181	13.35
9(22)	LIP6 (bn-m2-eqt-porder-o.df.t-parameters-00195)	0.3098	64.2
10(4)	LTI, Carnegie Mellon University (Lemur_CO_KStem_Mix02_Shrink01)	0.2953	73.02

UAms-CO-T-FBack (81.85% overlap) and UAms-CO-T-FBack-NoOverl (0% overlap), which are scored as 0.2636 and 0.3521, respectively. Another example may be the runs submitted by the University of Tampere (see Table 3). On the other hand, the runs submitted by RMIT: Hybrid_CRE (82.12% overlap), Hybrid_CRE_specific (0% overlap) and Hybrid_CRE_general (0% overlap) achieve scores of 0.2791, 0.2576 and 0.2540, respectively. The drop in effectiveness score suggests that when reducing overlap, the higher scoring nodes were actually removed from the ranking, leaving lower scoring nodes in the ranking and (presumably) filling the rest of the ranks with irrelevant nodes (provided the three runs are produced from the same baseline, of course).

Note that a detailed analysis of the system rankings produced by the two metrics is planned for a separate paper.

4 Conclusions

In this paper we investigated how closely the output of the two metrics, inex-2002 and nXCG, reflect the user satisfaction criteria defined within the INEX CO task. The results confirm the weaknesses of the inex-2002 metric reported in [4, 5], but show that with an appropriate quantisation function (e.g. when leaf nodes represent the best nodes) or with an arbitrary quantisation function when combined with a normalisation method, the inex-2002 metric is able to produce system rankings that match the evaluation criteria, provided no overlapping results are returned by the systems.

We also described and further developed the XCG metrics, which produced promising results in our metric reliability test. A weakness of the XCG metrics, however, is that they produce effectiveness scores for a given rank (or rank %) and not for recall. To address this issue, Gabriella Kazai is currently working on a version of the metric that is able to give recall related performance indicators. She is also working on an extension of the generalised Precion and Recall measures introduced in [7]. These will be published in the near future.

In the future, we also hope to be able to derive better user models and hence arrive at more accurate user satisfaction criteria based on the outcome of the INEX 2004 interactive track.

References

1. W. Cooper. Expected search length: A single measure of retrieval effectiveness based on the weak ordering action of retrieval systems. *American Documentation*, 19(1):30–41, 1968.
2. N. Gövert and G. Kazai. Overview of the INitiative for the Evaluation of XML Retrieval (INEX) 2002. In N. Fuhr, N. Gövert, G. Kazai, and M. Lalmas, editors, *Proceedings of the First Workshop of the INitiative for the Evaluation of XML Retrieval (INEX). Dagstuhl, Germany, December 8–11, 2002*, ERCIM Workshop Proceedings, pages 1–17, Sophia Antipolis, France, March 2003. ERCIM. http://www.ercim.org/publication/ws-proceedings/INEX2002.pdf.
3. K. Järvelin and J. Kekäläinen. Cumulated Gain-based evaluation of IR techniques. *ACM Transactions on Information Systems (ACM TOIS)*, 20(4):422–446, 2002.
4. G. Kazai. Report of the inex 2003 metrics working group. In N. Fuhr, M. Lalmas, and S. Malik, editors, *Proceedings of the 2nd Workshop of the INitiative for the Evaluation of XML retrieval (INEX), Dagstuhl, Germany, December 2003*, pages 184–190, April 2004.
5. G. Kazai, M. Lalmas, and A. de Vries. The overlap problem in content-oriented XML retrieval evaluation. In *Proceedings of the 27th Annual International ACM SIGIR Conference on Research and Development in Information Retrieval, Sheffield, UK, 2004.*, pages 72–79. ACM, July 2004.
6. G. Kazai, S. Masood, and M. Lalmas. A study of the assessment of relevance for the inex'02 test collection. In *Advances in Information Retrieval, Proceedings of the 26th European Conference on IR Research (ECIR), Sunderland, UK*, Lecture Notes in Computer Science. Springer, April 2004.

7. J. Kekäläinen and K. Järvelin. Using graded relevance assessments in IR evaluation. *Journal of the American Society for Information Science and Technology*, 53(13):1120–1129, 2002.
8. V. Raghavan, P. Bollmann, and G. Jung. A critical investigation of recall and precision. *ACM Transactions on Information Systems*, 7(3):205–229, 1989.
9. T. Tombros, B. Larsen, and S. Malik. The interactive track at INEX 2004. In N. Fuhr, M. Lalmas, S. Malik, and Z. Szlavik, editors, *Proceedings of the 3rd Workshop of the INitiative for the Evaluation of XML retrieval (INEX), Dagstuhl, Germany, December 2004*, 2005.
10. E. M. Voorhees. Overview of the TREC 2003 question answering track. In *Text REtrieval Conference, Gaithersburg*, 2003.

Component Ranking and Automatic Query Refinement for XML Retrieval

Yosi Mass and Matan Mandelbrod

IBM Research Lab,
Haifa 31905, Israel
{yosimass, matan}@il.ibm.com

Abstract. Queries over XML documents challenge search engines to return the most relevant XML components that satisfy the query concepts. In a previous work we described a component ranking algorithm that performed relatively well in INEX'03. In this paper we show an improvement to that algorithm by introducing a document pivot that compensates for missing terms statistics in small components. Using this new algorithm we achieved improvements of 30%-50% in the Mean Average Precision over the previous algorithm. We then describe a general mechanism to apply known Query Refinement algorithms from traditional IR on top of this component ranking algorithm and demonstrate an example such algorithm that achieved top results in INEX'04.

1 Introduction

While in traditional IR we are used to get back entire documents for queries, the challenge in XML retrieval is to return the most relevant components that satisfy the query concepts. The INEX initiative[4] sub classified this task into two sub tasks; Content only (CO) task and Content and Structure (CAS) task. In a CO task the user specifies queries in free text and the search engine is supposed to return the most relevant XML components that satisfy the query concepts. In a CAS task the user can limit query concepts to particular XML tags and to define the desired component to be returned using XPath[11] extended with an about() predicate.

In order to realize the problem in ranking XML components we first examine a typical class of IR engines that use *tf-idf* [8] to perform document ranking. Those engines maintain an inverted index in which they keep for each term among other things the number of documents in which it appears (*df*) and its number of occurrences in each document in the collection (*tf*). These statistics are then used to estimate the relevance of a document to the query by measuring some distance between the two. To be able to return a component instead of a full document search engines should modify their data structures to keep statistics such as *tf-idf* at the component level instead of at the document level. This is not a straight forward extension since components in XML are nested and the problem is how to keep statistics at the component level such that it handles components nesting correctly.

In INEX'03 we described a method [6] for component ranking by creating separate indices for the most informative component types in the collection. For example we

N. Fuhr et al. (Eds.): INEX 2004, LNCS 3493, pp. 73 – 84, 2005.

created an index for full articles, an index for all sections, for all paragraphs etc. This approach solved the problem of statistics of nested components since in each index we have now components from same granularity so they are not nested. While this approach solved the problem of nested components it introduced a deficiency that could distort index statistics. The problem is that the fine grained indices lack data that is outside their scope which is not indexed at all. For example the *articles* index contains 42,578,569 tokens while the *paragraphs* index contains only 31,988,622 tokens. This means that in the *paragraphs* index ~25% of the possible statistics is missing so for example a term with a low *df* based on the indexed tokens may actually be quite frequent outside the paragraphs so its actual *df* should be higher.

In this paper we describe a method to compensate for this deficiency using document pivot. Using this method we got a consistent improvement of 30%–50% in the mean average precision (MAP) for both INEX'03 and INEX'04 CO topics. On top of this improvement we achieved further improvement by applying Automatic Query Refinement (AQR) to the component ranking algorithm. AQR was studied in [7] in the context of traditional IR engines. The idea there is to run the query in two rounds where highly ranked results from the first round are used to add new query terms and to reweigh the original query terms for the second round. We show how to adopt such AQR algorithms on top of the XML component ranking algorithm.

The paper is organized as follows – in section 2 we describe the document pivot concept and in section 3 we describe how to adopt AQR methods from traditional IR to XML retrieval systems. In section 4 we describe our inverted index and our CO and CAS runs. We conclude in section 5 with discussion of the approaches and with future directions.

2 Component Ranking with Document Pivot

We start by briefing our component ranking approach from INEX'03 as described in [6] and then we show how it was improved using the document pivot concept. As discussed above the problem in XML component ranking is how to keep statistics at the component level such that it handles components nesting correctly. In [6] we solved that problem by creating different indices for the most informative component types. We created an index for articles, index for sections, index for sub sections and index for paragraphs. For simplicity we discuss now our approach for the CO topics.

For a given CO topic we run the query in parallel on the set of indices and get back a result set from each index with components of that index sorted by the relevance score. So we get a sorted list of articles, a sorted list of section and so on. We then described a method for comparing the different result sets so that we can merge the sets into a single sorted list of all component types. Why do we get different scores in each result set? Our scoring method is based on the vector space model where both the query Q and each document *d* are mapped to vectors in the terms space and the relevance of *d* to Q is measured as the cosine between them using the *tf-idf* statistics as described in Fig. 1 below.

$$score(Q,d) = \frac{\sum_{t_i \in Q \cap d} w_Q(t_i) * w_d(t_i) * idf(t_i)}{\|Q\| * \|d\|}$$

$$w_Q(t) = \frac{\log(TF_Q(t))}{\log(AvgTF_Q)} \qquad w_D(t) = \frac{\log(TF_d(t))}{\log(AvgTF_d)}$$

$$idf(t) = \log(\frac{\#DocumentsIntheCollection}{\#DocumentsContaining(t)})$$

Fig. 1. Document scoring function

$TF_Q(t)$ is the number of occurrences of t in Q and $TF_d(t)$ is the number of occurrences of t in d.

$AvgTF_Q$ is the average number of occurrence of all query terms in Q and $AvgTF_d$ is the average number of occurrence of all terms in d.

$\|Q\|$ is the number of unique terms in Q and $\|d\|$ is the number of unique terms in d, both scaled by the average document length in the collection.

It can be seen that while scores of components in each index are comparable to each other, scores in different indices are at a different scale. For example the *articles* index has 12,107 components so the *idf* of a relatively rare term is not very large compared to its *idf* in the *paragraphs* index which has 646,216 components. In addition the average document length (number of unique tokens) in the *articles* index is 900 while the average document length in the *paragraphs* index is 37. Since $\|d\|$ and $\|Q\|$ are scaled by the average document length then the denominator of scores in the *paragraphs* index is much lower than in the *articles* index. Combining the *idf* difference and the length normalization difference shows why scores of components in the *paragraphs* index are much higher than scores of components in the *articles* index.

In order to compare the scores in different result sets we described in [6] a normalization formula that ensures absolute numbers that are index independent. This is achieved by each index computing *score(Q,Q)* which is the score of the query itself as if it was a document in the collection. Since the score measures the cosine between vectors, then the max value is expected between two identical vectors. Each index therefore normalizes all its scores to its computed *score(Q,Q)*. The normalized results are then merged into a single ranked list consisting of components of all granularities.

While the approach of creating independent indices solved the problem of overlapping data it introduced another deficiency of missing data. The fine grained indices lack data that is outside their scope which is not indexed. For example the *articles* index contains 42,578,569 tokens while the *paragraphs* index contains only 31,988,622 tokens. The missing data in the fine grained indices can distorts the *idf* statistics of the collection and therefore may affect the quality of the results.

To fix that problem we use this year a concept first mentioned in [9] which uses a document pivot (DocPivot) factor to scale the final component score by the score of its containing article. The final score of a component with original score S_c and with its full article score S_a is then

DocPivot * S_a + (1 – DocPivot) * S_c.

Note that the idea of Pivoted document length normalization was first introduced in [10] but it was mentioned there in the context of normalizing scores inside a single index. We do apply pivoted normalization on ||Q||, ||d|| to compute Score(Q,d) as in Fig.1. on each index separately but we need the new DocPivot concept to scale results between the separate indices.

Assuming that the full *articles* index is the first index then the overall algorithm to return a result set for a given query Q is given in Fig. 2 below. Step c is the new step introduced by the DocPivot.

1 For each index i
   a. Compute the result set Res_i of running Q on index i
   b. Normalize scores in Res_i to [0,1] by normalizing to score(Q,Q)
   c. Scale each score by its containing article score from Res_0
2 Merge all Res_i's to a single result set Res composed of all components sorted by their score

Fig. 2. Component ranking algorithm

We experimented with several values of DocPivot on the 2003 CO topics using the inex_eval tool [5] with strict metric[1] and got the graph marked as 2003 in Fig. 3 below.

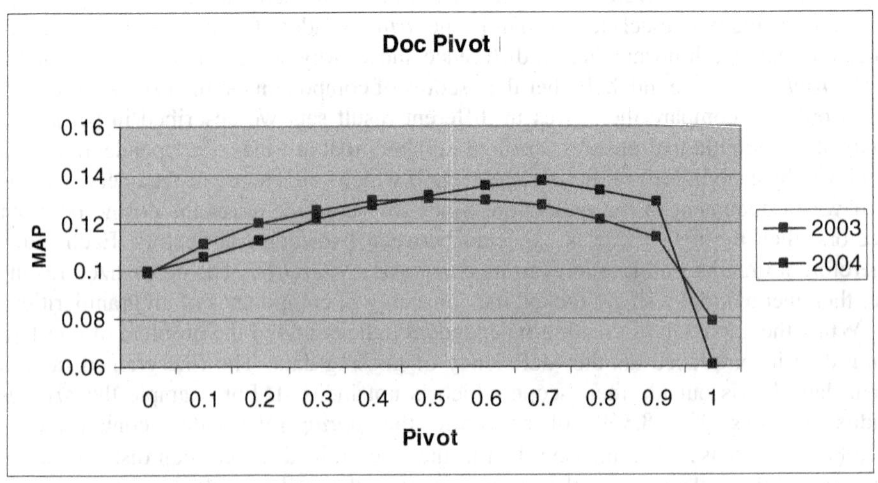

Fig. 3. Doc pivot on 2003/2004 data

[1] The strict metric considers only elements that were assessed as highly relevant.

The MAP with DocPivot = 0 is the result we achieved in our 2003 official submission. We can see that with DocPivot=0.5 we get improvements of 31% over the base 2003 run so we used that value for our 2004 runs.

Later when the 2004 assessments were available we tried those values on the 2004 CO topics using the same metric and got the best MAP for DocPivot = 0.7 (the 2004 graph in Fig. 3) which is 52% improvements over the base run with no DocPivot.

3 Automatic Query Refinement for XML

In this section we describe how to apply Automatic Query Refinement (AQR) on top of our XML component ranking algorithm. AQR was studied in [7] in the context of traditional IR engines. The idea is to run the query in two rounds where highly ranked results from the first round are used to add new query terms and to reweigh the original query terms for the second round. We show now a method to adopt such AQR algorithms on top of our XML component ranking algorithm.

Assume we have an AQR algorithm that can be used to refine query results. Since we have separate indices for different component granularities we can run the AQR algorithm on each index separately. The modified XML component ranking algorithm is described in Figure-4.

1 For each index i
   a. Compute the result set Res_i of running Q on index i
   b. Apply AQR algorithm on Res_i
   c. Normalize scores in Res_i to [0,1] by normalizing to score(Q,Q)
   d. Scale each score by its containing article score from Res_0
2 Merge all Res_i's to a single result set Res composed of all components sorted by their score

Fig. 4. Component ranking with AQR

We add step 1.b which is the query refinement step and the rest of the algorithm continues as in the simple case by normalizing and scaling scores in each index and finally merging the result sets.

We describe now a specific AQR algorithm that we used in INEX'04 and discuss some variants of its usage in our XML component ranking algorithm. The AQR algorithm we used is described in [2]. The idea there is to add Lexical Affinity (LA) terms to the query where a Lexical Affinity is a pair of terms that appear close to each other in some relevant documents such that exactly one of the terms appears in the query. The AQR is based on the information gain (IG) obtained by adding lexical affinities to the query. The IG of a lexical affinity L on a set of documents D with respect to a query Q denotes how much L separates the relevant documents in D from the non relevant documents for the query Q. IG is defined as:

$$IG_{Q,D}(L) = H_Q(D) - \left[\frac{|D^+|}{|D|} H_Q(D^+) + \frac{|D^-|}{|D|} H_Q(D^-) \right]$$

Fig. 5. Information Gain of a Lexical Affinity

where $D^+ \subseteq D$ is the set of documents containing L and $D^- \subseteq D$ is the set of documents not containing L. $H_Q(X)$ is the entropy (or degree of disorder) of a set of documents X and is defined as

$$H_Q(X) = -p_Q(X)\log(P_Q(X)) - (1 - p_Q(X))\log(1 - p_Q(X))$$

Fig. 6. Entropy of a group

where $p_Q(X)$ is defined as the probability of a document chosen randomly from X to be relevant to Q. Let $R^+ \subseteq D^+$ be the set of relevant documents in D^+ then $p_Q(D^+) = |R^+|/|D^+|$ and similarly $p_Q(D^-) = |R^-|/|D^-|$. The problem is that we don't know R^+ and R^- so we use the scoring function as an approximation for $p_Q(D^+)$ ($p_Q(D^-)$. We take $p_Q(D^+)$ to be sum of scores of documents in D^+ (a score is between 0 and 1) divided by the max sum of score they could get which is $|D^+|$. We do the same estimation for $p_Q(D^-)$. Note that $H_Q(D)$ is independent of L so to compare the IG of two LAs we don't have to compute it.

The AQR procedure works as follows: It gets the result set obtained by running the search engine on the query Q (algorithm step 1 in Figure-4) and additional 4 parameters ***(M, N, K, a)*** that are explained below. The AQR first constructs a list of candidate LAs that appear in the top ***M*** highly ranked documents from the result set. Then it takes D to be the set of the top ***N*** (N >> M) highly rank documents and finds the ***K*** LAs with the highest IG on that set D. Those LAs are then added to the query Q and their contribution to *score(Q, d)* for each d is calculated as given by Fig. 1. So for each such new LA we need to calculate its $w_Q(t) * w_d(t) * idf(t)$. Since the added LAs don't appear in the original query Q we take their $TF_Q(t)$ to be the given parameter ***a*** so $w_Q(t) = \alpha / \log(AvgTF_Q)$ for the newly added LAs. We can have several variants for using the above AQR algorithm in the XML component ranking algorithm.

1. The AQR procedure can be applied on each index separately using same (M, N, K, α) parameters or index specific (M, N, K, α) parameters. In this variant different LAs are added to the query for each index.

2. We can apply the first part of the AQR using (M, N, K) on the full *articles* index to find the best LAs. Then apply the last part of the AQR that does the re ranking (with the parameter α) on each index. using the LAs that were extracted from the *articles* index.

The motivation for the 2nd variant is that most informative LAs can be obtained on the full *articles* index since it has the full collection data. In section 4 we describe the (M, N, K, α) parameters used in our runs.

4 Runs Description

We describe now our indices setup and the runs we submitted for the CO, CAS and NLP tracks.

4.1 Index Description

Similar to last year[6] we have created six inverted indices for the most informative components which are {article, sec, ss1, ss2, {p+ip1}, abs}. We removed XML tags from all indices except from the {article} index where they were used for checking CAS topic constraints. Content was stemmed using a Porter stemmer and components with content smaller than 15 tokens[2] were not indexed in their corresponding index.

4.2 CO Runs

Each CO topic has 4 parts : <title>, <description>, <narrative> and <keywords>. This year we could use only the <title> for formulating the query to our search engine. Due to the loosely interpretation of topics as appear in [5] we ignored '+' on terms and we ignored phrase boundaries and instead we use the phrase's terms as regular terms. We still treated '-' terms strictly namely components with '-' terms were never returned.

For example topic 166

```
<title>+"tree edit distance" + XML - image </title>
```

is executed as

```
tree edit distance XML -image
```

We submitted three runs where two of them were ranked 1st and 2nd among the official INEX CO runs. See table 1 below.

4.2.1 Doc Pivot Run

In the run titled CO-0.5 we implemented the Component ranking algorithm as described in Figure-2 using DocPivot=0.5. This run was ranked 2nd in the aggregate metric.

4.2.2 AQR Run

In the run titled CO-0.5-LAREFIENMENT we implemented our AQR algorithm from Figure-4 using M= 20, N = 100, K = 5 and α = 0.9 on all indices. We have imple-

[2] We count 15 tokens without tags. This is roughly equivalent to counting 20 tokens with the tags which is a magic number we used last year and that was used by some other participants.

mented the first algorithm variant where each index computes its own LAs to add. This run was ranked 1st using the CO aggregate metric. We leave for future work experiments with more parameter settings with the two algorithm variants.

Table 1. CO table

TASK:CO			
rank	**Institute**	**avg**	**overlap(%)**
1.	IBM Haifa Research Lab(CO-0.5-LAREFIENMENT)	0.1437	80.89
2.	IBM Haifa Research Lab(CO-0.5)	0.1340	81.46
3.	University of Waterloo(Waterloo-Baseline)	0.1267	76.32
4.	University of Amsterdam(UAms-CO-T-FBack)	0.1174	81.85
5.	University of Waterloo(Waterloo-Expanded)	0.1173	75.62
6.	Queensland University of Technology(CO_PS_Stop50K_099_049)	0.1073	75.89
7.	Queensland University of Technology(CO_PS_099_049)	0.1072	76.81
8.	IBM Haifa Research Lab(CO-0.5-Clustering)	0.1043	81.10
9.	University of Amsterdam(UAms-CO-T)	0.1030	71.96
10.	LIP6(simple)	0.0921	64.29

Some example LAs that were added to queries:

1. For topic 162:
   Text and Index Compression Algorithms
   We got LA pairs (compress, huffman), (compress, gigabyte), (index, loss).
2. For topic 169:
   +"Query expansion" +"relevance feedback" +web
   We got (query, search), (relevance, search), (query, user), (query, result).

4.3 CAS Runs

We applied an automatic translation from XPath[11] to XML Fragments[1] which is the query language used in our search engine. XML Fragments are well-formed XML segments enhanced with

- '+/-' on XML tags and on content
- Phrases on content (" ")
- Parametric search on XML tag's value
- An empty tag (<>) that is used as parenthesis.

We can view any XML Fragment query as a tree[3] with the semantics that at each query node, '+' children must appear, '-' children should not appear and others are optional and only contribute to ranking. If a node doesn't have '+' children then at least one of its other (non '-') children must appear.

For example the query

```
<article>
    <abs>classification</abs>
    <sec>experiment compare</sec>
</article>
```

will return articles with *classification* under <abs> **or** with *experiment* or *compare* under <sec>. Note that the default semantics in XML Fragments is OR unless there are '+'s.

The same query with '+' on the tags -

```
<article>
    +<abs>classification</abs>
    +<sec>experiment compare</sec>
</article>
```

will return articles with *classification* under <abs> **and** with *experiment* or *compare* under <sec>.

Finally the query

```
<article>
    +<abs>classification</abs>
    <sec>experiment compare</sec>
</article>
```

will return only articles with *classification* under <abs>. Articles with *experiment* or *compare* under <sec> will be returned with higher ranking since the child <sec>experiment compare</sec> is optional.

The empty tag is used as a kind of parenthesis so the query

```
<title>
    <>+network +security</>
    <>+database +attributes</>
</title>
```

will return documents with *network* and *security* **or** with *database* and *attributes* under the <title> while the query

---

[3] For a query given as several disjoint fragments we add a dummy <root> node to make the all query a valid XML data.

```
<title>
    +<>network security</>
    +<>database attributes</>
</title>
```

will return documents with *network* or *security* **and** with *database* or *attributes* under its <title>.

The automatic transformation from an INEX modified XPath expression of the form

```
//path1[path1Predicates]//path2[path2Predicates]
```

to XML Fragments works as follows: It first creates a query node <path1> with two children: The first is a mandatory empty tag (+<>) surrounding path1Predicates and the second is the node <path2> prefixed with a '+'. The path1 and path2 Predicates are translated to nodes where 'about' predicates for the current node *('about(,. "text")')* are transformed to just *text* and about predicates for sibling nodes *('about(//path, "text")')* are transformed to *<path>text</path>*. For example the INEX CAS topic 131

```
<title>//article[about(.//au,"Jiawei Han")]//abs[about(.,"data mining")]</title>
```

is translated to the following XML Fragments query.

```
+<article>
   +<>
    <au>"jiawei han"</au>
   </>
   +<abs>
    +<>
         "data mining"
        "</>
   </abs>
</article>
```

To support AND/OR between XPath predicates we use the empty tag where predicates that are ANDed are transformed to XML Fragments under '+<>' tag and predicates that are ORed are transformed to XML Fragments under <> with no prefix. For example topic 134.

```
<title>//article[(about(.,"phrase search") OR about(.,"proximity search") OR
                    about(., "string matching")) AND
                (about(.,tries) OR about(.,"suffix trees") OR
                     about(.,"PAT arrays"))]//sec[about(.,algorithm)]
</title>
```

is transformed to

```
<article>
  +<>
   +<>
      <>"phrase search"</>
      <>"proximity search"</>
      <>"string matching"</>
   </>
   +<>
      <>"tries"</>
      <>"suffix trees"</>
      <>"pat arrays"</>
   </>
  </>
```

```
        +<sec>
          +<>algorithm</>
        </sec>
</article>
```

The interpretation of structure constraints in a CAS topic can vary from *Strict* interpretation (SCAS) where all structure constraints should be met to a loosely *Vague* interpretation (VCAS) where structure constraints are just a hint. In this year it was decided to follow the later VCAS flavor so in our runs we ignored the '+' on tags and similar to the CO case we ignored '+' on content and phrase boundaries. Ignoring '+' changes everything to OR semantics therefore the empty tags have no meaning and can be ignored. For example the above topic 131 is then equivalent to

```
<article>
        <au>jiawei han</au>
        <abs>data mining</abs>
</article>
```

We still keep the XML Fragments semantics that nodes with a single child must have that child so the above query will return only results which have *jiawei* or *han* under <au> or that have *data* or *mining* under the <abs>.

To decide which element to return we followed the XPath target element semantics that defines the last element in the XPath expression as the element to be returned up to the equivalent tags as defined in [5]. We run the CAS topics using a minor modification of step 1 in the algorithm in Figure-2 above: The *articles* index in addition to creating its result set also check the query constraints and mark valid components to be returned. The other indices then return in their results set only components that were marked valid by the *articles* index.

Obeying the target element constraint resulted in a low 38% overlap and as a result our official run got low MAP of 0.065 in the aggregate inex_eval metric[5]. It seems like assessors ignored the target elements as for example in the above topic 131 while <abs> was defined as the target element still many full articles were assessed as most relevant for that topic. Later we tried to weakness the target element constraint and return more elements and we got much better results of 0.120 MAP.

4.4 NLP Runs

We submitted one CO run and one CAS run. For the CO run we used the topic's <description> part and just applied the algorithm from Figure-2 with DocPivot=0.5. This run got MAP of 0.1286 using the aggregate inex_eval metrics[5]. For the CAS run we similarly used the topic's <description> with same DocPivot=0.5 but ignored the XPath target element as if it was a CO topic. This run got MAP of 0.05.

5 Discussion

We have presented two extensions to our last year's XML component ranking algorithm. The first extension introduces a document pivot that scales scores of components by the score of their containing article. This method achieved improvements of 31% over our base CO run in INEX'03 and 52% over our base CO run in INEX'04.

We then described an algorithm to apply existing AQR algorithms on top of our XML component ranking algorithm and demonstrated an example such AQR method using Lexical Affinities with Maximal Information Gain. Our two runs that implemented those extensions were ranked 1st and 2nd in the CO track. The space of possible AQR parameter combinations and the variants for their usage in XML is quite large and we still have to explore the best combination that would give best results. For Vague CAS (VCAS) we still need to find the correct balance of how much to constrain the structure and the target element. Some initial tests already improved our MAP by an order of magnitude over our official runs.

Acknowledgement

We would like to thank the INEX organizers for the assessment tool and for the inex_eval tool they have supplied.

References

1. Broder A.Z., Maarek Y., Mandelbrod M. and Y. Mass (2004): "Using XML to Query XML – From Theory to Practice". In Proceedings of RIAO'04, Avignon France, Apr , 2004.
2. Carmel D., Farchi E., Petruschka Y., Soffer A.: Automatic Query Refinement using Lexical Affinities with Maximal Information Gain. In Proceedings of the 25th Annual International ACM SIGIR Conference on Research and Development in Information Retrieval, 2002.
3. Carmel D., Maarek Y., Mandelbrod M., Mass Y., Soffer A.: Searching XML Documents via XML Fragments, In Proceedings of the 26th Annual International ACM SIGIR Conference on Research and Development in Information Retrieval, Toronto, Canada, Aug. 2003
4. INEX, Initiative for the Evaluation of XML Retrieval, http://inex.is.informatik.uni-duisburg.de
5. INEX'04 Participants area, http://inex.is.informatik.uni-duisburg.de:2004/internal/
6. Mass Y., Mandelbrod M.: Retrieving the most relevant XML Component, Proceedings of the Second Workshop of the Initiative for The Evaluation of XML Retrieval (INEX), 15-17 December 2003, Schloss Dagstuhl, Germany, pg 53-58
7. Ruthven I., Lalmas M. : A survey on the use of relevance feedback for information access systems, Knowledge Engineering Review, 18(1):2003.
8. Salton G. : Automatic Text Processing – The Transformation, Analysis and Retrieval of Information by Computer, Addison Wesley Publishing Company, Reading, MA, 1989.
9. Sigurbjornsson B., Kamps J., Rijke M. : An element based approach to XML Retrieval, Proceedings of the Second Workshop of the Initiative for The Evaluation of XML Retrieval (INEX), 15-17 December 2003, Schloss Dagstuhl, Germany, pg 19-26.
10. Singhal A., Buckley C., Mitra M.. : Pivoted document length normalization, *Proceedings of SIGIR'96,* pp 21--29, 1996.
11. XPath – XML Path Language (XPath) 2.0, http://www.w3.org/TR/xpath2

MultiText Experiments for INEX 2004

Charles L.A. Clarke and Philip L. Tilker

School of Computer Science, University of Waterloo, Canada
{claclark, pltilker}@plg.uwaterloo.ca

1 Introduction

This is the first year that the MultiText Group participated in INEX, submitting three runs for the content-only adhoc retrieval task. To generate these runs, we combined our existing experience and tools with the advice and ideas found in recent INEX papers [4, 1] to engineer a solid system capable of performing the basic task in a reasonable fashion.

2 Retrieval Methods

All runs used a version of the Okapi BM25 measure, augmented and tuned to meet the requirements of an XML retrieval task. One run (`Waterloo-Baseline`) used only the basic method, a second run (`Waterloo-Expanded`) added pseudo-relevance feedback, and a third (`Waterloo-Filtered`) added filtering to reduce overlap.

2.1 Basic Method

The MultiText system supports a number of facilities for querying XML and other structured document types, including generalized support for Okapi BM25 queries of the form

`rank` X `by` Y

where X is a sub-query specifying a set of document elements to be ranked and Y is a vector of sub-queries specifying individual retrieval terms.

For our INEX 2004 runs, the sub-query X specified a list of the following "acceptable" tags:

`sec p article ss1 bdy bb ip1 ss2 vt abs fig app bm li fm`

This list of acceptable tags was created manually from the collection and the 2003 relevance judgments, and only components with these tags were returned by the retrieval system. An acceptable tag identifies components that occur frequently in the collection, have a reasonable average length, and have many positive relevance judgments associated with them. Since the list was created manually, no specific thresholds were set for these criteria.

N. Fuhr et al. (Eds.): INEX 2004, LNCS 3493, pp. 85–87, 2005.

In general, terms in Y may be complex, containing proximity and structural constraints. However, for INEX 2004, Y was derived from the topic title simply by eliminating stopwords and negative terms (those starting with "-"), splitting phrases, and stemming the remaining terms with the Porter stemmer. For example, the title from topic 166

```
+"tree edit distance" + XML - image
```

became the four-term query

```
"$tree" "$edit" "$distance" "$xml"
```

where the "$" operator within a quoted string stems the term that follows it.

Our implementation of Okapi BM25 is based on the description of Robertson et al. [5] with parameter settings of $b = 0.80$, $k_1 = 10$, $k_2 = 0$ and $k_3 = \infty$. The values chosen for k_1 and b were the result of tuning over the INEX 2003 topics and judgments. The other parameter values are standard for our system. Specifically, given a term set Q, a component x is assigned the score

$$\sum_{t \in Q} w^{(1)} q_t \frac{(k_1 + 1)x_t}{K + x_t} \tag{1}$$

where

$$\begin{aligned} w^{(1)} &= \log\left(\frac{D - D_t + 0.5}{D_t + 0.5}\right) \\ D &= \text{number of documents in the corpus} \\ D_t &= \text{number of documents containing } t \\ q_t &= \text{frequency that } t \text{ occurs in the topic} \\ x_t &= \text{frequency that } t \text{ occurs in } x \\ K &= k_1((1 - b) + b \cdot l_x / l_{avg}) \\ l_x &= \text{length of } x \\ l_{avg} &= \text{average document length} \end{aligned}$$

For the purposes of computing D and D_t, a document was defined to be an `article`, and these term statistics were used for ranking all element types. After retrieval the results were filtered to eliminate very short elements (under 25 words) and elements with unusual path expressions, those with forms that did not appear in the INEX 2003 relevant set.

2.2 Pseudo-Relevance Feedback

Two runs (`Waterloo-Expanded` and `Waterloo-Filtered`) augmented this basic method with pseudo-relevance feedback. For both runs, we used the QAP passage-retrieval algorithm [2,3] to generate the top 25 passages from the INEX collection and the top 40 passages from a large Web collection. The top terms were extracted from these passages, re-weighted and added to the original query. In most respects we followed the procedure for our TREC Robust Track experiments described in the MultiText TREC 2003 paper [3], which may be consulted for further details.

2.3 Filtering for Element Overlap

In addition to pseudo-relevance feedback, one of our runs (`Waterloo-Filtered`) extended the basic method with filtering to reduce overlap. An element was eliminated from the final ranked list if it was entirely contained within a higher ranked element, or if it contained a higher ranked element covering at least 80% of its contents.

3 Results and Conclusion

For INEX 2004, our primary goal was to successfully complete the basic adhoc task, and we believe that we have satisfied this goal. Overall, we performed well under most measures, but we achieved our best performance under those quantization functions that emphasized exhaustivity, Unfortunately, both pseudo-relevance feedback and overlap filtering had a negative impact on performance. We were surprised by this result, and in future we plan to investigate this issue. Next year we hope to extend our participation to include other INEX tasks.

References

1. David Carmel, Yoelle S. Maarek, Matan Mandelbrod, Yosi Mass, and Aya Soffer. Searching XML documents via XML fragments. In *Proceedings of the 26th annual international ACM SIGIR conference on Research and development in informaion retrieval*, pages 151–158. ACM Press, 2003.
2. Charles L. A. Clarke, Gordon V. Cormack, and Thomas R. Lynam. Exploiting redundancy in question answering. In *Proceedings of the 24th annual international ACM SIGIR conference on Research and development in informaion retrieval*, pages 358–365, New Orleans, September 2001.
3. David L. Yeung, Charles L. A. Clarke, Gordon V. Cormack, Thomas R. Lynam, and Egidio L. Terra. Task-Specific Query Expansion (MultiText Experiments for TREC 2003). In *Proceedings of the Twelfth Text Retrieval Conference*, Gaithersburg, MD, 2003. National Institute of Standards and Technology.
4. Jaap Kamps, Maarten de Rijke, and Börkur Sigurbjörnsson. Length normalization in XML retrieval. In *Proceedings of the 27th annual international conference on Research and development in information retrieval*, pages 80–87. ACM Press, 2004.
5. S. E. Robertson, S. Walker, and M. Beaulieu. Okapi at TREC-7: Automatic ad hoc, filtering, VLC and interactive track. In *Proceedings of the Seventh Text REtrieval Conference*, Gaithersburg, MD, 1998. National Institute of Standards and Technology.

Logic-Based XML Information Retrieval for Determining the Best Element to Retrieve

Maryam Karimzadegan[1], Jafar Habibi[1], and Farhad Oroumchian[2]

[1] Department of Computer Engineering, Sharif University of Technology, Azadi Street, Tehran, Iran
{karimzadegan, habibi}@ce.sharif.edu
[2] University of Wollongong in Dubai, Dubai
FarhadOroumchian@uowdubai.ac.ae

Abstract. This paper presents UOWD-Sharif team's approach for XML information retrieval. This approach is an extension of PLIR which is an experimental knowledge-based information retrieval system. This system like PLIR utilizes plausible inferences to first infer the relevance of sentences in XML documents and then propagates the relevance to the other textual units in the document tree. Two approaches have been used for propagation of confidence. The first approach labeled "propagate-DS" first propagates the confidence from sentences to upper elements and then combines these evidences by applying Dempster-Shafer theory of evidence to estimate the confidence in that element. The second approach "DS-propagate" first applies the Dempster-Shafer theory of evidence to combine the evidences and then propagates the combined confidence to the parent element. The second approach performs relatively better than the first approach.

1 Introduction

The widespread use of Extensible Markup Language (XML) has brought up a number of challenges for information retrieval systems. These systems exploit the logical structure of documents instead of a whole document. In traditional information retrieval (IR), a document is considered as an atomic unit and is returned to a user as a query result. XML assumes a tree-like structure for the documents for example sentences, paragraphs, sections etc. Therefore XML retrieval not only is concerned with finding relevant documents but with finding the most appropriate unit in the document that satisfies a user's information need. A meaningful retrievable unit shouldn't be too small because in this case it might not cover all the aspects of users need (exhaustivity). It shouldn't be too large either because in this case there could be a lot of non-relevant information that are of no particular interest to a user's current information need (specificity). Therefore, XML retrieval is an approach for providing more focused information than traditionally offered by search engines when we know the structure of the documents[4].

We have used the INEX collection for evaluation of our XML retrieval system. The INEX document collection is made up of the full-texts, marked up in XML that

N. Fuhr et al. (Eds.): INEX 2004, LNCS 3493, pp. 88 – 99, 2005.

consists of 12,107 articles of the IEEE Computer Society's publications from 12 magazines and 6 transactions, covering the period of 1995-2002. Its size is about 494 megabytes. The collection contains scientific articles of varying length. On average an article contains 1,532 XML nodes, where the average depth of a node is 6.9. Overall, the collection contains over eight million XML elements of varying granularity (from table entries to paragraphs, sub-sections, sections and articles, each representing a potential answer to a user's query [5].

The INEX collection consists of two sets of queries: CO (content only) and CAS (Content and Structure). There are 40 CO and 40 CAS queries in INEX 2004. In CO topics, the retrieval system is expected to return a ranked list of the most relevant elements. In other words, the granularity of the response varies depending on the relevance of the element while in CAS queries; a retrieval system should return a ranked list of elements as specified in the topic. For more information about CO and CAS queries, one can refer to [14]. The focus of this paper is on CO topics.

This paper explores the possibility of using Human Plausible Reasoning [1] and theory of Dempster-Shafer [13] for combining evidences as a means of retrieving relevant units (elements) of documents. Collins and Michalski [2] developed the theory of Human Plausible Reasoning for question-answering situations. An experimental information retrieval system called PLIR which utilizes HPR is described in [8,9]. In [10], [11] and [6] the authors suggest some applications of the theory for adaptive filtering, intelligent tutoring and document clustering, respectively. All these implementations confirm the usefulness and flexibility of HPR for applications that need to reason about a user's information need. In this study, the HPR theory has been extended to accommodate XML information retrieval. This method utilizes Rich Document Representation [6] using single words, phrases, logical terms and logical statements that are captured from document contents. Dempster-Shafer theory have been applied to Structured Document Retrieval before [7], however, here it is used slightly differently as described below.

2 Basics of Human Plausible Reasoning

For approximately 15 years, Collins and his colleagues have been collecting and organizing a wide variety of human plausible inferences made from incomplete and inconsistent information [1]. These observations led to the development of a descriptive theory of human plausible inferences that categorizes plausible inferences in terms of a set of frequently recurring inference patterns and a set of transformations on those patterns. According to the theory, a specific inference combines an inference pattern with a transformation that relates the available knowledge to the questions based on some relationship (e.g. generalization, specialization, similarity or dissimilarity) between them. The primitives of the theory consist of basic expressions, operators and certainty parameters. In the formal notation of the theory, the statement "coffee grows in the Lianos" might be written:

$$\text{GROWS-IN (Lianos)} = \text{Coffee}, \gamma = 0.1$$

This statement has the *descriptor* GROWS-IN applied to the argument Lianos and the *referent* coffee. The certainty of the statement (γ) 0.1, since it declares a fact about the Lianos. The pair descriptor and argument is called a *term*. Expressions are terms associated with one or more referents. All descriptors, arguments and referents are nodes in (several) semantic hierarchies. Any node in the semantic network can be used as a descriptor, argument or referent when appropriate. Figure 1 demonstrates the basic elements of the core theory.

There are many parameters for handling uncertainty in the theory. There is no complete agreement on their computational definitions and different computer models have implemented them in different ways. The definition of the most important ones according to [1] is:

1. γ The degree of certainty or belief that an expression is true. This is applied to any expressions.
2. ϕ Frequency of the referent in the domain of the descriptor (e.g. a large percentage of birds fly). Applies to any non-relational statements.
3. τ Degree of typicality of a subset within a set. This is applied to generalization and specification statements.

Arguments a_1, a_2, f (a_1)
e.g. Fido ,collie, Fido's master
Descriptors d_1, d_2
e.g. Breed, color
Terms d_1 (a_1), d_2 (a_2), d_1 (d_2 (a_1))
e.g. breed(Fido), color(collie), color(breed(Fido))
Referents r_1, r_2, r_3, {r_1…}
e.g. collie, brown and white, brown plus other colors
Statements d_1 (a_1)= r_1: γ, ϕ
e.g. means-of-locomotion(bird)={fly…} :certain, high frequency(I am certain almost all birds fly)
Dependencies between terms d_1 (a_1) ←→ d_2 (f (a_1)): α,β,γ
e.g. latitude(place)←→average-temperature(place): moderate, moderate, (I am certain that latitude contains average temperature with moderate reliability, and that average temperature constrains latitude with moderate reliability)
Implication between statements d_1 (a_1)=r_1 ←→ d_2 (f (a_1))=r_2: α,β,γ
e.g. grain(place)={rice…}←→rainfall(place)=heavy: high, low certain

(I am certain that if a place produces rice, it implies the place has

heavy rainfall with high reliability, but that if a place has heavy rainfall it

Fig. 1. Basic Elements of the Core Theory

4. δ Dominance of a subset in a set (e.g. chickens are not a large percentage of birds but are a large percentage of barnyard fowl). That is applied to generalization and specification statements.
5. σ Degree of similarity of one set to another set. Sigma applies to similarity and dissimilarity statements.

This theory provides a variety of inferences and transforms that allow transformation of known knowledge (statements) into not known information (new statements). For more information on how to implement the theory, one can refer to [3].

3 Information Retrieval by Plausible Inferences

There are four elements in a logic-based IR system. Those are the description of documents, the representation of queries, a knowledge base containing domain knowledge and a set of inference rules. This study also acknowledges that retrieval is inference but relevance is not material implication [12]. A document is retrieved only if its partial description can be inferred from a query description. Thus the retrieval process is expanding a query description by applying a set of inference rules continuously on the description of the query and inferring other related concepts, logical terms and statements until locating a document or documents which are described partially by these concepts or logical terms or statements. In XML retrieval the smallest unit that is inferred is a sentence.

3.1 Document Representation

In this model, documents are represented in possible worlds by a partial set of single words, phrases, logical terms and logical statements, i.e., the representation of a document is not limited to the set of its representative phrases or logical terms and statements. Any concept that can be inferred from representation, by plausible reasoning using the given knowledge base, is also a representative of the document content. In its simplest form, a typical document such as Van Rijsbergen's 1986 article entitled "A Non-classical Logic for Information Retrieval" can be represented as follows:

1. REF (Information Retrieval) = {doc#l }
2. REF (Non-classical Logic) = {doc#l }
3. REF (Non-classical Logic(Information Retrieval)) = {doc#l }

The first statement indicates the concept Information Retrieval is a reference for doc#l. The second statement states that the concept Non classical Logic is a reference for doc#l. The third statement expresses that the term Non-classical Logic (Information retrieval) is a reference for doc#l.

3.2 Representing a Query as an Incomplete Statement

A query can be represented as an incomplete logical statement in which the descriptor is the keyword REF (reference) and its argument is the subject in which the user is interested. The referents of this statement i.e. the desired documents, are unknown. So, we should find the most suitable referent for this logical statement. A typical query in logical notation will have the form like this below:

REF (A-Subject)={?}

Therefore the retrieval process can be viewed as the process of finding referents and completing this incomplete sentence.

A query with a single phrase, such as "Content Retrieval Technique", can be formulated as:

REF(Content-based Retrieval Technique) = (?)

A query consisting of a sentence fragment can be treated as a regular text. Therefore it can be scanned for extracting its logical terms. For example, consider the topic number 197 from the INEX2004 [10] collection.

The query in figure 2 contains the sentence fragment "data compression in information retrieval systems". This query can be converted into a logical term, which is revealed by the proposition *in.* The query can be represented as:

REF(data compression (information retrieval system))= {?}

Queries with more than one concept or term can be represented as a set of simple queries and the system can retrieve a set of references for each one separately and then reexamine the sets by combining the confidence on references, which are members of more than one set. Then the sets can be joined and the resulting set can be sorted according to the confidence value.

3.3 Document Retrieval

The process of information retrieval in this system as mentioned above is about finding referents and completing an incomplete statement. The incomplete statement which is formed from the query has one of the following two formats:

- REF(c) = {?}
- REF(a(b)) = {?}

The above statements mean, we are interested in referents (references, documents) for the concept c or logical term a(b). The following steps describe the process of completing the above query statements.

Step 1- Simple Retrieval
Find references that are indexed by the concepts or terms in the query.

- Scan the query and extract single words, phrases and logical terms.
- Find all the references in the collection for the followings:

All the single words such as "Software" in the query.

All the phrases such as "information retrieval"

All the terms such as *a(b)* that are in query such as (coding algorithm(text compression)).

In the experiments, syntactic phrases of length 2 or 3 have been used.

Step 2 - Simple But Indirect Retrieval

Find references that are rewording of the logical term in query.

- find referents *c* for all the logical terms *a(b)* where *a(b)* = *{c}*.
- find all the references to the referents. For example *Fortran* is a referent for the logical term *Language (programming)* in the logical sentence: *Language (programming))=Fortran.*

The above statements means *Fortran* is a *programming language*. Therefore if query is about *programming languages*, system will return all the references for *Fortran*.

```
?xml version="1.0" encoding="ISO-8859-1"?>
<!DOCTYPE inex_topic SYSTEM "topic.dtd">
<inex_topic topic_id="197" query_type="CO" ct_no="178">
<title>"data compression" +"information retrieval"</title>
<description>We are interested in articles about usage data
compression in information retrieval systems, because IR systems are
very memory consuming, and these systems offer wide range of various
data to be compressed i.e. texts, index data, images, video
etc.</description>
<narrative>Our research team ARG (AmphorA Research Group) develops
experimental information retrieval system called AmphorA. The AmphorA
includes many retrieval techniques such as implementation of vector and boolean
queries, multidimensional indexing etc. Other research activity is background of
such system, which means data compression and storage for indexing and
querying algorithms. We are especially interested in word-based compression.
Article is considered relevant if it provides information about compression in IR
system. Compression means compression of text, index, query evaluation on
compressed index and text, image retrieval e.g. retrieval in JPEG compressed
images. Watermarking, straightforward storage of compressed images in database
etc. is considered as non-relevant article.</narrative>
<keywords>data, compression, information, retrieval, indexing, data
structure</keywords>
```

Fig. 2. CO Topic number 197 of INEX2004 collection

Step 3 - Use Relationships and Inferences

This step uses all the transforms and inference of the theory to convert the original concepts and/or logical statements into new statements and retrieve their references as the references of the query.

- find other referents such as *f* with SPEC, GEN and/or SIM relationship with referent *c* where f *{SPEC or GEN or SIM}* *c* in order to conclude *a(b)* = *{f}*. Then find all references indexed by f in the collection.

- find all the logical terms such as *d(e)* with mutual dependency relationship with term *a(b)* where a *(b)* ←→ *d(e)*. Find all references for *d(e)*.
- find all the logical statements such as *d(e)={b}* with mutual implication with statement *a(b)={c}* where *a(b)={c}* ←→ *d(e)={b}*. Find all references for new logical statements.

Step 3 is repeated as many times as necessary in order to find the best elements. Basically, the process is similar to rewriting query and looking for references for the new query.

Since a term, referent or sentence in a document could be reached through several different relationships or inferences, therefore a method for combining the confidence values attributed from these different evidences should be taken. For combining these confidence or uncertainty values, the Dempster-Shafer theory of evidence has been employed.

Step 4 - Propagation

Through the application of steps 1 through 3 the best possible sentence candidates will be recovered. However, documents have structures therefore the system needs to propagate the confidence in the sentences to the confidence in the other elements of this structure.

The inference depicted in figure 3 propagates the certainty value of a sentence to the paragraph that this sentence resides in. The first line represents our assumption that if a sentence is relevant to a concept then the paragraph that this sentence resides in is also relevant. The second line expresses the confidence on a specific sentence such as s1 to be relevant to some concept such as c1. The third sentence describes the importance of sentence s1 for the paragraph p1. The parameter δ_1 represents the dominance of the sentence among other sentences in the paragraph. We have assumed that the middle sentences in a paragraph are of less important than beginning and ending sentences. For that, we use a linear function with the slope of -1 from the first sentence till the middle sentence, and then the slope of the function increases to positive 1 from the middle sentence to the last sentence in the paragraph. The parameter μ_1 describes how much of the concepts in the paragraph are covered by the sentence s1. This parameter is estimated by "The number of concepts in sentence s1 divided by the total number of concepts in p1". The parameter A_1 represents acceptability of the sentence s1 being relevant to a concept c1 by the user population. The optimum value of this parameter could be learned during experiments. The rest are true for all cases. The inference estimates the confidence γ on paragraph p1 to be relevant to concept c1. This confidence is influenced by the confidence on the relevance of the sentence s1 to the query, the dominance of sentence s1 in the paragraph p1 and the amount of paragraph p1 which is covered by the sentence s1. The propagation does not stop at paragraph level and with the help of inferences similar to the one described in figure 3, it will continue until the document itself receives confidence values from its children. The SQRT function calculate square root of multiplication of its arguments.

Each element in the document structure may receive multiple confidence values. Sentences retrieved through different inferences will have a confidence value derived from each inference. Other elements receive different confidence values through propagation of the confidence values of their children. For combining these different values, we used the Dempster-Shafer theory of evidence. In sentence level, every inference returns a certainty value for each sentence of the document inferred by each term of the query.

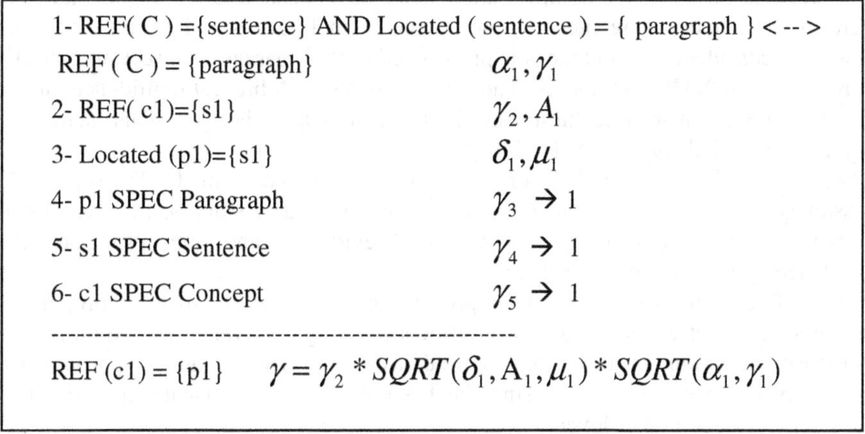

Fig. 3. Inference for Propagating the Certainty Value from a sentence to a paragraph

These certainty values are modeled by a density function $m : 2^{\Omega} \rightarrow [0,1]$ called a basic probability assignment (bpa).

$$m(\phi) = 0, \sum_{A \subset \Omega} m(A) = 1 \tag{1}$$

m(A) represents the belief exactly committed to A, that is the exact evidence that the sentence of the document is relevant to a query term. If there is positive evidence for relevance of a sentence of a document to a query term, then *m(A)>0*, and A is called a focal element. The focal element and *bpa* define a body of evidence. In this problem, we assume that focal elements are singleton sets. Each body of evidence is composed of the confidence on relevance of a document to each query term as estimated by inferences of plausible reasoning. Then,

$$m(\phi) = 0, m(\{doc_j\}) + m(T) = 1 \tag{2}$$

m(T) is referred to evidence that can not be assigned yet. The *m(T)* represents the uncertainty associated to the entire set of sentences of documents being relevant to a query term. Given a *bpa* m, the belief function is defined as the total belief provided by the body of evidence for relevance of a sentence of a document to a query term. Because the focal elements are singleton, then the belief function equates to the mass function. Dempster-Shafer rules for combination, aggregates two independent bodies of evidence defined within the same frame of discernment into one body of evidence. Since the focal elements are singleton, the combination function becomes simpler than Dempster's rules of combination. DS provides three functions for scoring of documents: mass, belief, and plausibility functions. For the first level, we compute the mass function to combine the evidences for one query term. In the second level, the evidence of each query part for different sentences of the documents should be combined to compute the final result. In this level, no preference is given to any of the query terms; therefore we have used the average function. These processes are repeated for each level (paragraph, section, …) of the documents.

In the first phase of experiments, first sentences with the highest confidence in their relevance to the user's information need have been inferred using plausible inferences. Then by using the inference depicted in figure 3 and Dempster-Shafer theory, the confidence in sentences is propagated to their paragraphs, sections and the entire document XML documents. Then the elements with highest confidence values are selected and put in order in a rank list to be shown to the user. This method of combining is called "propagate-DS" method.

We have used another method for combining the evidence named "DS-propagate". It assumes that, if more than one sentence relates to the user's query, first we should combine the evidences using DS theory of evidence, and then propagate the confidences gained to the higher levels.

The difference between these two approaches relies on the fact that, in "propagate-DS" approach, first we propagate the confidences to higher levels, then we utilize the DS theory for combining the evidences, whereas in the "DS-propagate" approach, we first combine the evidences by using the DS theory, then propagate the combined confidence value to higher level.

4 Experiments

We have experimented with two approaches for combining the evidences. The results based on average of all RP measures with comparison to other systems participating in INEX 2004 are depicted in figure 4 and figure 5, respectively. These figures depict the average of all RP measures in a standard 10 point Precision-recall chart. The results show that DS-propagate method entertains relatively higher precision than the Propagate-DS method. It seems that by using the DS theory first, then propagating the result to the higher levels, our precision will become higher. However, both methods performance is much lower than expected.

A number of other runs have been performed and the relevance judgments and evaluation metrics of INEX have been studied carefully after the INEX 2004 conference. In light of new knowledge of relevance and new results, a number of assumptions underlying this approach have been questioned. It has occurred to us that some of these assumptions may not be valid. For example, it was assumed that the smallest meaningful unit of interest for users is a sentence. However it was discovered that the runs with fewer sentences in their higher ranks (and with fewer sentences retrieved in general) have better performance than the runs that list the sentences higher than larger units such as paragraphs.

Another example is the assumption that users prefer seeing one element containing more information rather than viewing multiple smaller pieces of information each as a separate element. For example, if a paragraph has multiple relevant sentences, users would prefer to see the paragraph rather than to see each Individual sentence as a

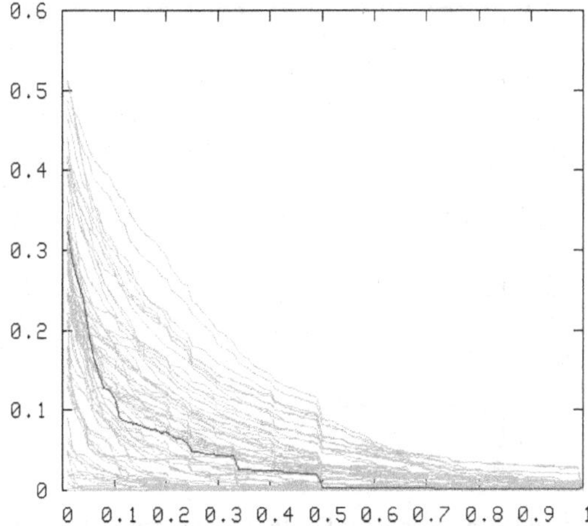

Fig. 4. Average of all RP measures for DS-propagate approach

separate line listed in the output. Therefore, in our runs we have eliminated sub-elements whenever their parent elements have higher confidence values than sub-elements. But this strategy does not correspond well with INEX metrics. Figure 6 depicts performance of a run where all the elements are included in the evaluation and no sub-element has been eliminated. This figure shows the average of all RP measures in a standard 10 point Precision-recall chart All elements (article, section, paragraph, sentences) regardless of their relationship have been ranked based on their confidence values. As seen in figure 6, this run (DS-propagate with all elements included) has produced better results than both of our original runs.

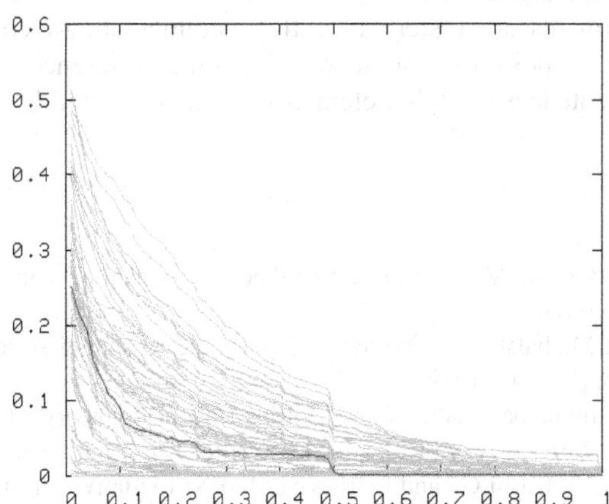

Fig. 5. Average of all RP measures for propagate-DS approach

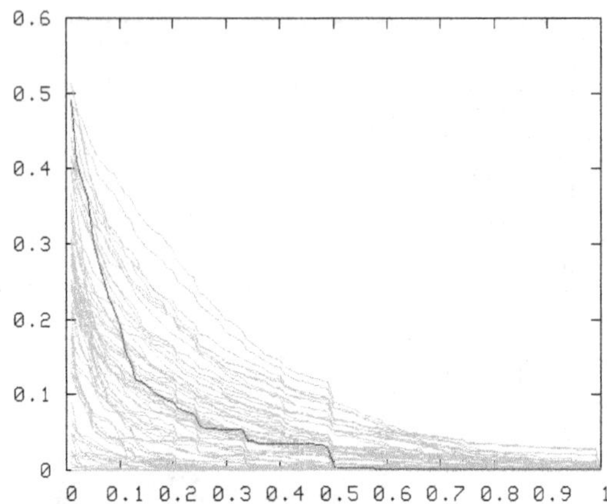

Fig. 6. Average of all RP measures for DS-Propagate approach considering all elements

5 Conclusion

We presented a novel approach and implementation for finding, scoring and ranking of the meaningful units of retrieval in the context of XML information retrieval. A new specialized inference is added to the inferences of PLIR system which uses Collins and Michalski theory of Human Plausible Reasoning in order to handle XML information retrieval. Then by using the DS theory of evidence, we have combined different confidence values coming from different sources to estimate the final confidence in each element of an XML document element.

The performances of our original runs have been understandably lower than our expectation. Currently we are analyzing the results of our experiments and questioning the assumptions underlying the development of our system. For the next year, other experiments are underway with other methods of combining evidences such as fusion. It is possible also to develop other inferences for propagation of confidence from sentences to higher elements of the document the document tree.

References

1. Collins A. and Burstejn M. H.: Modeling a theory of human plausible reasoning, *Artificial Intelligence III*, 1988.
2. Collins M. and Michalski R.: The logic of plausible reasoning A core theory, *Cognitive Science*, vol. 13, pp. 1-49, 1989.
3. Dontas k.: An implementation of the Collins-Michalski theory of plausible reasoning, Master's Thesis, *University of Tennessee*, Knoxville, TN, August 1987.
4. Fuhr N., Gövert N., Kazai G., and Lalmas M.: INEX: INitiative for the Evaluation of XML retrieval, In Ricardo Baeza-Yates, Norbert Fuhr, and Yoelle S. Maarek, editors, *Proceedings of the SIGIR 2002 Workshop on XML and Information Retrieval*, 2002.
5. http://inex.is.informatik.uni-duisburg.de:2004/ accessed 7th of Agust 2004.

6. Jalali A., Oroumchian F.: Rich document representation for document clustering, *Coupling Approaches, Coupling Media and Coupling Languages for Information Retrieval Avignon (Vaucluse)*, France, vol. 1, pp. 802-808, April 2004.
7. Lamlas M.: Dempster-Shafer's Theory of Evidence applied to the Structured Documents: modeling Uncertainty, *Proc. Of the 20^{h} ACM SIGIR Conference on Research and Development in Information Retrieval*, Philadelphia PA , pp. 110-118, 1997.
8. Oroumchian F.: Information retrieval by plausible inferences: an application of the theory of plausible reasoning of Collins and Michalski, *Ph.D. Dissertation, School Of Computer And Information Science, Syracuse University,* 1995.
9. Oroumchian F., Oddy R. N.: An application of plausible reasoning to information retrieval, *Proc. Of the 19th ACM SIGIR Conference on Research and Development in Information Retrieval*, Zurich , pp. 244-252, August 1996.
10. Oroumchian F., Arabi B., Ashori E.: Using plausible inferences and Dempster-shafer theory Of evidence for adaptive information filtering, *4th International Conference on Recent Advances in Soft Computing (RASC2002)*, Nottingham, United Kingdom, Dec 2002.
11. Oroumchian F., Khandzad B.: Simulating tutoring decisions by plausible inferences, *4th International Conference on Recent Advances in Soft Computing (RASC2002),* Nottingham, United Kingdom, Dec 2002.
12. Rijsbergen C. J.: Toward an information logic, In N. J. Belkin &C. J. Van Rijsbergen (Eds.), *Proceedings Of The 12th Annual International SIGIR Conference*, Cambridge, MA, 1989.
13. Shafer G. A.: Mathematical theory of evidence, *Princeton University Press*,1976.
14. Sigurbjörnsson B., Larsen B., Lalmas M., Malik S.: INEX 2003 guidelines for topic development, *In Proceeding of INEX 2003 Conference*, Schloss Dagstuhl, Dec 2003.

An Algebra for Structured Queries in Bayesian Networks

Jean-Noël Vittaut, Benjamin Piwowarski, and Patrick Gallinari

LIP6 Laboratoire d'Informatique de Paris 6,
8 rue du Capitaine Scott, 75015, Paris, France
{vittaut, bpiwowar, gallinar}@poleia.lip6.fr

Abstract. We present a system based on a Bayesian Network formalism for structured documents retrieval. The parameters of this model are learned from the document collection (documents, queries and assessments). The focus of the paper is on an algebra which has been designed for the interpretation of structured information queries and can be used within our Bayesian Network framework. With this algebra, the representation of the information demand is independent from the structured query language. It allows us to answer both vague and strict structured queries.

1 Introduction

Bayesian networks have been used by different authors for flat text information retrieval [2][9]. They have been shown to be theoretically well founded and different classical IR systems may be considered as particular cases of these BN-IR models. Recently, we proposed a BN model for structured IR retrieval [10][11][12]. This model allows taking into account local relations between the different elements of an XML document. It makes use of flat text IR models for computing local scores for document elements. BN inference is then used to compute a final score for the document elements. Inference on the BN variables allows combining in some way the relevance information computed for different document elements.

This paper describes the algebra we have developed for the interpretation of structured queries. It provides a representation of the query which is independent of any particular query language. The general algebra has been described in details in [13]. We show here how it can be adapted to the NEXI language used for INEX.

The paper is organized as follows. First we describe in section 2.1 an adaptation of the Okapi model which has been used as the local scorer for our BN system in the 2004 INEX evaluation. We briefly describe in section 2.2 the BN model and the use of Okapi within this BN. Results for CO queries are then presented in section 2.3. Section 3.1 describes the algebra used for the interpretation of the NEXI query language and its use for the VCAS queries of INEX. We finally present in section 3.2 the results obtained with this model on VCAS queries.

N. Fuhr et al. (Eds.): INEX 2004, LNCS 3493, pp. 100–112, 2005.

2 Content Only Queries

2.1 Okapi Model

We used Okapi as a standalone model and also as a local baseline model for Bayesian Networks. It allows us to compute a local score for each doxel (a document element) of the database. Then, this score is used to order the results (if we use the Okapi model alone) or as a source of evidence for Bayesian Networks.

In the Bayesian Network, the local scores provided by baseline models have to be interpreted as a probability (of relevance). So, we adapted Okapi [15] in order to:

- reach reasonable performances on the INEX corpus (and on a structured collection in general);
- compute a score which could be interpreted as a probability with this model.

The local score of a doxel x for a given query q , computed by the Okapi model, is defined by:

$$\text{Okapi}(q,x)=\sum_{j=1}^{\text{length}(q)}\omega_{j,x}\frac{(k_1+1)tf_{x,j}}{K_x+tf_{x,j}}\times\frac{(k_3+1)qtf_j}{k_3+qtf_j} \tag{1}$$

where k_1 and k_3 are constants, length (q) is the number of terms in query q. This formula is similar to classical Okapi except for the index x appearing in ω, K and tf. Okapi makes use of different statistics relative to the document collection such as term occurrences or mean document length. Since for Structured Information Retrieval (SIR) elements to be retrieved are doxels and not plain documents, these statistics have to be adapted. Values $\omega_{j,x}$ and K_x are defined as follows:

- $\omega_{j,x}=\log\left(\frac{N-n_j+0.5}{n_j+0.5}\right)$. In Okapi N is the number of documents in the collection and the n_j number of documents containing term j. There are different options for adapting these collection statistics to SIR. We will present here tests where these two values were defined respectively with respect to the classical document set ("document frequency") as in Okapi.
- $K_x=k_1\left((1-b)+b\frac{dl}{avdl}\right)$ where b is a constant and in Okapi dl is the document length and $avdl$ is the average document length. Here dl was replaced by the doxel length and one weighting scheme was tested for $avdl$: the average length taken respectively over all the doxels with the same tag ("tag").

We chose this peculiar weighting scheme as it allowed us to reach good performances when used by our BN model. As we said, we needed scores which can be interpreted as probabilities. Okapi score does not range between 0 and 1. The normalization of Okapi is discussed in [14] in the context of filtering, where it is proposed to make a regression of the original Okapi score via a logistic function. We used this idea here with the following transformation:

$$P\left(M_{\text{Okapi}}(x)=\mathrm{R} \mid q\right)=\frac{1}{1+e^{\alpha\times\text{Okapi}(q,x)/\text{length}(q)-\beta}} \tag{2}$$

This formula gives the normalized score for the local baseline variants of Okapi model. The α and β parameters were estimated on the whole INEX 2002 database. This score is dependant on the query length. Since the parameters of the logistic function should be valid for queries of varying length, this score was divided by the query length. We then computed the mean okapi score μ and the standard deviation σ for all the CO queries of INEX 2003. We then set α and β such that the probability $P\left(M_{\text{Okapi}}(x)=\mathrm{R} \mid q\right)$ is 0.5 when the score is μ and 0.75 when the score is $\mu+\sigma$. These values were chosen empirically.

This is different from [14] where the parameters of the regression are estimated for each query. This would not be realistic here because of the increased complexity of SIR.

2.2 Bayesian Networks

Model

Let us consider a hierarchically structured collection like the INEX corpus. Documents are organised in a category hierarchy with corpus as the root node, journal collections as its immediate descendents, followed by journals, articles etc. We view retrieval for such a collection as a stochastic process in which a user goes deeper and deeper in the corpus structure: the user starts its search at the "root node" of all categories, and then selects one or several categories in which relevant documents should be. For each category, he or she selects subcategories and/or documents within these categories. This process is iterated until the user has found relevant and highly specific doxels.

The BN structure we used directly reflects this document hierarchy and retrieval will follow the above stochastic process. We consider that each structural part within the hierarchy has an associated random variable. The root of the BN is thus a "corpus" variable, its children the "journal collection" variables, etc. The whole collection is thus modelled as a large BN which reflects the doxel hierarchy in the collection.

Each random variable in the BN can take its values in a finite set. Existing BN models for flat [2] or structured [8] documents use binary values $(R,\neg R)$. This is too limitative for SIR since quantifying an element relevance is more complex than for whole documents and should somewhat be related to the two dimensional scale (specificity, exhaustivity) proposed for INEX. We used a state space of cardinality 3, $V=\{I,B,E\}$ with:

1. I for Irrelevant when the element is not relevant;
2. B for Big when the element is marginally or fairly specific;
3. E for Exact when the element has a high specificity.

In this model, relevance is a local property in the following sense: if we knew that an element is relevant, not relevant or too big, the relevance value of its parent would not bring any new information on the relevance of one of its descendants.

For any element X and for a given query q, the probability $P(X = E, X\text{'s parent} = B \mid q)$ will be used as the final Retrieval Status Value (RSV) of this element. Using the simpler RSV $P(X = \mathrm{E} \mid q)$ led to poor performances with the BN. Our choice was partly motivated by the work of Crestani et al. [3][4] and by preliminary experiments.

Besides these variables, there are two more types of random variables in the BN. The first one corresponds to the information need, it is denoted Q and its realization is a query denoted q. Q is a vector of word frequencies taking its values in a multidimensional real space. This random variable is always observed (known). Document textual information is not directly modelled in this BN for complexity reasons. Instead a series of baseline IR models will be used to compute local relevance scores for each doxel given a query. For each local baseline model, this score will only depend on the doxel content and on the query. It is then independent on the context of the doxel in the XML tree. The global score for each doxel will then combine these local scores and will also depend on the doxel context in the BN – the parent's relevance. These local baseline models have been adapted from classical (flat) retrieval IR models. In the experiments presented here, one variant of the Okapi model was used for baseline: the okapi with standard document frequency and a length normalisation over elements with the same tag. In the BN model a random variable is associated to each local scorer and doxel. Let $M(X)$ denote the random variable associated to the local baseline model and doxel X and m its realization. As in classical IR this variable will take two values: R (relevant) and $\neg R$ (not relevant), i.e. $m \in \{R, \neg R\}$. The local relevance score at X given query q for the baseline model will be $P(M(X) = R \mid q)$. Note that it is straightforward to add new baseline models; in the following, all the formulas were adapted to the case where we have only one baseline model.

Based on the local scores $M(X)$ and on the BN conditional probabilities, BN inference is then used to combine evidence and scores for the different doxels in the document model. In our tree like model, the probability that element X is in state I, B or E depends on its parent state and on the fact that the local baseline models have judged the element as relevant or not relevant. The probability for X to be in a given state $v \in \mathrm{V}$ is then:

$$P(X = v \mid q) = \sum_{v_Y \in \mathrm{V}, m \in \{R, \neg R\}} P(X = v_X \mid Y = v_Y, M(X) = m) P(M(X) = m \quad (3)$$

In this expression, the summation is over all the possible values of v_Y and m ($\mathrm{v_Y}$ can take any value in $V = \{I, B, E\}$, and m can take values $R, \neg R$). The conditional probability is expressed as follows:

$$P(X = v_X \mid Y = v_Y, M = m) = F_X(\Theta, v_X, v_Y, m) = \frac{e^{\theta_{c_X, v_X, v_Y, m}}}{\sum_{v \in V = \{I, E, B\}} e^{\theta_{c_X, v, v_Y, m}}} \quad (4)$$

where the $\theta_{c_X,v_X,v_Y,m}$ are real values to be learned. There is one such parameter for each tag category c_X and value set v_X, v_Y, m . All the doxels sharing the same value set c_X, v_X, v_Y, m will share this θ parameter. The denominator ensures that conditional probabilities sum to 1.

Training Algorithm

In order to learn the parameters and to fit to a specific corpus, we used a training criterion based on the relative order of elements. We used all the assessed CO topics from the INEX 2003 dataset. The criterion to be minimised was:

$$Q(\Theta) = \sum_q w(q) \sum_{i,j} e^{(RSV(i,q)-RSV(j,q))s_q(i,j)} \tag{5}$$

where the weighted q summation is over the set of all training queries and the i and j ones are over the set of all doxels in the training set. $RSV(i,q)$ is the score of the element X_i and s_q is defined as follows:

$$s_q(i,j) = \begin{cases} -1 & \text{if } X_i \text{ is "better" than } X_j \text{ for query } q \ (X_i >_q X_j) \\ 1 & \text{if } X_j \text{ is "better" than } X_i \text{ for query } q \ (X_i <_q X_j) \\ 0 & \text{otherwise} \ (X_i =_q X_j) \end{cases} \tag{6}$$

The order (“better than”) between the elements depends on the assessments for a given query q. For instance, a highly specific and exhaustive element is “better than” a fairly exhaustive and highly specific one. We used the following partial order between assessments (from “best” to “worst”):

1. Highly specific and highly exhaustive
2. Highly specific and fairly exhaustive
3. Highly specific and marginally exhaustive
4. All other assessment including “not assessed”

The score of an element in the criterion formula is either $P(X = E \mid q)$ for the model BN1 or $P(X = E, X\text{'s parent} = B \mid q)$ for the model BN2. The latter is more complex but more related to our scoring algorithm. The weight $w(q)$ was chosen in order to normalize the contribution of different topics: even if the number of assessments were different, this normalization ensured that each topic had the same influence on the criterion. The criterion is minimal when all the elements are ordered according to our partial order.

In order to optimize the criterion, different gradient algorithms could be used. For the experiments we used a simple gradient descent algorithm where the learning rate (epsilon) was automatically set by a line search; for this latter, we use the Armijo algorithm. The number of steps was chosen so as to optimize the performance with respect to the generalized recall metric. For BN1, a maximum was reached after 195 iterations while for BN2 a maximum was reached after 700.

2.3 Experiments

Three official runs were submitted to INEX'04:

- **Okapi.** In this run, we used the Okapi weighting scheme; every volume (and not every doxel) in the INEX corpus was considered as a document while the average document length used in the Okapi formula was local: for every doxel, the average document length was the average length of the doxels with the same tag.
- **BN1.** In this run, we submitted the doxel retrieved with the BN which is described in 0. The former Okapi model was used for local model, $P(X = \mathrm{E} \mid q)$ was used as the score of an element for the learning process, and $P(X = E, X\text{'s parent} = B \mid q)$ was used as the score of an element. INEX tags were grouped in categories.
- **BN2.** In this run, we also submitted the doxel retrieved with the BN which was learnt with a different grouping of tag names. $P(X = E, X\text{'s parent} = B \mid q)$ was used as the score of an element both for learning and testing.

With respect to the experiments we have done the two previous years [10][12], this ranking criterion seems the most promising one – in INEX 2002 and 2003 we used a maximum likelihood algorithm (EM) [5] which was not well fitted to this task. However, the partial order should be refined so as to be more close to the "ideal" user related criterion.

Table 1. CO official runs

	Generalized recall	Average of all RP measures
Okapi	40.74	0.10
BN1	46.45	0.04
BN2	45.97	0.05

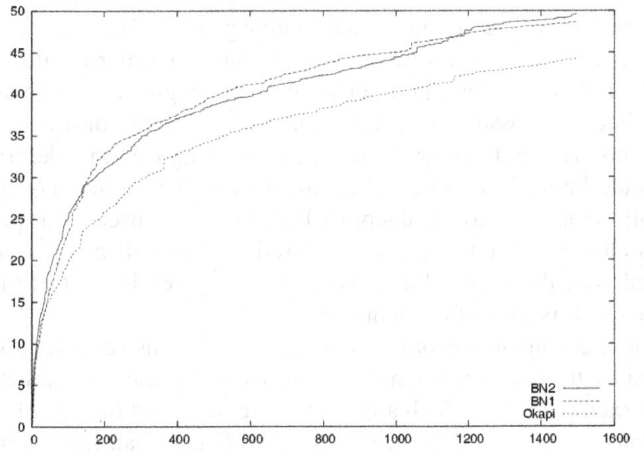

Fig. 1. CO official runs with generalized recall metric

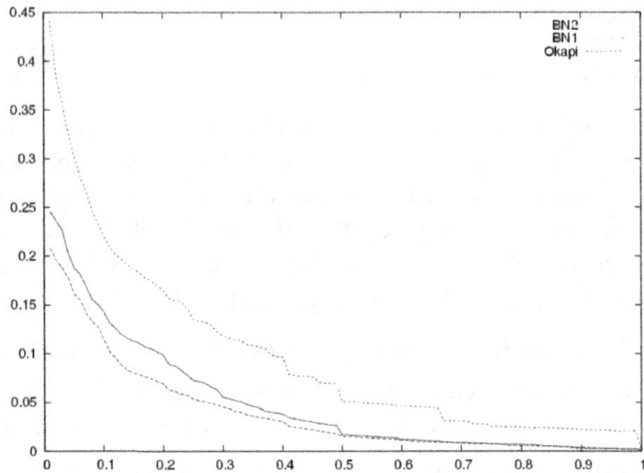

Fig. 2. CO official runs with the average of all RP measures

3 Content and Structure Queries

In this section, we present the algebra we have used to answer Vague Content and Structure Queries (VCAS) starting from the scores of BN Model or standalone Okapi model. We only give some elements to understand the way we use this algebra in the specific case of NEXI queries. A more detailed description of the algebra is given in [13]. At last, we give the results of the experiments on INEX 2004 for the Okapi model and Bayesian Networks.

3.1 Algebra

Introduction

In INEX, queries are expressed in a query language (NEXI) which is very similar to XPath in which a vague operator (about) is introduced in order to allow for queries in a similar fashion than in information retrieval. Such languages can be used to express query needs that mix possibly vague content and structure constraints. XPath is for XML documents what SQL is for databases: it is a language that describes which information should be retrieved from XML documents. In traditional databases, this request is usually mapped into an algebra which in turn is used as a query plan. This query plan is closely related to physical operations that will give the answers to the query. In databases, the result of a formula of the algebra is a set of tuples. In XML databases, the result is a set of elements.

Defining or choosing an algebra is very important to answer complex query needs. This is proved by the important number of works within the semi-structured database field, like for example [1][9]. Such approaches are also used in INEX [7]. Our algebra is closely related to the one defined by Fuhr and Grossjohan [6]. As in classical IR, SIR aim is to retrieve the set of document elements that fulfill a given query need. This query need is very often imprecise. The algebra we define here can be used to answers vague queries that have constraints on both content and structure and make use of the Bayesian Networks framework that we use for CO queries.

Algebra Description

Besides classical operators of the set theory like the intersection, the union and the complementary, our algebra uses structural operators like:

- $\overline{desc}_{/}(x)$ (descendant or self)
- $\overline{anc}_{/}(x)$ (ancestor or self)
- other operators which are not mentioned here because they are useless with the specification of NEXI language.

We denote X the set of all doxels. We introduce three functions:

1. *R(q)* which returns the set of doxels which are answers to the query need *q*. A doxel is in the set with a given probability.
2. $[comp(t, comparison\_op)]$ which returns the set of doxels x where $comparison\_op(x,t)$ is true. We have used $=, \neq, \leq, \geq, <, >$ as comparison operators.
3. *label (x)* which returns the label of the doxel (the tag name). The function $label^{-1}(l)$ returns the set of doxels which have a label *l* (This function is used for SCAS queries). In order to process VCAS queries, we can replace the latter function by a vague one called *invlabel (l)* which returns a set of labels with a given probability.

The algebra is defined on the set P(X) (the set of all the part of the set of doxels). We use the operator "$\circ$" to compose the different functions defined on P(X) which take values in P(X).

With all these operators and functions, we are able to answer structured queries.

Probabilistic Interpretation

In the previous section, *R(q)* returns the set of doxels that are answers to query *q*. In Information Retrieval (IR), the answers to a query are not well defined: the query is expressed in vague terms, and the real query need cannot be easily defined. We thus have to define $R(q)$ as a "*vague*" set in order to compute the answer to a query that contains predicates like *about*.

In our approach, as in the probabilistic interpretation of fuzzy sets [16], a set $A \subset X$ is not anymore defined strictly. We denote such a set by A_v (*v* for *vague*). A_v is defined by a probability distribution on subsets of X. The case where probability $P(A_v = A) = 1$ means that the set A_v is strict and not vague (the concept of fuzzy set is thus more general than the concept of classical set). An element a belongs to A_v with a probability $P(a \in A_v)$ which is formally defined by:

$$P(a \in A_v) = \sum_{A \subset X, a \in A} P(A_v = A) \tag{7}$$

We define recursively the fact that a doxel belongs to a vague set:

$$x \in \varphi(A_V) \equiv \bigvee_{x' \in X, x \in \varphi(\{x'\})} x' \in A_V \tag{8}$$

Lastly, intersection and union operators can also be transformed in logical formulas:

$$\begin{aligned} x \in A_V \cap B_V &\equiv (x \in A_V) \wedge (x \in B_V) \\ x \in A_V \cup B_V &\equiv (x \in A_V) \vee (x \in B_V) \end{aligned} \tag{9}$$

Algebraic Expression of a CAS Query

In order to convert a NEXI query into an algebraic expression, we briefly define the way we decompose the NEXI Queries used in INEX, which can be easily extended to XPath like queries.

A NEXI query is read from left to right. For instance, the NEXI query :

//article[about(., "bayesian networks")]//section[about(., "learning structure")]

could be used to express "in articles about Bayesian Networks, find sections that are about learning the structure of the network".

The different components are separated by two slashes "//" which are not within brackets. The query $// L_0 [F_0] // L_1 [F_1] ... // L_n [F_n]$ can be decomposed into $// L_i [F_i]$ elements, each such component being itself composed of three parts:

1. **The axis** (//). This is an abbreviation of the $/descendant-or-self::$ denoted axis in XPath. It defines a set with respect to a given doxel x. For the first component of the XPath, this set is defined by the document d. For the first component of an XPath within a filter, the set of selected doxels is evaluated with respect to the document d or to the filtered doxel. For any another component, the selection is made with respect to the set of doxels selected by the previous component;
2. **The label** (L_i) It filters the set of doxels selected by the axis and keep only those which have the label L_i. When the label is *, the "axis" set is not filtered;
3. **The filter** (F_i) that expresses a boolean condition on doxels. It returns the subset of those doxels which fulfill the boolean conditions expressed in the filter. An XPath can be used in the filter: it is relative to the context path and take the form of $.// L_0 // L_1 ... // L_n$. The filter is a condition which can be true or false for one doxel.

An algebraic expression is defined on $P(X)$. Each component of the query (either axis or label L_i or filter F_i) can be processed separately:

- An axis is transformed into the structural operator $\Psi_A(//) = \overline{desc/}$ except for the first component of the XPath which is transformed into $\Psi_A^{(0)}(//) = \overline{desc/}(d)$.
- A label (or a set of labels) L_i is transformed into a function Ψ_L that selects a subset of doxels which have a label L_i in the set:

$$\begin{array}{llll}\Psi_L(L_i): & \mathrm{P}(\mathrm{X}) & \mapsto \mathrm{P}(\mathrm{X}) \\ & X & \mapsto X \cap label^{-1}(L_i)\end{array}$$

where we handle the special case of * by defining $label^{-1}(*) = \mathrm{X}$

- As for the filter F_i, the transformation is more complex and is denoted Ψ_F:

$$\begin{array}{llll}\Psi_F(F_i): & \mathrm{P}(\mathrm{X}) & \mapsto \mathrm{P}(\mathrm{X}) \\ & X & \mapsto X \cap \Psi'_F(F_i)\end{array}$$

where Ψ'_F is the function which transforms a filter into the set of doxels that fulfill the conditions expressed in the filter.

With these notations, the query $p = // L_0[F_0] // L_1[F_1] ... // L_n[F_n]$ is the result of the evaluation of the algebraic expression:

$$\begin{array}{lll}\Psi(d,p) & = & \Psi_F(F_n)\circ\Psi_L(L_n)\circ\Psi_A(//) \\ & & \ldots \\ & & \circ\Psi_F(F_1)\circ\Psi_L(L_1)\circ\Psi_A(//) \\ & & \circ\Psi_F(F_0)\circ\Psi_L(L_0)\circ\Psi_A^{(0)}(//) \\ & = & \Psi'_F(F_n)\cap label^{-1}(L_n) \\ & & \overline{\cap\, desc/}\left(\begin{array}{l}\ldots \\ \overline{\cap\, desc/}\left(\begin{array}{l}\Psi'_F(F_1)\cap label^{-1}(L_1) \\ \overline{\cap\, desc/}\left(\begin{array}{l}\Psi'_F(F_0)\cap label^{-1}(L_0) \\ \overline{\cap\, desc/}(d)\end{array}\right)\end{array}\right)\end{array}\right)\end{array} \tag{10}$$

We do not detail here how Ψ'_F is evaluated.

3.2 Experiments

To compute the union or the intersection of two vague sets, we used the probabilistic and/or operators defined below:

- $P(a \in A \wedge b \in B) = P(a \in A)P(b \in B)$
- $P(a \in A \vee b \in B) = P(a \in A) + P(b \in B) - P(a \in A)P(b \in B)$

Table 2. VCAS official runs

	Generalized recall	Average of all RP measures
Okapi	33.14	0.05
BN1	27.97	0.05
BN2	31.67	0.04

Three official runs were submitted to INEX'04; the models we used to compute the probability of relevance are the same as in section 2.3.

The results are summarized in figures 3, 4 and in table 2. For generalized recall, Okapi model outperforms BN1 and BN2 models but not significantly. For CO, Okapi was below the BNs. For RP measures, results are similar for all models.

Our algebra can answer all INEX VCAS and also more complex structured queries. Nevertheless, the connection between CO queries and VCAS queries is not clear because the best model for CO queries is not the best one for VCAS queries. The Okapi model gives better results for structured queries than for content only queries. Moreover, the choice of union and intersection functions for aggregation has to be further investigated.

4 Conclusion

We introduced a BN model whose conditional probability functions are learnt from the data via a gradient descent algorithm. The BN framework has some advantages. Firstly, it can be used in distributed IR, as we only need the score of the parent element in order to compute the score of any its descendants. Secondly, it can use simultaneously different baseline models: we can therefore use specific models for non textual media (image, sound, etc.) as another source of evidence.

We have described the new algebra we have used in order to process content-and-structure queries. This algebra is a generic way to represent structured queries and can be easily used with the IR system based on Bayesian Networks we have developed.

Our system can answer CO and VCAS queries. The model has still to be improved, tuned and developed. In particular, we should improve the baseline models and fit them to the specificities of CO or VCAS queries. We showed that this algebra allows answering VCAS queries but we still have to investigate new ways of including vagueness in the structure of queries.

References

1. Abiteboul, S., Quass, D., McHugh, J., Widom, J., Wiener, J.L.: The lorel query language for semistructured data. International Journal on Digital Libraries, 1 (1997) 68–88
2. Callan, J., Croft, W.B., Harding, S.M.: The INQUERY Retrieval System. In A. Min Tjoa and Isidro Ramos, editors, Database and Expert Systems Applications, Proceedings of the International Conference, pages 78-83, Valencia, Spain, Springer-Verlag (1992)
3. Crestani, F., de Campos, L.M., Fernandez-Luna, J.M., Huete, J.F.: A multi-layered Bayesian network model for structured document retrieval, ECSQARU, LNAI 2711, Springer-Verlag (2003) 74-86
4. Crestani, F., de Campos, L.M., Fernandez-Luna, J.M., Huete, J.F.: Ranking Structured Documents Using Utility Theory in the Bayesian Network Retrieval Model, In SPIRE (String Processing and Information Retrieval), Brazil (2003) 168-182
5. Dempster, A.P., Laird, N.M., Rubin, D.B.: Maximum Likelihood from incomplete data via de EM algorithm. The Journal of Royal Statistical Society, 39 (1977) 1-37
6. Fuhr, N., Grossjohann, K.: XIRQL: A query language for information retrieval in XML documents. In W. B. Croft, D. J. Harper, D. H. Kraft, and J. Zobel, editors, The 24th International Conference on Research and Developmenent in Information Retrieval, New Orleans, Louisiana, USA, ACM (2001)

7. List, J., Mihajlovic, V., de Vries, A.P., Ramirez, G.: The TIJAX XML-IR system at INEX 2003. In N. Fuhr, M. Lalmas, and S. Malik, editors, INitiative for the Evaluation of XML Retrieval (INEX). Proceedings of the Second INEX Workshop, Dagstuhl, Germany (2003).
8. Myaeng, S.H., Jang, D.H., Kim, M.H. , Zhoo, Z.C.: A Flexible Model for Retrieval of SGML documents. In Proceedings of the 21st Annual International ACM SIGIR Conference on Research and Development in Information Retrieval, Melbourne, Australia, ACM Press, New York (1998) 138-140
9. Navarro, G., Baeza-Yates, R.: Proximal nodes: A model to query document databases by content and structure. ACM TOIS, 15 (1997) 401-435
10. Piwowarski, B., Faure, G.E., Gallinari, P.: Bayesian networks and INEX. In Proceedings of the First Annual Workshop of the Initiative for the Evaluation of XML retrieval (INEX), DELOS workshop, Dagstuhl, Germany ERCIM (2002)
11. Piwowarski, B., Gallinari, P.: A Bayesian Network for XML Information Retrieval: Searching and Learning with the INEX Collection, In Information Retrieval (2004)
12. Piwowarski, B., Vu, H.T., Gallinari, P.: Bayesian Networks and INEX'03. In INitiative for the Evaluation of XML Retrieval, Proceedings of the Second INEX Workshop (2003)
13. Piwowarski, B., Gallinari, P.: An algebra for probabilistic XML Retrieval. In The First Twente Data Management Workshop (2004)
14. Robertson, S.: Threshold setting and performance optimization in adaptive Filtering. Information Retrieval, 5 (2002) 239-256
15. Walker, S., Robertson, S.E.: Okapi/Keenbow at TREC-8. In E. M. Voorhees and D. K. Harman, editors, NIST Special Publication 500-246: The Eighth Text REtrieval Conference (TREC-8), Gaithersburg, Maryland, USA (1999)
16. Zadeh, L.A.: Fuzzy sets (1965)

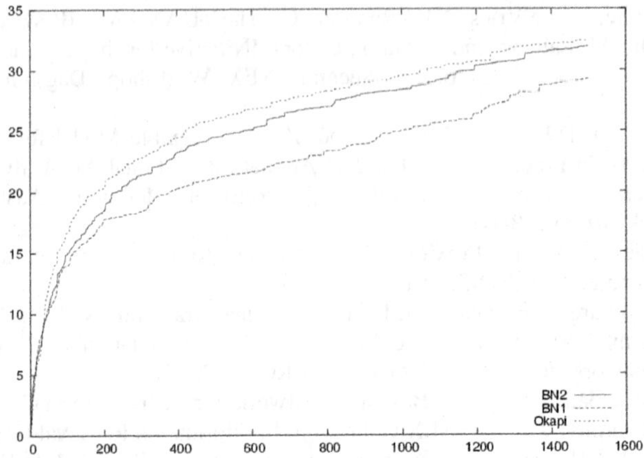

Fig. 3. VCAS official runs with generalized recall metric

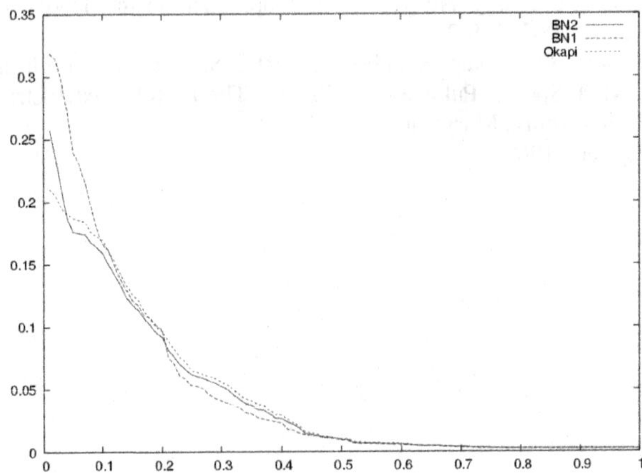

Fig. 4. VCAS official runs with the average of all RP measures

Complement remains $P(a \notin A) = 1 - P(a \in A)$. We have also tested min/max and Lukasievicz operators, but they were outperformed by the probabilistic operator.

In order to introduce vagueness into the query structure, we used the following labelling function:

$$invlabel(l) = \bigcup_{x \in X, label(x)=l} \{pa(x)\} \cup \{x\} \cup \{y \in X, pa(y) = x\} \qquad (11)$$

where we supposed that all the doxels from this set have the same probability of being labelled *l*. We have also tested the labelling function $label^{-1}(l)$, and other simple strategies to introduce vagueness into structure (not considering tag names), but they were outperformed by $invlabel(l)$.

IR of XML Documents – A Collective Ranking Strategy

Maha Salem[1], Alan Woodley[2], and Shlomo Geva[2]

[1] Faculty of Electrical Engineering, Computer Science and Mathematics,
University of Paderborn,
Warburger Str. 100, 33098 Paderborn, Germany
MahaSalem@web.de
[2] Centre for Information Technology Innovation,
Faculty of Information Technology,
Queensland University of Technology,
GPO Box 2434, Brisbane Q 4001, Australia
ap.woodley@student.qut.edu.au, s.geva@qut.edu.au

Abstract. Within the area of Information Retrieval (IR) the importance of appropriate ranking of results has increased markedly. The importance is magnified in the case of systems dedicated to XML retrieval, since users of these systems expect the retrieval of highly relevant and highly precise components, instead of the retrieval of entire documents. As an international, coordinated effort to evaluate the performance of Information Retrieval systems, the Initiative for the Evaluation of XML Retrieval (INEX) encourages participating organisation to run queries on their search engines and to submit their result for the annual INEX workshop. In previous INEX workshops the submitted results were manually assessed by participants and the search engines were ranked in terms of performance. This paper presents a Collective Ranking Strategy that outperforms all search engines it is based on. Moreover it provides a system that is trying to facilitate the ranking of participating search engines.

1 Introduction

Modern society unceasingly produces and uses information. To find the relevant information sought within the huge mass of information now available becomes ever more difficult. If information is supposed to be accessible it must be organised [1].

The specific nature of information has called for the development of many new tools and techniques for information retrieval (IR). Modern IR deals with storage, organisation and access to text, as well as multimedia information resources [2].

Within the area of information retrieval, keyword search querying has emerged as one of the most effective paradigms for IR, especially over HTML documents in the World Wide Web. One of the main advantages of keyword search querying is its simplicity – users do not have to learn a complex query language and can issue queries without any prior knowledge about the structure of the underlying data. Since the keyword search query interface is very flexible, queries may not always be precise and can potentially return a large number of query results, especially in large document collections. As a consequence, an important requirement for keyword search is to rank the query results so that the most relevant results appear first.

N. Fuhr et al. (Eds.): INEX 2004, LNCS 3493, pp. 113 – 126, 2005.

Despite the success of HTML-based keyword search engines, certain limitations of the HTML data model make such systems ineffective in many domains. These limitations stem from the fact that HTML is a presentation language and hence cannot capture much semantics. The XML (eXtensible Markup Language) data model addresses this limitation by allowing for extensible element tags, which can be arbitrarily nested to capture additional semantics. Information such as titles, references, sections and sub-sections are explicitly captured using nested, application specific XML tags, which is not possible using HTML.

Given the nested, extensible element tags supported by XML, it is natural to exploit this information for querying. One approach is to use sophisticated query languages based on XPath to query XML documents. While this approach can be very effective in some cases, a disadvantage is that users have to learn a complex query language and understand the schema of underlying XML.

Information retrieval over hierarchical XML documents, in contrast to conceptually flat HTML documents, introduces many new challenges. First, XML queries do not always return whole documents, but can return arbitrarily nested XML elements that contain the information needed by the user. Generally, returning the "deepest" node usually gives more context information, ignoring presentation or other superfluous nodes. Second, XML and HTML queries differ in how query results are ranked. HTML search engines usually rank entire documents partly based on their hyperlinked structure [3]. Since XML queries can return nested elements, not just entire XML documents, ranking has to be done at the granularity of XML elements, which requires complicated computing due to the fact that the semantics of containment links (relating parent and child elements) is very different from that of hyperlinks. As a consequence, traditional information retrieval techniques for computing rankings may not be directly applicable for nested XML elements [4].

This paper presents an approach for effective ranking of XML result elements in response to a user query by considering the results of several other search engines and producing a collective ranking on the basis of some sort of a vote. The hypothesis is that the resulting system will outperform all search engines delivering the results it is based on.

1.1 Overview of INEX

XML retrieval systems exploit the logical structure of documents, which is explicitly represented by the XML markup, to retrieve document components, instead of entire documents, in response to a user query. This means that an XML retrieval system needs not only to find relevant information in the XML documents, but also determine the appropriate level of granularity to return to the user, and this with respect to both content and structural conditions [5]. The expansion in the field of information retrieval caused the need to evaluate the effectiveness of the developed XML retrieval systems.

To facilitate research in XML information retrieval systems the **IN**itiative for the **E**valuation of **X**ML Retrieval (**INEX**) has established an international, coordinated effort to promote evaluation procedures for content-based XML retrieval. INEX provides a means, in the form of a large XML test collection and appropriate scoring scheme for the evaluation of XML retrieval systems [6]. The test collection consists of XML documents, predefined queries and assessments. Topics are the queries submitted to the retrieval systems. Their formats are based on the topics used in Text Retrieval Conference (TREC), however, they were modified to accommodate two types of topics used in INEX: **CO** (Content Only, queries that ignore document structure and only contain content requirements) and **CAS** (Content and Structure, queries whose stipulations explicitly refer to the documents' structure).

The scoring scheme is based upon two dimensions: *specificity* (reflects the relevancy of a particular XML component) and *exhaustiveness* (measures whether a relevant component contains suitable coverage). These values are quantised to the traditional metrics of *precision* (the probability that a result element viewed by a user is relevant) and *recall* (total number of known relevant components returned divided by the total number of known relevant components). In INEX two different quantisation functions are used to calculate the relevancy: $\mathbf{f}_{\mathbf{strict}}$ evaluates whether a component is highly focused and highly relevant. Alternatively, $\mathbf{f}_{\mathbf{generalised}}$ evaluates a component's degree of relevance. These metrics are combined to form a recall/precision curve.

Together they provide a means for qualitative and quantitative comparison between the various competitors participating at INEX. Each year the competitors' systems are ranked according to their overall effectiveness.

2 Ranking of Results

Ranking of results has a major impact on users' satisfaction with search engines and their success in retrieving relevant documents. While searches may retrieve thousands of hits, search engine developers claim their systems place items that best match the search query at the top of the results list.

Since users often do not have time to explore more than the top few results returned, it is very important for a search engine to be able to rank the best results near the top of all returned results. A study conducted by [7] indicates that 80% of users only view the first two pages of results. The user may consider a number of factors in deciding whether or not to retrieve a document. Regardless of relevance-ranking theory, users have an intuitive sense of how well the relevance ranking is working, and a key indicator of this intuitive satisfaction is the number of distinct query words that a document contains. For example, a document containing only two query words from an eight-word query should not be higher ranked than a document containing all eight words [8].

2.1 Collective Ranking

As described before, the INEX workshop is run once a year and is generally based on the following steps:

1. Participating organisations contribute topics (end user queries) and a subset of topics is selected for evaluation.
2. The topics are distributed to participants who run their search engines and produce a ranked list of results for each topic.
3. The results are pooled together (disassociated and duplicates eliminated).

4. The pooled results are individually assessed by the original topic contributors, who act as end users manually assessing the relevance of the results in terms of exhaustiveness and specificity.
5. The search engines are ranked in terms of performance (recall/precision) using several metrics.
6. Results are returned to participants who in turn write up and present their systems and discuss it at the workshop.

During the last two years the execution of step 4 (assessment of topics by human assessors) has emerged as a very time-consuming procedure which led to the idea of a "Collective Ranking Strategy". The idea is to take the entire set of results from all search engines and produce a collective ("committee") ranking by taking some sort of a vote. These approaches are often referred to as "data fusion" or "meta search".

The collectively ranked results are to be evaluated against the assessed pool of results (as determined by the human assessors). The hypothesis is that it may be possible to outperform any single system by taking account of the results from all systems. If this hypothesis is verified, then as a consequence manual assessment of pooled results by human assessors (step 4) may be no longer required. Instead, a relative comparison of submissions with the collective ranking results will be sufficient to derive a ranking of all search engines. Moreover, this would also prove the assumption that you can derive a better performing search engine by solely considering results of several other search engines.

2.2 Strategy

Several strategies were tested and the specifics of the Collective Ranking were determined. During the testing phase it became obvious that the simplest strategy led to best results. The eventually applied Collective Ranking Strategy is described by the following algorithm, which is to be applied separately for both CAS and CO topics:

For each topic $t_1 \dots t_n$:

For each submission $s_1 \dots s_m$ for topic t_i:

Take the top *x* result elements;

Assign a value $\mathbf{p}_i$ (points for ranking position) to each rank $r_i \in [1 \dots x]$ of the top *x* submitted result elements applying the following formula:

$$\mathbf{p}_i := (x - r_i) + 1;$$

Compute a total result element score **res_score**$_i$ for each unique submitted result element as follows (m being the number of submissions):

$$\forall \mathbf{x}_i \in \textbf{result elements:} \quad \textbf{res\_score}_i := \sum_{i=1}^{m} \mathbf{p}_i^{\,k}$$

Rank the result elements according to the assigned result element score res_score_i in descending order;

```
In the format of a submission file write the top 1500 re-
sult elements of the ranked list into the Collective Rank-
ing output file;
```

Within this algorithm, x ($\triangleq$ number of top ranked result elements taken from each submission for each topic) and k ($\triangleq$ weighting for $\mathbf{p_i}$) are variables whose optimal values are to be determined according to the best possible results in the testing phase.

The central idea of this strategy is to take into account both the number of *occurrences* and the *ranking* position of each result element submitted by the participants' search engines. With reference to the number of occurrences, the summation in the algorithm makes sure that, the more frequently an element occurs in the submitted result lists of various search engines, the higher it is rated and eventually ranked. This becomes evident considering an implication provided by the algorithm: If a particular result element is not returned in a search engine's top 100 results, it receives 0 points for the ranking position ($\mathbf{p_i}$). With respect to the consideration of the ranking position, the definition and incorporation of $\mathbf{p_i}$ (points for ranking position) makes sure that, the higher the ranking position of the same result element in each submitted result list is, the bigger the value $\mathbf{p_i}$ for each occurrence will be.

As the Collective Ranking is derived from a descending list of the top 1500 result element scores, the bigger the value $\mathbf{p_i}$ for each occurrence of a particular result element and as a consequence the bigger the result element score res_score_i (derived from the summation of $\mathbf{p_i}$) is, the better the final ranking position of this particular result element in the Collective Ranking will be.

3 Testing

The Collective Ranking algorithm was tested using different values for the variables x and k, in order to identify the optimal combination of these values, that is, the combination that produced the highest Mean Average Precision (MAP) for our committee submission. In the testing phase it became evident that the bigger the depth value x ($\triangleq$ number of top ranked result elements taken from each submission for each topic) is, the bigger the applied value for k ($\triangleq$ weighting for $\mathbf{p_i}$) is supposed to be in order to obtain optimal results. Furthermore, if $k = 0$, the Collective Ranking Strategy is equivalent to the Borda Count voting method discussed in [9].

The algorithm was also tested comparing results when considering all submissions and merely considering the top ten ranked submissions (as determined by INEX 2003), respectively. It became obvious that considering all submissions instead of solely considering those submissions ranked as the top ten in INEX 2003 led to better results while retaining the same values for x and k.

Figure 1 presents an example of the different effect on results when considering all submissions and only top ten submissions of INEX respectively. Figure 2 and 3 show examples of test results with different values for x and constant value for k and vice versa respectively.

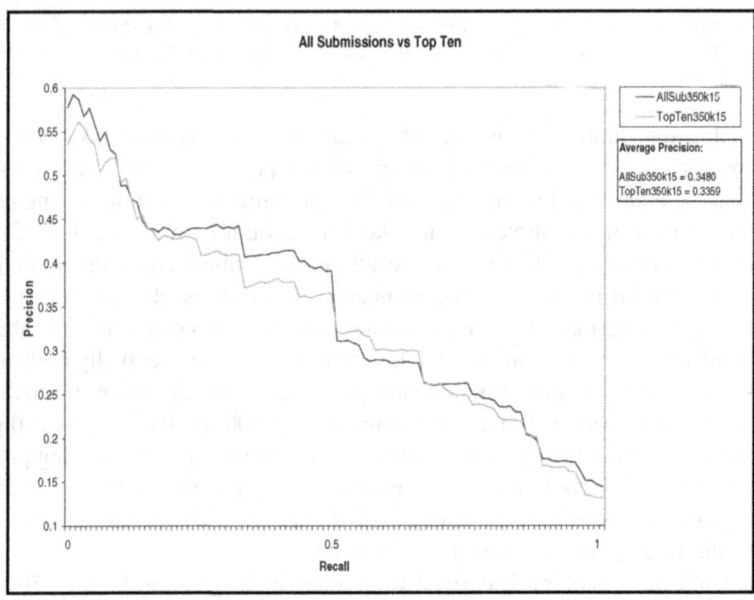

Fig. 1. Comparison of results considering all submissions / only top ten submissions of INEX

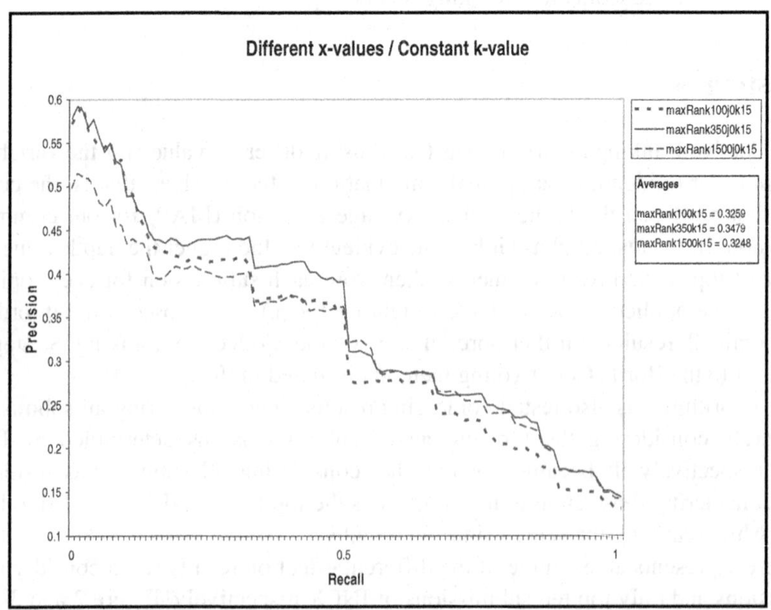

Fig. 2. Example of test results with different values for x and constant value for k

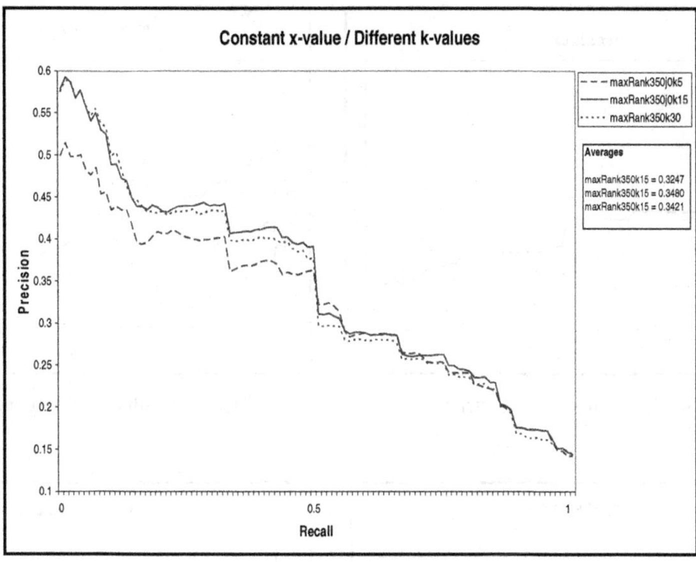

Fig. 3. Example of test results with constant value for x and different values for k

4 Results

After executing the described algorithm for both CAS and CO topics and submitting the obtained Collective Ranking result file to the INEX evaluation software the hypothesis was verified: The recall/precision curve as well as the average precision of the Collective Ranking outperformed all other systems' submissions.

In this context, best results for the different tasks and quantisations were achieved with the following values for x and k:

- CAS strict: $x = 400$ and $k = 18$
- CAS generalised: $x = 1000$ and $k = 30$
- CO strict: $x = 1500$ and $k = 39$
- CO generalised: $x = 1500$ and $k = 39$

Table 1. Comparison of best values of MAP achieved by Collect. Ranking and INEX 2003 participants (*Univ. of Amsterdam [10])

Task	Quantisation	Avg. Precision - Best Value	
		Participants	Collect. Ranking
CAS	Strict	0.3182*	0.3480
CAS	Generalised	0.2989*	0.3177
CO	Strict	0.1214*	0.1339
CO	Generalised	0.1032*	0.1210

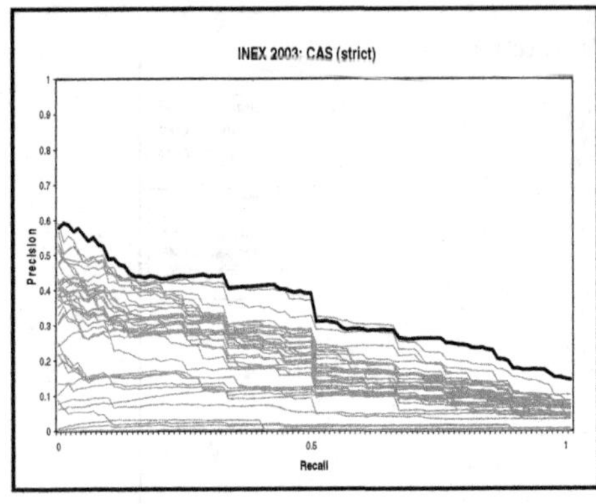

Fig. 4. Results – CAS (strict)

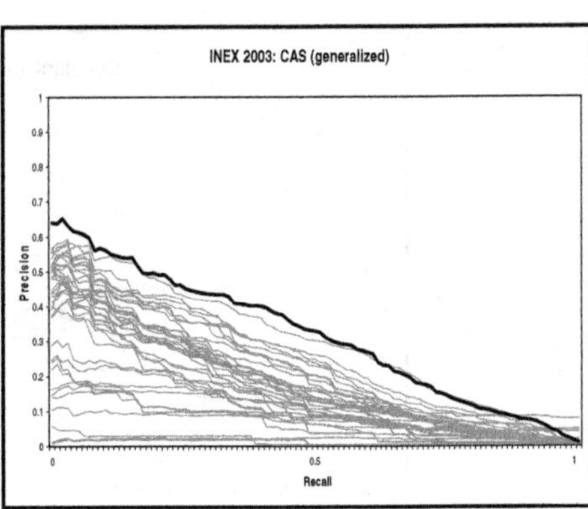

Fig. 5. Results – CAS (generalised)

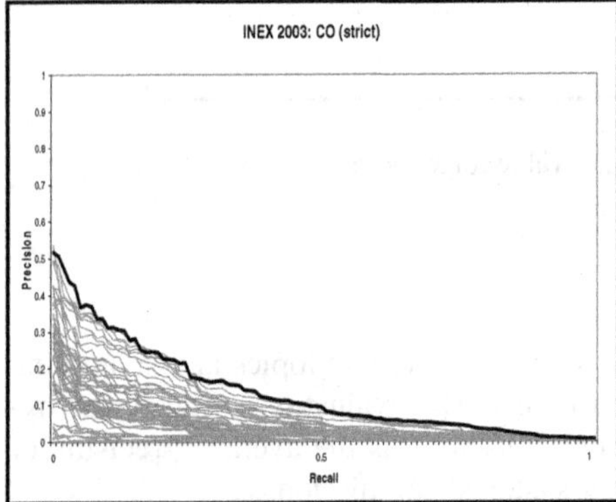

Fig. 6. Results – CO (strict)

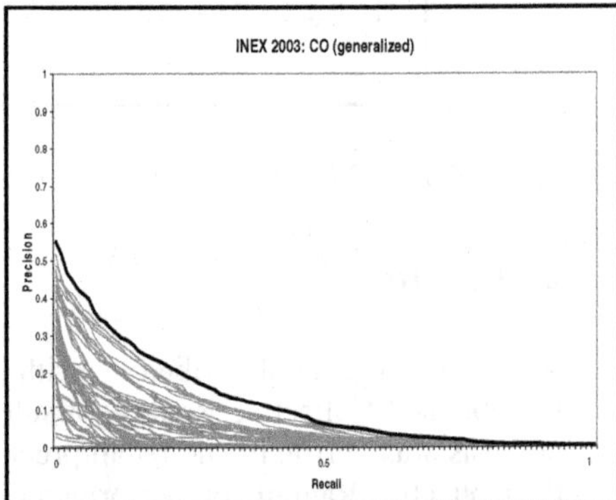

Fig. 7. Results – CO (generalised)

Table 1 displays the best values of average precision achieved by the Collective Ranking in comparison with the best ranked submissions of participants in INEX 2003.

The Precision/Recall curves represented in Figures 4 to 8 demonstrate the performance of the Collective Ranking (displayed in dark bold) in comparison with all other submissions of INEX 2003 (displayed in light grey).

5 Outlook and Future Work

The development and implementation of a Collective Ranking Strategy as presented in this paper and the results obtained establish a basis for copious future work. This chapter gives an overview of challenges and ideas of approaches for further research on this topic.

5.1 Realistic Assessment

In order to identify the extent of possible improvement regarding the Collective Ranking, a programme indicating the notionally maximum performance was implemented, which is based on the following idea:

During the assessment process of the INEX workshop human assessors determine the relevancy of result elements returned by the participants' systems and pooled together in the pool of results in terms of exhaustiveness and specificity. While exploring the XML files of the INEX document collection with respect to the result elements returned for a certain topic, assessors may add elements of the XML files that were not returned by any participating system but, however, are considered relevant to the pooled results. This procedure yields a pool of results referred to as the "Official Perfect Pool of Results", which provides the basis for the INEX Official Assessment Files that are required for the evaluation of the search engines' performance. These assessment files suggest an "idealish" ranking of particular result elements for each topic representing a guideline for the assessment of the actually returned results. This ranking is referred to as "idealish" since elements from some relevant articles might not be included in the top 100 results from any submission, hence are not in the pool of results at all. Adding these elements to the pool would make it theoretically possible to achieve an even better performance. However, due to the fact that some result elements contained in those idealish assessment files are manually added and not returned by any single system, it is not realistic to expect the search engines to actually retrieve these result elements. Therefore, it is equally unlikely that the Collective Ranking system could perform as good as the official ideal results, since it is solely based on the results actually returned by the participants' search engines.

In order to set a more realistic benchmark to identify the (theoretically) best possible performance of the Collective Ranking system, a so-called "Realistic Perfect Pool of Results" is to be established. The appendant programme developed to derive the required Realistic Assessment Files eliminates all result elements not actually submitted by any participant's search engine from the "idealish" Official Perfect Pool of Results.

Figures 8 to 11 display the performance of the Collective Ranking system compared with the precision/recall curves of the "Official Perfect" (displayed as bold grey line) and "Realistic Perfect" Results (displayed as a dotted line). They reveal the remarkably big capability of improvement regarding the Collective Ranking Strategy. Note that for both the strict quantisations, the "Official Perfect" curve is a horizontal line with precision equal to 1 for all recall values.

Surveying these results it is particularly striking to see that the precision/recall curves of the Realistic Perfect Results are remarkably better performing than the Collective Ranking, although the Realistic Perfect "system" avails itself of the same source – solely consisting of result elements returned by INEX participants – that is also available for the Collective Ranking system. This emphasises the crucial importance of successful ranking of returned results and therefore represents a point of origin for further examinations.

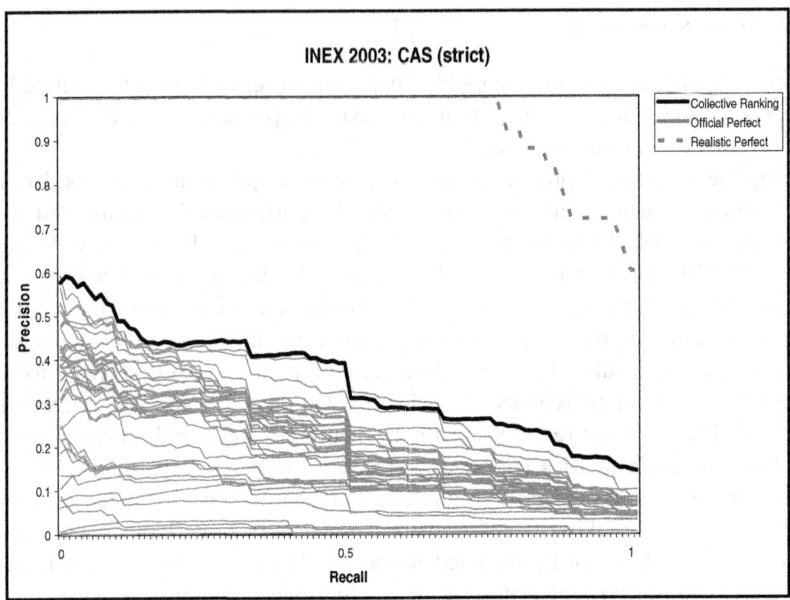

Fig. 8. Collective Ranking compared with "Official Perfect" and "Realistic Perfect" results (CAS – strict)

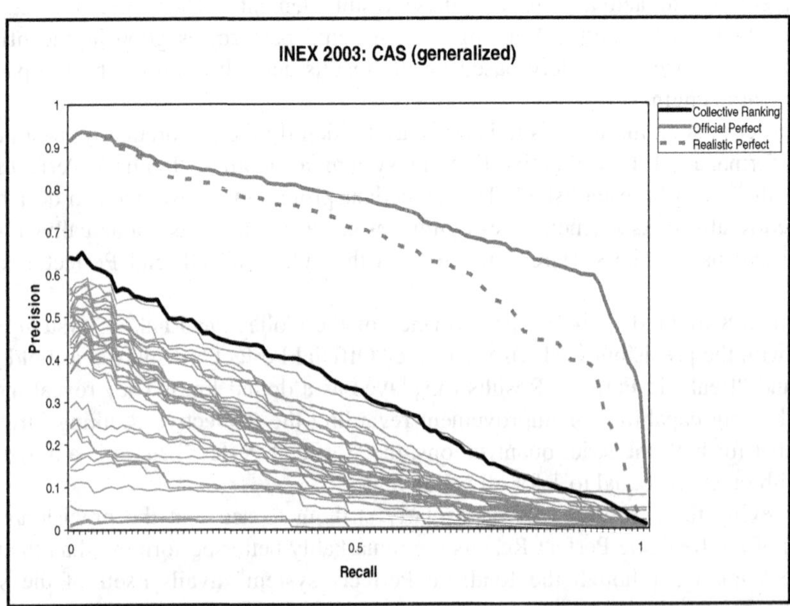

Fig. 9. Collective Ranking compared with "Official Perfect" and "Realistic Perfect" results (CAS – generalised)

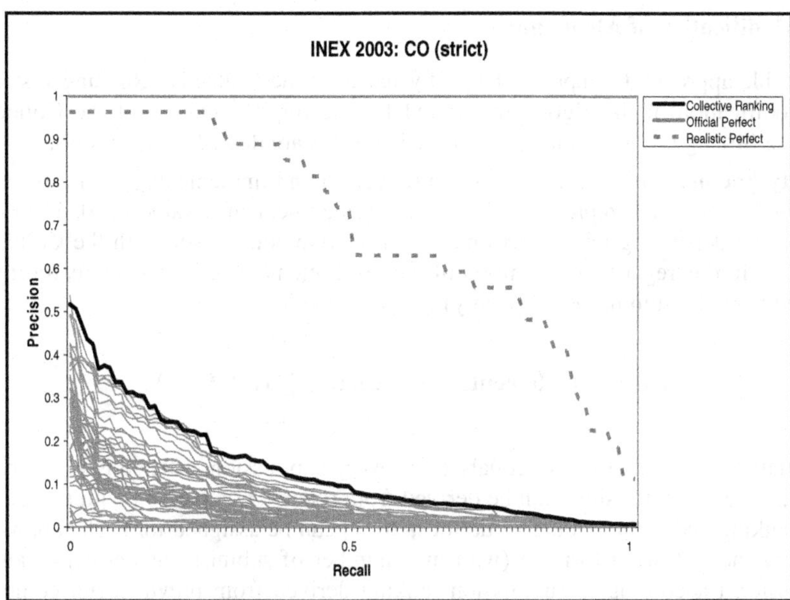

Fig. 10. Collective Ranking compared with "Official Perfect" and "Realistic Perfect" results (CO – strict)

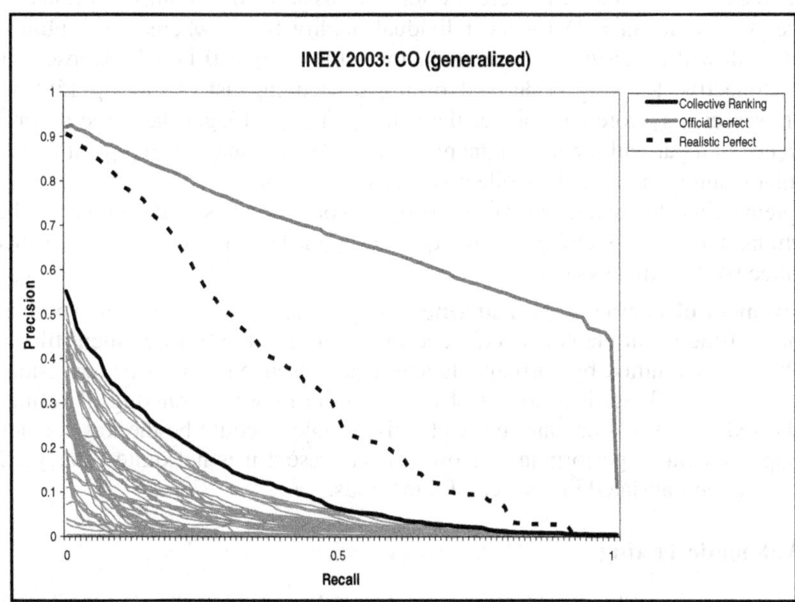

Fig. 11. Collective Ranking compared with "Official Perfect" and "Realistic Perfect" results (CO – generalised)

5.2 Modification of Algorithm

A possible approach to improve the performance of the Collective Ranking system is the modification of the algorithm applied for the implementation of the Collective Ranking Strategy. In this context two practical ideas are described as follows:

Quality Factor: The main idea is the introduction and implementation of a so-called Quality Factor which represents an iterative assignment of a value $\mathbf{q_i}$ (0, 1] to each submission depending on its performance in relative comparison with the Collective Ranking. In this regard the definition of the result element score res_score_i (currently derived from the summation of $\mathbf{p_i}$ only) would be the following:

$$\forall \mathbf{x_i} \in \textbf{result elements: } \mathbf{res\_score_i} := \sum_{i=1}^{m} (\mathbf{p_i}^{k} * \mathbf{q_i}^{j}) \qquad (1)$$

Initially, for the first run $\mathbf{q_i}$ equals 1 for every submission. After this initial run, a first ranking of submissions can be derived from relative comparison with the Collective Ranking and an individual value for $\mathbf{q_i}$ (0, 1] can be assigned for each submission applying the following formula (with m = number of submissions and sr_i = rank of submission i according to submission ranking derived from previous run compared with Collective Ranking):

$$\mathbf{q_i} := (\mathbf{m} - \mathbf{sr_i} + \mathbf{1}) \ / \ \mathbf{m} \qquad (2)$$

This means for example, if there are ten submissions, the submission ranked first achieves the value ($\mathbf{q_i}$ = 1) for its individual quality factor whereas the submission ranked tenth will be assigned a quality factor value of ($\mathbf{q_i}$ = 0.1) only. Consequently, as the Collective Ranking is derived from a descending list of the top 1500 result element scores res_score_i, the bigger the value $\mathbf{p_i}$ and the bigger the value $\mathbf{q_i}$ for each occurrence of a particular result element is, the better the final ranking position of this particular result element in the Collective Ranking will be.

Implementing the idea of a quality factor $\mathbf{q_i}$ would emphasise the impact of better performing submissions and as a consequence might lead to a better performance of the Collective Ranking system.

Improvement of Participants' Ranking: As the Realistic Pool results have revealed that most of the result elements contained in the official INEX assessment files have actually been submitted by participants and as a consequence must be accessible for the Collective Ranking, it becomes obvious that an improved ranking of results for both the INEX submissions and the Collective Ranking could be the key for noticeable improvement of performance. However, at present it is not quite clear yet how this idea can be translated into successful methods.

5.3 Automatic Testing

At this stage, values identified best for *x* and *k* applied in the Collective Ranking programme are based on results derived from experimental testing. However, since possible values for *x* can range from 1 to 1500 and appropriate values for *k* can theoretically range from 0 to infinite, it was not possible to test all possible combinations of these two values. Therefore it is conceivable that better "optimal" combinations may be identified by using automated testing methods which in turn requires the assignment of an adequate implementation.

5.4 Automatic Assessment

At the present time the INEX Assessment Files that are used for the evaluation of submissions are derived from assessments conducted by human assessors who work through the INEX document collection to identify relevant result elements. Since this has emerged as a very time-consuming procedure, future work and development with respect to the Collective Ranking could benefit the INEX workshop at such a rate that human assessments might eventually be replaced by assessment and ranking of submissions derived from a relative comparison of those submissions with the Collective Ranking. For this purpose, however, Automatic Assessment Files are to be established within the scope of further research and testing.

6 Conclusion

The results achieved within the scope of this research project by the development and implementation of a Collective Ranking Strategy may benefit the future procedure of the INEX workshop since – although not yet a suitable substitute for human assessments of results – a ranking of participating search engines can now be derived without manual assessment.

The hypothesis stated at the beginning of this project, suggesting that it may be possible to outperform any single system by taking account of the results from all systems was verified. Moreover it was proven that an outperforming search engine can be developed on the basis of other search engines' results. However, the results derived from the implementation of the Realistic Pool Assessment Programme revealed that there is still much room for improvement. Therefore, ample research on the reasons for the performance of the Collective Ranking system will be required in order to identify means to improve the current results.

However, the baselines at INEX are relatively low at present, and it is questionable whether the Collective Ranking Strategy will still lead to the same results after bringing up the baselines. There exists some work revealing that meta search or data fusion methods do not seem to provide extra benefit when the systems being combined all work very well [11].

These conclusions will provide a basis for further research on this topic, especially for the automatic assessment and ranking of search engines, and may be considered a starting point for the exploration of new challenges regarding ranking strategies within this area of modern Information Retrieval.

References

[1] B. C. Vickery. "The Need for Information". In Techniques of Information Retrieval, p 1, London, 1970.

[2] G. G. Chowdhury. "Basic concepts of information retrieval systems". In Introduction to Modern Information Retrieval, pp 1-2, London, 2004.

[3] S. Brin, L. Page. "The Anatomy of a Large-Scale Hypertextual Web Search Engine", WWW Conf., 1998.

[4] L. Guo, F. Shao, C. Botev, J. Shanmugasundaram. "Ranked Keyword Search over XML Documents", p.1, San Diego, CA, June 9-12, 2003.

[5] N. Fuhr and S. Malik. "Overview of the Initiative for the Evaluation of XML Retrieval (INEX) 2003". In INEX 2003 Workshop Proceedings, pp 1-11, Schloss Dagstuhl, Germany, December 15-17, 2003.

[6] N. Fuhr, N. Gövert, G. Kazai and M. Lalmas. "Overview of the Initiative for the Evaluation of XML Retrieval (INEX) 2002". In Proceedings of the First Workshop of the INitiative for the Evaluation of XML Retrieval (INEX), pp 1-15, Schloss Dagstuhl, Germany, December 9-11, 2002.

[7] Jansen, J. Bernard, A. Spink, J. Bateman, T. Saracevic. "Real Life Information Re-trieval: a Study of User Queries on the Web". In SIGIR Forum 32 No. 1, pp. 5-17, 1998.

[8] M. B. Koll. "Automatic Relevance Ranking: A Searcher's Complement to Indexing" . In Indexing, Providing Access to Information: Looking Back, Looking Ahead, Pro-ceedings of the 25th Annual Meeting of the American Society of Indexers, pp 55-60, Alexandria, VA, May 20-22, 1993. J. A. Aslam and M. Montague. "Models for Metasearch". In Proc. of

[9] the 24th Annual International ACM SIGIR Conf. on Research and Development in Information Retrieval, pp 276-284, 2001.

[10] B. Sigurbjornsson, J. de Rijke, M. Kamps. An Element-based Approach to XML Retrieval. In INEX 2003 Workshop Proceedings, pp 19-26, Schloss Dagstuhl, Ger-many, December 15-17, 2003.

[11] S. Beitzel, A. Chowdhury, O. Frieder, N. Goharian, D. Grossman, and E. Jensen. "Disproving the Fusion Hypothesis: An Analysis of Data Fusion via Effective Informa-tion Retrieval Stategies". In ACM Eighteenth Symposium on Applied Computing (SAC), Melbourne, Florida, March, 2003.

TRIX 2004 – Struggling with the Overlap

Jaana Kekäläinen[1], Marko Junkkari[2], Paavo Arvola[2], and Timo Aalto[1]

[1] University of Tampere, Department of Information Studies,
33014 University of Tampere, Finland
{jaana.kekäläinen, timo.aalto}@uta.fi
[2] University of Tampere, Department of Computer Sciences,
33014 University of Tampere, Finland
marko.junkkari@cs.uta.fi, paavo.arvola@uta.fi

Abstract. In this paper, we present a new XML retrieval system prototype employing structural indices and a *tf*idf* weighting modification. We test retrieval methods that a) emphasize the *tf* part in weighting and b) allow overlap in run results to different degrees. It seems that increasing the overlap percentage leads to a better performance. Emphasizing the *tf* part enables us to increase exhaustiveness of the returned results.

1 Introduction

In this report, we present an XML retrieval system prototype, TRIX (Tampere retrieval and indexing system for XML), employing structural indices and a *tf*idf* weighting modification based on BM25 [3], [10]. The system is aimed for full scale XML retrieval. Extensibility and generality for heterogeneous XML collections have been the main goals in designing TRIX. This prototype is able to manipulate content_only (CO) queries but not content_and_structure (CAS) queries. However, with the CO approach of TRIX we achieved tolerable ranking for VCAS runs in INEX 2004.

One idea of XML is to distinguish the content (or data) element structure from stylesheet descriptions. From the perspective of information retrieval, stylesheet descriptions are typically irrelevant. However, in the INEX collection these markups are not totally separated. Moreover, some elements are irrelevant for information retrieval. We preprocessed the INEX collection so that we removed the irrelevant parts from the collection. The main goal of the preprocessing of the INEX collection was to achieve a structure in which the content element has a natural interpretation. In the terminology of the present paper, the content element means an element that has own textual content. The ranking in TRIX is based on weighting the words (keys) with a *tf*idf* modification, in which the length normalization and *idf* are based on content elements instead of documents.

The overlap problem is an open question in XML information retrieval. On one hand, it would be ideal that the result list does not contain overlapping elements [7]. On the other hand, the metrics of INEX 2004 encourage for a large overlap among results. In this paper, we introduce how the ranking of runs depends on the degree of overlap. For this, we have three degrees of overlap:

N. Fuhr et al. (Eds.): INEX 2004, LNCS 3493, pp. 127 – 139, 2005.

1. No overlapping is allowed. This means that any element is discarded in the ranking list if its subelement (descendant) or superelement (ancestor) is ranked higher in the result list.
2. Partial overlapping is allowed. The partial overlapping means that the immediate subelements and superelement are not allowed in the result list relating to those elements which have a higher score.
3. Full overlapping is allowed.

In this report we present the performance of two slightly different scoring schemes and three different overlapping degrees for both CO and VCAS tasks. The report is organized as follows: TRIX is described in Section 2, the results are given in Section 3, and discussion and conclusions in Sections 4 and 5 respectively.

2 TRIX 2004

2.1 Indices

The manipulation of XML documents in TRIX is based on the structural indices [4]. In the XML context this way of indexing is known better as Dewey ordering [11]. To our knowledge the first proposal for manipulating hierarchical data structures using structural (or Dewey) indices is found in [9]. The idea of structural indices is that the topmost element is indexed by ⟨1⟩ and its immediate subelements by ⟨1,1⟩, ⟨1,2⟩, ⟨1,3⟩ etc. Further the immediate subelements of ⟨1,1⟩ are labeled by ⟨1,1,1⟩, ⟨1,1,2⟩ ⟨1,1,3⟩ etc. This kind of indexing enables analyzing any hierarchal data structure in a straightforward way. For example, the superelements of the element labeled by ⟨1,3,4,2⟩ are found from indices ⟨1,3,4⟩, ⟨1,3⟩ and ⟨1⟩. In turn, any subelement related to the index ⟨1,3⟩ is labeled by ⟨1,3,ξ⟩ where ξ is a non-empty subscripts of the index.

In TRIX we have utilized structural indices in various tasks. First, documents and elements are identified by them. Second, the structure of the inverted file for elements is based on structural indices. Third, algorithms for degrees of overlapping are based on them. A detailed introduction to Dewey ordering in designing and manipulating inverted index is given in [1].

2.2 Weighting Function and Relevance Scoring

The content element is crucial in our weighing function. In this study, the content element is an element that has own textual content but none of its ancestors possess own textual content. Content elements are index units. For example, if the paragraph level is the highest level in which text is represented then paragraphs are manipulated as content elements and their descendants are not indexed. Content elements are chosen automatically for each document in the indexing process.

In TRIX the weighting of keys is based on a modification of the BM25 weighting function [3], [10]. Related to a single key *k* in a CO query the weight associated with the element *e* is calculated as follows:

$$w(k,e) = \frac{kf_e}{kf_e + v \cdot ((1-b) + b \cdot l\_norm(k,e))} \cdot \frac{\log\left(\frac{N}{m}\right)}{\log N} \quad (1)$$

where

- kf_e is the number of times k occurs in element e,
- m is the number of content elements containing k in the collection,
- N is the total number of content elements in the collection,
- v and b are constants for tuning the weighting,
- $l\_norm(k,e)$ is a normalization function defined based on the ratio of the number (ef_c) of all descendant content elements of the element e, and the number (ef_k) of descendant content elements of e containing k. If the element e is a content element then $l\_norm(k,e)$ yields the value 1. Formally, the length normalization function is defined as follows:

$$l\_norm(k,e) = \begin{cases} 1, \text{if } e \text{ is a content element} \\ efc / \sqrt{efk}, \text{otherwise} \end{cases} \quad (2)$$

The weighting formula 1 yields weights scaled into the interval [0,...,1].

TRIX does not support proximity searching for phrases. Instead, we require that each key k_i ($i \in \{1,\ldots,n\}$) in a phrase p ="$k_1,\ldots,k_n$" must appear in the same content element. This is a very simple approximation for weighting of phrases but it works well when content elements are short – such as paragraphs and titles.

Related to the element e the weight of the phrase p is is calculated as follows:

$$w(p,e) = \frac{\min(p,e)}{\min(p,e) + v \cdot ((1-b) + b \cdot lp\_norm(p,e))} \cdot \frac{\log\left(\frac{N}{m_p}\right)}{\log N} \quad (3)$$

where

- min(p,e) gives the lowest frequency among the keys in p in the element e,
- m_p is the number of content elements containing all the keys in p.
- v, b, N and ef_c have the same interpretation as in formula 1.
- *lp_norm* where ef_p is the number of descendant content elements of e containing all the keys in p,

$$lp\_norm(p,e) = \begin{cases} 1, \text{if } e \text{ is a content element} \\ ef_c / \sqrt{ef_p}, \text{otherwise} \end{cases} \quad (4)$$

In CO queries, a query fragment or sub-query (denoted by *sq* below) is either a key or phrase with a possible +/- prefix. The '+' prefix in queries is used to emphasize the importance of a search key. In TRIX the weight of the key is increased by taking a square root of the weight:

$$w(+sq,e) = \sqrt{w(sq,e)} \quad (5)$$

The square root increases the weight related to the element e and the query fragment sq (either k or p) because the weight of a query fragment is scaled between 0 and 1.

The '-' prefix in queries denotes an unwanted key. In TRIX the weight of such a key is decreased by changing the weight to its negation. For any key or phrase sq the minus expression $-sq$ is weighted by the negation of the original weight as follows:

$$w(-sq,e) = -w(sq,e) \tag{6}$$

In other words, unwanted query fragments are manipulated in the interval [-1,0].

For combination of query fragments (with a possible +/- subscript) two operation have been implemented: average and a fuzzy operation called Einstein's sum [8]. Using the average the weight $w(q,e)$ related to the CO query $q = sq_1 \ldots sq_n$ is formulated as follows:

$$w(q,e) = \frac{\sum_{i=1}^{n} w(sq_i,e)}{n} \tag{7}$$

The other implemented alternative, Einstein's sum (denoted by $\oplus$), means that two weights w_1 and w_2 are combined as follows:

$$w_1 \oplus w_2 = \frac{w_1 + w_2}{1 + w_1 \cdot w_2} \tag{8}$$

Unlike the average the operation $\oplus$ is associative, i.e. $w_1 \oplus w_2 \oplus w_3 = (w_1 \oplus w_2) \oplus w_3 = w_1 \oplus (w_2 \oplus w_3)$. Thus, the weight (denoted by w') of a CO query $q = sq_1\ sq_2 \ldots sq_n$ can be calculated follows:

$$w'(q,e) = w(sq_1,e) \oplus w(sq_2,e) \oplus \cdots \oplus w(sq_n,e)$$

To illustrate this function we apply it to topic 166 (+"tree edit distance" +xml -image) for an element e:

w'(+"tree edit distance" +xml -image, e)

First, Equation 9 is applied as follows:

w(+"tree edit distance", e) $\oplus$ w(+xml, e) $\oplus$ w(-image, e) (9)

Then, Equations 5 and 6 are used (sqrt means square root in Equation 5)

sqrt(w("tree edit distance", e)) $\oplus$ sqrt(w(xml, e)) $\oplus$ -w(image, e)

Now, w("tree edit distance", e) is calculated using Equation 3 and the others using Equation 1.

2.3 Implementation

The TRIX is implemented in C++ for Windows/XP but the implementation is aimed for UNIX/LINUX as well. In implementing the present TRIX prototype we have paid attention for effective manipulation of XML data structures based on structural indices. However, the efficiency has not been the main goal of TRIX.

The TRIX prototype has two modes: online mode and batch mode. In the online mode the user can run CO queries in the default database (XML collection). The batch mode enables running a set of CO queries. In this mode queries are saved in a text file. Running the CO queries of INEX 2004 in the batch mode takes about 40 minutes in a sample PC (Intel Pentium 4, 2.4 GHz, 512MB of RAM). The weights are calculated at query time for every element. The size of the inverted index is 174 MB.

The command-based user interface of the TRIX prototype is tailored for testing various aspects of XML information retrieval. This means that a query can be run with various options. For example, the user can select:

- the method (average or Einstein's sum) used in combining the query term weights,
- the degree of overlap (no overlapping, partial overlapping or full overlapping), and
- the values of the constants.

For example, the command string

```
TRIX -e -o b=0.1 queries2004co.txt
```

means that Einstein's sum is used for combining weights (parameter -e), full overlapping is allowed (parameter -o) and the *b* is 0.1. Finally, queries2004co.txt denotes the file from which the query set, at hand, is found. Actually, there is no assumption of ordering for the parameters of a query. For example, the command string

```
TRIX -o queries2004co.txt b=0.1 -e
```

is equivalent with the previous query.

The online mode of TRIX is chosen by the command

```
TRIX
```

After this command the user may give his/her query, e.g.:

```
+"tree edit distance" +xml -image
```

3 Data and Results

We preprocessed the INEX collection so that from a retrieval point of view irrelevant parts were removed. As irrelevant content we considered elements consisting of non-natural language expressions, e.g. formulas, abbreviations, codes. We classified irrelevant parts into three classes. First, there are elements which possess relevant content but the tags are irrelevant. Tags which only denote styles, such as boldface or italic, inhere in this class. These tags were removed but the content of elements was maintained. Second, there are elements whose content is irrelevant but their tags are necessary in order to maintain the coherent structure of documents. For example we appraised the content of <sgmlmath> and <tmath> elements to inhere in this class. Third, there are elements having irrelevant content whose tags are not necessary in structural sense. These elements, such as <doi> and <en>, were removed. The selection of the parts to be removed was done by researchers, the removal was automatic.

For INEX 2004 we submitted both CO and VCAS runs though our system actually supports only CO queries. In both cases, the title field was used in automatic query construction. Phrases marked in titles were interpreted as 'TRIX phrases' in queries, i.e. all the phrase components were required to appear in the same element. In addition, all the components were added as single keys to queries. For example, topic 166 is formulated into a query as follows:

```
+"tree edit distance" +xml -image tree edit distance
```

In VCAS queries the structural conditions were neglected and all keys were collected into a flat query. Word form normalization for the INEX collection and queries was Porter stemming, and a stoplist of 419 words was employed.

3.1 Tuning Constants

Setting the values of the constants v and b in the weighting function has an impact on the size of elements retrieved. For analyzing this impact, v was tested with values 1 and 2, and b was varied between 0 and 1. The value $v = 2$ gave better performance than $v = 1$, and the former is thus used as default now on. We ran the CO queries using average scoring, no-overlap and full overlap with different values of b. Then, the result lists were analyzed for the percentage of different element types at document cut-off values (DCV) 100 and 1500. Our categorization was rather coarse; percentages of articles, sections, abstracts, paragraphs and others ware calculated in the result lists. Category *section* contains sections and 'equivalent elements' (see [5]); category *paragraph* contains paragraphs and equivalent elements. Only DCV 100 is reported below because DCV 1500 gave very similar results.

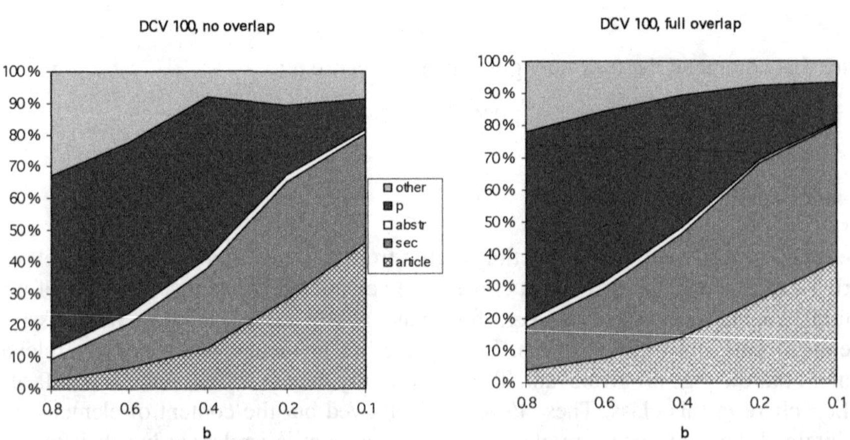

Fig. 1. Percentages of elements of different size in the result sets when b is varied

Figure 1 illustrates the change in the size of retrieved elements when *b* is varied between 0.8 and 0.1. The percentage of the smaller units increases from *b* value 0.1 to *b* value 0.8. In other words large *b* values promote small elements and the small b values promote large elements. This is due to strengthening the *tf* part in the weighting scheme by weakening length normalization. Although our categorization is rough and the category 'other' includes also large elements, the trend is visible. The change is apparent with and without overlap. In our official submissions *b* was 0.4. However, later tests revealed, that *b* value 0.1 gives better performance. Results with both values of *b*, 0.1 and 0.4, are reported in the following sections.

3.2 CO Runs

The evaluation measure used in INEX 2004 was precision at standard recall levels (see [2]) with different quantizations for relevance dimensions (see Relevance Assessment Guide elsewhere in these Proceedings). In the strict quantization only those elements that are highly exhaustive and highly specific are considered relevant, others non-relevant. In other quantization functions elements' degree of relevance is taken into account by crediting elements according to their level of specificity and exhaustiveness. (For details of metrics, see [12] or Evaluation metrics 2004 in these Proceedings.) The results are based on the topic set with relevance assessements for 34 topics. Our official submissions were:

1. CO_avrg: run using *w* weighting (average) with no overlapping when $b = 0.4$,
2. CO_Einstein: run using *w'* weighting (Einstein's sum) with no overlapping when $b = 0.4$,
3. CO_avrg_part_overlap: run using *w* weighting with partial overlapping when $b = 0.4$.

The results for 1 and 2 were so similar that we report the results based on average only. Further, in our official submissions two overlap degrees were tested: no overlapping and partial overlapping. Later on we added the full overlapping case.

Table 1. Mean average precision (MAP) and ranking of CO runs with average scoring

	b	MAP	Rank
No overlapping	0.4	0.0198	45
	0.1	0.0239	42
Partial overlapping	0.4	0.0443	31
	0.1	0.0487	25
Full overlapping	0.4	0.0831	11
	0.1	0.0957	10

Aggregate precision values, given in Table 1, are macro-averages over the different quantizations used in INEX 2004. Table 1 shows the effect of different overlaps and tuning of *b* to aggregate precision and rank. Decreasing *b* has a slight positive effect on the aggregate score and rank. When the different metrics are considered, it is obvious that small b values enhance the dimension of exhaustiveness at specificity's expense. Figures 4 - 5 in Appendix show P-R-curves for CO runs with specificity- and exhaustiveness-oriented quantizations. In case of specificity-oriented quantization (Figures 4a-b and 5 a-b) average precision decreases as b decreases. Figures 4c-d and 5c-d in the appendix show an exhaustiveness-oriented quantization, and there average precision increases as b decreases. The mean average precision figures with all quantizations for our official submissions are given in Table 2.

Table 2. MAP figures for University of Tampere official CO submissions, $b = 0.4$

	MAP						
	strict	gen.	so	s3_e3 21	s3_e3 2	e3_s32 1	e3_s3 2
CO_avg	0.022	0.016	0.015	0.016	0.017	0.026	0.026
CO_Einstein	0.023	0.016	0.015	0.014	0.017	0.034	0.029
CO_avg_po	0.044	0.041	0.041	0.039	0.042	0.051	0.054

The effect of overlap is more substantial: allowing the full overlapping changes the aggregate rank from 45th to 11th when $b = 0.4$, or from 42nd to 10th when $b = 0.1$. Figure 2 illustrates the increase in the aggregate score when overlap percentage increases. (No overlap 0%; partial overlap 40%/44%; full overlap 63%/69%. Compare also Figures 4a and 5a, and 4b and 5b, etc. in Appendix). Whether the change in the result lists is desirable from the user's point of view is questionable because it means returning several overlapping elements from the same document in a row.

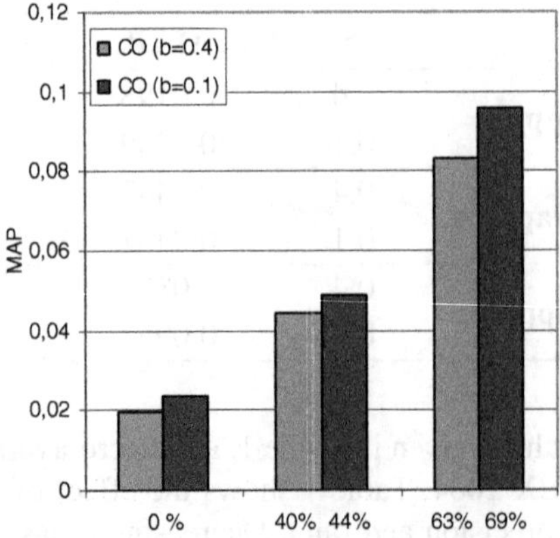

Fig. 2. Mean average precision and overlap percentage of CO runs with average scoring

3.3 VCAS Runs

The results of the VCAS runs are very similar to CO runs. Decreasing *b* value gives better exhaustivity-oriented results but impairs specificity. Increasing the overlap enhances effectiveness. Both these tactics have a positive effect on the aggregate score (see Table 3).

Table 3. Mean average precision and ranking of VCAS runs with average scoring

	b	MAP	Rank
No overlapping	0.4	0.269	30
	0.1	0.031	30
Partial overlapping	0.4	0.038	25
	0.1	0.042	22
Full overlapping	0.4	0.061	11
	0.1	0.075	7

Figure 3 shows the overlap percentages for different VCAS runs. Also here the benefits of allowing the overlap are evident though not as strong as with CO queries.

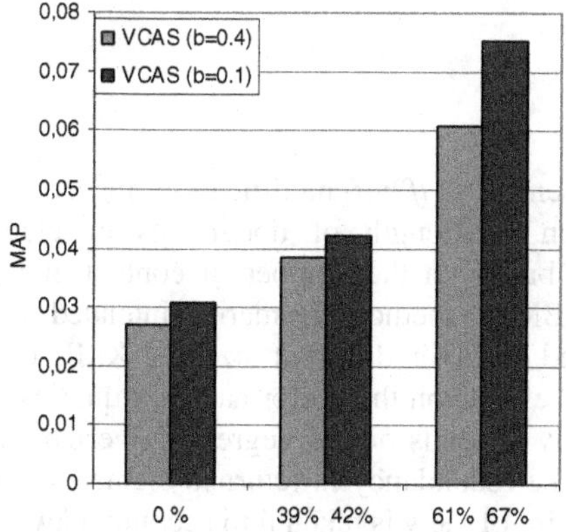

Fig. 3. Mean average precision and overlap percentage of CAS runs with average scoring

4 Discussion

In INEX 2004 University of Tampere group was struggling with the overlap. Our basic design principle was not to allow overlap in the result lists. Because of the structural indices of our system overlap is easy to eliminate. However, the reports of the previous INEX workshop led us to test effectiveness of partial overlap. Because of improved performance, we tested several runs with and without overlap, and allowing full overlap yielded the best performance. Nevertheless, the overlap percentage, showing the percentage of elements that have either a superelement or a subelement ranked higher in the result list, is almost 70 in case of full overlap. This means that in the result list of 10 elements only 3 elements are 'totally new' for the user. It seems that the INEX metrics encourage returning overlapping elements though this might not be beneficial for the user. Our original idea of eliminating overlap was supported by an alternative measure, addressing the problem of overlapping relevant elements, proposed in [6]. The measure, XCG, ranked our runs without overlap higher than runs with overlap.

Our retrieval system, TRIX, employs a modification of *tf*idf* weighting. The number of content subelements is used in element length normalization. In the present mode, TRIX only supports CO queries but we aim at introducing a query language for content and structure queries. Because only titles of the topics – providing a very terse description of the information need – were allowed in query construction, and we did not expand the queries, a mediocre effectiveness was to be expected. Since TRIX does not support querying with structural conditions we submitted VCAS runs processed similarly as CO runs. Surprisingly our success with the VCAS task was not worse than with the CO task. However, if structural conditions are not considered when assessing the relevance, it is understandable that CO and VCAS tasks resemble each other.

Our further work with TRIX is aimed at introducing a query expansion or enhancing module. Incapability to deal with short content queries is a well-known disadvantage. Also, a CAS query language allowing also document restructuring is under construction.

5 Conclusion

In this paper we presented a *tf*idf* modification for XML retrieval. Instead of normalization based on the length of documents or elements we proposed a normalization function based on the number of content elements. We have shown how the well-known BM25 method, primarily intended to full-text information retrieval, can be applied to favor different sizes of XML elements. This sizing of result elements also has effects on the performance of queries. As our study indicates the performance strongly depends on the degree of overlap when such metrics as in INEX 2004 are used. The redundancy in returned elements might not serve the user. Therefore, if the user point of view is taken into account, nåw measures are needed.

Acknowledgments

This research was supported by the Academy of Finland under grant number 52894.

References

1. Guo, L., Shao, F., Botev, C. and Shanmugasundaram, J.: XRANK: Ranked Keyword Search over XML Documents. In: Proc. of ACM SIGMOD 2003, San Diego, CA (2003) 16-27

2. Gövert, N., and Kazai, G. Overview of the INitiative for the Evaluation of XML retrieval (INEX) 2002. In: Proc. of the First Workshop of the Initiative for the Evaluation of XML Retrieval (INEX), (2002), pp. 1-17. Retrieved 27.1.2005 from http://qmir.dcs.qmul.ac.uk/inex/Workshop.html
3. Hawking, D., Thistlewaite, P., and Craswell, P. ANU/ACSys TREC-6 experiments. In: Proc. of TREC-6, (1998). Retrieved 10.3.2004 from http://trec.nist.gov/pubs/trec6/papers/anu.ps
4. Junkkari, M. PSE: An object-oriented representation for modeling and managing part-of relationships. Journal of Intelligent Information Systems, to appear.
5. Kazai, G. Lalmas, M, and Malik, S. INEX´03 guidelines for topic developmen. In: INEX 2003 Workshop Proc., (2003), pp. 192-199. Retrieved 21.1.2005 from http://inex.is.informatik.uni-duisburg.de:2003/internal/downloads/INEXTopicDevGuide.pdf
6. Kazai, G., Lalmas, M., and de Vries, A.P. Reliability tests for the XCG and INEX-2002 metrics. In INEX 2004 Workshop Pre-Proc. (2004), pp. 158-166. Retrieved 18.1.2005 from http://inex.is.informatik.uni-duisburg.de: 2004/pdf/INEX2004PreProceedings.pdf
7. Kazai, G., Lalmas, M., and de Vries, A.P. The overlap problem in content-oriented XML retrieval evaluation. In Proc. of the 27th Annual International ACM SIGIR Conference on Research and Development in Information Retrieval, Sheffield, UK, (2004), pp.72-79.
8. Mattila, J.K. Sumean Logiikan Oppikirja: Johdatusta Sumean Matematiikkaan. Art House, Helsinki, (1998).
9. Niemi, T. A seven-tuple representation for hierarchical data structures. Information systems, 8, 3 (1983), 151-157.
10. Robertson S.E., Walker, S., Jones, S., Hancock-Beaulieu, M.M., and Gatford, M. Okapi at TREC-3. In: NIST Special Publication 500-226: Overview of the Third Text REtrieval Conference (TREC-3), (1994). Retrieved 21.11.2004 from http://trec.nist.gov/pubs/trec3/papers/city.ps.gz
11. Tatarinov, I., Viglas, S.D., Beyer, K., Shanmugasundaram, J., Shekita, E., and Zhang, C. Storing and querying ordered XML using a relational database system. In Proc. of the SIGMOD Conference, (2002), pp. 204-215.
12. de Vries, A.P, Kazai, G., and Lalmas, M. Evaluation metrics 2004. In INEX 2004 Workshop Pre-proc., (2004), pp. 249-250. Retrieved 18.1.2005 from http://inex.is.informatik.uni-duisburg.de:2004/pdf/INEX2004PreProceedings.pdf

Appendix

Precision-Recall Curves for CO Queries

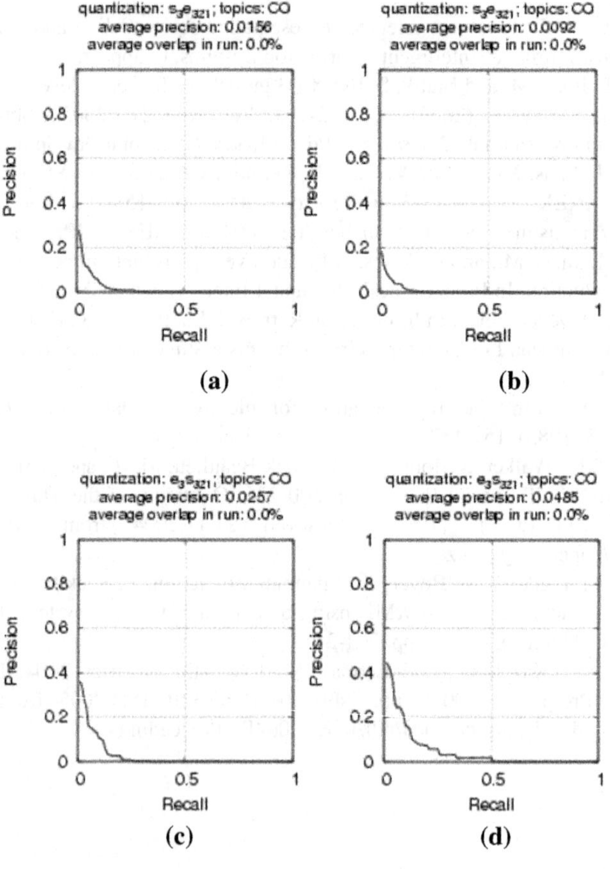

Fig. 4. CO without overlap. Quantization: s_3e_{321} (a) $b = 0.4$, rank 39/70; (b) $b = 0.1$, rank 46/70. Quantization e_3s_{321} (c) $b = 0.4$, rank 45/70 ; (d) $b = 0.1$, rank 39/70

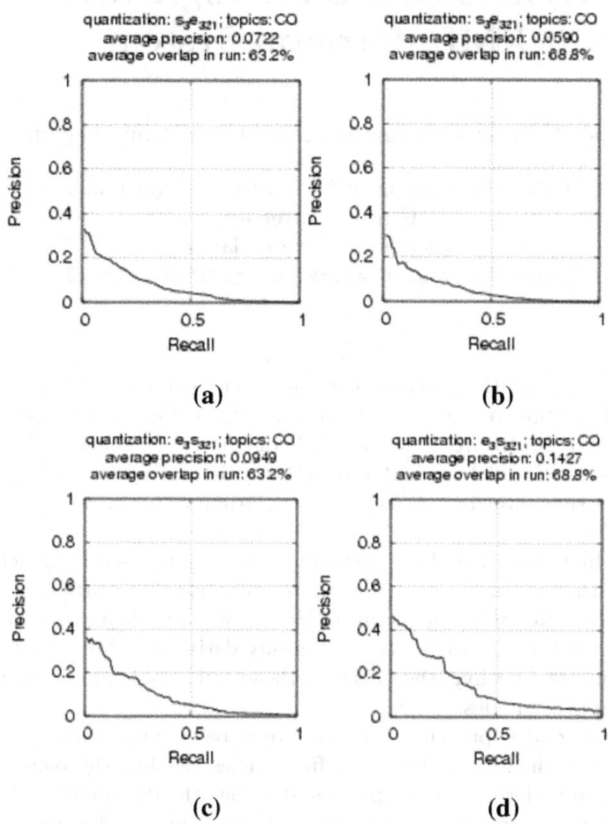

Fig. 5. CO with full overlap. Quantization: s_3e_{321} (a) $b = 0.4$, rank 8/70; (b) $b = 0.1$, rank 12/70. Quantization: e_3s_{321} (c) $b = 0.4$, rank 17/70; (d) $b = 0.1$, rank 11/70

The Utrecht Blend: Basic Ingredients for an XML Retrieval System

Roelof van Zwol, Frans Wiering, and Virginia Dignum

Centre for Content and Knowledge Engineering,
Utrecht University,
Utrecht, The Netherlands
{roelof, frans.wiering, virginia}@cs.uu.nl

Abstract. Exploiting the structure of a document allows for more powerful information retrieval techniques. In this article a basic approach is discussed for the retrieval of XML document fragments. Based on a vector-space model for text retrieval we aim at investigating various strategies that influence the retrieval performance of an XML-based IR system.

The first extension of the system uses a schema-based approach that assumes that authors tag their text to emphasise on particular pieces of content that are of importance. Based on the schema used by the document collection, the system can easily derive the children of mixed content nodes. Our hypothesis is that those child nodes are more important than other nodes.

The second approach discussed here is based on a horizontal fragmentation of the inverse document frequencies, used by the vector space model. The underlying assumption states that the distribution of terms is related to the semantical structure of the document. However, we observed that the IEEE collection is not a good example of semantic tagging.

The third approach investigates how the performance of the retrieval system can improve for the 'Content Only' task by using a set of a-priori defined cut-off nodes that define 'logical' document fragments that are of interest to a user.

1 Introduction

The upcoming XML standard as a publishing format provides many new challenges. One of these challenges, the scope of INEX [2], is the retrieval of structured documents. This requires new techniques that extend current developments in text retrieval. Not only should an XML retrieval system be equipped with an adequate text retrieval strategy, it is also required that the system is capable to include the document structure into the retrieval process.

The structure of the XML document is not only used to refine the query formulation process, it also allows to retrieve more accurate the relevant pieces of information that a user is interested in. For the ad hoc track of INEX, two

N. Fuhr et al. (Eds.): INEX 2004, LNCS 3493, pp. 140–152, 2005.

tasks are defined that examine these aspects: the *Content Only* (CO) task and the '*Vague Content and Structure* (VCAS) task [5]. The aim of both tasks is to retrieve relevant document fragments. The difference lays in the query formulation. The CO task uses only a keyword specification, as commonly used for text retrieval and the well-known Internet search engines. The VCAS task, however, alsouses the document structure for the query formulation, using the NEXI specification [9]. NEXI is an Xpath-like query language, that allows both structural and content-based constraints to be specified for a typical user information request on a structured document collection.

The challenge is thus to build the best content-based XML retrieval system that allows for the retrieval of relevant text fragments, while taking the structure of the XML documents into account. Our personal aim is more modest, since we are primarily interested in the effect of our hypothesis on the retrieval performance of an XML retrieval system. Therefore we have built a retrieval system, that is based on the vector space model for text retrieval and use a strict interpretation of the structural constraints, formerly referred to as the *strict content and structure* (SCAS) task [3].

We have three hypothesis that we want to put to the test. First of all our aim is to investigate whether the retrieval performance of our default XML retrieval system can be improved by taking into account that the author uses markup (structure) to emphasise on particular pieces of text that are of extra importance, i.e. bold/italic text, itemised lists, or enumerations. Focusing on the XML structure, examples of these text fragments are typically found within *mixed-content* nodes. The content model of a mixed-content node contains a mixture of text and child-elements. Using the DTD or XML-schema definition the content type of nodes can easily be determined. In this article we refer to this as the *schema-based* run.

Another hypothesis that we want to investigate here, takes into account that some terms will occur more often within certain XML document fragments, than in other document fragments. We expect that adjusting the term weights by taking this distribution into account will increase the performance of the ranking of the retrieval strategy. This hypothesis has already been tested successfully in the context of XML and semantical schemas [10]. The vector space model consists of two components: a document statistic, i.e. the term frequency (tf), and a collection statistic, i.e. the inverse document frequency (idf). These two statistics are calculated for each term in the document collection. However, the inverse document frequencies are no longer calculated over the entire document, but for small text fragments. Assume now that some terms occur less frequently in abstract, than in other parts of the document. As a result the idf, and thus the term weight, of those terms is valued relatively low compared to other terms in the abstract. Using a fragmented document frequency, where the idf is calculated per XML element name corrects this problem. Our experience is that for semantically tagged XML documents an increase in retrieval performance can be achieved, when the query consists of two or more query terms [10]. We refer to this approach as the *fdf* run.

The third hypothesis focuses on the CO task. For the CO task it is not specified in the query, which document fragments should be returned by the system. Returning entire documents as the result of a query will result in a low performance according to the specificity quantisation [4], since it is likely that only small portions of the XML document will contain relevant information. To deal with this we have defined a cutoff node set, that consists of XML elements that provide a partial logical view on the XML document. When retrieving XML document fragments this node set is used to return smaller fragments, that have a higher specificity of the content in relation to the query terms. We refer to this strategy as the *cutoff* run.

1.1 Organisation

In the remainder of this article we first discuss the approach used to index the XML collection in Section 2. In Section 3 the different retrieval strategies for querying XML documents is discussed for the different runs that we have submitted for INEX 2004. The results of our system are presented in Section 4, together with the unofficial runs that we computed with improved performance of the vector space model. Finally we come to our conclusions in Section 5.

2 Indexing the XML Collection

To index the IEEE XML document collection the XML structure of each document is analysed and a text retrieval strategy is implemented. In Section 2.1 the indexing of the index structure is discussed, while in Section 2.2 the text retrieval component is described.

2.1 Processing XML Structures

To index the XML collection the structure of each document is analysed as follows. The nodes are numbered using the method described in Table 1. This resembles an approach adopted by others [6], however we have chosen not to number the individual terms within a text fragment, but to refer to a text fragment as a whole.

Furthermore we keep track of parent-child relations for each node. All node information is stored in the `Element` table, as shown in Table 2. This table

Table 1. XML example illustrating the numbering of nodes

<ElementA>^{1}
    TextFragmentA^{2}
    <ElementB>^{3}TextFragmentB^{4}</ElementB>^{5}
    <ElementC>^{6}TextFragmentC^{7}</ElementC>^{8}
    <ElementB/>^{9}
    TextFragmentD^{10}
</ElementA>^{11}

Table 2. Internal data structure

Document

id	uri

Element

id	name	parent	document	path	start	end

Textfragment

id	parent	position	length	document

Term

content	fragment	tf	tfidf

contains the following information about element nodes: A unique id, the element name, a reference to its parent, a pointer to the document containing the element, and the unique path leading to the element node. Finally, for each element node the start and end positions are stored, as explained above.

Whenever the indexer encounters a text fragment, a new id is generated and stored in the table `TextFragment`. A reference to the parent node, its position in the document, the number of terms, i.e. the length, and a pointer to the document URI is stored. The text fragment is then handed to the text indexer.

2.2 Processing Text Fragments

The text retrieval component of our indexing system is based on vector space model [1]. This component analyses the rather small text fragments according to the following steps:

- **pre-processing.** A number of basic text operations are called during the pre-processing step. Among these are lexical cleaning, stop word removal and stemming [1].
- **indexing.** Using a bag of terms approach the frequencies of the terms occurring in the text fragment are calculated. After processing a text fragment, all the terms are stored in the `Term` table. For each term, its content, a reference to the corresponding text fragment and the term frequency is stored in the database.
- **post-processing.** Once all documents have been indexed the collection statistics are calculated. For each unique term in the collection the inverse document frequency is calculated as:

$$idf(t) = log(\frac{N}{n(t)}), \tag{1}$$

with N being the total number of unique terms, and $n(t)$ the number of text fragments in which term t occurs.

Later on, we also used a normalised tf factor [8]. The ntf factor reduces the range of the contributions from the term frequency of a term. This is done by compressing the range of the possible tf factor values. The ntf factor is used with the belief that mere presence of a term in a text should have a default weight. Additional occurrences of a term could increase the weight of the term to some maximum value. To compute this factor we used:

$$ntf(t) = 0.5 \ + \ 0.5 \ * \ \frac{tf(t)}{max \ tf(t)} \tag{2}$$

$tf(t)$ contains the raw term frequency for the term, while $max\ tf(t)$ provides the maximum term frequency found in that text fragment.

The tfidf for each term in `Term` is then calculated as:

$$tfidf(t) = \frac{tf(t) * idf(t)}{l} \tag{3}$$

Where l is the length of the text fragment. Please note that this is not a standard way to normalise the term weights for the length of the text fragments.

3 Querying the XML Collection

For INEX we submitted six runs, as discussed below. They all use the same vector space model, with the exception of the fdf runs. Furthermore, we believe that this implementation of the vector-space model leaves plenty of room for improvement. When discussing the results, we will show some simple modifications that improve the retrieval performance of our system. Our interest in this experiment focuses mainly on the effect of using different XML-based mechanisms for calculating the relevances of the document fragments retrieved by our system. The official runs computed for the INEX 2004 topic set are described below.

3.1 Content and Structured XML Retrieval

The so called vague content and structure (VCAS) topics are defined using the NEXI specification [9]. Our system implements the NEXI grammar for these types of topics and evaluates the NEXI queries by following the path expressions and narrowing down the possible set of results. In fact our system enforces that the path constraints defined by the topic are computed in a strict fashion, according to the SCAS specification. We computed the following three runs for the VCAS ad hoc task:

- **33-VCAS-default.** Our default approach to compute a ranking of the retrieved documents simply determines a set of possible document fragments for the first structural constraint, and assigns a textual relevance of ‘0’ to them. If a filter clause is available, this set is narrowed down, according to the conditions defined in the filter. If an *about*-clause is defined within that filter, a relevance ranking of the document fragments is obtained by the system.

Table 3. NEXI example: INEX 2004, topic 132

$//article[about(.//abs, classification)]//sec[about(., experiment\ compare)]$

This basic approach is followed for all VCAS runs submitted. The variance between the runs is determined by the implementation of the *about*-clause. Consider for example the following NEXI-query, presented in Table 3.

During the first step a set of `article`-fragments is retrieved, having a relevance score of '0'. The next step is to evaluate the *about*-filter, narrowing down the set of articles to those containing an `abstract`, which contains the word '*classification*'. The relevances computed by the about function are then summed and associated with the corresponding `article`-fragments. For this set, the second path-constraint is computed, which in this case results in a set of `sec`-nodes, which inherit the relevances computed for the parent `article` nodes. Again the about-filter is evaluated and the relevances are added to the existing relevance scores of the retrieved `sec` nodes.

For the default run the relevances for the document fragment are simply calculated by filtering all the relevant terms from the `TERM` table, using only the *positive* query terms. The relevance for each document fragment, defined in the offset of the about clause, is then calculated by summing over the terms of the text fragments that are contained within the start- and end position of the document fragment.

- **33-VCAS-schema.** The structural constraints for this run are computed similar to the default run. However the about function uses a weighing function, that increases the weight of those nodes which are considered of more importance.

  The underlying hypothesis is that authors writing text use markup to emphasise on particular pieces of content that they find of more importance. Simple examples are those text fragments containing bold and italic text. A reader's attention is automatically drawn whenever a bold or italic text fragment is seen. In XML, this markup is typically found within *mixed-content* nodes. Mixed content nodes are nodes that allow both text fragments and additional markup to be used in a mixed context. In our case, we are interested in the set of child nodes found within such *mixed-content* nodes. Using the DTD, or XML-schema definition this node set can be easily computed. To compute the relevances of the XML document fragments the system first has to derive the set with text fragments containing relevant terms. If one or more ancestor nodes are contained in the set with mixed-content nodes a multiplication factor, i.e. 2, 4, 8, or ..., is added to the weight of that text fragment, depending on the number of mixed-content nodes that are found. Next, the relevance for each document fragment is calculated by summing over the terms of the text fragments that are contained within the start- and end position of the document fragment.

- **33-VCAS-fdf.** This run uses an alternative way of calculating the term weights. The vector space model uses a combination of two statistics to calculate the term weights, i.e. the term frequencies and the inverse document frequencies. The inverse document frequency is a collection measure, that determines how frequently a term occurs in different documents of the collection. For the 'fragmented document fragments'-run (fdf) we have used a fragmented version of the inverse document frequencies (ifdf).

  The underlying assumption for this fragmentation is that if the XML structure of the document is not merely based on presentation, but defines a semantic structure for the content contained in the document, it is likely that some terms, associated with the semantic structure will appear more often in certain document fragments than other terms.

  For example, in text fragments discussing cultural information about a destination, the term '*church*' is more likely to appear, than in text fragments that discuss sports activities[1]. Consider now the following information request: 'Find information about basketball clinics in former churches', the term church is an important query term in this search, however the *idf* for the query term '*church*' will be relatively low if the document collection contains both cultural- and sports descriptions of destinations. We have found that the retrieval performance improves significantly [10], when using the fdf approach. The retrieval strategy, based on the ifdf, is capable of ranking the relevant documents higher in the ranking, if the query consists of two or more query terms. In fact, increasing the amount of query terms will result in a higher retrieval performance.

3.2 Content Only XML Retrieval

For the CO task we have defined four runs.

- **33-CO-default.** The content only runs are mainly driven by the text retrieval component. The positive query terms defined for each content only topic are used to find relevant text fragments. The term weights found in each text fragment are summed over the corresponding parent node of each text fragment.

  In the next step the result set is grouped and summed per document. As a result the smallest common document fragment that can be retrieved for each document is returned as the result of a query. This approach ensures that no redundancy is possible between the document fragments retrieved by the system.

  This approach has two advantages: no redundancy in the retrieved document fragments, and the retrieved fragments should score high on the ex-

[1] This example is based on the Lonely Planet collection, where the tagging of content is semantically organised[10].

haustiveness measure. This also introduces the drawback of this approach: together with the relevant information a lot of 'garbage' is retrieved, resulting in poor performance from a specificity point of view.

- **33-CO-schema.** This run is a combination of runs 33-CO-default and 33-VCAS-schema. It uses the multiplication scheme for the children of the mixed-content nodes, and the combinational logic as defined for the default approach described above. In this way, for each document the smallest document fragment is returned that contains all relevant text fragments.
- **33-CO-cutoff.** From a user point of view not all document fragments that can be retrieved are logical units. To facilitate this, we have defined a set of nodes that provide the users logical document fragments. The aim here is to find a balance between the exhaustiveness and specificity measures. For the IEEE collection we have defined a cutoff-node set containing five nodes: $fm, abs, sec, bib, article$. The article element forms the root node of many documents and should always be there, to prevent losing documents from the result set.

  After retrieving the relevant text fragments, the parent nodes are retrieved and (child) results merged into larger document fragments, until a node is found that is contained in the set with cutoff-nodes.
- **33-CO-fdf.**[2] This run is also a combination of two other runs: 33-VCAS-fdf, and 33-CO-default. Instead of the default tfidf weights this run uses the tfifdf index, as explained in Section 3.1

4 Results

In this section we will first present the results CO task and then the results for the VCAS task. Before diving into the evaluation of the results, we have two issues to address that highly affected the retrieval performance. First of all, we did not allow overlapping elements in the result set, and secondly we used a SCAS interpretation, which also reduces the possible candidate elements for the resultset. All plots and measures were calculated using the on-line evaluation tool [7].

4.1 CO Task

We first discuss the results of the official run for the CO task in Section 4.1. To improve on the performance for the CO task we need a better retrieval strategy for the text retrieval component.

Official Runs. Figure 1 gives an overview of the performance of our CO runs. The *CO-default*-run performed best when evaluated using the strict quantisation

[2] For the official INEX runs, this approach was left out, since only six runs per participant were permitted.

INEX 2004: CO-default

quantization: strict; topics: CO
average precision: 0.0010
rank: 62 (69 official submissions)

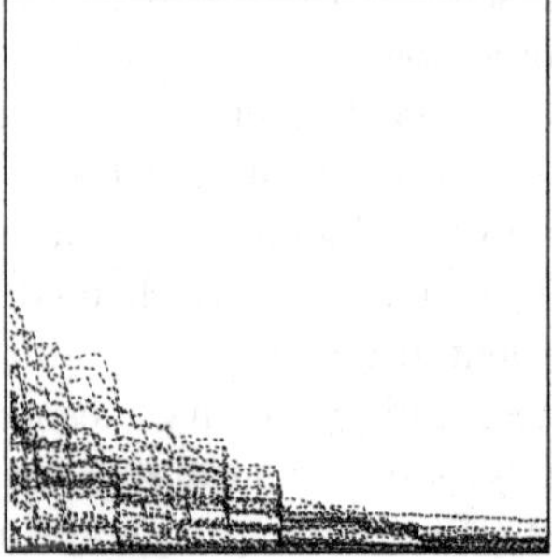

INEX 2004: CO-schema

quantization: e3$_s$32; topics: CO
average precision: 0.0192
rank: 45 (69 official submissions)

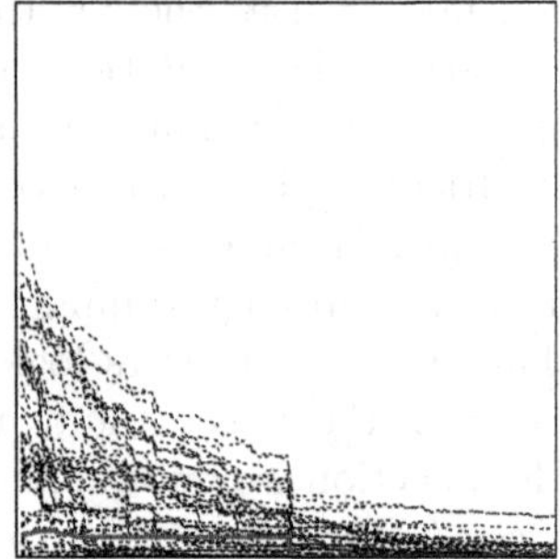

INEX 2004: CO-cutoff

quantization: s3$_e$32; topics: CO
average precision: 0.0009
rank: 62 (69 official submissions)

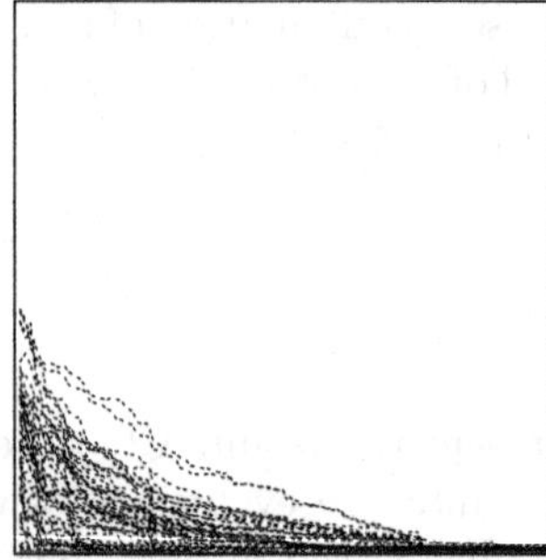

Fig. 1. Official runs for the CO task - best performances

measure. Slightly better performed the run *CO-schema*, while using the e3_s32 quantisation, which illustrates that this approach is best used, when searching for exhaustive document fragments. On the other hand, the *CO-cutoff*-run performed best for the s3_e32 quantisation measure. This was expected, since the aim of this approach was to return smaller logical document fragments, that would score better on the specificity scale.

These aspects are better illustrated in Figure 2, 3, 4, and 5. The average over all RP measures is showed in the top-left corner. On average, the best performance with the official runs was obtained with *CO-schema*, while the *CO-cutoff*-run performed worst. Surprisingly however, the run *CO-cutoff* performed best when looking at the expected ratio of relevance (bottom-right) for the generalised recall, and slightly better when evaluation is based on the specificity quantisation. The top-right graph shows that for the CO task, it makes sense to

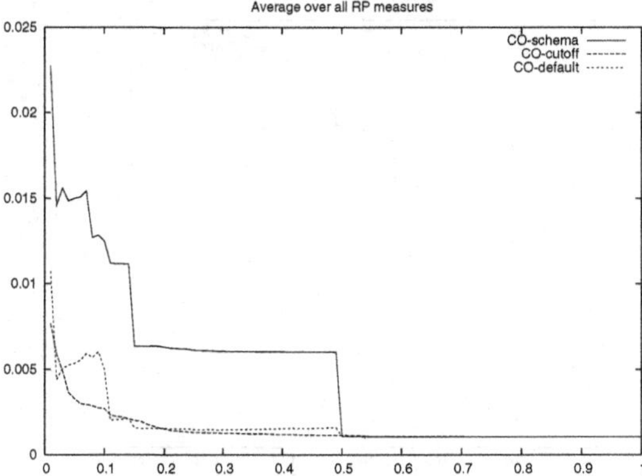

Fig. 2. Official runs for the CO task (a)

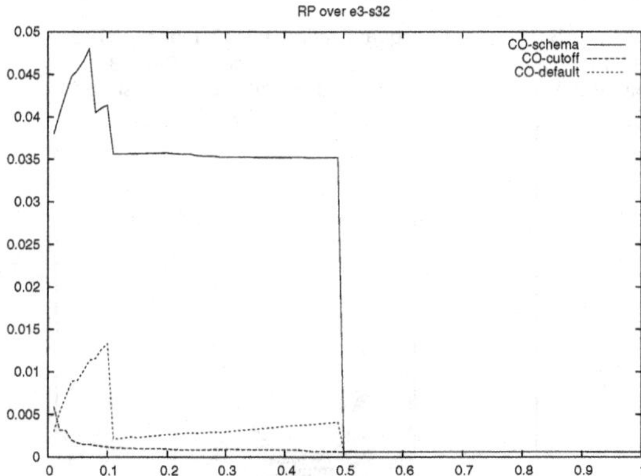

Fig. 3. Official runs for the CO task (b)

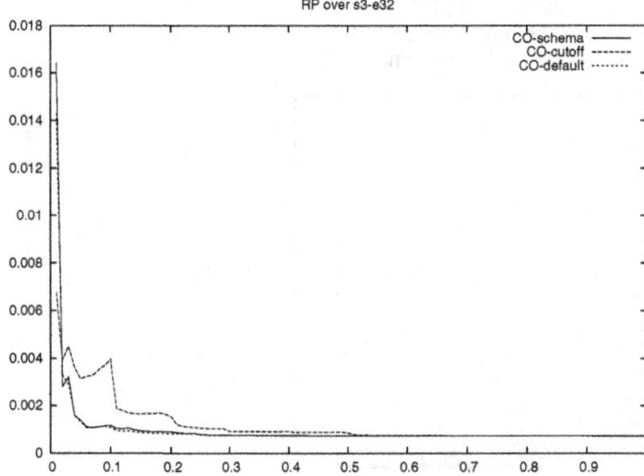

Fig. 4. Official runs for the CO task (c)

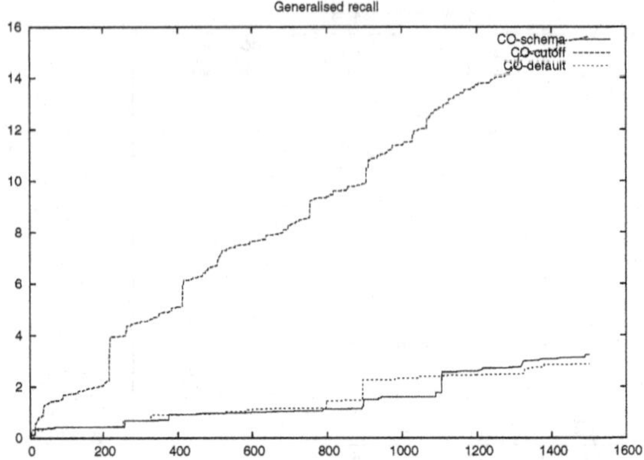

Fig. 5. Official runs for the CO task (d)

INEX 2004: VCAS-default

quantization: s3$_e$32; topics: VCAS
average precision: 0.0219
rank: 37 (52 official submissions)

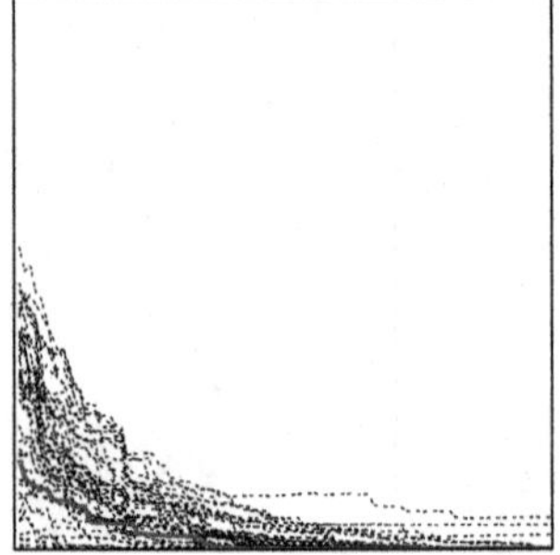

INEX 2004: VCAS-schema

quantization: e3$_s$32; topics: VCAS
average precision: 0.0218
rank: 38 (52 official submissions)

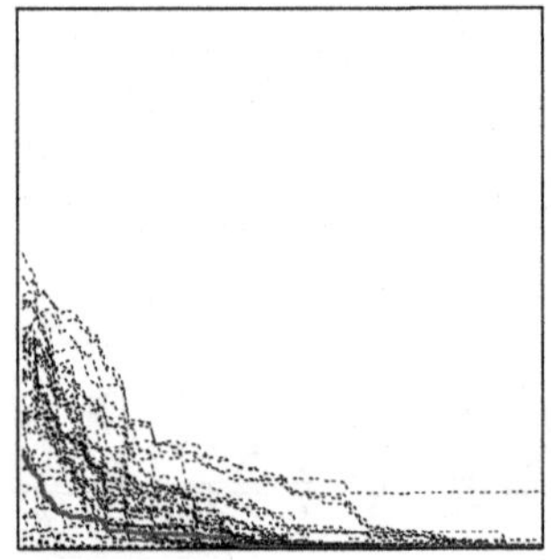

INEX 2004: VCAS-fdf

quantization: s3$_e$32; topics: VCAS
average precision: 0.0221
rank: 36 (52 official submissions)

Fig. 6. Official runs for the VCAS task - Best performances

include the markup added by the author to emphasise certain terms in the text into the ranking process.

4.2 VCAS Task

Figure 6 gives an overview of the performance of our VCAS runs. The *VCAS-default*-run performed best when evaluated using the s3e32 quantisation measure. Not surprising, since the implementation of our system uses the strict content and structure approach. The same is true for the *VCAS-fdf*-run. For the *VCAS-schema*-run the best performance is gained using the exhaustiveness quantisation measure. The differences between the runs however are marginal.

5 Conclusions

Our goal within INEX was to investigate the influence of the three hypothesis on the retrieval performance. Obviously our system does not belong to the top performing systems. This is mainly caused by two important factors: we did not allow overlapping elements in the result set, and we used a SCAS interpretation, which also reduces the possible candidate elements for the result set.

The comparison the schema-based run with thedefault run, clearly showed that if authors use markup to emphasise on particular pieces of content that they find of more importance, it makes sense to increase the weights of those document fragments to improve the retrieval performance. The results show that more relevant document fragments are ranked higher in the result list.

On the other hand we can increase the specificity of the retrieved document fragments, by using a so called cutoff node set. The system then returns smaller document fragments that are more relevant for the given topic. Whereas our default run returns rather large document fragments, containing the all the relevant document fragments of one physical document.

Finally, the runs that were using the fragmented document frequencies (fdf) did not increase the retrieval performance of our system. We feel that this is mainly caused by the absence of a semantical markup of the content of the IEEE document collection. However, many of the XML document collections that are currently available are based on logical and presentation tagging, rather then semantical tagging. Extending these documents with a semantical markup, will allow for more meaningful structured document retrieval. Besides that we expect that the retrieval performance for the FDF run will also improve, as shown in the past for different document collections.

References

1. R. Baeza-Yates and B. Ribeiro-Neto. *Modern Information Retrieval.* ACM Press, 1999.
2. N. Fuhr, N. Kazai, and M. Lalmas. INEX: Initiative for the evaluation of XML retrieval. In *In Proceedings of the ACM SIGIR 2000 Workshop on XML and Information Retrieval*, 2000.

3. N. Fuhr, S. Malik, and M. Lalmas. Overview of the initiative for the evaluation of xml. In *In Proceedings of the Second INitiative for the Evaluation of XML Retrieval (INEX) Workshop*, pages 1–11, Decmber 2003.
4. G. Kazai. Report of the inex'03 metrics working group. In *In Proceedings of the Second INitiative for the Evaluation of XML Retrieval (INEX) Workshop*, pages 184–190, Dagstuhl, Germany, 2003.
5. M. Lalmas and S. Malik. Inex 2004 retrieval task and result submission specification, June 2004. http://inex.is.informatik.uni-duisburg.de:2004/internal/pdf/INEX04_Retrieval_Task.pdf.
6. J. A. List and A. P. de Vries. CWI at inex 2002. In *Proceedings of the First Workshop of the INitiative for the Evaluation of XML Retrieval (INEX)*, 2002.
7. S. Malik and M. Lalmas. http://inex.lip6.fr/2004/metrics/official.php, 2004.
8. G. Salton and C. Buckley. Term-weighting approaches in automatic text retrieval. *Information Processing and Management*, 24(5):513–523, 1988.
9. A. Trotman and R. A. O'Keefe. The simplest query language that could possibly work. In *Proceedings of the Second Workshop of the INitiative for the Evaluation of XML retrieval (INEX)*, 2004.
10. R. van Zwol. *Modelling and searching web-based document collections.* Ctit ph.d. thesis series, Centre for Telematics and Information Technology (CTIT), Enschede, the Netherlands, 26 April 2002.

Hybrid XML Retrieval Revisited

Jovan Pehcevski[1], James A. Thom[1], S.M.M. Tahaghoghi[1], and Anne-Marie Vercoustre[2]

[1] School of CS and IT, RMIT University, Melbourne, Australia
{jovanp, jat, saied}@cs.rmit.edu.au
[2] INRIA, Rocquencourt, France
anne-marie.vercoustre@inria.fr

Abstract. The widespread adoption of XML necessitates structure-aware systems that can effectively retrieve information from XML document collections. This paper reports on the participation of the RMIT group in the INEX 2004 ad hoc track, where we investigate different aspects of the XML retrieval task. Our preliminary analysis of CO and VCAS relevance assessments identifies three XML retrieval scenarios: *Original*, *General* and *Specific*. Further analysis of the relevance assessments under the General retrieval scenario reveals two categories of CO and VCAS topics: *Broad* and *Narrow*. We design runs that follow a hybrid XML approach and implement two retrieval heuristics with different levels of overlap among the answer elements. For the Original retrieval scenario we show that the overlap CO runs outperform the non-overlap CO runs, and the VCAS run that uses queries with structural constraints and no explicitly specified target element performs best. In both CO and VCAS cases, runs that implement the retrieval heuristic that favours less specific over more specific answer elements produce most effective retrieval. Importantly, we present results which show that, for the General retrieval scenario where users prefer less specific and non-overlapping answers to their queries, the choice of using a plain full-text search engine is a very effective choice for XML retrieval.

1 Introduction

Two types of retrieval topics are explored in the INEX 2004 ad hoc track: Content-Only (CO) topics and Vague Content-And-Structure (VCAS) topics. Forty CO topics are used in the CO sub-track, while thirty-five VCAS topics are investigated in the VCAS sub-track.

CO topics do not refer to the existing document structure. An XML retrieval system using these topics may return elements with varying sizes and granularity, prompting a revisit of the issue of *length normalisation* for XML retrieval [4]. Moreover, a large proportion of overlapping result elements may be expected, since the same textual information in an XML document is often contained by more than one element. This *overlap problem* is particularly apparent during evaluation, where the "overpopulated and varying recall base" [6] contains a substantial number of mutually overlapping elements.

N. Fuhr et al. (Eds.): INEX 2004, LNCS 3493, pp. 153–167, 2005.

Strict Content-And-Structure (SCAS) topics enforce restrictions on the existing document structure and explicitly specify the target element (such as article, section, or paragraph). The structural conditions in a VCAS topic, however, need not be strictly matched. This means that not only are the restrictions on document structure *vague*, but also that the target element could be any element considered *relevant* to the information need. Thus, the same retrieval strategies for CO topics may also be used for VCAS topics, since CO topics may be considered as *loosely restricted* VCAS topics.

We undertake a preliminary analysis of the INEX 2004 CO and VCAS relevance assessments to identify the types of highly relevant elements. Arising from our analysis we identify many cases where, for a particular CO/VCAS topic and an XML document, several layers of elements in the document hierarchy (such as `article`, `bdy`, `sec` and `ss1`) have all been assessed as highly relevant. It then follows that this overlap problem is not only an evaluation problem, but it is also a serious retrieval problem, since the choice of the *preferable units of retrieval* for a CO/VCAS topic becomes a non-trivial one. For instance, given an overlapping recall base, an XML retrieval system that returns overlapping answer elements is likely to exhibit better performance than a system that returns non-overlapping answers. However, the former system will obviously retrieve and present a substantial amount of redundant information, which raises the question: is this what users really want?

Different evaluation metrics — which typically aim at modelling different user behaviours — have been proposed for XML retrieval, but only some of them attempt to address the overlap problem [6]. To investigate this and other similar aspects of XML retrieval, from the above analysis we distinguish between three *scenarios* of XML retrieval: the *Original* retrieval scenario, where all the highly relevant (and possibly mutually overlapping) elements are considered; the *Specific* retrieval scenario, where only the *most specific* highly relevant elements are considered; and the *General* retrieval scenario, where only the *least specific* highly relevant elements are considered. Unlike the Original retrieval scenario, the latter two scenarios allow for non-overlapping recall base. Indeed, in the absence of more realistic user models for XML retrieval, the Specific retrieval scenario reflects users that prefer specific, more focused answers for their queries, whereas the General retrieval scenario models users that prefer more encompassing answers for their queries.

Further analysis of the CO and VCAS relevance assessments under the General retrieval scenario reveals two categories of retrieval topics, which we call *Broad* and *Narrow*. We observed in our previous work that an XML retrieval system appears to behave differently when its performance is measured against different categories of CO topics [8]. Indeed, this has also been experimentally shown to be true for a fragment-based XML retrieval system [3]. Thus, distinguishing between different categories of topics — whether it applies to CO or VCAS — is likely to be useful information during retrieval.

The system we use for the ad hoc track in INEX 2004 follows a *hybrid XML approach*, utilising the best features of Zettair[1] (a full-text search engine) and eXist[2] (a native XML database). The hybrid approach is a "fetch and browse" [1] retrieval approach, where full articles considered likely to be relevant to a topic are first retrieved by Zettair (the *fetch* phase), and then the most specific elements within these articles are extracted by eXist (the *browse* phase) [8].

The above approach resulted in rather poor system performance for the CO topics in INEX 2003, where Zettair performed better than our initial hybrid system. We have since developed a retrieval module that utilises the structural information in the eXist list of answer elements, and identifies and ranks *Coherent Retrieval Elements* (CREs). The hybrid system with the CRE module more than doubles the retrieval effectiveness of Zettair [8]. We show elsewhere that this hybrid-CRE system also produces performance improvements for the INEX 2003 SCAS topics [7]. Different retrieval heuristics may be used by the CRE module, mainly to determine the final rank of each CRE.

For the INEX 2004 CO sub-track, we use our hybrid system to explore which CRE retrieval heuristic yields the best retrieval performance, and to investigate whether — under different retrieval scenarios and topic categories — having non-overlapping answer elements has an impact on system performance.

For the INEX 2004 VCAS sub-track, we also investigate which retrieval choice — plain queries; queries with structural constraints and no explicitly specified target element; or queries with both structural constraints and a target element — results in more effective VCAS retrieval. Different retrieval scenarios and topic categories are also used for this investigation.

The remainder of this paper is organised as follows. In Section 2 we present our analysis of the INEX 2004 relevance assessments, both for the CO and the VCAS retrieval topics. A detailed description of the runs we consider for the CO and the VCAS sub-tracks is provided in Section 3. In Section 4 we present the evaluation results of our CO and VCAS runs. These results reflect different retrieval scenarios, which are based on our analysis of the INEX 2004 relevance assessments. We conclude in Section 5 with a brief discussion of our findings.

2 Analysis of INEX 2004 Relevance Assessments

Some names in the XML document collection include: `article` for a full article; `abs` and `bdy` for article abstract and article body; `sec`, `ss1` and `ss2` for section and subsection elements; and `p` and `ip1` for paragraph elements. Analysing the INEX 2004 CO and VCAS relevance assessments, we observe that since neither case restricts the answer elements, the final answer list may contain elements of different types and of varying sizes and granularity. We expect that `article` elements may represent preferable answers for some topics, while for other topics more specific elements may be preferable over `article` elements.

[1] `http://www.seg.rmit.edu.au/zettair/`

[2] `http://exist-db.org/`

```
<file file="ic/2000/w4036">
 <path path="/article[1]" E="3" S="3"/>
 . . . . .
 <path path="/article[1]/bdy[1]" E="3" S="3"/>
 . . . . .
 <path path="/article[1]/bdy[1]/sec[3]" E="3" S="3"/>
 <path path="/article[1]/bdy[1]/sec[3]/ss1[1]" E="3" S="3"/>
 <path path="/article[1]/bdy[1]/sec[3]/ss1[2]" E="3" S="3"/>
 <path path="/article[1]/bdy[1]/sec[3]/ss1[3]" E="3" S="3"/>
 . . . . .
 <path path="/article[1]/bdy[1]/sec[4]" E="3" S="3"/>
 <path path="/article[1]/bdy[1]/sec[4]/ss1[2]" E="3" S="3"/>
 . . . . .
</file>
```

Fig. 1. An extract from the INEX 2004 CO relevance assessments (CO topic 176)

2.1 CO Relevance Assessments

Figure 1 shows an extract from the INEX 2004 CO relevance assessments for the CO topic 176. Values for the two INEX relevance dimensions, *exhaustivity*[3] (how many aspects of the topic are covered in the element), and *specificity*[4] (how specific to the topic is the element), are assigned to an `article` and elements within `article` for assessing their relevance to a CO topic.

In our analysis we focus on *highly relevant* elements. For a given topic, these are elements that have been assessed as both highly exhaustive and highly specific (E3S3) elements. In Fig. 1 there are eight such elements, including the article itself. These answer elements represent the most useful retrieval elements, even though there is a substantial amount of overlap between them. Following our previous analysis of INEX 2003 relevance assessments [8], we identify two distinct types of highly relevant elements: *General* and *Specific*. Unlike the INEX definitions for exhaustivity and specificity, the definitions for General and Specific elements result from our analysis as follows [8].

General
"For a particular article in the collection, a *General* element is the least-specific highly relevant element containing other highly relevant elements". Based on this definition, `article[1]` is the only General element in the example of Fig. 1. However, an article may contain several General elements if the article as a whole is not highly relevant. Figure 2 shows a tree representation of all the highly relevant elements shown in Fig. 1. The General element is the element shown in the ellipse.

[3] E represents the level of exhaustivity (values between 0-3).

[4] S represents the level of specificity (values between 0-3).

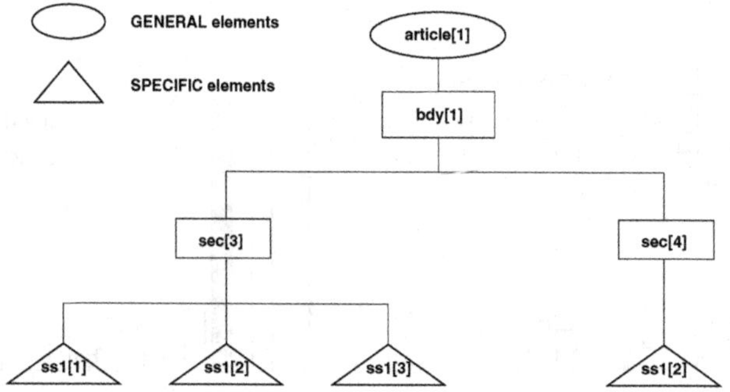

Fig. 2. A tree-view example of GENERAL versus SPECIFIC elements

Specific
"For a particular article in the collection, a *Specific* element is the most-specific highly relevant element contained by other highly relevant elements". In Fig. 2, the Specific elements are the elements shown in triangles.

When there is only one highly relevant element in an article, that element is both a General and a Specific element.

There are 40 CO topics in INEX 2004 (numbers 162–201). We use version 3.0 of the INEX 2004 relevance assessments, where 34 of the 40 CO topics have their relevance assessments available. Of these, 9 topics do not contain highly relevant (E3S3) elements. Consequently, a total of 25 CO topics are used.

In the following analysis, we focus on those highly relevant elements that appear in more than half the CO topics (that is, elements that appear in 12 or more CO topics). We choose this because we want to eliminate the outlier elements that may occur very frequently, but these occurrences are distributed across a few CO topics (such as 297 occurrences distributed across 6 topics for the `it` element). Figure 3(a) shows the frequency of highly relevant elements (including full articles) that appear in more than half the CO topics. The figure shows three distinct scenarios: the *Original* retrieval scenario, where all highly relevant elements are considered; the *General* retrieval scenario, where only General elements are considered, and the *Specific* retrieval scenario, where only Specific elements are considered. The x-axis contains the names of the six most frequent highly relevant elements (under the Original retrieval scenario). The y-axis contains the number of occurrences of each element.

Under the Original retrieval scenario, `p` and `sec` elements occur most frequently, with 691 and 264 overall occurrences, respectively. The `ss1` and `ip1` elements come next, followed by `article` and `bdy` with 99 and 89 occurrences. The latter suggests that in most cases when a `bdy` element was assessed as highly relevant, the parent `article` is also likely to have been assessed as highly relevant too.

Under the General retrieval scenario, `sec` elements are most frequent with 103 overall occurrences, followed by `article` elements with 99 occurrences; however, the `article` occurrences are distributed across 16 topics, whereas there are 15

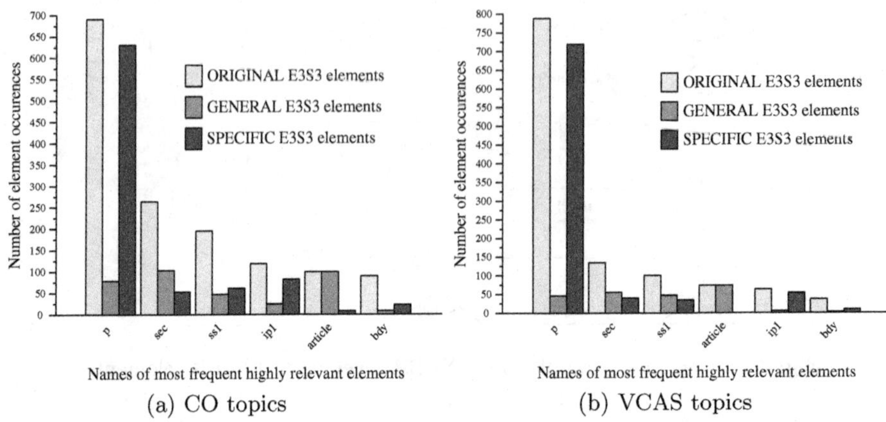

(a) CO topics (b) VCAS topics

Fig. 3. Number of occurrences of highly relevant elements that appear in more than half the INEX 2004 CO and VCAS topics, for three distinct retrieval scenarios. In each CO/VCAS case, the Original retrieval scenario is used to determine the element ordering

topics where `sec` elements occur. There are 8 cases (occurring across 6 topics) where a `bdy` was assessed as highly relevant, but the parent `article` was *not* assessed as highly relevant.

The last scenario shown in Fig. 3(a) is the Specific retrieval scenario. As expected, the situation changes here in favour of the more specific elements, with `p` elements being most frequent. The `ip1`, `ss1`, `sec` and `bdy` elements come next, followed by only 8 occurrences of `article` elements. The 8 occurrences are distributed across 4 topics, where these `article` elements were the most specific elements assessed as highly relevant.

The above statistics provide an interesting insight of what might happen when the performance of an XML retrieval system is evaluated against three distinct XML retrieval scenarios. For instance, under the General retrieval scenario one would expect that a full-text search engine could solely be used for effective XML retrieval, given that the full article is the second most frequent highly relevant element. The above information may therefore be appropriately utilised by XML retrieval systems, particularly because distinct retrieval scenarios favour different types of highly relevant elements.

Topic Categories. In the following analysis we consider the General retrieval scenario. Our aim is to distinguish those CO topics that are mostly about less specific highly relevant elements (such as `article` and `bdy`), from those that are mostly about more specific highly relevant elements (such as `sec` and `p`). Consider Fig. 4: a point on this graph represents a CO topic. The x-axis shows the total number of General `article` and `bdy` elements for a CO topic, whereas the y-axis shows the total number of General elements other than `article` and `bdy`. For example, the CO topic 183 depicted at coordinates (23,11) contains 23 General `article/bdy` elements and 11 General elements other than `article/bdy`.

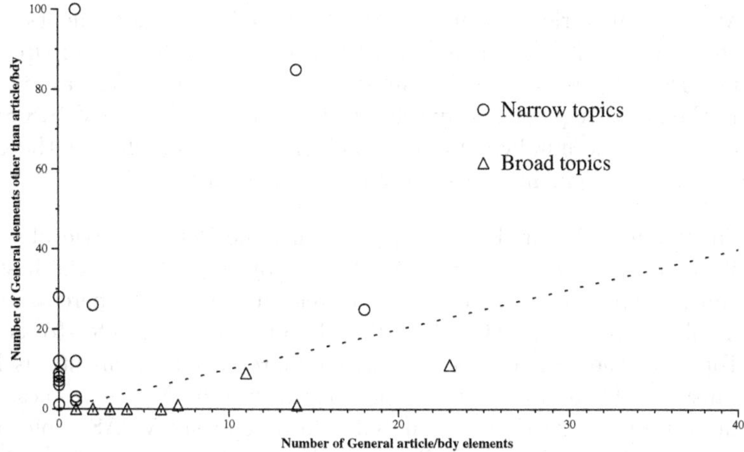

Fig. 4. Categories of INEX 2004 CO topics under the General retrieval scenario

We use this graph to identify two categories of INEX 2004 CO topics. Topics in the first category, shown as triangles on the graph and located below the dashed line, favour less specific elements as highly relevant answers. There are 9 such topics (numbers 164, 168, 175, 178, 183, 190, 192, 197 and 198). We refer to these as *Broad* topics.

Topics in the second category, shown as circles on the graph, favour more specific elements as highly relevant answers. There are 16 such topics. We refer to these as *Narrow* topics.

The above topic categorisation cannot easily be derived under the other two scenarios, that is, under either the Original or the Specific retrieval scenario. However, we also observed that four Broad topics (numbers 168, 178, 190 and 198) clearly belong to the Broad category even under these two scenarios.

2.2 VCAS Relevance Assessments

There are 35 VCAS topics in INEX 2004 (numbers 127-161). We use version 3.0 of the INEX 2004 relevance assessments, where 26 (out of 35) VCAS topics have their relevance assessments available. Of these, 4 topics do not contain highly relevant (E3S3) elements, and so we limit our analysis to a total of 22 VCAS topics.

Figure 3(b) shows the frequency of highly relevant elements that appear in more than half the VCAS topics. The figure also shows the three distinct scenarios: Original, General and Specific.

Since the VCAS relevance assessments have been done in much the same way as those for the CO topics, it is not surprising that Fig. 3(a) and Fig. 3(b) are similar. In both assessment cases, the frequency of `p` elements (under the Original and Specific retrieval scenarios) is far greater than that of all the other elements. However, the frequencies of `article` and `bdy` elements in the VCAS case differ from the frequencies of the same elements in the CO case. Under the VCAS Original retrieval scenario, the number of `article` elements is much greater than that of the `bdy` elements (73 `article` occurrences compared to 36 `bdy` occurrences). Under the VCAS General retrieval scenario, the `article` elements are the most frequent highly relevant elements. Under the VCAS Specific retrieval scenario, the number of `article` elements is zero, whereas there are 9 highly relevant `bdy` elements (distributed across 3 topics).

Topic Categories. As for the CO topics, we use the General retrieval scenario to identify two categories of INEX 2004 VCAS topics. Topics in the first category favour less specific elements as highly relevant answers. There are 6 such topics (numbers 130, 131, 134, 137, 139 and 150), which we refer to as *Broad* topics. Topics in the second category favour more specific elements as highly relevant answers. There are 16 such topics, referred to as *Narrow* topics.

An interesting observation is that only two out of six VCAS topics of the Broad category (137 and 139) explicitly ask for retrieving `article` or `bdy` elements in their titles (that is, these elements represent their *target* elements). This is not the case with the other four Broad topics, where two topics ask for `sec` (134 and 150), one asks for `abs` (131), and one asks for `p` (130).

The above analysis clearly shows that highly relevant elements for VCAS topics do not necessarily represent target elements. We believe that distinguishing between categories of VCAS topics is, similarly as for the CO topics, important information that an XML retrieval system should utilise.

3 Runs Description

The following sections provide a detailed description of our runs for each (CO and VCAS) sub-track.

3.1 Background

Most of the runs we consider for the INEX 2004 ad hoc track use a system that follows a hybrid XML retrieval approach. The system implements the best retrieval features from Zettair and eXist [8]. To further increase the system's retrieval effectiveness, an additional module that identifies and ranks Coherent Retrieval Elements (CREs) is used.

A CRE is defined as follows. The list of matching elements, extracted by eXist, is an article-ordered list. This list is processed by considering a pair of matching elements, starting from the first element down to the second last. In each step, a CRE is identified as the most specific ancestor of the two matching elements that constitute the pair [8]. To determine the ranks of CREs in the final answer list, the CRE module in our system uses a combination of the following XML-specific retrieval heuristics:

1. The number of times a CRE appears in the absolute path of each matching element in the eXist answer list — more matches (`M`) or fewer matches (`m`);
2. The length of the absolute path of the CRE, taken from the root element — longer path (`P`) or shorter path (`p`); and

3. The ordering of the XPath sequence in the absolute path of the CRE — nearer to the beginning (B) or nearer to the end (E).

There are 16 possible CRE heuristic combinations, since the first two heuristics can be applied in any order, and the third heuristic is complementary to the other two and is always applied at the end. We have found that for the INEX 2003 test set, the best results are obtained when using the MpE heuristic combination [8]. With MpE, less specific elements are ranked higher than more specific elements.

However, we have also observed that different CRE heuristic combinations may be more suitable for different XML retrieval scenarios, where retrieving more specific elements early in the ranking (such as with using the PME heuristic) produces better results. We implement and compare these two retrieval heuristics in different runs for the ad hoc track in INEX 2004.

3.2 CO Sub-track

For the CO sub-track we consider the following runs.

- `Zettair` – using the full-text search engine as a baseline run.
- `Hybrid_MpE` – using the hybrid system with the MpE heuristic combination in the CRE module.
- `Hybrid_MpE_NO` – using the hybrid system, with the MpE heuristic combination, and no overlap among the elements in the final answer list.
- `Hybrid_PME` – using the hybrid system with the PME heuristic combination in the CRE module.
- `Hybrid_PME_NO` – using the hybrid system, with the PME heuristic combination, and no overlap among the elements in the final answer list.

Our goals are threefold. First, we aim to explore which heuristic combination yields the best performance for the hybrid system under different retrieval scenarios. Second, we aim to investigate the impact of overlapping answer elements on system performance. Thus, the two cases of non-overlap runs, `Hybrid_MpE_NO` and `Hybrid_PME_NO`, implement different non-overlap strategies: the former allows less specific elements to remain in the list and removes all the other (contained) elements, whereas the latter retains more specific elements, and removes all the other (encompassing) elements. Finally, by comparing the hybrid runs with the baseline run, we aim to better understand the issues surrounding the CO retrieval task.

3.3 VCAS Sub-track

For the VCAS sub-track we consider the following runs.

- `Zettair` – using the full-text search engine as a baseline run.
- `Hybrid_CO_MpE` – using the hybrid system with the MpE heuristic combination in the CRE module. The structural constraints and the target element of each VCAS topic are removed, leaving only plain query terms.

- `Hybrid_CO_PME` – using the hybrid system with the `PME` heuristic combination in the CRE module. As with the previous run, each VCAS topic is treated as a CO topic.
- `Hybrid_VCAS_MpE` – using the hybrid system with the `MpE` heuristic combination in the CRE module. The target element of each VCAS topic is not explicitly specified (that is, it is allowed to have any granularity), while the structural constraints are strictly matched.
- `Hybrid_VCAS_PME` – using the hybrid system with the `PME` heuristic combination in the CRE module. As with the previous run, the structural constraints remain, while the target element is allowed to represent any element.
- `Hybrid_CAS` – using the initial hybrid system (without the CRE module), where the structural constraints and the target element of each VCAS topic are strictly matched.

We aim to achieve several goals through these VCAS runs. First, we aim to investigate which query choice (`CO`, `VCAS` or `CAS`) results in more effective VCAS retrieval. Second, for the hybrid runs using the CRE module and a particular query choice, we aim to identify the best choice of retrieval heuristic. Finally, by comparing the hybrid runs with the baseline run, we wish to empirically determine whether we can justify using a plain full-text search engine in the VCAS retrieval task.

4 Experiments and Results

In INEX 2004, an evaluation metric with different quantisation functions is used to evaluate the retrieval effectiveness of XML systems [5]. Since our focus is on highly relevant elements, we use the strict quantisation function (E3S3) in our experiments.

For each of the retrieval runs, the resulting answer list for a CO/VCAS topic comprises up to 1500 articles or elements within articles. To measure the overall performance of each run, two standard information retrieval measures are used with the strict quantisation function: *Mean Average Precision* (MAP), which measures the ability of a system to return highly relevant (E3S3) elements, and *Precision at 10* (P@10), which measures the number of highly relevant (E3S3) elements within the first 10 elements returned by a system. In the following we describe results obtained by evaluating the retrieval effectiveness of our runs — under different retrieval scenarios — for each CO and VCAS sub-track.

4.1 CO Sub-track

Original CO Retrieval Scenario. Table 1(a) shows evaluation results for the CO retrieval runs under the Original retrieval scenario. Values for the best runs are shown in bold. Several observations can be drawn from these results.

First, for overlap runs using the hybrid system, the `MpE` heuristic yields better performance than the `PME` heuristic. This result shows that under the Original CO retrieval scenario, systems that prefer retrieving less specific over more specific answer elements yield better performance.

Table 1. Performance results of INEX 2004 CO and VCAS runs when using the strict quantisation function and the Original retrieval scenario. For each run, an overlap indicator shows the percentage of overlapping elements in the answer list. Values for the best runs are shown in bold

CO run	**%Ovp**	**Original** MAP	**Original** P@10
`Zettair`	0	0.049	0.073
`Hybrid_MpE`	82.2	**0.124**	**0.103**
`Hybrid_MpE_NO`	0	0.051	0.076
`Hybrid_PME`	82.1	0.081	0.100
`Hybrid_PME_NO`	0	0.047	0.088

(a) CO runs

VCAS run	**%Ovp**	**Original** MAP	**Original** P@10
`Zettair`	0	0.052	0.119
`Hybrid_CO_MpE`	78.3	0.101	0.104
`Hybrid_CO_PME`	78.2	0.034	0.096
`Hybrid_VCAS_MpE`	67.8	**0.103**	**0.154**
`Hybrid_VCAS_PME`	67.8	0.045	0.142
`Hybrid_CAS`	5.4	0.032	0.142

(b) VCAS runs

Second, the non-overlap hybrid runs perform worse than the corresponding overlap hybrid runs. This is very likely to be a result of the "overpopulated" CO recall base, and reflects the inability of the strict quantisation function to cope with the overlap problem. We revisit the latter comparison in the next section (the General CO retrieval scenario), where a non-overlapping recall base is considered for evaluation.

Last, all the hybrid runs perform better on average than the baseline run. However, we observe that the baseline run is very competitive with the non-overlap hybrid runs, and, when the `MAP` measure is used for evaluation it even performs better than the non-overlap `Hybrid_PME` run. Since the answer list of the non-overlap `Hybrid_PME` run contains more specific (and non-overlapping) elements, the last result again confirms that retrieving more specific answer elements leads to poor system performance under this retrieval scenario.

The graph in Fig. 5(a) shows recall/precision curves for the two overlap hybrid runs and the baseline run. For low recall (0.1 and less), `Zettair` outperforms `Hybrid_PME`, although its performance gradually decreases and reaches zero for 0.5 (and higher) recall. Overall, `Hybrid_MpE` performs best and is substantially better than `Hybrid_PME`.

General CO Retrieval Scenario. In the following analysis, we use the General CO retrieval scenario to compare the performance of the two `Hybrid_MpE` runs (overlap and non-overlap) with `Zettair` (the baseline run).

The General retrieval scenario reflects a non-overlapping recall base, since the relevance assessments allow an article to only contain General elements. Moreover, our previous analysis has also distinguished different categories of CO topics. Thus, the performance of the above runs are also compared across three topic categories: the *All topics* category, with all the 25 CO topics, and the *Broad* and the *Narrow* categories, with 9 and 16 CO topics, respectively.

Table 2 shows the evaluation results for each run. Two observations are clear in the cases of *All* and *Broad* topic categories: first, with both `MAP` and `P@10`

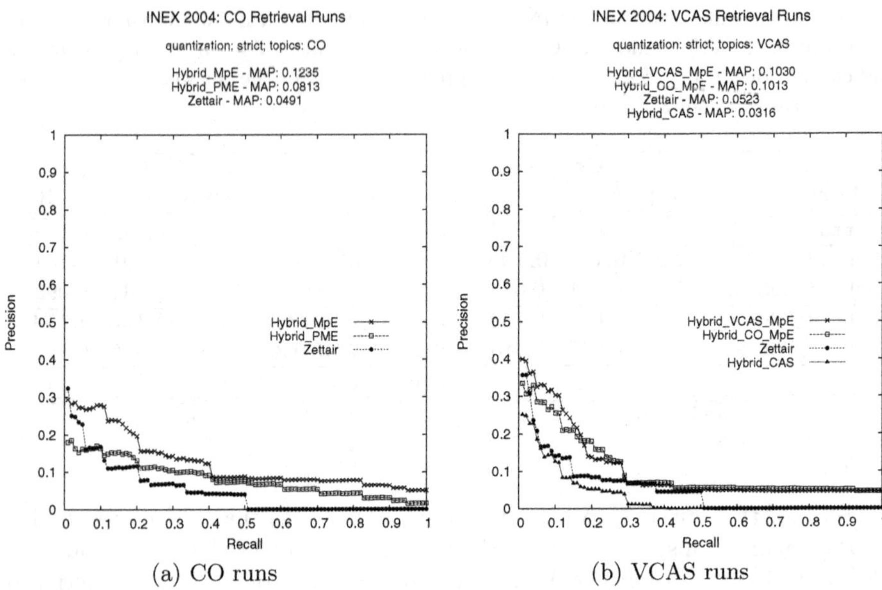

(a) CO runs (b) VCAS runs

Fig. 5. Evaluation of the INEX 2004 CO and VCAS retrieval runs when using the strict quantisation function and the Original retrieval scenario

measures `Zettair` performs best, although with `P@10` the non-overlap hybrid run (`MpE_NO`) performs the same as `Zettair`; and second, unlike for the case of overpopulated recall base (the Original retrieval scenario), the non-overlap hybrid run substantially outperforms the overlap hybrid run. These results show that, when a non-overlapping CO recall base is used for evaluation, the strict quantisation function can safely be used to reliably evaluate XML retrieval systems. Thus, systems that return overlapping answer elements (or redundant information) perform worse than systems that return non-overlapping answer

Table 2. Performance results of three INEX 2004 CO runs when using the strict quantisation function and different CO topic categories. The General retrieval scenario is used. For each run, an overlap indicator shows the percentage of overlapping elements in the answer list. Values for the best runs are shown in bold

		General					
		All topics		**Broad topics**		**Narrow topics**	
CO run	**%Ovp**	MAP	P@10	MAP	P@10	MAP	P@10
`Zettair`	0	**0.154**	**0.073**	**0.364**	**0.211**	0.036	0.024
`Hybrid_MpE`	82.2	0.126	0.050	0.240	0.056	**0.062**	**0.048**
`Hybrid_MpE_NO`	0	0.152	**0.073**	0.359	**0.211**	0.036	0.024

elements. More specifically, the choice of using a full-text search engine results in very effective XML retrieval under this scenario.

In the case of *Narrow* topic category, the overlap hybrid run performs best, whereas the performance of the other two runs is the same. The latter result shows that a different topic category needs a different choice of optimal retrieval parameters.

4.2 VCAS Sub-track

Original VCAS Retrieval Scenario. Table 1(b) shows evaluation results for the VCAS retrieval runs under the Original retrieval scenario. Values for the best runs are shown in bold. Several observations can be drawn from these results.

First, the `Hybrid_CAS` run (where structural constraints and the target element of a VCAS topic are strictly matched) performs worse than the other hybrid runs. Of these, the `Hybrid_VCAS` runs (the choice of strict structural constraints and no explicit target element) perform better than the `Hybrid_CO` runs (the choice where plain text queries are used). The former results can partly be explained from our analysis of the VCAS relevance assessments (see Section 2.2), which showed that highly relevant elements for VCAS topics do not necessarily represent their target elements. The latter results, however, show that the choice to strictly follow the structural constraints in the VCAS topics results in more effective retrieval than the choice of using only plain text queries.

Second, as with CO topics the `MpE` heuristic in the hybrid runs yields better performance than the `PME` heuristic. This shows that even with VCAS topics retrieving less specific over more specific answer elements is better.

Last, the hybrid runs perform better overall than the baseline run, except when using the `MAP` measure, where `Zettair` performs better than `Hybrid_CAS` and the two hybrid-`PME` runs. These results again confirm that, under the Original VCAS retrieval scenario, systems that prefer retrieving more specific answer elements and explicitly specify the target element in their queries exhibit poor performance.

The graph in Fig. 5(b) shows recall/precision curves for the three hybrid runs (`CO`, `VCAS` and `CAS`) and the baseline run (`Zettair`). The `VCAS` run performs best, particularly for low recall (0.2 and less), however its performance is almost identical to that of the `CO` run for 0.3 (and higher) recall. Figure 5(b) also shows that, when highly relevant elements are the target of retrieval, `Zettair` clearly outperforms the `Hybrid_CAS` run.

General VCAS Retrieval Scenario. In the following analysis, we use the General retrieval scenario to compare the performance of the three hybrid VCAS runs (query choices `CO`, `VCAS` and `CAS`) with `Zettair`. The three VCAS topic categories are also used in this analysis: the *All* category, with all the 22 VCAS topics, and the *Broad* and *Narrow* categories, with 6 and 16 VCAS topics, respectively.

Table 3 shows the evaluation results for each run. One observation is very clear: for each VCAS topic category (with both `MAP` and `P@10` measures), `Zettair` outperforms all the other runs. This is a very interesting observation, since the unit of retrieval in Zettair is a full article, and queries used are plain content-

Table 3. Performance results of four INEX 2004 VCAS runs when using strict quantisation function and different VCAS topic categories. The General retrieval scenario is used. For each run, an overlap indicator shows the percentage of overlapping elements in the answer list. Values for the best runs are shown in bold

		General					
		All topics		Broad topics		Narrow topics	
VCAS run	**%Ovp**	MAP	P@10	MAP	P@10	MAP	P@10
`Zettair`	0	**0.192**	**0.119**	**0.625**	**0.367**	**0.029**	**0.045**
`Hybrid_CO_MpE`	78.3	0.128	0.035	0.417	0.100	0.020	0.015
`Hybrid_VCAS_MpE`	67.8	0.128	0.046	0.412	0.100	0.021	0.030
`Hybrid_CAS`	5.4	0.061	0.085	0.162	0.233	0.023	0.040

only queries. These results show that under this retrieval scenario, applying a full-text search engine may be a better choice than an XML-specific retrieval approach.

5 Conclusions

In this paper we have reported on our participation in the ad-hoc track of INEX 2004. We have designed and submitted different runs for each CO and VCAS sub-track to investigate different aspects of the XML retrieval task.

The results of our preliminary analysis of the INEX 2004 CO and VCAS relevance assessments have identified many cases of mutually overlapping elements in the recall base. This finding, which is also known as the *overlap problem*, turns out to be not only an evaluation problem, but also a serious retrieval problem. Indeed, we have shown that in what we call the Original retrieval scenario, the strict quantisation function is not capable of dealing with the overlap problem. Efforts are being made, however, in the direction of unifying existing INEX metrics into a robust evaluation metric which aims at addressing this problem [6].

The two different XML retrieval scenarios, General and Specific, which were identified as a result of our analysis, model different user behaviours; we have shown that the preferred retrieval parameters — such as the choice of retrieval heuristic, level of element overlap or query type — vary depending on which user model is used. Moreover, distinguishing between existing topic categories can, in some retrieval scenarios, influence the choice of these parameters.

For the CO sub-track, we have shown that under the General retrieval scenario where users prefer less specific and non-overlapping answers, a full-text search engine alone can satisfy users' information needs. Our hybrid system, which is also capable of retrieving less specific and non-overlapping answers, is another effective alternative. However, our results have also shown that distinguishing between different categories of retrieval topics is very useful for the General CO retrieval scenario. Indeed, depending on the topic category, using a retrieval heuristic capable of retrieving more focused — and possibly overlapping — answers may be a better choice.

For the VCAS sub-track, we have shown that under the same General retrieval scenario, the same choice of using a full-text search engine — which ignores all the structural constraints and target elements — is very effective. Unlike for the General CO retrieval scenario, the choice of optimal retrieval parameters is not affected by a VCAS topic category.

It is our hope that this work will aid better understanding of the different aspects of the XML retrieval task, and ultimately lead to more effective XML retrieval.

References

1. Y. Chiaramella, P. Mulhem, and F. Fourel. A Model for Multimedia Information Retrieval. Technical report, FERMI ESPRIT BRA 8134, University of Glasgow, April 1996.
2. N. Fuhr, M. Lalmas, and S. Malik, editors. *INitiative for the Evaluation of XML Retrieval (INEX). Proceedings of the Second INEX Workshop. Dagstuhl, Germany, December 15–17, 2003*, March 2004.
3. K. Hatano, H. Kinutan, M. Watanabe, Y. Mori, M. Yoshikawa, and S. Uemura. Keyword-based XML Fragment Retrieval: Experimental Evaluation based on INEX 2003 Relevance Assessments. In Fuhr et al. [2], pages 81–88.
4. J. Kamps, M. de Rijke, and B. Sigurbjoernsson. Length Normalization in XML Retrieval. In *Proceedings of the 27th Annual International ACM SIGIR Conference on Research and Development in Information Retrieval. Sheffield, UK, July 25–29, 2004*, pages 80–87, 2004.
5. G. Kazai. Report on the INEX2003 Metrics working group. In Fuhr et al. [2], pages 184–190.
6. G. Kazai, M. Lalmas, and A. P. de Vries. The Overlap Problem in Content-Oriented XML Retrieval Evaluation. In *Proceedings of the 27th Annual International ACM SIGIR Conference on Research and Development in Information Retrieval. Sheffield, UK, July 25–29, 2004*, pages 72–79, 2004.
7. J. Pehcevski, J. A. Thom, and A.-M. Vercoustre. Enhancing Content-And-Structure Information Retrieval using a Native XML Database. In *Proceedings of The First Twente Data Management Workshop (TDM'04) on XML Databases and Information Retrieval. Enschede, The Netherlands, June 21, 2004*, pages 24–31, 2004.
8. J. Pehcevski, J. A. Thom, and A.-M. Vercoustre. Hybrid XML Retrieval: Combining Information Retrieval and a Native XML Database. *Journal of Information Retrieval: Special Issue on INEX (to appear)*, 2004.

Analyzing the Properties of XML Fragments Decomposed from the INEX Document Collection

Kenji Hatano[1], Hiroko Kinutani[2], Toshiyuki Amagasa[1],Yasuhiro Mori[3], Masatoshi Yoshikawa[3], and Shunsuke Uemura[1]

[1] Nara Institute of Science and Technology, Japan
[2] Ochanomizu University, Japan
[3] Nagoya University, Japan

Abstract. In current keyword-based XML fragment retrieval systems, various granules of XML fragments are returned as retrieval results. The number of the XML fragments is huge, so this adversely affects the index construction time and query processing time of the XML fragment retrieval systems if they cannot extract only the answer XML fragments with certainty. In this paper, we propose a method for determining XML fragments that are appropriate in keyword-based XML fragment retrieval. This would help to improve overall performance of XML fragment retrieval systems. The proposed method utilizes and analyzes statistical information of XML fragments based on a technique of the dynamics of terminology in quantitative linguistics. Moreover, our keyword-based XML fragment retrieval system runs on a relational database system. In this paper, we briefly explain the implementation of our system.

1 Introduction

Extensible Markup Language (XML) [5] is becoming widely used as a standard document format in many application domains. In near future, a great variety of documents will be produced in XML. Therefore, in a similar way to the development of Web search engines, XML information retrieval systems will become very important tools for users wishing to explore XML documents.

In the research area of XML retrieval, it is important to develop a method for retrieving fragments of XML documents. XQuery [4], proposed by the World Wide Web Consortium (W3C), is known as a standard query language for XML fragment retrieval. Using XQuery, users can issue a flexible query consisting of both keywords and XPath notations. If users already have knowledge of the structure of XML documents, users can issue XQuery-style queries for XML fragment retrieval. Consequently, we can state that XQuery is suitable for searching for data in XML documents[1].

[1] In this paper, we refer to this type of XML documents as *data-centric* XML documents.

N. Fuhr et al. (Eds.): INEX 2004, LNCS 3493, pp. 168–182, 2005.

At the same time, the XML Query Working Group has been developing powerful full-text search functions [3, 2] for XQuery. This is because there are many *document-centric* XML documents like articles in XML form, including structured information such as the names of authors, date of publication, sections, and sub-sections, as well as unstructured information such as the text content of the articles. However, document-centric XML documents like these have different XML schemas in each digital library, making it impossible to comprehend the structure of XML documents or to issue a formulated query like XQuery into XML fragment retrieval systems. Therefore, XML information retrieval systems should employ a much simpler form of query such as keyword search services without utilizing XQuery-style queries. Keyword search services enable users to retrieve needed information by providing a simple interface to information retrieval systems. In short, it is the most popular information retrieval method because users need to know neither a query language nor the structure of XML documents.

Considering the above background of XML fragment retrieval, it is not surprising that much attention has recently been paid to developing a keyword-based XML fragment retrieval system. Such systems usually decompose document-centric XML documents into XML fragments by using their markup and then generate an index of decomposed fragments for searching. In spite of their systems' simple approach to XML fragment retrieval, this method enables the user to retrieve XML fragments related to keyword-based queries fairly well. However, XML documents are decomposed as much as possible by using their markup; thus index construction time and query processing time are too long compared with current document retrieval systems. This is because returning various granules and the huge number of XML fragments as retrieval results adversely affects processing time unless XML fragment retrieval systems can extract only the answer XML fragments with certainty.

We believe that the XML fragments required for keyword-based fragment retrieval make up only a part of the decomposed fragments from document-centric XML documents. In short, there is a certain type of XML fragments that are never returned as retrieval results regardless of the issued keyword-based queries. In particular, extremely small XML fragments are unlikely to become retrieval results of keyword-based queries from the viewpoint of information retrieval research. Therefore, we could perform XML fragment retrieval more efficiently than with current systems if we could eliminate inappropriate fragments in XML fragment retrieval from the index file. To cope with this problem, we have to determine which XML fragments are appropriate in the XML fragment retrieval extracted from document-centric XML documents.

In this paper, we propose a method for determining the appropriate XML fragments needed to efficiently search XML fragments. Our method utilizes and analyzes statistical information of XML fragments decomposed from original documents based on a technique of the dynamics of terminology in quantitative linguistics. Our proposal holds the promise of not only reducing index construction time and query processing time of XML fragment retrieval systems but also dealing with many types of document-centric XML documents, since statistical information does not depend on the structures of XML documents. We also perform some experiments to verify the effectiveness of our proposal.

2 Research Issues

There are two main types of keyword-based XML fragment retrieval systems. In this paper, we refer to these as *data-centric type* and *document-centric type* for convenience. The former is based on structured or semi-structured database systems with keyword proximity search functions that are modeled as labeled graphs, where the edges correspond to the relationship between an element and a sub-element and to IDREF pointers [1, 13, 16]. Dealing with XML documents as XML graphs facilitates the development of keyword-based information retrieval systems that are able to perform the retrieval processing efficiently. The latter type has been developed in the research area of information retrieval [9, 12], and it enables us to retrieve XML fragments without indicating the element names of XML documents. The major difference between these two types of XML fragment retrieval systems is in the data characteristics of their retrieval targets. In short, we assume that the former type focuses mainly on XML documents that have a data-centric view, whereas the latter type deals with those having a document-centric view. At the same time, almost all XML fragment retrieval systems currently assume the existence of the DTD of XML documents in either field of research. It is true that DTD enhances the retrieval accuracy and query processing time of their systems. However, there are some problems associated with searching heterogeneous XML fragments on the Web. Thus, other types of XML retrieval systems that do not utilize DTD are required. Consequently, XML fragment retrieval systems in the future will have to deal with heterogeneous XML documents whose structures are not uniform.

To meet the needs of the new architectures for XML fragment retrieval systems, we have been developing a keyword-based XML fragment retrieval system [15]. Our system focuses on retrieval of document-centric XML documents rather than that of data-centric ones, and it does not utilize any information on elements of the XML documents, whereas almost all existing XML fragment retrieval systems take advantage of this information for querying and indexing XML documents. In our approach, XML documents must be decomposed into their fragments, and the decomposed fragments are utilized to generate an index file. XML is a markup language, thus XML documents can be automatically decomposed into their fragments by using their markup [19]. However, this gives rise to an unmanageable profusion of XML fragments. In other words, it takes a very long time to construct an index file and to search for XML fragments related to a keyword-based query. For this reason, it is critical to avoid inspecting all decomposed XML fragments, by focusing on the XML fragments that are appropriate to the XML fragment retrieval, in order to reduce index construction time and query processing time. In the next section, we explain the method for determining the appropriate fragments in XML fragment retrieval based on a technique of the dynamics of terminology in quantitative linguistics.

3 Analysis of INEX Test Collection

Our research group has been analyzing the statistical information of the INEX document collection since last year. According to our analysis, it was notable that variances in the statistical information, especially the variance in the length of XML fragments, were too large. Therefore, we have focused on the length of XML fragments. In our INEX 2003 paper [14], we regarded small XML fragments as inappropriate ones in XML fragment retrieval and verified the practicality of our proposal by using recall-precision curves. However, we simply sketched an outline of our proposal and did not show strong reasons for adopting it. Consequently, in this section, we show the practical justification of our proposal.

3.1 Properties of XML Fragments

The Dynamics of Terminology in Quantitative Linguistics. In our INEX 2003 paper, we determined a threshold for the length of XML fragments, thus regarding XML fragments below this threshold as inappropriate for XML fragment retrieval. However, this approach required a large number of experiments to determine the threshold, so it was inappropriate for developing a large-scale XML fragment retrieval system. Therefore, we have to determine the threshold systematically.

It is well known that statistical information on XML fragments, such as the number of tokens, length of XML fragments, and so on, is useful for determining the thresholds. The examination of the relationships among the constituent elements and the type of conceptual combinations used in the construction of the terminology permits deep insights into the systematic thought processes underlying term creation. And the powerful interaction of linguistic possibilities and the limitation of conceptual entities are offered by the quantitative analysis of the patterns of the growth of terminology. In the dynamics of terminology in quantitative linguistics, statistical information is often used. This is because analyzing the statistical information helps us to discover some rules in a document set, and the discovery of such rules is essential for constructing a sound basis of a theory of terminology. In this research area, it is thought that conducting an examination to discover rules is similar to finding out the systematic processes underlying a document set. For this reason, we employ a technique of the dynamics of terminology to determine the threshold by using the number of tokens and XML fragments as statistical information[17]. Needless to say, not only the number of tokens and XML fragments but also other mathematical or algebraic information can be utilized as statistical information. The reason for using such statistical information is that it can be extracted easily when our XML fragment retrieval system simultaneously analyzes XML documents and decomposes them into fragments.

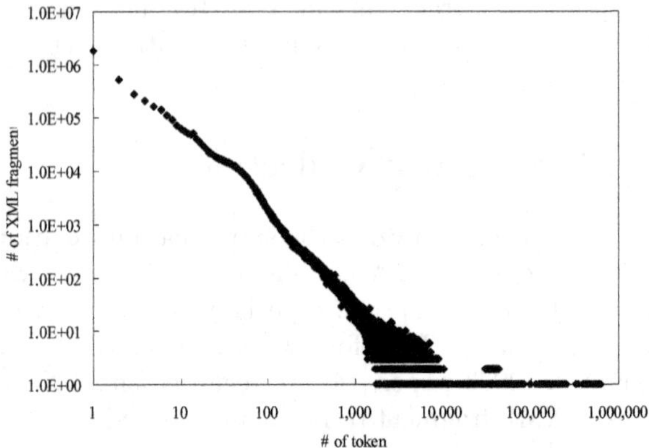

Fig. 1. Relationship between n and $N(n)$

By adopting a technique of quantitative linguistics, we can determine the threshold systematically.

Determining Appropriate XML Fragments. In the research area of quantitative linguistics, capturing properties of a document set is performed by analyzing statistical information. Utilizing the number of tokens and documents as statistical information, we can find a correlation between number of tokens and number of XML fragments with the same number of tokens. However, a small minority of documents have no relationship with the statistical information, so it is said that such documents have an anomalous property. Therefore, it is understood that such documents are not appropriate for capturing the properties of the document set and should be disregarded in capturing properties.

This concept can be utilized for determining inappropriate fragments in XML fragment retrieval. In short, if we are able to define a function between pieces of statistical information, XML fragments that do not follow the function can be regarded as inappropriate XML fragments. It is difficult to explain the process of determining inappropriate XML fragments on a conceptual basis, so we describe the process using the following example.

Figure 1 shows log-log plots of the relationship between the number of tokens and XML fragments of the INEX document collection, where n is the number of tokens in each XML fragment and $N(n)$ is the number of XML fragments that contain n tokens. This figure shows that the property of the INEX document collection is similar to that of Web document collection, since the log-log plots follow Zipf's distribution (or power-law distribution) [20]. Therefore, it is reasonable that statistics information of the INEX document collection follows Zipf's distribution. However, it is difficult to determine whether XML fragments, in general, follow Zipf's distribution.

From a statistical point of view in the dynamics of terminology, it can be said that the gaps between the plots in Figure 1 cause a harmful effect on statistical information. Therefore, statistical information in plots with gaps is not used

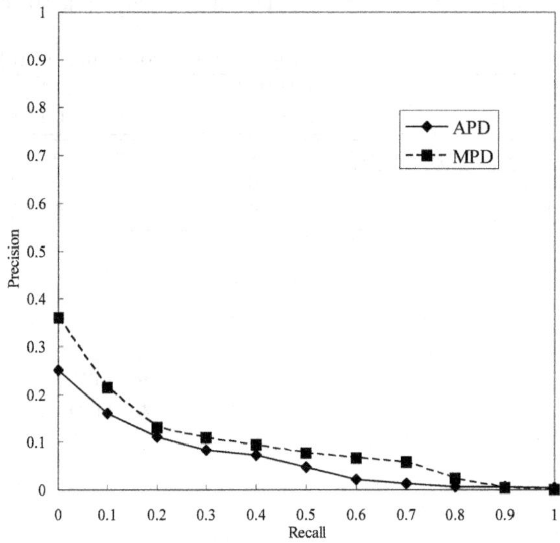

Fig. 2. Recall-precision curves based on the INEX 2003 relevance assessment

for capturing the property of the document set. In short, we consider the XML fragments in these plots with gaps to be inappropriate in XML fragment retrieval because we cannot capture the property of the document set accurately. As a result, we defined the appropriate fragments in XML fragment retrieval as the XML fragments in the plots in Figure 1 whose number of tokens is no smaller than 10 nor larger than 10,000 in the case of adopting the INEX document collection. This definition is sensible, because small XML fragments are not informative enough and large ones are too informative for users in keyword-based queries, and thus small/large XML fragments are unlikely to be answers to the CO-topics.

Verification of XML Fragments' Properties. In order to verify the validity of a technique from the dynamics of terminology, we performed some experiments using the INEX 2003 relevance assessment. In these experiments, we measured average precisions, index construction time, query processing time, and the number of indexed XML fragments of the following two types of index files in our XML fragment retrieval system: the index files of all XML fragments (APD) and those of the XML fragments other than the inappropriate fragments described in 3.1 (MPD).

Figure 2 shows the recall-precision curves based on the INEX 2003 relevance assessment. We initially expected that the recall-precision curves of APD and MPD would be very close to each other, since the fragments that were judged as inappropriate in XML fragment retrieval did not rank in the top 1,500 of all fragments. However, the recall-precision curve of MPD was higher than originally expected. Therefore, we think that the method proposed in 3.1 does not deteri-

Table 1. Comparison of APD with MPD in INEX 2003 relevance assessment

	# of fragments	index construction (s)
APD	8,224,053	513,878
MPD	1,011,202	109,115
	query processing (s/topic)	**average precision**
APD	17.66	0.0707
MPD	5.27	0.1038

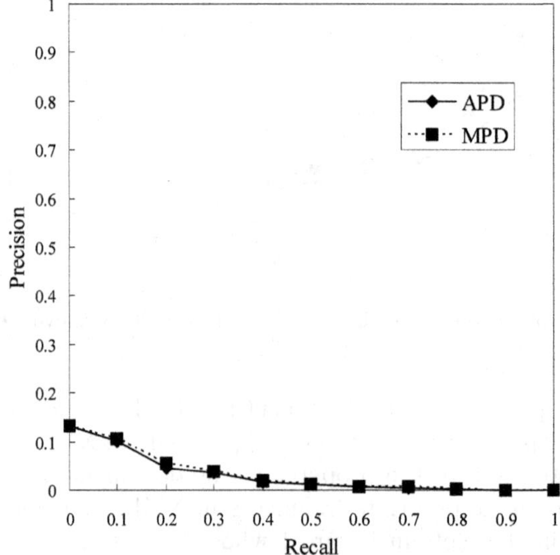

Fig. 3. Recall-precision curves based on the INEX 2004 relevance assessment

orate the retrieval accuracy of XML fragment retrieval systems. In addition, the number of indexed XML fragments was significantly reduced by adopting our method, thus also reducing index construction time and query processing time (see Table 1).

As shown above, the proposed method is useful not only in reducing index construction time and query processing time but also in improving the retrieval accuracy of an XML fragment retrieval system. Therefore, the proposed method is also suitable for the INEX 2004 relevance assessment.

3.2 Experiments Using INEX 2004 Relevance Assessment

Proposed method applied to the INEX 2003 relevance assessment worked well for reduction of index construction time and query processing time; thus we apply it to the INEX 2004 relevance assessment.

Figure 3 shows the recall-precision curves based on the INEX 2004 relevance assessment. Unlike the case of using the INEX 2003 relevance assessment, the recall-precision curves of APD and MPD were very close to each other. The

Table 2. Success ratios of our method (worst 5)

topic ID	$(E, S) = (2, 3)$			$(E, S) = (3, 2)$			$(E, S) = (3, 3)$			total
	miss	all	success ratio	miss	all	success ratio	miss	all	success ratio	
187	378	554	0.32	1,028	1,463	0.30	646	848	0.25	0.50
166	9	15	0.40	5	48	0.90	27	62	0.56	0.76
192	5	42	0.88	0	0	N/A	1	10	0.90	0.81
194	3	4	0.25	0	5	1.00	4	11	0.64	0.83
179	0	6	1.00	3	5	0.40	0	0	N/A	0.88

XML fragments that were judged as inappropriate in XML fragment retrieval based on the proposed method did not rank in the top 1,500 of all fragments; therefore, the recall-precision curves were almost the same. Moreover, average precisions in the INEX 2004 relevance assessment were smaller than those in INEX 2003. Our XML fragment retrieval system tends to retrieve relatively small XML fragments, so it could not retrieve large XML fragments whose root node is `article`, `bdy`, or `fm`. As a result, the exhaustivity of our system tends to be small, while its specificity tends to be large and average precision becomes small. This characteristic of our XML fragment retrieval system has negative effects on average precision; therefore, we have to propose a new term weighting scheme for XML fragment retrieval. Currently, some term weighting schemes, including ours, are already published[21, 6, 10, 9, 11]; however, they are not suitable for XML fragments that overlap each other. Consequently, we will have to adopt another weighting scheme that is suitable for XML fragment retrieval[2].

In order to investigate the problems of the proposed method, we also calculated the number of indexed XML fragments by using the proposed method relative to the number of answer XML fragments in the relevance assessment.

Table 2 shows the success ratio, which is the ratio of the number of answer XML fragments indexed by the proposed method relative to the number of all answer XML fragments. In this table, we show the topic IDs whose success ratios were in the bottom five topics. Almost all success ratios of CO-topics of the INEX 2003/2004 relevance assessments were more than 90%; however, only the success ratios of these topics listed in Table 2 were remarkably low. In topic 185, especially, the higher the exhaustivity and the specificity, the smaller the success ratio. Moreover, the number of fragments that were inappropriate in our method but were answers in the relevance assessment was extremely large. In our opinion, there is a tendency that keyword-based queries (CO-topics) are used to retrieve such document fragments that just contain specified keywords, and not for searching fragments that are most suitable for the users' intention. If this concept is valid, the CO-topics whose answers contain small XML fragments

[2] Length normalization of XML fragments [18] is one of the term weighting schemes in XML fragment retrieval. We believe that not only normalization of the length of XML fragments but also the frequencies of tokens in XML fragments are important for improving the average precision of our system.

Table 3. Comparison of APD with MPD in INEX 2004 relevance assessment

	query processing (s/topic)	average precision
APD	25.48	0.0263
MPD	13.03	0.0286

should not be used for the relevance assessment in XML fragment retrieval. Consequently, we think that not only the controversial issue of the term weighting scheme for XML fragment retrieval but also inappropriate CO-topics for the INEX relevance assessment cause the low average precision of our system.

On the other hand, the number of indexed XML fragments was significantly reduced by adopting our method in the manner done for INEX 2003, so the query processing time was reduced as shown in Table 3. Therefore, XML fragment retrieval systems could perform index construction and query processing more efficiently than current systems if we adopted our method.

3.3 Discussion About the Method

Through the experiments on INEX 2003 and 2004 relevance assessments, we found that index construction time and query processing time were reduced by adopting our method based on the dynamics of terminology in quantitative linguistics. Moreover, the average precision of an XML fragment retrieval system adopting our method did not become worse. As a result, the proposed method helps to improve the performance of XML fragment retrieval systems. We are now working to improve the average precision of our XML fragment retrieval system. We expect that a novel term weighting scheme for XML fragment retrieval and a phrase match function will enable us to improve the average precision of our XML fragment retrieval system.

4 Implementing XML Fragment Retrieval System on Relational XML Database

It goes without saying that not only accuracy but also performance is an essential aspect of an XML fragment retrieval system. In fact, this is not an easy task because we have to deal with several millions of fragments extracted from document collection. In our project, we have been attempting to develop an XML fragment retrieval system based on relational databases. The reason for using relational databases is that we can utilize a variety of techniques, such as query optimization, storage management, and top-k ranking, to speed up the process of XML fragment retrieval.

This section describes our first attempt at constructing such an XML fragment retrieval system. The system is based on a path-based relational XML database system, XRel [22], that is used for storing and retrieving XML documents by using off-the-shelf relational databases. In fact, we make an extension to XRel, which originally supports XPath as its basic query language, for supporting IR queries including CO- and CAS-topics.

4.1 An Overview of XRel

The Basics. XRel [22] is a scheme to realize XML databases on top of off-the-shelf relational databases. Using XRel, we can store any well-formed (or valid) XML documents in a relational database and can retrieve XML fragments from the database by using XPath expressions.

For storing XML documents, we shred the documents into small fragments so that they can be stored in relational tuples. Actually, we take a path-based approach, in which each node in an XML tree, such as element node, attribute node, and text node, is extracted and stored in a relational table with its *simple path expression* from the root and the *region* in the document. Here, a region is represented as a pair of integers (*start*, *end*), where *start* and *end* represent the starting and ending byte positions of the node in the XML file, respectively. This information is necessary and sufficient to retain the topology of an XML tree, and we can therefore achieve lossless decomposition of XML documents into flat relational tables. An important notice here is that, for given regions, we can detect the relationships among XML nodes, such as ancestor, descendant, precedes, and follows, by applying a subsumption theorem[3][22, 7]. Optionally, *depth*, which represents the depth of a node from the root, may be added as the third dimension in a region. In this case, we can additionally detect parent and child relations.

Schema Design. The components extracted from an XML document are stored in relational tables. Actually, there are countless ways to design the relational schema. In XRel, we decided to use four kinds of tables according to the node types, namely, *Element*, *Attribute*, *Text*, and *Path*. In addition, metadata about XML files, such as location, size, and identifier, are stored in the *Document* table. The actual schema definition of the tables are as follows:

```
Document (docID, filepath, length)
Element (docID, elementID, parentID, depth, pathID, start, end, index,
    reindex)
Attribute (docID, elementID, pathID, start, end, value)
Text (docID, elementID, pathID, start, end, value)
Path (pathID, pathexp)
```

In this definition, metadata are stored in the *Document* table with unique IDs. Also, all possible path expressions are stored in the *Path* table as character strings with their unique IDs. The other tables refer to these values in terms of `docID` and `pathID` attributes. For the *Element* table, each element node is stored with its document ID (`docID`), path expression (`pathID`), and region (`start`, `end`, and `depth`). Additionally, `elementID`, which is the unique identifier of an element node, is included for efficiency reasons, although this information is not mandatory. Likewise, `parentID`, which refers to the `elementID` of its parent node, is defined so that parent nodes can be easily reached. The `index` (`reindex`)

[3] Node x is an ancestor (descendant) of node y iff the region of x subsumes (is subsumed by, respectively) the region of y.

```
<vol no="1">
  <article>
    <title>TITLE1</title>
    <body>The first content.</body>
  </article>
  <article>
    <title>TITLE2</title>
    <body>The second <em>content.</em></body>
  </article>
</vol>
```

Fig. 4. An example XML document

attribute represents the (reverse) ordinal of nodes that share the same parent and the same path expression, and it is used to speed up positional predicates, such as `/book/author[2]` (`/book/author[-2]`). For the *Attribute* and *Text* tables, all attributes, except for `value`, act as in the *Element* table. The `value` attribute is used to store textual values of attribute and text nodes.

Figure 5 demonstrates how an XML document in Figure 4 is decomposed and stored in the relational tables.

Query Processing in XRel. For query retrieval, XRel supports XPath core, which is a subset of XPath [8], as its query language. Simply speaking, XPath core permits using "/" and "//" as location steps and using typical predicate expressions. Given an XPath core expression, XRel translates it into an equivalent SQL query that operates on the relational tables. The point here is that the translated query can be processed solely by the underlying relational database system. Then, the query result is obtained in the form of a result table, which is, in turn, reconstructed as the resultant XML fragments. For example, an XPath core query, "`//article/title[2]`," can be expressed as:

```
SELECT e1.docID, e1.st, e1.ed
FROM Path p1, Element e1
WHERE p1.pathexp LIKE '#%/article#/title'
AND e1.pathID = p1.pathID AND e1.idx = 2
ORDER BY e1.docID, e1.st
```

We do not go into the details due to the limitations of space, but more complicated queries containing node tests and/or predicates can be expressed in this way[22].

4.2 Supporting IR Queries in XRel

Statistics. Although the above tables are sufficient for processing XPath core queries, when considering INEX tasks, we need more information regarding IR statistics in order to support IR queries like in CO- and CAS-topics. To this end, we are attempting to maintain the statistics of XML nodes, in addition to the basic tables of XRel. These values include TF-IDF scores (including several variations), numbers of descendant elements, and various kinds of statistics. The concrete definition of the relational tables is as follows:

(a) Document

docID	filepath	length
0	"/path/to/foo.xml"	203

(c) Attribute

docID	elemID	pathID	st	ed	value
0	0	1	1	1	"1"

(b) Element

docID	elemID	parID	depth	pathID	st	ed	idx	reidx
0	0	-1	1	0	0	202	1	1
0	1	0	2	2	15	98	1	2
0	2	1	3	3	29	49	1	1
0	3	1	3	4	55	85	1	1
0	4	0	2	2	102	195	2	1
0	5	4	3	3	116	136	1	1
0	6	4	3	4	142	182	1	1
0	7	6	4	5	159	175	1	1

(d) Text

docID	elemID	pathID	st	ed	value
0	2	3	36	41	"TITLE1"
0	3	4	61	78	"The first content."
0	5	3	123	128	"TITLE2"
0	6	4	148	158	"The second "
0	7	5	163	170	"content."

(e) Path

pathID	pathexp
0	"#/vol"
1	"#/vol#/@no"
2	"#/vol#/article"
3	"#/vol#/article#/title"
4	"#/vol#/article#/body"
5	"#/vol#/article#/body#/em"

Fig. 5. A storage example of XRel

```
Token (docID, elementID, nodeFlag, token, articleNo, tf, tfidf,
      tfidfMG, tfief, tfipf, tfOrder)
DescendantElementNum (docID, elementID, elementName, count)
ElementStatistics (docID, elementID, sentenceNum, termFreq,
      tokenFreq, wordFreq)
```

Let us take a closer look at the definitions. The *Token* table is for storing every occurrence of a distinct token. A token is stored with the document ID, element ID, and article ID where it appears, term frequency (`tf`), and several variations of term scores (`tfidf`, `tfidfMG`, `tfief`, and `tfipf`). `tfOrder` is used for ordering the tuples in the descending order of `tf`, so as to speed up table scans. The *DescendantElementNum* table maintains the number of descendant elements for each element. The *ElementStatistics* table is for storing various kinds of statistics regarding elements, such as the numbers of elements, term frequencies, token frequencies, and word frequencies.

Processing CO-Topics. Using the above tables as well as the basic XRel tables, we can express any CO-topic in the form of `[key_1, ..., key_l, +plus_1, ..., +plus_m, -minus_1, ..., -minus_n]`, as an SQL query:

```
SELECT docID, elementID, SUM(t.tfidf) result
FROM token t
WHERE t.token IN ('key_1', ..., 'key_l')
GROUP BY docID, elementID
HAVING (SELECT COUNT(*)
        FROM token
        WHERE token IN ('minus_1', ..., 'minus_n')
        AND t.docID = token.docID
        AND t.elementID = token.elementID ) = 0
AND
       (SELECT COUNT(*)
        FROM token
        WHERE token IN ('plus_1', ..., 'plus_m')
        AND t.docID = token.docID
        AND t.elementID = token.elementID ) = m
ORDER BY result DESC;
```

As can be seen, the calculation of TF-IDF is implemented in terms of an aggregation function. It should also be noted that, in the translated query, "+key" and "-key" are expressed in terms of a HAVING clause. The resulting query is sorted in descending order of TF-IDF scores, by the ORDER BY clause.

In the same way, we can express CO-topics with phrase match by using the `value` attribute in the *Text* table. However, this may not be realistic from the viewpoint of efficiency, due to the fact that the cost for approximate matching in SQL is quite expensive. Consequently, a naive implementation would cause serious performance degradation. Actually, we may need an additional index that supports full-text search of text contents to deal with phrase matching.

4.3 Discussions About the Implementation

As discussed above, our system currently only supports XPath core and CO queries, and we thus need to accomplish further development to extend its ability and improve system performance. We are now working to improve overall system performance. In our scheme, we use a novel technique to reduce the number of result candidates. Also, we are working to achieve support of CAS- (VCAS-) topics. Efficient execution of top-k ranking in CO- and CAS-topics is another important issue.

5 Conclusion

In this paper, we proposed a method for determining XML fragments that are appropriate in keyword-based XML fragment retrieval based on the dynamics of terminology. Through some experimental evaluations in 3.1, 3.2, we found that proposed method helps to improve the performance of our XML fragment retrieval system. Moreover, we applied our XML fragment retrieval system on a relational database system, which enabled us to reduce the query processing time of our system. If we implemented a phrase match function in our system, we could expect to improve average precision. Currently, we also have the problem of finding a term weighting scheme that is suitable for XML fragment retrieval and query optimization with a ranking function on relational database systems. These problems are the immediate tasks of our project, so we intend to solve these tasks in the near future. As an original approach, we are focusing on XML fragment retrieval without scheme information; accordingly we are going to address these problems with a view to the heterogeneous collection track of the INEX project.

Acknowledgments

This work is partly supported by the Ministry of Education, Culture, Sports, Science and Technology (MEXT), Japan, under grants #15200010, #16016243 and #16700103.

References

1. S. Agrawal, S. Chaudhuriand, and G. Das. DBXplorer: A System for Keyword-Based Search over Relational Databases. In *Proc. of the 18th International Conference on Data Engineering*, pages 5–16. IEEE CS Press, Feb./Mar. 2002.
2. S. Amer-Yahia, C. Botev, S. Buxton, P. Case, J. Doerre, D. McBeath, M. Rys, and J. Shanmugasundaram. XQuery 1.0 and XPath 2.0 Full-Text. `http://www.w3.org/TR/xmlquery-full-text/`, July 2004. W3C Working Draft 09 July 2004.
3. S. Amer-Yahia and P. Case. XQuery 1.0 and XPath 2.0 Full-Text Use Cases. `http://www.w3.org/TR/xmlquery-full-text-use-cases/`, July 2004. W3C Working Draft 09 July 2004.
4. S. Boag, D. Chamberlin, M. F. Fernandez, D. Florescu, J. Robie, and J. Siméon. XQuery 1.0: An XML Query Language. `http://www.w3.org/TR/xquery`, Oct. 2004. W3C Working Draft 29 October 2004.
5. T. Bray, J. Paoli, C. M. Sperberg-McQueen, E. Maler, and F. Yergeau. Extensible Markup Language (XML) 1.0 (Third Edition). `http://www.w3.org/TR/REC-xml`, Feb. 2004. W3C Recommendation 04 February 2004.
6. J.-M. Bremer and M. Gertz. XQuery/IR: Integrating XML Document and Data Retrieval. In *Proc. of the 5th International Workshop on the Web and Databases (WebDB2002)*, pages 1–6. June 2002.
7. S.-Y. Chien, V. J. Tsotras, C. Zaniolo, and D. Zhang. Storing and querying multiversion XML documents using durable node numbers. In *Proc. of the 2nd International Conference on Web Information Systems Engineering*, pages 270–279. 2001.
8. J. Clark and S. DeRose. XML Path Language (XPath) Version 1.0. `http://www.w3.org/TR/xpath`, Nov. 1999. W3C Recommendation 16 November 1999.
9. S. Cohen, J. Mamou, Y. Kanza, and Y. Sagiv. XSEarch: A Semantic Search Engine for XML. In *Proc. of 29th International Conference on Very Large Data Bases*, pages 45–56. Morgan Kaufmann, Sep. 2003.

10. C.J. Crouch, S. Apte and H. Bapat. Using the Extended Vector Model for XML Retrieval. In *Proc. of the 1st Workshop of the Initiative for the Evaluation of XML Retrieval (INEX)*, pages 95–98. ERCIM, March 2003.
11. H. Cui, J.-R. Wen and T.-S. Chua. Hierarchical Indexing and Flexible Element Retrieval for Structured Document. In *Proc. of the 25th European Conference on Information Retrieval Research (ECIR2003)*. pages 73–87, April 2003.
12. N. Gövert, N. Fuhr, M. Abolhassani, and K. Großjohann. Content-Oriented XML Retrieval with HyREX. In *Proc. of the First Workshop of the Initiative for the Evaluation of XML Retrieval*, pages 26–32. ERCIM, Mar. 2003.
13. L. Guo, F. Shao, C. Botev, and J. Shanmugasundaram. XRANK: Ranked Keyword Search over XML Documents. In *Proc. of the 2003 ACM SIGMOD International Conference on Management of Data*, pages 16–27. ACM Press, June 2003.
14. K. Hatano, H. Kinutani, M. Watanabe, Y. Mori, M. Yoshikawa, and S. Uemura. Keyword-based XML Portion Retrieval: Experimental Evaluation based on INEX 2003 Relevance Assessments. In *Proc. of the Second Workshop of the Initiative for the Evaluation of XML Retrieval*, pages 81–88. Mar. 2004.
15. K. Hatano, H. Kinutani, M. Yoshikawa, and S. Uemura. Information Retrieval System for XML Documents. In *Proc. of the 13th International Conference on Database and Expert Systems Applications*, volume 2453 of *LNCS*, pages 758–767. Springer, Sep. 2002.
16. V. Hristidis, Y. Papakonstantinou, and A. Balmin. Keyword Proximity Search on XML Graphs. In *Proc. of the 19th International Conference on Data Engineering*, pages 367–378. IEEE CS Press, Mar. 2003.
17. K. Kageura. *The Dynamics of Terminology*. John Benjamins, 2002.
18. J. Kamps, M. de Rijke, and B. Sigurbjörnsson. Length Normalization in XML Retrieval. In *Proc. of the 27th Annual International ACM SIGIR Conference on Research and Development in Informaion Retrieval*, pages 80–87. ACM Press, July 2004.
19. M. Kaszkiel and J. Zobel. Passage Retrieval Revisited. In *Proc. of the 20th Annual International ACM SIGIR Conference on Research and Development in Information Retrieval*, pages 178–185. ACM Press, July 1997.
20. J. Nielsen. Do Websites Have Increasing Returns? `http://www.useit.com/alertbox/9704b.html`, Apr. 1997. Jakob Nielsen's Alertbox for April 15, 1997.
21. D. Shin, H. Jang and H. Jin. BUS: An Effective Indexing and Retrieval Scheme in Structured Documents In *Proc. of the 3rd ACM Conference on Digital libraries (DL'98)*, pages 235–243. June 1998.
22. M. Yoshikawa, T. Amagasa, T. Shimura, and S. Uemura. XRel: A Path-Based Approach to Storage and Retrieval of XML Documents using Relational Databases. *ACM Transactions on Internet Technology*, 1(1):110–141. June 2001.

A Voting Method for XML Retrieval

Gilles Hubert[1,2]

[1] IRIT/SIG-EVI, 118 route de Narbonne, 31062 Toulouse, cedex 4
[2] ERT34, Institut Universitaire de Formation des Maîtres, 56 av. de l'URSS, 31400 Toulouse
hubert@irit.fr

Abstract. This paper describes the retrieval approach proposed by the SIG/EVI group of the IRIT research centre in INEX'2004 evaluation. The approach uses a voting method coupled with some processes to answer content only and content and structure queries. This approach is based on previous works we leaded in the context of automatic text categorization.

1 Introduction

The development of systems to perform searches in collections constituted of XML (eXtensible Markup Language) documents [3] has become a need since the use of XML is growing. Consequently, a growing number of systems intend to provide means to retrieve relevant components among XML documents. XML retrieval systems need to take into account content and structural aspects.

Regarding the variety of proposed XML retrieval systems it is interesting to evaluate their effectiveness. For that, the INitiative for the Evaluation of XML retrieval (INEX) provides a testbed and scoring methods allowing participants to evaluate and compare their results.

Underlying approaches of systems participating to INEX can be classified in two categories [5] : model-oriented approaches and system-oriented approaches. Model-oriented approaches gather notably approaches based on language models [11], [8], [1] or other probabilistic models [14] which obtained good results in 2003. System-oriented approaches extend textual document retrieval system adding XML-specific processing. Various systems in this category [10], [6], [13], [16] obtained good results in 2003.

In this paper, we present an IR approach initially applied to automatic categorization of structured documents according to concept hierarchies and its evolution brought for XML retrieval notably within the context of INEX.

Section 2 is a short presentation of the INEX initiative 2004 edition. Section 3 presents the initial context in which the method was initiated and its first application within INEX in 2003. The evolutions made to this approach for INEX 2004 are described in section 4. Section 5 presents the submitted runs and the obtained results. In section 6 we conclude analyzing the experiment and considering future works.

N. Fuhr et al. (Eds.): INEX 2004, LNCS 3493, pp. 183 – 195, 2005.

2 The INEX Initiative

2.1 Collection

The INEX documents correspond to approximately 12,000 articles of the IEEE Computer Society's publications from 1995 to 2002 marked up in XML. All the documents respect the same DTD. The collection gathers over eight millions XML elements of varying length and granularity (ex. title, paragraph or article).

2.2 Queries

INEX introduces two types of queries:

- CO (Content Only) queries describe the expected content of the XML elements to retrieve.
- CAS (Content and Structure) queries combine content and explicit references to the XML structure using a variant of Xpath [4]. CAS topics contain indications about the structure of expected XML elements and about the location of expected content.

Both CO and CAS topics are made up of four parts: topic title, topic description, narrative and keywords.

Within the ad-hoc retrieval task, two types of tasks are defined: (1) the CO task, using CO queries, (2) the VCAS task, using CAS queries, for which the structural constraints are considered as vague conditions.

3 A Voting Method in Information Retrieval

The approach we proposed is derived from a process we first defined for textual document categorisation [7], [2]. Document categorisation intends to link documents with pre-defined categories. Our approach focuses on categories organised as taxonomy. The original aspect of our approach is that it involves a voting principle instead of a classical similarity computing. The association of a text to categories is based on the Vector Voting method [12]. The voting process evaluates the importance of the association between a given text and a given category.

This method is similar to the HVV method (Hyperlink Vector Voting) used within the Web context to compute the relevance of a Web page regarding the web sites referring to it [9]. In our context, the initial strategy considers that the more the category terms appear in the text, the more the link between the text and this category is strong. Thus, this method relies on terms describing each category and their automatic extraction from the document to be categorised. The result is a list of categories annotating each document.

For INEX'2003, this categorisation process has been applied. Every XML component has been processed as a complete document. Every topic has been considered as a category of a flat taxonomy. The result was a list of topics corresponding to each

XML component. It was then reversed and reordered to fit the INEX format of results.

Results obtained for the submitted runs [15] have led us to improve the process to suit a retrieval process. The axes of this evolution have been as follows:

- inverse the voting process to estimate the relevance of each XML component according to each topic,
- modify the voting function to take into account the great variations of element sizes and to take into account topic treatment rather than category treatment,
- integrate the aggregation aspect of an XML element (i.e. elements composed of relevant elements),
- integrate structural constraint processing for CAS topics.

4 Evolution of the Voting Method Within INEX

The approach we proposed is derived from a process we first defined for textual document categorisation [7], [2]. Document categorisation intends to link documents with pre-defined categories. Our approach focuses on categories organised as taxonomy. The original aspect of our approach is that it involves a voting principle instead of a classical similarity computing. The association of a text to categories is based on the Vector Voting method [12]. The voting process evaluates the importance of the association between a given text and a given category.

4.1 INEX Collection Pre-processing

From the INEX collection point of view, the documents are considered as sets of text chunks identified by xpaths. For each XML component, concepts are extracted automatically and saved with the xpath identifying the XML component in which they appear and the number of occurrences in the component. Concept extraction involves notably stop word removal. Optionally, some processes can be applied to concepts such as stemming using Porter's algorithm. For INEX'2004 experiments all XML tags except text formatting tags (bold, italic, underline) have been taken into account. From the topic point of view, although our method can use all the parts constituting CO and CAS topics, we used only the title part for the INEX'2004 experiments as requested. For both topic types, stop words are removed and optionally terms can be stemmed using Porter's algorithm.

4.2 Voting Function

The voting function must take into account the importance in the XML element of each term describing the topic and the importance of each term in the topic representation. We have studied different voting functions and the one providing the best results is described as follows:

$$Vote(E,T) = \sum_{\forall t \in T} F(t,E) \cdot \frac{F(t,T)}{S(T)}$$

where

T is the topic

E is an XML element

$F(t,E)$ This factor measures the importance of the term t in the XML element E. F(t,E) corresponds the number of occurrences of the term t in the element E.

$\frac{F(t,T)}{S(T)}$ This factor measures the importance of the term t in the topic representation T. F(t,T) corresponds to the number of occurrences of the term t in the topic T and S(T) corresponds to the size (number of terms) of T.

The voting function combines two factors: the presence of a term in the element and the importance of this term in the topic.

4.3 Scoring Function

The voting function is coupled with a third factor representing the importance of the topic presence within the XML element.

The final function (scoring function) that computes the score of an XML element regarding a given topic is the following:

$$Score(E,T) = Vote(E,T) \cdot f(\frac{NT(T,E)}{S(T)})$$

where

$\frac{NT(T,E)}{S(T)}$ This factor measures the presence rate of terms representing the topic in the text (importance of the topic). S(T) corresponds to the number of terms in the topic representation T and NT(T,E) corresponds to the number of terms of the topic T that appear in the XML element E.

Applying a function f to the third factor (i.e. the presence rate of terms representing the topic in the text) aims at varying the influence of this factor on the scoring function. We tried different functions f, for example the initial function was the exponential (i.e. $f(\frac{NT(T,E)}{S(T)}) = e^{\frac{NT(T,E)}{S(T)}}$).

4.4 Additional Processes for Both CO and CAS Topics

The scoring function is completed with the notion of *coverage*. The aim of the coverage is to ensure that only documents in which the topic is represented enough will be selected for this topic. The coverage is a threshold corresponding to the percentage of terms from a topic that appears in a text. For example, 50% of coverage implies that at least half of the terms describing a topic have to appear in the text of a document to select it.

$$\text{If } \frac{NT(T,E)}{S(T)} \geq CT \quad \text{then} \quad Score(E,T) = Vote(E,T) \cdot f(\frac{NT(T,E)}{S(T)})$$

$$\text{else} \quad Score(E,T) = 0.0$$

where CT is a real constant (CT≥0.0) corresponding to the coverage threshold.

The hierarchical structure of XML has to be taken into account. The hypothesis on which is based our system is that an element containing a component selected as relevant is also relevant. Our system takes into account this hypothesis propagating the score of an element to the elements it composes. The score propagated to the composed elements is decreased applying a reducing factor.

$$\forall\, E_a \text{ ancestor of } E \quad \text{and} \quad d(E_a,E)\cdot\alpha<1$$
$$Score(E_a,T) = Score(E_a,T) + (1 - d(E_a,E)\cdot\alpha)\cdot Score(E,T)$$

where

α is a constant coefficient and E is an XML element

$d(E_a,E)$ is the distance between E_a and E in the xpath associated to E (e.g. in the xpath /article/bdy/s/ss1/p the distance between p and bdy is equal to 3 i.e. d(bdy,p)=3).

This process tends to consider a composed element less relevant than the element it is composed of. However, an element composed of several relevant elements can obtain a score greater than one of its components.

The hypothesis chosen for INEX is quite different notably due to relevance dimensions: exhaustivity and specificity. Considering exhaustivity, a composed element is considered at least as relevant as the most relevant of its components. Considering specificity, the relevance of an element composed of several relevant components is less or equal to the relevance of the most relevant component. It would be interesting to evaluate the impact of this difference of relevance propagation on the retrieval results of our system.

In addition, in INEX, terms constituting a topic title can have either the prefix + or -. The sign + is used to emphasize a concept and – denotes an unwanted concept. The + and – signs do not have strict semantics but just indicate preferences wished by the topic's author. An element containing a term prefixed by – in the topic title can be judged relevant to the information need. In the same way, an element judged relevant to the information need even if it does not contain the term prefixed by + in the topic title.

To take into account the possibility of having prefixed terms, a coefficient is associated to each term. A coefficient is fixed for each case: term not prefixed, term with the prefix + and term with the prefix -.

$$Vote(E,T) = \sum_{\forall t \in T} sc(t,T) \cdot F(t,E) \cdot \frac{F(t,T)}{S(T)}$$

where

sc(t,T) = a if t has the prefix – in the topic

sc(t,T) = b if t has no prefix in the topic

sc(t,T) = c if t has the prefix + in the topic

a, b, c are real constants.

4.5 Specific Processes for CAS Topics

On one hand, we take into account different types of constraints on content. Structural constraints on xpath of elements which are expected to contain keywords (e.g. about(.//p,'+authorization +"access control" +security') and constraints on the year of the article .(e.g. //yr <='2000') are taken into account. These kinds of structural constraints on content gathered all the constraints appearing in the CAS topics of INEX'2004. The voting method applied to CO topics has been extended to take into account such constraints as follows:

$$Vote(E,T) = \sum_{\forall t \in T} (1+\beta) \cdot F(t,E) \cdot \frac{F(t,T)}{S(T)}$$

where

if E matches a structural constraint defined on t then $\beta>0.0$

else $\beta=0.0$

On the other hand, an additional step identifies the structural constraints on target elements indicated in CAS topics. All the structural constraints defined on target elements of topics are taken into account and stored to be processed in a post-voting step to enrich the results issued from the voting step.

For VCAS evaluation, the target constraint specified in the topic does not have to be strictly verified. The constraint is rather regarded as a hint for expected results without eliminating the elements which do not satisfy the target constraint.

To take into account these principles, the score associated to the elements of the results that match the expected xpaths are increased. A factor is applied to the score of matching elements as follows:

If R matches X then $Score(E,T) = \gamma \cdot Vote(E,T) \cdot f(\frac{NT(T,E)}{S(T)})$ where $\gamma>1.0$

where

R is the location path (xpath) of the element E from the root of the document

X is the location path (xpath) defined as the target constraint in the topic.

5 Experiments

5.1 Experiment Setup

Our experiments aim at evaluating the efficiency of the evolution given to the voting function and the coefficient adjustments resulting from training performed on the INEX'2003 assessment testbed. The training phase only concerns system processes applied to both CO and CAS topics.

Three runs based on the voting method were submitted to INEX'2004. Two runs were performed on CO topics and one run was performed on CAS topics. The runs on CO topics differ from the function f used in the voting method.

The run labelled VTCO2004TC35xp400sC-515 uses the voting function:

$$Score(E,T) = Vote(E,T) \cdot \varphi^{(\frac{NT(T,E)}{S(T)})} \quad \text{where } \varphi=400.$$

The run labelled VTCO2004TC35p4sC-515 uses the voting function:

$$Score(E,T) = Vote(E,T) \cdot \left(\frac{NT(T,D)}{S(T)}\right)^{\lambda} \quad \text{where } \lambda=4.$$

The run on CAS topics labelled VTCAS2004C35xp200sC-515PP1 uses the voting function:

$$Score(E,T) = Vote(E,T) \cdot \varphi^{(\frac{NT(T,E)}{S(T)})} \quad \text{where } \varphi=200.$$

The coefficient taking into account structural predicates associated to searched concepts was fixed to 1.0 (i.e. the vote of an element regarding a given concept is doubled when the element matches the structural constraint associated to the concept). The coefficient taking into account structural predicates for expected results was fixed to 2.0 (i.e. the score of an element matching the structural predicate is doubled). The values of these two coefficients were fixed arbitrarily.

For all submitted runs the other parameters of the scoring function were the same. Coverage threshold was fixed to 35% (i.e. more than a third of terms describing the topic must appear in the text to keep the XML component). Coefficients applied to take into account the signs '+' and '-' used to emphasise a concept or to denote an unwanted one were fixed to:

- +5.0 for concepts marked with '+' (the vote of these concepts increases the score of the elements in which they appear),
- -5.0 for concepts marked with '-' (the vote of these concepts reduces the score of the elements in which they appear),
- 1.0 for unmarked concepts.

The coefficient α used to propagate a component score through the hierarchical structure of the XML document was fixed to 0.1.

The values of the parameters are those which gave the best results during a training phase done with INEX'2003 CO topics.

5.2 Results

The following table shows the preliminary results of the three runs based on the voting method:

Table 1. Results of the 3 runs performed using the voting method

Run	Aggregate score	Rank
VTCO2004TC35xp400sC-515	0.0783	13/70
VTCO2004TC35p4sC-515	0.0775	15/70
VTCAS2004TC35xp200sC-515	0.0784	5/51

The results of the two runs for CO topics are detailled in the following table:

Table 2. Detailed results of the 2 runs for CO topics

	VTCO2004TC35xp400sC-515		VTCO2004TC35p4sC-515	
Quantisation	**Average precision**	**Rank**	**Average precision**	**Rank**
strict	0.0778	18/70	0.0759	19/70
generalised	0.0683	14/70	0.0682	15/70
so	0.0559	16/70	0.0564	15/70
s3_e321	0.0395	22/70	0.0400	21/70
s3_e32	0.0508	17/70	0.0508	17/70
e3_s321	0.1456	10/70	0.1424	11/70
e3_s32	0.1106	11/70	0.1083	13/70

For CO topics, the run which has obtained the best results is the run labelled VTCO2004TC35xp400sC-515. The best measures have been obtained with e3s321 quantisation. Average precision is equal to 0.1456, placing the run at the 10th rank. The run labelled VTCO2004TC35p4sC-515 has obtained values slightly lower for most of the quantisations. Only the best results obtained for CO topics are presented in the following graphs that is to say run VTCO2004TC35xp400sC-515 for e3s321 quantisation.

For CAS topics, the run VTCAS2004TC35xp200sC-515PP1 has been ranked at the 5th place. The results of the run are detailled in the following table:

The best measures have been obtained for quantisations strict, e3s321 and e3s32 for which the run is ranked 5. The following figures present the results corresponding to the strict quantisation and e3s321 quantisation.

Table 3. Detailed results of the run for CAS topics

	VTCAS2004TC35xp200sC-515PP1	
Quantisation	**Average precision**	**Rank**
strict	0.1053	5/51
generalised	0.0720	6/51
so	0.0554	9/51
s3_e321	0.0462	12/51
s3_e32	0.0644	10/51
e3_s321	0.1162	5/51
e3_s32	0.0892	5/51

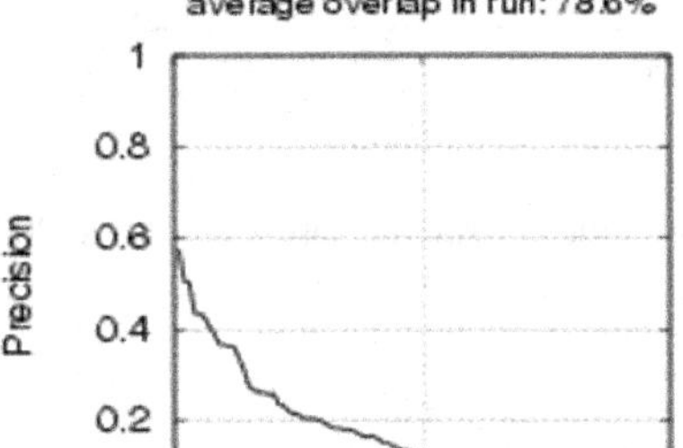

Fig. 1. Precision/Recall curve of the CO run labelled VTCO2004TC35xp400sC-515 for e_3s_{321} quantisation

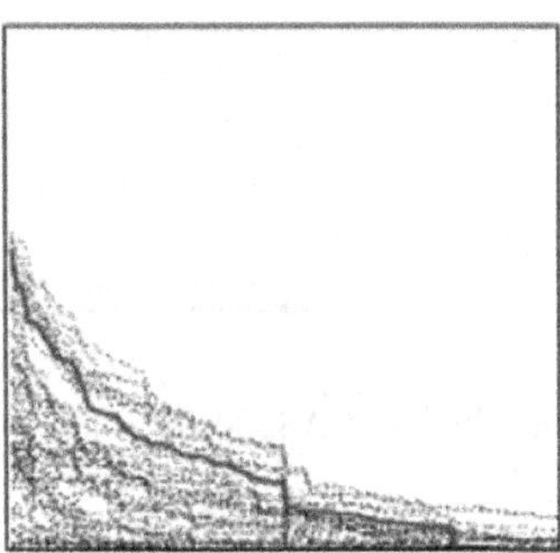

Fig. 2. Rank of the CO run labelled VTCO2004TC35xp400sC-515 for e_3s_{321} quantisation

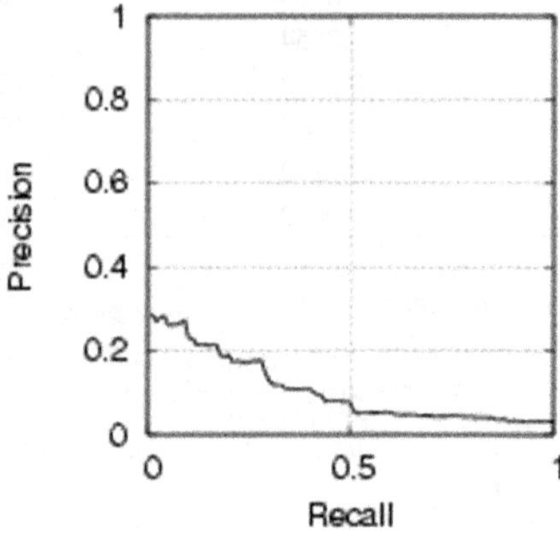

Fig. 3. Precision/Recall curve of the VCAS run labelled VTCAS2004TC35xp200sC-515PP1 for strict quantisation

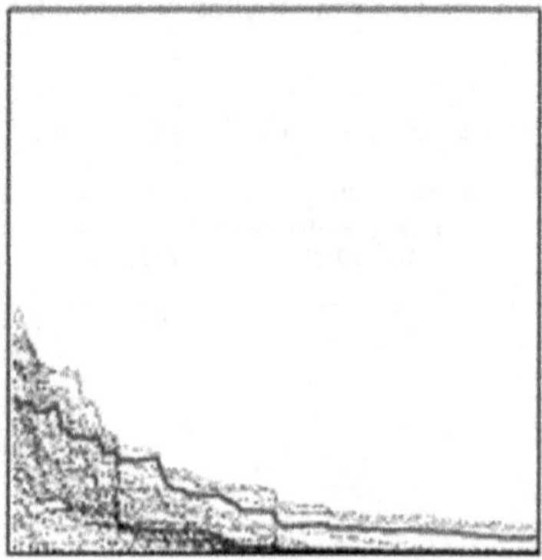

Fig. 4. Rank of the VCAS run labelled VTCAS2004TC35xp200sC-515PP1 for strict quantisation

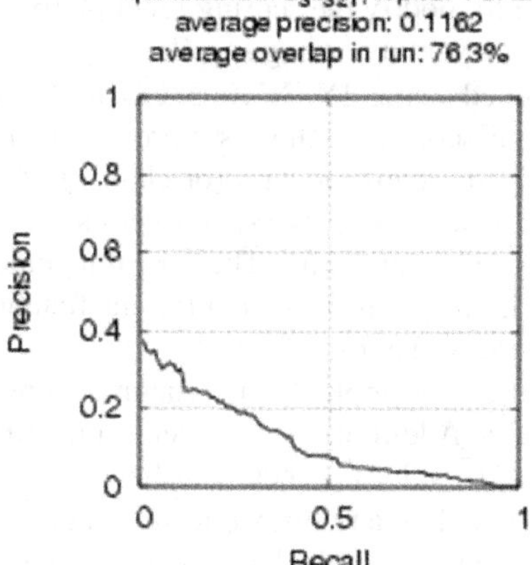

Fig. 5. Precision/Recall curve of the VCAS run labelled VTCAS2004TC35xp200sC-515PP1 for e_3s_{321} quantisation

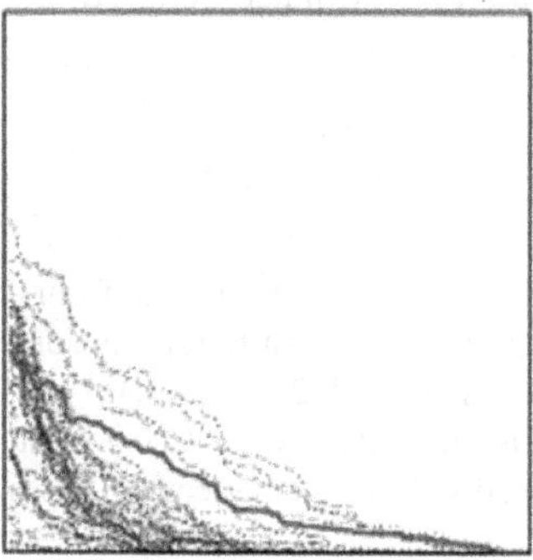

Fig. 6. Rank of the VCAS run labelled VTCAS2004TC35xp200sC-515PP1 for e_3s_{321} quantisation

6 Discussion and Future Works

Regarding the experiments that were performed and the obtained results we can notice that:

- the chosen functions and parameters for the scoring method tend to support exhaustivity rather than specificity. Indeed, the importance of the factor measuring the representation of the topic (i.e. NT(T,E)/S(T)) dominates in the scoring function and this factor is related to the exhaustivity relevance. It would be interesting to modify the scoring function to increase the number of elements judged as relevant regarding specificity.

- The measures obtained using INEX'2003 CO topics were globally better. This suggests that our scoring method is more efficient on certain queries. It would be interesting to identify a class (or classes) of queries for which the function works better, a class (classes) of queries for which the function is less efficient and to understand why. The function could evolve to extend its efficiency to other kinds of queries or different functions could be applied regarding different query classes.
- The values of coefficients applied for structural constraint matching have been fixed arbitrarily. Additional experiments on INEX'2004 CAS topics will help us to adjust the values of these coefficients.
- Evaluate the profit of adding a relevance feedback process to our method. On one hand, feedback from first ranked elements of the assessments can be performed. This is the process chosen this year in the relevance feedback track. On the other hand, we plan to integrate a feedback process using first ranked elements of a first search using our system.

Acknowledgments

Research outlined in the paper is part of the project QUEST: Query reformulation for structured document retrieval, PAI Alliance N°05768UJ. However, this publication only reflects the author's view.

References

1. Abolhassani, M., Fuhr, N.: Applying the Divergence from Randomness Approach for Content-Only Search in XML Documents. 26th European Conference on IR Research (ECIR), Lecture Notes in Computer Science vol. 2997 (2004) 409-419
2. Augé, J., Englmeier, K., Hubert, G., Mothe, J. : Catégorisation automatique de textes basée sur des hiérarchies de concepts. 19ième Journées de Bases de Données Avancées (BDA) Lyon (2003) 69-87
3. Bray, T., Paoli, J., Sperberg-McQueen, C. M., Maler, E., Yergeau, Y.: Extensible Markup Language (XML) 1.0 (Third Edition). W3C Recommendation., http://www.w3.org/TR/REC-xml/ (2004)
4. Clark, J., DeRose, S.: XML Path Language (XPath). W3C Recommendation, http://www.w3.org/TR/xpath.html (1999).
5. Fuhr, N., Maalik, S., Lalmas, M.: Overview of the INitiative for the Evaluation of XML Retrieval (INEX) 2003. Proceedings of the Second INEX Workshop, Dagstuhl, Germany (2004) 1-11
6. Geva, S., Leo-Spork, M.: XPath Inverted File for Information Retrieval. INEX 2003 Workshop Proceedings, (2003) 110-117

7. IRAIA: Getting Orientation in Complex Information Spaces as an Emergent Behaviour of Autonomous Information Agents. European Information Societies Technology, IST-1999-10602, (2000-2002).
8. Kamps, J., de Rijke, M., Sigurbjörnsson, B.: Length normalization in XML retrieval. Proceedings of the 27th International Conference on Research and Development in Information Retrieval (SIGIR). New York NY, USA, (2004) 80-87
9. Li, Y.: Toward a qualitative search engine. IEEE Internet Computing, vol. 2 n°4, (1998) 24-29
10. List J., Mihajlovic V., de Vries A. P., Ramirez G., Hiemstra D.: The TIJAH XML-IR system at INEX 2003. INEX 2003 Workshop Proceedings, (2003) 102-109
11. Ogilvie, P., Callan J.: Using Language Models for Flat Text Queries in XML Retrieval. Proceedings of the Second INEX Workshop. Dagstuhl, Germany, (2004) 12-18
12. Pauer, B., Holger, P.: Statfinder. Document Package Statfinder, Vers. 1.8, (2000)
13. Pehcevski, J., Thom J., Vercoustre, A.M.: Enhancing Content-And-Structure Information Retrieval using a Native XML Database. Proceedings of The First Twente Data Management Workshop on XML Databases and Information Retrieval (TDM'04), Enschede, The Netherlands, (2004)
14. Piwowarski B., Vu H.-T., Gallinari P.: Bayesian Networks and INEX'03. Proceedings of the Second INEX Workshop. Dagstuhl, Germany, (2003) 33-37
15. Sauvagnat, K., Hubert, G., Boughanem, M., Mothe, J.: IRIT at INEX 2003. Proceedings of the Second INEX Workshop. Dagstuhl, Germany, (2003) 142-148
16. Trotman, A., O'Keefe, R. A.: Identifying and Ranking Relevant Document Elements. INEX 2003 Workshop Proceedings, (2003) 149-154

Mixture Models, Overlap, and Structural Hints in XML Element Retrieval

Börkur Sigurbjörnsson[1], Jaap Kamps[1,2], and Maarten de Rijke[1]

[1] Informatics Institute, University of Amsterdam
[2] Archives and Information Studies, Faculty of Humanities, University of Amsterdam

Abstract. We describe the INEX 2004 participation of the Informatics Institute of the University of Amsterdam. We completely revamped our XML retrieval system, now implemented as a mixture language model on top of a standard search engine. To speed up structural reasoning, we indexed the collection's structure in a separate database. Our main findings are as follows. First, we show that blind feedback improves retrieval effectiveness, but increases overlap. Second, we see that removing overlap from the result set decreases retrieval effectiveness for all metrics except the XML cumulative gain measure. Third, we show that ignoring the structural constraints gives good results if measured in terms of mean average precision; the structural constraints are, however, useful for achieving high initial precision. Finally, we provide a detailed analysis of the characteristics of one of our runs. Based on this analysis we argue that a more explicit definition of the INEX retrieval tasks is needed.

1 Introduction

We follow an Information Retrieval (IR) approach to the Content-Only (CO) and Vague-Content-And-Structure (VCAS) ad hoc tasks at INEX. In our participation at INEX 2004 we built on top of our element-based approach at INEX 2003 [10], and extended our language modeling approach to XML retrieval.

Specifically, we addressed the following technological issues, mainly to obtain a statistically more transparent approach. For our INEX 2003 experiments we combined article and element scores outside our language modeling framework. That is, we calculated scores separately for articles and elements, and then updated the element scores by taking into account the score of the surrounding article. This year, we implemented a proper mixture language model, incorporating evidence from both the XML elements and the article in which they occur. Furthermore, at INEX 2003 we estimated the language model of the collection by looking at statistics from our overlapping element index. For our INEX 2004 experiments we estimate this collection model differently, by looking at statistics from our article index. The main change in our blind feedback approach, compared to last year, is that this year we perform query expansion based on an element run, whereas last year we performed the expansion based on an article

N. Fuhr et al. (Eds.): INEX 2004, LNCS 3493, pp. 196–210, 2005.

run. All our runs were created using the ILPS extension to the Lucene search engine [7,3].

Our main research questions for both tasks were twofold. First, we wanted to investigate the effect of blind feedback on XML element retrieval. Second, we wanted to cast light on the problem of overlapping results; in particular, we investigate the effect of removing overlapping results top-down from a retrieval run. A third, additional research question only concerns the VCAS task: we investigate the difference between applying a content-only approach and a strict content-and-structure approach.

The remainder of this paper is organized as follows. In Section 2 we describe our experimental setup, and in Section 3 we provide details on the official INEX 2004 runs. Section 4 presents the results of our experiments, and in Section 5 we analyze the characteristics of one of our runs. In Section 6 we conclude.

2 Experimental Setup

2.1 Index

Our approach to XML retrieval is IR-based. We calculate a retrieval score for an element by using a mixture model which combines a language model for the element itself, a model for the surrounding article, and a model for the whole collection. To estimate the language models we need two types of inverted indexes, one for the XML elements and another for the full XML articles. The two indexes have a somewhat different purpose. The element index functions as a traditional inverted index used to retrieve elements. The article index, on the other hand, is used for statistical estimates only. Furthermore, we maintain a separate index of the collection structure.

Element Index. We index each XML element separately. The indexing unit can be any XML element, ranging from small elements such as words in italics (⟨`it`⟩) to full blown articles (⟨`article`⟩). For each element, all text nested inside it is indexed. Hence, the indexing units overlap (see Figure 1). Text appearing in a particular nested XML element is not only indexed as part of that element, but also as part of all its ancestor elements.

Article Index. Here, the indexing unit is a complete XML document containing all the terms appearing at any nesting level within the ⟨`article`⟩ tag. Hence, this is a standard inverted index as used for traditional document retrieval.

Both the element and the article index were word-based: we applied case-folding, and stop-words were removed using the stop-word list that comes with the English version on the Snowball stemmer [12], but other than that words were indexed as they occur in the text, and no stemming was applied.

Structure Index. The structure of the collection is indexed using a relational database. To index the XML trees we use pre-order and post-order information of the nodes in the XML trees [1].

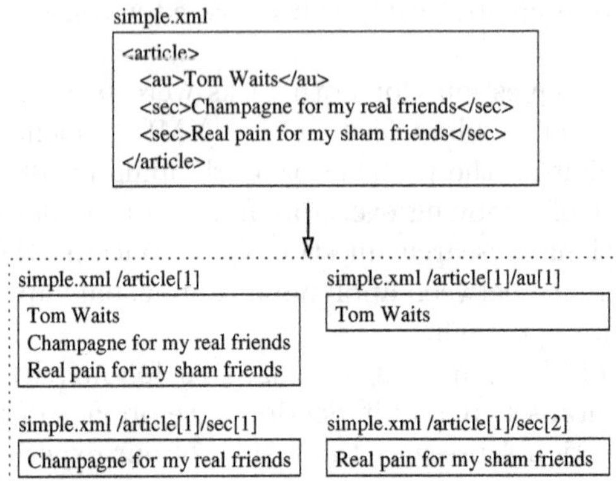

Fig. 1. Figure of how XML documents are split up into overlapping indexing units

2.2 Query Processing

For both the CO and the VCAS task we only use the ⟨`title`⟩ part of the topics. We remove words and phrases bounded by a minus-sign from the queries; other than that, we do not use the plus-signs, or phrase marking of the queries.

For the CAS topics we have a NEXI tokenizer which can decompose the query into a set of `about` functions [11]. If there is a disjunction in a location-path, we break it up into a disjunction of about functions. That is,

`about(.//(abs|kwd), xml)` (1)

becomes

`about(.//abs,xml) or about(.//kwd,xml).` (2)

If there are multiple about functions with the same scope we merge them into a single one. That is,

`about(., broadband) or about(., dial-up)` (3)

becomes

`about(., broadband dial-up).` (4)

For some of the VCAS runs we ignore the structural constraints and use only a collection of content query terms. That is, from the query

`//article[about(.,sorting)]//sec[about(.,heap sort)]` (5)

we collect the query terms

`sorting heap sort.` (6)

We will refer to these as the *full content queries.*

2.3 Retrieval Model

All our runs use a multinomial language model with Jelinek-Mercer smoothing [2]. We estimate a language model for each of the elements. The elements are then ranked according to their prior probability of being relevant and the likelihood of the query, given the estimated language model for the element:

$$P(e|q) \propto P(e) \cdot P(q|e). \tag{7}$$

We assume query terms to be independent, and rank elements according to:

$$P(e|q) \propto P(e) \cdot \prod_{i=1}^{k} P(t_i|e), \tag{8}$$

where q is a query made out of the terms $t_1, \ldots, t_k$. To account for data sparseness we estimate the element language model by taking a linear interpolation of three language models: one for the element itself, one for the article that contains the element, and a third one for the collection. That is, $P(t_i|e)$ is calculated as

$$\lambda_e \cdot P_{mle}(t_i|e) + \lambda_d \cdot P_{mle}(t_i|d) + (1 - \lambda_e - \lambda_d) \cdot P_{mle}(t_i), \tag{9}$$

where $P_{mle}(\cdot|e)$ is a language model for element e; $P_{mle}(\cdot|d)$ is a language model for document d; and $P_{mle}(\cdot)$ is a language model of the collection. The parameters λ_e and λ_d are interpolation factors (smoothing parameters). We estimate the language models, $P_{mle}(\cdot|\cdot)$ and $P_{mle}(\cdot)$, using maximum likelihood estimation. For the element model we use statistics from the element index; for the document model we use statistics from the article index; and for the collection model we use document frequencies from the article index.

The language modeling framework allows us to easily model non-content features. One of the non-content features that proved to be useful during our experiments for INEX 2003 is document length [4]. Specifically, we assign a prior probability to an element e relative to its length in the following manner:

$$P(e) = \frac{|e|}{\sum_e |e|}, \tag{10}$$

where $|e|$ is the size of an element e.

2.4 Query Expansion

We have been experimenting with blind feedback in every edition of INEX so far, focusing on query expansion for the content-only task exclusively. Initially, we experimented with Rocchio-style reweighting to select up to 10 terms from the top 10 documents [9]. In INEX 2002 we observed that query expansion with Rocchio on the article index gave intuitively useful expanded queries, leading to the kind of improvements that are familiar from article retrieval [5]. However, expanding queries based on the top 10 retrieved XML elements seemed not to work due to the short and overlapping elements in the top 10 results. Hence, we decided to expand queries on the article index, and then run the expanded queries against the element index. This did, indeed, give us a boost for the 2002 topics, but, alas, substantially lowered our score for the 2003 topics [10].

Our analysis of the failure of article-index based feedback in INEX 2003 was that the terms were useful, but highly unlikely to occur in the proper element. An example is getting prominent author names from the bibliography, which are relevant and useful retrieval cues but generally do not appear in a paragraph (maybe in the author field, or the bibliography).[1]

We decided to go back to the idea of doing blind feedback on the XML element index. This has the advantage of conservatism, the initially retrieved top 10 elements will keep their high ranking, but the problem of overlap in the initial result set remains. In pre-submission experiments, Ponte's language modeling approach to feedback [8] proved more robust, and improved performance on the 2003 topics.

3 Runs

In this section we describe our runs submitted for INEX 2004. All our runs use the language modeling framework described in the previous section. For all runs we use a two level smoothing procedure: we smooth against both the article and the collection. Our collection model uses the document frequencies from the article index. For computing the likelihood of a term given an element, see Equation 9, we use the following parameter settings for all runs: $\lambda_e = 0.1$ and $\lambda_d = 0.3$. All runs also use the same length prior settings in Equation 10. All the runs that use blind feedback use the language modeling approach [8], and consider the top 15 elements as pseudo relevant, and expand the query with up to 5 additional terms.

3.1 Content-Only Runs

Baseline (UAms-CO-T). This run uses the mixture language model approach and parameter settings as described above.

Feedback (UAms-CO-T-FBack). This run uses the same model and parameters as the previous run. Additionally, it uses blind feedback to expand the queries, as described above.

No Overlap (UAms-CO-T-FBack-NoOverl). This run uses the same model, parameters and feedback approach as the previous run. Additionally, overlapping results are filtered away. The filtering is done in a top-down manner. That is, the result list is processed from the most relevant to the least relevant element. A result is removed from the result list if its content overlaps with the content of an element that has been processed previously.

---

[1] We have been planning to incorporate context (i.e., tags in which term occurs) into our model, but this would requires some CAS features for the CO runs that are non-trivial to implement.

Table 1. Average scores for our submissions, with the best scoring run in italics. The first two rows (MAP, P@10) are results of using `trec_eval` and strict assessments. The next three rows are results of using `inex_eval`. Finally, we list the XCG scores that have been released and the set-based overlap in the runs. (Left): Our CO runs. (Right): Our VCAS runs

	CO-Runs			VCAS-Runs		
Measure	Baseline	Feedback	No Overlap	CO-style	XPath-style	No Overlap
MAP	0.1142	*0.1216*	0.0385	*0.1377*	0.0811	0.0621
P@10	*0.1680*	0.1600	0.1000	0.1818	*0.2591*	0.1121
strict	0.1013	*0.1100*	0.0332	*0.1260*	0.0735	0.0582
generalized	0.0929	*0.1225*	0.0198	*0.1167*	0.0451	0.0330
so	0.0717	*0.1060*	0.0149	*0.0912*	0.0472	0.0282
XCG	–	0.2636	*0.3521*	–	–	–
Overlap	72.0%	81.8%	0.0%	77.8%	18.8%	0.0%

3.2 Vague Content-and-Structure Runs

CO-style (UAms-CAS-T-FBack). This run uses the full-content version of the queries. The run is identical to CO-Feedback, except for the topics, of course.

No Overlap (UAms-CAS-T-FBack-NoOverl). This run uses the full-content version of the queries. The run is identical to CO-No-Overlap.

XPath-style (UAms-CAS-T-XPath). This run is created using our system for the INEX 2003 Strict Content and Structure task. It uses both content and structural constraints. Target constraints are interpreted as strict. We refer to [11] for a detailed description of the retrieval approach used. The run uses the exact same approach and settings as the run referred to as "Full propagation run" in that paper.

4 Results and Discussion

In this section we present the results of our retrieval efforts. Result analysis for XML retrieval remains a difficult task: there are still many open questions regarding how to evaluate XML element retrieval. A plethora of measures has been proposed, but still the problem has not been resolved. We will present results for a number of the suggested measures and try to interpret the flow of numbers. All results are based on version 3.0 of the assessments.

4.1 Content-Only Task

For the content-only task we focus on two issues, effect of blind feedback and overlap removal.

Blind Feedback. From Table 1 (Left) we see that the run which uses blind feedback outperforms the normal run on all metrics except for early precision.

Table 2. Tag-name distribution of retrieved elements. We only list the most frequently occurring elements

Tag-name	Baseline	Feedback	No Overlap
article	27.2%	14.3%	46.1%
bdy	21.2%	12.3%	5.7%
sec	16.6%	16.9%	7.1%
p	7.8%	17.2%	12.8%

Note also that the overlap in the feedback run is somewhat higher than for the baseline. Unfortunately, we do not have the XCG score for our baseline run. It is thus not clear how the less overlapping baseline compares to the feedback run for that measure.

The changing overlap percentage is just one of a larger set of changes brought about by applying blind feedback. Table 2 shows the distribution of retrieved elements over the most common elements. We see that by applying blind feedback, our retrieval focus changes from mostly retrieving articles and bodies, to retrieving more sections and paragraphs. We have thought of two possible explanations for this behavior. First, our retrieval model is sensitive to query length. The effect of our normal length prior decreases as the queries get longer.[2] When we expand our queries we make them longer and consequently decrease the effect of the length prior. Second, the increased overlapping might be caused by the fact that we use pseudo-relevant elements to calculate feedback terms. The goal of the added feedback terms is to attract similar content as in the pseudo-relevant elements. Obviously, the elements that overlap with the pseudo-relevant elements have to some extent very similar content.

Overlap Removal. Let's now take a look at a more striking difference in overlap. Namely for our feedback run with and without the list-based removal of overlapping elements. We go from having more than 80% overlap to having none at all. The removal of overlap is appreciated by neither of the two traditional metrics `trec_eval` or `inex_eval`. The XML Cumulative Gain (XCG) [6] measure is however clearly sympathetic to the removal of overlap. It is interesting to note that from Table 2 we see that almost half of the elements in our non-overlapping run are full articles.

It is tricky to draw strong conclusions from these observations. The `_eval` measures on the one hand and XCG on the other, seem to evaluate different tasks. The `_eval` measures evaluate a "system-oriented" task where the main goal is to find relevance and overlap is (and should be) rewarded. The XCG measure on the other hand evaluates a "user-oriented" task where overlap is not (and should not be) rewarded. We will return to this point at the end of Section 5.

[2] Previously, we have shown that a more radical length bias is essential to achieve good results [4]. Those experiments were performed using both the title and description fields of the topics.

4.2 Vague Content-and-Structure Task

For the VCAS task we focus on the difference between two styles of retrieval: CO and XPath. Table 1 (right) shows the results for our VCAS runs, using the different metrics. We see that the CO-style run clearly outperforms the XPath-style run with respect to all the MAP-oriented metrics. When we look at early precision, however, we see a clear distinction in favor of the XPath-style run. This finding is very much in-line with our intuition: the main reason behind adding structural constraints to content queries is to make them more precise.

The CAS topics can be divided into classes based on the extent to which structure is being used. We define 4 classes.

Restricted Search. This category has topics in which structure is only used as a granularity constraint. The topic is an ordinary content-only topic, where the search is restricted to particular XML elements. There is a filter on the target element having no nested path constraint. A typical example of such a topic is to restrict the search to sections:

```
//sec[about(., ''xxx'')].
```

Contextual Content Information. This category is similar to the *Restricted Search* category, but now there is a (simple) filter on the path constraint. I.e., there is a content restriction on the environment in which the requested element occurs. A typical example of such a topic is to have a content restriction on the whole article in which the requested sections occur, this may look like:

```
//article[about(., ''xxx'')]//sec[about(., ''yyy'')].
```

Search Hints. This category contains topics with a complex filter in which a nested path occurs, but the element targeted by the nested paths resides inside the requested element. I.e., the user provides a particular retrieval cue to the system. A typical example of such a topic may be, when interested in a whole article on a topic, to tell the system to look for certain terms to appear in the abstract, this may look like:

```
//article[about(., ''xxx'') and about(.//abs, ''yyy'')].
```

Twig Hints. The fourth and last category deals with topics with a nested path that targets elements that are disjoint from the requested element. This is called a tree pattern query or a 'twig.' Here, the user is really exploiting her knowledge of the structure of the documents, and conditions the retrieval of elements on the content found along other paths in the document tree. I.e., the condition is evaluated against parts of the text that are not being returned to the user as a result. E.g., the similar retrieval cue on the abstract, may still make sense for a user looking for sections, which may look like:

```
//article[about(.//abs, ''xxx'')]//sec[about(., ''yyy'')].
```

Table 3. Scores for different categories of CAS topics. Scores are calculated using `trec_eval` and the strict assessments. The number of assessed topics per class is stated in brackets

	Restricted Search (5)		Contextual Content (5)		Search Hints (4)		Twig Hints (8)	
	MAP	P@10	MAP	P@10	MAP	P@10	MAP	P@10
CO	*0.1454*	0.2000	*0.1009*	0.1000	*0.3231*	0.2250	0.0631	0.2000
XPath	0.1254	*0.3000*	0.0319	*0.1200*	0.0504	*0.3500*	*0.0994*	*0.2750*

Table 3 shows the evaluation results for different topic classes. We can see that the XPath-style approach gives better early precision for all the topic classes. Only for the most complex class of topics gives XPath-style a better MAP than CO-style approach. It is interesting to note that, in terms of MAP, the two approaches are competitive for both the simplest and most complex topics. For the two middle-classes, however, the MAP scores for the CO-style run are superior by a margin.

5 Per-Topic Analysis

In this section we look at the per-topic results for our content-only baseline. Throughout this section, we will try to come up with necessary and sufficient conditions for successful XML element retrieval. Our main aim is to try to understand better how our XML retrieval system works. All experiments in this section are performed using the `trec_eval` program and the strict version of the assessments.

Figure 2 shows the precision scores for the individual topics. It is striking that for most of the topics, our performance is very poor. We score reasonably for only a handful of topics. The first questions that arise are: 'What is going wrong?' and 'What is going right?' The answers are far from obvious, since there are so many possibilities. We start by considering the core task of XML retrieval, namely, finding the relevant elements. This seems to be a combination of two problems. On the one hand we need to find relevance. On the other, we need to

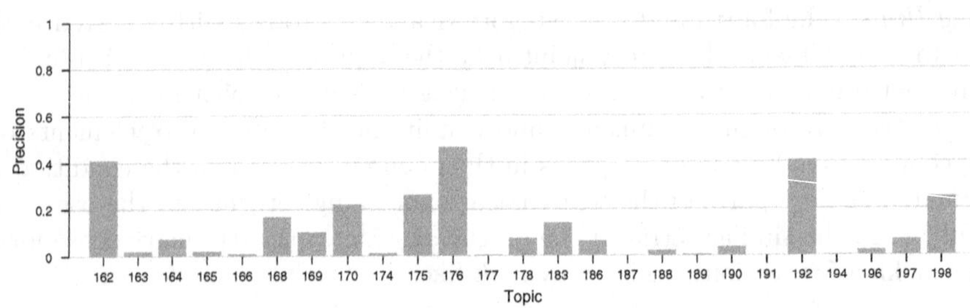

Fig. 2. Precision of our baseline for individual topics

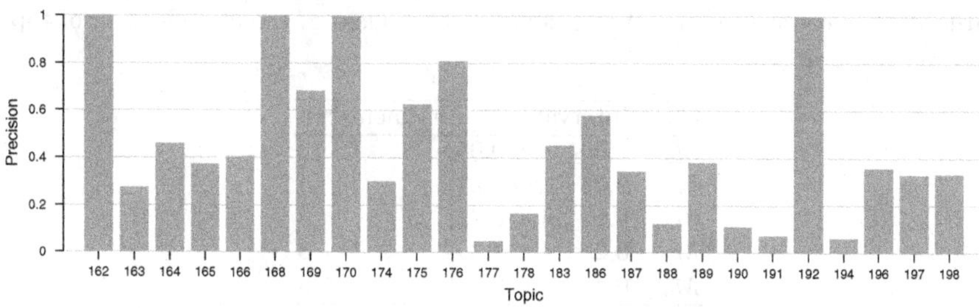

Fig. 3. Precision of document retrieval based on element score

find the appropriate granularity of results. We will thus start with an obvious, or at least intuitive, hypothesis.

– Our difficulty is more with finding the right unit, than finding the relevance.

We investigate this hypothesis by trying to take the granularity problem out of the equation and see what happens. We create an article retrieval run, based on our official element run. We simply assign to an article, the score of its highest scoring element. Similarly, we define a new set of article assessments from the *strict* element assessments. A document is considered relevant if, and only if, it contains an element which is both highly exhaustive and highly specific. Figure 3 shows the precision of our new document run. In comparison to Figure 2, Figure 3 looks much more promising.

Of course, one important difference between the two evaluations is the recall base. In the case of elements, there are millions of elements that can possibly be retrieved. In the case of documents, however, the recall base "only" consists of thousands of documents. While XML element retrieval is a "needle in the haystack problem," XML document retrieval is merely a "pencil in the drawer problem." Hence, the score in the two figures are not at all comparable.

What we can do, however, is to look at topics where we did not find the appropriate elements and see if we are at least finding elements in the right documents. If we look at the recall of our element run, retrieving up to 1,500 elements per topic, we see that we find 903 out of 2,589 relevant elements (35%). The recall of the document run tells us that we find elements from 273 out of 279 articles which contain an element which is highly specific and highly exhaustive (98%). This is a clear indication that, while we may not be finding the right elements, we are at least in the neighborhood.

The differences in scoring from one topic to another may come as no great surprise. At the INEX 2004 workshop, it was reported that assessor agreement at the element level is extremely low for the strict assessments. This would imply that it is difficult to get much higher retrieval scores, unless some measures are taken to try to increase assessor agreement. The same study revealed that, even using a liberal measure of agreement at the document level, the agreement was still no more than 20%. Viewed in this light, the document retrieval scores of Figure 3 are surprisingly high.

Table 4. The count of topics that belongs to each class of the classification of topics based on retrieval score

Class	Interval	Element-run
M_0	$0.0 \leq x < 0.05$	12
M_1	$0.05 \leq x < 0.1$	4
M_2	$0.1 \leq x < 0.2$	3
M_3	$0.2 \leq x < 0.3$	3
M_5	$0.4 \leq x < 0.5$	3

Table 5. Relation between retrieval score and the number of elements assessed as relevant. (Left): Assessment statistics for different topic classes. (Right): Topics classified by the number of relevant elements (vertical). The number of topics in each class is shown in brackets. For each class we look at the distribution over score classes (horizontal)

	# assessments			
	avg	median	min	max
M_0	125.6	33.5	4	848
M_1	212.5	128.0	13	581
M_2	58.3	10.0	2	163
M_3	8.3	4.0	3	18
M_5	10.7	10.0	5	17

	score classes (%)				
# rel.	M_0	M_1	M_2	M_3	M_5
1-10 (7)	14.3	–	28.6	28.6	28.6
11-20 (6)	50.0	16.7	–	16.7	16.7
21-40 (4)	100.0	–	–	–	–
41-80 (2)	50.0	50.0	–	–	–
> 80 (6)	50.0	33.3	16.7	–	–

Let's now look in more detail at our element retrieval run. We would like to understand better the scoring behavior of our system. When do we succeed? When do we fail? We try to analyze this by looking at the following hypotheses:

- Our system scores well if, and only if, few elements are assessed relevant;
- Our system scores well if, and only if, the assessor likes somewhat large elements;
- Our system scores well if, and only if, the recall base of the topic is overlapping.

In order to test these hypotheses we divide the topics into 5 classes, based on the precision of our baseline element retrieval run for the individual topics. Table 4 shows the topic classification. Our hypotheses so-far only consider the relation between assessments and scores. The more interesting, and more challenging, task is to relate queries and scores: this remains as future work.

Let's look at our first hypothesis: *Our system scores well if, and only if, few elements are assessed relevant.* Table 5 shows the relation between assessment count and retrieval score of our baseline system. The left table shows average, median, minimum and maximum number of relevant elements for each of our score classes. This table supports one direction of the hypothesis. That is, for the topics where our system scores high, there are relatively few elements assessed relevant, at most 18. The other direction of our hypothesis is however not

Table 6. Relation between size bias in assessments and retrieval effectiveness. (Left): The first column defines the topic classes. Then, for each class of topics, the numbers in columns 2–6 represent the percentage of assessed elements having the tag-name in the column heads. (Right): We look at sets of topics having at least 10% of their assessments of a particular tag-name (vertical). Number of topics is in brackets. For each set we look at the distribution over score classes (horizontal)

	tag-names (%)				
	article	bdy	sec	ss1	Σ
M_0	2.3	2.0	5.8	5.3	15
M_1	4.2	3.9	15.2	9.3	33
M_2	12.6	10.9	22.3	14.3	60
M_3	12.0	12.0	16.0	12.0	52
M_5	9.4	12.5	12.5	25.0	59

	score classes (%)				
$\geq$ 10%	M_0	M_1	M_2	M_3	M_5
article (9)	11.1	22.2	22.2	22.2	22.2
bdy (9)	22.2	11.1	22.2	22.2	22.2
sec (17)	35.3	17.6	11.8	17.6	17.6
ss1 (11)	45.5	9.1	18.2	9.1	18.2
$\Sigma \geq 60\%$ (9)	44.4	11.1	22.2	11.1	11.1

supported by the data. While low assessment count seems to be necessary for high score, it is not sufficient. This can be seen from Table 5 (right). There are quite a few topics that have few assessments ($\leq$ 20), but our system does not score well. Note, however, that we can quite safely say that if there are many assessments then our system will score badly.

We now turn to our second hypothesis: *Our system scores well if, and only if, the assessor likes somewhat large elements.* We look at the 6 most frequent tag-names appearing in the assessments. We will define 4 of them to be "somewhat large," namely article, bdy, sec and ss1. We refer to the set of these tag-names as Σ. The other two frequent tag-names, p and it, we do not regard as "somewhat large." First we try to see if it is true that *if our system scores well then the assessor likes somewhat large elements.* Table 6 (left) shows, for each score class, the percentage of assessments belonging to the most frequent "somewhat large" tag-names. For the topics with the highest precision, M_5, we see that almost 60% of the relevant elements belongs to Σ. For the next two classes the percentage is 52% and 60%, respectively. For the classes of topics where we score lower than 0.1 the percentage is 33% and 15%, respectively. So far the data seems to give some support for our hypothesis. Let's now look at the other direction: *if the assessor likes somewhat large elements then our system scores well.* This direction is not supported by the data, however. We take a look at the "somewhat large" elements and for each element-type we look at the topics for which 10% or more of the relevant elements have the particular tag-name. Table 6 (right) shows, for each tag-name the distribution of those topics over our score-based classes. The bottom line of the table shows the distribution of the topics for which more than 60% of assessments have tag-names from Σ. The topics are relatively evenly distributed over our score-based classes and thus does not support that direction of our hypothesis.

Now it's time for our third hypothesis: *Our system scores well if, and only if, the recall base of the topic is overlapping.* Table 7 shows the relation between system scoring and overlapping recall base. The left table shows for each of the

Table 7. Relation between overlapping recall base and retrieval effectiveness. (Left): For each score class, the distribution of topics over overlap classes. (Right): For each overlap class, the distribution of topics over score classes. The count of topics in each overlap class is in brackets

	overlapping recall-base (%)				
	0-20	21-40	41-60	61-80	81-100
M_0	8.3	16.7	33.3	16.7	25.0
M_1	–	–	25.7	–	75.0
M_2	33.3	–	33.3	33.3	–
M_3	–	–	–	66.7	33.3
M_5	33.3	–	–	66.7	–

	score classes (%)				
	M_0	M_1	M_2	M_3	M_5
0-20 (3)	33.3	–	33.3	–	33.3
21-40 (2)	100	–	–	–	–
41-60 (6)	66.7	16.7	16.7	–	–
61-80 (7)	28.6	–	14.3	28.6	28.6
81-100 (7)	42.9	42.9	–	14.3	–

score classes, the distribution over overlapping classes. We can see that for two-thirds of our best scoring topics, the overlap is 61–80%. We can thus say that if we score well then there is rather high overlap in the recall base. As with our other hypotheses the other direction is not supported by the data. High overlap in the recall base does not lead to high scoring for our system. What we can say, however, is that if the overlap is rather high (60–80%), we score quite well. For the overlap classes above and below, we score poorly.

What have we learned from the analysis in this section? We have seen that divergence in scores is very great from one topic to another. We have argued that this might be due to lack of assessor agreement. This disagreement is possibly an artifact of a combination of the unclear nature of the XML element retrieval task and the complex assessment procedure. Bluntly, assessors must perform an unclear task with machinery that is too complex to use.

We have also seen some characteristics of the topics where we score well: there are few relevant elements, the elements are fairly long and quite overlapping. While we could say that the first two characteristics are, respectively, understandable and intuitive, we might be tempted to judge the third one as disappointing and contrary to the whole purpose or XML element retrieval. But before we make such judgments we should recall what the task at hand was.

In the analysis above, we have made some crucial assumptions. We defined a particular task by fixing the assessments and evaluation metric. Based on those assumptions we have tried to analyze the performance of our system. For most test collections, this would not raise any methodological questions. The assessment procedure and evaluation metrics are usually not subject to debate. In the INEX case, those issues are far from being settled. The assessments, the metrics, and, in particular, the interplay between assessments and metrics, are all open questions. We think, however, that the kind of analysis that we carried here may yield valuable insights into what is happening under the hood of an XML element retrieval engine. If we can explain why we are unhappy with the reasons why a system scores well, we can more precisely pinpoint the flaws of the evaluation methodology. In this case we might be unhappy about the fact that for our high scoring topics the overlap in the recall-base is high.

This brings us to the question whether overlap in the recall base is good or bad. The _eval measures seem to say it is good, but XCG seems to disagree. It is easy to disagree on this matter. From a user perspective overlap is bad because it puts additional effort on the user who has to look at the same material over and over again (depending, of course, also on the mode of presentation in the interface). From a test collection perspective overlap may be desirable because it is necessary to get a complete pool of relevant elements and we need to be able to reward near misses.

The different perspectives seem to advocate two different retrieval tasks. Currently, it is unclear where the INEX task stands relative to those two. In some sense it seems to be trying to play both roles at the same time. Is this actually possible? One of the urgent priorities for the INEX community is to clearly and unambiguously define what the actual retrieval task is.

6 Conclusions

In this paper, we documented our experiments at the INEX 2004 ad hoc retrieval track. We used a document-element mixture model for processing content-only queries and a more complex mixture approach for handling content-and-structure queries. We investigated the effectiveness of element-based query expansion, and found that it improved retrieval effectiveness. Adding feedback, however, increased overlap. Unfortunately, we do not have access to an implementation of the XCG measure to see how this affects user-oriented evaluation. We investigated the impact of non-overlap on the runs, and found that returning overlapping results leads to far superior scores on all measures, except the recently proposed XCG measure where it was inferior by quite a margin. The radical difference between the measures suggest that they are measuring the quality of two radically different tasks.

We argue that a more explicit definition of the INEX element retrieval task is needed. Our results for the VCAS task showed that, if evaluated in terms of mean average precision, the content-oriented-based approach is clearly superior to a more structured processing of the content-and-structure topics. From the vantage point of a retrieval system, our experiments highlighted the great similarity between the CO and VCAS tasks. If, on the other hand, we evaluate in terms of early precision, the tables turn. Structural processing is superior to looking only at content. This indicates that the great added value of structural constraints is to improve initial precision.

Informed by an analysis of the scoring behavior of one of our runs, we have argued that it is very important for the INEX community to use the data collected to date to clarify the complete INEX process, from the retrieval task, through assessment procedure, to evaluation.

Acknowledgments

Jaap Kamps was supported by the Netherlands Organization for Scientific Research (NWO), under project number 612.066.302. Maarten de Rijke was supported by grants from NWO, under project numbers 365-20-005, 612.069.006, 612.000.106, 220-80-001, 612.000.207, 612.066.302, 264-70-050, and 017.001.190.

References

1. T. Grust. Accelerating XPath Location Steps. In *Proc. SIGMOD*, pages 109–120. ACM Press, 2002.
2. D. Hiemstra. *Using Language Models for Information Retrieval.* PhD thesis, University of Twente, 2001.
3. ILPS. The ILPS extension of the Lucene search engine, 2004. `http://ilps.science.uva.nl/Resources/`.
4. J. Kamps, M. de Rijke, and B. Sigurbjörnsson. Length normalization in XML retrieval. In *Proceedings of the 27th Annual International ACM SIGIR Conference on Research and Development in Information Retrieval, (SIGIR 2004)*, pages 80–87, 2004.
5. J. Kamps, M. Marx, M. de Rijke, and B. Sigurbjörnsson. The importance of morphological normalization for XML retrieval. In *Proceedings of the First Workshop of the INitiative for the Evaluation of XML retrieval (INEX)*, pages 41–48. ERCIM Publications, 2003.
6. G. Kazai, M. Lalmas, and A. de Vries. The overlap problem in content-oriented XML retrieval evaluation. In *SIGIR '04: Proceedings of the 27th Annual International Conference on Research and Development in Information Retrieval*, pages 72–79. ACM Press, 2004.
7. Lucene. The Lucene search engine, 2004. `http://jakarta.apache.org/lucene/`.
8. J. Ponte. Language models for relevance feedback. In W. Croft, editor, *Advances in Information Retrieval*, chapter 3, pages 73–96. Kluwer Academic Publishers, Boston, 2000.
9. J. Rocchio, Jr. Relevance feedback in information retrieval. In *The SMART Retrieval System: Experiments in Automatic Document Processing*, chapter 14, pages 313–323. Prentice-Hall, Englewood Cliffs NJ, 1971.
10. B. Sigurbjörnsson, J. Kamps, and M. de Rijke. An Element-Based Approch to XML Retrieval. In *INEX 2003 Workshop Proceedings*, pages 19–26, 2004.
11. B. Sigurbjörnsson, J. Kamps, and M. de Rijke. Processing content-oriented XPath queries. In *Proceedings of the Thirteenth Conference on Information and Knowledge Management (CIKM 2004)*, pages 371–380. ACM Press, 2004.
12. Snowball. The Snowball string processing language, 2004. `http://snowball.tartarus.org/`.

GPX – Gardens Point XML Information Retrieval at INEX 2004

Shlomo Geva

Centre for Information Technology Innovation,
Faculty of Information Technology,
Queensland University of Technology,
Queensland 4001, Australia
s.geva@qut.edu.au

Abstract. Traditional information retrieval (IR) systems respond to user queries with ranked lists of relevant documents. The separation of content and structure in XML documents allows individual XML elements to be selected in isolation. Thus, users expect XML-IR systems to return highly relevant results that are more precise than entire documents. In this paper we describe the implementation of a search engine for XML document collections. The system is keyword based and is built upon an XML inverted file system. We describe the approach that was adopted to meet the requirements of Content Only (CO) and Vague Content and Structure (VCAS) queries in INEX 2004.

1 Introduction

The widespread use of Extensible Markup Language (XML) documents in digital libraries has lead to development of information retrieval (IR) methods specifically designed for XML collections. Most traditional IR systems are limited to whole document retrieval; however, since XML documents separate content and structure, XML-IR systems are able to retrieve the relevant portions of documents. This means that users interacting with XML-IR system will potentially receive highly relevant and highly precise material. However, it also means that XML-IR systems are more complex than their traditional counterparts, and many challenges remain unsolved. These issues were specifically addressed at INEX 2002 and INEX 2003, with marked improvement in performance of most systems.

Since all systems base retrieval on keywords, one would expect that most system would be able to identify the same set of documents in response to a query on several keywords. The key difference between systems is therefore in the ranking of these documents. Often it is possible to identify many thousands of elements that contain at least some of a given set of keywords. The trick is to rank the elements and select the top 1500 elements. There are four important issues to be resolved with respect to IR in an XML collection:

1. Accurate efficient selection of elements satisfying the containment constraints.
2. Accurate efficient selection of elements that satisfy the structural constraints.
3. The assignment of scores to matching elements.
4. The assignment of scores to antecedents of selected elements.

N. Fuhr et al. (Eds.): INEX 2004, LNCS 3493, pp. 211 – 223, 2005.

Steps 1 to 3 are common to ordinary text collection IR systems, except that the unit of retrieval has finer granularity (XML element). Step 4 is an additional step that is required in the context of XML oriented IR. Rather than identify relevant documents, the XML IR system is required to select and score elements at different levels of granularity.

This paper presents a system that attempts to provide a solution to the selection and ranking question, while at the same time provide an effective and efficient search engine that is based on an inverted file scheme.

First we discuss the internal storage of the XML collection and present a database structure that is aimed at increasing the efficiency of the system. Then we discuss a re-formulation of the queries as a set of sub-queries, and describe the identification of leaf level elements that contain keywords. We describe the retrieval and scoring process of individual elements. We then discuss the ranking scheme that is used to propagate scores to antecedent elements at coarser granularity. Finally we present benchmark test results using the INEX 2003 XML collection, and the 2004 official results assessments.

2 Query Interpretation

INEX provides a test collection of over 12,000 IEEE journal articles, a set of queries and a set of evaluation metrics. Two types of queries are used in INEX 2004: CO and VCAS. Content Only (CO) queries ignore document structure and only contain content stipulations. In contrast Vague Content and Structure (VCAS) queries explicitly express both content and structural requirements. Both CO and CAS queries are expected to return appropriately sized elements – not just whole documents, and all queries are loosely interpreted with respect to structural and containment constraints – the overriding goal is to satisfy the user's information need rather than the strict query formulation.

2.1 The format of NEXI Queries

Examples of the two types of queries, CO and VCAS, are depicted in Figures 1 and 2:

```
<inex_topic topic_id="XX" query_type="CO">
  <title>
      "multi layer perceptron" "radial basis func-
      tions" comparison
  </title>
  <description>
      The relationship and comparisons between radial
      basis functions and multi layer perceptrons
  </description>
</inex_topic>
```

Fig. 1. CO Query

```
<inex_topic topic_id="XX" query_type="CAS">
  <title>
      //article[about(.,information retrieval)]//
      sec[about(.,compression)]
  </title>
  <description>
      Find sections about compression in articles about
      information retrieval.
  </description>
</inex_topic>
```

Fig. 2. CAS Query

Both the *description* and *title* elements express the user's information needs. The description expresses users' need in a natural language (e.g. English). The title expresses users' information need in either a list of keywords/phrases (CO) or as a formal XPath-like language (CAS) called Narrowed Extended XPath I (NEXI) [4].

The syntax of NEXI is similar to XPath, however, it NEXI only uses XPath's descendant axis step, and extends XPath by incorporating an 'about' clause to provide an IR-like query. NEXI's syntax is **//A[about(//B,C)]** where **A** is the context path, **B** is the relative path and **C** is the content requirement. Conceptually each **'about'** clause in a NEXI query represents an individual information request. So conceptually the query

//A[about(//B,C)]//X[about(//Y,Z)]

contains two requests:

//A[about(//B,C)]

and

//A//X[about(//Y,Z)].

However, in NEXI only elements matching the leaf (i.e. rightmost) **'about'** clause, the second request here, are flagged as of direct interest to the user. We refer to these requests and elements as 'return requests' and 'return elements'. Elements that match the other **'about',** clauses, the first request here, are used to support the return elements in ranking. We refer to these requests and elements as 'support requests' and 'support elements'. It should be noted that under VCAS rules, the vague interpretation of queries allows the return of elements whose XPath signature does not strictly conform to the query specification. The structural constraints are regarded as retrieval hints, much in the same way that keywords are regarded as retrieval hints.

2.2 Processing NEXI Queries

Once NEXI queries are input into the system they are converted into an intermediate language called the RS query language. The RS query language converts NEXI queries to a set of information requests:

Instruction | Retrieve Filter | Search Filter | Content

Instruction: Either 'R' or 'S', corresponding to 'return' or 'support' component.

Retrieve Filter: A logical XPath expression that describes which elements should be retrieved by the system. Often this correlates to context path of a NEXI query, so, in the query *//A[about(//B,C)]* the retrieve filter is *//A*.

Search Filter: A logical XPath expression that describes which elements should be searched by the system. Often this correlates to relative path of a NEXI query, so, in the query *//A[about(//B,C)]* the search filter is *//A//B*.

Figure 3 is an example of the queries introduced in Figure 1 and Figure, 2 when converted to RS queries.

RS Query 1:

R|//*|//*| relationship, comparisons, radial basis functions, multi layer perceptrons

RS Query 2:

R|//article//sec|//article//sec|compression
S|//article|//article| information retrieval

Fig. 3. Examples of RS Queries

3 XML File Inversion

In our scheme each term in an XML document is identified by 3 elements. File path, absolute XPath context, and term position within the XPath context. The file path identifies documents in the collection; for instance:

C:/INEX/ex/2001/x0321.xml

The absolute XPath expression identifies a leaf XML element within the document, relative to the file's root element:

/article[1]/bdy[1]/sec[5]/p[3]

Finally, term position identifies the ordinal position of the term within the XPath context.

One additional modification that we adopted allowed us to support queries on XML tag attributes. This is not a strictly content search feature, but rather structure oriented search feature. For instance, it allows us to query on the 2nd named author of an article by imposing the additional query constraint of looking for that qualification in the attribute element of the XML author element. The representation of attribute values is similar to normal text with a minor modification to the XPath context representation – the attribute name is appended to the absolute XPath expression. For instance:

article[1]/bdy[1]/sec[6]/p[6]/ref[1]/@rid[1]

Here the character '@' is used to flag the fact that "rid" is not an XML tag, but rather an attribute of the preceding tag <ref>. An inverted list for a given term, omitting the File path and the Term position, is depicted in table 1.

In principle at least, a single table can hold the entire cross reference list (our inverted file). Suitable indexing of terms can support fast retrieval of term inverted lists. However, it is evident that there is extreme redundancy in the specification of partial absolute XPath expressions (substrings). There is also extreme redundancy in full absolute XPath expressions where multiple terms in the same document share the same leaf context (e.g. all terms in a paragraph). Furthermore, many XPath leaf contexts exist in almost every document (e.g. /article[1]/fm[1]/abs[1]).

We have chosen to work with certain imposed constraints. Specifically, we aimed at implementing the system on a PC and base it on the Microsoft Access database engine. This is a widely available off-the-shelf system and would allow the system to be used on virtually any PC running under any variant of the standard Microsoft Windows operating system. This choice implied a strict constraint on the size of the database – the total size of an Access database is limited to 2Gbyte. This constraint implied that a flat list structure was infeasible and we had to normalise the inverted list table to reduce redundancy.

The structure of the database used to store the inverted lists is depicted in Figure 5. It consists of 4 tables. The ***Terms*** table is the starting point of a query on a given term. Two columns in this table are indexed - The ***Term*** column and the ***Term_Stem*** column. The ***Term_Stem*** column holds the Porter stem of the original term. The ***List_Position*** is a foreign key from the ***Terms*** table into the ***List*** Table. It identifies the starting position in the inverted list for the corresponding term. The ***List_Length***

Table 1. XPath Inverted List

Context **XPath**
article[1]/bdy[1]/sec[6]/p[6]/ref[1]
article[1]/bdy[1]/sec[6]/p[6]/ref[1]/@rid[1]
article[1]/bdy[1]/sec[6]/p[6]/ref[1]/@type[1]
article[1]/bm[1]/bib[1]/bibl[1]/bb[13]/pp[1]
article[1]/bm[1]/bib[1]/bibl[1]/bb[14]/pdt[1]/day[1]
article[1]/bm[1]/bib[1]/bibl[1]/bb[14]/pp[1]
article[1]/bm[1]/bib[1]/bibl[1]/bb[15]
article[1]/bm[1]/bib[1]/bibl[1]/bb[15]/@id[1]
article[1]/bm[1]/bib[1]/bibl[1]/bb[15]/ti[1]
article[1]/bm[1]/bib[1]/bibl[1]/bb[15]/obi[1]

is the number of list entries corresponding to that term. The ***List*** table is (transparently) sorted by Term so that the inverted list for any given term is contiguous. As an aside, the maintenance of a sorted list in a dynamic database poses some problems, but these are not as serious as might seem at first, and although we have solved the problem it is outside the scope of this paper and is not discussed any further.

A search proceeds as follows. Given a search term we obtain a starting position within the List table. We then retrieve the specified number of entries by reading sequentially. The inverted list thus obtained is *Joined* (SQL) with the ***Document*** and ***Context*** tables to obtain the complete de-normalised inverted list for the term. The retrieval by ***Term_Stem*** is similar. First we obtain the Porter stem of the search term.

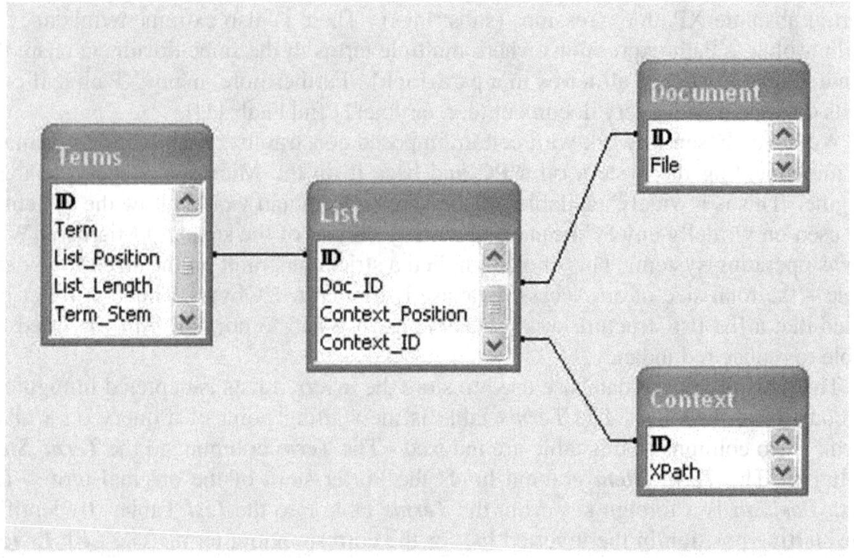

Fig. 4. Schema for XML Inverted File

Then we search the list by ***Term_Stem*** – usually getting duplicate matches. All the lists for the duplicate hits on the ***Terms*** table are then concatenated. Phrases and other proximity constraints can be easily evaluated by using the ***Context_Position*** of individual terms in the ***List*** table. With this normalization the database size was reduced to 1.6GByte and within the Microsoft Access limits.

4 Ranking Scheme

Elements are ranked according to a relevance judgment score. In our scheme leaf and branch elements need to be treated differently. Data usually occurs at leaf elements, and thus, our inverted list mostly stores information about leaf elements. A leaf element is considered candidate for retrieval if it contains at least one query term. A branch node is candidate for retrieval if it contains a relevant child element. Once an element (either leaf or branch) is deemed to be a candidate for retrieval its relevancy judgment score is calculated. A heuristically derived formula (Equation 1) is used to calculate the relevance judgment score of leaf elements. The same equation is used for both return and support elements. The score is determined from query terms contained in the element. It penalises elements with frequently occurring query terms (frequent in the collection), and it rewards elements with evenly distributed query term frequencies within the elements.

Equation 1: Calculation of a Leaf Element's Relevance Judgment Score

$$L = K^{n-1} \sum_{i=1}^{n} \frac{t_i}{f_i} \qquad (1)$$

Here n is the number of unique query terms contained within the leaf element, N is a small integer (we used K=5). The term K^{n-1} scales up the score of elements having multiple distinct query terms. The system is not sensitive to the value of K – we experimented with K=3 to 10 with little difference in results. The sum is over all terms where t_i is the frequency of the ith query term in the leaf element and f_i is the frequency of the ith query term in the collection. This sum rewards the repeat occurrence of query terms, but uncommon terms contribute more than common terms.

Once the relevance judgment scores of leaf elements have been calculated, they can be used to calculate the relevance judgment score of branch elements. A naïve solution would be to just sum the relevance judgment score of each branch relevant children. However, this would ultimately result in root (i.e. article) elements accumulating at the top of the ranked list, a scenario that offers no advantage over document-level retrieval. Therefore, the relevance judgment score of children elements should be somehow decreased while being propagated up the XML tree. A heuristically derived formula (Equation 2) is used to calculate the scores of intermediate branch elements.

Equation 2: Calculation of a Branch Element's Relevance Judgment Score

$$R = D(n) \sum_{i=1}^{n} L_i \qquad (2)$$

Where:

n = the number of children elements
$D(n)$ = 0.49 if n = 1
0.99 Otherwise
L_i = the ith return child element

The value of the decay factor D depends on the number of relevant children that the branch has. If the branch has one relevant child then the decay constant is 0.49. A branch with only one relevant child will be ranked lower than its child. If the branch has multiple relevant children the decay factor is 0.99. A branch with many relevant children will be ranked higher than its descendants. Thus, a section with a single relevant paragraph would be judged less relevant than the paragraph itself, but a section with several relevant paragraphs will be ranked higher than any of the paragraphs.

Having computed scores for all result and support elements, the scores of support elements are added to the scores of the corresponding result elements that they support. For instance, consider the query:

//A[about(.//B,C)]//X[about(.//Y,Z)]

The score of a support element **//A//B** will be added to all result elements **//A//X//Y** where the element **A** is the ancestor of both **X** and **Y**.

Finally, structural constraints are only loosely interpreted. So elements are collected regardless of compliance with the structural stipulations of the topic. So in the example above, ancestors or descendents of **Y** may be returned, depending on their score and final rank.

5 Assessment Against 2003 Data

We conducted experiments against the INEX 2003 query set and evaluation metrics. The results from 2003 INEX queries were submitted into the official INEX evaluation program that calculated the recall/precision graphs. We tested the system against the SCAS and against the CO data. It should be noted that unlike the 2004 VCAS queries, in the case of 2003 SCAS queries only results that strictly satisfy the structural constraints are permissible. Therefore, the test against the SCAS set was only useful in assessing the utility of the search engine in identifying return elements, but not in testing the selection of antecedent elements. The 2003 CO data however allowed us to test this approach.

The results from the INEX 2003 data were encouraging. We were able to obtain results that were better than the best official runs in both the CO and the SCAS track under the strict metric, and very close to the best results under the generalised metric. Figures 5 to 8 depict the retrieval results of our unofficial test runs against the 2003 data.

6 Assessment Against 2004 Data

The system was implemented in C# and run under Windows XP. We tested the system in both CO and VCAS tasks. The entire sets of queries from each of the tasks were evaluated in about 30 minutes on a Pentium M 1.6 MHz processor with 1GB RAM. We have submitted 3 official runs in each of the tracks. We have used the same 3 run strategies in both tasks as follows. The basic run was as described in section 4. A second run eliminated from the search any keyword with a frequency greater than 50,000 in the INEX collection. This almost halved the time it took to evaluate all the queries. Our results from tests on the 2003 data indicated that this would have little impact on the final result and indeed this is confirmed by the 2004 results (see figures 10 and 11). The third run was used to test a slightly different ranking approach. We have changed the decay factor in Equation 2 as follows:

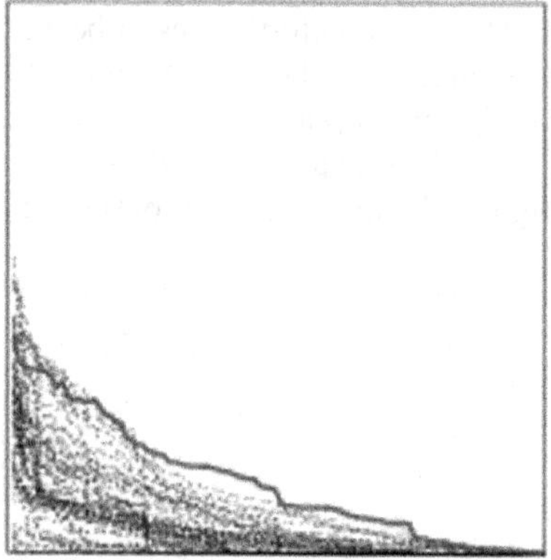

Fig. 5. CO run evaluation

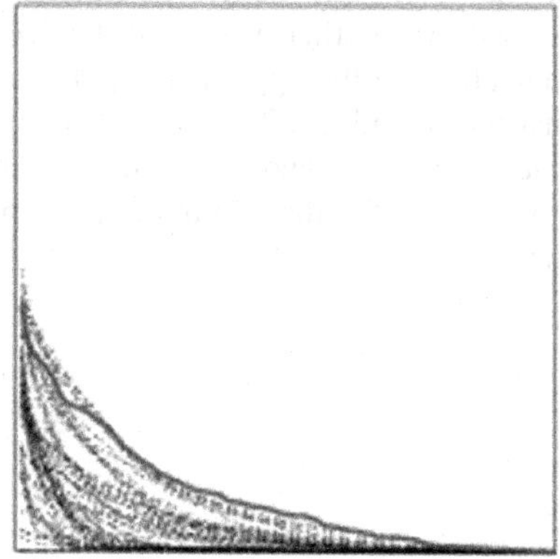

Fig. 6. CO run evaluation

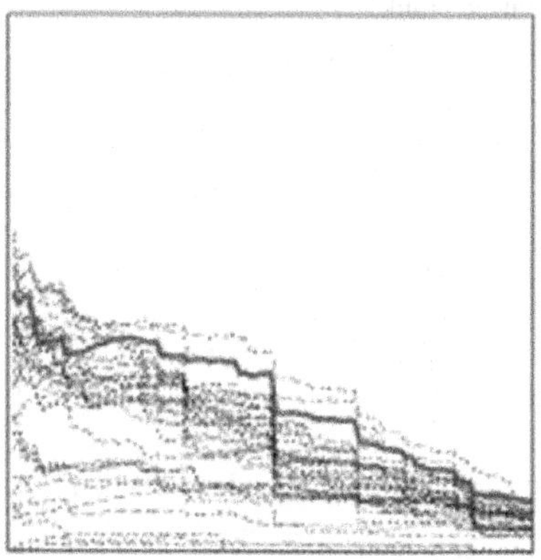

Fig. 7. SCAS run evaluation

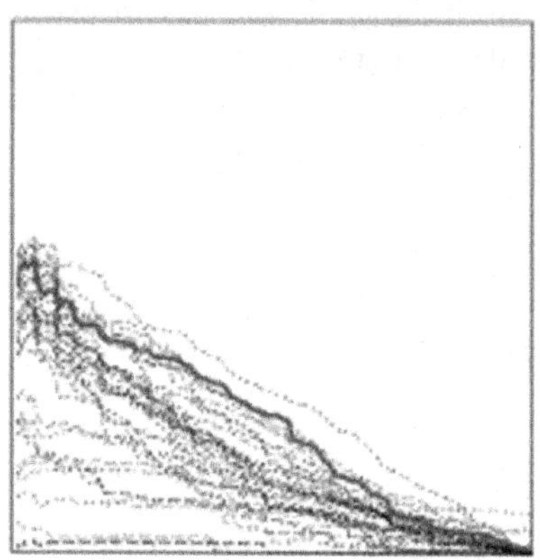

Fig. 8. SCAS run evaluation

$$D(n) = \begin{cases} 0.25 & \text{if } n = 1 \\ 0.49 & \text{otherwise} \end{cases}$$

This means that more specific elements are preferred. It takes the accumulation of several children before a parent element accumulates a score higher than its children scores. Our experiments against 2003 data revealed that this strategy worked best against metrics that preferred specificity over exhaustivity. We have not used stemming, but used plural/singular expansion of search terms.

The results of the INEX 2004 benchmark are depicted in figures 9 to 12. It can be seen that it did not make a great difference to the overall ranking whether stopping was used, or whether we varied the decay factor. This is a comforting result because it indicates that the approach is not sensitive to the "magic numbers" that we used in Equations 1 and 2. The best result was obtained when stopping keywords at frequency above 50K and using the standard ranking strategy (equations 1 and 2).

The results for the CO track are depicted in figures 13 to 14, and we observe the same pattern.

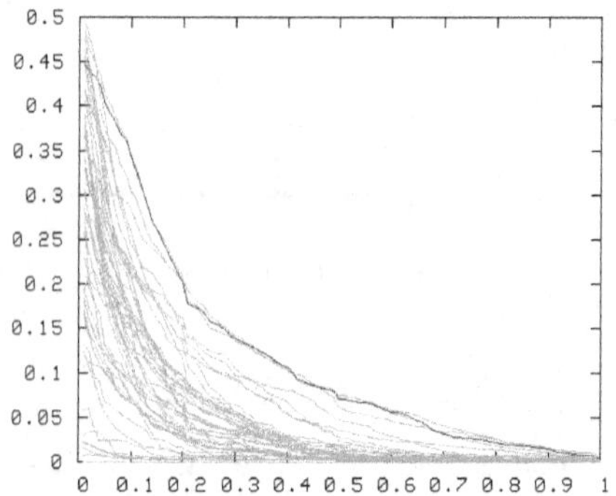

Fig. 9. VCAS evaluation, stopping words with frequency greater than 50,000 in the collection (rank: 1)

Fig. 10. VCAS evaluation, standard configuration (rank: 2)

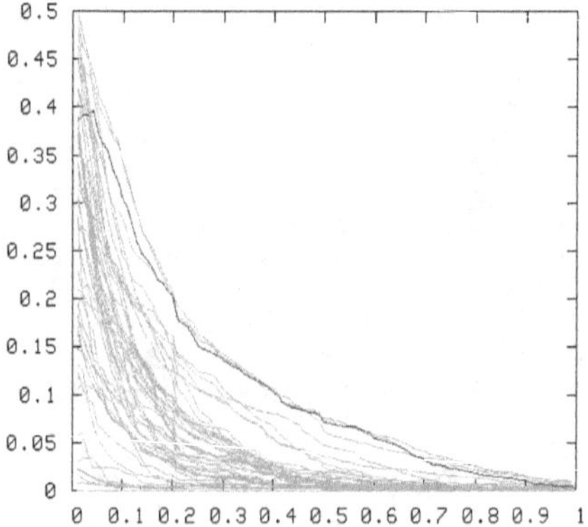

Fig. 11. VCAS run evaluation, stopping words with frequency greater than 50,000, Decay factor 0.49 / 0.25 (rank: 3)

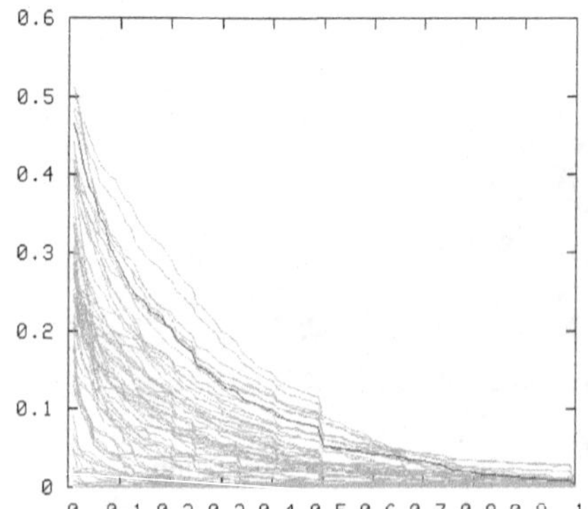

Fig. 12. CO evaluation standard configuration (rank: 7)

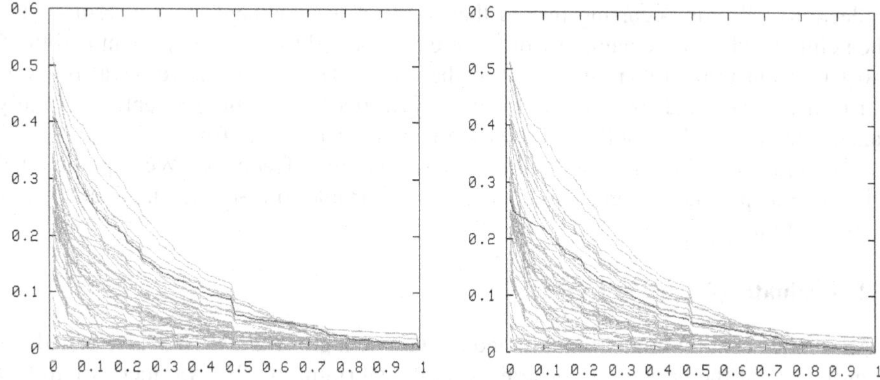

Fig. 13. CO run evaluation, stopping words with frequency greater than 50,000 in the INEX collection (rank: 6)

Fig. 14. CO run evaluation, stopping words with frequency greater than 50,000, Decay factor 0.49 or 0.25 (rank: 12)

7 Unofficial Submissions

Several other unofficial submissions were used to test additional techniques. We have tested the utility of blind feedback and of evaluating VCAS topics as if they were CO topics.

7.1 Blind Feedback

Blind feedback was performed as follows. First a retrieval run was performed. Then the top 10 result elements were extracted. All the words in these elements were collected and stop words eliminated (words occurring more than 50,000 times in the

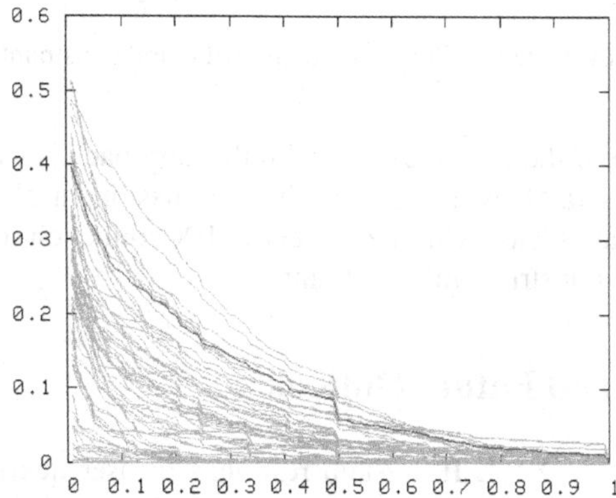

Fig. 15. CO topics evaluated with blind feedback using the top 10 elements (unofficial rank: 8)

collection). Words occurring in less than 20% of leaf elements in the results were then eliminated. The remaining words were then sorted by frequency count and the 5 most frequent terms (at most) added to the topic. Then a second retrieval run was performed. As usual, the idea is to identify words that occur frequently in highly ranked elements. The results of this experiment are depicted in figure 15.

The results are similar to those obtained without blind feedback. We experimented with various parameters on 2003 data, but were unable to discover an advantageous configuration.

7.2 Evaluating VCAS as CO

CAS queries contain both structural and containment constraints. We have tested the significance of the structural constraints by transforming the VCAS queries into CO queries. This is easily done by collecting all the keywords from all the about clauses to form a CO title elements for the topic. One would expect degradation in performance, but the question is to what extent performance will degrade. Figure 16 depicts the performance of a VCAS as CO evaluation.

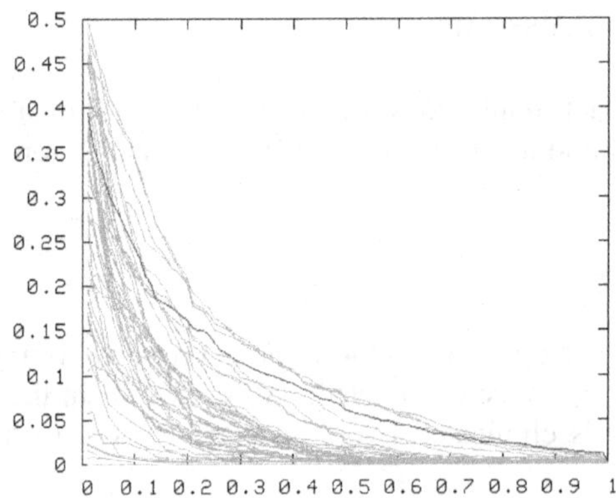

Fig. 16. VCAS evaluated as CO by removing structural constraints (unofficial rank 5th)

The performance of the search engine with this approach is surprisingly good. The average precision is 0.09, which places the submission in 5th position overall. It seems to suggest that at least with the current INEX collection there is relatively little advantage to specifying structural constraints.

8 Conclusions and Future Outlook

This paper presents an XML IR system responds to user queries with relevant and appropriately sized results in a timely manner. The approach is based on simple inverted lists indexing and on simple heuristics in ranking. Despite its simplicity our system produces results that are comparable with the best alternatives at INEX.

Future work will concentrate on improving the ranking strategy, improving the blind feedback implementation, the use of ontology for query expansion, and on natural language processing.

The system had been implemented as a massively distributed IR system and we are looking forward to an opportunity to evaluate it against a Terabyte size collection.

References

1. N. Fuhr and S. Malik : Overview of the Initiative for the Evaluation of XML Retrieval (INEX) 2003. In *INEX 2003 Workshop Proceedings*, Schloss Dagstuhl, Germany, December 15-17, (2003) 1-11.
2. B. Sigurbjornsson, J. Kamps, M. de Rijke, An Element-based Approach to XML Retrieval, In INEX 2003 Workshop Proceedings, Schloss Dagstuhl, Germany, December 15-17 (2003) 19-26.
3. Trotman, A. and O'Keefe, "The Simplest Query Language That Could Possibly Work", In INEX 2003 Workshop Proceedings, Schloss Dagstuhl, Germany, December 15-17 (2003) 167-174, 2004.
4. A. Trotman and B. Sigurbjörnsson, *Narrowed Extended XPath I (NEXI)*, http://www.cs.otago.ac.nz/postgrads/andrew/2004-4.pdf, 2004.
5. R. J. Van Rijsbergen, R. J., Information Retrieval, Butterworths, Second Edition, 1979.

Hierarchical Language Models for XML Component Retrieval

Paul Ogilvie and Jamie Callan

Language Technologies Institute,
School of Computer Science,
Carnegie Mellon University
{pto, callan}@lti.cs.cmu.edu

Abstract. Experiments using hierarchical language models for XML component retrieval are presented in this paper. The role of context is investigated through incorporation of the parent's model. We find that context can improve the effectiveness of finding relevant components slightly. Additionally, biasing the results toward long components through the use of component priors improves exhaustivity but harms specificity, so care must be taken to find an appropriate trade-off.

1 Introduction

Language modeling approaches have been applied successfully to retrieval of XML components in previous INEX evaluations [1][2][3][4][5]. In [4] and [5], the authors presented a hierarchical language model for retrieval of XML components. These works proposed that each document component be modeled by a language model estimated using evidence in the node and its children nodes. The work here extends the model to include the parent node's model in estimation, which allows for some context and is called shrinkage.

New experiments using this model are presented that examine the role of shrinkage introduced in this work and the use of the prior probabilities popularized by [3] for the evaluation of Content-Only queries. Our experiments show that shrinkage provides a modest boost in performance. Prior probabilities can have a strong effect in biasing results, particularly in improving exhaustivity (finding all relevant text) while at the same time harming specificity (finding the best component within the hierarchy). A prior based on the square of the length of text contained in a component and its children was found to be most effective.

Section 2 presents the model of documents and Section 3 describes how document components are ranked. Experimental methodology and results are presented in Sections 4 and 5. Related work is discussed in Section 6 and Section 7 concludes the paper.

2 Modeling Documents with Hierarchical Structure

Hierarchically structured documents may be represented as a tree, where nodes in the tree correspond to components of the document. From the content of the

N. Fuhr et al. (Eds.): INEX 2004, LNCS 3493, pp. 224–237, 2005.

document, a generative distribution may be estimated for each node in the tree. The distribution at a node may be estimated using evidence from the text of the node, the children's distributions, or the parent's distribution, and so on.

Representing hierarchically structured documents in this manner is simple and flexible. In this approach we combine the evidence from the various components in the document using the document structure as guidance. This model uses linear interpolation to combine the evidence from the component, its children components, and its parent component. The model below is similar to previous work by the authors [4][5], but is extended to allow for the inclusion of a component's context within the document.

More formally, the hierarchical structure of the document is represented by a tree, each vertex $v \in \mathcal{V}$ in the tree corresponding to a document component. Directed edges in the tree are represented as a list of vertex pairs $(v_i, v_j) \in \mathcal{E}$ when v_i is the parent of v_j. *Parent*, *children* and *descendants* functions may be defined as:

$$parent\left(v_j\right) = v_i : \left(v_i, v_j\right) \in \mathcal{E}$$

$$children\left(v_i\right) = \left\{v_j : \left(v_i, v_j\right) \in \mathcal{E}\right\}$$

$$descendants\left(v_i\right) = \left\{\begin{array}{c} v_j : v_j \in children\left(v_i\right) \text{ or} \\ \exists v_k \in children\left(v_i\right) \\ \text{s.t. } v_j \in descendants\left(v_k\right) \end{array}\right\}$$

As stated above, the generative model for a component may be estimated using a linear interpolation of the model estimated directly from the component, its children's models, and its parent model. Estimation of the generative models for the components of a document is a three step process. First, a smoothed generative model is θ_{v_i} estimated from the observations of the component in the document v_i that does not include evidence of children components:

$$\begin{aligned} P\left(w\left|\theta_{v_i}\right.\right) = {} & \left(1 - \lambda^u_{v_i}\right) P\left(w\left|MLE\left(v_i\right)\right.\right) \\ & + \lambda^u_{v_i} P\left(w\left|\theta_{type(v_i)}\right.\right) \end{aligned} \tag{1}$$

This model estimates a distribution directly from observed text within the document component. The $\theta_{type(v_i)}$ model is a collection level background model for smoothing these estimates. The background model is sometimes referred to as a "universal" model, hence the u in λ^u. The *type* function may be used to specify document component specific models, as the language in titles may be different from other text, or it may simply return one language model for all components, which would provide larger amounts of text for the estimation of the corpus model.

The next step is to estimate the intermediate θ'_{v_i} model, from the bottom up to the top of the tree:

$$P\left(w\left|\theta'_{v_i}\right.\right) = \lambda^{c'}_{v_i} P\left(w\left|\theta_{v_i}\right.\right) + \sum_{v_j \in children(v_i)} \lambda^{c}_{v_j} P\left(w\left|\theta'_{v_j}\right.\right), \tag{2}$$

$$1 = \lambda^{c'}_{v_i} + \sum_{v_j \in children(v_i)} \lambda^{c}_{v_j}$$

This model incorporates the evidence from the children nodes. If the λ^c parameters are set proportional to the length of the text in the node, as in

$$\begin{aligned} \lambda^{c'}_{v_i} &= \frac{|v_i|}{|v_i| + \sum_{v_k \in descendants(v_i)} |v_k|} \\ \lambda^{c}_{v_j} &= \frac{|v_j| + \sum_{v_k \in descendants(v_j)} |v_k|}{|v_i| + \sum_{v_k \in descendants(v_i)} |v_k|} \end{aligned} \tag{3}$$

where $|v_i|$ is the length in tokens of the text in node v_i not including tokens in its children, θ'_{v_i} is equivalent to a flat text model estimated from the text in node v_i interpolated with a background model. However, this choice of parameters is not required, and the weight placed on a child node may be dependent on the node's type. For example, the text in title nodes may be more representative than the body of a document, so a higher weight on the title model may improve retrieval performance.

After the estimation of θ'_{v_i}, the θ''_{v_i} models used for ranking the components are estimated from the root of the tree down:

$$\begin{aligned} P\left(w\left|\theta''_{v_i}\right.\right) = &\left(1 - \lambda^{p}_{parent(v_i)}\right) P\left(w\left|\theta'_{v_i}\right.\right) \\ &+ \lambda^{p}_{parent(v_i)} P\left(w\left|\theta''_{parent(v_i)}\right.\right) \end{aligned} \tag{4}$$

Incorporating the parent model in this way allows the context of the component within the document to influence the language model. Incorporating a parent's language model in this way is referred to as shrinkage. In [6], McCallum and Nigam introduced shrinkage to information retrieval in the context of text classification. Classes were modeled hiearchically in this work. Class language models were estimated from the text in the documents assigned to the class, and all ancestor language models in the class hierarchy. The hierarchical model for classes used in [6] is very similar to the model of documents presented in this proposal. The difference in model estimation in this work is the application of shrinkage to document models, rather than class models.

The choice of linear interpolation parameters λ may depend upon the task and corpus. Ideally, the choice of these parameters would be set to maximize some measure of retrieval performance through automated learning.

A set of rankable items, document components that may be returned by the system, $\mathcal{R}$ must also be defined for the document. For the hierarchical model presented here, $\mathcal{R}$ may be any subset of $\mathcal{V}$.

2.1 Example

The estimation process described above may be clarified through describing the process for an example document. The example document is a well known children's poem encoded in XML:

```
<poem id='p1'>
    <title> Little Jack Horner </title>
    <body>
        Little Jack Horner
        Sat in the corner,
        Eating of Christmas pie;
        He put in his thumb
        And pulled out a plumb,
        And cried, <quote> What a
            good boy am I! </quote>
    </body>
</poem>
```

There are four components of this document, corresponding to the poem, title, body, and quote tags. Let us now assign labels to these components v_1 to the poem, v_2 to the title component, v_3 to the body component, and v_4 to the quote. The structure of the document may be drawn, as in Figure 1 or be described as a set of vertices and edges:

$$\begin{aligned}
\mathcal{G} &= (\mathcal{V}, \mathcal{E}) \\
\mathcal{V} &= \{v_1, v_2, v_3, v_4\} \\
\mathcal{E} &= \{(v_1, v_2), (v_1, v_3), (v_3, v_4)\}
\end{aligned}$$

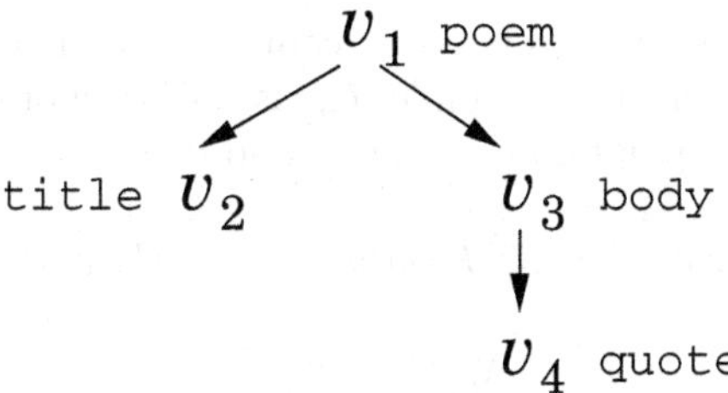

Fig. 1. The tree representing document structure for "Little Jack Horner"

Not all components of the document may be rankable items. A set of rankable items must be defined. In our example, perhaps only the poem and the body of the poem are considered rankable items: $\mathcal{R} = \{v_1, v_3\}$.

The estimation process is illustrated in Figure 2. First, smoothed θ_{v_i} models are estimated for each vertex using the text occurring in the document component corresponding to the vertex. Note that "What a good boy am I!" is not

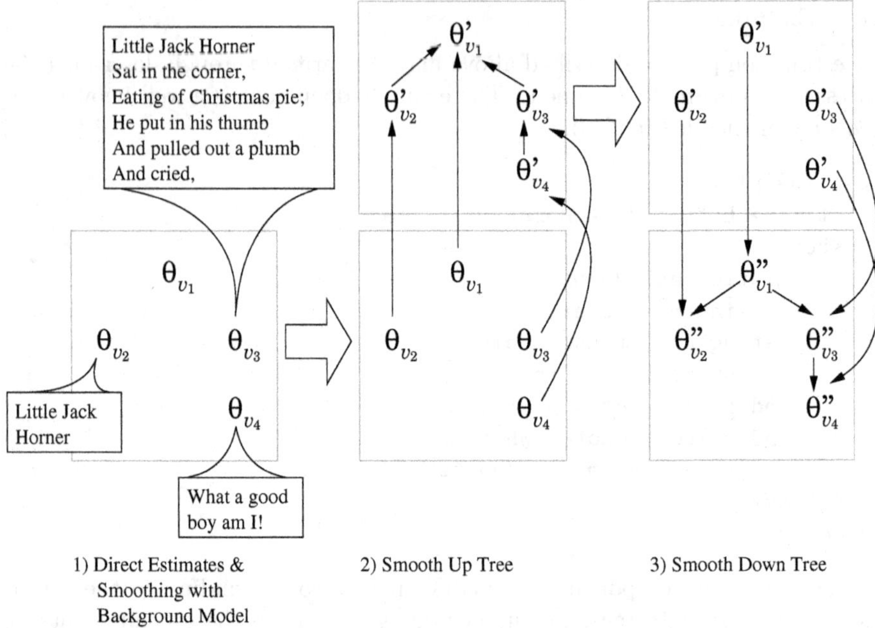

Fig. 2. The estimation process for "Little Jack Horner"

used for the estimation of θ_{v_3}, it is only used in the estimation for the model of v_3's child node v_4:

$$P\left(w\left|\theta_{v_i}\right.\right)=\left(1-\lambda_{v_i}^u\right)P\left(w\left|MLE\left(v_i\right)\right.\right)+\lambda_{v_i}^u P\left(w\left|\theta_{type(v_i)}\right.\right) \tag{5}$$

Next, the θ'_{v_i} models are estimated by combination of the θ_{v_i} model and the θ' models of v_i's children. For example, θ'_{v_3} is an interpolation of θ_{v_3} and θ'_{v_4}. Similarly, θ'_{v_1} is an interpolation of θ_{v_1}, θ'_{v_2}, and θ'_{v_3}:

$$\begin{aligned}
P\left(w\left|\theta'_{v_1}\right.\right)&=\lambda_{v_1}^{c'}P\left(w\left|\theta_{v_1}\right.\right)+\lambda_{v_2}^{c}P\left(w\left|\theta'_{v_2}\right.\right)\\
&\quad+\lambda_{v_3}^{c}P\left(w\left|\theta'_{v_3}\right.\right)\\
P\left(w\left|\theta'_{v_2}\right.\right)&=P\left(w\left|\theta_{v_2}\right.\right)\\
P\left(w\left|\theta'_{v_3}\right.\right)&=\lambda_{v_3}^{c'}P\left(w\left|\theta_{v_3}\right.\right)+\lambda_{v_4}^{c}P\left(w\left|\theta'_{v_4}\right.\right)\\
P\left(w\left|\theta'_{v_4}\right.\right)&=P\left(w\left|\theta_{v_4}\right.\right)
\end{aligned} \tag{6}$$

Finally, the θ''_{v_i} models used in ranking are estimated by interpolating the θ'_{v_i} model with the $\theta''_{parent(v_i)}$ model. In the example, θ''_{v_1} is simply taken as θ'_{v_1} as v_1 has no parent. The other vertices do have parents, and θ''_{v_3} is an interpolation of θ'_{v_3} and θ''_{v_1}:

$$\begin{aligned} P\left(w\left|\theta''_{v_1}\right.\right) &= P\left(w\left|\theta'_{v_1}\right.\right) \\ P\left(w\left|\theta''_{v_3}\right.\right) &= \left(1-\lambda^p_{v_1}\right) P\left(w\left|\theta'_{v_3}\right.\right) + \lambda^p_{v_1} P\left(w\left|\theta''_{v_1}\right.\right) \end{aligned} \tag{7}$$

We can expand the equations for these rankable items to use only θ models as follows:

$$\begin{aligned} P\left(w\left|\theta''_{v_1}\right.\right) &= \lambda^{c'}_{v_1} P\left(w\left|\theta_{v_1}\right.\right) + \lambda^{c}_{v_2} P\left(w\left|\theta_{v_2}\right.\right) \\ &\quad + \lambda^{c}_{v_3}\left(\lambda^{c'}_{v_3} P\left(w\left|\theta_{v_3}\right.\right) + \lambda^{c}_{v_4} P\left(w\left|\theta_{v_4}\right.\right)\right) \\ P\left(w\left|\theta''_{v_3}\right.\right) &= \left(1-\lambda^p_{v_1}\right)\left(\lambda^{c'}_{v_3} P\left(w\left|\theta_{v_3}\right.\right) + \lambda^{c}_{v_4} P\left(w\left|\theta_{v_4}\right.\right)\right) \\ &\quad + \lambda^p_{v_1} P\left(w\left|\theta''_{v_1}\right.\right) \\ &= \left(1-\lambda^p_{v_1}+\lambda^p_{v_1}\lambda^c_{v_3}\right) \\ &\quad \left(\lambda^{c'}_{v_3} P\left(w\left|\theta_{v_3}\right.\right) + \lambda^{c}_{v_4} P\left(w\left|\theta_{v_4}\right.\right)\right) \\ &\quad + \lambda^p_{v_1}\left(\lambda^{c'}_{v_1} P\left(w\left|\theta_{v_1}\right.\right) + \lambda^{c}_{v_2} P\left(w\left|\theta_{v_2}\right.\right)\right) \end{aligned} \tag{8}$$

3 Ranking Items for Queries

This section describes how rankable items are ordered for queries. Ordering of items is based on the query-likelihood model, where items are ranked by the probability of generating the query. It is also desirable to provide support for structured queries as well, which will be discussed.

3.1 Queries

Rankable items across documents for flat text queries may simply be ordered by $P\left(Q\left|\theta''_{v_i}\right.\right)$, where

$$P\left(Q\left|\theta''_{v_i}\right.\right) = \prod_{w \in Q} P\left(w\left|\theta''_{v_i}\right.\right)^{tf(w,Q)} \tag{9}$$

This is the natural adaptation of query-likelihood [7][8] [9][10][11] to the model.

There are many cases where it is desirable to place constraints on where the query terms appear in the document structure of a representation. This can be done by constraining which θ_{v_i} distribution generates the terms. For example, consider the NEXI [12] query

```
//poem[about(.//title, Horner)]
```

which requests poem components where the title component is about 'Horner'. The NEXI query language was developed as a simple adaptation of XPath to information retrieval. All example queries in this proposal will be expressed in NEXI. For our example document with a single representation, instead of measuring $P\left(\text{'Horner'}\left|\theta''_{v_1}\right.\right)$, corresponding to the probability the poem component generated the query term 'Horner', $P\left(\text{'Horner'}\left|\theta''_{v_2}\right.\right)$ is used. $P\left(\text{'Horner'}\left|\theta''_{v_2}\right.\right)$ measures the probability that the title component generated 'Horner'.

There are cases where a structural constraint on the query may be applicable to multiple components. Consider the query:

```
//document[about(.//paragraph, plum)]
```

Most documents contain many paragraphs. Which distribution is chosen to generate 'plum'? Many reasonable options are applicable. One approach may create a new distribution estimated as a combination of all of the θ''_{v_i} distributions corresponding to paragraph components. Another approach may take the θ''_{v_i} distribution corresponding to paragraph nodes that maximizes the probabity of generating 'plum', which is the approach taken here.

Constraining the generating distribution in this manner is a strict interpretation of the constraints expressed in the query (as in previous SCAS tasks). The ranking items as described above requires that only poems be returned as results and that they contain titles. Note that through the use of smoothing, 'Horner' is not required to be present in the title. However, if the structural constraints are intended as hints to relevance (as in the VCAS task), then this approach can only return a subset of relevant items. Loose interpretation of structural constraints is something that remains a challenge and will be investigated as a part of future work.

3.2 Priors

Query independent information about relevant documents is not uncommon and may be useful for ranking purposes. For example, there may be a tendency for longer documents to be more likely to be relevant than short documents. This information may be leveraged through the use of priors, which are a belief independent of the query that the document may be relevant. They are incorporated to ranking within the generative framework using Bayes rule:

$$\begin{aligned} &P\left(v_i \text{ is Rel}\left|Q, g\left(v_i\right)=a\right.\right) \\ &\propto \frac{P\left(Q\left|v_i \text{ is Rel}, g\left(v_i\right)=a\right.\right)}{P\left(v_i \text{ is Rel}\left|g\left(v_i\right)=a\right.\right)} \\ &\approx P\left(Q\left|\theta''_{v_i}\right.\right) P\left(v_i \text{ is Rel}\left|g\left(v_i\right)=a\right.\right) \end{aligned} \tag{10}$$

where $g(v_i)$ is a function of the rankable item such as the length of v_i and $P(Q|\theta''_{v_i})$ is assumed representative of $P(Q|v_i \text{ is Rel}, g(v_i) = a)$. Theoretically, the prior probability $P(v_i \text{ is Rel}|g(v_i) = a)$ can be estimated from training data. However, in practice the prior is not a true prior probability estimate as it is often used to correct a bias in the ranking function at the same time as incorporating the prior belief that v_i is relevant. This makes the choice of how $P(v_i \text{ is Rel}|g(v_i) = a)$ is estimated somewhat of a fine art, rather than a theoretically driven process.

4 Methodology

All experiments use a local adaptation of the Lemur [13] toolkit for XML retrieval. Two databases were built - one using the Krovetz stemmer [14], and one without stemming. A stopword list of around 400 words was used for both databases. Our prior INEX paper [5] describes most adaptations to index structures and basic retrieval algorithms used presently.

Since then, some query nodes for structured retrieval have been added. We presently only support *AND* clauses, *about* clauses, and path constraints. Numeric constraints are ignored by the retrieval system. *OR* clauses are converted to *AND* clauses, temporarily sidestepping the issue of how the *OR* probabilities are computed. *NOT* clauses are dropped from the query, as are terms with a '-' in front of them. Different clauses of the queries are given equal weight. Phrase constraints are dropped, but the words are kept. A '+' in front of a query term is ignored. Basically, all queries are converted to contain only *AND* clauses with path constraints and about clauses. For example, query 66 is converted from

```
//article[.//fm//yr < 2000]
   //sec[about(., 'search engines')]
```

to

```
//article//sec[about(., search engines)]
```

The graph structures used were taken directly from the XML structure of the document. All components were considered rankable items. The weight placed on the collection model λ^u is 0.2 and when using shrinkage, λ^p is set to 0.1. A single background model estimated from all text in the collection was used. Estimation of θ' models use $\lambda^{c'}$ and λ^c set according to Equation 3. These parameters were chosen by experimentation on the INEX 2003 topics.

The prior probabilities used in experiments are all based on the aggregated length of a component may take the following form:

- *linear* – $P(v_i \text{ is Rel}|length(v_i) = x) \propto x$
- *square* – $P(v_i \text{ is Rel}|length(v_i) = x) \propto x^2$
- *cubic* – $P(v_i \text{ is Rel}|length(v_i) = x) \propto x^3$

where

$$length(v_i) = |v_i| + \sum_{v_k \in descendants(v_i)} |v_k| . \tag{11}$$

5 Experiments

This section describes some experiments with variations of the system. The discussion in this section centers on the content-only topics. Figure 3 examines the effects of prior probabilities on the strict measure and the specificity oriented measure for content-only topics. The runs in this figure used the Krovetz stemmer and a shrinkage parameter $\lambda^p = 0.1$. The use of more extreme length priors generally resulted in noticeable improvements to the strict measure but at a sacrifice to the specificity oriented measure. Results for more configurations and measures are presented in Table 5. The trends in Figure 3 are confirmed in the table. The more extreme the prior, the higher the exhaustivity and the lower the specificity. Using a more extreme prior also reduced overlap in the result lists, as these runs had distinct biases toward long components. For the rest of the discussion in this section, a linear prior was chosen as a good trade-off between improved exhaustivity and harmed specificity.

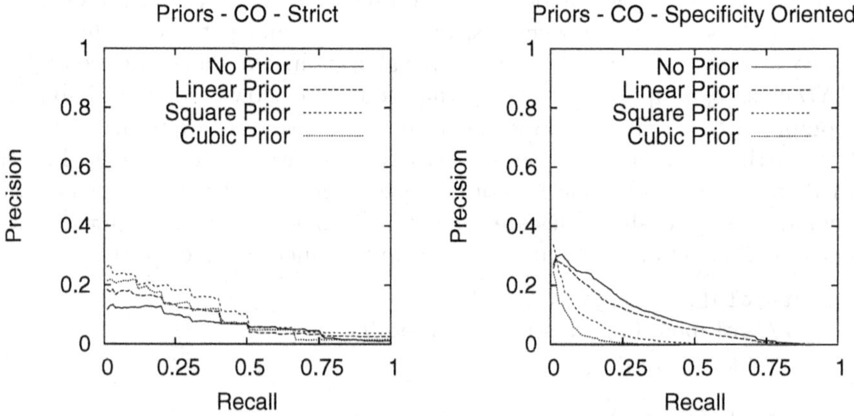

Fig. 3. More extreme length priors can greatly improve performance under strict evaluation, but at a sacrifice to specificity oriented evaluation

Next, some experiments using different shrinkage parameters are explored. For these runs, only the system using the Krovetz stemmer and a linear prior was explored. Figure 4 demonstrates that small values of λ^p boost precision modestly for both strict and specificity oriented measures. A non-zero shrinkage parameter did seem to help, and using too large a parameter hurt precision at low recall. The bottom half of Table 5 contains more evaluation measures and parameter settings. Small settings for the shrinkage parameter can improve performance across all measures, but these results may not be significant.

This section concludes with a brief discussion of the content-and-structure runs. Our original submission had a bug which allowed a component to be returned in the result list multiple times (with different supporting components).

Table 1. Run performance for Content-Only topics

Official	λ^p	Stemmer	Prior	Strict	Generalized	SO	s3 e321	e3 s321
YES[1]	0.0	-	-	0.0640	0.0728	0.0655	0.0541	0.0806
NO	0.0	-	linear	0.0896	0.0770	0.0650	0.0564	0.1234
NO	0.0	-	square	0.1224	0.0448	0.0318	0.0236	0.1864
NO	0.0	-	cubic	0.0902	0.0226	0.0167	0.0130	0.1367
YES[2]	0.1	-	-	0.0675	0.0908	0.0897	0.0771	0.0769
NO	0.1	-	linear	0.0688	0.0829	0.0721	0.0640	0.1055
NO	0.1	-	square	0.1268	0.0480	0.0344	0.0262	0.1885
NO	0.1	-	cubic	0.0927	0.0230	0.0173	0.0139	0.1380
YES[3]	0.1	Krovetz	-	0.0667	0.0947	0.0941	0.0835	0.0776
NO	0.1	Krovetz	linear	0.0817	0.0882	0.0770	0.0663	0.1191
NO	0.1	Krovetz	square	0.1129	0.0445	0.0330	0.0252	0.1721
NO	0.1	Krovetz	cubic	0.0859	0.0200	0.0151	0.0117	0.1324
NO	0.000	Krovetz	linear	0.0745	0.0771	0.0651	0.0561	0.1173
NO	0.025	Krovetz	linear	0.0874	0.0867	0.0748	0.0632	0.1315
NO	0.050	Krovetz	linear	0.0849	0.0885	0.0765	0.0654	0.1315
NO	0.075	Krovetz	linear	0.0830	0.0889	0.0775	0.0667	0.1255
NO	0.100	Krovetz	linear	0.0817	0.0882	0.0770	0.0663	0.1191
NO	0.125	Krovetz	linear	0.0682	0.0840	0.0734	0.0632	0.1076
NO	0.150	Krovetz	linear	0.0591	0.0761	0.0670	0.0573	0.0915

[1]Lemur_CO_NoStem_Mix02 [2]Lemur_CO_NoStem_Mix02_Shrink01
[3]Lemur_CO_KStem_Mix02_Shrink01

Official	λ^p	Stemmer	Prior	Overlap	Aggregate
YES[1]	0.0	-	-	66.7	0.0651
NO	0.0	-	linear	72.6	0.0809
NO	0.0	-	square	47.1	0.0881
NO	0.0	-	cubic	41.7	0.0629
YES[2]	0.1	-	-	74.8	0.0774
NO	0.1	-	linear	73.4	0.0772
NO	0.1	-	square	46.3	0.0910
NO	0.1	-	cubic	40.5	0.0641
YES[3]	0.1	Krovetz	-	73.0	0.0807
NO	0.1	Krovetz	linear	72.6	0.0853
NO	0.1	Krovetz	square	46.2	0.0861
NO	0.1	Krovetz	cubic	40.4	0.0625
NO	0.000	Krovetz	linear	72.4	0.0764
NO	0.025	Krovetz	linear	72.1	0.0877
NO	0.050	Krovetz	linear	72.3	0.0881
NO	0.075	Krovetz	linear	72.5	0.0869
NO	0.100	Krovetz	linear	72.6	0.0853
NO	0.125	Krovetz	linear	72.8	0.0781
NO	0.150	Krovetz	linear	73.0	0.0685

[1]Lemur_CO_NoStem_Mix02
[2]Lemur_CO_NoStem_Mix02_Shrink01
[3]Lemur_CO_KStem_Mix02_Shrink01

This bug has been fixed, and a comparison of the official runs and the bug-fixes are in Table 5. The runs using query structure took a strict interpretation of constraints and as such, it is not surprising that they did poorly for the VCAS task. Our best performing run did not use any structure in the query.

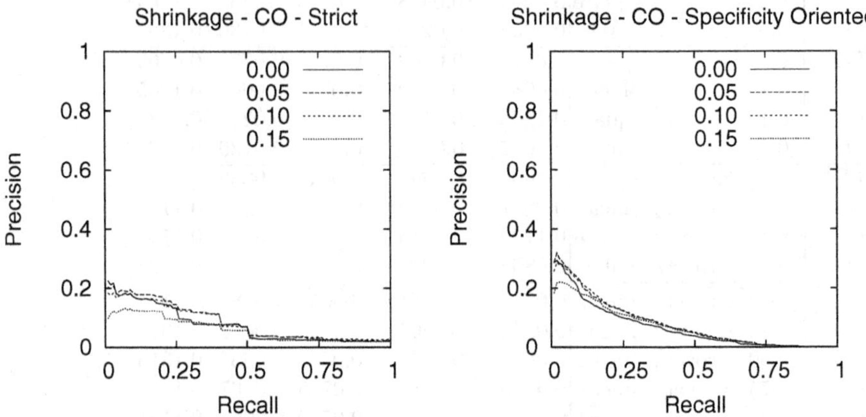

Fig. 4. Very small shrinkage parameter values boost precision moderately at mid-recall ranges for strict evaluation and across the range for specificity oriented evaluation

All non-structural constraints were removed from the query so that keywords present in the about clauses remained. This was then treated as a flat text query and run using the configuration for CO topics. The use of prior probabilities was investigated, and it was found that the trade-off between exhaustivity and specificity observed for CO held for VCAS as well. However, there does seem to be a preference for shorter components in the VCAS task, as the square prior hurt performance across the board, while the linear prior improved performance.

Table 2. Run performance for Content-and-Structure topics

Official	Structure	λ^p	Prior	Strict	Generalized	SO	s3 e321	e3 s321	Overlap	Aggregate
YES[1]	NO	0.1	-	0.0710	0.0746	0.0759	0.0834	0.0700	74.0	0.0759
NO	NO	0.1	Linear	0.0889	0.0847	0.0804	0.0819	0.0949	69.9	0.0864
NO	NO	0.1	Square	0.0585	0.0468	0.0377	0.0359	0.0836	48.3	0.0217
YES[2]	YES	0.0	-	0.0468	0.0180	0.0166	0.0253	0.0419	2.4	0.0325
NO (fix)	YES	0.0	-	0.0616	0.0276	0.0309	0.0409	0.0413	4.6	0.0459
YES[3]	YES	0.1	-	0.0466	0.0199	0.0177	0.0249	0.0457	2.4	0.0339
NO (fix)	YES	0.1	-	0.0621	0.0274	0.0302	0.0409	0.0418	4.8	0.0460

[1]Lemur_CAS_as_CO_NoStem_Mix02_Shrink01 [2]Lemur_CAS_NoStem_Mix02
[3]Lemur_CAS_NoStem_Mix02_Shrink01

6 Related Work

Much of the current work in XML component retrieval can be found in these proceedings and in [15][16], so only highly related works will be discussed here.

The Tijah system [1] also uses generative models for retrieval of XML components. They do not explicitly model the hierarchical relationship between components when estimating language models. Instead, they estimate a language model for each component using the text present in it and its children. This is equivalent to our model when $\lambda^p = 0$ and $\lambda^{c'}$ and λ^c are set according to Equation 3. They also incorporate prior probabilities using a log-normal and a linear component length prior. To provide context in the scoring of a component, they average the component score with the document score. For structured queries, constraints on structure are processed similarly. However, for *OR* clauses, the maximum of the scores is taken, while the minimum is taken for *AND* clauses. A system configuration for vague evaluation of structured queries is realized using query rewrites.

Kamps, Sigurbjörnsson, and de Rijke [3] [2] also work within the language modeling framework. Like [1], they do not explicitly model hierarchical relationship between document components when estimating the language model for a component. Rather than estimating the background model using a maximum likelihood estimator, they use an estimate based on element frequencies. They present experiments using a linear, square, and cubic component length prior, and also experiment with a cut-off filtering out short components. As with [1], their model is comparable to our model when $\lambda^p = 0$ and $\lambda^{c'}$ and λ^c are set according to Equation 3. For processing structured queries, [2] describes an approach that combines query rewrites with strict interpretation of the query.

7 Conclusions

This paper described experiments using hierarchical language models for modeling and ranking of XML document components. It extended previous work to incorporate context through the use of shrinkage, which helps modestly for flat text queries. A very small choice for the shrinkage parameter was found to be best for retrieval. This paper also presented experiments using length based priors. A prior probability proportional to the length of the component was found to be most effective across a number of measures.

For vague content and structure queries, where structure is intended only as a hint to the retrieval system, we found that ignoring structure in the query was better than taking a strict interpretation of the structural constraints. This is much like using a flat text query. As with the content only queries, a linear length prior was found to improve performance, but the vague content and structure queries may have a preference for shorter components than the content only queries on average.

Future experiments will examine use of the structural constraints in the content and structure queries as hints for relevance within the framework. More experimentation with how the shrinkage parameter is set will be performed, as well as different approaches to setting the interpolation parameters for the combination of evidence from child nodes.

Acknowledgments

This research was sponsored by National Science Foundation (NSF) grant no. CCR-0122581. The views and conclusions contained in this document are those of the author and should not be interpreted as representing the official policies, either expressed or implicit, of the NSF or the US government.

References

1. List, J., Mihajlovic, V., Ramirez, G., Hiemstra, D.: The tijah xml-ir system at inex 2003. In: INEX 2003 Workshop Proceedings. (2003) 102–109
2. Sigurbjörnsson, B., Kamps, J., de Rijke, M.: Processing content-and-structure queries for xml retrieval. In: Proccedings of the First Twente Data Management Workshop. (2004) 31–38
3. Kamps, J., de Rijke, M., Sigurbjörnsson, B.: Length normalization in xml retrieval. In: Proceedings of the Twenty-Seventh Annual International ACM SIGIR Conference on Research and Development in Information Retrieval. (2004) 80–87
4. Ogilvie, P., Callan, J.: Language models and structured document retrieval. In: Proceedings of the First Workshop of the INitiative for the Evaluation of XML Retrieval (INEX). (2003)
5. Ogilvie, P., Callan, J.P.: Using language models for flat text queries in xml retrieval. In: Proc. of the Second Annual Workshop of the Initiative for the Evaluation of XML retrieval (INEX), Dagstuhl, Germany (2003)
6. McCallum, A., Nigam, K.: Text classification by bootstrapping with keywords, em and shrinkage. In: Proceedings of the ACL 99 Workshop for Unsupervised Learning in Natural Language Processing. (1999) 52–58
7. Ponte, J., Croft, W.: A language modeling approach for information retrieval. In: Proceedings of the 21st Annual International ACM SIGIR Conference on Research and Development in Information Retrieval, ACM Press (1998) 275–281
8. Hiemstra, D.: Using language models for information retrieval. PhD thesis, University of Twente (2001)
9. Zhai, C., Lafferty, J.: A study of smoothing methods for language models applied to information retrieval. ACM Transactions on Information Systems **2** (2004)
10. Song, F., Croft, W.: A general language model for information retrieval. In: Proceedings of the Eighth International Conference on Information and Knowledge Management. (1999)
11. Westerveld, T., Kraaij, W., Hiemstra, D.: Retrieving web pages using content, links, URLs, and anchors. In: The Tenth Text REtrieval Conf. (TREC-10), NIST SP 500-250. (2002) 663–672
12. Trotman, A., Sigurbjörnsson, B.: Narrow Extended XPath I. Technical report (2004) Available at http://inex.is.informatik.uni-duisburg.de:2004/.
13. Lemur: The Lemur Toolkit for Language Modeling and Information Retrieval. (http://lemurproject.org/)

14. Krovetz, R.: Viewing morphology as an inference process. In: Proceedings of the 16th Annual International ACM SIGIR Conference on Research and Development in Information Retrieval, ACM (1993) 191–202
15. Fuhr, N., Goevert, N., Kazai, G., Lalmas, M., eds.: Proceedings of the First Workshop of the INitiative for the Evaluation of XML Retrieval (INEX), ERCIM (2003)
16. Fuhr, N., Maalik, S., Lalmas, M., eds.: Proc. of the Second Annual Workshop of the Initiative for the Evaluation of XML retrieval (INEX), Dagstuhl, Germany (2003)

Ranked Retrieval of Structured Documents with the S-Term Vector Space Model

Felix Weigel[1], Klaus U. Schulz[1], and Holger Meuss[2]

[1] Centre for Information and Language Processing (CIS), University of Munich (LMU), Germany
[2] European Southern Observatory (ESO), Headquarter Garching, Germany

Abstract. This paper shows how the s-term ranking model [1] is extended and combined with index structures and algorithms for structured document retrieval to enhance both the effectiveness of the model and the retrieval efficiency. We explain in detail how previous work on ranked and exact retrieval can be integrated and optimized, and which adaptions are necessary. Our approach is evaluated experimentally at the INEX workshop 2004 [2]. The results are encouraging and give rise to a number of future enhancements.

1 Introduction

The retrieval and ranking of structured text documents has by now become an IR discipline in its own right. As more and more documents are available in ever growing web repositories, digital libraries, and intranet knowledge bases, performance both in terms of the ranking effectiveness and the retrieval efficiency is paramount. When searching the relevant parts of millions of documents occupying hundreds of megabytes, naive solutions often turn out to be inadequate. Many sophisticated ranking models for structured documents have been proposed [3,4,1,5,6,7], most of which are based on the traditional *tf·idf* model for "flat" text documents [8]. Two key issues in the adaption of *tf·idf* to structured data are (1) the *document boundary problem*, i.e. the question which units of the data are to be treated as coherent pieces of information, and (2) the *structural similarity problem*, which concerns methods for quantifying the distance of a document to a given query. While the first problem is intrinsic to structured documents whose hierarchical nature blurs the physical boundaries imposed by a file system, the second problem arises in "flat" retrieval as well. However, similarity measures for structured documents necessarily make assumptions concerning the documents to be ranked, hence both problems are tightly linked.

The second aspect of performance, efficiency, seems to be a greater concern in the field of exact (i.e., unranked) retrieval of structured documents. However, ongoing work [9,10,7,11] investigates how to integrate effective ranking techniques with data structures and algorithms used in exact retrieval. In this paper, we follow the approach adopted in [9] and integrate the *s-term* ranking model [1] with the *Content-Aware DataGuide (CADG)* index [10], which stores additional information needed for computing relevance scores. As a further enhancement, an

N. Fuhr et al. (Eds.): INEX 2004, LNCS 3493, pp. 238–252, 2005.

efficient structural join [12] is applied during relevance computation. To increase the effectiveness of the original s-term model, we extend it with IR features such as order and distance constraints on term occurrences and Boolean constraints on textual and structural conditions. We also report on a first experimental evaluation of the extended model at INEX 2004 [2].

The paper proceeds as follows: Section 2 reviews the original s-term model in a nutshell. Section 3 explains the data structures and algorithms used in our implementation, as well as the extensions to the model. Section 4 presents and discusses the results from INEX 2004. Section 5 briefly reviews some of the related work cited above. Section 6 concludes with future work.

2 S-Term Vector Space Model

The *s-term vector space model* [1] combines the vector space model (VSM) [8] with Kilpeläinen's tree matching approach [13] to retrieving structured documents. The key concepts in the VSM, *document*, *query* and *term*, are adapted so as to cover both the structural and the textual dimension of the data. To this end, documents, queries and – most notably – terms are modelled as labelled trees in [1]. Note that the resulting *structured terms (s-terms)* are in general subtrees of queries and documents, labelled with both element names and "flat" terms (i.e., ordinary unstructured keywords as known from traditional IR). As a special case, an s-term representing a "flat" term consists of a single labelled text node. Each s-term contained in a query may be weighted to reflect its contribution to the underlying information need. In [1] it is shown that with suitable weights for query terms, the s-term vector space model can simulate both the traditional VSM for "flat" documents and the tree matching approach.

Like in the original VSM, documents are described by document vectors whose weight components are computed from the distribution of s-terms in the collection, using the *tf·idf* method [8]. The definition of the *inverse document frequency idf* is related to the notion of documents to be retrieved in response to a query, and hence to the document boundary problem (see Sect. 1). The s-term vector space model addresses this issue by introducing the concept of a *logical document* (as opposed to the *physical documents* in the collection), which applies to any subtree of the document tree. In other words, any subtree of the document tree can be an answer to a query, provided its root has the same label as the query root. Thus the document boundary problem is solved at query time.

The s-term model supports ranking of partial matches to a query. Both violations to structural and textual query conditions are tolerated, although by default the structure is regarded as a weaker criterion than the keywords in the query. More precisely, query keywords occurring in a structural context which does not satisfy the query still contribute to the relevance of a document. Conversely, documents which lack a particular query keyword but contain matches to other parts of the query (i.e., other s-terms not containing the missing "flat" term) are still considered relevant. Adjusting the weights of individual s-terms in the query, the user tunes the model more towards structure or keyword matching.

2.1 Data Model

Both *documents* and *queries* are conceived as unordered labelled trees in the s-term vector space model. Order conditions are not considered, and the original s-term model draws no distinction between the parent/child relation and the more general ancestor/descendant relation between document nodes (but see Sect. 3.1). Besides documents and queries, [1] defines *structured terms (s-terms)* and the frequency of their occurrences in documents. The notion of s-terms can be viewed as a generalization of the "flat" terms known from traditional IR, which are simply words (or word compounds). By contrast, a structured term is an unordered tree whose nodes are labelled with element names or "flat" terms, as illustrated in Fig. 1.

A query q *contains* an s-term s if s is a full subtree of q.[1] For instance, the query in Fig. 1 contains the six s-terms s_0 to s_5 corresponding to the non-shaded parts of the insets on the right. An s-term s is said to *occur* in a document d if there is an embedding f from s to d respecting the labels and ancestor/descendant relationships. The document node $f(root(s))$ (where $root(s)$ denotes the root of a tree or s-term s) is called an *occurrence* or *match* of s in a document. Note that the concept of occurrence in documents, relying on tree embedding, is somewhat weaker than that of containment in a query: an occurrence of an s-term in a document may have descendants which do not match any query node. (In particular, the same document node may be an occurrence of different s-terms.) Any logical document in which at least one s-term contained in q occurs is an *answer* to q. Note that the occurring term need not be the *root s-term* (the largest s-term contained in q, e.g., s_0 in Fig. 1). Intuitively, an answer is any subtree of the document tree which (1) has the same label as the query root and (2) contains an occurrence of a full query subtree (but see the discussion on *target elements* in Sect. 3.4).

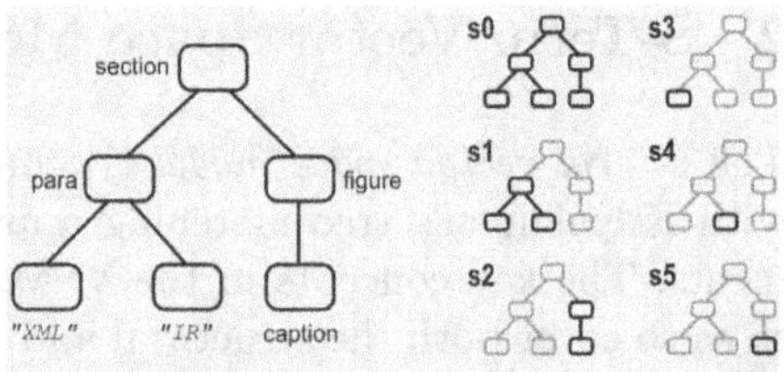

Fig. 1. Query tree with six s-terms

2.2 Similarity of Queries and Documents

Computation of term weights. The two *tf·idf* components *term frequency* and *inverse document frequency* and the resulting *weight* of a term in a document are defined as follows:

$$tf_{s,d} := \frac{freq_{s,d}}{maxfreq_d}$$

$$idf_s^t := log\frac{|D^t|}{df_s} + 1$$

$$w_{s,d}^t := tf_{s,d} \cdot idf_s^t$$

[1] By a *full subtree* of a tree T we mean a subtree of T that has one of the nodes of T as its root and contains all children and descendants of that node as children and descendants. Hence the number of full subtrees equals the number of nodes in T.

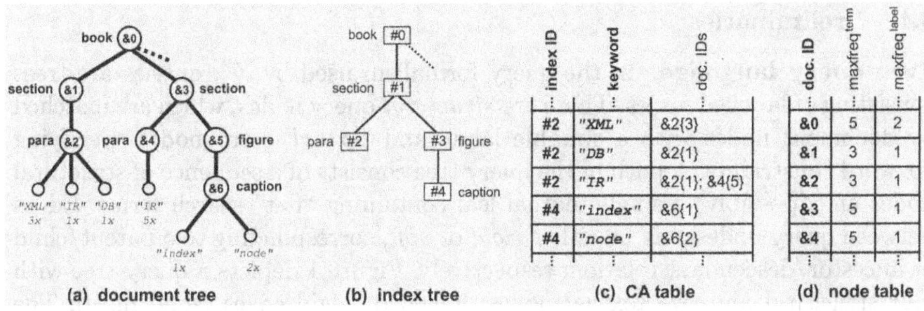

Fig. 2. Indexing a document collection with the IR-CADG for s-term evaluation

Like in the VSM, the *term frequency* $tf_{s,d}$ indicates how often a given s-term s occurs in a given document d. The *raw term frequency* $freq_{s,d}$ is normalized with the *maximal term frequency* $maxfreq_d$, i.e. the maximal number of occurrences of any s-term in d. As [1] points out, $maxfreq_d$ is bounded by the maximal number of occurrences of any element name or "flat" term in d. In the second definition, D^t is the set of logical documents of type t, i.e. with the same label t as the query root. The *inverse document frequency* idf_s^t is defined in terms of the number $|D^t|$ of logical documents and the number df_s^t of logical documents in D^t containing the structured term s. Thus only logical documents of a particular type specified in the query (e.g., section in Fig. 1) contribute to the inverse document frequency. Both $tf_{s,d}$ and idf_s^t together determine the weight $w_{s,d}^t$ of a given term s in a given logical document d of type t, as defined above.

Computation of relevance scores. Finally, each document d of type t is conceptually described by a document vector $\underline{d}$ consisting of term weights $w_{s,d}^t$ for all terms s. The similarity ϱ of a document d w.r.t. to a query q is determined by the dot product $\varrho_{d,q} := \underline{d} \bullet \underline{q}$ where $\underline{q}$ is the vector of all query term weights (0 for s-terms not contained in q). Note that there is no need to compute all document vectors and store them at indexing time. Instead only those term weights which contribute to the final result are calculated during query evaluation.

3 Implementation

We integrated the s-term vector space model with the retrieval system X^2 [14,15], which uses a *Content-Aware DataGuide (CADG)* [10,9] as path index for efficiently computing *Complete Answer Aggregates (CAA)* [16,17], a data structure for structured query results. Section 3.1 describes how the CADG and CAA were adapted for s-term evaluation and summarizes the query formalism, as well as necessary modifications to the original ranking model. Based on these preliminaries, Sect. 3.2 then discusses the bottom-up tree matching algorithm replacing the original algorithm used by X^2. Section 3.3 describes the computation of relevance scores for logical documents. Section 3.4 sketches further features of our implementation extending both the X^2 system and the original s-term model.

3.1 Preliminaries

Tree query language. In the query formalism used by X^2, queries are trees consisting of labelled nodes. There are *structural* query nodes, which are matched by document nodes with a suitable label, and *textual* query nodes specifying keyword constraints. A path in the query tree consists of a sequence of structural nodes and (possibly) a single textual leaf containing "flat" search terms. Edges between query nodes may be either *rigid* or *soft*, corresponding to a parent/child or ancestor/descendant relation, respectively. Figure 1 depicts a query tree with four structural and two textual nodes, linked by rigid edges (solid lines). The original s-term model, which ignores the parent/child relation, is easily adapted to the distinction of soft and rigid edges.

Structural query nodes may be labelled with any number of alternative element names, or else a wildcard matching any element name. Textual query nodes may specify more than one search term in a logical disjunction or conjunction. A conjunction is either unordered or ordered. In the latter case, an optional minimal and maximal token distance may be specified for any two consecutive terms. Section 3.4 describes order and distance constraints in more detail. As a special case, the implementation of phrase search as required by the NEXI query language [18] is built upon this feature. To support another NEXI construct which was missing in X^2, we integrated Boolean expressions over sibling query nodes. Allowing for partial s-term matches, this affects the way occurrences are counted, as explained in Sect. 3.4.

IR-CADG index. We slightly extended the original CADG index [10] used by X^2 to obtain an *Integrated Ranking CADG (IR-CADG)* for the s-term vector space model. Similar adaptions of the CADG index to other ranking models [4,3,6,7] are described in previous work [9]. Figure 2 *(b)* and *(c)* depict the data structures of the IR-CADG for the sample document in *(a)*, whose leaf nodes contain one or more occurrences of different "flat" terms. The index consists of an index tree *(b)*, residing entirely in main memory, and a *Content/Annotation Table (CA Table)* stored in a relational database system *(c)*. As can be seen in the figure, a single path in the index tree – e.g., the one leading to index node #2 in *(b)* – represents all identical label paths in the documents – in this case, the two book/section/para paths reaching the document nodes &2 and &4 in *(a)*. (We say that these document nodes are *referenced by* #2.) Compared to the document tree, the index tree therefore has a path structure which is typically extremely small and far less redundant. This motivates its use as a compact structural summary for schema browsing and path matching [19,14].

Keywords are indexed in the CA Table *(c)*, which maps a given index node ID, representing a label path, and a "flat" term to the list of document nodes with that same label path which contain occurrences of that same term. Unlike the original CADG, the IR-CADG for the s-term vector space model also records how often the term occurs in the document node. This node-specific occurrence count, which we henceforth refer to as the *local term frequency* tf^{loc}, is stored with each document node ID in the CA Table (in Fig. 2 *(c)*, the integers in curly braces). Section 3.3 explains how raw term frequencies are computed from the local term frequencies in the CA Table. During index creation, for each document node being indexed the maximal number of occurrences of any element name ($maxfreq^{label}$) and any "flat" term ($maxfreq^{term}$) in its subtree is calculated. The values are needed for normalizing the raw term frequency (see Sect. 3.3). Since X^2 internally uses a *node table* for storing document-node specific information (such as byte offsets in XML source files etc.), we simply add columns for $maxfreq^{label}$ and $maxfreq^{term}$ to the node table.

Complete Answer Aggregates. A *Complete Answer Aggregate (CAA)* is a compact data structure for representing the complete set of answers (document subtrees) retrieved in response to a structured query. (Its properties are analyzed in [16], along with an algorithm for computing CAAs in polynomial time.) As shown in Fig. 3, a CAA A_q has the same overall structure (shaded edges) as the corresponding tree query q (see Fig. 1), representing each structural or textual query node by a dedicated *slot* containing that query node's matches. For instance, in Fig. 3 the document node &6 is the only match to the query node labelled caption in Fig. 1, whereas the *"IR"* node has two matches (&2 and &4). Besides document nodes, the CAA temporarily stores pointers to index nodes during query evaluation (omitted in the figure).

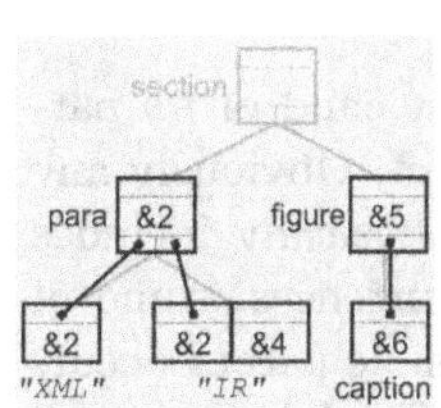

Fig. 3. CAA for the query in Fig. 1

Unlike flat lists of answer documents in traditional IR, CAAs provide a structured view on the matching subtrees in the document collection. As shown e.g. in the lower left part of Fig. 3, document nodes in different slots are typically linked to each other (black edges), reflecting (part of) the relations in their tree neighbourhood. In exact (non-ranked) retrieval, from each match in a slot of the CAA at least one match can be reached in each of the other slots by following these links. This is because a subtree of the document collection which does not comprise matches to all query nodes fails to satisfy the full set of query constraints, therefore being inadmissible in exact retrieval. By contrast, our implementation of the tree matching algorithm with s-term ranking (see Sect. 3.2) may produce partly filled CAAs like the one shown in Fig. 3 which contains only document subtrees matching the smaller s-terms s_1 to s_5, but no match to the root s_0.

In the following, the term *logical document root* refers to all document nodes in the set D^t. The index nodes referencing any such document node are called *logical index roots*.

3.2 Tree Matching Algorithm

The following tree matching algorithm computes a modified CAA as described above. Occurrences of smaller s-terms are obtained before those of larger s-terms in a bottom-up strategy. This is preferable to a top-down strategy since occurrences of a complex s-term invariably include occurrences of all subterms of that s-term in the document collection. From these subterm occurrences the occurrences of more complex s-terms can easily be derived in a step-wise process.

The core of the s-term tree matching algorithm is given in Listing 1. The procedure *evalSTerm* visits all nodes in the query tree in a depth-first traversal, recursively processing the subtrees of complex s-terms (lines 18 to 20). When a query leaf is reached, recursion halts and the occurrences of the corresponding leaf s-term in the documents are fetched from disk (*occurrence fetching*, line 24), along with their respective local term frequencies tf^{loc} (see the previous subsection). The CADG allows textual leaves representing "flat" terms and structural leaves representing element names to be treated alike, as postulated in [1]. All fetched document nodes are stored in the CAA slot corresponding to the query leaf, together with pointers to (1) their referencing index node and (2) the lowest of their logical index roots (as defined above; there may be multiple logical document and index roots in case of a recursive schema). The logical document and index roots are fetched once before the recursive matching procedure is called.

At this point the occurrences of the current s-term need to be propagated upwards along the query path in order to collect a set of candidate occurrences for the parent query node (*path matching*, line 29), or else to verify existing ones (*path joining*, line 31). In the following we assume that query nodes are processed in preorder. Different query plans (based e.g. on the selectivity of terms or labels associated with the query nodes) are ignored for the sake of simplicity.

Path matching. If the current query node r is the leftmost child of its parent r_p, no candidate occurrences for r_p have been collected yet. Obviously any occurrence of the parent s-term (the s-term rooted at r_p) physically includes occurrences of all child s-terms below r_p . These child occurrences, some of which are already known in the incarnation for r, hint at possible parent occurrences yet to be confirmed (so-called *occurrence candidates*). Candidates are all matches to the parent query node which are ancestors (in case of a soft edge, or parents for a rigid edge) of a child occurrence in the same logical document. The label and level constraints involved are first checked in the index (remember each child occurrence comes with its referencing index node and lowest logical index root). Only for ancestor (parent) index nodes which are descendants of the lowest logical index root and match the parent query node, the corresponding ancestor (parent) document nodes are determined and passed back to the calling incarnation. If document nodes must be fetched from disk, this may save many needless I/O operations for nodes which do not match the parent query node. Along with the referencing index nodes, the occurrence candidates for the parent query node are stored in the CAA before undergoing path joining and further upward propagation and finally producing the occurrences of the root s-term s_0.

Path joining. When visiting child nodes other than the leftmost one, a previous path matching step has already collected candidate occurrences for the parent query node r_p, some of which may not contain occurrences of the current child r'. Ruling out these false candidates is the aim of the path joining step (unless

```
// evalSTerm: recursively evaluates an s-term
// → r: the root query node of the s-term to be evaluated
// → i: the IR-CADG to be used for evaluation
// ⇄ A: the CAA holding the query result
proc evalSTerm (r: QueryNode, i: IR-CADG, A: CAA)

  // get hold of the parent query node and slot
  r_p := the parent of r
  a_p := the slot corresponding to s_p in A

  // create a new slot for r in A
  a := a new slot corresponding to r in A
  a.parent := a_p

  // recursively process inner s-terms
  C := r.children
  if C = ∅ then
    for all r_c ∈ C do
      call evalSTerm (r_c, i, A)
    end for

  // recursion anchor: process leaf s-terms
  else
    call i.fetchOccurrences (r, a)
  end if

  // trigger path matching or joining
  if r is the leftmost child of r_p then
    call matchPath (r_p, a_p, r, a, i, A)
  else
    call joinPath (r_p, a_p, r, a, i, A)
  end if

end proc
```

Listing 1. Recursive s-term evaluation

Boolean child constraints are enabled, see Sect. 3.4). The candidates for r_p to be kept are those which have at least one descendant (in case of a soft edge, or child for a rigid edge) among the occurrences of r'. Again, this condition is checked for the corresponding index nodes first, which may save the manipulation and comparison of huge sets of document nodes. Only if an index node referencing occurrence candidates of the parent s-term has a descendant (child) among the index nodes referencing occurrences of the current child s-term, the corresponding occurrence candidate sets are compared to rule out some of the parent candidates. When the last child query node has been processed, the remaining parent candidates are confirmed as occurrences of the parent s-term, ready to enter a new propagation phase until the query root is reached.

3.3 Relevance Computation

When tree matching is over, the computed CAA contains the occurrences of all s-terms in the query, as mentioned in Sect. 3.1. Each occurrence e of a "flat" s-term s' comes with its local term frequency $tf^{loc}_{s',e}$ as defined in Sect. 3.1. For s-terms s'' involving node labels, $tf^{loc}_{s'',e}$ is fixed to 1 in the original model since any such s-term can occur only once in the same document node (the occurrence being defined as the document node itself, see Sect. 2.1). A modified definition of $tf^{loc}_{s'',e}$ for the use with Boolean child constraints is given in Sect. 3.4. Note that the root slot of the CAA contains only logical document roots which are occurrences of the root s-term (i.e. the whole query tree), a subset of the set D^t fetched for tree matching. However, relevance scores are computed for all members of D^t since logical documents containing only smaller s-terms are also part of the query result, even though their roots are missing in the CAA.

According to Sect. 2.2, the weight $w^t_{s,d}$ quantifying the relevance of an s-term s w.r.t. a document d of type t, is calculated from the following four frequencies:

$$\begin{aligned} \mathit{freq}_{s,d} &: \text{number of occurrences of } s \text{ in } d \\ \mathit{maxfreq}_d &: \text{max. number of occurrences of any term in } d \\ |D^t| &: \text{number of logical documents of type } t \\ \mathit{df}_s &: \text{number of logical documents of type } t \text{ containing occurrences of } s \end{aligned}$$

While $|D^t|$ is immediately available, determining the value of $\mathit{maxfreq}_d = max(\mathit{maxfreq}_d^{term}, \mathit{maxfreq}_d^{label})$ requires access to the node table, but only for those logical document roots d' with $\mathit{freq}_{s,d'} > 0$. The raw term frequencies *freq* are computed in a linear ancestor/descendant join of all logical document roots and all s-term occurrences from the CAA (see below). An array F of frequency vectors iteratively accumulates the *freq* values for all terms and documents during the join. Let F_s denote the frequency vector for term s and $F_{s,d}$ its component for the logical document root d. For each pair $\langle d, e\rangle$ joining d with a descendant e of d containing an occurrence of the s-term s, the term frequency $F_{s,d}$ is incremented by $tf^{loc}_{s,e}$. After the join, F contains a raw term frequency $\mathit{freq}_{s,d}$ for each s-term s and each document d it occurs in. The document frequency df_s equals the length of the frequency vector F_s.

3.4 Further Features

Linear ancestor/descendant join. As explained in Sect. 3.3, the computation of term weights involves a join of logical document roots and s-term occurrences. We implemented a $|q|$-way join, where $|q|$ is the number of s-terms in the query q, with an ancestor stack similar to the *stack-tree join* proposed in [12]. The stack serves to keep track of "active" members of the list of potential ancestors, whose subtree may contain some of the potential descendants to be checked next. This technique guarantees that the join is performed in time linear in the number of potential ancestor and descendant nodes involved, i.e. $\mathcal{O}(|D^t| + |A_q|)$ where $|A_q|$ is the number of occurrences stored in the aggregate A_q.

Target elements. In Sect. 2.1, the set of answers to a structured query q is defined as a subset of the set of logical documents induced by the label of $root(q)$. In some cases, however, it may be more useful to retrieve specific parts of logical documents while keeping the query-specific document concept intact. In our implementation, we extended the original s-term model by introducing the notion of a *target element*, which specifies which kind of document nodes are to be retrieved as answers to a given query q. This is done by marking a single node in the query tree for q as being the target element $target(q)$ of q. As a consequence, matches to the target element are either logical document roots or descendants of a logical document root. Note that the use of target elements typically makes the query result more specific; e.g., the user may be given individual paragraphs in response to a query which otherwise returns articles.

As a special case, the query root $root(q)$ and the target element $target(q)$ may be identical, such that entire logical document are retrieved as described before. Otherwise the query is evaluated as follows. First the subtree q_{target} of q rooted at $target(q)$ is evaluated in isolation, i.e. with $target(q)$ as root node specifying "logical subdocuments" to be retrieved in response to this part of the original query q. Ranking of the matches to $target(q)$ takes place as described in Sect. 3.3. In a second step, the remaining part q_{root} of q (i.e., the entire query tree except the subtree rooted at $target(q)$) is evaluated in the same way. During evaluation, each match e to $target(q)$ is associated with the set R_e of roots of logical documents containing e. As mentioned in the previous paragraph, $R_e \neq \emptyset$ for all such occurrences of the target element. Finally, the relevances score of any given match e to $target(q)$ computed in the first step is *biased* with the relevance scores of all elements in R_e, in order to capture both the relevance of e w.r.t. q_{target} and the relevance of the containing logical document(s) w.r.t. q_{root}. Many biasing methods are conceivable; currently we simply calculate the relevance of an occurrence e of $target(q)$ w.r.t. q as $\varrho_{e,q} := \varrho_{e,q_{target}} \cdot \sum_{e' \in R_e} \varrho_{e',q_{root}}$. The effectiveness of this extension to the original s-term model depends largely on the choice of suitable target elements, an issue which we have not yet examined in detail.

Boolean constraints on tree queries. Any complex s-term, represented by an inner node r in the query tree, may be constrained by an arbitrarily nested Boolean expression involving (1) atoms representing the smaller s-terms rooted at r's child nodes and (2) the Boolean operators $\{\wedge, \vee, \neg\}$. Replacing the default conjunctive interpretation of child query nodes in tree matching, the Boolean constraints allow individual s-terms to be treated as optional, alternative, or negated. For instance, if the root of the query tree in Fig. 1 is constrained by the expression $(s_1 \vee s_2)$, the s-term s_0 is matched by any subtree of the document tree in Fig. 2 *(a)* where either s_1 or s_2 occurs (or both). The root slot of the CAA in Fig. 3 then contains two occurrences of s_0, namely &1 and &3.

The semantics of Boolean child constraints entails modifications of both the ranking model (see next paragraph) and the tree matching algorithm described in Sect. 3.2. During evaluation of an s-term s, the path join procedure *joinPath* is only called when the child constraint β_s associated with s is a simple conjunction of child atoms (the default tree matching behaviour, see line 31 in Listing 1). Otherwise matches to all child subtrees below s are stored in the CAA by repeated calls to *matchPath*, as in line 29 of Listing 1. The child constraint β_s is evaluated after all children of s have been processed, i.e. immediately below line 20 in the incarnation for $r = s$, unless (1) β_s is a simple conjunction of child atoms, which is catered for by the calls to *joinPath*, or (2) β_s is a simple disjunction of child atoms, in which case all (even partial) occurrences stored in the slot a corresponding to r trivially match s. If none of these conditions holds, β_s is evaluated recursively for each occurrence in a. Subexpression involving a Boolean operator are interpreted recursively in the obvious way. As recursion anchor, an atom representing a child s-term s_c of s evaluates to $\top$ iff the current occurrence of s in a is linked to one or more occurrences of s_c in the corresponding child slot of a.

As mentioned in Sect. 3.3, if an s-term s involving node labels occurs in a document node e, its local term frequency $tf^{loc}_{s,e}$ is fixed to 1 in the original s-term model. By contrast, when using Boolean child constraints we would like to quantify how close a – possibly partial – occurrence matches s. To this end, we redefine the local term frequency $tf^{loc}_{s,e}$ to be either 1 (see above) or equal to the number of atoms in β_s evaluating to $\top$ for e, whatever value is greater. For instance, consider two occurrences e, e' of s and $\beta_s = (s_1 \vee s_2)$ for child terms s_1, s_2 of s. Assuming that only the subtree rooted at e contains occurrences of both s_1 and s_2, $tf^{loc}_{s,e} > tf^{loc}_{s,e'}$ according to the new definition, which accounts for the fact that e satisfies more (non-Boolean) constraints specified by s. As a special case, all full occurrences of s (i.e., those which would satisfy a Boolean constraint of the form $(s_1 \wedge \ldots \wedge s_j)$ where j is the number of children of s) have the same local term frequency. In this sense, our adaption of the s-term model to Boolean child constraints generalizes the original model.

Order/distance constraints on keyword conjunctions. We extended the query language of the X^2 system to support order and distance constraints on binary conjunctions of "flat" terms specified in a textual query node. For instance, the expression `"XML [1,3] node"` requires matching document nodes to contain an occurrence of the keyword *"XML"*, followed by an occurrence of the keyword *"node"*, such that both occurrences are separated by at most two tokens. Either value in the `[`*min*`,`*max*`]` pair may be omitted; as special cases, `"XML [,] node"` specifies an ordered conjunction without distance constraints, and `"XML node"` is a shorthand for `"XML [1,1] node"` (i.e., a simple phrase search for directly adjacent tokens). Note that distance constraints in X^2 queries imply that the conjunction of terms is ordered. By contrast `"XML , node"` specifies an unordered conjunction of both terms (with arbitrary distance). Expressions of either type (i.e., "s_1 `[`*min*`,`*max*`]` s_2" and "s_1 `,` s_2") may be chained together, implicitly forming a left-associative nested conjunction. The expression `"XML [,3] node , IR [5,] rank"`, e.g., selects document nodes containing (1) occurrences of *"XML"* and *"node"* in that order, separated by at most two tokens, and (2) an occurrence of *"IR"* anywhere in the textual content (possibly even between the former two occurrences), and (3) an occurrence of *"rank"* at least four tokens after the rightmost of the former three occurrences.

Since order and distance constraints apply only to term occurrences within the same document node, they are easily integrated with the index procedure *fetchOccurrences*. To this end, each occurrence of a "flat" term s in a document node e is associated with a list of *token position offsets* in the CA Table, omitted in Fig. 2 *(c)*, which indicate the number of tokens preceding the first occurrence of s in e as well as the number of tokens between any two consecutive occurrences of s in e. As an example, consider a leaf node whose textual content is *"to be or not to be"*. The respective lists of token position offsets of all keywords are: *"to"* $\langle 1, 4\rangle$, *"be"* $\langle 2, 4\rangle$, *"or"* $\langle 3\rangle$, and *"not"* $\langle 4\rangle$. (For the sake of the example, assume these terms are not treated as stop-words.) If a term occurs directly after a stop-word (which is not stored in the CA Table) or after a child node (in case of mixed content), the token position of that occurrence is incremented by one to avoid erroneous phrase matching.[2]

When matching a binary conjunction of the "flat" terms s_1 and s_2, two CA Table entries are intersected to identify all nodes containing co-occurrences of both terms. Order and distance constraints are checked on the two lists of token position offsets associated with any document node in the intersection. Those nodes satisfying the constraints for s_1 and s_2 keep only the list of token position offsets for the second term, reduced to the occurrences which justify the match. Thus in a nested expression involving a third term s_3, the constraint check for the subsequent binary conjunction operates on (1) a list of token position offsets representing matches to the conjunction of s_1 and s_2 and (2) a list of token position offsets for s_3. This corresponds to the aforementioned left-associative interpretation of chained term conjunctions.

4 Experiments and Evaluation

We evaluated our implementation of the s-term vector space model at the third workshop of the *Initiative for the Evaluation of XML Retrieval (INEX)* [2] in 2004. Queries in both the *Vague Content And Structure (VCAS)* and *Content Only (CO)* tracks were submitted to X^2 after automatic translation into the system's query language. As general results, we observe that (1) the model performs reasonably well for structured queries (VCAS), occupying a position 26 among the 52 participants (position 12 in the best case), and (2) there is considerable room for optimizations which have not been considered yet. The plots in Fig. 4 show the recall/precision graph for the s-term vector space model (black line) and all other approaches (shaded lines). The left plot averages over all quantisation methods, whereas the right plot shows only the method with the best s-term model performance (*RPng with overlap and strict quantisation*).

[2] For instance, the expression `"XML node"` is matched neither by *"XML and node"* nor by *"XML <i>root</i> node"*. Obviously, phrase matching across mixed content may be desirable in cases such as *"XML <br/> node"*.

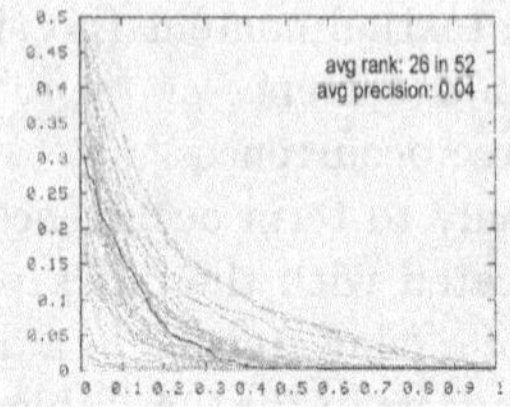

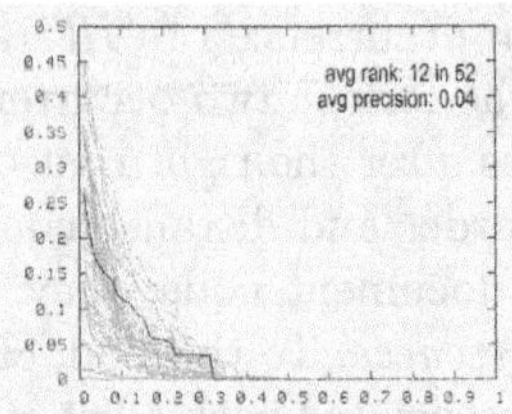

Fig. 4. VCAS performance (left: avg. over all quantisations; right: best case)

Fixed vs. flexible target element. Among the features presented in Sect. 3.4, the parameter with the greatest impact on ranking performance is the choice of the target element. In the course of this work we tested two simple strategies: either the target element is fixed to be identical with the query root (*fixed target element*), or the target element is determined in an XPath-style as the lowest structural query node outside predicates (*semi-flexible target element*). Figure 5 illustrates how performance degradates when only logical documents are returned as answers to VCAS queries (left column), compared to a semi-flexible choice of the target element (right column). While in the average over all quantisation methods the difference is nine ranks, the impact is even higher (16 positions) for the *s3e32* quantisation which favours answers with high specificity (not shown in the figure). As could be expected, answers which are constantly at the article level are often fairly unspecific, including many irrelevant nodes.

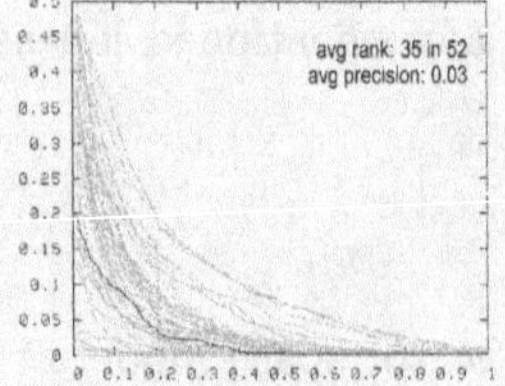

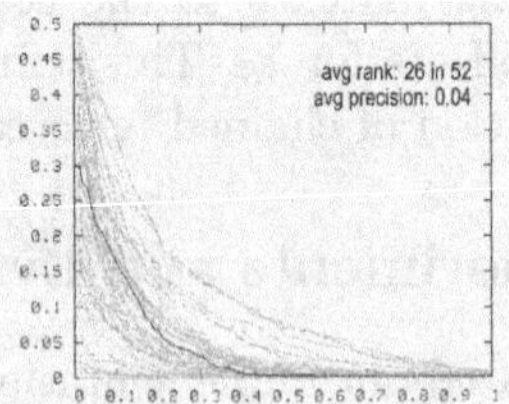

Fig. 5. Fixed vs. flexible target element (VCAS)

Structured vs. flat retrieval. Finally, the plots in Fig. 6 compare the performance of the s-term vector space model in the VCAS and CO tracks. Note that both plots are based on results for fixed target elements only, which explains the low overall precision of the s-term results. For CO queries, the target element was fixed to an article node containing the actual "flat" query. As can be seen in the right plot, the s-term model performs worse than almost 75% of all participants of the CO track, whereas in structured document retrieval (VCAS) it is closer to two thirds even without a flexible target element. This is not astounding given that the core concept of the model, the s-term, relies on the structure of the query. Obviously, in the absence of structural hints as to which elements the user expects, the choice of the target element needs dedicated strategies.

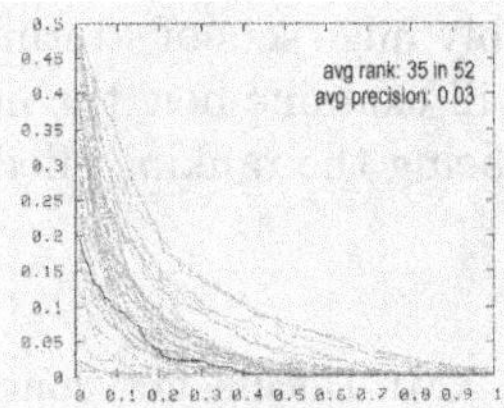

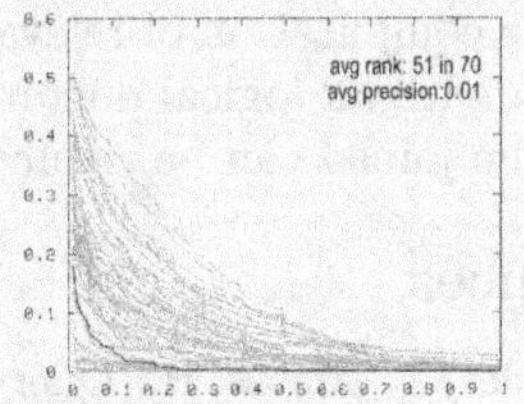

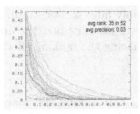

Fig. 6. Structured (VCAS) vs. flat (CO) retrieval

5 Related Work

Previous work [9] describes in detail how to adapt the CADG index to four models for structured documents [4,3,6,7]. In Sect. 3.1 of this work the CADG is modified along these lines in order to obtain an IR-CADG for the s-term model. In terms of the *Path/Term/Node (PTN) hierarchy* proposed in [9], which specifies how an index structure stores information for relevance ranking, the IR-CADG described in Sect. 3.1 contains only *Path/Term/Node*-specific information.

Ranking models have different concepts of *idf* for structured documents, an issue related to the document boundary problem (Sect. 1). [9] distinguishes a *structured idf*, which counts only documents satisfying structural *and* textual constraints, and a strictly term-specific *flat idf*. The s-term model, with its definition of logical documents, features a structured *idf*. In [9] it is argued that under certain circumstances, this is closer to the user's information need.

6 Conclusion and Future Work

In this work, we extended the s-term vector space model [1] for ranked retrieval of structured documents, with a number of useful features such as Boolean constraints on tree queries, order and distance constraints on search terms (including phrase search), and the specification of target elements. We also described data structures and algorithms for the retrieval and ranking of structured documents using the s-term model in combination with the IR-CADG index [9,10] and showed how the adaption of state-of-the-art techniques for exact retrieval can complement our work, thus integrating effective ranking with efficient retrieval. Finally, we evaluated the ranking performance of our s-term implementation at INEX 2004 [2]. The results show that while the model performs reasonably well for Vague Content And Structure (VCAS) queries in these first tests, there is also a fair potential for optimization, especially for Content Only (CO) queries.

Future work on the model and the implementation may include, among others, a truly *flexible target element* definition which dynamically determines document nodes to be retrieved as query results, even when no hints are given in the query, and a substantial simplification of the s-term model in order to reduce the computational effort of relevance ranking. While the former issue targets the effectiveness of the model, the latter is motivated by the observation that during the computation of relevance scores possibly huge sets of s-term matches are joined with all logical document roots. We will examine how the number of nodes to be joined can be reduced without sacrificing the ranking effectiveness.

References

1. Schlieder, T., Meuss, H.: Querying and Ranking XML Documents. Journal of the American Society for Information Science and Technology **53** (2002)
2. INEX: Initiative for the Evaluation of XML Retrieval. Available at `http://inex.is.informatik.uni-duisburg.de:2004` (2004)
3. Fuhr, N., Großjohann, K.: XIRQL: A Query Language for Information Retrieval in XML Documents. In: Research and Development in Information Retrieval. (2001)
4. Wolff, J.E., Flörke, H., Cremers, A.B.: Searching and Browsing Collections of Structural Information. In: Proc. IEEE Forum on Research and Technology Advances in Digital Libraries. (2000)
5. Schlieder, T.: Similarity Search in XML Data using Cost-Based Query Transformations. In: Proc. 4th Intern. Workshop on the Web and Databases. (2001)
6. Theobald, A., Weikum, G.: The Index-Based XXL Search Engine for Querying XML Data with Relevance Ranking. In: Proc. 8th Int. Conf. on Extending Database Technology. (2002)
7. Shin, D., Jang, H., Jin, H.: BUS: An Effective Indexing and Retrieval Scheme in Structured Documents. In: Proc. 3rd ACM Int. Conf. on Digital Libraries. (1998)
8. Salton, G.: The SMART Retrieval System – Experiments in Automatic Document Processing. Prentice Hall Inc., Englewood Cliffs, NJ. (1971)
9. Weigel, F., Meuss, H., Schulz, K.U., Bry, F.: Content and Structure in Indexing and Ranking XML. In: Proc. 7th Int. Workshop on the Web and Databases. (2004)
10. Weigel, F., Meuss, H., Bry, F., Schulz, K.U.: Content-Aware DataGuides: Interleaving IR and DB Indexing Techniques for Efficient Retrieval of Textual XML Data. In: Proc. 26th European Conf. on Information Retrieval. (2004)
11. Sacks-Davis, R., Arnold-Moore, T., Zobel, J.: Database Systems for Structured Documents. In: Proc. Int. Symposium on Advanced Database Technologies and Their Integration. (1994)
12. Al-Khalifa, S., Jagadish, H.V., Koudas, N., Patel, J.M., Srivastava, D., Wu, Y.: Structural Joins: A Primitive for Efficient XML Query Pattern Matching. In: Proc. 18th IEEE Int. Conf. on Data Engineering. (2002)
13. Kilpeläinen, P.: Tree Matching Problems with Applications to Structured Text Databases. PhD thesis, University of Helsinki (1992)
14. Meuss, H., Schulz, K.U., Weigel, F., Leonardi, S., Bry, F.: Visual Exploration and Retrieval of XML Document Collections with the Generic System X^2. Journal of Digital Libraries, Special Issue on Information Visualization Interfaces (2004)
15. Meuss, H.: Logical Tree Matching with Complete Answer Aggregates for Retrieving Structured Documents. PhD thesis, University of Munich (2000)
16. Meuss, H., Schulz, K.U.: Complete Answer Aggregates for Tree-like Databases: A Novel Approach to Combine Querying and Navigation. ACM Transactions on Information Systems **19** (2001)
17. Meuss, H., Schulz, K., Bry, F.: Towards Aggregated Answers for Semistructured Data. In: Proc. 8th Int. Conf. on Database Theory. (2001)
18. Trotman, A., Sigurbjörnsson, B.: Narrowed Extended XPath I (2004)
19. Goldman, R., Widom, J.: DataGuides: Enabling Query Formulation and Optimization in Semistructured Databases. In: Proc. 23rd Int. Conf. on Very Large Data Bases. (1997)

Merging XML Indices

Gianni Amati, Claudio Carpineto, and Giovanni Romano

Fondazione Ugo Bordoni,
Via Baldassarre Castiglione 59, 00142, Rome, Italy
{gba, carpinet, romano}@fub.it

Abstract. Using separate indices for each element and merging their results has proven to be a feasible way of performing XML element retrieval; however, there has been little work on evaluating how the main method parameters affect the results. We study the effect of using different weighting models for computing rankings at the single index level and using different merging techniques for combining such rankings. Our main findings are that (i) there are large variations on retrieval effectiveness when choosing different techniques for weighting and merging, with performance gains up to 102%, and (ii) although there does not seem to be any best weighting model, some merging schemes perform clearly better than others.

1 Introduction

We focus on the Content Only (CO) task and try to extend information retrieval (IR) techniques to deal with XML documents. As each XML document is formed by several nested elements and the goal is to retrieve the most relevant elements, IR ranking models must be expanded with element level statistics. However, at INEX 2003, Mass and Mandelbrod [8] showed that, for XML documents, the use of classical IR statistics involving element and term frequencies is not straightforward and may easily lead to inconsistencies and errors, due to the nesting of elements.

To overcome this problem, one can compute weights at the most specific level and propagate such weights upwards using augmentation factors [5]. Another approach, which does not rely on user parameters, is to use a separate index for each type of elements and compute rankings at the single index level. Such rankings are then merged to return a combined result [8].

In this paper we aim at experimenting with the latter approach, extending previous work in two directions. Our goal is to study whether the choice of the weighting model and the merging technique affect the retrieval performance of XML indices in the INEX environment, and to evaluate relative merits and drawbacks of different parameter choices.

We consider three weighting models with a different theoretical background that have proved their effectiveness on a number of tasks and collections. The three models are deviation from randomness [3], Okapi [12], and statistical language modeling [14].

N. Fuhr et al. (Eds.): INEX 2004, LNCS 3493, pp. 253–260, 2005.

The merging problem is tackled by combining the relevance scores associated with each index through different normalization techniques. We consider five schemes; namely, normalization by query score, maximum score, standard norm, sum norm, and Z-score norm.

In the following we first present the weighting models and the normalization schemes. Then we describe the experimental setting and discuss the results. Finally, we provide some conclusions.

2 Weighting Models

For the ease of clarity and comparison, the document ranking produced by each weighting model is represented using the same general expression, namely as the product of a document-based term weight by a query-based term weight:

$$sim(q,d) = \sum_{t \in q \wedge d} w_{t,d} \cdot w_{t,q}$$

Before giving the expressions for $w_{t,d}$ and $w_{t,q}$ for each weighting model, we report the complete list of variables that will be used:

f_t	the number of occurrences of term t in the collection
$f_{t,d}$	the number of occurrences of term t in document d
$f_{t,q}$	the number of occurrences of term t in query q
n_t	the number of documents in which term t occurs
D	the number of documents in the collection
λ_t	the ratio between f_t and D
T	the number of terms in the collection
l_d	the length of document d
l_q	the length of query q
avr_l_d	the average length of documents in the collection

2.1 Okapi

To describe Okapi, we use the expression given in [12]. This formula has been used by most participants in TREC and CLEF over the last years.

$$w_{t,d} = \frac{(k_1+1) \cdot f_{t,d}}{k_1 \cdot \left[(1-b) + b\,\frac{l_d}{avr\_l_d}\right] + f_{t,d}}$$

$$w_{t,q} = \frac{(k_3+1) \cdot f_{t,q}}{k_3 + f_{t,q}} \cdot \log_2 \frac{D - n_t + 0.5}{n_t + 0.5}$$

2.2 Statistical Language Modeling (SLM)

The statistical language modeling approach has been proposed in several papers, with many variants (e.g., [7], [10]). Here we use the expression given in [14], with Dirichlet smoothing.

$$w_{t,d} = \log_2 \frac{f_{t,d} + \mu\frac{f_t}{T}}{l_d + \mu} - \log_2 \frac{\mu}{l_d + \mu} - \log_2 \frac{f_t}{T} + \frac{l_q}{|q \wedge d|} \cdot \log_2 \frac{\mu}{l_d + \mu}$$

$$w_{t,q} = f_{t,q}$$

2.3 Deviation from Randomness (DFR)

Deviation from randomness has been successfully used at TREC, for the Web track [1], and CLEF , for the monolingual tasks [2]. We use the model GL2 and it is best described in [3].

$$w_{t,d} = \left(\log_2(1 + \lambda_t) + f^*_{t,d} \cdot \log_2 \frac{1+\lambda_t}{\lambda_t}\right) \cdot \frac{f_t + 1}{n_t \cdot (f^*_{t,d} + 1)}$$

$$w_{t,q} = f_{t,q}$$

with

$$f^*_{t,d} = f_{t,d} \cdot \log_2 \left(1 + \frac{c \cdot avr\_l_d}{l_d}\right)$$

The parameter c can be set automatically, as described by He and Ounis [6].

3 Merging Methods

Most of IR work on method combination has focused on merging multiple rankings with overlapping documents, whereas combining disjoint rankings has not received much attention. If training information is available, one can learn cut-off values for each ranking [13] or give a value to each index [4]. As in this case we did not have access to prior data (this is our first participation in INEX), we use combination techniques that do not require such data.

One simple approach would be to combine the original scores into a large ranked list, without modifying the scores. However, such an approach would not work, due to the different scales of the scores yielded by each index. In fact, the relevance scores used in our experiments are not probabilities and the statistics on which they are based are relative to indices of varying size. Thus, the scores need to be normalized, and the merging problem essentially becomes a normalization problem.

Normalization can be done in different ways (see for instance [9]). We test five approaches, which feature different properties in terms of shift and scale invariance and outlier tolerance. Such approaches are detailed in the following.

3.1 Q

The raw scores of the elements retrieved in response to query Q by index i are divided by $sim(q, q)$, which is the score of the query itself (as if it were a document in the index) according to the weighting model of index i. This technique, denoted here by Q, has been used in [8].

3.2 Max

The raw scores are divided by the maximum score in the corresponding index. Note that each index will produce one element with normalized score = 1. In the combined ranking, these topmost elements are ordered according to their original value. This normalization scheme will be referred to as *Max.*

3.3 MinMax

This scheme consists of shifting the minimum raw score to zero and scaling the maximum to one, i.e.

$$\frac{score - minimum}{maximum - minimum}$$

This scheme will be denoted by *MinMax.*

3.4 Sum

A normalized score is obtained by shifting the minimum raw score to zero and the sample sum to one; i.e.,

$$\frac{score - minimum}{\sum_N scores \; - \; N \cdot minimum}$$

This scheme will be denoted by *Sum.*

3.5 Z-Score

This is the classical *standard score*, denoted *Z-score.* It is derived by subtracting the sample mean from raw scores and then dividing the difference by the sample standard deviation, i.e.,

$$\frac{score - mean}{\sigma}.$$

4 Experimental Setting

As also pointed out in [8], the great majority of highly relevant elements are taken from the set: {article, bdy, abs, sec, ss1, ss2, p, ip1}, because they represent more meaningful results for a query. We intended to build a separate index for each of these types; however, a bug in the program for building the indices of more specific types (i.e., paragraphs) and a tight schedule prevented us from doing so. In the experiments reported here we use only 5 types of elements: {article, abs, sec, ss1, ss2 }. Even the runs actually submitted by us to INEX for evaluation had the same limitation.

Each index was built as follows. We identifed the individual words occurring in the elements of interest, ignoring punctuation and case; thus, a strict single-word indexing was used. The system then performed word stopping and word stemming, using Porter algorithm [11].

At run time, we ran each INEX 2004 CO topic against all 5 indices and computed the ranking associated with each index. Only the title topic statement was considered. For each query and for each index, we then computed three rankings, one for each weighting model. The choice of the parameters involved in the weighting models was as follows.

DFR $c = 2$
Okapi $k_1 = 1.2$, $k_3 = 1000$, $b = 0.75$
SLM $\mu = 1000$

Then, for each query, we merged the index level rankings of each weighting model using the five normalization schemes described above.

5 Results

We computed in all 15 rankings, i.e., three weighting models times five normalization schemes. In order to evaluate the retrieval effectiveness, we focus on strict relevance; i.e., on highly exaustive and specific (E3S3) elements. This choice was partly motivated by the importance of this task for an XML information retrieval system, partly by the observation that a E3S3 relevance judgement may better reflect the will of the assessor rather than the rules enforced by the evaluation system, which were found to produce a proliferation of small irrelevant elements labeled as (partially) relevant.

The results are shown in Table 1; performance was measured using average precision averaged on the 25 topics with nonempty E3S3 elements.

Before discussing the results, we would like to make one general comment about the absolute value of the strict quantization figures at INEX 2004. Our impression is that the results have been penalized by a large number of elements that have probably been mistakenly labeled as strictly relevant (E3S3) for some topics. For instance, there are as many as 288 E3S3 "it" elements and 68 E3S3 "tmath" elements associated with one single topic. Also, the 55% of all E3S3 elements (i.e., 1429 out of 2589 elements) is associated with only two topics. Even though evaluation of precision may not be so much affected by these spurious elements, because they will probably not be highly ranked by the retrieval systems, this will definitely downweight the recall part of the evaluation measures.

Table 1. Average precision (strict quantization) by weighting method and by normalization scheme

	DFR	Okapi	SLM
Q	0.0695	0.0769	0.0927
Max	0.0903	0.0963	0.0931
MinMax	0.0853	0.0911	0.0848
Sum	0.0713	0.0806	0.0492
Z-score	0.1018	0.0987	0.0938

Turning to the relative behaviour of the different methods tested in the experiments, the results in Table 1 show that there was a huge variability in retrieval effectiveness. The worst performance was obtained by the pair SLM/Sum, with an average precision of 0.0492; the best performance by the pair DFR/Z-score, with an average precision of 0.1018 (+ 102%). Incidentally, the submitted runs were obtained using DFR with Q, with official scores very similar to that reported here (0.0695).

If we look at the behaviour of the weighting models when the normalization scheme is kept constant, we see that no weighting model clearly won. DFR achieved the best results for Z-score, Okapi for Max, MinMax, and Sum, and SLM for Q. In most cases (i.e., for Max, MinMax, and Z-score), the results were comparable.

The results for the normalization schemes reveal a more interesting pattern. The most important finding is that Z-score achieved the best performance for each weighting model, with notable performance improvements over the results obtained by the other normalization schemes using the same weighting model. In particular, for DFR, the average precision grows from 0.0695 with Q to 0.1018 with Z-score, and for Okapi, it grows from 0.0769 with Q to 0.0987 with Z-score.

The results in Table 1 also show that Max was consistently ranked as the second best normalization scheme for each weighting model, although with more comparable performance improvements than Z-score. The other three normalization schemes showed a mixed behaviour.

The results presented so far were obtained considering the full set of relevance judgements. As our system only deal with five types of elements, all the other relevant elements cannot be actually retrieved. So it may be interesting to see what happens if we remove from the relevance set all the elements other than those used by the system. This should give an idea about the results that this method might obtain if we expanded the number of indices to include at least the body and paragraph elements. On the other hand, it must be considered that not all indices are alike; chances are that there are proportionally fewer small elements (e.g., paragraphs) that are relevant, so it may be more difficult to find them.

If we consider only the elements dealt with by our system, we get 614 E3S3 elements (rather than 2589). In Table 2, we show the retrieval effectiveness of the weighting/merging methods relative to such a restricted set of E3S3 elements, in which only the elements {article, abs, sec, ss1, ss2 } have been kept.

If we compare the results in Table 1 with those in Table 2, we see that passing from unrestricted to restricted relevance judgements roughly doubles the retrieval performance. The improvement might seem smaller than one might expect by judging from the decreasing in the number of relevant elements. Consider that the system retrieves the same elements in the same order in both situations, so the change in average precision only depends on the different number of relevant elements per query. As this number roughly reduces to one fourth (from 2589 to 614), it may be somewhat surprising to see that the average precision just doubled, rather than becoming four times greater. In fact, we checked that most of the relevant elements other than those considered by our system are concentrated in a very small number of topics. For instance, 323 out of the 691 E3S3 paragraphs are associated with just one query.

The results in Table 2 confirm the main findings obtained for the unrestricted relevances. The main differences are that DFR achieved the best performance for two normalization schemes rather than for one and that the performance variations were slightly less marked.

Table 2. Average precision (strict quantization) by weighting method and by normalization scheme on the restricted relevances

	DFR	Okapi	SLM
Q	0.1352	0.1500	0.1673
Max	0.1716	0.1791	0.1651
MinMax	0.1594	0.1654	0.1479
Sum	0.1520	0.1517	0.0911
Z-score	0.2080	0.2033	0.1807

On the whole, our results suggest that while the different weighting models achieved comparable retrieval performance the normalization schemes differed considerably, with Z-score showing a superior performance. This raises the question of why Z-score worked better. One explanation is that Z-score is based on aggregate statistics, which are more robust (e.g., with respect to outliers). However, this is not completely satisfying, because Sum is also based on aggregate statistics and it did not score so well. A better understanding of why some methods perform better than others would probably require a deeper analysis of the ranking data.For instance, as standard scores are especially appropriate for data that are normally distributed, one can hypothesize that the ranking data follow this distribution.

Our results also suggest that certain combinations of weighting and merging work particularly well (e.g., DFR and Z-score) or particularly badly (e.g., SLM and Sum); an analysis of the mutual relationships between weighting models and merging schemes is another issue that deserves more investigation.

6 Conclusions

The main indication of our experiments is that there is much scope for improving the performance of XML retrieval based on separate indices. We showed that an appropriate choice of the weighting model and normalization scheme may greatly improve the retrieval effectiveness of this technique.

One direction for future work is to use more queries and evaluation measures, incorporating past statistics about distribution of relevant elements across element types to improve combination of results. As one shortcoming of using separate indices is that the relationships between the elements in different indices are not taken into account, future work will also consider how to discriminate between nested retrieval results.

References

1. Amati, G. , Carpineto, C., Romano, G.: FUB at TREC-10 Web Track: A Probabilistic Framework for Topic Relevance Term Weighting. In *Proceedings of the 10th Text REtrieval Conference (TREC-10), NIST Special Publication 500-250*, pages 182–191, Gaithersburg, MD, USA, 2001.
2. Amati, G. , Carpineto, C., Romano, G.: Comparing Weighting Models for Monolingual Information Retrieval. In *Working Notes for the CLEF 2003 Workshop*, pages 169–178, Trondheim, Norway, 2003.
3. Amati, G., van Rijsbergen, C. J.: Probabilistic Models of Information Retrieval Based on Measuring Divergence From Randomness. *ACM Transactions on Information Systems*, 20(4):357–389, 2002.
4. Callan, J. P., Lu, Z.,Croft, W. B.: Searching Distributed Collections with Inference Networks. In *Proceedings of the 18th Annual International ACM SIGIR Conference on Reasearch and Development in Information Retrieval*, pages 21–28, Seattle, Washington, USA, 1995.
5. Fuhr, N., GrossJohann, K.: XIRQL: A Query Language for Information Retrieval in XML Documents: In *Proceedings of SIGIR 2001*, pages 172–180, New Orleans, LA, USA,, 2001.
6. He, B., Ounis, I.: A Refined Term Frequency Normalisation Parameter Tuning Method by Measuring the Normalisation Effect. To appear in the 27th European Conference on Information Retrieval (ECIR 05).
7. Hiemstra, D., Kraaij, W.: Twenty-one at TREC-7: Ad Hoc, Cross-Language Track: In *Proceedings of the 7th Text Retrieval Conference (TREC-7), NIST Special Publication 500-242*, pages 227–238, Gaithersburg, MD, USA, 1998.
8. Mass, Y., Mandelbrod, M.: Retrieving the Most Relevant XML Components: In *Proceedings of the INEX 2003 Worksop*, pages 53–58, Schloss Dagsthul, Germany, 2003.
9. Montague, M., Aslam, J.: Relevance Score Normalization for Metasearch: In *Proceedings of the 10th International ACM Conference on Information, Knowledge Management*, pages 427–433, Atlanta, Georgia, USA, 2001.
10. Ponte, J., Croft, W. B.: A Language Modeling Approach to Information Retrieval. In *Proceedings of the 21st Annual International ACM SIGIR Conference on Reasearch, Development in Information Retrieval*, pages 275–281, 1998.
11. Porter, M. F.: An Algorithm for Suffix Stripping. *Program*, 14:130–137, 1980.
12. Robertson, S. E., Walker, S., Beaulieu, M. M.: Okapi at TREC-7: Automatic Ad Hoc, Filtering, VLC, and Interactive track. In *Proceedings of the 7th Text Retrieval Conference (TREC-7), NIST Special Publication 500-242*, pages 253–264, Gaithersburg, MD, USA, 1998.
13. Voorhees, E., Gupta, N., Johnson-Laird, B.: Learning Collection Fusion Strategies. In *Proceedings of the 18th Annual International ACM SIGIR Conference on Reasearch, Development in Information Retrieval*, pages 172–179, Seattle, Washington, USA, 1995.
14. Zhai, C., Lafferty. J.: A Study of Smoothing Methods for Language Models Applied to Ad Hoc Information Retrieval. In *Proceedings of the 24th Annual International ACM SIGIR Conference on Research, Development in Information Retrieval*, pages 334–342, New Orleans, LA, USA, 2001.

DocBase – The INEX Evaluation Experience

Sriram Mohan[1] and Arijit Sengupta[2]

[1] Computer Science Department, Indiana University,
Bloomington, IN 47405, USA
srmohan@cs.indiana.edu

[2] Information Systems Department, Kelley School of Business,
Indiana University, Bloomington, IN 47405, USA
asengupt@indiana.edu
http://www.kelley.iu.edu/asengupt

Abstract. Can a system designed primarily for the purpose of database-type storage and retrieval be used for information-retrieval tasks? This was one of the questions that led us to participate in the INEX 2004 initiative. DocBase, a prototype database system developed initially for SGML, and adapted to work with XML, was used for the purpose of answering the queries. DocBase uses DSQL, an adaptation of SQL to provide a mechanism for querying XML using existing database and indexing technologies. The INEX evaluation experience was encouraging - although it did show the limitations of database query languages for classic information retrieval tasks, it also demonstrated that several interesting results can be obtained by using database query languages for information retrieval, especially for queries involving both content and structure. Our results demonstrate the adaptability and scalability of a database system for processing IR queries.

1 Introduction

Database management systems (DBMS) are designed for the purpose of efficient management of data in low-level storage devices. DBMS technology excels in the processing of transactions in multi-user environments, ensuring the quality and integrity of data in the presence of adverse conditions such as concurrent access and modification, as well as unpredicted system failure. DBMS provides high level languages and models to design, understand, and manipulate the data. On the other hand, the process of information retrieval is concerned with the extraction of the most relevant information from a data repository, with very little assistance from users. The classic information retrieval method is keyword search, where the objective is to retrieve information using just a few keywords. A critical question is whether these two apparently diverse technologies can be brought together for the purpose of retrieving information from future document repositories? What can each field learn from the other? What can each field use to better achieve its goals with knowledge from the other field? Such questions drove us to test DocBase, a system primarily designed for the purpose of SQL-like query processing on documents, in the INEX framework.

N. Fuhr et al. (Eds.): INEX 2004, LNCS 3493, pp. 261–275, 2005.

XML is fast becoming one of the most commonly used document representation formats. In less than ten years of its conception, it has become the leading technology for document representation for the next generation of applications. One of the primary differences between XML and other document formats (*e.g.*, word processing formats, HTML) is that XML incorporates logical structure in the documents. XML embeds additional structural information (meta-data) with the text content of the documents. XML applications need to appropriately utilize this structure for the purpose of information retrieval. This provides a potential for improving the recall and relevance of retrieved information when content is mixed with structure in the query. However, when a user searches only for content without the structure, such structural information may not be immediately useful. The retrieval application however can use such structure to improve recall by utilizing past searches and other statistical information gathered over time.

1.1 Differences Between DBMS and IR

Databases have always used structure in searches. In fact, a database search that looks for keywords anywhere in the database is an extremely complex query, not immediately supported in most current database management systems. Such searches, even if implemented, are a challenge to execute efficiently. However, since underneath the document structures in XML, the data is predominantly textual, one can potentially improve the types of retrieval operations that are possible, by using database-type searches. We intend to determine the types of functionality that we gain when a database query language is used for the purpose of information retrieval of both structure and content.

Databases make efficient use of low level storage indexes such as B+ trees to retrieve data quickly. Indexes are used in information retrieval as well (*e.g.*, "Inverted tree index" [1, 2], Patricia tree index [3]). The main difference between index use in databases and IR lies in the fact the IR indexes are used for full-text retrieval, whereas database indexes are used for speeding up retrieval in specific structures.

The rest of the paper is organized as follows. In the rest of this section, we motivate our participation in the INEX initiative. Section 2, introduces the DocBase system, and subsequently Section 3, introduces DSQL, the query language used by DocBase, and Section 4 describes how it can be used for the purpose of information retrieval. Section 5 describes how the data was prepared for indexing, and Section 6 describes how DocBase was adapted to work as an IR engine for the data. Section 7 presents the relevance and timing results and we conclude with a discussion on the lessons learned from this experience in Section 8.

1.2 Motivation

The power of a DBMS comes from its ability to perform data manipulation and management. But if the underlying data is essentially static, i.e., changes are not frequently made to the data, then the use of databases for retrieval purposes

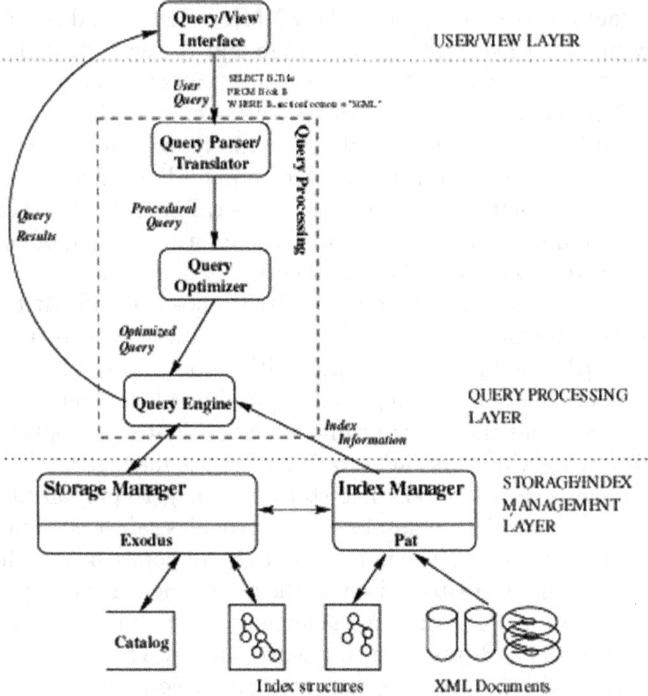

Fig. 1. The DocBase Architecture

might seemingly introduce more overhead than efficiency. However, the fact that a database query language potentially has the capability of restructuring and creating new structures while retrieving information, can still be useful for the purpose of information retrieval. Such creation and restructuring of information in ad hoc queries is not typically available in IR. Because of the efficient use of storage, indexes, and corresponding retrieval methods, database retrieval is typically highly efficient and scalable to very high volumes of data.

The motivation behind this work can be briefly stated as: (i) to identify areas where a database language could augment and potentially improve information retrieval methods, and (ii) to determine areas where a database query language can itself be altered and augmented to allow the possibility of information retrieval. This paper presents our findings from the INEX evaluation initiative from the perspective of the above objectives, and to show how some of the advantages and disadvantages of database technologies for information retrieval applied to the use of DocBase as an IR engine.

2 DocBase – A Database for Documents

DocBase is a research prototype system, developed in 1997 as part of a Ph.D. dissertation [4]. Although originally developed for the purpose of querying SGML documents, DocBase was modified to allow XML indexing and retrieval as well. The primary intent of DocBase is the storage and retrieval of structured data. The storage is handled by one of several possible storage manager components, while the retrieval is handled by an internal query engine, that uses an external indexing system if available. The DocBase architecture block diagram is shown in Figure 1. Users specify queries using a command-line interface, or by using QBT (Query By Templates), a specialized graphical interface for the purpose of querying structured data using the shape of the information [5], or by specifying the query in DSQL - DocBase's internal query language [6].

DocBase uses a 3-layer architecture similar to most DBMS. At the top layer (user/view layer) sits the query interface which allows users to specify queries using DSQL or QBT, and provides the user with a view of the result of the query. In the middle is the query processing layer, which includes a query parser, a rudimentary optimizer, and the query engine which evaluates the optimized query. At the lowest level is the physical storage and index management layer. There are two components in this layer. The storage manager component deals with keeping track of the data in the database, and provides safe access, modification, and management of the data. The index management component includes one or more indexes that can be created based on the data. The current implementation of DocBase uses Exodus, a storage management system developed in Wisconsin [7] and OpenText's Pat [8] software to create indexes. The query processing in DocBase is performed by (i) parsing the query and decomposing it into algerbaic atomic operations, (ii) optimizing the query to separate operations that can be performed using the created indexes, and the operations that require external processing. The individual operations are performed and composed as much as possible, and the intermediate results are combined in memory for the purpose of final packaging to the view layer.

3 DSQL – An SQL for Documents

DSQL is the query language used in DocBase and is entirely based on SQL, and has all the properties of SQL that make SQL the most popular database language today. DSQL uses the same syntax as SQL, and in fact, we can prove that DSQL queries are syntactically equivalent to the corresponding SQL queries, when the underlying data structure is flat. For flat structures, DSQL does not introduce any additional complexity over SQL - and has the same PTIME and LOGSPACE complexity as SQL. However, when the embedded structure is available and relevant, DSQL allows the creation and traversal of such structure, and hence DSQL queries can be used with advantages in the information retrieval context.

DSQL has the same basic structure as SQL, with recognizable `SELECT`, `FROM` and `WHERE` clauses for retrieval, and `GROUP BY`, `HAVING` and `ORDER BY` clauses for grouping and ordering the results. Moreover, queries can be nested using the standard `IN`, `EXISTS` or `NOT EXISTS` sub queries. As in SQL, only the `SELECT` and the `FROM` clauses are required. The other clauses are optional. Also, multiple

SELECT queries can be combined using standard set operations (Union, Intersect, Minus). The following section describes in detail the above constructs of DSQL.

3.1 The SELECT Clause

The SELECT clause in DSQL has the same major structure as SQL. The main difference is that it can create complex structures, and can traverse paths. To keep the language simple and close to SQL, generation of attributes has not been included in the base language. In fact, the formal specification of the language uses a form of XML known as ENF (Element Normal Form) [9], that ensures that any XML document with attributes can be re-written without the use of attributes and vice versa. DSQL provides a rudimentary element construction technique by specifying the element name and its contents within <>. Some examples of the select clause are given below:

```
SELECT *
SELECT output<*>
SELECT result<B.title, B.author>
SELECT booklist<B.author, books<B.title, B.year>>
```

The SELECT clause allows the creation of structures with arbitrary levels of nesting. Notice that grouping is not inherent in this specification and is, instead, the task of the GROUP BY clause.

3.2 The FROM Clause

The FROM clause allows the specification of the source of the information. The FROM clause can use URL sources, as well as aliased sources within the database. Some examples of the FROM clause are given below:

```
FROM books.xml B
FROM books.xml B, authors.xml A
FROM http://www.mycompany.com/docs/invoices.xml V, V..items I
```

3.3 The WHERE Clause

WHERE conditions in DSQL are similar to those in SQL. The main difference in semantics is due to paths, *i.e.*, all expressions in DSQL are path expressions, so operators are often set operators. For example, consider the following query:

```
SELECT result<B.title>
FROM bibdb..book B
WHERE  B.title = 'Extending SQL'
```

The WHERE expression evaluates to true if the path expression yields a singleton set containing an atom identical to 'Extending SQL'. Set membership operations such as in and contains are also available in DSQL.

3.4 Grouping and Ordering Clauses

SQL has several ways of specifying post query formatting and layout generation. The following are the grouping and ordering specifications in DSQL:

- `ORDER BY` (sorting): DSQL has the same semantics for ORDER BY as SQL. The expressions in the `SELECT` clause can be ordered by expressions in the ORDER BY clause, regardless of whether or not the ordering expressions appear in the `SELECT` clause, as long as the expressions are logically related, i.e., an ordering is possible using the ordering expression.
- Aggregate functions: DSQL supports the same five basic aggregate functions as SQL (`sum, count, min, max, avg`).
- `GROUP BY`: In DSQL, `GROUP BY` is a restructuring operation but unlike SQL, the aggregate function is optional. Moreover, multiple GROUP BY clauses can be specified for a single SELECT query.
- `IN/EXISTS/NOT EXISTS`: As in SQL, queries can be nested using sub queries. The semantics of sub queries remains the same in DSQL.

4 Information Retrieval Tasks Using DSQL

Section 6 describes how the INEX CO and CAS queries were performed in DocBase. Queries specified using the INEX format need to be first translated to DSQL before they can be evaluated in DocBase. Here we quickly motivate the translation process of the queries, and the reasoning for such alteration of the queries. We also discuss how such alteration potentially alters the semantics of the queries.

4.1 Keyword-Based or Content-Only (CO) Queries

DocBase technically, does not allow completely structure-free keyword based queries. Structure-free queries are difficult, and are not supported in standard database query languages such as SQL. With an immediate glance, it may be construed that DSQL also is unable to perform keyword-based queries. DSQL queries must specify where the keywords are being searched for, and what to retrieve as the result of the search.This implies that along with keywords, the queries should also include the structure regions of the documents where these keywords must be found. In the case keywords may appear anywhere in the document, the query must specify the bounding structure as the top level of the document, which is often termed the "root node" or the "root element" of the document. This is made possible by the hierarchical structure of XML. Of course, in the case of multiple documents, this implicitly assumes that all the documents where information is sought from have the same structure, or at the least, the same root element. In the case the repository contains documents with different root elements, a disjunction of these root elements must be specified in the query, so a completely structure-independent query may not be possible. Note that XPath uses the concept of a structure-independent root element (the '/' element) which can be used for this purpose. However, DocBase does not support this "super-root" element.

DSQL and other database query languages do not have a mechanism to specify the actual "point of match" of a search keyword. For example, if the query is a search for the keyword "XML" in a document repository, the database search might retrieve the documents that contain the keyword "XML", whereas an IR technique will retrieve all points of match of the keyword. Obviously, the number of matches retrieved by the database retrieval will be less than the number of matches retrieved by the IR method, although the documents retrieved by the database method will still contain all the matches returned by IR.

If the content-only query includes multiple keywords, potentially combined using boolean expressions, the actual "point of match" may not be easily identifiable, since one match might span several match points within same document and possibly across different structural regions. For example, a search on "XML or Information retrieval" may result in some documents where both the keywords appear in potentially different regions of the document. In such cases, it is not immediately apparent which of these match points is the actual result of the search. In the database search, the return point is always specified in the query, and hence always well-defined.

CO queries are translated to DSQL by simply searching for all the keywords bounded by the root element, and returning the root element as the retrieved element as well. So, for example, for a search in a poetry database (root element "poem") if the CO search is *'love' AND 'heart' AND NOT 'hate'*, then the equivalent DSQL Query is:

```
Select poem
From   poetry
Where  poem = 'love' and poem = 'heart' and not poem = 'hate'
```

The return region can be varied depending on what level of detail should be shown in the result, although the semantics of the query might change slightly based on what is returned. Actual translation of selected INEX queries will be shown in Section 6.

4.2 Content and Structure (CAS) Queries

CAS queries are more natural in databases. In such queries, the content that is being searched for is augmented with the logical region of the document where the content should be found. For example, Searching for "XML" in "document title" should result in documents where the the keyword "XML" appears in the document title. DSQL is better designed for the purpose of performing such queries. However, the same limitations regarding retrieving the actual point of match still apply. For CAS queries, a "point of match" is potentially more problematic, since the semantics of the language must determine whether the match should return the position of the keyword or the structure where the match was obtained (the position of the document title or the position of the keyword "XML" in the above example). The requirement in DSQL of always specifying the region to retrieve leads to more concrete semantics for such queries.CAS Queries are translated to DSQL using a logical translation of the CAS conditions into conditions in the WHERE clause. Actual translations of selected INEX CAS queries are shown in Section 6.

4.3 Approximation

Like any other database query language, DSQL queries are very rigid. If the query asks for "XML", the retrieved results would only have "XML". There is never any approximation, never any semantics associated with the search keywords. For example, the result will not contain documents with the phrase "Extensible Markup Language", although semantically they are the same. Several information retrieval methods incorporate such semantics in searches, so that the results not only contain the documents using the exact search, but also documents containing approximate searches. Moreover, if the search condition is long, such as "complexity analysis of computationally complete query languages", information retrieval techniques may use a disjunction of keywords and phrases from the search phrase to retrieve the result. DSQL does not have such functionality, so for searches involving such long search phrases, we often divided up the search phrase into multiple keywords, and used a conjunction of these keywords, instead of a disjunction, so that only documents containing all the chosen keywords would be matched. Searches in DSQL are, however, always partial searches, so a search for "XML" would retrieve "XML database systems" as well.

4.4 Ranking

Ranking is another aspect where database languages are lacking. In database terminology, a data instance either matches a query or it doesn't, and the query simply returns the items in the database that match the query conditions. However, ranking of the results is an important aspect of information retrieval. DocBase has no way of ranking the retrieved results. This is definitely an area where database systems and languages need to improve in order to provide enough value in information retrieval.

5 Preparing and Indexing the INEX Data

DocBase is capable of using any index structure that is appropriate for text and tree-based searches. The current implementation of DocBase uses OpenText 5 "PAT" indexing engine [8]. The INEX data was parsed by the built-in tagged document parser of OpenText Parser, and the required catalog entries were created in order to enable querying of the INEX data using DocBase. Because of the nature of the Pat indexes, most of the tree traversals can be performed by DocBase except those of an immediate child or immediate parent. Since the version of Open Text used was somewhat dated and did not have direct support for XML, the INEX data needed some preprocessing to enable it to be queried using DocBase. The following section will briefly explain the processes that were carried out on the INEX data collection to reach the "Query - Capability" state.

5.1 Indexing the Data Using Patricia Trees

The Design of DocBase focused on query processing capabilities, so incorporating new data in DocBase usually involves specifying a number of required

Table 1. A Sample Data Dictionary Control File

```
<Text>
  <MfsFiles>
    <FileMap>inex</FileMap>
    <FilterChain>
      <FileGroup>
        <MfsDir>./xml/an/1995</MfsDir>
        <MfsFile>*.xml</MfsFile>
        <MfsExpand>file</MfsExpand>
      </FileGroup>
    </FilterChain>
  </MfsFiles>
</Text>
```

configuration parameters. These parameters have to be specified using several predefined control files created specifically for this purpose. Patricia trees can handle different kinds of database formats with differing indexing schemes available to best suit the chosen data format. DocBase assumes that all the available data is in ASCII format and needs the following 3 control files:

1. Data Dictionary Control File: The Data dictionary control file is used to define the location of the database files and other database specific information. The control file consists of a number of segments each of which is specific to a different property of the associated database. Since we are dealing with ASCII format or in other words textual data, the only segment that needs to be modified is the Text control segment delineated by the `<Text>` `</Text>` tags in the data dictionary. Within the text control segment, one has to specify the source directories containing the actual data files and the format for the same. A sample Data Dictionary control file is shown in Table 1.
2. Region Tags Control File: The region tags control file is used in cases where the source data has tags delimiting various regions in the text on which source queries will be performed. This is required for indexing efficiency, since not all XML tags used in the document would be suitable for searching, and hence providing a small set of indexable tags would improve the efficiency of the searches. The tags specified in the region tags file are used to generate region indices that can be used to facilitate text queries that search for phrases within specified regions. Although tags not specified in the region index would still be searchable, region searches are much more efficient when a region index is created. In order to automatically generate this region file, we used a small XSL script that runs through the DTD/Schema associated with the source data and automatically determines the tags that are present in the document.
3. Regions Configuration Control File: The regions configuration file consists of one or more region segments, one for each tag file in use. This control file is used to specify the output format from the indexing structure(For Example

ASCII) and also the name of the tag file whose contents are used to build the data region indices.

It is easy to generate the Pat Indices for the source data once the above configuration files have been generated. DocBase makes use of the predefined "dbbuild" command to generate the indices. The current implementation of DocBase also creates a detailed catalog of objects in the database, including a binary representation of the document structure and a list of the different types of objects (*e.g.,* documents, DTDs, stored queries, auxiliary join indices and temporary structures) etc. The catalog has to be updated to reflect the newly indexed INEX data collection. Once the index has been created and cataloged the INEX data collection reaches the "Query Capability" state.

6 The INEX Retrieval Evaluation Process

As described in Section 4, INEX CO and CAS queries need to be translated for them to be executed in DocBase using DSQL. The translation process is fairly straight forward, as described earlier. For CO queries, the WHERE clause contain the keywords bounded by the root level element of the documents (article in the case of INEX). The returned element is typically the root element as well, which unfortunately returns the complete article. We altered the returned element in some of the queries to find more specific items in the article (the title of the article, for example). See Table 2 for a selection of the queries in INEX format, along with their DSQL equivalent.

CAS queries are translated using a logical translation of the Structural conditions. In the case all conditions are on the same structure, a single alias is created in the FROM clause, and conditions for all of the searched query words are used in the WHERE clause. However, when nested structures are used, multiple aliases need to be declared in the FROM clause to capture the nesting, and

Table 2. CO Topics and Equivalent DSQL Queries

	Candidate Topic	DSQL Equivalent
162	Text and Index "Compression Algorithms"	Select i From inex.article i Where i="text" and i="index" and i="compression algorithm"
166	+"tree edit distance" + XML	Select i From inex.article i Where i="edit distance" and (i ="XML" or i="xml") and (i ="tree")
178	"Multimedia Retrieval"	Select i.fm.tig.atl From inex.article i Where i="multimedia retrieval"

Table 3. CAS Topics and Equivalent DSQL Queries

	Candidate Topic	DSQL Equivalent
127	//sec//(p|fgc)[about(., Godel Lukasiewicz and other fuzzy implication definitions)]	Select s From inex.sec s Where (s.fgc ="Godel Lukasiewicz" and s.fgc="fuzzy logic") or (s.p ="Godel Lukasiewicz" and s.p="fuzzy logic)"
133	//article[about(.//fm//tig//atl, Query) and about(.//st, optimization)]	Select i From inex.article i Where i.fm.tig.atl="Query" and i..st="optimization"
137	//article [about(.//abs, "digital library") or about(.//ip1, "digital library")]	Select i From inex.article i Where i..abs="digital library" and i..ipl="digital library"

the WHERE clause needs to appropriately use the alias for the specific search condition. Once again, long search phrases can be split into several small keywords or phrases. Some selected CAS queries from INEX and their translations are shown in Table 3.

7 INEX Evaluation Results

Using the translation process described in Section 6 the INEX queries were converted to equivalent queries in DocBase. We were able to convert all the 75 Queries (40 CO and 35 CAS) successfully into DSQL revealing the capability and applicability of DSQL and DocBase as a querying platform for XML databases. This section details the relevance and timing results obtained while executing the above queries on DocBase.

7.1 Relevance Results

The INEX initiative has some restrictions on the format of each run submission. Each run submission must consist of the file from which that particular result was obtained and the XPath expression that can be evaluated to obtain that specific result instance. DocBase relies heavily on its indexing mechanism to perform data retrieval. The INEX restrictions demanded changes in the code to obtain the results in the desired format. The indexes were retraced back to the source data file for each result instance that matched the query conditions. But because of the design of the system the XPath corresponding to matched components cannot be determined (in many queries such an XPath is even impossible - most XQuery results cannot be evaluated with an XPath). So the runs for each candidate topic reveals the filename, and a system specific unique offset generated using the Patricia trees indexing mechanism instead of the XPath expression for each result

Table 4. Modified Query Output to meet INEX Requirements


```
<topic-id="127"><result>
 <file>./xml/an/2001/a1057.xml</file>
 <path><![CDATA[12421643<st>LECTURES AT
THE HISTORY CENTER<st>...]]> </path> </result><result>
 <file>./xml/an/2001/a1057.xml</file>
 <path><![CDATA[12421967<st> consultant,
author, and "technomad"<st>...]]></path> </result> </topic-id>
```


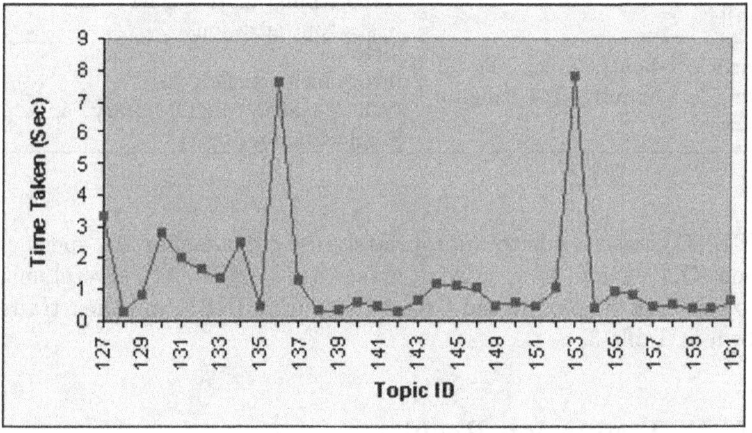

Fig. 2. INEX Content and Structure Queries on DocBase

instance. This was necessary because database queries use indexes that enable the query engine to access the data directly at the index points, without having to explicitly navigate the tree structure. So although the result still contains the relevant document regions, the actual path of the tree used for navigating to that region is not returned by the query. In addition, the INEX initiative requires that only the first 1500 results to be generated and that for each result instance, only the relevant portion be returned. The query evaluation engine was appropriately updated to meet the conditions.See Table 4 for details.

As mentioned earlier, relevance ranking is not a forte of database query languages. The retrieval engine ensures that all retrieved results correspond to the query and since no semantic alterations were performed on the query, all results are treated as equally relevant (a drawback with using database techniques).

7.2 Timing Results

The queries were executed on our test server platform - a Sun Enterprise 250 (2 * Ultrasparc II 400 Mhz, 4x34GB RAID disk with RAID disabled and 2048MB RAM). The primary indexing engine used for the tests was Open Text Pat, and an installation of the Sybase database was used as an auxiliary storage manager.

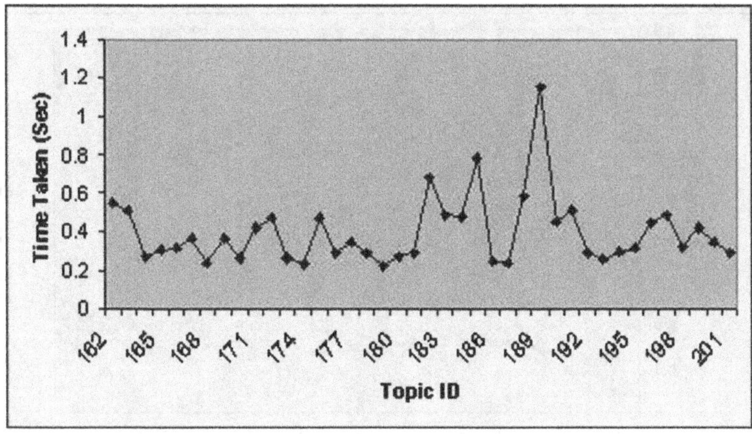

Fig. 3. INEX Content Only Queries on DocBase

On average CAS queries took 1.33 seconds while CO queries took 0.395 seconds. The standard deviations for the same were 1.80 and 0.179 seconds respectively. Most of the queries performed within the acceptable range except for two queries which took approximately 7 seconds to execute. These queries are also responsible for the slightly elevated mean of CAS queries. Careful analysis of the topics in question reveal that those queries had a conjunction of very specific search conditions on widely different structures.

Figures 3 and 2 demonstrate that most queries, whether involving only content, or both content and structure, can be efficiently executed by DocBase. Because of the indexing technique, DocBase achieves a very high retrieval speed, and hence, potentially multiple queries can be executed to create more relevant and ranked results.

7.3 Scalability Results Using XMark

The timing results on the INEX data clearly show the efficiency of DocBase. However, without a discussion of scalability, the real impact of a database management system cannot be felt. Although not part of the INEX process, we evaluated DocBase for scalability against the XMark Benchmark Suite [10]. XMark provides a data generator called "xmlgen" which can generate documents of differing sizes (controlled by a scaling factor) modeling a real world auction web site. We evaluated DocBase on standard XMark Benchmark queries using different scaling factors ranging from 0.1(Document size is 10 MB) to 1.0 (Document Size is .1GB). The time (See Figure 4) taken by DocBase to evaluate the queries compares favorably to the 4 systems reported in [10]. Further DocBase scales very well as the size of the database increases from 10 MB. The results show that even with a ten-fold increase in data size, the query time only increased linearly, a fact that clearly demonstrates the scalability of DocBase.

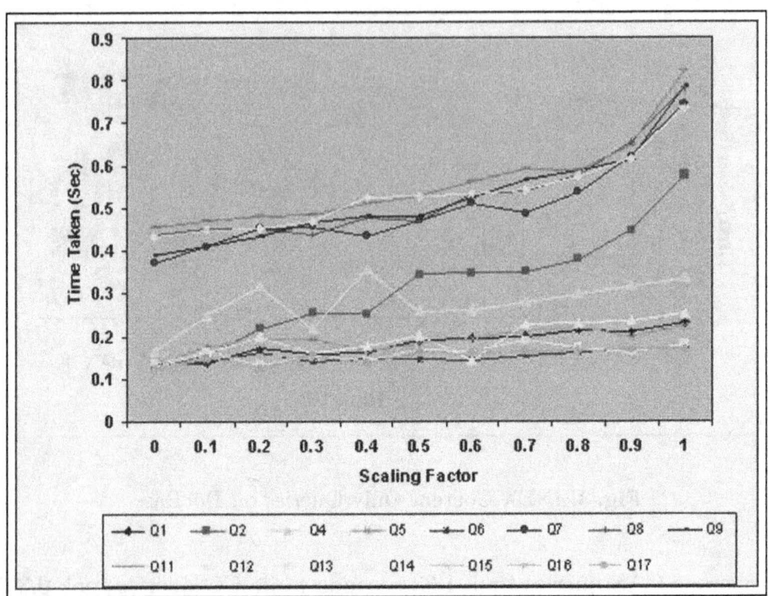

Fig. 4. XMark Benchmark Queries on DocBase

8 Discussion and Conclusion

The INEX evaluation experience with DocBase was an extremely useful learning process and helped demonstrated that with XML, it is possible for database systems and languages to come closer to fulfilling traditional IR tasks. Similarly IR engines can be augmented with the security, stability, and scalability of databases by taking advantage of the transaction processing principles seen in DBMS. Databases and information retrieval are not orthogonal principles, but can coexist and use the lessons learned from decades of research to improve the fields. With the advent of XML, databases and IR have come a step closer. The new XML full-text recommendation from W3C clearly is a step in that direction. The results from our INEX evaluation process does show that there are still limitations in a database language to provide ranking and relevance, but this is certainly a place where database languages can be augmented to achieve such effects. Similarly, IR languages can be augmented to be more specific about the retrieval scope, and become more first-order complete by allowing constructs like sub queries. We believe that XML databases will provide the opportunity for both database and information retrieval applications to co-exist, processing the same data repository, and providing value-added functionality to both methods.

References

1. Salton, G.: Developments in automatic text retrieval. Science **253** (1991) 974–980
2. Tomasic, A., Garcia-Molina, H., Shoens, K.: Incremental updates of inverted lists for text document retrieval. SIGMOD RECORD **23** (1994) 289–300

3. Gonnet, G.H., Baeza-Yates, R.: Lexicographical indices for text: Inverted files vs pat trees. Technical Report TR-OED-91-01, University of Waterloo (1991)
4. Sengupta, A.: DocBase - A Database Environment for Structured Documents. PhD thesis, Indiana University (1997)
5. Sengupta, A., Dillon, A.: Query by templates: A generalized approach for visual query formulation for text dominated databases. In Aho, A., ed.: Proceedings: Symposium on Advanced Digital Libraries, Library of Congress, Washington, DC, IEEE/CESDIS, IEEE Computer Scociety Press (1997) 36–47
6. Sengupta, A., Dalkilic, M.: DSQL - an SQL for structured documents. Lecture Notes in Computer Science **2348** (2002) 757–760 Proceedings of the 14th International Conference on Advanced Information Systems Engineering (CAISE'02), Toronto, Canada.
7. Carey, M.J., DeWitt, D.J., Frank, D., Graefe, G., Muralikrishna, M., Richardson, J.E., Shikita, E.J.: The architecture of the EXODUS extensible DBMS. In Dittrich, K.R., Dayal, U., eds.: Proceedings, 1996 International Workshop on Object-Oriented Database Ssytems, Pacific Grove, California, USA, IEEE-CS (1986) 52–65
8. Open Text Corporation Waterloo, Ontario, Canada: Open Text 5.0. (1994)
9. Layman, A.: Element-normal form for serializing graphs of data in XML. Based in part on an earlier paper, Serializing Graphs of Data in XML, by A. Bosworth, A. Layman, M. Rys, in XML Europe '99, Granada, April 1999 (1999)
10. Schmidt, A.R., Waas, F., Kersten, M.L., Carey, M.J., Manolescu, I., Busse, R.: XMark: A Benchmark for XML Data Management. In: Proceedings of the International Conference on Very Large Data Bases (VLDB). (2002)

TIJAH at INEX 2004 Modeling Phrases and Relevance Feedback

Vojkan Mihajlović[1], Georgina Ramírez[2], Arjen P. de Vries[2], Djoerd Hiemstra[1], and Henk Ernst Blok[1]

[1] University of Twente,
P.O. Box 217, 7500 AE Enschede, The Netherlands
{v.mihajlovic, d.hiemstra, h.e.blok}@utwente.nl
[2] Centre for Mathematics and Computer Science,
P.O. Box 94079, 1090GB Amsterdam, The Netherlands
{georgina, arjen}@cwi.nl

Abstract. This paper discusses our participation in INEX using the TIJAH XML-IR system. We have enriched the TIJAH system, which follows a standard layered database architecture, with several new features. An extensible conceptual level processing unit has been added to the system. The algebra on the logical level and the implementation on the physical level have been extended to support phrase search and *structural* relevance feedback. The conceptual processing unit is capable of rewriting NEXI content-only and content-and-structure queries into the internal form, based on the retrieval model parameter specification, that is either predefined or based on relevance feedback. Relevance feedback parameters are produced based on the data fusion of result element score values and sizes, and relevance assessments. The introduction of new operators supporting phrase search in score region algebra on the logical level is discussed in the paper, as well as their implementation on the physical level using the pre-post numbering scheme. The framework for structural relevance feedback is also explained in the paper. We conclude with a preliminary analysis of the system performance based on INEX 2004 runs.

1 Introduction

In our research for INEX 2004 we extended the TIJAH system to support more advanced IR techniques, namely phrase search and relevance feedback. The TIJAH system follows a layered database architecture, consisting of a conceptual, a logical, and a physical level. Each level has been built upon a different data model and has its own operators. The top level is based on the NEXI query language [10]. A NEXI query is first translated (at the conceptual level) into an internal query representation that closely resembles the NEXI query language, but enriched with some additional operators. The translation process is based on the retrieval model specification. The conceptual query is then transformed into a score region algebra (SRA) query plan [7] on the logical level of the TIJAH

N. Fuhr et al. (Eds.): INEX 2004, LNCS 3493, pp. 276–291, 2005.

system. SRA views XML as a collection of regions and not as a tree-like structure, and operators in the SRA are based on the region containment relation and on region frequency counts to support vague containment conditions. The logical query plan is transformed into the physical plan (via Monet interpreter language - MIL) that is executed in the MonetDB database kernel [1].

The TIJAH system that we use for INEX 2004 is an extended version of the TIJAH system used in 2003 [6]. Each level of the TIJAH database system has been extended to support phrase search and relevance feedback. Thus, the conceptual level is capable of handling phrases and supports relevance feedback specification. New operators have been introduced into the score region algebra to support phrase modeling and relevance feedback specification and the physical level has been enriched with new functions that implement phrase search. Furthermore, a fully automatic query rewriting unit has been developed at the conceptual level capable of transforming original NEXI queries into proper conceptual queries based either on the retrieval model specification or on the relevance feedback data.

The retrieval model used for the NEXI *about* function is essentially the same as the one used for INEX 2003 [6]. We calculate the relevance of a document component (i.e., XML element), following the idea of independence between the relevance on exhaustivity and the relevance on specificity. The relevance on exhaustivity is estimated using the language modeling approach to information retrieval [4]. The phrase model is kept orthogonal to the unigram language model for single terms, similarly to [9], and we used variants of the n-gram ($n > 1$) language model to see if and in what degree phrases can contribute to the TIJAH system effectiveness. The relevance on specificity is assumed to be related to the component length (e.g., following a log-normal distribution).

This paper presents our approaches for two out of five tracks defined for INEX 2004, namely the ad-hoc track and the relevance feedback track. For the ad-hoc track, we developed approaches for both the content-only (CO) and the vague content-and-structure (VCAS) subtasks. Different models have been implemented in the TIJAH system for these subtasks. Moreover, the TIJAH system supports the specification of relevance feedback parameters and a simple model for relevance feedback on structure has been implemented in our system.

The following section gives a global overview of the TIJAH system architecture. Section 3 describes the capabilities of a conceptual level of our system performing different NEXI query rewriting and expansions. Section 4 specifies an extension of score region algebra for phrase handling and explains how these expressions are mapped into efficient operations on the physical level. Section 5 describes the incorporation of relevance feedback on structure in our system. The paper concludes with a discussion of the experiments performed with the TIJAH system for the two INEX ad-hoc search tasks (CO and CAS) and for the INEX relevance-feedback task.

2 TIJAH System Architecture

The TIJAH XML-IR system follows a traditional three-level database architecture consisting of a conceptual, logical, and physical level. Although the concept has been well known in the database field for about thirty years, we introduced some modifications in the architecture to bridge the gap between traditional DBMSs and IR systems.

2.1 Conceptual Level

As a base for the conceptual level we used the Narrowed Extended XPath (NEXI) query language [10] as proposed by the INEX community in 2003. The NEXI query language supports only a subset of the XPath syntax and extends XPath with a special *about* function that ranks XML elements by their estimated relevance to a textual query. As such, the invocation of the *about* function can be regarded as the instantiation of a retrieval model.

Throughout the paper we will use two NEXI examples, one taken from the INEX CAS topic 149:

```
//article[about(.//(abs|kwd), "genetic algorithm")]
                      //bdy//sec[about(., simulated annealing)]
```

and the other from INEX CO topic 166:

```
+"tree edit distance" +XML -image
```

During query processing a (conceptual) NEXI query language expression is encoded into an internal representation that closely resembles the original query in its structure, and all manipulations are done on this internal representation. As a result of the processing on the conceptual level we obtain a conceptual query representation.

2.2 Logical Level

The difference on the logical level of traditional DBMSs and our system is in that we enhanced it with an algebra that takes into account the specific (i.e., nested) structure of the modeled data, i.e., XML in our case, to enable high level reasoning about the query specification and algebraic optimization. Since the algebra supports region score manipulation and ranked retrieval we named it score region algebra (SRA).

The basic score region algebra operators that involve score manipulations are depicted in Table 1[1]. We assume that the default value for score attribute is 1. Note that the probabilistic containment operators $\sqsupset_p$, $\not\sqsupset_p$, ►, and ◄ copy the region start, end, type, and name attribute values from the left operand region set (R_1) to the result region set, while the score attribute of the result set (p) gets its value based on the containment relation among regions in the left and regions in the right operand as well as their respective score values. The

[1] We used a slightly different notation than in [6]. For more extensive coverage of our score region algebra we refer to [7].

Table 1. Region algebra operators for score manipulation

Operator	Operator definition
$\sigma_{t=type,n=name}(R)$	$\{r \| r \in R \wedge t = type \wedge n = name\}$
$R_1 \sqsupset_p R_2$	$\{r \| r_1 \in R_1 \wedge (s,e,n,t) := (s_1,e_1,n_1,t_1) \wedge p := p_1 \times f_{\sqsupset}(r_1,R_2)\}$
$R_1 \not\sqsupset_p R_2$	$\{r \| r_1 \in R_1 \wedge (s,e,n,t) := (s_1,e_1,n_1,t_1) \wedge p := p_1 \times f_{\not\sqsupset}(r_1,R_2)\}$
$R_1 \blacktriangleright R_2$	$\{r \| r_1 \in R_1 \wedge (s,e,n,t) := (s_1,e_1,n_1,t_1) \wedge p := p_1 \times f_{\blacktriangleright}(r_1,R_2)\}$
$R_1 \blacktriangleleft R_2$	$\{r \| r_1 \in R_1 \wedge (s,e,n,t) := (s_1,e_1,n_1,t_1) \wedge p := p_1 \times f_{\blacktriangleleft}(r_1,R_2)\}$
$R_1 \sqcap_p R_2$	$\{r \| r_1 \in R_1 \wedge r_2 \in R_2 \wedge (s_1,e_1,n_1,t_1) = (s_2,e_2,n_2,t_2)$ $\wedge (s,e,n,t) := (s_1,e_1,n_1,t_1) \wedge p := p_1 \otimes p_2\}$
$R_1 \sqcup_p R_2$	$\{r \| r_1 \in R_1 \wedge r_2 \in R_2 \wedge ((s,e,n,t) := (s_1,e_1,n_1,t_1)$ $\vee (s,e,n,t) := (s_2,e_2,n_2,t_2)) \wedge p := p_1 \oplus p_2\}$

definitions of the set-like operators ($\sqcap_p$ and $\sqcup_p$) are similar to the definitions of basic set intersection and set union operators, i.e., the result region start, end, type and name are obtained the same way as for set intersection and union operators, except that the result score value for regions is defined based on the score values of regions in the left and right operand region set.

In the definition of score operators we introduced four abstract scoring functions: $f_{\sqsupset}$, $f_{\not\sqsupset}$, $f_{\blacktriangleright}$, and $f_{\blacktriangleleft}$, as well as two abstract operators: $\otimes$ and $\oplus$, that define the retrieval model. For the $\oplus$ operator we assume that there exists a default value for the score (denoted with d), and in case the region r_1 is not present in the region set R_2 the score is computed as $p = p1 \oplus d$ and in case the region r_2 is not present in the region set R_1 the score is computed as $p = d \oplus p_2$.

The functions $f_{\sqsupset}$, $f_{\not\sqsupset}$, $f_{\blacktriangleright}$, and $f_{\blacktriangleleft}$, applied to a region r_1 and a region set R_2, result in the numeric value that takes into account the score values of all regions r_2 ($\in R_2$) and the numeric value that reflects the structural relation between the region r_1 and the region set R_2. The abstract $\otimes$ operator specifies how scores are combined in an **and** expression, while the $\oplus$ operator defines the score combination in an **or** expression inside the NEXI predicate. The exact instantiation of these functions and operators is done on the physical level as can be seen in the next section.

2.3 Physical Level

The SRA is defined as an XML specific logical algebra and can be implemented easily with relational operators [6, 11, 2]. Since we used the MonetDB on the physical level the last step on the logical level of the TIJAH system is a translation to Monet Interpreter Language (MIL). The MIL query plan is executed using MIL primitives that define the manipulation over Monet binary tables (BATs) [1].

The physical level is based on a pre-post numbering scheme [3] and the containment join operators ($\bowtie_{\sqsupset}$ and $\bowtie_{\sqsubset}$) introduced in [6]. In the specification of our retrieval model we first introduce three auxiliary functions at the physical level. These functions are used to compute the term frequency - $tf(r, R)$, the collection frequency - $cf(R)$ and the length prior - $lp(r)$. Variable λ represents the smoothing parameter for the inclusion of background statistics, μ is the mean value of the logarithmic distribution of the desired size for the element, and ρ is the variance (in our case set to 1) for the log-normal prior. These auxiliary functions can be implemented using two physical operators: a size operator $size(r)$ that returns the size of a selected region r, and a count operator $|R|$ that returns the number of regions in a region set R.

Function $tf(r, R)$ computes the term frequency of a term region set R, i.e., a set containing only regions representing a single term, in a region r, while function $cf(tm, R)$ computes the collection frequency of a term tm in the collection. They are computed as:

$$tf(r, R) = \frac{|R \bowtie_{\sqsubset} r|}{size(r)}, \quad cf(term, R) = \frac{|\sigma_{t=term, n=tm}(\mathcal{C})|}{size(Root)} \tag{1}$$

where tm is the name of a region $r \in R$, C denotes the set of all regions in XML collection, and *Root* represents the region that is not contained by any other region in the collection (i.e., the region corresponding to the top node of the entire XML tree).

To define the length prior of the region r we used either the size of the element: $lp(r) = size(r)$, the standard element prior: $lp(r) = \log(size(r))$, or the log-normal distribution:

$$lp(r) = \frac{e^{-((\log(size(r))-\mu)^2/2\rho^2)}}{size(r)\rho\sqrt{2\pi}} \tag{2}$$

Although in our framework arbitrary implementations of abstract functions can be introduced on the physical level, for INEX 2004 we followed the language model [4] and the conclusion drawn from numerous experiments last year [6]. The abstract scoring functions defined in our region algebra, $f_{\sqsupset}(r, R)$ and $f_{\not\sqsupset}(r, R)$, implement the about function specified in NEXI, while $f_{\blacktriangleright}(r, R)$ and $f_{\blacktriangleleft}(r, R)$ specify the score propagation in nested regions:

$$f_{\sqsupset}(r, R) = \lambda tf(r, R) + (1-\lambda)cf(tm, R), \quad f_{\not\sqsupset}(r, R) = 1-(\lambda tf(r, R) + (1-\lambda)cf(tm, R)),$$

$$f_{\blacktriangleright}(r, R) = \frac{\sum_{r_i \in r \bowtie_{\sqsupset} R}(size(r_i) * p_i)}{\sum_{r_i \in r \bowtie_{\sqsupset} R} size(r_i)}, \quad f_{\blacktriangleleft}(r, R) = \sum_{r_i \in r \bowtie_{\sqsubset} R} p_i \tag{3}$$

In this paper we take the simple approach for the score combination operators where $\otimes$ is implemented as a product of two score values, and $\oplus$ as the sum of scores (with the default value $d = 1$), as it shows good behavior for retrieval.

3 Query Rewriting

Upgrading the TIJAH system used previous year for INEX [6], we developed a fully automatic approach for translating NEXI queries, first into internal conceptual representation and later into logical algebra. The structure of the conceptual query translator is depicted in Figure 1. The conceptual level of the TIJAH system consists of three processing units: the query preprocessor, the

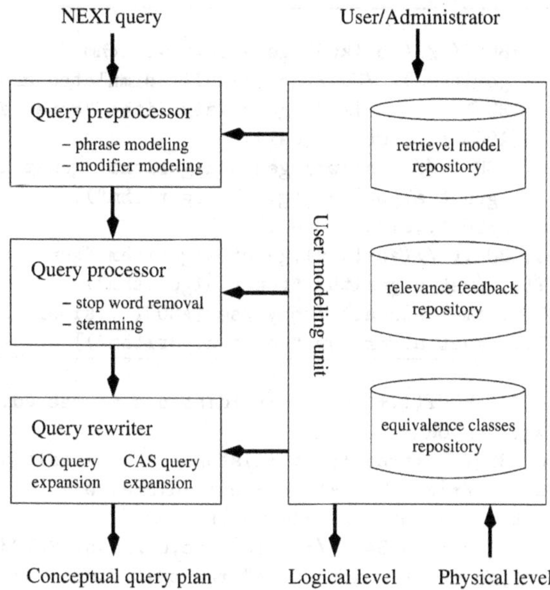

Fig. 1. The conceptual level of the TIJAH system

query processor, and the query rewriter; and three user modeling units: the retrieval model repository, the relevance feedback repository, and the equivalence classes repository[2].

The retrieval model repository and relevance feedback repository form the input to the preprocessing unit. How the data from the repository is interpreted depends on a specification in the user modeling unit. The retrieval model repository in the TIJAH system currently only stores the parameters of a retrieval model, i.e., the smoothing parameter λ for the language model used for retrieval, and the desired size of the retrieved element for estimating the relevance on specificity.

Handling Phrases and Modifiers. The query preprocessing unit rewrites NEXI queries based on a user specification on handling phrases and modifiers. Thus, users can specify whether phrases should be considered as phrases or as a set of terms in the query, and whether term and phrase modifiers ('+', and '−') should be considered during the query execution. The result of our example CAS query with phrases can be seen in Figure 2 as CAS query 1.

Stop Word Removal and Stemming. The standard IR query processing consisting of query stop word removal and stemming is done by the processing

[2] The equivalence classes repository represents a repository that should support retrieval from heterogeneous collections and is still not fully supported in the TIJAH system.

CAS queries:

```
1. ROOT//article[ABOUT(.//(abs|kwd),genetic algorithm
      "genetic algorithm")]//bdy//sec[ABOUT(.,simulated annealing)]
2. ROOT//article[ABOUT(.//(abs|kwd),genet algorithm "genet algorithm")]
      //bdy//sec[ABOUT(.,simul anneal)]
3. ROOT//article[ABOUT(.//(abs|kwd),genet algorithm "genet algorithm")
      AND ABOUT(.,genet algorithm "genet algorithm")]
      //bdy//sec[ABOUT(.,simul anneal)]
4. ROOT//article[ABOUT(.//(abs|kwd),genet algorithm "genet algorithm")
      AND ABOUT(.,genet algorithm "genet algorithm")
      AND ABOUT(.,simul anneal)]//bdy//sec[ABOUT(.,simul anneal)
      AND ABOUT(.,genet algorithm "genet algorithm")]
```

CO queries:

```
1. ROOT//article//*[ABOUT(.,+tree +edit +distance +"tree edit distance"
      +XML -image)]PRIOR
2. ROOT//article[ABOUT(.,+tree +edit +distance +"tree edit distance"
      +XML -image)]//*[ABOUT(.,+tree +edit +distance
      +"tree edit distance" +XML -image)]PRIOR
3. ROOT//journal[MATCH(tp,0.34)]//*[MATCH(sec,0.22) or MATCH(p,0.18)]
      [ABOUT(.,+tree +edit +distance +"tree edit distance"
      +XML -image)]PRIOR(856)
```

Fig. 2. The conceptual query representations generated from the NEXI queries

unit. We used the standard Porter stemmer and a publicly available stop word list consisting of 429 stop words. Stemming and stop word removal are applied based on a user specification (in the user modeling unit). In Figure 2 CAS query 2 depicts the outcome of the processing unit in case stemming would have been performed.

Query Expansion. The last step in conceptual query processing is query rewriting and expansion. The conceptual query rewriting unit distinguishes between NEXI content-only (CO) and content-and-structure (CAS) queries.

NEXI CO queries are transformed into CAS queries according to the user specification. For instance, the CO query can be translated in two ways:

- we are looking for any relevant XML element in any of the articles in the collection, including the articles themselves, as depicted in CO query 1 in Figure 2, [3] or
- we are looking for any relevant element in an article (including article elements themselves) that is about the topic specified, as depicted in CO query 2 in Figure 2.

The `PRIOR` in the conceptual query representation denotes that we use the relevance on specificity (i.e., result element size) in computing the final score of

[3] In the TIJAH system, `//*` is treated as `descendant_or_self::node`.

XML elements. The default is a length prior while for the log-normal prior the mean size should be specified (see CO example 3 in Figure 2).

Since NEXI CAS queries specify the element that should be retrieved as a result, query rewriting can only be about structural constraints in the *about* clause and about term distribution in different *about* clauses. Therefore, we applied two simple rules to enable elementary CAS query rewriting:

- relaxing the constraint that terms or phrases must be contained by the XML elements specified in the structural part of the *about* clause, as depicted in CAS query 3[4] in Figure 2;
- further relaxing the structural constraints and allowing that terms or phrases in each subquery are also added to the other subqueries (similarly as we had in the TIJAH 2003 approach [6]), as shown in Figure 2, CAS query 4.

4 Phrase Modeling

For phrase modeling we follow the ideas introduced by Song and Croft [9], where authors individualized unigram and bigram language models and combined them in an independent way. We slightly modified their approach and used two interpretations:

- combination of n-gram LMs is modeled as an equally weighted sum: $P(t_1, .., t_{n-1}, t_n|e) = P_1(t_1|e) + P_2(t_1, t_2|e) + ... + P_n(t_1, t_2, ..., t_n|e)$, and
- combination of n-gram LMs is modeled as a product: $P(t_1, .., t_{n-1}, t_n|e) = P_1(t_1|e) \times P_2(t_1, t_2|e) \times ... \times P_n(t_1, t_2, ..., t_n|e)$.

In our approach the expression $P_i(t_1, t_2, ..., t_i|e)$ gives the probability that the XML element e contains the phrase "t_1 t_2 ... t_i".

To be able to model phrases in region algebra we had to extend SRA to support phrase specification and more advanced score manipulation operators. For such a purpose we introduced a complex selection operator and additional containment operator defined in Table 2.

Table 2. Complex selection and containment operators

Operator definitions
$\sigma_{t=type, n=name_1\ adj\ n=name_2\ adj\ ...\ adj\ n=name_n}(R) = \{r|(r_1 \in R \wedge r_2 \in R \wedge t_2 = t_1 = type \wedge n_1 = name_1 \wedge n_2 = name_2 \wedge e_1 = s_2 - 1 \wedge (s, e, n, t, p) := (s_1, e_2, n_2, adj, p_2)) \vee ... \vee (r_1 \in R \wedge r_2 \in R \wedge\ ...\ \wedge r_n \in R \wedge t_n = ... = t_2 = t_1 = type \wedge n_1 = name_1 \wedge n_2 = name_2 \wedge ... \wedge n_n = name_n \wedge e_1 = s_2 - 1 \wedge e_2 = s_3 - 1 \wedge ... \wedge e_{n-1} = s_n - 1 \wedge (s, e, n, t, p) := (s_1, e_n, n_n, adj, p_n))\}$
$R_1 \sqsupset_{\odot} R_2 = \{r|r_1 \in R_1 \wedge (s, e, n, t) := (s_1, e_1, n_1, t_1) \wedge p := p_1 \times f_{\sqsupset_{\odot}}(r_1, R_2)\}$

The first operator makes a union of all adjacent sub-regions in the region set that have the same type attribute. The name attributes of these new regions

[4] Note that the stemming has been applied in the query processing.

take the names of the regions from the second operand, while their type is now changed to adj. Following this approach and using xp as a shorthand for any arbitrary SRA expression formed during the NEXI to SRA query translation, phrase 'texttttree edit distance" can be transformed into the following logical expressions:

$$xp \sqsupset_{\odot} \sigma_{t=term,n='tree'\ adj\ n='edit'\ adj\ n='distance'}(R)$$

Here, xp denotes an arbitrary SRA expression formed during the NEXI to SRA query translation.

The operator $\sqsupset_{\odot}$ defines how relevance scores from regions with distinct region name attributes (i.e., regions with adjacent terms of different length) are combined to form the resulting score value for regions in the left operand ($r_1 \in R_1$). The definition of function $f_{\sqsupset_{\odot}}$ is similar to the definition of function $f_{\sqsupset}$ in Equation 3 except that it treats adjacent regions with different name attributes in isolation and combines them based on the specifications of the operators $\otimes$ and $\oplus$, i.e., multiplying or summing them, respectively.

Furthermore, the scaling operator ($\circledast$) is introduced in the SRA to model terms with and without modifier '+'. The operator definition is as follows: $R_1 \circledast num = \{r | r_1 \in R_1 \wedge (s, e, n, t) := (s_1, e_1, n_1, t_1) \wedge p := (p_1 * num)\}$. This operator scales down the terms (regions) that are not marked with '+' and, therefore, considered not so important, and scales up terms (regions) marked with '+' that are considered important terms. In our approach important terms are scaled with a *num* value that is double the *num* value for not so important terms.

Based on the defined operators we can now translate the conceptual query representation into the logical query plan. For example, if we consider the first part of query 1 in Figure 2:

```
ROOT//article[ABOUT(.//(abs|kwd), genetic algorithm "genetic algorithm")]
```

we can express it in SRA as:

$$\texttt{ARTICLE} \blacktriangleright (((\texttt{(ABS} \sqcup_p \texttt{KWD)} \sqsupset_p \texttt{GENETIC)} \circledast 0.5) \sqcap_p$$
$$(((\texttt{ABS} \sqcup_p \texttt{KWD)} \sqsupset_p \texttt{ALGORITHM)} \circledast 0.5) \sqcap_p (((\texttt{ABS} \sqcup_p \texttt{KWD)} \sqsupset_{\odot} \texttt{GEN\_ALG)} \circledast 0.5))$$

Here we used ABS instead of $\sigma_{t=entity,n='abs'}$, KWD instead of $\sigma_{t=entity,n='kwd'}$, GENETIC instead of $\sigma_{t=term,n='genetic'}$, ALGORITHM instead of $\sigma_{t=term,n='algorithm'}$, and GEN_ALG instead of $\sigma_{t=term,n='genetic'\ adj\ n='algoithm'}$.

For the phrase modeling on the physical level we implemented two variants of the function $f_{\sqsupset_{\odot}}$, based on [9] and functions in Equation 1, as defined below:

$$f_{\sqsupset_{\odot}}(r, R) = \prod_{R_i} \eta tf(r, R_i) + (1 - \eta) cf(R_i) \tag{4}$$

$$f_{\sqsupset_{\odot}}(r, R) = \sum_{R_i} \eta tf(r, R_i) + (1 - \eta) cf(R_i) \tag{5}$$

Here, R_i is a set of regions (r_i) that have the same region name attribute (n_i). The sum and the product is defined over all sets R_i with different region names in R. Parameter η is used to specify the influence of foreground and background statistics for different adjacent regions in the region set.

5 Relevance Feedback

Our approach for the relevance feedback track is based on the idea that knowledge of relevant components provides implicit structural *hints* that may help improve the performance of the content-oriented queries. We use a two-step procedure to implement this idea:

- First, we extract the *structural relevance* of the top-ranked elements according to the relevance assessments provided by the test collection;
- Second, the content-oriented query is rewritten into a structured one and the priors of the system are tuned based on the relevance feedback information. Then, the new structured query is evaluated in the TIJAH system.

In the following subsections, we define these two steps and explain their implementation in the TIJAH XML-IR system.

5.1 Extracting Structural Information

How to extract the *structural relevance* from the top relevant elements is a difficult problem. The semantics of the relevance assessments should be analyzed in depth to decide which type of *structural hints* should be extracted from the different relevant components and to define what is the best interpretation for the different relevance combinations.

In our first attempt to model the *structural relevance* of a query, we use the *journal* and the *XML tag* name information from the top-ranked elements as well as their relevance values. We also use the size of these elements to update the length prior for the next iteration in the relevance feedback cycle. We believe that with a good combination of these *hints* we can considerably improve the performance of the content oriented results. In Section 6 we give a preliminary analysis of the results of this approach.

The reminder of this section details how the structural information from the top-ranked elements and the results from relevance assessments on exhaustivity and specificity are used to rewrite the query for the next iteration in a relevance feedback process.

Journal Name. The content of the INEX collection consists of eighteen different journals. Each of these journals contains articles discussing a different computer science related field. We believe that when a component is assessed as relevant for a given topic, the journal it belongs to will contain elements with a similar content information. Therefore, we want to use this information to give a prior to the elements that are contained in that journal.

As an example, consider the relevance assessments for this year. If we consider only highly exhaustive and highly specific elements, marked with (3,3), we find that most of the topics have less than 3 relevant journals. That means, that likely, these are the journals that discuss the topic. Therefore, it is easy to imagine that other elements from these journals will also contain relevant information for that specific topic.

We decided to model the *journal prior* information according to the following formula:

$$P(J) = a + b \cdot \frac{\sum_{r \in top_{20} \sqsubseteq J} E_r}{3 \cdot |\{r \in top_{20} | E_r > 0\}|} + (1 - a - b) \cdot \frac{|J \sqsupseteq top_{20}|}{20}, \tag{6}$$

where E_r is the exhaustivity value of the relevant top 20 components ($r \in top_{20}$) that belong ($\sqsubseteq$ and $\sqsupseteq$, respectively) to the journal J and a and b are weighting parameters used to tune the importance of this information.

Note that we only use the exhaustivity information to get a prior for the journal. We argue that if a component is somewhat exhaustive, it means that the journal it belongs to is likely to be about the topic need, i.e., to contain the desired information specified in the query (whatever the specificity for that component is). We also reward the journals that have a higher number of elements in the top 20 ranked elements (see the third part of the sum in the equation).

XML Tag Names. The goal of using the element names for relevance feedback is to push up in the ranked result list the kind of elements we already know to be relevant for the topic ("make sense to be retrieved") and to push down the ones that are not.

For modeling the information on the XML tag names extracted from the top-ranked elements (e), we use a similar approach as for the journals (Equation 6):

$$P(e) = a + b \cdot \frac{\sum_{r \in top_{20} \sqsubseteq e} E_r + S_r}{6 \cdot |\{r \in top_{20} | E_r \cdot S_r > 0\}|} + (1 - a - b) \cdot \frac{|e \in top_{20}|}{20} \tag{7}$$

In this case, we also take into account the *specificity* scale (S_r) as it gives information on the size of the element: i.e, if the element was large enough or too small for the information need.

Size. We use the size information to tune the length prior of our retrieval model for the next iteration. We believe that elements similar in length to those that are assessed as relevant have a higher likelihood to be the ones that the user is looking for. Nevertheless, it is not easy to combine the sizes of the top components to estimate a *desired* size to be retrieved.

We decided to use the following formula to define the *desired size* given the elements (r) in the top 20:

$$DesiredSize = \frac{\sum_{r \in top_{20}} size(r) \times SizeModifier_r}{\sum_{r \in top_{20}} sgn(SizeModifier_r)}, \tag{8}$$

where $SizeModifier_r$ is defined as:

$$SizeModifier_r = \begin{cases} 1 & \text{if } (E_r, S_r) \in \{(2,2),(3,3)\} \\ 0 & \text{if } (E_r, S_r) \in \{(1,1),(0,0)\} \\ \frac{3 - E_r + S_r}{3} & \text{otherwise} \end{cases} \tag{9}$$

We based this formula on the assumption that very specific components that are not very exhaustive (i.e., $S_r > E_r$) are likely to be too small to answer the information need and, on the other hand, highly exhaustive components that are not very specific (i.e., $E_r > S_r$) are likely to be too large as an answer. In case there are no relevant elements in the 20 top-ranked elements, or the relevant elements are marginally exhaustive and marginally specific, i.e., marked with (1,1), we use a default value for desired size. We also experimented with the following, simpler, estimation of the $SizeModifier_r$ than in Equation 9:

$$SizeModifier_r = \begin{cases} 0 & \text{if } (E_r, S_r) \in \{(1,1),(0,0)\} \\ \frac{S_r}{E_r} & \text{otherwise} \end{cases} \qquad (10)$$

5.2 Rewriting and Evaluating the Query

After the information extraction on the structural information of the relevant elements and its fusion with the relevance assessments on exhaustivity and specificity, in the first step, the information is stored in the relevance feedback repository[5]. The information is used to rewrite the CO query and evaluate it in the TIJAH system. Assuming that in the relevance feedback repository for topic 166 the journal name specification is `tp` with a relevance prior 0.34, element names are `sec` and `p` with relevance prior values 0.22 and 0.18, respectively, and estimated element size is 856, the conceptual query after rewriting will look like the query given in Figure 2 as CO query plan 3. The `MATCH(e_name,imp)` is used to denote that the elements in the `e_name` have the higher probability to be relevant answers to a query than other elements, and the value `imp` gives their respective relevance prior.

The `MATCH` expression in the conceptual query representation is translated into a combination of a selection and scaling operators on the logical level. For example, query excerpt:

```
xp[MATCH(sec,0.22) or MATCH(p,0.18)]
```

is expressed on the logical level as:

$$xp \sqcap_p ((\sigma_{n='sec',t=entity}(C) \circledast 1.22) \sqcup (\sigma_{n='p',t=entity}(C) \circledast 1.18))$$

where C is the collection of all regions (all XML elements and terms in the collection). These operators are further translated into a physical query plan as defined in the previous sections.

6 Experiments

In this section we give an overview of the experiments we did with the TIJAH XML-IR system and present our results (official and additional runs) for the ad-hoc retrieval task (CO and CAS) and the relevance feedback task.

[5] Currently the computation and specification of these values are not completely integrated into the TIJAH system.

Table 3. CO experimentation runs: basic language model without length prior. Effects of supporting phrases. The 'n-gram' column indicates the kind of combination for the n-gram LMs and the $\odot$ column indicates the way the scores within a region are combined for a final score (Equations 4 and 5)

Run	λ	n-gram	$\odot$	avg. MAP	overlap
$R_{comp_{nophr}}$	0.35	-	-	0.0446	49.4%
$R_{comp_{phr1}}$	0.35	product	product	0.0437	51.1%
$R_{comp_{nophr}}$	0.5	-	-	0.0496	52.3%
$R_{comp_{phr2}}$	0.5	product	sum	**0.0502**	82.8%
$R_{comp_{phr3}}$	0.5	sum	sum	0.0470	82.1%

6.1 INEX Ad-Hoc Track

This year we used a completely new implementation on the physical level of our system, we designed different experiments to evaluate which would be the best parameters for the retrieval model as well as to check if the scenarios used in previous years would produce the same performance on the new implementation.

CO Queries. For the CO task we designed two main experiments: The first one evaluates the effect of supporting phrases in the TIJAH XML-IR system as explained throughout the paper. Results of these runs are shown in Table 3. The different columns show the different approaches used to model the phrase search (see Section 4 for details). According to the results, supporting phrase search improved the retrieval performance in only one of the runs. Note that this improvement is partially positive as the overlap increased considerably too.

The second experiment was designed to evaluate the effect of including a length prior in the retrieval model. We defined several priors and applied them to the best of our runs. The results are shown in Table 4. In the first four runs, the length prior consists on removing from the result list the elements smaller than a certain threshold. The last two runs use a log normal and a log standard distribution to model the length prior. We can see that, whatever the prior is, the performance of the original run improves. As we saw already in previous years, a log standard distribution works best in our case, reaching a MAP of 1.4 in one of the metrics.

VCAS Task. For the VCAS task, we designed three different scenarios. The first one, R_{strict} treats the structural constraints of a query strictly and all the result components must exactly match these structural constraints. The second and the third one, R_{relax} and R_{all}, implement the relaxations of the structural constraints explained in Section 3, and shown in queries 3 and 4 in Figure 2. The results of these runs are shown in Table 5. Even if the improvement for the first relaxation (second row) is not significant, we can see in the precision and recall graphs that the relaxation of the structural constraints leads to better precision for this run. Contrary to last year, the second relaxation by using all the terms

Table 4. Additional CO experimentation runs: Length priors

Run	length prior	Avg MAP	overlap
$R_{comp_{05}}$	none	0.0496	52.3%
$R_{comp_{cut5}}$	$res > 5$	0.0534	51.8%
$R_{comp_{cut10}}$	$res > 10$	0.0578	53.2%
$R_{comp_{cut25}}$	$res > 25$	0.0635	55.4%
$R_{comp_{cut50}}$	$res > 50$	0.0645	57%
$R_{comp_{logn}}$	log normal	0.0526	51.1%
$R_{comp_{logs}}$	log standard	**0.0985**	73.6%

Table 5. Official VCAS experiment runs. Note that results in R_{all} have been modified due to an implementation error in the submitted ones

Run	Avg MAP	overlap
R_{strict}	0.0624	22.8%
R_{relax}	**0.0694**	24.3%
R_{all}	0.0588	23.9%

in all the about clauses did not performed as expected. Further analysis should determine if this is just an effect of the different topics for this year or if, in general, the relaxation is not appropriate for our purposes.

6.2 INEX Relevance-Feedback Track

The aim of the experiments submitted for the relevance feedback task is to identify which combination of the different structural and size information works better. The MAPs obtained with the different combinations experimented and their results are shown in Table 6.

Table 6. Official Relevance Feedback runs. Note that baseline runs are the result of removing the descendants of the top 20 elements from the original CO runs. Relevance feedback is applied on the residual collections of these runs, after freezing the top 20 elements. S1 and S2 refer to the size information extracted using Equations 9 and 10, respectively, J refers to journal information and XT to XML tag information

baseline	S1	S1+J	S1+XT	S2	S2+J	J	S1+J+XT	XT	XT+J
0.0405	0.0406	**0.0416**	0.0406						
0.0431				0.0429	0.0448	**0.0450**			
0.0456							0.0482	**0.0486**	0.0468

The results show that none of the combinations improves significantly the performance of our system. Further experimentation is required to see whether different values for the parameters of the formulas presented will give a better performance or some other interpretation of the relevance assessments should be done.

7 Conclusions and Future Work

Our participation in INEX is characterized by applying a fully systematic approach able to support different retrieval tasks identified as ad-hoc tasks (CO and CAS) with simple user modeling and relevance feedback. We investigated the influence of phrases in the retrieval model with respect to the retrieval effectiveness. Furthermore, we experimented with straightforward approaches to (blind) *structural* relevance feedback. Future research includes more extensive experimenting in the area of phrase search and relevance feedback, applying new models for incorporating different aspects of relevance feedback information, and taking more advanced methods for phrase search, by adapting IR approaches such as classifier-thing bigrams [5], by using the WWW as N-gram training data [12], by using vocabulary clustering [8], etc., to XML phrase modeling. Finally, we aim to improve the efficiency of the system on, both memory and CPU wise, using rewriting and optimization rules on the logical level as well as by applying horizontal fragmentation and encoding of the data into more compact structures on the physical level.

References

1. P. Boncz. *Monet: a Next Generation Database Kernel for Query Intensive Applications.* PhD thesis, CWI, 2002.
2. T. Grust, S. Sakr, and J. Teubner. XQuery on SQL Hosts. In *Proceedings of the 30th Int'l Conference on Very Large Data Bases (VLDB)*, 2004.
3. T. Grust and M. van Keulen. Tree Awareness for Relational DBMS Kernels: Staircase Join. In H. M. Blanken, T. Grabs, H.-J. Schek, R. Schenkel, and G. Weikum, editors, *Intelligent Search on XML*, volume 2818 of *Lecture Notes in Computer Science/Lecture Notes in Artificial Intelligence (LNCS/LNAI)*, pages 179–192. Springer-Verlag, Berlin, New York, etc., August 2003.
4. D. Hiemstra. *Using Language Models for Information Retrieval.* PhD thesis, University of Twente, Twente, The Netherlands, 2001.
5. M. Jiang, E. Jensen, S. Beitzel, and S. Argamon. Choosing the Right Bigrams for Information Retrieval. In *Proceeding of the Meeting of the International Federation of Classification Societies*, 2004.
6. J. List, V. Mihajlović, A. de Vries, G. Ramirez, and D. Hiemstra. The TIJAH XML-IR System at INEX 2003. In *Proceedings of the 2nd Initiative on the Evaluation of XML Retrieval (INEX 2003)*, ERCIM Workshop Proceedings, 2004.
7. V. Mihajlović, D. Hiemstra, H. E. Blok, and P. M. G. Apers. An XML-IR-DB Sandwich: Is it Better with an Algebra in Between? In *Proceedings of the SIGIR workshop on Information Retrieval and Databases (WIRD'04)*, pages 39–46, 2004.
8. R. Rosenfeld. Two Decades of Statistical Language Modeling: Where do we go from here? In *Proceedings of the IEEE*, 2000.
9. F. Song and W. B. Croft. A General Language Model for Information Retrieval. In *Proceedings of the eighth international Conference on Information and Knowledge Management*, pages 316–321, 1999.

10. A. Trotman and R. A. O'Keefe. The Simplest Query Language That Could Possibly Work. In N. Fuhr, M. Lalmas, and S. Malik, editors, *Proceedings of the Second Workshop of the INitiative for the Evaluation of XML retrieval (INEX)*, ERCIM Publications, 2004.
11. M. van Keulen. Relational Approach to Logical Query Optimization of XPath. In *Proceedings of the 1st Twente Data Management Workshop (TDM'04) on XML Databases and Information Retrieval*, pages 52–58, 2004.
12. X. Zhu and R. Rosenfeld. Improving Trigram Language Modeling With the World Wide Web. In *Proceedings of the International Conference on Acoustics, Speech, and Signal Processing*, pages 533–536, 2001.

Flexible Retrieval Based on the Vector Space Model

Carolyn J. Crouch, Aniruddha Mahajan, and Archana Bellamkonda

Department of Computer Science,
University of Minnesota Duluth,
Duluth, MN 55812,
(218) 726-7607
ccrouch@d.umn.edu

Abstract. This paper describes the current state of our system for structured retrieval. The system itself is based on an extension of the vector space model initially proposed by Fox [5]. The basic functions are performed using the Smart experimental retrieval system [11]. The major advance achieved this year is the inclusion of a flexible capability, which allows the system to retrieve at a desired level of granularity (i.e., at the element level). The quality of the resultant statistics is largely dependent on issues (in particular, ranking) which have yet to be resolved.

1 Introduction

Our original goal when we began our work with INEX in 2002 was to assess the utility of Salton's vector space model [12] in its extended form for XML retrieval. Familiarity with Smart [11] and faith in its capabilities led us to believe that it might prove useful in this environment. Early results [2, 3] led us to believe that such a system could be utilized for XML retrieval if particular problems (e.g., flexible retrieval, ranking issues) could be solved. During 2002, much effort was spent on the translation of documents and topics from XML to internal Smart format and then back again into INEX reporting format. In 2003, we produced an operational system, but it did not include a flexible component (that is, it could only retrieve at the document level). During 2004, query formulation (for both CO and CAS queries) was completely automated. CAS queries received special attention to insure that all conditions of the query were met [1]. Our major improvement was the design and implementation of a flexible capability which allows the system to retrieve elements at various degrees of granularity [10]. Investigations with respect to relevance feedback in a structured environment were initiated.

We now have a system which, we believe, has the potential to function well in the XML environment. Significant issues, which stand to impact results markedly, remain open to investigation. These include, in particular, ranking and length normalization.

2 Background

One of the basic models in information retrieval is the vector space model, wherein documents and queries are represented as weighted term vectors. The weight as-

N. Fuhr et al. (Eds.): INEX 2004, LNCS 3493, pp. 292 – 302, 2005.

signed to a term is indicative of the contribution of that term to the meaning of the document. Very commonly, *tf-idf* weights [13] or some variation thereof [14] are used. The similarity between vectors (e.g., document and query) is represented by the mathematical similarity of the corresponding term vectors.

In 1983, Fox [5] proposed an extension of the vector space model—the so-called extended vector space model—to allow for the incorporation of objective identifiers with content identifiers in the representation of a document. An extended vector can include different classes of information about a document, such as author name, date of publication, etc., along with content terms. In this model, a document vector consists of a set of subvectors, where each subvector represents a different class of information. Our current representation of an XML document/query consists of 18 subvectors (*abs, ack, article_au_fnm, article_au_snm, atl, au_aff, bdy, bibl_atl, bibl_au_fnm, bibl_au_snm,, bibl_ti, ed_aff, ed_intro, kwd, pub_yr, reviewer_name, ti, vt*) as defined in INEX guidelines. These subvectors represent the properties of the document or article. Of the 18, eight are subjective, that is, contain content-bearing terms: *abs, ack, atl, bdy, bibl_atl, bibl_ti, ed_intro, kwd* (abstract, acknowledgements, article title, body, title of article cited in the bibliography, title of publication containing this article [i.e., journal title], editorial introduction, and keywords, respectively). Similarity between extended vectors in this case is calculated as a linear combination of the similarities of the corresponding subjective subvectors. (The objective subvectors serve here only as filters on the result set returned by CAS queries. That is, when a ranked set of elements is retrieved in response to a query, the objective subvectors are used as filters to guarantee that only elements meeting the specified criteria are returned to the user.)

Use of the extended vector model for document retrieval normally raises at least two issues: the construction of the extended search request [4, 6] and the selection of the coefficients for combining subvector similarities. For XML retrieval, of course, the query is posed in a form that is easily translated into an extended vector. The second problem—the weighting of the subvectors themselves—requires some experimentation. Experiments performed with the 2003 INEX topic set identified the following subjective subvectors as being particularly useful for retrieval: *abs, atl, bdy, bibl_atl, kwd.* We found our best results were obtained with subvector weights of 1, 1, 2, 2, and 1, respectively. (The three remaining subjective subvectors received 0 weights.) More investigation is required in this area with respect to the 2004 topics.

Another issue of interest here is the weighting of terms within subjective subvectors. Experiments indicated that the best results were achieved for the 2003 topics with the respect to both article and paragraph indexings when *Lnu.ltu* term weighting [15] was used. Our 2004 results are based on *Lnu.ltu* term weighting, as defined below:

$$\frac{(1 + \log(tf)) \,/\, (1 + \log(\text{average } tf))}{(1 - \text{slope}) * \text{pivot} + \text{slope} * (\#\text{ unique terms})}$$

where *tf* represents term frequency, slope is an empirically determined constant, and pivot is the average number of unique terms per document, calculated across the entire collection.

3 System Description

Our system handles the processing of XML text as follows:

3.1 Parsing

The documents are parsed using a simple XML parser available on the web.

3.2 Translation to Extended Vector Format

The documents and queries are translated into Smart format and indexed by Smart as extended vectors. We selected the paragraph as our basic indexing unit in the early stages. Thus a typical vector in this system (based on a paragraph indexing) consists of a set of subjective and objective subvectors with a paragraph in the *bdy* subvector. (Other indexing units were later added to include section titles, tables, figure captions, abstracts, and lists.) *Lnu-ltu* term weighting is applied to all subjective subvectors.

3.3 Initial Retrieval

Retrieval takes place by running the queries against the indexed collection using Smart. The queries used in the initial retrieval are simple (rather than extended) vector queries. That is, each query consists of search terms distributed only in the *bdy* subvector. The result is a list of *elements* (paragraphs) ordered by decreasing similarity to the query. Consider all the elements in this list with a non-zero correlation with the query. Each such element represents a terminal node (e.g., paragraph) in the body of a document with some relationship to the query.

3.4 Flexible Retrieval

A basic requirement of INEX is that the retrieval method must return to the user components of documents or elements (i.e., abstract, paragraphs, sub-sections, sections, bodies, articles, figure titles, section titles, and introductory paragraphs) rather than just the document itself. The object is to return the most relevant element(s) in response to a query. Thus a good flexible system should return a mixture of document components (elements) to the user. These elements should be returned in rank order. The method to determine rank should incorporate both exhaustivity (relevance) and specificity (coverage).

Our flexible retrieval module (which we call Flex), is designed as follows. It takes as input a list of elements (e.g., paragraphs), rank-ordered by similarity to the query as determined by Smart in the initial retrieval stage. Each such element represents a leaf of a tree; each tree represents an article in the document collection. (The query at this stage, used to determine correlation with a paragraph, is a simple subvector query; that is, it consists only of search terms distributed in the *bdy* subvector.)

Consider Figure 1, which represents the tree structure of a typical XML article. The root of the tree is the article itself, whereas the leaf nodes are the paragraphs. Flexible retrieval should return relevant document components (e.g., <sec>, <ss1>, <ss2>, <p>, <bdy>, <article>) as shown in Figure 1. In order to determine which components or elements of a tree to return, the system must first build the tree

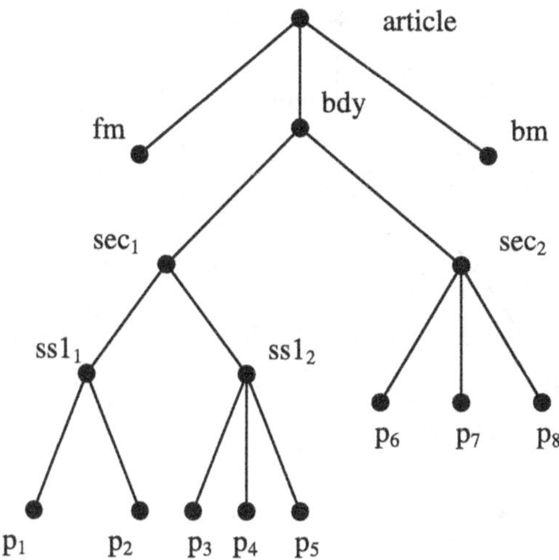

Fig. 1. Tree Structure of a Typical XML Document

structure and then populate the tree by assigning a value to each non-terminal node in the tree. (The value in this case represents a function of exhaustivity and specificity.)

Flex takes a bottom-up approach. All leaf elements having non-zero correlations with the query have already been assigned similarity values by Smart. Consider the set of all such leaf elements which belong to the same tree. For a particular query, trees are constructed for all articles with leaves in this set. To construct the trees (and deal with the issue of specificity [coverage]), at each level of the tree, the number of siblings of a node must be known. The process is straight-forward. Suppose for example in Figure 1 that p_1, p_2, and p_7 were retrieved as leaf elements of the same tree. Flex would then build the tree represented in Figure 2. Any node on a path between a retrieved terminal node and the root node (*article*) is a valid candidate (element) for retrieval.

Building the tree is simple; populating it is not. We have weights (similarity values) associated with all terminal nodes. We consider each such value representative of that node's exhaustivity (e-value) with respect to the query. A question that arises at this point is how to produce a corresponding value representing specificity (s-value) for this node. Our current approach assigns an s-value equal to the e-value for that node. Since all the elements in question here (i.e., the terminal nodes) are relatively small in terms of the number of word types contained therein, this appears to be a reasonable initial approach.

Now that all the terminal nodes of the document tree have associated e-values and s-values, populating the tree (i.e., assigning e- and s-values to the rest of the nodes) begins. For every leaf node, we find its parent and determine the e- and s-values for that parent. The values of a parent are dependent on those of its children (i.e., relevance is propagated up the tree, whereas coverage may diminish as a function of the

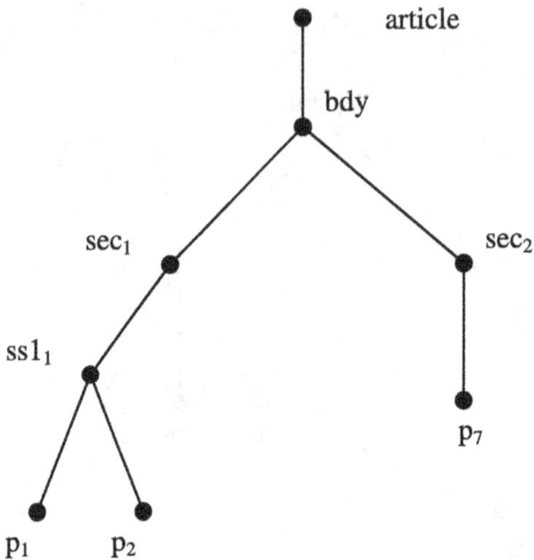

Fig. 2. Tree of Relevant Elements

total number of children [relevant and non-relevant] of a node). The process continues until all the nodes on a path from a leaf to the root (the *article* node) have been assigned e- and s-values. .

After all trees have been populated (and we have e- and s-values associated with each node of each tree), one major problem remains. How can we produce a rank-ordered list of elements (document components) from these populated trees? We need a method which ranks the document components on the basis of e- and s-value. We considered a number of approaches. Our current method uses a simple function of e- and s-value to produce a single value for ranking. (The description given here presents the logical view of Flex; see [10] for a detailed view of Flex implementation.)

3.5 Rank Adjustment

Once a rank-ordered list of elements is produced by Flex, we can undertake the final step in the retrieval process. Initial retrieval produces a set of terminal node elements (paragraphs) having some relationship with the query. Flex produces the expanded set of elements (subsections, sections bodies) associated with those terminal nodes. Taken together, this is the set of potentially relevant elements associated with the query.

Up to this point, only the *bdy* subvector has been utilized in the retrieval process. We can now use the remaining subjective subvectors to adjust the ranking of the element set. By correlating the extended vector representation of the query with the extended vector representation of each element in the returned set, another and potentially more accurate ranking is produced. This step, rank adjustment, is not yet implemented in our current system.

Once a rank-ordered list is produced, the elements are reported for INEX evaluation.

4 Experiments

In the following sections, we describe the experiments performed with respect to the processing of the CO and CAS topics, respectively. In all cases, we use only the topic title as search words in query construction. Term weighting is *Lnu.ltu* in all cases. All indexing is done at the paragraph (basic indexing unit) level unless otherwise specified. No rank adjustment is performed.

4.1 Using CO Topics

Our initial experiments using flexible retrieval were performed using the 2003 topic set. We used several simple methods for calculating e- and s-values and propagating these values up the tree. Our 2004 results are based on one of those methods, wherein the e-value of a node is calculated as the sum of the e-values of its children whereas its s-value is the average of the s-values of its children. Final ranking of a node is based on the product of its e-value and s-value. (The calculation of e- and s-values, their propagation, and the ranking of results will be a focus of attention in the coming year.)

Results indicated that flexible retrieval produced an improvement over document retrieval for the 2003 topic set. The approach was subsequently applied to the 2004 topic set as seen in Table 1. Results achieved by flexible retrieval (labeled Flex) are compared with the results retrieved by the same *Lnu.ltu* weighted query set against various *Lnu.ltu* weighted indexings of the documents (at the article, section, subsection, and paragraph levels, respectively). These results improve to 0.06 (average precision-recall) when the input to Flex is filtered so that trees are built only when a terminal node (paragraph) occurs in one of the top 500 documents retrieved by the query in an article-based indexing. The last entry in Table 1 utilizes an all-element index (an indexing of document elements at all levels of granularity—the union of the article, section, subsection, and paragraph indices). See Figure 3 for more detail.

Table 1. CO Processing (2004 Topic Set)

Indexing	Avg Recall-Precision	Generalized Recall
Article	0.02	4.04
Sec	0.02	28.89
Subsec	0.03	26.57
Para	0.03	32.94
Flex (on para)	0.05	34.94
All Elem	0.06	38.31

It is worth noting that filtering the input to Flex, which with respect to a specific query reduces the number of trees built and ensures that each such tree represents a document in the top (in this case, 500) documents retrieved by that query, produces a average recall-precision of 0.06—the same value produced by a search of the all-element index.

4.2 Using CAS Topics

We process CAS topics in much the same fashion as CO topics, with some important exceptions. During pre-processing of the CAS queries, the subjective and objective portions of the query and the element to be returned (e.g., abstract, section, paragraph) are identified.

Depending on its syntax, a CAS query can be divided into parts, which can be divided into subparts depending on the number of search fields. Further subdivision, depending on the presence of plus or minus signs (representing terms that should or should not be present) preceding a search term, is also possible. CAS preprocessing splits the query into the required number of parts, each of which is processed as a separate Smart query. For example, suppose the query specifies that a search term is to be searched for in field 1. If the field to be searched is an objective subvector, the search term is distributed in that subvector. If the search field specifies a specific subjective subvector, the search term is distributed in that subvector, otherwise the search takes place in the paragraph subvector. The result in this last case is a set of elements (terminal nodes) returned by the Smart search which is used as input to Flex. Flex produces a ranked set of elements (terminal, intermediate, and/or root nodes) as the final output of this small search. After all subsearches associated with the query are complete, the final result set is produced (i.e., the original query is resolved). The element specified for return in the original query is then returned from each element in the result set. See [1] for more details.

CAS processing using flexible retrieval based on a paragraph indexing was applied using the 2004 CAS topic set. The first entry in Table 2 reports the result. In this experiment, the structural constraints specified in the query are strictly maintained (i.e., only the element specified by the query is returned). That is, Flex is run on the para graph indexing, objective constraint(s) applied, and the element specified is returned from that result set. The second entry in this table shows the result when no structural constraints are maintained (that is, all relevant elements, regardless of type, are returned from the result set). The next two entries duplicate experiments 1and 2, but instead of running Flex on the paragraph index retrieve on the all element index. The last

Table 2. CAS Processing (2004 Topic Set)

Indexing	Avg Recall-Precision	Generalized Recall
Flex (on para) constraints maintained	0.04	27.99
Flex (on para) constraints ignored	0.04	9.93
All Elem constraints maintained	0.02	18.33
All Elem constraints ignored	0.02	13.40
All Elem CAS as CO	0.05	36.30

experiment reports on results obtained by relaxing the conditions specified in the query. It treats a CAS query essentially as if it were a CO query. Instead of breaking the query into subqueries and processing each part separately, it combines the search terms and searches the all element index with the combined terms. See Figure 4 for more detail.

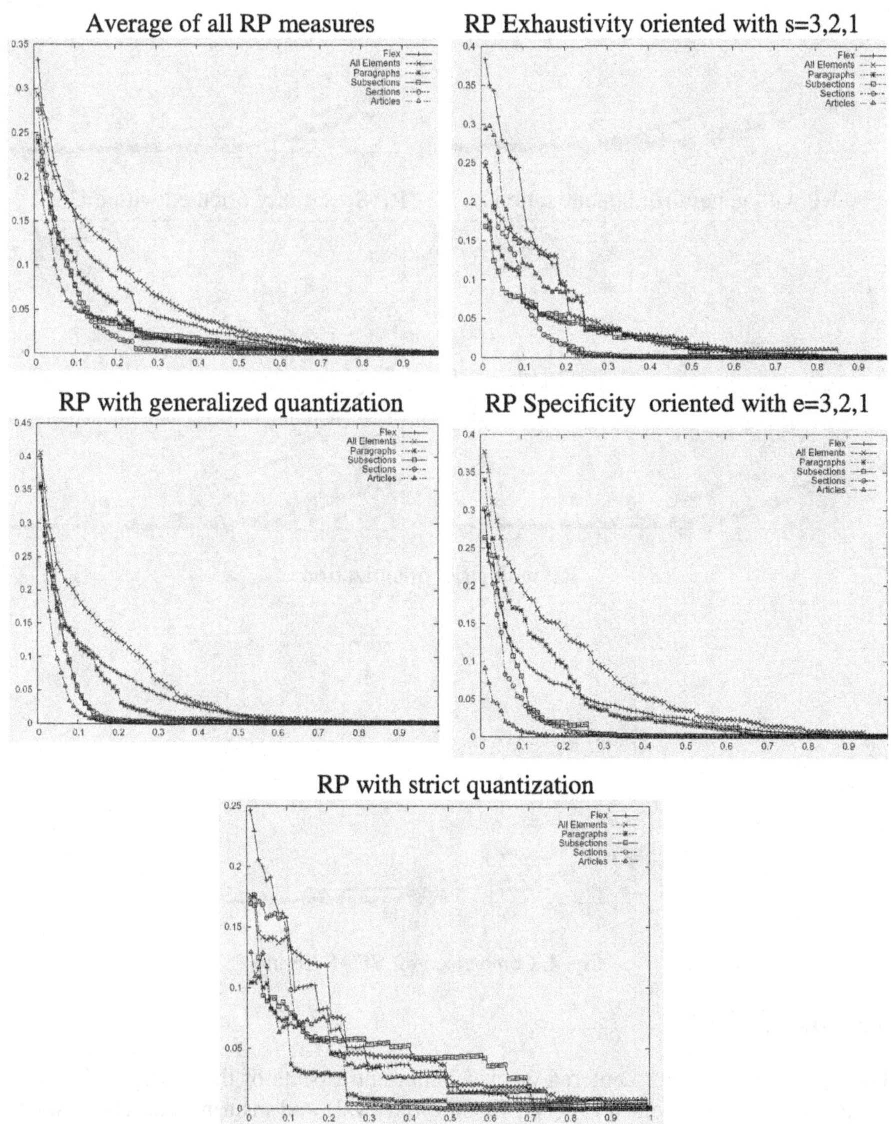

Fig. 3. Comparison of CO Results

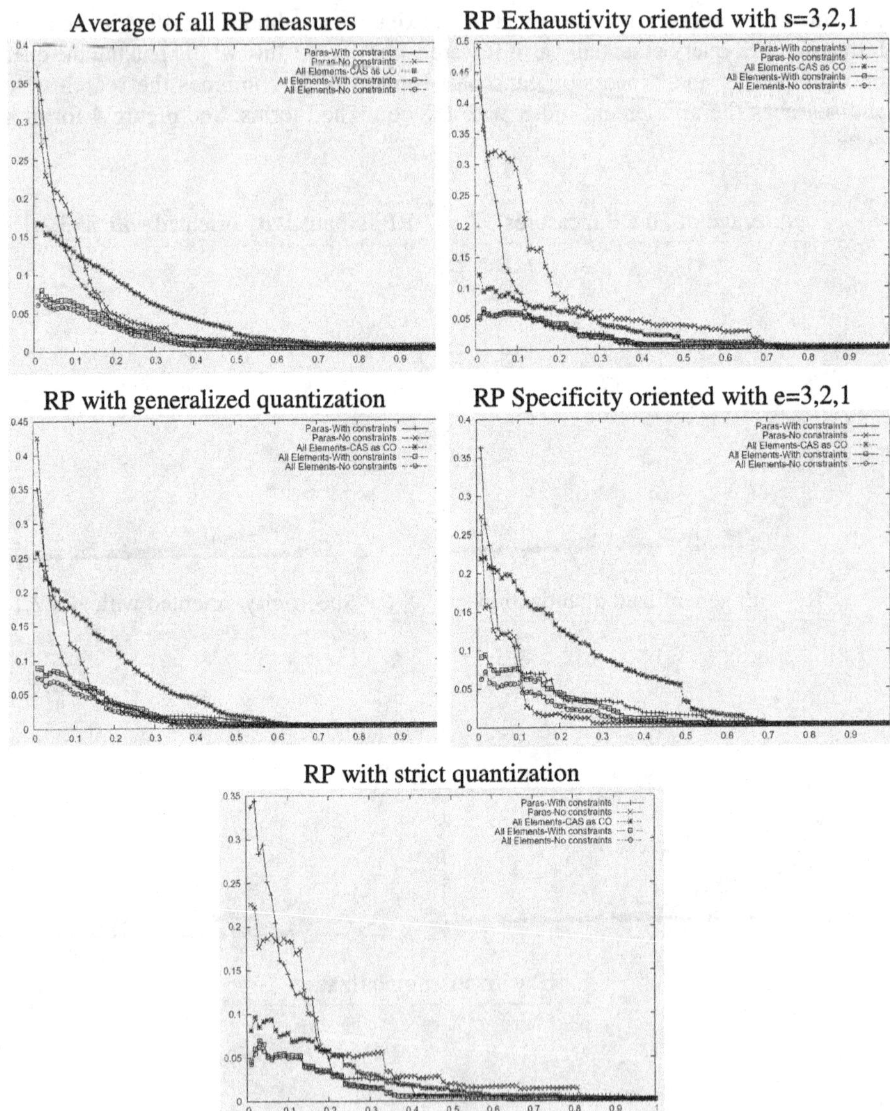

Fig. 4. Comparison of VCAS Results

4.3 Results

During 2004, our work centered on two important aspects of the INEX ad hoc task: retrieving at the element level (i.e., flexible retrieval) and insuring that the result returned from a CAS search met the search requirements (thus producing improvements under SCAS but not necessarily under VCAS). We note that our 2004 results are not competitive (as opposed to 2003 when we were only able to retrieve at the article level). This year, with flexible retrieval based on a paragraph indexing, our current ranking scheme favors the return of smaller elements rather than larger ones. Yet as Kamps, *et.al.* [8] clearly show, in 2003 the probability of relevance increased with element length. Our method of propagating values and ranking elements needs to take this into consideration. It appears that using an all element index improves results. However, the very large index required, the redundancy within it, and the inefficiencies of storage and search time which result leave us to conclude that flexible retrieval, which produces a result dynamically based on a single index, is preferred if it can produce even a comparable result.

4.4 Relevance Feedback in INEX

The importance and value of relevance feedback in conventional information retrieval have long been recognized. Incorporating relevance feedback techniques within the domain of structured retrieval is an interesting challenge.

Working within the constraints of our system, the first question which arises is how to translate the exhaustivity and specificity values associated with each INEX element into an appropriate measure of relevance in our system. Conventional retrieval views relevance assessment as binary. In INEX, we have a range of values for exhaustivity and a corresponding set of values for specificity. There are many possibilities to consider when mapping these values to relevance.

As an initial approach, we decided simply to recognize as relevant those paragraphs with e-values of 3. In other words, we recognize as relevant to the query all elements that are highly exhaustive (disregarding other combinations). We were interested in determining the feasibility of this approach, which depends strongly on having enough of these elements available in the top ranks of retrieved elements. We completed a run using Rocchio's algorithm ($\alpha = \beta = 1$, $\gamma = 0.5$) on a paragraph index with the relevance assessments of the top 20 paragraphs used when constructing the feedback query. The query set consisted of the CO queries in their simple form with search terms distributed in the *bdy* subvector only. The result of the feedback iteration is a set of paragraphs rank-ordered by correlation with the query. The feedback iteration produces an average recall-precision of 0.03 compared to 0.02 in the base case. Flex is then run on this set to produce the associated elements, yielding an aggregate score of 0.04. We look forward to producing more experiments and results next year.

5 Conclusions

Our system, as a result of work done in the past year, is now returning results at the element level, i.e., retrieving at the desired level of granularity. The incorporation of a flexible retrieval facility is required before meaningful INEX experiments can take place. However, there are a number of problems still to be solved with this system, including in particular the propagation of e- and s-values upwards through the document hierarchy and the ranking of elements based on those values. Various approaches have been suggested [7, 9]. Much of our work in the coming year will focus on this issue. A good working result is important, since regardless of how well it does everything else, in the end all results depend on the system's ability to retrieve good elements. We believe that the initial retrieval through Smart produces valid terminal nodes with meaningful e-values. How well we build on this foundation will determine the final utility of the system.

A second area of interest is the extension of relevance feedback techniques to structured retrieval. There are many interesting questions to be addressed in this area in the coming year.

References

[1] Bellamkonda, A. Automation of Content-and-Structure query processing. Master's Thesis, Dept. of Computer Science, University of Minnesota Duluth (2004). http://www.d.umn.edu/cs/thesis/bellamkonda.pdf

[2] Crouch, C., Apte, S., and Bapat, H. Using the extended vector model for XML retrieval. In *Proc of the First Workshop of the Initiative for the Evaluation of XML Retrieval (INEX)*, (Schloss Dagstuhl, 2002), 99-104.

[3] Crouch, C., Apte, S. and Bapat, H. An approach to structured retrieval based on the extended vector model. In *Proc of the Second Workshop of the Initiative for the Evaluation of XML Retrieval (INEX)*, (Schloss Dagstuhl, 2003), 87-93.

[4] Crouch, C., Crouch, D. and Nareddy, K. The automatic generation of extended queries. In *Proc. of the 13th Annual International ACM SIGIR Conference*, (Brussels, 1990), 369-383.

[5] Fox, E. A. Extending the Boolean and vector space models of information retrieval with p-norm queries and multiple concept types. Ph.D. Dissertation, Department of Computer Science, Cornell University (1983).

[6] Fox, E., Nunn, G. and Lee, W. Coefficients for combining concept classes in a collection. *In Proc. of the 11th Annual International ACM SIGIR Conference*, (Grenoble, 1988), 291-307.

[7] Fuhr, N. , and GrossJohann, K. XIRQL: A query language for information retrieval in XML documents. In *Proc of the 24th Annual International ACM SIGIR Conference*, (New Orleans, 2001), 172-180.

[8] Kamps, J., de Rijke, M., and Sigurbjornsson, B. Length normalization in XML retrieval. *In Proc of the 27th Annual International ACM SIGIR Conference* (Sheffield, England, 2004), 80-87.

[9] Liu, S., Zou, Q., and Chu, W. Configurable indexing and ranking for XML information retrieval. *In Proc of the 27th Annual International ACM SIGIR Conference* (Sheffield, England, 2004), 88-95.

[10] Mahajan, Aniruddha. Flexible retrieval in a structured environment. Master's Thesis, Dept. of Computer Science, University of Minnesota Duluth (2004). http://www.d.umn.edu/ cs/thesis/mahajan.pdf

[11] Salton, G. *Automatic information organization and retrieval.* Addison-Wesley, Reading PA (1968).

[12] Salton, G., Wong, A., and Yang, C. S. A vector space model for automatic indexing. *Comm. ACM* 18, 11 (1975), 613-620.

[13] Salton, G. and Buckley, C. Term weighting approaches in automatic text retrieval. In *IP&M* 24, 5 (1988), 513-523.

[14] Singhal, A. AT&T at TREC-6. In *The Sixth Text REtrieval Conf (TREC-6)*, NIST SP 500-240 (1998), 215-225.

[15] Singhal, A., Buckley, C., and Mitra, M. Pivoted document length normalization. In *Proc. of the 19th Annual International ACM SIGIR Conference*, (Zurich,1996), 21-19.

Relevance Feedback for XML Retrieval

Yosi Mass and Matan Mandelbrod

IBM Research Lab,
Haifa, 31905, Israel
{yosimass, matan}@il.ibm.com

Abstract. Relevance Feedback (RF) algorithms were studied in the context of traditional IR systems where the returned unit is an entire document. In this paper we describe a component ranking algorithm for XML retrieval and show how to apply known RF algorithms from traditional IR on top of it to achieve Relevance Feedback for XML. We then give two examples of known RF algorithms and show results of applying them to our XML retrieval system in the INEX'04 RF Track.

1 Introduction

Relevance Feedback (RF) was studied e.g. in [6, 7] in the context of traditional IR engines that return full documents for a user query. The idea is to have an iterative process where results returned by the search engine are marked as relevant or not relevant by the user and this information is then fed back to the search engine to refine the query. RF algorithms can be also used for Automatic Query Refinement (AQR) by applying an automatic process that marks the top results returned by the search engine as relevant for use by subsequent iterations.

In [5] we described an algorithm for XML component ranking and showed how to apply existing AQR algorithms to run on top of it. The Component ranking algorithm is based on detecting the most informative component types in the collection and creating separate indices for each such type. For example in the INEX[3] collection the most informative components are articles, sections and paragraphs. Given a query Q we run the query on each index separately and results from the different indices are merged into a single result set with components sorted by their relevance score to the given query Q. We showed then in [5] that we can take advantage of the separate indices and apply existing AQR methods from traditional IR on each index separately without any modification to the AQR algorithm.

In this paper we show how further to exploit the separate indices to achieve Relevance Feedback for XML by applying existing RF algorithms with real user feedback to the base component ranking algorithm. Why is it different than applying Automatic Relevance Feedback? The difference lies in the data on which the relevance feedback input is given. In AQR the process is automatic hence it can be done on the top N results (N is a given constant) of each index separately before merging the results. In a real user feedback scenario the user does the feedback on the merged results and assuming assessment of at most the top N results then we have feedback on N results

N. Fuhr et al. (Eds.): INEX 2004, LNCS 3493, pp. 303 – 310, 2005.

from all indices together. It can happen that most of the feedback came from few indices but still we would like to use the feedback to improve results from other indices as well. This is explained in details in section 2 below.

The paper is organized as follows: In section 2 we describe a general method to apply existing RF algorithms on top of the component ranking algorithm. Then in section 3 we discuss two specific RF algorithms and demonstrate their usage to XML retrieval using the method from section 2. In section 4 we report experiments with those algorithms for the INEX RF track and we conclude in section 5 with summary and future directions.

2 Relevance Feedback for XML Retrieval

In [5] we described an algorithm for XML component ranking and showed how to apply existing AQR algorithms on top of it. The base algorithm is described in Fig. 1 below.

1. For each index i
   a. Compute the result set Res_i of running Q on index i
   b. Normalize scores in Res_i to [0,1] by normalizing to score(Q,Q)
   c. Scale each score by its containing article score from Res_0
2. Merge all Res_i to a single result set Res composed of all components sorted by their score

Fig. 1. XML Component ranking

We brief here the algorithm steps while full details can be found in [5]. In step 1 we run the given query on each index separately (step a) and then normalize result scores in each index to be able to compare scores from different indices (step b). We then apply a DocPivot scaling (step c) and finally in step 2 we merge the results to a single sorted result set of all components.

Since we have separate indices for different component granularities we showed in [5] that we can modify the above algorithm with an AQR procedure by adding a new step between 1.a and 1.b in which we apply the given AQR algorithm on each index separately.

Applying real user feedback is somewhat more complicated than applying AQR since the feedback is given on the merged result set and not on results from each index separately. Assuming that the user can assess at most N results then we have feedback on the top N results from all indices together. Those N results can all come form a single index or from few indices but we still want to use this feedback to improve results from all indices. Moreover we would like to do it without modifying the RF algorithms. We do this by applying the base component ranking algorithm as in Fig. 1 above and then continue with the algorithm in Fig. 2 below.

3. Take the top N results from Res and given their assessments extract R (Relevants) and the NR (Not relevants) from the top N.
4. For each index i
   a. Apply the RF algorithm on (R, NR, Res_i) with any other needed RF specific params and refine Q to Q'
   b. Compute the result set Res'_i of running Q' on index i
   c. Normalize scores in Res'_i to [0,1] by normalizing to score(Q',Q)
   d. Scale each score by its containing article score from Res'_0
5. Merge all Res'_i to a single result set Res' composed of all components sorted by their score
6. Freeze the original top N from Res as the top N in Res'

Fig. 2. XML Component ranking with RF

The algorithm in Fig. 2 describes a single iteration of applying an RF algorithm on our component ranking algorithm. The algorithm works as follows; In step 3 we use the top N results from the merged results and based on the user feedback we select the subset of relevant (R) and non relevant (NR) components. Note that in a traditional RF algorithm the R and NR components are of same type as the collection (namely, full documents) while here they come from different component types so for each index some of them may be of different granularities than components in that index. We claim that the fact that a component is relevant or not relevant for the query can be used in a typical RF algorithm regardless to its granularity. In the next section we demonstrate two specific RF algorithms and show that at least for them the above claim holds.

So in step 4 we just apply the existing RF algorithm on each of our indices separately where we give it the R and NR components as if they came from that index. The result is a refined query Q' (step 4.a) and then similar to the AQR case the new query is used to generate a new result set Res_i for each index. Results are then scaled by the DocPivot as described in [5] and finally the different result sets are merged (step 5) to a single result set of all component types.

To be able to measure the contribution of an RF iteration over the original query we take in step 6 the seen top N components and put them back as the top N in the final merged result. We then remove them from rest of Res' if they appear there again. In the next section we demonstrate two example RF algorithms that we applied on our XML component ranking using the algorithm from Fig. 2 above.

3 Example Usages of RF Algorithms for XML

In this section we describe two RF algorithms known from IR and we show how we applied them on top of our XML component ranking algorithm.

3.1 Rocchio for XML

The Rocchio algorithm [6] is the first RF algorithm that was proposed for the Vector Space Model[8]. The idea in the Vector Space model is that both the documents and the query are represented as vectors in the space generated by all tokens in the collection (assuming any two tokens are independent). The similarity of a document to a query is then measured as some distance between two vectors, usually as the cosine of the angle between the two.

The Rocchio formula tries to find the optimal query; one that maximises the difference between the average of the relevant documents and the average of the non-relevant documents with respect to the query. The Rocchio equation is given in Fig. 3 below.

$$Q' = \alpha Q + \beta/_{n_1} \sum_{i=1}^{n_1} R_i - \gamma/_{n_2} \sum_{i=1}^{n_2} NR_i$$

Fig. 3. The Rocchio equation

Q is the initial query, Q' is the resulted refined query, $\{R_1, \ldots R_{n1}\}$ are the set of relevant documents and $\{NR_1, \ldots, NR_{n2}\}$ are the non-relevant documents. Since Q, $\{R_i\}$, and $\{NR_i\}$ are all vectors then the above equation generates a new vector Q' that is close to the average of the relevant documents and far from the average of the non-relevant documents. The α, β, γ are tuning parameters that can be used to weight the effect of the original query and the effect of the relevant and the non-relevant documents. The Rocchio algorithm gets an additional parameter *k* which is the number of new query terms to add to the query.

Note that step 4.a in Fig. 2 above is composed in the Rocchio case from two sub steps; In the first sub step new terms are added to the query and then the original query terms are reweighed. We can therefore apply to the first sub step in the Rocchio case two embedding variants into our XML component ranking –

1. Compute the new query terms only in the main index[1] and use them for other indices as well.
2. Compute a different set of new terms to add for each index separately.

In section 4 we report experiments we did with the Rocchio algorithm in our XML component ranking algorithm.

3.2 LA Query Refinement for XML

In [5] we described a general method to modify our component ranking algorithm with Automatic Query Refinement and described results for an example such AQR algorithm based on [1]. The idea there is to add to the query Lexical Affinity (LA) terms that best separate the relevant from the non relevant documents with respect to

---

[1] We always assume the the first index contains the full documents.

a query Q. A Lexical Affinity is a pair of terms that appear close to each other in some relevant documents such that exactly one of the terms appears in the query. We summarize here the various parameters that are used in the LA Refinement procedure while full details can be found in [5]. The procedure gets 4 parameters ***(M, N, K, α)*** where ***M*** denotes the number of highly ranked documents to use for constructing a list of candidate LAs. ***N*** (N >> M) is the number of highly rank documents to be used for selecting the best ***K*** LAs (among the candidate LAs) which have the highest Information Gain. Those LAs are then added to the query Q and their contribution to *score(Q, d)* is calculated as described in details in [5]. Since they don't actually appear in the query Q we take their TF_Q to be the given parameter **α**.

This LA Refinement algorithm can be used with real user feedback and can be plugged as a RF module in our component ranking algorithm as in Fig. 2 above. In section 4 we describe experiments we did with that algorithm for XML retrieval.

4 Runs Description

We describe now the runs we submitted for the RF track - one for the Rocchio implementation and one for the LA refinement.

4.1 Rocchio Runs

As discussed above the Rocchio algorithm is based on the Vector Space scoring model. Since our component ranking algorithm is also based on that model then we could easily plug the Rocchio algorithm into our component ranking as in Fig. 2 above. In our implementation a document *d* and the query *Q* are represented as vectors as in Fig. 4 below.

$$d = (w_d(t_1),\dots,w_d(t_n)),\ w_d(t_i) = tf_d(t_i) * idf(t_i)$$
$$Q = (w_Q(t_1),\dots,w_Q(t_n)),\ w_Q(t_i) = tf_Q(t_i) * idf(t_i)$$

Fig. 4. Document and Query vectors

Where $tf_Q(t)$ is a function of the number of occurrences of *t* in *Q*, $tf_d(t)$ is a function of the number of occurrences of *t* in *d* and *idf(t)* is a function of the inverse document frequency of *t* in the index (exact functions details are described in [5]).

Given α, β, γ we define the Gain of a token *t* as

$$G(t) = \beta/_{n_1} \sum_{i=1}^{n_1} w_{R_i}(t) - \gamma/_{n_2} \sum_{i=1}^{n_2} w_{NR_i}(t)$$

Fig. 5. Gain of a token

where $w_{R_i}(t)$ are the weights of *t* in each relevant component R_i and $w_{NR_i}(t)$ are the weights of *t* in each non-relevant component NR_i as defined in Fig. 4. It is easy to see that tokens with the highest Gain are the ones that maximize the optimal query Q' as defined by the Rocchio equation in Fig. 3 above.

So in the RF step (4.a) in Fig. 2 above we compute *G(t)* for each new token *t* in the top N components that is not already in Q. We then select the *k* tokens with the maximal Gain as the terms to be added to the query Q.

We run a single Rocchio iteration where we compute the new tokens to add only on the main index (first variant from sec 3.1 above). We tried with N = 20, $\alpha = 1$, $\beta = \{0.1, \ldots, 0.9\}$, $\gamma = \{0.1, \ldots, 0.9\}$ and k = 3 on our base CO algorithm. The Mean Average Precision (MAP) values we got using the inex_eval aggregate metric for 100[2] results are summarized in Fig. 6.

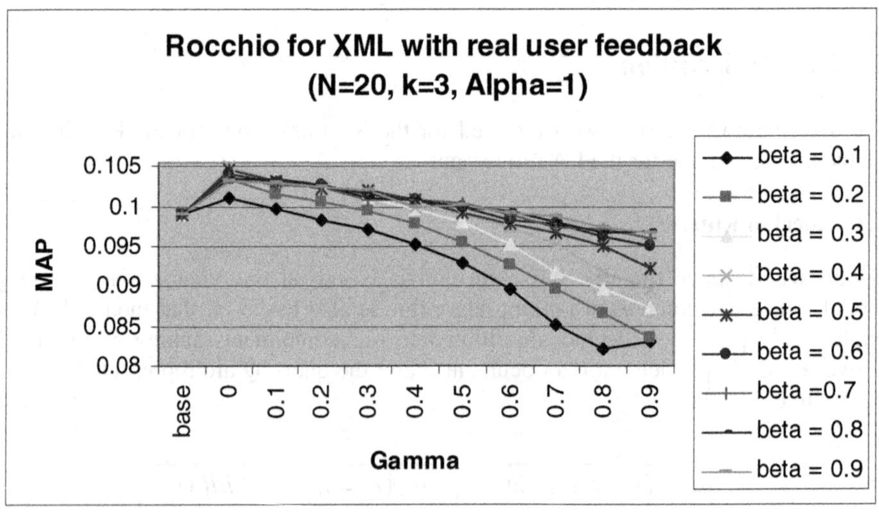

Fig. 6. Rocchio for XML

The Figure shows graphs for the different values. We can see that the value for γ = 0.1 gives best results for all γ values. The best MAP was achieved at γ = 0.8 which is what we sent for the RF track.

We see that we get very minor improvement (~5%) over the base run. A possible reason can be the Freezing method of the top N results which leave many possible Non-relevant components in the top N so the effect of RF is only for components at rank N+1 and lower.

[2] Note that the results here are for a run with 100 results so the MAP is lower then the 0.134 value we got in our official INEX submission for 1500 results. Note also that the MAP values in this graph are lower than those achieved in Fig. 7 for LA Refinement as those in Fig. 7 were calculated for 1500 results.

4.2 LA Refinement Runs

Fig. 7 summarizes our experiments with the LA procedure parameters (M, N, K, α). In all experiments we fixed M = 20 and we selected out of the top 20 components from our base run those that were assessed as relevant (highly exhaustive-highly specific). We then used those components for extracting the set of candidate LAs to add to the query. The figure below shows are results for fixing K = 5 namely we select the best 5 LAs to be added to the query. The figure shows 4 graphs for different values of N (100, 200, 300, 400) and each graph shows the MAP achieved for α values at the range 0.4-1.3.

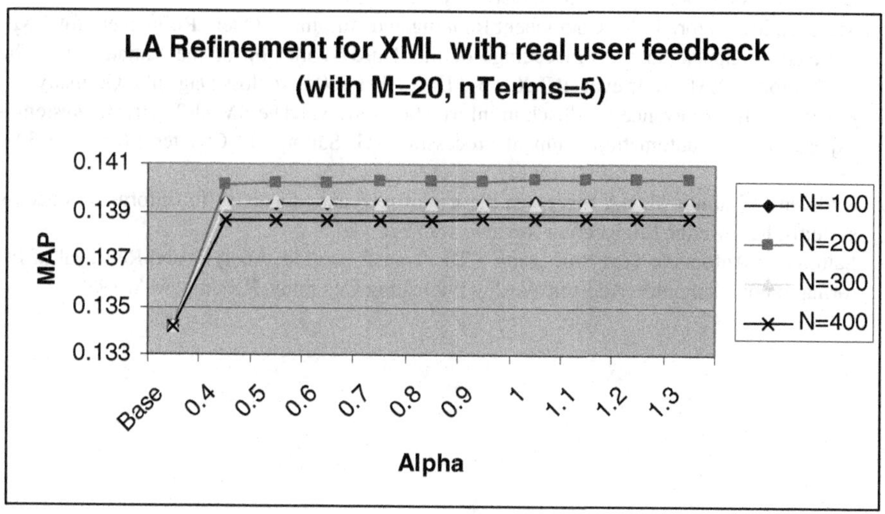

Fig. 7. LA runs with fixed M=20, K=5 and varying N, α

We can see that the base run with no RF got MAP=0.134 and actually all graphs achieved improvement over that base run. The best results were achieved for N=200 (N is the number of documents to use for selecting the best LAs) but it was not significantly different from other parameter combinations we have tried.

5 Discussion

We have presented an XML retrieval system and showed how to run RF algorithms on top of it to achieve relevance feedback for XML. We then demonstrated two example RF algorithms and reported their usage for the XML RF track. We got relatively small improvements in the Mean Average Precision (MAP) with those algorithms and we still need to explore if it's an algorithm limitations or a possible problem in the metrics used to calculate the MAP.

References

1. Carmel D., Farchi E., Petruschka Y., Soffer A.: Automatic Query Refinement using Lexical Affinities with Maximal Information Gain. Proceedings of the 25th Annual International ACM SIGIR Conference on Research and Development in Information Retrieval, 2002.
2. Carmel D., Maarek Y., Mandelbrod M., Mass Y., Soffer A.: Searching XML Documents via XML Fragments, SIGIR 2003, Toronto, Canada, Aug. 2003
3. INEX, Initiative for the Evaluation of XML Retrieval, http://inex.is.informatik.uni-duisburg.de
4. Mass Y., Mandelbrod M.: Retrieving the most relevant XML Component, Proceedings of the Second Workshop of the Initiative for The Evaluation of XML Retrieval (INEX), 15-17 December 2003, Schloss Dagstuhl, Germany, pg 53-58
5. Mass Y., Mandelbrod M. : Component Ranking and Automatic Query Refinement for XML retrieval, to appear in the Proceedings of the Third Workshop of the Initiative for The Evaluation of XML Retrieval (INEX), 6-8 December 2004, Schloss Dagstuhl, Germany
6. Rocchio J. J. : Relevance Feedback in information retrieval The SMART retrieval system – experiements in automatic document processing, (G. Salton ed.) Chapter 14 pg 313-323, 1971.
7. Ruthven I., Lalmas M. : A survey on the use of relevance feedback for information access systems, Knowledge Engineering Review, 18(1):2003.
8. Salton G. : Automatic Text Processing – The Transformation, Analysis and Retrieval of Information by Computer, Addison Wesley Publishing Company, Reading, MA, 1989.

A Universal Model for XML Information Retrieval

Maria Izabel M. Azevedo[1], Lucas Pantuza Amorim[2], and Nívio Ziviani[3]

[1] Department of Computer Science, State University of Montes Claros, Montes Claros, Brazil
izabel@dcc.ufmg.br
[2] Department of Computer Science, State University of Montes Claros, Montes Claros, Brazil
lucaspantuza@yahoo.com.br
[3] Department of Computer Science, Federal University of Minas Gerais, Belo Horizonte, Brazil
nivio@dcc.ufmg.br

Abstract. This paper presents an approach for extending the vector space model (VSM) to perform XML retrieval. The model is extended to support important aspects of XML structural and semantic information such as element nesting level, matching tag names in the query and the collection and the relation between tag names and content of an element. Potential use of the model for heterogeneous as well as for the unstructured collection is also shown. We compared our model with the standard vector space model and obtained a gain for unstructured and structured queries. For unstructured collections the vector space model effectiveness is preserved.

1 Introduction

Studying the structure of a XML [3] document we can observe special aspects on its information organization: the hierarchical structure corresponding to the nesting of elements in a tree and the presence of *markups that describes their content* [1]. The first one is important for information retrieval because the words on different levels of the XML tree may have different importance for expressing the information content in the whole tree. Moreover, if markup describes its content, it must have been conceived semantically related to the information it delimits. This makes the second aspect especially important.

Another important aspect on XML documents is that it introduces a new retrieval unit. We do not have only documents and collections anymore. Now we have elements that can be inside of another element and also contain many others. Consequently, the unit of information to be returned to users can vary. If one element satisfies a query so its ancestor or descendant may also satisfy. Besides, with XML documents, the user can propose queries that explore specific elements.

In the XML environment there are two types of queries, those with structural constraints, called CAS (Content and Structure), and those without constraints called CO (Content Only) [5]. In this paper we propose an extension of the vector space model [8] that considers both aspects (nested structure and markup that describes content) of

N. Fuhr et al. (Eds.): INEX 2004, LNCS 3493, pp. 311 – 321, 2005.

XML structure. This will be done in order to improve the vector space model result for CO and CAS queries, processing retrieval units of varying lengths.

Although the extended model has been conceived to explore the semantic relation between XML markups and content of an element, we demonstrate that it can be applied to non-XML documents. In this case, the vector space model effectiveness will be preserved. It can also be applied to homogeneous collections, where homogeneous structures do not always allow appropriate semantic relation between markups and content of an element. Consequently, our model has universal application, achieve in complete automatic process.

The rest of the paper is organized as follows: Section 2 describes the extension to the vector space model presenting the factor that will explore XML characteristics. Section 3 shows the model applications to different collections. Section 4 presents the results and section 5 concludes the paper.

2 XML Retrieval Using the Vector Space Model

In this section, we introduce the retrieval model. A retrieval unit is defined and also the new *fxml* factor, used to explore XML characteristics.

2.1 Retrieval Units

The first challenge we face when studying XML Information Retrieval is what will be the ideal retrieval unit to be returned to the user, the one that best solve his information needs. In one XML document, there are many possibilities: we can return a whole document or any of its sub-elements. But, what is the best one? The answer depends on the user query and the content of each element. Related work, as [2] and [6], index pre-defined elements as retrieval units.

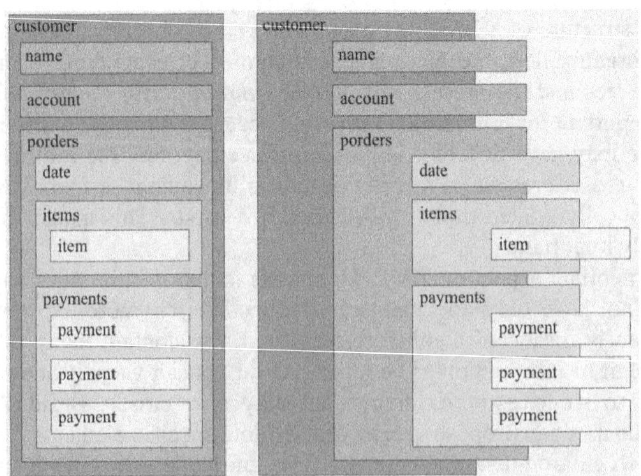

Fig. 1. Retrieval units

In our model we evaluate all possible combinations of elements for each query. To make it possible we should index all components as an information unit. In the example of Fig. 1, our original collection will be expanded from 1 document and 10 sub-elements to 11 retrieval units, each one with an entry in the inverted list. The statistic of each element will consider all the text inside of its sub-elements.

2.2 Vector Space Model Applied to XML Retrieval

From the vector space model, we have that the relevance of document D to query Q, $\rho(Q,D)$, is given by the cosine measure [7]:

$$\rho(Q,D) = \sum_{ti \in Q \cap D} \frac{w_Q(ti) * w_D(ti)}{\|Q\| * \|D\|} \tag{1}$$

where,

- ti is a term in the collection;
- $W_Q(ti)$ is the weight of the query and does not affect the ranking;
- $W_D(ti)$ is the weight of the document and is given by

$$w_D(ti) = log(tf(ti)) * log(N/df(ti)). \tag{2}$$

To adapt this model to XML documents we introduce changes that express their characteristics, as follows. First, we will consider each element as a new retrieval unit. $tf(ti)$ is taking for each of them, becoming $tf(ti,e)$, so:

- $tf(ti,e)$ is the number of occurrences of a term ti in a element e;
- $df(ti)$ is the number of elements that contain ti;
- N is the total number of elements in the collection.

```
<customer id="C1"/>
  <name> JOHN DOE </name>
  <account id="A1"> 1894654 </account>
  <porders>
     <porder id="PO1" acct="A1">
       <items>
         <item id="I1"> shoes </item>
       </items>
       <payments>
         <payment id="P1">due january 15 </payment>
         <payment id="P2">due january 20 </payment>
         <payment id="P3">due february15 </payment>
       </payments>
     </porder>
  </porders>
</customer>
```

Fig. 2. One XML Document

Now, we consider the nested structure of a XML document. One term will be counted for elements where it appears in textual content and for the ancestor elements of *e*, as showed bellow for the example XML document in Fig. 2.

Thus:

- *tf(*`january, payment id = "P1"`*)* = 1;
- *tf(*`january, payment id = "P2"`*)* = 1;
- *tf(*`january, payments`*)* = 2;
- *df(*`january`*)* = 3.

So *ρ(*`january,payments`*)* will be greater than *ρ(*`january,payment`*)*. As elements in a higher level in the XML tree include the contents of sub-elements, *tf(ti,e)* will increase. This problem has been treated in [2], using the concept of augmentation. We will apply this idea, using a factor (*fnh*) that will reduce the weight of terms contribution depending on their position on XML tree as explained later on.

2.3 Retrieval Model Extension

At this point, we have already defined how the standard vector space model statistics will be calculated, just adapting them to the new retrieval unit, present on XML documents. In the following, we will describe one new factor (*fxml*), which will explore XML characteristics pointed in the introduction, assigning different weights for each term. Thus:

$$\rho(Q, D) = \sum ti \in Q \cap D \frac{w_Q(ti) * w_D(ti, e) * fxml(ti, e)}{\|Q\| * \|D\|} \tag{3}$$

where,

$$fxml(ti,e) = fnh(ti,e) * fstr(ti,e) * focr(ti,e) \cdot \tag{4}$$

The Nesting Factor, denoted by fnh, expresses the relevance of terms considering their position on the XML tree, and is given by:

$$fnh(ti,e) = 1/(1+nl) \tag{5}$$

where,

- *nl* is the number of levels from element *e* to its sub-element containing term *ti*.

The nesting factor can vary between the following two values:

- *fnh(ti,e)* = 1, for terms directly in element *e*,
- *fnh(ti,e)* = 1/*nd*, *nd* being the depth of the XML tree.

This factor will reduce the term contribution for distant elements (upwards) in XML tree.

The Structure Factor, denoted by *fstr*, expresses how the query structural constraints are satisfied by the context[1] of an element and is given by:

$$fstr(ti,e) = (common\_markups + 1)/(nr\_qmarkups + 1) \tag{6}$$

where,

- *common_markups* is the number of markups present in the query structural constraints and also in the context of element *e* that contains *ti*;
- *nr_qmarkups* is the number of markups in the query structural constraints.

The structure factor can vary from the following to values:

- *fstr(ti,e)* = 1/(*nr_qmarkups*+1), when no structural constraints appears in the context of *ti*,
- *fstr(ti,e)* = 1, when all query's structural constraints markups appears in the context of *ti*.

This factor will valorize a context that better satisfies structural constraints present in the query. It is important on the CAS query, where users express elements that will better fit their information need. For CO queries it will be equal to 1, and will not influence the relevance equation.

The last factor, Co-occurrence Factor, denoted by *focr*, expresses the semantic relation between markups and their content, and is given by:

$$focr(ti,e) = cf(ti,e) * idf(ti) * N * icf(e) \tag{7}$$

where,

- *cf(ti,e)* is the number of times the markup of element *e*, denoted by *m*, delimits a textual content containing term *ti*. In other words, number of co-occurrences of term *ti* and markup *m* in the collection;
- *idf(ti,e)* is the inverse of the number of elements *e* that contain *ti*;
- *icf(e)* is the inverse of the number of times markup *m* appears in the collection;
- *N* is the total number of elements in the collection.

Then, *cf(ti,e)*idf(ti,e)*, is the reason between the number of times term *ti* appears with *m* for the numbers of elements containing *ti* in the collection. And *icf(e)*N*, express the popularity of markup *m* in the collection. So, the co-occurrence factor takes into account the co-occurrence of terms and markups, considering the popularity of markups. Concluding, the XML factor (*fxml*) explores XML characteristics looking for the semantic of terms, looking for information behind words.

3 Applications of the Extended Model

In this section we show the application of our model in unstructured, homogeneous and heterogeneous collections, analyzing the fxml factor.

[1] Context is the element position on the XML tree, represented by its complete path, from the root to the element containing the textual content.

3.1 Non-XML Documents

Considering that a real world collection may contain XML documents and non-XML documents, we will demonstrate that the same model can be applied on those documents, preserving the vector space model effectiveness.

Examining Formula 3, we conclude that to satisfy this condition, XML factor must be equal to 1. To demonstrate it, we will consider that the whole content of a non-XML document will be delimited by one special markup, for example `<article>` and `</article>`. This special markup will convert a non-XML document in a XML document, with only one element. So it will be processed as any other XML document, but XML factor will be equal to 1.

Next we will analyze each of the three *fxml* factors, for non-XML documents.

Fnh. In one non-XML document there is only one level where all textual content is, so $nl = 0$ and *fnh(ti,e)* will be equal to 1.

Fstr. For a non-XML document, the numerator will be equal to 1 because it has no markup, the denominator will depend on the query type. Thus:

- For CO: *q_markups* = 0 and *fstru(ti,e)* = 1;
- For CAS: *nr_qmarkups* may vary depending on the number of structural constraints in the query.

One non-XML document will never satisfy the CAS query structural constraints because it is not structured, then its relevance will be decreased compared with those that can satisfy query constraints.

Focr. For one non-XML:

- *cf(ti,e)*, the number of times *ti* appears with markup *m*, will be the number of times *ti* appears in the collections because all documents have the same special markup `<article>` and only this markup. So *cf(ti,e)* is the inverse of *idf(ti)*, making *cf(ti,e)*idf(ti)* = 1;
- *icf(e)*, the inverse number of times markup *m* appears in the collection, will be equal 1/*N*, the number of documents in the collection, because all documents in the collection will have the same special markup `<article>`. So *N*icf(e)* will be equal 1, making *focr(ti,e)* =1.

Non-XML documents are a special case and the model will converge to the vector space model.

3.2 Homogeneous Collections

A homogeneous collection is defined as a collection where all documents have the same DTD. In this section we will analyze the implications it has on our model. We now discuss each of the three *fxml* factor, for homogeneous Collections.

Fnh. This factor will affect the relevance of elements, reducing the term contribution for distant elements (upwards) in XML tree.

Fstr. This factor will be analyzed only for CAS queries because for CO queries it will be always 1, as stated in Section 4.

As all documents have the same DTD, they have the same elements and so *fstr(ti,e)* will be equal for all elements. Any document will have the same probability to have an element return to user. Within one document, those elements with more similarity with the query structural constraints will have greater relevance. Also they will have better chance to be returned to the user.

Focr. In homogeneous collections, all documents have the same markups, and not always there will be an appropriated semantic relation between markups and the content of an element. Examining INEX [4] homogeneous collections, for example, we observe that its markups describe information structure (`<p>`, `<bdy>`, `<fm>`, `<bm>`) rather than information content. So this factor, will probably not affect much the relevance ranking.

3.3 Heterogeneous Collection

A heterogeneous collection is defined as a collection where documents may have different DTD. Our Model does not use any information that comes from DTD. It just indexes elements, terms and markups, collecting statistics that measure the relation between them, so we do not need to make any change in dealing with heterogeneous collections. But it is important to analyze how the heterogeneity of markups will influence the relevance ranking of our model. We now discuss each of the three *fxml* factor, for heterogeneous Collections.

Fnh. This factor will affect the relevance of elements, reducing the term contribution for distant elements (upwards) in XML tree.

Fstr. As stated before, this factor is always 1 for CO query. So let us analyze CAS queries. CAS queries impose a structural constraint, and will have greater relevance to those elements that satisfy them. So, documents with DTDs similar to the structure of the query will be ranked first. If a user asks for:

```
//article[about(.//author, John Smith)],
```

one element as:

```
<author> John Smith </author>,
```

or even

```
<author>
   <first name> John</first name>
   <last name> Smith</last name>
</author>,
```

will be better ranked than one as

```
<title> John Smith Biography </title>.
```

The reason is because the first two have markups present in the structure constraint of the query and the third has not. This will come across the information need of the user.

But one element with a markup <author> will be better ranked than one with <writer> on its DTD. It happens because both markups have the same semantic, but they are not equal and only <author> is present in the structure constraint of the query. It will affect the ranking, but will not avoid that the element with <writer> can be returned to the user.

Focr. This factor tries to explore the fact that markups describe their content. Considering that in a heterogeneous collection different DTD will allow better relation between each document structure and its content, it will help to explore different meanings of the same words in different contexts.

But here appears the following language problem: which markup is semantically closer to John Smith, <author> or <writer>? <author> or <autor> ?

Factor *focr* also ponders the frequency of markups in the collection by *N*icf(e)*. So, if <author> is more widespread than <writer> and <autor>, it will have more chance to appear with John Smith. But it will be compensated by *icf(e)*, in a similar way that common terms in one collection will be reduced by *idf(t)*, in standard vector space model.

Concluding, our model can deal with heterogeneous collections, to answer unstructured or structured queries. The model uses statistical measures of markups and terms, and do not need to map the structure of one DTD onto the others.

4 Results

The proposed model was run over the homogeneous and heterogeneous INEX collections [4]. For the homogeneous collection, the effect of each term of *fxml* factor was observed.

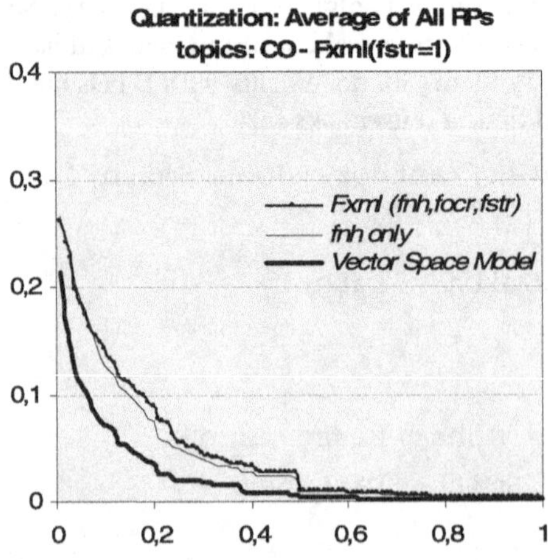

Fig. 3. Recall/Precision Curves comparing Vector Space Model and Adapted Model

The *fnh* factor as expected, improves considerably the vector space model effectiveness as expected, as shown in Fig. 3. Upwards elements accumulate all sub-elements contribution and without this consideration many of them would have been better ranked than more important sub-elements.

We also compared different values of Fnh, concluding that when it changes for elements in different levels of a XML tree, then precision improves a little bit. Subsequently, we introduced the Focr factor and observed a small improvement, observe the small improvement as shown in Fig. 4, which can be imputed to the fact that in homogeneous collections this factor will not vary much, because all documents have the same structure.

For CAS queries the factor Fstr was introduced and also caused some improvement as shown in Fig. 5.

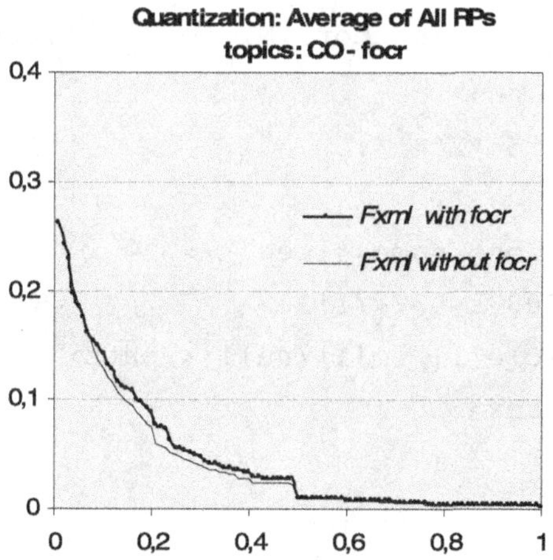

Fig. 4. Recall/Precision Curves changes with *Focr*

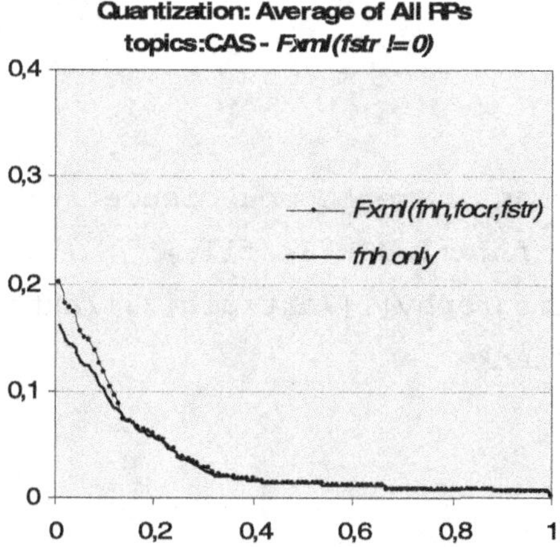

Fig. 5. Recall/Precision Curves changes with *Fstr*

CAS queries results are worse than CO results. It raises a question: can the structure constraint of a query help to improve the precision of the results? To answer this question we should compare the results of CAS queries using fstr, which uses structure information to improve performance, with the results without it, for the same set of queries. Fig. 5 confirms that structure constraint of a query improves precision. So, why CAS queries results are worst? Maybe because the CAS queries express a more specific information need, and receive more strict assessment. But this question remains open.

We submitted runs to the INEX Iniciative for heterogeneous collections, but as its assessments were not concluded, we have no Recall/Precision Curves. It follows a sample of an answer to a query showing results from many sub-collections, confirming that our model can deal with different DTDs.

For query:

```
//article[about(.//author, Nivio Ziviani)],
```

we get the following answer:

```
<topic topic-id="2"> ...
<result>
  <subcollection  name="ieee" />
  <file>co/2000/ry037</file>
  <path>/article[1]/fm[1]/au[1]</path>
  <rank> 3</rank>
</result> ...
<result>
  <subcollection  name="dblp" />
  <file>dblp</file>
  <path>/dblp[1]/article[177271]/author[4]</path>
  <rank> 6</rank>
  </result> ...
<result>
  <subcollection  name="CompuScience" />
  <file>exp-dxf1.xml.UTF-8</file>
  <path>/bibliography[1]/article[23]/author[1]</path>
  <rank> 30</rank>
</result>
 ...
<result>
  <subcollection  name="hcibib" />
```

```
  <file>hcibib</file>
  <path>/file[1]/entry[229]/article[1]/author[1]</path>
  <rank> 139</rank>
</result>
```

5 Conclusions and Future Work

We have shown a universal model for dealing with information retrieval on XML documents. It can be applied to non-XML documents, homogeneous and heterogeneous collections, to answer structured (CAS – content and structured) and no-structured (CO – content only) queries. The major contribution of this work is its universal application, achieved in a completely automatic process.

All introduced factors behave as expected and our results are close to the average of other INEX participants. The average precision stays around 0.05 for CO and 0.04 for CAS queries and needs to be improved, demanding further investigation. *Fstr* factor should be better adjusted to query constraints. For an appropriated assessment of *Focr* factor it would be better to have a real heterogeneous collection, with documents from different knowledge areas, as biology, geography, etc., and including XML documents originated from databases.

References

1. S. Abiteboul, P. Buneman and D. Suciu. *Data on the Web – From Relations to Semistructured Data in XML.* Mogan Kaufmann Publishers, San Francisco, California, 2000, pp. 27-50.
2. M. Abolhassani, K. Grobjohann and N. Fuhr. Content-oriented XML Retrieval with HyREX. In *INEX 2002 Workshop Proceedings*, Duisburg, 2002, pp.26-32.
3. T. Bray, J. Paoli, C. M. Sperberg-McQueen and E. Maler. *Extensible Markup Language (XML) 1.0.* 2nd ed. http://www.w3.org/TR/REC-xml, Cct 2000. W3C Recommendation 6 October 2000.
4. N. Fuhr and M. Lalmas. *INEX document Collection.* http://inex.is.informatik.uni-duisburg.de:2004/internal/, Duisburg, 2004.
5. G. Kazai, M. Lalmas and S. Malik. INEX'03 Guidelines for Topic Development. In *INEX 2003 Workshop Proceedings*, Duisburg, 2003 pg. 153-154.
6. M. Mandelbrod and Y. Mass. Retrieving the most relevant XML Components. In *INEX 2003 Workshop Proceedings*. Duisburg, 2003, pp. 58-64.
7. B. Ribeiro-Neto e R. Baeza-Yates. *Modern Information Retrieval.* Addison Wesley, 1999, pp. 27-30.
8. G. Salton e M. E. Lesk. *Computer evaluation of indexing and text processing*. Journal of the ACM. 15(1), 1968, pp. 8-36.

Cheshire II at INEX '04: Fusion and Feedback for the Adhoc and Heterogeneous Tracks

Ray R. Larson

School of Information Management and Systems,
University of California, Berkeley, California, USA, 94720-4600
ray@sims.berkeley.edu

Abstract. This paper describes the retrieval approach used by UC Berkeley in the adhoc and heterogeneous tracks for the 2004 INEX evaluation. As in previous INEX evaluations, the main technique we are testing is the fusion of multiple probabilistic searches against different XML components using both Logistic Regression (LR) algorithms and a version of the Okapi BM-25 algorithm in conjunction with Boolean constraints for some elements. We also describe some additional experiments, subsequent to INEX that promise further improvements in results.

1 Introduction

In this paper we describe the document and component fusion approaches used by U.C. Berkeley for INEX 2004, the results from our official INEX submissions, and the results of subsequent analysis and re-testing. This work is based upon and extends the work described in the special INEX issue of the Journal of Information Retrieval[9]. In addition we will discuss the approach taken for INEX Heterogeneous track.

The basic approach that we use for the INEX 2004 retrieval tasks is based on some early work done in TREC, where it was found that fusion of multiple retrieval algorithms provided an improvement over a single search algorithm[14, 2]. Later analyses of these fusion approaches[10, 1] indicated that the greatest effectiveness improvements appeared to occur between relatively ineffective individual methods, and the fusion of ineffective techniques, while often approaching the effectiveness of the best single IR algorithms, seldom exceeded them for individual queries and never exceeded their average performance. In our analysis of fusion approaches for XML retrieval[9], based on runs conducted after the 2003 INEX meeting, we conducted analyses of the overlap between result sets across algorithm and also examined the contributions of different XML document components to the results.

The remainder of the paper is organized as follows: we will first discuss the algorithms and fusion operators used in our official INEX 2004 adhoc runs and for the heterogeneous track. Then we will look at how these algorithms and operators were used in the various submissions for the adhoc and heterogeneous tracks, and finally we will examine the results and discuss directions for future research.

N. Fuhr et al. (Eds.): INEX 2004, LNCS 3493, pp. 322–336, 2005.

2 The Retrieval Algorithms and Fusion Operators

In [9] we conducted an analysis of the overlap between the result lists retrieved by our Logistic Regression algorithm and the Okapi BM-25 algorithm. We found that, on average, over half of the result lists retrieved by each algorithm in these overlap tests were both non-relevant *and* unique to that algorithm, fulfilling the main criteria for effective algorithm combination suggested by Lee[10]: that the algorithms have similar sets of relevant documents and different sets of non-relevant. This section is largely a repetition of the material presented in [9] with additional discussion of the re-estimation of the LR parameters for different XML components and indexes used in the INEX 2004 tests.

In the remainder of this section we describe the Logistic Regression and Okapi BM-25 algorithms that were used for the evaluation and we also discuss the methods used to combine the results of the different algorithms. The algorithms and combination methods are implemented as part of the Cheshire II XML/SGML search engine [7, 8, 6] which also supports a number of other algorithms for distributed search and operators for merging result lists from ranked or Boolean sub-queries. Finally, we will discuss the re-estimation of the LR parameters for a variety of XML components of the INEX test collection.

2.1 Logistic Regression Algorithm

The basic form and variables of the *Logistic Regression* (LR) algorithm used was originally developed by Cooper, et al. [4]. It provided good full-text retrieval performance in the TREC ad hoc task and in TREC interactive tasks [5] and for distributed IR [6]. As originally formulated, the LR model of probabilistic IR attempts to estimate the probability of relevance for each document based on a set of statistics about a document collection and a set of queries in combination with a set of weighting coefficients for those statistics. The statistics to be used and the values of the coefficients are obtained from regression analysis of a sample of a collection (or similar test collection) for some set of queries where relevance and non-relevance has been determined. More formally, given a particular query and a particular document in a collection $P(R \mid Q, D)$ is calculated and the documents or components are presented to the user ranked in order of decreasing values of that probability. To avoid invalid probability values, the usual calculation of $P(R \mid Q, D)$ uses the "log odds" of relevance given a set of S statistics, s_i, derived from the query and database, such that:

$$\log O(R \mid Q, D) = b_0 + \sum_{i=1}^{S} b_i s_i \tag{1}$$

where b_0 is the intercept term and the b_i are the coefficients obtained from the regression analysis of the sample collection and relevance judgements. The final ranking is determined by the conversion of the log odds form to probabilities:

$$P(R \mid Q, D) = \frac{e^{\log O(R|Q,D)}}{1 + e^{\log O(R|Q,D)}} \tag{2}$$

Based on the structure of XML documents as a tree of XML elements, we define a "document component" as an XML subtree that may include zero or more subordinate XML elements or subtrees with text as the leaf nodes of the tree. For example, in the XML Document Type Definition (DTD) for the INEX test collection defines an article (marked by XML tag *<article>*) that contains front matter (*<fm>*), a body (*<bdy>*) and optional back matter (*<bm>*). The front matter (*<fm>*), in turn, can contain a header *<hdr>* and may include editor information (*<edinfo>*), author information (*<au>*), a title group (*<tig>*), abstract (*<abs>*) and other elements. A title group can contain elements including article title (*<atl>*) the page range for the article (*<pn>*), and these in turn may contain other elements, down to the level of individual formatted words or characters. Thus, a component might be defined using any of these tagged elements. However, *not all possible components are likely to be useful* in content-oriented retrieval (e.g., tags indicating that a word in the title should be in italic type, or the page number range) therefore we defined the retrievable components selectively, including document sections and paragraphs from the article body, and bibliography entries from the back matter (see Table 3).

Naturally, a full XML document may also be considered a "document component". As discussed below, the indexing and retrieval methods used in this research take into account a selected set of document components for generating the statistics used in the search process and for extraction of the parts of a document to be returned in response to a query. Because we are dealing with not only full documents, but also document components (such as sections and paragraphs or similar structures) derived from the documents, we will use C to represent document components in place of D. Therefore, the full equation describing the LR algorithm used in these experiments is:

$$\begin{aligned}\log O(R \mid Q, C) = \\ & b_0 + \left(b_1 \cdot \left(\frac{1}{|Q_c|}\sum_{j=1}^{|Q_c|} \log qtf_j\right)\right) \\ & + \left(b_2 \cdot \sqrt{|Q|}\right) \\ & + \left(b_3 \cdot \left(\frac{1}{|Q_c|}\sum_{j=1}^{|Q_c|} \log tf_j\right)\right) \\ & + \left(b_4 \cdot \sqrt{cl}\right) \\ & + \left(b_5 \cdot \left(\frac{1}{|Q_c|}\sum_{j=1}^{|Q_c|} \log \frac{N - n_{t_j}}{n_{t_j}}\right)\right) \\ & + \left(b_6 \cdot \log |Q_d|\right)\end{aligned} \tag{3}$$

Where:

Q is a query containing terms T,
$|Q|$ is the total number of terms in Q,

$|Q_c|$ is the number of terms in Q that also occur in the document component,
tf_j is the frequency of the jth term in a specific document component,
qtf_j is the frequency of the jth term in Q,
n_{t_j} is the number of components (of a given type) containing the jth term,
cl is the document component length measured in bytes.
N is the number of components of a given type in the collection.
b_i are the coefficients obtained though the regression analysis.

This equation, used in estimating the probability of relevance in this research, is essentially the same as that used in [3]. The b_i coefficients in the "Base" version of this algorithm were estimated using relevance judgements and statistics from the TREC/TIPSTER test collection. In INEX 2004 we used both this Base version and a version where the coeffients for each of the major document components were estimated separately and combined through component fusion. The coefficients for the Base version were $b_0 = -3.70, b_1 = 1.269, b_2 = -0.310, b_3 = 0.679, b_4 = -0.021, b_5 = 0.223$ and $b_6 = 4.01$. We will discuss the re-estimated coefficients for the various document components and indexes later in this section.

2.2 Okapi BM-25 Algorithm

The version of the Okapi BM-25 algorithm used in these experiments is based on the description of the algorithm in Robertson [12], and in TREC notebook proceedings [13]. As with the LR algorithm, we have adapted the Okapi BM-25 algorithm to deal with document components :

$$\sum_{j=1}^{|Q_c|} w^{(1)} \frac{(k_1+1)tf_j}{K+tf_j} \frac{(k_3+1)qtf_j}{k_3+qtf_j} \tag{4}$$

Where (in addition to the variables already defined):
K is $k_1((1-b)+b \cdot dl/avcl)$
k_1, b **and** k_3 are parameters (1.5, 0.45 and 500, respectively, were used),
$avcl$ is the average component length measured in bytes
$w^{(1)}$ is the Robertson-Sparck Jones weight:

$$w^{(1)} = \log \frac{\left(\frac{r+0.5}{R-r+0.5}\right)}{\left(\frac{n_{t_j}-r+0.5}{N-n_{t_j}-R-r+0.5}\right)}$$

r is the number of relevant components of a given type that contain a given term,
R is the total number of relevant components of a given type for the query.

Our current implementation uses only the *a priori* version (i.e., without relevance information) of the Robertson-Sparck Jones weights, and therefore the $w^{(1)}$ value is effectively just an IDF weighting. The results of searches using our implementation of Okapi BM-25 and the LR algorithm seemed sufficiently different to offer the kind of conditions where data fusion has been shown to be be most effective [10], and our overlap analysis of results for each algorithm (described in the evaluation and discussion section) has confirmed this difference and the fit to the conditions for effective fusion of results.

2.3 Boolean Operators

The system used supports searches combining probabilistic and (strict) Boolean elements, as well as operators to support various merging operations for both types of intermediate result sets. Although strict Boolean operators and probabilistic searches are implemented within a single process, using the same inverted file structures, they really function as two parallel *logical* search engines. Each logical search engine produces a set of retrieved documents. When a only one type of search strategy is used then the result is either a probabilistically ranked set or an unranked Boolean result set. When both are used within in a single query, combined probabilistic and Boolean search results are evaluated using the assumption that the Boolean retrieved set has an estimated $P(R \mid Q_{bool}, C) = 1.0$ for each document component in the set, and 0 for the rest of the collection. The final estimate for the probability of relevance used for ranking the results of a search combining strict Boolean and probabilistic strategies is simply:

$$P(R \mid Q, C) = P(R \mid Q_{bool}, C) P(R \mid Q_{prob}, C) \quad (5)$$

where $P(R \mid Q_{prob}, C)$ is the probability of relevance estimate from the probabilistic part of the search, and $P(R \mid Q_{bool}, C)$ is the Boolean. In practice the combination of strict Boolean "AND" and the probablistic approaches has the effect of restricting the results to those items that match the Boolean part, with ranking based on the probabilistic part. Boolean "NOT" provides a similar restriction of the probabilistic set by removing those document components that match the Boolean specification. When Boolean "OR" is used the probabilistic and Boolean results are merged (however, items that only occur in the Boolean result, and not both, are reweighted as in the "fuzzy" and merger operations described below.

A special case of Boolean operators in Cheshire II is that of proximity and phrase matching operations. In proximity and phrase matching the matching terms must also satisfy proximity constraints (both term order and adjacency in the case of phrases). Thus, proximity operations also result in Boolean intermediate result sets.

2.4 Result Combination Operators

The Cheshire II system used in this evaluation provides a number of operators to combine the intermediate results of a search from different components or indexes. With these operators we have available an entire spectrum of combination methods ranging from strict Boolean operations to fuzzy Boolean and normalized score combinations for probabilistic and Boolean results. These operators are the means available for performing fusion operations between the results for different retrieval algorithms and the search results from different different components of a document. We will only describe one of these operators here, because it was the only type used in the evaluation reported in this paper.

The MERGE_CMBZ operator is based on the "CombMNZ" fusion algorithm developed by Shaw and Fox [14] and used by Lee [10]. In our version we take the normalized scores, but then further enhance scores for components appearing in both lists (doubling them) and penalize normalized scores appearing low in a single result list, while using the unmodified normalized score for higher ranking items in a single list.

2.5 Recalculation of LR Coefficients for Component Indexes

Using LR coefficients derived from relevance analysis of TREC data for INEX is unlikely to provide the most effective performance given the differences in tasks, queries and their structure, and relevance scales.

In order to begin to remedy this we have re-estimated the coefficients of the Logistic regression algorithm based on the INEX 2003 relevance assessments. In fact, separate formulae were derived for each of the major components of the INEX XML document structure, providing a different formula for each index/component of the collection. These formulae were used in only one of the official *ad hoc* runs submitted for the INEX 2004 evaluation, in order to have a basis of comparison with the fusion methods used in INEX 2002 and 2003. In this section we focus on the re-estimation and the values obtained for the new coefficients. Later we will this discuss the effectiveness of the new coefficients (or rather, the *lack* of effectiveness when used without supplementary adjustments) and several possible reasons for it.

For re-estimation purposes we submitted the INEX 2003 CO queries using the "Base" LR algorithm, which was the best performing LR-only experiment as reported in [9] (which was able to obtain 0.0834 *mean average precision* under the strict quantization, and 0.0860 under the generalized quantization). In addition we performed separate runs using only searches on single indexes (which may combine multiple document elements, as described in Tables 2 and 4). For all of these runs we captured the values calculated for each of the variables described in equation 4 for each document element retrieved. Then the *strict* relevance/non-relevance of each of these documents was obtained from the INEX 2003 relevance judgements and the resulting relevance/element data was analyzed using the SPSS logistic regression procedure to obtain re-estimations of the variable coefficients (b_i) in equation 4. The resulting coefficients for the various components/indexes are shown in Table 1, where the "Base" row is the default TREC-estimated coefficients and the other rows are the estimates for the named index. Not all indexes were reestimated because they (e.g., pauthor) tend to be used as purely Boolean criteria, or were components of another index and/or not present in all articles (e.g., kwd).

Testing these new coefficients with the INEX 2003 queries and relevance judgements we were able to obtain a mean average precision of 0.1158 under the strict metric and 0.1116 for the generalized metric, thus exceeding the best fusion results reported in [9]. However, the data used for training the LR model was obtained using the relevance data associated with the same topics, and it appears very likely that the model may be *over-trained* for that data, or that a different set of variables needs to be considered for XML retrieval.

3 INEX 2004 Adhoc Approach

Our approach for the INEX 2004 adhoc task was quite similar to that used for INEX 2003 runs. This section will describe the indexing process and indexes used, and also discuss the scripts used for search processing. The basic database was unchanged from last year's. We will summarize the indexing process and the indexes used in the adhoc task for reference in the discussion.

3.1 Indexing the INEX Database

All indexing in the Cheshire II system is controlled by an SGML Configuration file which describes the database to be created. This configuration file is subsequently used in search processing to control the mapping of search command index names (or Z39.50 numeric attributes representing particular types of bibliographic data) to the physical index files used and also to associated component indexes with particular components and documents. This configuration file also includes the index-specific definitions for the Logistic Regression coefficients (when not defined, these default to the "Base" coefficients shown in Table 1).

Table 2 lists the document-level (/article) indexes created for the INEX database and the document elements from which the contents of those indexes were extracted. These indexes (with the addition of proximity information the are the same as those used last year. The *abstract, alltitles, keywords, title, topic* and *topicshort* indexes support proximity indexes (i.e., term location), supporting phrase searching.

As noted above the Cheshire system permits parts of the document subtree to be treated as separate documents with their own separate indexes. Tables 3 & 4 describe the XML components created for INEX and the component-level indexes that were created for them.

Table 3 shows the components and the path used to define them. The component called COMP_SECTION consists of each identified section or subsection (<sec> ... </sec> or <ss*>... </ss*>) in all of the documents, permitting each individual section of an article to be retrieved separately. Similarly, each of the COMP_BIB, COMP_PARAS, and COMP_FIG components, respectively, treat

Table 1. Re-Estimated Coefficients for The Logistic Regression Model

Index	b_0	b_1	b_2	b_3	b_4	b_5	b_6
Base	-3.700	1.269	-0.310	0.679	-0.021	0.223	4.010
topic	-7.758	5.670	-3.427	1.787	-0.030	1.952	5.880
topicshort	-6.364	2.739	-1.443	1.228	-0.020	1.280	3.837
abstract	-5.892	2.318	-1.364	0.860	-0.013	1.052	3.600
alltitles	-5.243	2.319	-1.361	1.415	-0.037	1.180	3.696
sec_words	-6.392	2.125	-1.648	1.106	-0.075	1.174	3.632
para_words	-8.632	1.258	-1.654	1.485	-0.084	1.143	4.004

Table 2. Cheshire Article-Level Indexes for INEX

Name	Description	Contents
docno	Digital Object ID	//doi
pauthor	Author Names	//fm/au/snm, //fm/au/fnm
title	Article Title	//fm/tig/atl
topic	Content Words	//fm/tig/atl, //abs, //bdy, //bibl/bb/atl, //app
topicshort	Content Words 2	//fm/tig/atl, //abs, //kwd, //st
date	Date of Publication	//hdr2/yr
journal	Journal Title	//hdr1/ti
kwd	Article Keywords	//kwd
abstract	Article Abstract	//abs
author_seq	Author Seq.	//fm/au@sequence
bib_author_fnm	Bib Author Forename	//bb/au/fnm
bib_author_snm	Bib Author Surname	//bb/au/snm
fig	Figure Contents	//fig
ack	Acknowledgements	//ack
alltitles	All Title Elements	//atl, //st
affil	Author Affiliations	//fm/aff
fno	IEEE Article ID	//fno

Table 3. Cheshire Components for INEX

<table>
<tr><th>Name</th><th>Description</th><th>Contents</th></tr>
<tr><td>COMP_SECTION</td><td>Sections</td><td>//sec|//ss1|//ss2|//ss3|//ss4</td></tr>
<tr><td>COMP_BIB</td><td>Bib Entries</td><td>//bib/bibl/bb</td></tr>
<tr><td>COMP_PARAS</td><td>Paragraphs</td><td>//ilrj|//ip1|//ip2|, //ip3|//ip4|//ip5|
//item-none|//p|//p1|//p2|//p3|fi//tmath|//tf</td></tr>
<tr><td>COMP_FIG</td><td>Figures</td><td>//fig</td></tr>
<tr><td>COMP_VITAE</td><td>Vitae</td><td>//vt</td></tr>
</table>

each bibliographic reference (<bb> ... </bb>), paragraph (with all of the alternative paragraph elements shown in Table 3), and figures (<fig> ... </fig>) as individual documents that can be retrieved separately from the entire document.

Table 4 describes the XML component indexes created for the components described in Table 3. These indexes make individual sections (COMP_SECTION) of the INEX documents retrievable by their titles, or by any terms occurring in the section. These are also proximity indexes, so phrase searching is supported within the indexes. Bibliographic references in the articles (COMP_BIB) are made accessible by the author names, titles, and publication date of the individual bibliographic entry, with proximity searching supported for bibliography titles. Individual paragraphs (COMP_PARAS) are searchable by any of the terms in the paragraph, also with proximity searching. Individual figures (COMP_FIG) are indexed by their captions, and vitae (COMP_VITAE) are indexed by keywords within the text, with proximity support.

Table 4. Cheshire Component Indexes for INEX †Includes all subelements of paragraph elements

Component or Name	Description	Contents
COMP_SECTION		
sec_title	Section Title	//sec/st
sec_words	Section Words	//sec
COMP_BIB		
bib_author	Bib. Author	//au
bib_title	Bib. Title	//atl
bib_date	Bib. Date	//pdt/yr
COMP_PARAS		
para_words	Paragraph Words	*†
COMP_FIG		
fig_caption	Figure Caption	//fgc
COMP_VITAE		
vitae_words	Words from Vitae	//vt

Almost all of these indexes and components were used during Berkeley's search evaluation runs of the 2004 INEX topics. The official submitted runs and scripts used in INEX are described in the next section.

3.2 INEX '04 Official Adhoc Runs

Berkeley submitted 5 retrieval runs for the INEX 2004 adhoc task, three CO runs and 2 VCAS runs. This section describes the individual runs and general approach taken in creating the queries submitted against the INEX database and the scripts used to do the submission. The paragraphs below briefly describe Berkeley's INEX 2004 runs.

Berkeley_CO_FUS_T_CMBZ (FUSION): This run uses automatic query generation with both Okapi BM-25 and Logistic regression retrieval algorithms combined using a score-normalized merging algorithm (MERGE_CMBZ). Results from multiple components where combined using MERGE_CMBZ as well. Separate retrieval of Articles, Sections and paragraphs were combined using score normalized merges of these results. Only Titles were used in generating the queries, which also included Boolean operations for proximity searching and "negated" terms. This run was based on the most effective fusion method found in our post-INEX 2003 analysis and reported in [9] and was intended as a baseline for comparison with the other runs.

Berkeley_CO_FUS_T_CMBZ_FDBK (FEEDBACK): This run is fundamentally the same as the previous run, with the addition of "blind feedback" where the <kwd> elements from top 100 results were extracted and the top 30 most frequently occurring keyword phrases were used as an addition to the base query generated by the initial query.

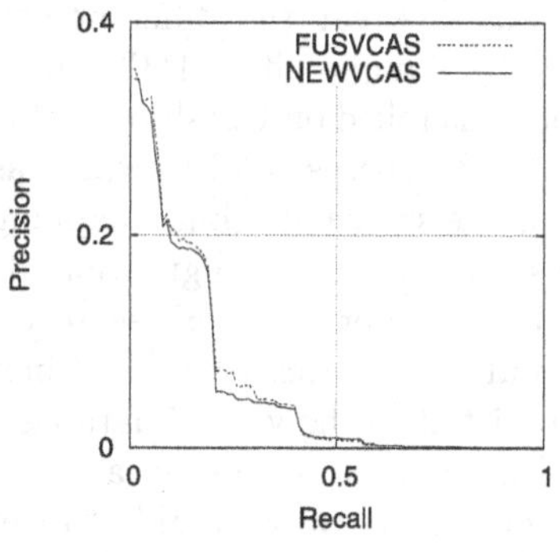

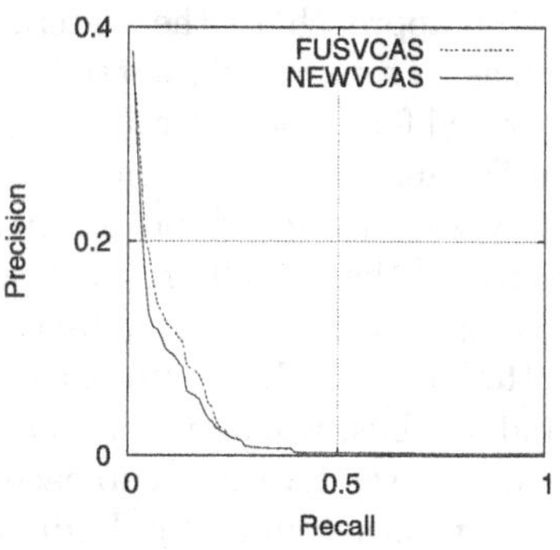

Fig. 1. Berkeley VCAS Runs – Strict (left) and Generalized (right) Quantization

Berkeley_CO_PROB_T_NEWPARMS (NEWPARMS): This run used automatic query generation with *only* the Logistic regression retrieval algorithm where the new coefficients for each of the indexes, as noted in Table 1, were used.

Berkeley_VCAS_FUS_T_CMBZ (FUSVCAS): This was a VCAS automatic run using automatic query generation from the NEXI title expression, and like the Berkeley_CO_FUS_T_CMBZ run, uses both Logistic Regression and the Okapi BM-25 ranking. Results from multiple components where combined using MERGE_CMBZ merging of results.

Berkeley_VCAS_PROB_T_NEWPARMS (NEWVCAS): This run also uses automatic query generation and is very similar to the NEWPARMS CO run above. Results from multiple components in this VCAS run were combined using the MERGE_CMBZ merger operator, as in the NEWPARMS CO run. This run used *only* the LR algorithm with the new LR coefficients as shown in Table 1.

Query Generation and Contents. All of the Cheshire client programs are scriptable using Tcl or Python. For the INEX test runs we created scripts in the Tcl language that, in general, implemented the same basic sequence of operations as described in the INEX 2003 paper[7]. For VCAS-type queries, the NEXI specification was used to choose the indexes (and components) to be searched, and the RESTRICT operators described above were used to validate proper nesting of components. For each specified "about" clause in the XPath, a merger of phase, keyword, Boolean and ranked retrieval was performed, depending on the specifications of the NEXI query.

3.3 INEX '04 Heterogeneous Track Runs

The Hetergeneous Track for INEX 2004 is attempting to test the ability to perform searches across multiple XML collections with different structures and contents. The evaluation results are still pending, so they cannot be discussed here. In this section we briefly describe the approach taken for the track and the system features used in the implementation.

Our approach to the Heterogeneous Track was to treat the different collections as separate databases with their own DTDs (simple "flat" DTDs were generated for those collections lacking them). The runs relied on Cheshire's "Virtual Database" features, in which multiple physical databases can be treated as if they were a single database. In addition we used the search attribute mapping features of the Z39.50 protocol, so that each physical database configuration file could specify that some subset of tags was to be used for "author" searches, another for "title", etc., for each as many of the index types described in Tables 2 and 4. Thus, when an "author" search was submitted to the virtual database, the query was forwarded to each of the physical databases, processed, and the results returned in a standardized XML "wrapper". Thus we were able to run scripts similar to those used for the adhoc track "CO" runs against the virtual database requesting the LR algorithm and obtain a result from all of the physical databases sorted by their estimated probability of relevance. In effect, the "Virtual Search" implements a form of distributed search using the Z39.50 protocol.

The only difficulty in this implementation was that all collections consisted of a single XML "document", including one of the databases where that single document was 217Mb in size. We ended up treating each of the main sub-elements of these "collection documents" as separate documents (another feature of Cheshire). The difficulty was then generating the actual full XPath for the elements in order to report results. This was eventually handled by a script that, in most cases, was able to infer the element from the internal document ID, and in the case of the 217Mb document (with multiple different subelements for the collection document) this involved matching each of the subtypes in separate databases. Until the evaluation is complete, we won't know whether this mapping was actually accurate.

4 Evaluation of Adhoc Submissions

The summary average precision results for the runs described above are shown in Table 5. The table includes an additional row (...POST_FUS_NEWPARMS) for an unofficial run that essentially used the Berkeley_CO_FUS_T_CMBZ structure

Table 5. Mean Average Precision for Berkeley INEX 2004

Run Name	Short name	Avg Prec (strict)	Avg Prec (gen.)
...._CO_FUS_T_CMBZ	FUSION	0.0923	0.0642
...._CO_FUS_T_CMBZ_FDBK	FEEDBACK	0.0390	0.0415
...._CO_PROB_T_NEWPARMS	NEWPARMS	0.0853	0.0582
...._VCAS_T_CMBZ	FUSVCAS	0.0601	0.0321
...._VCAS_PROB_T_NEWPARMS	NEWVCAS	0.0569	0.0270
...POST_FUS_NEWPARMS	POSTFUS	0.0952	0.0690

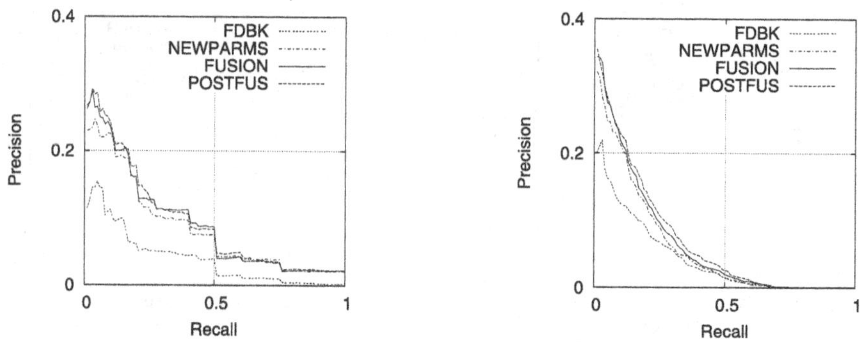

Fig. 2. Berkeley CO Runs – Strict and Generalized Quantization

of combining LR and Okapi searching along with the new LR coefficients. This combination performed a bit better than any of the official runs. (However, see the next section about subsequent additional tests using pivoted component probabilities of relevance).

Figure 1 shows, respectively, the Recall/Precision curves for strict and generalized quantization of each of the officially submitted Berkeley "VCAS" runs. Figure 2 shows, respectively, the Recall/Precision curves for strict and generalized quantization of each of the officially submitted Berkeley "CO" runs. No Berkeley runs appeared in the top ten for all submitted runs. None of these runs was in the top 10, though the "FUSION" run was close (ranked 14th in aggregate score).

Our attempt at "blind feedback" performed very poorly (which was expected, given that it was very much a last-minute attempt, and we had no time to attempt to determine the optimal number of records to analyze or the number of retrieved <kwd> phrases to include in the reformulated query). More interesting was the fact that the re-estimated LR parameters, when used alone did not perform as well as the basic fusion method. However, when combined with in a fusion approach the new coeffients do improve the results over the basic Fusion method using the "Base" coefficients.

4.1 Additional Tests and Evaluation

Work reported at the INEX 2004 meeting by Mass and Mandelbrot[11] of the IBM Haifa Research Lab involving "pivoting" component weights by scaling them against the document-level weights for the same query appeared to offer a significant improvement in performance for the vector-space based algorithm used there. A similar pivot approach was reported by Sigurbjornsson, Kamps, and Rijke in the INEX 2003 Workshop Proceedings[15] in conjunction with a language model approach. We decided to apply the pivoted normalization method described in Mass and Mandelbrod[11] to the estimated probabilities for each component adjusted by the document-level probabilities returned by the new LR model parameters. We scale the estimated component probability of relevance based on a "Pivot" parameter, and the estimated probability of relevance for

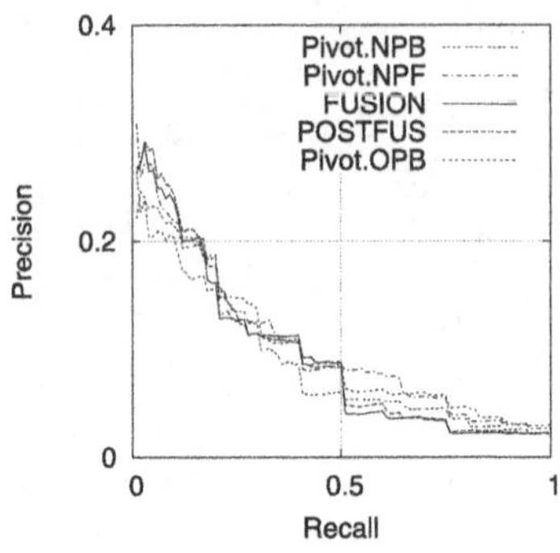

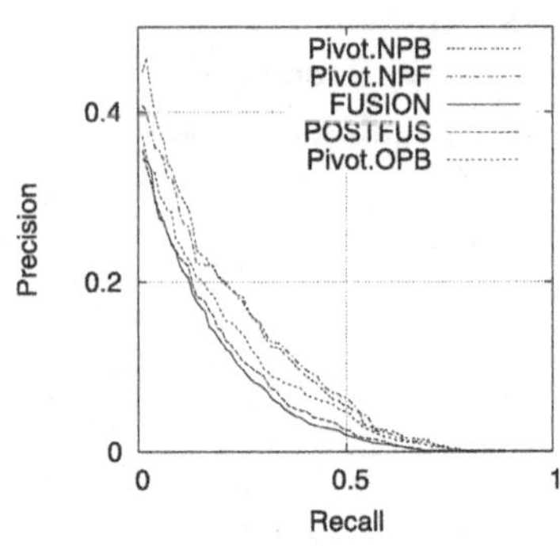

Fig. 3. – Strict (left) and Generalized (right) Quantization for Post-Official Tests

Table 6. Mean Average Precision for Additional Tests

Short name	Avg Prec (strict)	Avg Prec (gen.)	Avg Prec (aggr.)
PivotNPB	0.0901	0.1028	0.1146
PivotNPF	0.0961	0.0888	0.1108
PivotOPB	0.0849	0.0771	0.0944
POSTFUS	0.0952	0.0690	0.0819
FUSION	0.0923	0.0642	0.0776

the same search performed against the entire document. Formally, we estimate a new probability of relevance for the component, $P(R \mid Q, C')$, such that:

$$P(R \mid Q, C') = Pivot \cdot P(R \mid Q, D) + (1.0 - Pivot) \cdot P(R \mid Q, C) \qquad (6)$$

where $P(R \mid Q, C)$ is the original estimated probability of relevance for the component and $P(R \mid Q, D)$ is the estimated probability of relevance for the full document.

Table 6 shows the results of testing several variations of this "pivoted probabilities" approach. In all cases the article-level probability of relevance used for $P(R \mid Q, D)$ in equation 6 was taken from a search using the "topic" index described in Table 2. In all of the pivoted tests, the pivot value used was 0.70, the same value suggested by Mass and Mandelbrod in [11].

In Table 6 "PivotNPB" is an LR run using the new LR coefficients described above, with only the full text indexes of the section and paragraph component types described in Tables 3 and 3, along with the <article> and <bdy> tags. (That is, the same elements as used for the official runs, but not combining the results from multiple indexes on the elements.) The "PivotNPF" test is similar to the PivotNPB test, employing the new LR coefficients, but here the multiple index combinations used in the official runs were used for each component. The "PivotOPB" test is also similar to the PivotNPB test, except the old LR coefficients were used for all components and for the article-level probabilities

$P(R \mid Q, D)$. The "POSTFUS" and "FUSION" tests (the best performing tests from Table 5) were described in the previous section and are included in Table 6 for reference and comparison.

As can be seen in Table 6 the pivoted probabilities provide a considerable increase in the generalized performance metric over the FUSION and POSTFUS tests. The table also includes the "aggregate metric" merging all of the INEX 2004 metrics. The PivotNPB test provided the best generalized and aggregate metric performance, and the best performing test for the strict metric was the PivotNPF. Thus, with the addition of the pivoted element scores, the new LR coefficients do provide a noticeable increase in performance over the old coefficients. This is recent work and we not yet performed significance tests on the results, nor have we experimented with different settings for the pivot value.

5 Conclusions and Future Directions

We still need to perform a number of analyses of alternative combinations, but it appears that the re-estimated LR coefficients, although not as effective as the submitted FUSION approach when LR alone is used (without additional enhancement), do provide additional improvement when combined in a similar fusion approach, and when used alone with the addition of a document pivot as described in the previous section. However this improvement comes at the cost of a large increase in overlap between the returned elements. For example, the overlap for the FUSION test was 57.0640, while the overlap for the PivotNPB test was 92.03, suggesting that the primary effect of the pivot method is to promote elements with strong document matches in the ranking.

Our preliminary attempt at using blind feedback, with only assigned keywords in articles, doesn't appear to offer a benefit, though we plan to experiment a bit further using the framework developed for the "relevance feedback" track. Now with two years of usable and comparable relevance evaluations for INEX we can once again re-estimate the LR parameters from the INEX 2003 results and now test on the 2004, and also examine variations on the document pivot to attempt to determine optimal values for weighing elements vis a vis documents.

In addition we want to experiment with applying the score pivot approach to the Okapi algorithm and to new fusion combinations of LR and Okapi, combined with pivoted score normalization.

References

1. S. M. Beitzel, E. C. Jensen, A. Chowdhury, O. Frieder, D. Grossman, and N. Goharian. Disproving the fusion hypothesis: An analysis of data fusion via effective information retrieval strategies. In *Proceedings of the 2003 SAC Conference*, pages 1–5, 2003.
2. N. Belkin, P. B. Kantor, E. A. Fox, and J. A. Shaw. Combining the evidence of multiple query representations for information retrieval. *Information Processing and Management*, 31(3):431–448, 1995.

3. W. S. Cooper, F. C. Gey, and A. Chen. Full text retrieval based on a probabilistic equation with coefficients fitted by logistic regression. In D. K. Harman, editor, *The Second Text Retrieval Conference (TREC-2) (NIST Special Publication 500-215)*, pages 57–66, Gaithersburg, MD, 1994. National Institute of Standards and Technology.
4. W. S. Cooper, F. C. Gey, and D. P. Dabney. Probabilistic retrieval based on staged logistic regression. In *15th Annual International ACM SIGIR Conference on Research and Development in Information Retrieval, Copenhagen, Denmark, June 21-24*, pages 198–210, New York, 1992. ACM.
5. R. R. Larson. TREC interactive with cheshire II. *Information Processing and Management*, 37:485–505, 2001.
6. R. R. Larson. A logistic regression approach to distributed IR. In *SIGIR 2002: Proceedings of the 25th Annual International ACM SIGIR Conference on Research and Development in Information Retrieval, August 11-15, 2002, Tampere, Finland*, pages 399–400. ACM, 2002.
7. R. R. Larson. Cheshire II at INEX: Using a hybrid logistic regression and boolean model for XML retrieval. In *Proceedings of the First Annual Workshop of the Initiative for the Evaluation of XML retrieval (INEX)*, pages 18–25. DELOS workshop series, 2003.
8. R. R. Larson. Cheshire II at INEX 03: Component and algorithm fusion for XML retrieval. In *INEX 2003 Workshop Proceedings*, pages 38–45. University of Duisburg, 2004.
9. R. R. Larson. A fusion approach to XML structured document retrieval. *Journal of Information Retrieval*, 2005. (in press).
10. J. H. Lee. Analyses of multiple evidence combination. In *SIGIR '97: Proceedings of the 20th Annual International ACM SIGIR Conference on Research and Development in Information Retrieval, July 27-31, 1997, Philadelphia*, pages 267–276. ACM, 1997.
11. Y. Mass and M. Mandelbrod. Component ranking and automatic query refinement for xml retrieval. In *INEX 2004 Workshop Pre-Proceedings*, pages 134–140. University of Duisburg, 2004.
12. S. E. Robertson and S. Walker. On relevance weights with little relevance information. In *Proceedings of the 20th annual international ACM SIGIR conference on Research and development in information retrieval*, pages 16–24. ACM Press, 1997.
13. S. E. Robertson, S. Walker, and M. M. Hancock-Beauliee. OKAPI at TREC-7: ad hoc, filtering, vlc and interactive track. In *Text Retrieval Conference (TREC-7), Nov. 9-1 1998 (Notebook)*, pages 152–164, 1998.
14. J. A. Shaw and E. A. Fox. Combination of multiple searches. In *Proceedings of the 2nd Text REtrieval Conference (TREC-2), National Institute of Standards and Technology Special Publication 500-215*, pages 243–252, 1994.
15. B. Sigurbjrnsson, J. Kamps, and M. de Rijke. An element-based approach to xml retrieval. In *INEX 2003 Workshop Proceedings*, pages 19–26. University of Duisburg, 2004.

Using a Relevance Propagation Method for Adhoc and Heterogeneous Tracks at INEX 2004

Karen Sauvagnat and Mohand Boughanem

IRIT-SIG, 118 route de Narbonne,
F-31062 Toulouse Cedex 4, France

Abstract. This paper describes the evaluation of the XFIRM system in INEX 2004 framework. The XFIRM system uses a relevance propagation method to answer queries composed of content conditions and/or structure conditions. Runs were submitted to the ad-hoc (for both CO and VCAS task) and heterogeneous tracks.

1 Introduction

Long documents may have heterogeneous content from different domains. In that case, selecting a whole document as answer unit is not necessary useful for the user. He/she may require document parts, which are of higher precision and finer granularity. XML documents, combining structured and unstructured (i.e.) text data, allow the processing of information at another granularity level than the whole document.

The challenge in IR context is to identify and retrieve relevant parts of the document. In other words, the aim is to retrieve the most exhaustive and specific information units answering a given query.

The approach we used for our participation at INEX 2004 is based on a relevance propagation method implemented in XFIRM system. The idea of relevance propagation (or augmentation) is also undertaken in [1], [5], [4]. In our approach, all leaf nodes are used as a starting point of the proagation, because even the smallest leaf node can contain relevant information (it can be a *title* or *sub-title* node for example). Advantages of such an approach are twofold: the index process can be done automatically, without any human intervention and the system will be so able to handle heterogeneous collections automatically; and secondly, even the most specific query concerning the document structure will be processed, since all the document structure is stored.

In this paper, we present the experiments we carried out in INEX'2004. Section 2 presents the XFIRM model, namely the data representation model and the associated query language. Section 3 describes the search approach used for the ad-hoc track for both CO and VCAS sub-tasks and section 4 presents the XFIRM model in the heterogeneous track context.

N. Fuhr et al. (Eds.): INEX 2004, LNCS 3493, pp. 337–348, 2005.

2 The XFIRM Model

2.1 Data Representation

Logical Data Representation Model. A structured document sd_i is a tree, composed of simple nodes n_j, leaf nodes ln_j and attributes a_j.

Structured document: $sd_i = (tree_i) = (n_{ij},\ ln_{ij},\ a_{ij})$
This representation is a simplification of Xpath and Xquery data model [3], in which a node can be a document, an element, text, a namespace, an instruction or a comment.

In order to easy browse the document tree and to quickly find ancestors-descendants relationships, the XFIRM model uses the following representation of nodes and attributes, based on the Xpath Accelerator approach [6]:

Node: $n_{ij} = (pre, post, parent, attribute)$
Leaf node: $ln_{ij} = (pre, post, parent, \{t_1, t_2, \ldots, t_n\})$
Attribute: $a_{ij} = (pre, val)$
A node is defined thanks to its pre-order and post-order value (*pre* and *post*), the pre-order value of its parent node (*parent*), and depending on its type (simple node or leaf node) by a field indicating the presence or absence of attributes (*attribute*) or by the terms it contains ($\{t_1, t_2, \ldots, t_n\}$). A simple node can either contain other simple nodes, leaf nodes, or both. This last case is not really a problem, because as each node owns a *pre* and *post* order value independently of its type (simple node or leaf node), the reconstruction of the tree structure can be done in an easy way. An attribute is defined by the pre-order value of the node containing it (*pre*) and by its value (*val*). Pre-order and post-order values are assigned to nodes thanks respectively to a pre-fixed and post-fixed traversal of the document tree (see [12] for having an example).

If we represent nodes in a two-dimensions space based on the *pre* and *post* order coordinates, we can exploit the following properties, given a node n:

- all ancestors of n are to the upper left of n's position in the plane
- all its descendants are to the lower right,
- all preceding nodes in document order are to the lower left, and
- the upper right partition of the plane comprises all following nodes (regarding document order)

Xpath Accelerator is well-suited for the navigation in XML documents with Xpath expressions. In contrast to others path index structures for XML, it efficiently supports also path expressions that do not start at the document root. Moreover, this data representation allow the processing of all XML documents, without necessarily knowing their DTD. This implies the ability of the model to process *heterogeneous* collections.

Physical Data Representation Model. As explained in our previous work [9], all data are stored in a relational database.

The *Path Index* (PI) allows the reconstruction of the document structure (thanks to the Xpath Accelerator model): for each node, its type, and its pre and post-order values are stored. The *Term Index* (TI) is a traditional inverted file, i.e. for each term, the index stores the nodes containing it and its positions in the different nodes. The *Element Index* (IE) describes the content of each leaf node, i.e. the total number of terms and also the number of different terms it contains, and the *Attribute Index* (AI) gives the values of attributes.

Finally, the *Dictionary* (DICT) provides for a given tag the tags that are considered as equivalent. It is useful in case of heterogeneous collections (i.e. XML documents with different DTD) or in case of documents containing similar tags, like for example, *title* and *sub-title*. This index is built manually.

2.2 The XFIRM Query Language

A query language is associated to the model, allowing queries with simple keywords terms and/or with structural conditions [11].

The user can express hierarchical conditions on the document structure and choose the element he/she wants to be returned (thanks to the *te:* (target element) operator).

Examples of XFIRM queries:
(i) // te: p [weather forecasting systems]
(ii) // article[security] // te: sec ["facial recognition"]
(iii) // te: article [Petri net] //sec [formal definition] AND sec [algorithm efficiency]
(iv) // te: article [] // sec [search engines]
respectively mean that *(i)* the user wants paragraphs about *weather forecasting* systems, *(ii)* sections about *facial recognition* in articles about *security*, *(iii)* articles about *Petri net* containing a section giving a *formal definition* and another section talking about *algorithm efficiency*, and *(iv)* articles containing a section about search engines. When expressing the eventual content conditions, the user can use simple keywords terms, eventually preceded by + or - (which means that the term should or should not be in the results), and connected with boolean operators. Phrases are also processed by the XFIRM system.

Concerning the structure, the query syntax allows the formulation of vague path expressions. For example, the user can ask for *"article[]//sec[]"* (he/she so knows that article nodes have sections nodes as descendants), without necessarily asking for a precise path, i.e. *article[]/bdy[]/sec[]*. Moreover, thanks to the Dictionary index, the user does not need to express in his/her query all the equivalent tags of the requested tag. He/she can ask for example for a *section* node, without referring he/she is also interested in *sec* nodes. User can also express conditions on attribute values, as explained in [11].

3 Ad-Hoc Task

This year, within the ad-hoc retrieval task, two sub-tasks were defined: the Content-Only (CO) task and the Vague Content-and-Structure (VCAS) task.

3.1 Answering CO Queries

CO queries are requests that ignore the document structure and contain only content related conditions, e.g. only specify what a document/component should be about (without specifying what that component is). In this task, the retrieval system has to identify the most appropriate XML elements to be returned to the user.

Query Processing. The first step in query processing is to evaluate the relevance value of leaf nodes ln according to the query. Let $q = t_1, \ldots, t_n$ be this query. Relevance values are computed thanks to a similarity function called $RSV_m(q, ln)$ (Retrieval Status Value), where m is an IR model. The XFIRM system authorizes the implementation of many IR models, which will be used to assign a relevance value to leaf nodes. As shown in [10], a simple adaptation of the $tf - idf$ measure to XML documents seems to perform better in case of content and structure queries. So:

$$RSV_m(q, ln) = \sum_{i=1}^{n} w_i^q * w_i^{ln} \tag{1}$$

with $w_i^q = tf_i^q * ief_i$ and $w_i^{ln} = tf_i^{ln} * ief_i$.

And where:

- tf_i is the term frequency in the query q or in the leaf node ln
- ief_i is the inverse element frequency of term i, i.e. *log (N/n+1)+1*, where n is the number of leaf nodes containing i and N is the total number of leaf nodes.

In our model, each node in the document tree is assigned a relevance value which is function of the relevance values of the leaf nodes it contains. Terms that occur close to the root of a given subtree seems to be more significant for the root element that ones on deeper levels of the subtrees. It seems so intuitive that the larger the distance of a node from its ancestor is, the less it contributes to the relevance of its ancestor. This affirmation is modeled in our propagation formula by the use of the $dist(n, ln_k)$ parameter, which is the distance between node n and leaf node ln_k in the document tree, i.e. the number of arcs that are necessary to join n and ln_k. The relevance value r_n of a node n is computed according the following formula:

$$r_n = \sum_{k=1..N} \alpha^{dist(n, ln_k)} * RSV(q, ln_k) \tag{2}$$

where ln_k are leaf nodes being descendant of n and N the total number of leaf nodes being descendant of n.

To avoid selecting nodes that do not supply information (like *title* nodes for example), we introduce the following rule: *Let n be a node and ln_i, $i \in [1..N]$ be its descendant leaf nodes having a non-zero relevance score. Let L be the sum of the length of ln_i (i.e. the sum of the number of ln_i terms). If L is smaller than a given value x, n will be considered as not relevant.* This rule can be formalised as follows:

$$r_n = \begin{cases} \sum_{k=1..N} \alpha^{dist(n,ln_k)} * RSV(q, ln_k) \ if \ L > x \\ 0 \ else \end{cases} \tag{3}$$

$$where \ L = \sum_{i=1..N} length(ln_i) \ with \ RSV(q, ln_i) > 0 \tag{4}$$

Experiments and Results. Table 1 shows the obtained results with different values of α and L. All runs were performed using the title field of topics. Our official run is in bold characters.

Average precision decreases when factor L is considered (run *xfirm_co_05_25_o* processed with $L = 25$ obtains lower precision than runs precessed with $L = 0$). This surprising observation can be mainly explained by the fact that some very small elements may have been judged relevant during the INEX assessments although they do not supply information.

Run *xfirm_co_05_25_wo* was processed without any node overlap. Results (for all metrics) are lower, because of the *overpopulated recall-base* [8].

Run *xfirm_co_1_0_o* is processed with α set to 1, which is equivalent to do a simple sum of leaf nodes relevance weights without down-weighting them during propagation. As a consequence, highest nodes in the document structure have a higher relevance value and are better ranked than deeper nodes (because they have a greater number of leaf nodes as descendants). As highest nodes in the document structure are also the biggest ones, the specificity criteria of the CO task is not respected. However, results are still relatively good, which is quite surprising. The same observation can be done on XFIRM results on INEX 2003 CO topics.

In a general manner, performances are lower than those obtained with the same parameters on the INEX 2003 CO topics, even for the "old" metrics. We need to conduct more experiments to evaluate the impact of all our parameters on each metric.

3.2 Answering VCAS Queries

The VCAS (Vague Content and Structure) task consists in content-oriented XML retrieval based on content-and-structure (CAS) queries, where the structural constraints of a query can be treated as vague conditions. CAS queries are topic statements, which contain explicit references to the XML structure, and

Table 1. Average precision of our runs over all quantizations for CO topics

Run	α	L	Average precision	Overlap	Rank
xfirm_co_05_25_o	**0.5**	**25**	**0.0660**	**77,4%**	**19/70**
xfirm_co_06_0_o	0.6	0	0.0758	81,8%	17/70
xfirm_co_09_0_o	0.9	0	0.0754	83.8%	17/70
xfirm_co_1_0_o	1	0	0.0781	83.8%	
xfirm_co_05_25_wo	0.5	25	0.0143	0%	48/70

explicitly specify the contexts of the users interest (e.g. target elements) and/or the contexts of certain search concepts (e.g. containment conditions). The idea behind the VCAS sub-task is to allow the evaluation of XML retrieval systems that aim to implement approaches, where not only the content conditions within a user query are processed with uncertainty but also the expressed structural conditions.

Query Processing. A VCAS query evaluation in XFIRM is carried out as follows:

1. INEX (NEXI) queries are translated into XFIRM queries.
2. XFIRM queries are decomposed into sub-queries and elementary sub-queries.
3. relevance values are then evaluated between leaf nodes and the content conditions of elementary sub-queries.
4. relevance values are propagated in the document tree to answer to the structure conditions of elementary sub-queries.
5. sub-queries are processed thanks to the results of elementary sub-queries.
6. original queries are evaluated thanks to upwards and downwards propagation of the relevance weights.

Query Translation
The transformation of INEX CAS queries to XFIRM queries was fairly easy. Table 2 gives some correspondences.

Table 2. Transformation of NEXI topics into XFIRM queries

Topic	NEXI	XFIRM
138	//article [about(.,operating system) and about(.//sec,thread implementation)]	// te: article [operating system] // sec [thread implementation]
145	//article[about(.,information retrieval) // p[about(.,relevance feedback)]	//article [information retrieval] // te: p [relevance feedback]
156	//article[about(.//abs,"spatial join")]// bdy // sec [about(.,"performance evaluation")]	//article[] AND abs["spatial join"] // te: sec ["performance evaluation"]

Query Decomposition
Each XFIRM query can be decomposed into sub-queries SQ_i as follows:

$$Q = //SQ_1//SQ_2//\ldots//te: SQ_j//\ldots//SQ_n \quad (5)$$

Where *te:* indicates the tag name of the target element. Each sub-query SQ_i can then be re-decomposed into elementary sub-queries $ESQ_{i,j}$, eventually linked with boolean operators and of the form:

$$ESQ_{i,j} = tg[q] \tag{6}$$

Where tg is a tag name and $q = \{t_1, \ldots, t_n\}$ is a set of keywords, i.e. a content condition. For example, topic 156 is decomposed as follows:

SQ_1=article[ ] AND abs["spatial join"]
    $ESQ_{1,1}$=article[ ]
    $ESQ_{1,2}$=abs["spacial join"]
SQ_2=sec["performance evaluation"]

Evaluating Leaf Nodes Relevance Values
As for CO topics, formula 1 is used.

Elementary Sub-queries $ESQ_{i,j}$ Processing
The relevance values assigned to leaf nodes are then propagated upwards in the document tree until nodes having the asked tag name are found. The result set of an elementary sub-query *tg[q]* is so composed of nodes having *tg* as tag name (or having a tag name equivalent to *tg* according to the DICT index) and their associated relevance values, which are obtained thanks to the propagation.

Formally, the result set $R_{i,j}$ of $ESQ_{i,j}$ is a set of pairs *(node, relevance)* defined as follows:

$$\begin{aligned} R_{i,j} = \{ & (n, r_n)/n \in construct(tg) \\ & and\ r_n = F_k(RSV_m(q, nf_k), dist(n, nf_k)) \} \end{aligned} \tag{7}$$

Where:

- r_n is the relevance weight of node n
- the *construct(tg)* function allows the creation of the set of all nodes having *tg* as tag name
- the $F_k(RSV_m(q, nf_k), dist(n, nf_k))$ function allows the propagation and aggregation of relevance values of leaf nodes nf_k,descendants of node n, in order to form the relevance value of node n. This propagation is function of distance $dist(n, nf_k)$ which separates node n from leaf node nf_k in the document tree (i.e. the number of arcs that are necessary to join n and nf_k).

In our INEX 2004 experiments, we choose to use the following function:

$$\begin{aligned} & F_k(RSV_m(q, nf_k)\ ,\ dist(n, nf_k)) \\ & \qquad = \sum_k \alpha^{dist(n,nf_k)} * RSV(q, nf_k) \end{aligned} \tag{8}$$

α is set to 0.9, which is the optimal value for experiments presented in [12] on INEX 2003 SCAS topics.

Sub-queries SQ_i Processing
Once each $ESQ_{i,j}$ has been processed, sub-queries SQ_i are then evaluated as explained below. Let R_i be the result set of SQ_i.

- if sub-query SQ_i is composed of one elementary sub-query $ESQ_{i,j}$ then the result set of SQ_i is the same than the one of $ESQ_{i,j}$

$$If\ SQ_i = ESQ_{i,j},\ then\ R_i = R_{i,j} \tag{9}$$

- if sub-query SQ_i is composed of elementary sub-queries $ESQ_{i,j}$ linked by the Boolean operator AND, the result set of SQ_i is composed of nodes being the nearest common ancestors of nodes belonging to the result sets of elementary sub-queries $ESQ_{i,j}$. The associated relevance values are obtained thanks to propagation functions. Formally,

$$\begin{aligned} If\ SQ_i = ESQ_{i,j}\ \ AND\ \ ESQ_{i,k}, \\ then\ R_i = R_{i,j} \oplus_{AND} R_{i,k} \end{aligned} \tag{10}$$

with $\oplus_{AND}$ defined as follow:

Definition 1. *Let $N = \{(n, r_n)\}$ and $M = \{(m, r_m)\}$ be two sets of pairs (node, relevance).*

$$\begin{aligned} N\ \oplus_{AND} M = \{(l, r_l)/\ l\ is\ the\ nearest\ common\ ancestor \\ of\ m\ and\ n,\ or\ l = m\ (respectively\ n)\ if\ m \\ (resp\ .n) is\ ancestor\ of\ n\ (resp.\ m), \\ \forall m, n\ being\ in\ the\ same\ document\ and \\ r_l = aggreg_{AND}(r_n, r_m,, dist(l, n), dist(l, m))\} \end{aligned} \tag{11}$$

Where $aggreg_{AND}(r_n, r_m, dist(l, n), dist(l, m)) = r_l$ defines the way relevance values r_n and r_m of nodes n and m are aggregated in order to form a new relevance r_l.

According to the results obtained in [12] for the INEX'2003 SCAS topics, we use the following function in this year experiments:

$$\begin{aligned} aggreg_{AND}(r_n, r_m\ , dist(l, n), dist(l, m)) \\ = \tfrac{r_n}{dist(l,n)} + \tfrac{r_m}{dist(l,m)} \end{aligned} \tag{12}$$

- if sub-query SQ_i is composed of elementary sub-queries $ESQ_{i,j}$ linked by the Boolean operator OR, the result set of SQ_i is an union of the result sets of elementary sub-queries $ESQ_{i,j}$.

$$\begin{aligned} If\ SQ_i = ESQ_{i,j}\ \ OR\ \ ESQ_{i,k}, \\ then\ R_i = R_{i,j} \oplus_{OR} R_{i,k} \end{aligned} \tag{13}$$

with $\oplus_{OR}$ defined as follow:

Definition 2. *Let $N = \{(n, r_n)\}$ and $M = \{(m, r_m)\}$ be two sets of pairs (node, relevance).*

$$\begin{aligned} N \oplus_{OR} M = \{(l, r_l)\quad /l = n \in N\ and\ r_l = r_n \\ or\ l = m \in M\ and\ r_l = r_m\} \end{aligned} \tag{14}$$

Whole Query Processing

The result set of sub-queries SQ_i are then used to process the whole query. In this query, a target element is specified, as defined above.

$Q = //SQ_1//SQ_2//\ldots//te : SQ_j//\ldots//SQ_n$

The aim in whole query processing will be to propagate the relevance values of nodes belonging to the results sets R_i of sub-queries SQ_i to nodes belonging to the result set R_j, which contains the target elements. Relevance values of nodes belonging to R_i where $i \in [1\ldots j-1]$ are propagated downwards in the document tree, while relevance values of nodes belonging to R_i where $i \in [j+1\ldots n]$ are propagated upwards. This is obtained thanks to the non-commutative operators Δ and ∇ defined below:

Definition 3. *Let $R_i = \{(n, r_n)\}$ and $R_{i+1} = \{(m, r_m)\}$ be two sets of pairs (node, relevance).*

$$\begin{aligned} R_i \Delta R_{i+1} &= \{(n, r_n)/n \in R_i \; is \; descendant \; of \; m \in R_{i+1} \\ &\quad and \;\; r_n = prop\_agg(r_n, r_m, dist(m, n))\} \end{aligned} \quad (15)$$

$$\begin{aligned} R_i \nabla R_{i+1} &= \{(n, r_n)/n \in R_i \; is \; ancestor \; of \; m \in R_{i+1} \\ &\quad and \;\; r_n = prop\_agg(r_n, r_m, dist(m, n))\} \end{aligned} \quad (16)$$

Where $prop\_agg(r_n, r_m, dist(m, n)) \rightarrow r_n$ allows the aggregation of relevance weights r_m of node m and r_n of node n according to the distance that separates the 2 nodes, in order to obtain the new relevance weight r_n of node n .

The result set R of a query Q is thus defined as follows :

$$\begin{aligned} R &= R_j \nabla (R_{j+1} \nabla (R_{j+2} \nabla \ldots)) \\ R &= R_j \Delta (R_{j-1} \Delta (R_{j-2} \Delta \ldots)) \end{aligned} \quad (17)$$

For the experiments presented here and according to the results obtained in [12], we use:

$$prop\_agg(dist(m, n), r_n, r_m) = \frac{r_n + r_m}{dist(n, m)} \quad (18)$$

Experiments and Results. We processed several runs, using different Dictionary indexes. This way, we are able to control the notion of *uncertainty* on structure constraints.

Table 3 shows the average precisions of all runs. All runs were performed using the title field of topics. Our official runs are in bold characters.

Equivalencies in the *INEX Dict* are given in the INEX guidelines [7]. For example, *ss1, ss2, and ss3* nodes are considered as equivalent to *sec* nodes. Equivalencies are then gradually extended in the other DICT indexes. For example, *sec, ss1, ss2, ss3* nodes and *p* nodes are considered as equivalent in DICT1,

Table 3. Average precision of our runs over all quantizations for VCAS topics

Run	Dict	Average precision	Overlap	Rank
xfirm_vcas_09_vague	**INEX**	**0.0346**	**17,8%**	**26/51**
xfirm_vcas_09_vague_dict	**DICT1**	**0.0475**	**38,5%**	**16/51**
xfirm_vcas_09_vague_dict2	DICT2	0.0686	62,6%	8/51
xfirm_vcas_09_vague_dict3	DICT3	0.0694	68,3%	7/51

whereas in DICT3 *sec, ss1, ss2, and ss3* nodes are equivalent to both *p* and *bdy* nodes. The use of a very extended DICT index increases the percentage of nodes overlap but increases also the average precision. This is not really surprising because as the structure conditions are treated with uncertainty, the recall-base obtained during the assessments is overpopulated, as it is the case for the CO task.

4 Heterogeneous Track

4.1 Motivation

The idea behind the heterogeneous track is that an information seeker is interested in semantically meaningful answers irrespectively to the structure of documents.

The Het collection consists in documents from different sources and thus with different DTDs (one can cite the original INEX Collection, the Computer Science database of FIZ Karlsruhe or the Digital Bibliography and Library Project in Trier). The additional collections are mainly composed of bibliographic references. Documents' sizes are also very "heterogeneous" : smallest documents have a few Kb whereas the biggest is 300 Mb.

Heterogeneous collection raises new challenges: (i) for CO queries, DTD-independent methods should be developed; (ii) for CAS queries, there is the problem of mapping structural conditions from one DTD onto other (possibly unknown) DTDs. Methods from federated databases could be applied here, where schema mappings between the different DTDs are defined manually. However, for a larger number of DTDs, automatic methods must be developed, that can for exampel be based on ontologies.

This year, different topic types were defined for answering the different retrieval challenges in heterogeneous collections [2]:

- CO queries;
- BCAS (Basic CAS) queries : these topics focus on the combination of singular structural constraints with a content-based constraint;
- CCAS (Complex CAS) queries : they are the het track equivalent of the CAS topics of the ad-hoc track, specified using the NEXI language;
- ECCAS (Extended Complex CAS) queries : these topics assume that the user is able to express th probability of the likelihood of a given structural constraint.

4.2 Experiments

As this is the first year the het track is proposed in INEX framework, the track was mainly explorative. Participants to the Het track proposed 10 Co topics, 1 BCAS topic and 13 CCAS topics.

As the index structure of XFIRM is designed to handle heterogeneous collections, the indexing process was quite easy. We submitted one run per topic category. For CO queries, we used the same formula as for the ad-hoc task. For BCAS and CCAS queries, a new Dict index was built manually, comparing the different DTDs.

Results are not known yet.

5 Perspectives

For this year INEX evaluation campaign, we have submitted runs for both the ad-hoc task and the heterogeneous track. Runs were performed with the XFIRM system using a propagation method.

Results obtained for the CO task are lower than those obtains with the same parameters on INEX 2003 CO topics. Results obtained for the VCAS track are relatively good comparing to other participants when using a very extended Dictionary index. In both cases, we need to conduct more experiments to evaluate the impact of all our parameters on all INEX metrics.

Concerning the Heterogeneous track, the task this year was mainly explorative. Runs we submitted were performed using a Dictionary index built manually by comparing the different DTDs. Some het challenges are still open: how can we build a Dictionary index automatically? Do we need to adapt our formulas for taking into account the gap between document sizes of the different collections?

References

1. V. N. Anh and A. Moffat. Compression and an ir approach to xml retrieval. In *Proceedings of INEX 2002 Workshop, Dagstuhl, Germany*, 2002.
2. V. Dignum and R. van Zwol. Guidelines for topic development in heterogeneous collections. Guidelines of INEX 2004, 2004.
3. M. Fernandez, A. Malhotra, J. Marsh, M. Nagy, and N. Walsh. Xquery 1.0 and xpath 2.0 data model. Technical report, World Wide Web Consortium (W3C), W3C Working Draft, may 2003.
4. N. Gövert, M. Abolhassani, N. Fuhr, and K. Grossjohann. Content-oriented xml retrieval with hyrex. In *Proceedings of the first INEX Workshop, Dagstuhl, Germany*, 2002.
5. T. Grabs and H. Scheck. ETH zürich at INEX: Flexible information retrieval from XML with powerdb-xml. In *Proceedings of the first INEX Workshop, Dagstuhl, Germany*, 2002.
6. T. Grust. Accelerating xpath location steps. In *Proceedings of the 2002 ACM SIGMOD International Conference on Management of Data, Madison, Wisconsin, USA*. In M. J. Franklin, B. Moon, and A. Ailamaki, editors, ACM Press, 2002.

7. Guidelines for topic development. Proceedings of INEX 2003, Dagstuhl, Germany, december 2003.
8. G. Kazai, M. Lalmas, and A. P. de Vries. The overlap problem in content-oriented XML retrieval evaluation. In *Proceedings of SIGIR 2004, Sheffield, England*, pages 72–79, July 2004.
9. K. Sauvagnat. Xfirm, un modèle flexible de recherche d'information pour le stockage et l'interrogation de documents xml. In *Proceedings of CORIA'04 (COnférence en Recherche d'Information et Applications), Toulouse, France*, pages 121–142, march 2004.
10. K. Sauvagnat and M. Boughanem. The impact of leaf nodes relevance values evaluation in a propagation method for xml retrieval. In R. Baeza-Tates, Y. Marek, T. Roelleke, and A. P. de Vries, editors, *Proceedings of the 3rd XML and Information Retrieval Workshop, SIGIR 2004, Sheffield, England*, pages 13–22, July 2004.
11. K. Sauvagnat and M. Boughanem. Le langage de requête xfirm pour les documents xml: De la recherche par simples mots-clés *à* l'utilisation de la structure des documents. In *Proceedings of Inforsid 2004, Biarritz, France*, may 2004.
12. K. Sauvagnat, M. Boughanem, and C. Chrisment. Searching XML documents using relevance propagation. In A. Apostolico and M. Melucci, editors, *SPIRE 04, Padoue, Italie*, pages 242–254. Springer, 6-8 october 2004.

Building and Experimenting with a Heterogeneous Collection

Zoltán Szlávik and Thomas Rölleke

Queen Mary University of London, London, UK
{zolley, thor}@dcs.qmul.ac.uk

Abstract. Today's integrated retrieval applications retrieve documents from disparate data sources. Therefore, as part of INEX 2004, we ran a heterogeneous track to explore the experimentation with a heterogeneous collection of documents. We built a collection comprising various sub-collections, re-used topics (queries) from the sub-collections and created new topics, and participants submitted the results of retrieval runs. The assessment proved difficult, since pooling the results and browsing the collection posed new challenges and requested more resources than available. This reports summarises the motivation, activities, results and findings of the track.

1 Introduction

A heterogeneous track has been part of INEX 2004. The task of the track was to explore how to build and maintain a testbed, how to create topics, and how to perform retrieval runs, assessment and evaluation.

1.1 Motivation

Before 2004, the INEX collection has been a collection of XML documents with a single DTD. However, in practical environments, XML retrieval requires to deal with XML documents with different DTDs, because a collection comprises documents of different purpose, authors and sources. Further, information in practical environments is spread over XML documents, relational databases, and other data source formats. Therefore, we included in INEX 2004 a heterogeneous track (also known as het track) that addressed the heterogeneity of a collection.

A heterogeneous collection poses a number of challenges:

- For content-only (CO) queries, approaches for homogeneous and well-typed collections can make direct use of the DTD. The DTD can be used, for example, for identifying what element type is reasonable to present in the retrieval result. In a heterogeneous collection, we might have several or no DTD's, and retrieval methods independent of DTD are essential, and DTD mappings might be useful.
- For content-and-structure (CAS) queries, there is the problem of mapping structural conditions to different sub-collections. If we consider structural

N. Fuhr et al. (Eds.): INEX 2004, LNCS 3493, pp. 349–357, 2005.

conditions as useful, then a DTD-based mapping of structural conditions is essential for CAS queries. Methods known for federated databases could be applied here. We can distinguish between manual, semi-automatic or fully automatic methods for creating the schema mappings.
- When performing retrieval runs, the retrieval algorithms need to merge the results retrieved from different sub-collections. For an experimental point of view, we can compare global strategies that know the whole collection with local strategies that make only use of the knowledge that can be derived per sub-collection. The latter strategies are probably closer to what we meet in reality.
- The content of a relational database can be represented in an XML document (collection, respectively). The question is whether the retrieval of relational databases via XML is beneficial.

The goal of the INEX het track was to set up a test collection, and investigate the new challenges.

This track aims to answer, among others, the following research questions:

- For CO queries, what methods are feasible for determining elements that would be reasonable answers? Are pure statistical methods appropriate and sufficient, or are ontology-based approaches also helpful?
- What methods can be used to map structural criteria such that they can be applied (make sense) for a collection for which the DTD might be different or even not known!?
- Should mappings focus on element names (types) only, or also deal with element content?
- Should the data be organized (and indexed) as a single collection of heterogeneous documents, or is it better to treat het coll as a set of homogeneous sub-collections?
- Are evaluation criteria developed for homogeneous collections also suitable for heterogeneous collections, or should other criteria and metrics be applied?

Since this was the first year of the heterogeneity track, the focus of the activities was on making a test collection available to participants, create some topics and perform retrieval runs and assessment, and apply evaluation measures.

The emphasis was on investigating the How to do it, with a detailed look at individual topics and runs, and the technicalities involved. A statistical measure was not the aim of the first year of het track.

1.2 Activities

The participants of this track carried out the following activities:

- Construction of a heterogeneous test collection (sometimes called het coll): We used the current INEX corpus, and added various sub-collections including DBLP, HCIBIB, Berkeley lib, Duisburg bibdb, and QMUL bibdb (the latter an XML representation of a relational database). The collection is maintained at http://inex.is.informatik.uni-duisburg.de:2004/internal/hettrack/.

- Selection of 20 CO and CAS queries from the existing INEX body and creation of four new topics. The topics were selected and created with the aim to retrieve documents from several sub-collections.
- INRIA has developed and experimented with a tool, XSum, for graphically representing XML documents; one of the main purposes of the tool was to enable the user to grasp the structure and aspect of various XML datasets, with or without a DTD.[1]
- Retrieval runs on the heterogeneous collection for this set of queries (see appendix).
- The assessment has been not carried out yet, due to technical problems and restricted resources. The aim is to join the het coll with the relevance assessment tool used for the INEX IEEE collection.
- For the evaluation, we aim at a qualitative (query-and-run-oriented) analysis rather than a quantitative average-oriented analysis of results.

Based on the results and experience gained in 2004, a larger and quantitative het track can be carried out in following years.

2 Collection Creation

Table 1 shows the sub-collections that were used this year.

Table 1. Sub-collections used in 2004

Collection	MB(unpacked)	Number of elements
IEEE Computer Society	494	8.2M
Berkeley	33.1	1194863
CompuScience	313	7055003
bibdb Duisburg	2.08	40118
DBLP	207	5114033
hcibib	30.5	308554
qmul-dcs-pubdb	1.05	23436

From creating the sub-collections, we learned the following:

1. For a larger scale het track, methods and tools are needed for managing a set of sub-collections. With restricted resources, the management of 5-10 sub-collections is achievable but more sub-collections require tools and resources.
2. Sub-collections come with syntax errors (non-tidy XML). It is best to correct those errors centrally and "by hand", but keep a carefully maintained log of the changes made.

[1] Currently, XSum represents the XML elements and attributes structure within an XML document, statistics such as numbers of elements on a given path. The tool is developed in Java, and freely available.

3 Topic Creation

Given the objectives of the het track, four types of topics have been proposed in the topic creation guideline:

1. CO (Content Only Topics): Since CO queries do not take structural information into account. This type had not been found challenging, but any CO query used in the ad-hoc track could be used in the het track and gave similar results (because the test collection used for the ad-hoc track is part of the het track).
2. BCAS (Basic Content and Structure Topics): This type of topics focuses on the combination of singular structural constraints with a content-based constraint. The aim is synonym matches for structural constraints.
3. CCAS (Complex Content and Structure Topics): are the het track equivalent of the CAS topics of the ad-hoc track, specified used the NEXI language. The aim is to enable transformations and partial mappings of the topic path upon the different collections in het track, without losing the IR component of the topic.
4. ECCAS (Extended Content and Structure Topics): extended CCAS to enable the specification of the correctness path transformation and mapping probabilities.

3.1 Re-used Topics

Twenty topics were selected from the ad-hoc topics to re-use in het track. After examining the ad-hoc topics, 10 CO topics were selected that probably contain results not only in the IEEE (also referred to and used as inex-1.3 and inex-1.4) sub-collection. 10 CAS topics were also selected. The main criterion was that topics should possibly have relevant results in more sub-collections. Selected CAS topics were identified as CCAS het track topics.

3.2 New Topics

Four new topics (see B) were created by participants of which three topics are CCAS and one is BCAS.

4 Retrieval Runs

The main difference between a mono- and a heterogeneous track is that sub-collections are specified in the run submissions. In order to be able to examine results with respect to the considered sub-collections, a slightly modified version of the ad-hoc track's submission format has been proposed (see C).

Actually, the consideration of sub-collections poses some major research question, since we cannot assume that each run considers all sub-collections:

1. How do we pool results from runs if some runs considered a sub-collection X and other runs considered a sub-collection Y?
2. How does an evaluation measure deal with the incompleteness of runs?

Another issue is the assignment of topics to participants. Is it useful to assign topics under strict rules and supervision, trying to make sure that sub-collections are covered equally, and the same number of runs is performed per topic, etc? Or is it the nature of heterogeneous track that this effort is not justified and is rather to be replaced by a random assignment?

5 Assessment and Evaluation

During the preparation for assessment and evaluation, we identified the following two main challenges:

1. Browsing the results and the collection. The browsing tool X-Rai was initially developed for the IEEE collection only, and currently cannot handle larger sub-collection files, even the QMUL sub-collection with its 1.05MB, efficiently. Therefore, the two smallest sub-collections (bibdbpub and qmuldcsdbpub) were converted into many small files, and made available for browsing.
2. Pooling. The aforementioned problem also affected the pooling procedure, as the format of submission runs could not be exactly used for pooling. The other challenge in pooling was that, unlike the ad hoc track runs, het track runs could consider various sets of sub-collections, and there has not been a straightforward method to create pools from this kind of source, e.g. "use the first 150 results in each run" method may create larger pools for sub-collections having more elements in the top-ranked results and small for those having less.

6 Summary and Conclusions

The first year of het track established a heterogeneous collection, reused and created topics, and performed retrieval runs. The assessment and evaluation is currently outstanding.

The discussion among the participants and the work carried out raised the following questions:

1. What makes the heterogeneity of a collection? The current het coll is viewed as little heterogeneous since it consists "only" of XML documents, and all documents are about computer science literature. Can we measure heterogeneity?
2. How can we manage many and large sub-collections? In particular creating the browsing facilities for the sub-collections and the assessment proved difficult. Can we easily split (and possibly merge files)?
3. Topics and retrieval runs relate only to some sub-collections. Topics might have been created and runs might have been performed without considering the whole collection. How is this incompleteness captured in an evaluation?

Het track has established a collection and experience about how to do it and where the difficulties are. INEX is now ready for the next phase of het track, and it can re-use and extend the existing collection and pay particular attention to the efficient inclusion of new sub-collections into the whole process.

A Topic Format

```
<!ELEMENT inex_topic (title,
   content_description,
   structure_description,
   narrative,keywords)>
<!ATTLIST inex_topic
  topic_id   CDATA  #REQUIRED
  query_type CDATA  #REQUIRED
>

<!ELEMENT title (#PCDATA)>
<!ELEMENT content_description   (#PCDATA)>
<!ELEMENT structure_description   (#PCDATA)>
<!ELEMENT narrative     (#PCDATA)>
<!ELEMENT keywords      (#PCDATA)>
```

B Het Track Topics

Topic created by IRIT:

```
<?xml version="1.0" encoding="ISO-8859-1"?>
<inex_topic topic_id="1" query_type="BCAS">
  <title>
    //bb[about(.,"PhD thesis amsterdam")]
  </title>
  <content_description>
    I'm looking for bibliography entries concerning
    PhD thesis obtained at the university of Amsterdam
  </content_description>
  <structure_description>
    I'm looking for full references of PhD thesis: it
    means that results elements should contain the author,
    the title,the year and the school/city where the PhD
    thesis was obtained.
  </structure_description>
  <narrative>
    I'm maybe interested in working in Amsterdam next year
    and I would like to know what are the research subjects
    in the city. I think that a way to obtained this information
    (in the collections we have) is to see what are the subjects
    of the PhD thesis obtained in Amsterdam.
  </narrative>
```

```
  <keywords>
    phD thesis, university, amsterdam
  </keywords>
</inex_topic>
```

Topic created by UMONTES:

```
<?xml version="1.0" encoding="ISO-8859-1"?>
<inex_topic topic_id="2" query_type="CCAS">
  <title>
    //article[about(.//author, nivio ziviani)]
  </title>
  <content_description>
    We are seeking for works with Nivio Ziviani as one of its authors
  </content_description>
  <structure_description>
    Title is a tag identifying works title and author is a
    tag identifying who wrote those works. They are usually part of
    front matter of a document, or part of  bottom matter  in a
    bibliography reference or can be an item in a volume index.
  </structure_description>
  <narrative>
    We are seeking for works with Nivio Ziviani as one of its
    authors. We want to catalogue all Nvio Ziviani works, so any
    reference, index entry , abstract or complete article will be
    relevant, but biography works  will not.
  </narrative>
  <keywords>
    Nivio Ziviani
  </keywords>
</inex_topic>
```

Topic created by RMIT:

```
<?xml version="1.0" encoding="ISO-8859-1"?>
<inex_topic topic_id="3" query_type="CCAS">
  <title>
    //article[about(.//abs, Web usage mining) or
    about(.//sec, "Web mining" traversal navigation patterns)]
  </title>
  <content_description>
    We are looking for documents that describe capturing and mining
    Web usage, in particular the traversal and navigation patterns;
    motivations include Web site redesign and maintenance.
  </content_description>
  <structure_description>
    Article is a tag identifying a document, which can also be
    represented as a book tag, an inproceedings (or incollection)
```

```
    tag, an entry tag, etc. Abs is a tag identifying abstract of
    a document, which can be represented as an abstract tag, an abs
    tag, etc. Sec is a tag identifying an informative document
    component, such as section or paragraph. It can also be represented
    as sec, ss1, ss2, p, ip1 or other similar tags.
  </structure_description>
  <narrative>
    To be relevant, a document must describe methods for capturing
    and analysing web usage, in particular traversal and navigation
    patterns. The motivation is using Web usage mining for site
    reconfiguration and maintenance, as well as providing recommendations
    to the user. Methods that are not explicitly applied to the Web
    but could apply are still relevant.
    Capturing browsing actions for pre-fetching is not relevant.
  </narrative>
  <keywords>
    Web usage mining, Web log analysis, browsing pattern,
    navigation pattern, traversal pattern, Web statistics, Web design,
    Web maintenance, user recommendations.
  </keywords>
</inex_topic>
```

Topic created by LIP6:

```
<?xml version="1.0" encoding="ISO-8859-1"?>
<inex_topic topic_id="4" query_type="CCAS">
  <title>
    //article[about(.,"text categorization") and
    (about(.//fm//au, "David D. Lewis")
    or about(.//bib//au, "David D. Lewis"))]
  </title>
  <content_description>
    I am looking for documents about text categorization which
    have been written by David D. Lewis, or related work from other authors.
  </content_description>
  <structure_description>
    The tags which are used in this topic come from the DTD of the
    ad hoc task collection. Article is a tag identifying a document,
    which can also be represented as a book tag, an inproceedings
    (or incollection) tag, an entry tag, etc. Fm is a tag identifying
    the header of a document which usually contains title, authors...
    Bib is a tag identifying the bibliography of a document.
    Au is a tag identyfying an author name.
  </structure_description>
  <narrative>
    To be relevant, a document must describe text categorization methods.
    It must have been written by David D. Lewis or must contain
    a bibliography entry with David D. Lewis.
  </narrative>
```

```
  <keywords>
    Text categorization, Text classifier
  </keywords>
</inex_topic>
```

C Run Format

```
<!ELEMENT inex_het_track_submission (description, topic+)>
<!ATTLIST inex_het_track_submission
participant-id CDATA #REQUIRED
run-id CDATA #REQUIRED
query (automatic | manual) #REQUIRED
topic-part  (T|D|K|TD|TK|DK|TDK)    #IMPLIED
task  CDATA  #IMPLIED
>

<!ELEMENT description (#PCDATA)>

<!ELEMENT topic (subcollections, result*)>
<!ATTLIST topic
topic-id CDATA #REQUIRED
>
<!ELEMENT subcollections (subcollection+)>
<!ELEMENT result (subcollection, file, path, rank?, rsv?)>
<!ELEMENT subcollection EMPTY>
<!ATTLIST subcollection name CDATA #REQUIRED>

<!ELEMENT file (#PCDATA)>
<!ELEMENT path (#PCDATA)>
<!ELEMENT rank (#PCDATA)>
<!ELEMENT rsv (#PCDATA)>
```

D Submitted Runs

- IRIT submitted 3 runs. One run is for CCAS, one for CO and one for BCAS topics. Files contain results for all the 24 het track topics. Various groups of sub-collections were considered for topics.
- RMIT submitted results of three different approaches, all approaches were applied to all topic types and topics (9 files - file groups of 3 - one file is for a specific approach, specific topic type (CCAS,CO,BCAS)). Various groups of sub-collections were considered for topics, often all sub-collections were used.
- UBERKELEY submitted 2 runs, used all CO topics, 12 (i.e. all but one) CCAS topics. All sub-collections were considered.
- UMONTES submitted 6 runs, 3 runs for all CO topics, 3 for all 'VCAS' (CCAS and BCAS together) topics, considered 5 sub-collections.
- UNIDU submitted 3 runs, considered only topic no. 1 (as CO) and used 3 sub-collections.

A Test Platform for the INEX Heterogeneous Track

Serge Abiteboul[1], Ioana Manolescu[1], Benjamin Nguyen[3], and Nicoleta Preda[1,2]

[1] INRIA Futurs & LRI, PCRI, France
firstname.lastname@inria.fr
[2] LRI, Université de Paris-Sud, France
[3] PRiSM, Université de Versailles Saint-Quentin, France

Abstract. This article presents our work within the INEX 2004 Heterogeneous Track. We focused on taming the structural diversity within the INEX heterogeneous bibliographic corpus.

We demonstrate how semantic models and associated inference techniques can be used to solve the problems raised by the structural diversity within a given XML corpus. The first step automatically extracts a set of *concepts* from each class of INEX heterogeneous documents. An *unified set of concepts* is then computed, which synthesizes the interesting concepts from the whole corpus. Individual corpora are connected to the unified set of concepts via *conceptual mappings*. This approach is implemented as an application of the KADOP platform for peer-to-peer warehousing of XML documents. While this work caters to the structural aspects of XML information retrieval, the extensibility of the KADOP system makes it an interesting test platform in which components developed by several INEX participants could be plugged, exploiting the opportunities of peer-to-peer data and service distribution.

1 Context

Our work is situated in the context of the INEX Heterogeneous Track (which we will denote as *het-track* throughout this paper). The het-track is very young: it has been held in 2004 for the first time. The het-track has built a collection of *heterogeneous data sets*, all representing bibliographic entries structured in different XML dialects. In keeping with the INEX terminology, throughout this paper, we will use the term *heterogeneous* to qualify a set of XML documents featuring different sets of tags (or conforming to different DTDs), and this shall not cause confusion.

The het-track collection includes:

- Berkeley: library catalog of UC Berkeley in the areas of computer and information science. The particularity of this data set is to include *several* classifications or codes for each entry.
- CompuScience: Computer Science database of FIZ Karlsruhe.
- BibDB Duisburg: Bibliographic data from the Duisburg university.
- DBLP: The well-known database and logical programming data source.

N. Fuhr et al. (Eds.): INEX 2004, LNCS 3493, pp. 358–371, 2005.

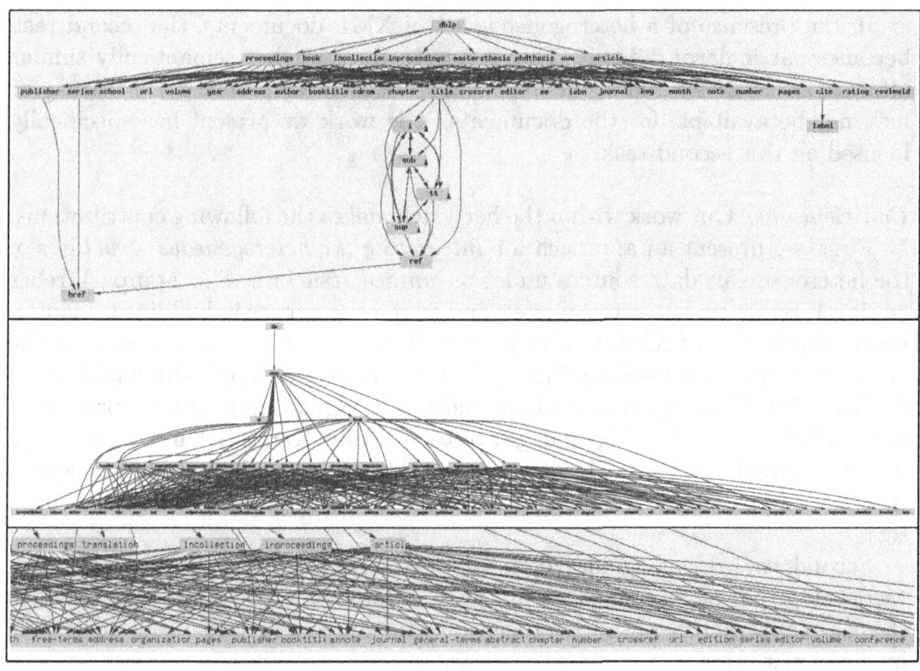

Fig. 1. XSum drawing of the DBLP DTD (top), Duisburg DTD (middle), and zoom-in on Duisburg DTD articles (bottom)

- HCIBIB: Bibliographic entries from the field of Human-Computer Interaction.
- QMUL: Publications database of QMUL Department of Computer Science.

A set of topics have also been proposed, which are largely similar (in structure and scope) to those formulated within the relevance feedback track. The topics include:

- *Content-only (CO)* topics, of the form "database query". The answer given by an IR engine to a CO topic consists of XML fragments pertinent to the specified keywords.
- *Content-and-structure (CAS)* topics, such as
  //article[about(.//body, "XML technology")]
  The answer given by an IR engine to a CAS topic consists of XML fragments pertinent to the specified keywords, and using the structure criteria of the topic as hints.

Answering an IR query on a structurally heterogeneous corpus raises two main challenges. First, the relevance of a data fragment for a given keyword or set of keywords must be computed; this task is no different from the main relevance assessment track. Second, the structural hints present in the topic, in the case of CAS topics, must be taken into account.

In the presence of a heterogeneous set of XML documents, the second task becomes particularly difficult. This is due to the fact that semantically similar information is structured in different XML dialects; furthermore, DTDs may or may not be available for the documents. The work we present has specifically focused on this second task.

Contributions. Our work within the het-track makes the following contributions.

First, we present an approach for *integrating the heterogeneous structures* of the heterogeneous data sources under an *unified structure*. This approach relies on simple semantic-based techniques, and on our experience in building semantic-based warehouses of XML resources [2, 3]. The result of this integration on the het-track corpus is *a unified DTD, and a set of mappings* from individual sources to this DTD. CAS topics against the het-track corpus can now be expressed in terms of the unified DTD, and get automatically translated into a union of topics over each data set. Thus, solving a CAS topic on a heterogeneous corpus is reduced to solving several CAS topics against the individual component data sets.

Second, we present XSum [20], a free XML and DTD visualization tool, that we developed as part of our work in INEX. XSum helped us get acquainted with the complex structure of the heterogeneous collection, and devise semi-automatic integration strategies.

Finally, we outline the architecture of a peer-to-peer platform for processing XML queries or IR searches, over a set of distributed, potentially heterogeneous XML data sources. This platform has the advantage of being *open* and *inherently distributed*, allowing to take advantage of the data sources and capabilities of each peer in the network in order to solve a given query or search. In particular, we show this platform may be used as a testbed for the XML IR methodologies developed within the het-track, by allowing to test and combine the various implementations of the about functions developed by INEX participants.

This document is structured as follows. Section 2 describes our semantic-based approach for XML information retrieval over a heterogeneous corpus. Section 3 details the result we obtained by applying this approach on the INEX het-track corpus. Section 4 outlines the peer-to-peer generic platform we propose, and describes how it could be used as a testbed for the het-track in the future. Section 5 compares our work with related ones, while Section 6 draws our conclusion and outlines future work.

2 Approach

Dealing with structural diversity in heterogeneous sources has been a topic of research in the field of databases and in particular of *data integration*; the basic concepts in this area can be found, e.g., in [16]. The purpose of a data integration system is to provide the user the illusion of a single, integrated database, on which the user can pose queries (in our case, IR queries, or topics). Behind the uniform interface, the system will process these queries by translating them into the formats specific to each data source, processing them separately, and integrating the results into a single one.

Traditionally, data integration operates at the level of *schemas*. A source schema characterizes the structure of each data source, and an integrated schema is provided to the user. This approach has been thoroughly investigated in the case of relational data sources and schemas [11, 6].

In the case of heterogeneous, complex, potentially schema-less data sources, this approach is no longer applicable. Instead, we chose to draw from the experience obtained in *semantic-based data integration* [6, 5], to integrate sources pertinent to a specific domains, such as the het-track corpus, under a single *conceptual model*. The building bricks of our conceptual model are:

- *Concepts*, which are the notions of relevance for a given application. For instance, in the het-track corpus, useful concepts are: publication, author, etc.
- *IsA* relationships represent specialization relationships between concepts. For instance, book IsA publication represents the fact that books are a kind of publication. IsA relationships are also known under the name of *hyponymy*.
- *PartOf* relationships represent composition (aggregation) relationships between concepts. For instance, title PartOf book represents the fact that a title is a component of a book. PartOf relationships are also known under the name of *meronymy*.

Since its inception, XML has been hailed as a *self-descripting* data format: since the set of markup tags is by definition extensible, typical XML applications use semantically meaningful tag names. This was part of the indended usage for XML in data management, and indeed this choice is made in most popular XML applications. An outstanding example is XSL, the XML-based stylesheet language: an XSL program is written based on a set of XML types with meaningful names, such as if/else, apply-templates, select etc. An inspection of the DTDs found on the "XML Cover Pages" leads to the same conclusion: XML flexibility is typically exploited to encode meaning into tag names. Furthermore, tag nesting is often used to reflect nesting of application objects. Thus, while tags by themselves are insufficient to capture complex application semantics, they are at least a first step in that direction.

As a consequence of this "pseudo-semantic description" approach, in several data management applications the need arises for integrating data sources of which we only know their XML syntax (or their DTDs). This approach has been taken for instance in [5], and has been further studied and refined in [8].

Thus, our approach starts by extracting a conceptual model from each source. For the sources for which DTDs are available, the process is straightforward: we extract a concept for each type in the DTD, including element and attributes (among which we do not make a distinction). For sources for which DTDs are not available, we start by extracting a "rough" DTD, including all elements and attributes. Whenever we encounter in the data an element labeled l_1 as a child of an element labeled l_2, we mention in the DTD that the type l_1 can appear as a child of the type l_2. After having extracted this DTD, we compute from it a set of concepts as in the previous case.

At the end of this stage, we have obtained a set of conceptual data source models. Our purpose then is to construct a unified conceptual model characterizing all sources, and mappings between each conceptual model to the unified one.

Extracting the Unified Conceptual Model. To build the unified conceptual model, we identify groups of concepts (each one in different conceptual source models) that represent semantically similar data items. We do this in a semi-automatic manner, as follows.

First, the names of concepts from different source models are compared for similarity, to identify potential matches. This is done automatically, with the help of WordNet [7]. We have used WordNet outside the peer; it can be easily wrapped as a Web service local to the integration peer. If simple matches such as the one between book (DBLP) and book (HCI BIB) can be automatically detected, more subtle ones such as the similarity between editor (HCI BIB) and Edition (Berkeley) require the usage of tools such as WordNet. Having identified clusters of concepts which potentially represent the same thing, we create one concept in the unified model, for each cluster of source model concepts above a given similarity threshold; human intervention is required at this point in setting the similarity threshold.

At the end of this process, it may happen that some source model concepts have not been clustered with any others. This may be the case, for instance, of concepts called Fld012, Fld245, etc. from the Berkeley data source. These concepts are difficult to cluster, since their names (standing for Field number 012, Field number 245, etc.) do not encapsulate the meaning of the concept, instead, this meaning is included in plain-text comments preceding to the corresponding element type definition. To deal with such concepts, we need to capture the DTD comments preceding the type definition, and feed those descriptions to the word similarity-based clustering. This way, we may learn that Fld245 stands for "Title Statement", and cluster Fld245 with similarly named concepts from other DTDs.

Once the clusters of similar (and supposedly semantically close) concepts have been extracted, we create a concept for each such cluster, in the unified conceptual model.

Extracting Mappings Between the Source and Unified Conceptual Models. We add an IsA relationship going from each source model concept, to the unified model concept that was derived from its clusters. If a source model participates to several clusters, this may yield several IsA relationships.

3 Contributions

In this section, we report on the results that we obtained in our work in the framework of the het-track.

3.1 Unified Model for the Het-Track Corpus

In this section, we discuss the techniques used to construct a unified DTD in order to query the documents of the heterogeneous track. An important factor is that the documents are all about the same application domain: scientific bibliography. Five of them are quite verbose, and the labels are self descriptive, while one (Berkeley data set) has labels that convey no semantic signification whatsoever. Some examples of such labels would be: Fld001, Fld002, etc.

In this article, we do not take into account this DTD, therefore the unified DTD we propose does not include elements from the Berkeley data set for the moment. We report on our experience with the Berkeley data set, based on using our XSum tool, in Section 6.

The method used in order to determine a unified DTD is the following :

- We first of all create mappings between elements whose tags are similar, which feature similar children element types, but that originate from different DTDs. For instance, we might find two article elements, one from DBLP, the other from BibDB Duisburg. If there are several elements with the same (or very similar) type definition in multiple DTDs, we group them all together. These are one to one mappings, and the output of this phase is a group of clusters of syntactically close elements.
- For each cluster, we then check the parent nodes, and group them together in a new parent cluster.
- For all these automatically constructed clusters, we manually check the correctness of these groupings, and cho0se a name for the cluster, generally of the form nameOfElementC.

We provide the unified DTD on our website [18].

Using the unified DTD: The Unified DTD is to be used when asking queries over the heterogeneous data set. The querying mechanism is as follows.

- The INEX queries must be written taking into account the unified DTD. The names of the elements appearing in the unified DTD should be used to formulate queries against the whole het-track corpus. We call such a query a *generic query*.
- The generic query is then converted into specific queries, with a specific structure for each database, and the queries are then run seperately on all the databases.
- Given the unified DTD, the answers returned are clustered together in a common structure, in order to use only a single DTD for browsing means.

3.2 XSum: A Simple XML Visualization Tool

We have developed a simple XML visualization tool, called *XSum* (for *XML Summary Drawer*). XSum can be used in two ways.

Drawing Path Summaries. Given an XML document, XSum extracts a tree-shaped structural summary of the document, and draws it. This structural summary contains a node for each distinct path in the input document [13], and is

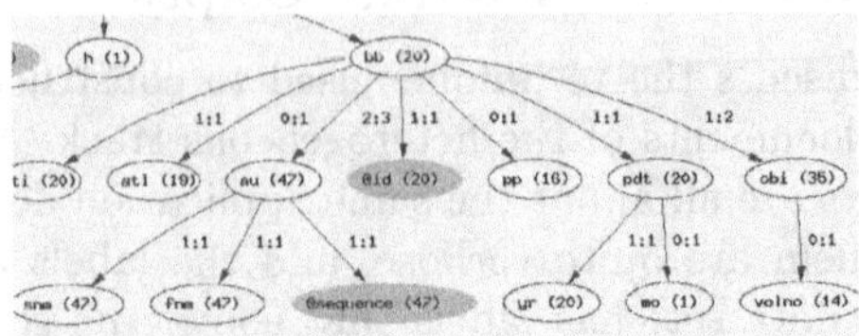

Fig. 2. Fragment of a path summary computed from an article in the INEX main corpus (IEEE CS)

the equivalent of a strong DataGuide [9] for XML data (DataGuides were initially proposed for graph-structured OEM data). XSum enhances this structural representation with:

– Node counts: XSum records the number of nodes on a given path in the XML document, and correspondingly may show this number in the summary node corresponding to that path.
– Leaf types: XSum attempts to "guess" the type (String, integer or real number), of each leaf node (which can be either a text node, or an attribute value), and depicts the corresponding node in a color reflecting its type.
– Edge cardinalities: for every path p/l, where p is a path and l is a label, XSum records the minimum and maximum number of children on path p/l that an element on path p may have. This holds also for text children.

A sample summary representation produced by XSum from a XML-ized article from the INEX IEEE CS corpus is depicted in Figure 2. The fragment shown here reflects the references at the end of an article, including authors, titles, and publication information for the relevant references. If a an element type is recursive, the summary drawn by XSum will unfold the recursion: it will construct several nodes corresponding to the recursive type, nested within each other, up to the maximum nesting level actually encountered in the data.

Drawing DTDs. When given a DTD, XSum draws a simple graph, representing each attribute or element type from the DTD as a node, and adding an edge from a node to another whenever a type may appear inside another in the DTD. If a an element type is recursive, the DTD graph will only include one node for this type, and that node will participate in a cycle.

Figure 1 shows the drawing extracted by XSum from: the DBLP DTD, the DTD of the Duisburg data source, and a zoomed-in fragment around the node corresponding to the "article" type in the Duisburg data source.

Structural Clusterering of DTDs. Graphs corresponding to DTDs tend to have relatively few nodes, but large number of edges, crossing each other in the drawing (as shown in Figure 1), which may make the image difficult to read. To cope with this problem, we have devised a *structural DTD clustering technique* which reduces the number of nodes (and edges) in a DTD graph. The clustering is performed as follows. All DTD nodes sharing the same set of parents are clustered together; an edge is drawn between two clusters, if some nodes in the parent cluster are parents of all the nodes in the child cluster. Notice that the structural clustering performed by XSum takes place *within* a single DTD; it has nothing in common with the semantic clustering performed *across* DTDs and described in the previous section.

Clustered DTD graphs are much more readable than simple DTD graphs. As an example, Figure 3 shows the clustered graph produced for the Duisburg DTD. This readability comes at the price of some loss of precision (since they do no longer show the exact set of parents of each node).

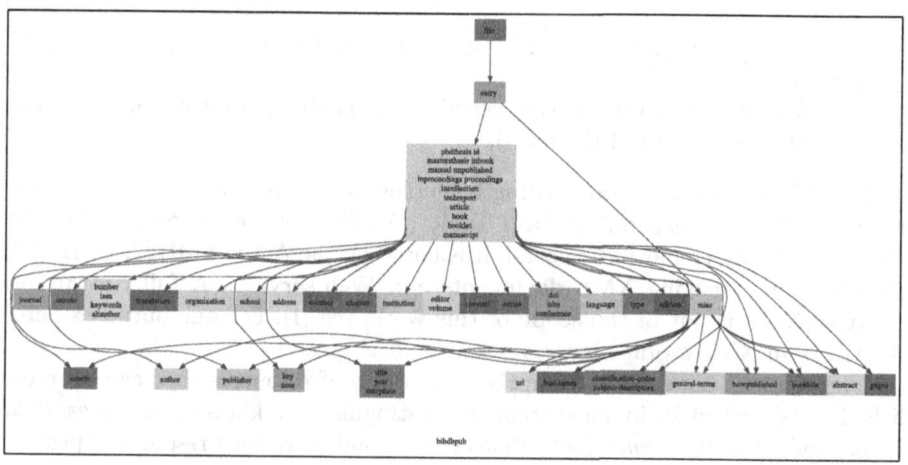

Fig. 3. Clustered DTD graph for the Duisburg data set

From our experience using XSum with the INEX standard and heterogeneous corpus, we draw some remarks. Both DTD and summary drawings tend to be large for documents of the complexity we are dealing with, typically larger than the screen or a normal printer format. Understanding the image requires "sliding" over it to see one part at a time. To simplify path summaries, we have introduced in XSum options allowing to omit leaf nodes and/or cardinality annotations, which simplifies the graphs. To simplify DTD graphs, we introduced structural clustering. We welcome the feedback of INEX participants on how to enhance XSum's XML and DTD drawing logic, to produce more helpful images.

XSum is implemented in Java, and is based on GraphViz, a well-known free graph drawing library developed at AT&T. XSum is freely available for download from [20].

Further Info and Graphs. The graphs produced by XSum, for all DTDs in the het-track corpus, are available at [18].

4 The KadoP Platform

In this section, we briefly describe the KADOP peer-to-peer XML resources management platform, which serves as the framework for our work. A more detailed presentation can be found in [3].

The KADOP platform allows constructing and maintaining, in a decentralized, P2P style, a warehouse of *resources.* By resource, we mean: data items, such as XML or text documents, document fragments, Web services, or collections; semantic items, such as simple hierarchies of concepts; and relationships between the data and semantic items. KADOP's functionality of interest to as are:

- *publishing* XML resources, making them available to all peers in the P2P network;
- *searching* for resources meeting certain criteria (based on content, structure as well as semantics of the data).

KADOP leverages several existing technologies and models. First, it relies on a state-of-the art Distributed Hash Table (DHT) implementation [19] to keep the peer network connected. Second, it is based on the ActiveXML (AXML) [17] platform for managing XML documents and Web services. A full description of ActiveXML is out of the scope of this work, see [1]. For our purposes here, AXML is an XML storage layer, present on each peer.

The KADOP data model comprises the types of resources that can be published and searched for in our system. We distinguish two kinds of resources: *data items*, and *semantic items. Data items* correspond to various resource types:

- A *page* is an XML document. Pages may have associated *DTDs* or *XML schemas* describing their type; we treat DTDs as sources of semantic items (see further). Other formats such as PDF can be used; we ignore them here.
- We consider data with various granularities. Most significantly, we model: *page fragments*, that is, results of an XML query on a page, and *collections*, as user-defined sets of data items. Collections can be viewed as an extension of the familiar concept of Web navigator bookmarks: they are defined by the user who gives them a name, and can gather in a collection any kind of data items which, from the viewpoint of the user, logically belong together. Inside pages, we also consider element *labels*, attribute *names*, and *words*.
- Finally, a *web service* is a function taking as input types XML fragments, and returning a typed XML fragment.

Any data item is uniquely identified by an PID (peer ID) and a name. The PID provides the unique name (logical identifier) of the peer that has published the data item, and where the item resides; names allow distinguishing between data items within the peer. Data items are connected by PartOf relationships, in the natural sense: thus, a word is part of a fragment, a fragment part of a page etc. Furthermore, any type of data items can be part of collections. A data item residing on one peer may be part of a collection defined on another peer (just like for bookmarks, adding a page to a collection does not entail its replication).

Semantic items consist of *concepts*, connected by two types of relationships: IsA, and PartOf. A graph of concepts, connected via IsA or PartOf links, is called a *concept model.* We derive a source concept model from each particular data source, as described in Section 2.

InstanceOf statements connect data items with concepts. In particular, all elements from an XML document, of given type τ (obtained as the result of the XPath expression $//\tau$), are implicitly connected by InstanceOf statements to the concept derived from the type τ.

The KADOP query language allows retrieving *data items*, based on constraints on the data items, and on their relationship with various concepts. Queries are simple tree patterns, and return the matches found for a single query

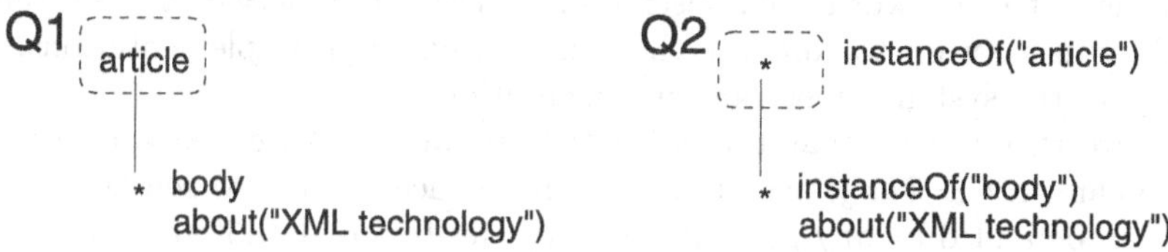

Fig. 4. Sample KADOP queries

node (in the style of XPath and the CAS INEX topics). For instance, the query in Figure 4 at left allows retrieving all "article" elements such that they have a "body" element, and the body is about XML technology. This corresponds to the sample CAS topic in Section 1. The dashed box designates the node for which matches will be returned.

Such a query, however, needs specific element tag names for its nodes. In the case of the heterogeneous corpus, such queries are no longer helpful, due to the presence of different element tag names corresponding to semantically similar data objects.

The approach we take for solving INEX heterogeneous CAS topics is based on the unified conceptual model. The idea is to drop name conditions from the queries, and instead use conditions of the form "instanceOf c", where c is a concept from the unified model. On our example query, this leads to the KadoP query at right in Figure 4, where we assume that "article" and "body" are part of the unified conceptual model. This query is processed as follows:

1. The elements directly declared as instance of the concepts "article" and "body" are found.
2. We search for concepts c_a such that c_a IsA "article", and concepts c_b such that c_b IsA "body". This will lead to retrieving all the concepts from the source concept models, which have been mapped to the unified concepts "article" and "body".
3. We search for elements declared as instances of the concepts c_a and c_b obtained as above.

These steps lead to matching the structural conditions posed by the CAS query against the heterogeneous corpus. They do not, however, apply the "about" condition, since implementing this condition is out of the scope of our work. We next explain how others' implementations of the "about" function could be plugged in our work.

Integrating "about" Functions. In the KADOP framework, "about" can be integrated as a Web service, offered by one or several peers. The implementation of this function is typically complex. From the KADOP perspective, all that is needed is that one or several participants make available a Web service named "about", obeying to a well-defined interface. Then, the KADOP query processor can invoke one of these services to evaluate the pertinence of an XML fragment for a given set of keywords. The user may specify which service to use; this is helpful when we want to compare the results of different implementations. Or, she may let the system choose an implementation.

It is worth stressing that the KADOP framework is based on a concept of *openness* and *extensibility*: new data sets, new concepts, or new semantic statements can be added by any participant, and refer to any data item on any peer. Finally, the KADOP framework is by nature distributed: any Web service (thus, any "about" function) can be invoked on XML fragments originating from any peer.

5 Related Work

We have proposed in this paper a method of integrating heterogeneous DTDs related to the same domain, into a unified DTD. Our work is related to projects on semi-automatic schema matching. In the domain of semi-automatic schema matching, we may distinguish three main research directions related to our work:

- given two schemas S_1 and S_2, compute the matching that associates label elements in schema S_1 with other label elements in schema S_2.
- given two schemas S_1 and S_2, create mappings between the elements of S_1 and the elements of S_2 in the form of views.
- given a set of schemas, generate one or more integrated schemas.

Our approach is related to the first direction as mappings between two DTD sources are derived based on the semantic and syntactic resemblance between nodes. The KADOP query engine exploits not only mappings between the unified DTD and each DTD source, but also mappings between two DTD source schemas.

We have proposed a semi-automatic method of computing a unified DTD. This work, related to the third research direction, is based on clustering similar elements. As related integrating schemas system based on clustering techniques, we mention ARTEMIS [4].

The particularity of our integration problem consists in the type of our input schemas: DTD schemas. These schemas do not have rich semantics associated with the edges between concept nodes. In the XSum project, we are now investigating, heuristics in order to add more semantic information to the DTD structure. Conceived first as a method of pretty drawing a DTD, we have defined a clustering method that has good properties of grouping related concepts together. This is interesting, because it implies that semantic relationships between nodes may be verified on a smaller graph instance. Other heuristics that transform the DTD-s into ER database schemas have been investigating in [6], [14], [12].

For the het-track collection, we have defined a single (unified) abstract schema, and mappings between concepts in the in the unified DTD and concepts in the various DTD sources, as each DTD was referring to the same topic.

In the case of a collection that contains schemas and resources of different domains (which may be the case of a peer to peer application), we may build a tool that semi-automatically defines unified DTDs by clustering DTDs of the same domain. We may benefit of works done in the ONION [15] project, that is heavily based on the existence of rich semantic relationships between the nodes of the schemas.

The second research direction hasn't been investigated in this paper, although the KADOP query language may handle mappings in the form of a concept node in the DTD associated to a view (KADOP query). An automatic method of deriving such mappings may benefit of works done in Xyleme [6] (path to path mappings), or CLIO [10].

6 Conclusion and Perspectives

We have presented our work focused on building an unified DTD for the data sets of the het-track. We have produced an unified DTD including all but the Berkeley data set, and we have developed a simple XML visualization tool which helped us get acquainted with the various data sets. We have furthermore presented an approach for formulating CAS INEX topics against a heterogeneous data corpus, based on our KADOP platform.

Our next step is merging the DTD of the Berkeley data set into the unified DTD.Aas explained in Section 3.1, the tag names encountered in this data set are meaningless; however, tag meaning can be found in comments appearing in the DTD, just before the element type definition appearing in the DTD. We attempted to cluster the DTD, but we were not able to parse it; thus, we extracted our own DTD, and clustered this one. We made several remarks.

First, the original DTD features much more element types (around 700) than the data set actually uses (around 200). Thus, the extracted DTD is easier to grasp.

Second, in some cases on the Berkeley data set, our structural clustering criteria has (quite surprisingly) clustered nodes representing semantically similar things. For instance, we obtained a cluster of 8 nodes representing variants of a publication's title, and a cluster of 33 nodes representing various numerical publication codes. However, in other cases, our parent-based clustering has grouped together nodes that do not *represent similar things*, but *are part of the same data subset*: namely, there is a "Main" cluster, grouping nodes such as Fld100 ("Main entry, personal name") and Fld111 ("Main entry, meeting name"), although personal and meeting names do not stand for the same thing. In this case, semantic clustering (using the comments, since the tag names themselves are meaningless) will disagree with structural clustering. Semantic clustering may correctly group "Main entry, personal name" with Fld700 ("Added entry, personal name"), since they represent similar things. However, this is only our intuition; a librarian's viewpoint may be quite different.

Third, we noticed also a (single, small) cluster where neither the tags, nor the accompanying comments convey any useful information. This is the case of a set of fields whose comments read "XXX Local Holdings Information for 9XXX"; we do not expect automatic processing of such data to yield meaningful results.

In a more general perspective, we intend to develop our approach into an easy-to-use integration platform, in order to include any other bibliographical semi-structured databases.

Acknowledgements. The authors are grateful to the anonymous INEX referee, whose careful comments helped improve the readability of the paper.

References

1. Serge Abiteboul, Omar Benjelloun, and Tova Milo. The ActiveXML project: an overview. Gemo research report no. 344, 2004.
2. Serge Abiteboul, Gregory Cobéna, Benjamin Nguyen, and Antonella Poggi. Construction and maintenance of a set of pages of interest (SPIN). In *Bases de Donnees Avancees*, Evry, 2002. Informal proceedings only.
3. Serge Abiteboul, Ioana Manolescu, and Nicoleta Preda. Constructing and querying a peer-to-peer warehouse of XML resources. In *Proceedings of the Semantic Web and Databases Workshop (in collaboration with VLDB)*, Toronto, CA, 2004.
4. Silvana Castano, Valeria De Antonellis, and Sabrina De Capitani di Vimercati. Global viewing of heterogeneous data sources. *IEEE Transactions on Knowledge and Data Engineering*, 13(2):277–297, 2001.
5. Sophie Cluet, Pierangelo Veltri, and Dan Vodislav. Views in a large scale XML repository. In *VLDB*, pages 271–280, 2001.
6. Claude Delobel, Chantal Reynaud, Marie-Christine Rousset, Jean-Pierre Sirot, and Dan Vodislav. Semantic integration in Xyleme: a uniform tree-based approach. *IEEE Data and Knowledge Engineering*, 44(3):267–298, 2003.
7. Christine Fellbaum. *WordNet: An Electronic Lexical Database.* MIT Press, 1998.
8. Gloria Giraldo. Automatic ontology construction in mediator systems. Ph.D. thesis, University of Orsay, France, 2005.
9. R. Goldman and J. Widom. Dataguides: Enabling query formulation and optimization in semistructured databases. In *VLDB*, pages 436–445, Athens, Greece, 1997.
10. Laura M. Haas, Renée J. Miller, B. Niswonger, Mary Tork Roth, Peter M. Schwarz, and Edward L. Wimmers. Transforming Heterogeneous Data with Database Middleware: Beyond Integration. *IEEE Data Engineering Bulletin*, 22(1):31–36, 1999.

11. Alon Y. Levy. Logic-based techniques in data integration. *Logic Based Artificial Intelligence*, 2000.
12. Jayant Madhavan, Philip A. Bernstein, and Erhard Rahm. Generic schema matching with Cupid. In *The VLDB Journal*, pages 49–58, 2001.
13. I. Manolescu, A. Arion, A. Bonifati, and A. Pugliese. Path Sequence-Based XML Query Processing. In *Bases de Données Avancées (French database conference)*, Montpellier, France, 2004. Informal proceedings only.
14. P. Mitra, G. Wiederhold, and J. Jannink. Semi-automatic integration of knowledge sources. In *Proc. of the 2nd Int. Conf. On Information FUSION'99*, 1999.
15. Prasenjit Mitra, Gio Wiederhold, and Martin Kersten. A graph-oriented model for articulation of ontology interdependencies. *Lecture Notes in Computer Science*, 1777:86, 2000.
16. Gio Wiederhold. Mediators in the architecture of future information systems. *IEEE Computer*, pages 38–49, 1992.
17. The ActiveXML home page. Available at www.activexml.net, 2004.
18. Gemo and PRiSM at the INEX heterogeneous track. Available at www-rocq.inria.fr/gemo/Gemo/Projects/ INEX-HET, 2004.
19. The FreePastry system. Available at www.cs.rice.edu/CS/Systems/Pastry/FreePastry/, 2001.
20. XSum: The XML Summary Drawer. Available at www-rocq.inria.fr/gemo/Gemo/Projects/SUMMARY, 2004.

EXTIRP 2004: Towards Heterogeneity

Miro Lehtonen

Department of Computer Science,
P. O. Box 68 (Gustaf Hällströmin katu 2b),
FI–00014 University of Helsinki, Finland
Miro.Lehtonen@cs.Helsinki.FI

Abstract. The effort around EXTIRP 2004 focused on the heterogeneity of XML document collections. The subcollections of the heterogeneous track (het-track) did not offer us a suitable testbed, but we successfully applied methods independent of any document type to the original INEX test collection. By closing our eyes to the element names defined in the DTD, we created comparable runs and discovered improvement in the results. This was anticipated evidence for our hypothesis that we do not need to know the element names when indexing the collection or when returning full-text answers to the Content-Only type queries. Some problematic areas were also identified. One of them is score combination which enables us to combine elements of any size into one ranked list of results given that we have the relevance scores of the leaf-level elements. However, finding a suitable score combination method remains part of our future work.

1 Introduction

One of our goals for the INEX 2004 project was to adapt our system to support heterogeneous XML collections without losing the retrieval accuracy achieved in 2003. Our system for XML retrieval — EXTIRP — has now been successfully modified: it is independent of any document type and, based on tests with the topics of 2003, the accuracy has even improved. However, not all components of EXTIRP adjusted to the changes equally well. For example, the score combination algorithm of EXTIRP showed its weakness in a significant decline in average precision. Consequently, the best result sets were those that consisted of disjoint answers at the finest level of granularity. Another factor having a negative impact on EXTIRP 2004 was the lack of manpower, due to which we gave up a previous success story: query expansion.

During the course of the year, the research on heterogeneous XML collections was added to the number of fields where documents as a whole are too big for their users and use cases, e.g. to be indexed for information retrieval or displayed in a browser window, and where algorithms are needed for dividing the documents into fragments. We analysed a selection of existing algorithms that detect fragments inside documents and observed which properties could be applied to heterogeneous XML documents. Based on the analysis, we developed a novel method for dividing the collection into equi-sized fragments.

N. Fuhr et al. (Eds.): INEX 2004, LNCS 3493, pp. 372–381, 2005.

This paper is organised as follows. XML terminology and related vocabulary have had various interpretations in the history of INEX. Section 2 clarifies the terminology that is necessary in order to fully understand the rest of the paper. In Section 3, EXTIRP is briefly described. The problem of documents that are too big to be easily handled is addressed in Section 4, and the challenge of score combination in Section 5. Our runs for 2004 topics are described in Section 6 after which we draw conclusions in Section 7.

2 Common Misconceptions

The purpose of this section is to make our paper accessible to readers who are not familiar with XML terminology. Because of the confusion with vocabulary, the INEX document collection is often misrepresented; see [1, 2]. We will now explain what the collection looks like to XML-oriented people in order to have a common terminological basis with the reader.

XML documents in INEX. An *XML Document* is the biggest logical unit of XML. It can be stored in several XML files which are part of the physical structure of the document. When parsed into DOM[1] trees, each XML document only has one Document Node in the tree. The DOM trees representing the whole INEX collection have 125 Document Nodes because the collection consists of 125 XML documents. Each XML document contains one volume of an IEEE journal. It is misleading to look at the physical structure of the document collection which includes over 12,000 files, as most of the files contain an external entity instead of a whole XML document.

INEX articles. The concept of a *document* has changed because of XML. A document is no longer considered the atomic unit of retrieval. However, XML should have no effect on the concept of an *article*. It is true that there are 12,107 `article` elements in the document collection, but the number of actual articles is smaller. According to the common perception, many article elements do not have article content. Instead, they contain a number of other papers such as errata, lists of reviewers, term indices, or even images without any text paragraphs.

INEX tags. The specification for XML[2] defines three different kind of tags: start tags, end tags, and empty element tags. A DTD does not define any tags, but it does define *element types*. In the XML documents, though, each non-empty element contains two different tags. Counting the different tags in the collection (361) is very different from counting the different element type definitions in the DTD (192), different element types inside the article elements (178), or different element types in the whole collection (183).

Number of content models. The content models of the collection are defined in the DTD. Each element type definition contains the name of the element

[1] http://www.w3.org/DOM/
[2] http://www.w3.org/TR/REC-xml/

followed by its content model. Altogether 192 content models are defined in the DTD, but only 65 of those are different. Of the 65 different content models, only 59 appear in the articles of the collection. For example, the content models of element types `journal` and `books` are not allowed in article content, and elements such as `couple`, `line`, and `stanza` are not included in the collection at all.

DTD-independent methods. One of the goals of the het-track has been the development of DTD-independent methods. However, methods that are independent of the DTD are necessary only when no DTD is available. The problem of documents with several different DTDs or schema definitions is far more common. Methods that are independent of the document type may require the presence of a DTD or a schema definition in order to make the most of it. For example, link relations inside one document are easily resolved with a DTD by reading which attributes are of the ID type and which are of the type IDREF or IDREFS. Moreover, the independence of the DTD does not exclude the dependence on a schema definition. Because the lack of a DTD does not increase the amount of heterogeneity in the collection but different document types do, methods independent of document types suffice for heterogeneous XML collections.

3 System Overview

EXTIRP specialises in full-text search of XML documents and does not support any structural conditions in the queries. Only full-text is indexed, and only full-text is queried. It is thus natural to focus on CO-type topics when evaluating our system.

EXTIRP uses two static indices: an inverted word index and an inverted phrase index. The *key* in the word index is the identifier of a stemmed word and the corresponding *value* contains a list of XML fragment identifiers indicating where in the collection the word occurs. The phrase index contains similar information about those phrases that are considered *Maximal Frequent Sequences* [3].

Before the static indices are built, we divide the document collection into document fragments which results in a collection of disjoint fragments. Each fragment represents the smallest atomic unit of content that can be retrieved. In other words, only the finest level of granularity is indexed. The fragments are not leaf nodes in the document tree but whole sub-trees that contain element and text nodes. How the indexed fragments are selected is described in Section 4 in more detail.

Upon query processing, two normalised similarity scores are computed for each fragment: word similarity and phrase similarity. These two scores are aggregated into a Retrieval Status Value (RSV), according to which the fragments are ranked. At this point, the result list contains a ranked list of relatively small answers for each query. By combining the scores of these fragments, we can replace them with bigger fragments in the list. For example, the score of a section is computed using the scores of each child element, e.g. a paragraph, inside the section. If the section seems more relevant than the paragraphs in the light of RSVs, the paragraph-size fragments are replaced with the particular section-size fragment and ranked accordingly. By combining the scores of adjacent fragments, all the scores are propagated upward in the document hierarchy all the way to the article level. This process has turned out to be remarkably challenging with the fragment collections of 2004.

A more detailed description of the 2003 version of EXTIRP was presented in the INEX Workshop in 2003 [4]. A novelty in EXTIRP 2004 is its independence of any document type. The major changes from 2003 are described in Section 4.2.

4 Division into Fragments

The INEX test collection of IEEE journals is organised into 125 volumes, each of which is represented by the logical unit of storage called an XML document. The character sizes of the volumes vary between 405,832 and 7,385,546 characters, which in most cases is considered too coarse of a granularity in XML retrieval. A finer granularity level has to be reached if smaller units for indexing and retrieval are required.

In recent research, several different purposes have been presented for dividing structured documents into fragments. We will first look into the state of the art and see whether these algorithms could be applied to XML retrieval. Then we will describe how EXTIRP selects the fragments to be indexed.

4.1 Related Work

Ramaswamy et al. presented a fragment detection algorithm motivated by performance issues [5]. Web pages were divided into fragments according to certain criteria, e.g. how many other fragments share its content, whether it is maximal or content of another fragment, and how frequently the content is updated in comparison with other fragments on the web page. A minimum size was also set on the qualifying fragments which were considered cost-effective cache units. This algorithm is not directly applicable to a static collection of XML documents because we cannot measure any lifetime characteristics in an unchanging set of documents. Moreover, the potential fragments in the INEX test collection are unique and not shared among other fragments. Some noteworthy details in their studies include the *minimum size of a detected fragment* which is used to exclude the smallest segments of web pages from being detected as candidate fragments. The values of 30 bytes and 50 bytes seemed reasonable in their experiments. Note also the unit of the minimum size: it is not the number of words, terms, or tokens but simply the bytesize which roughly corresponds to the number of characters in the element content.

In 1999, Jon Kleinberg introduced the HITS algorithm [6] that categorises web pages into *hubs* and *authorities*. A page with a good collection of links has a high hub score whereas a popular page or an authoritative source of information has a high authority score. However, hubs rarely contain links related to a single topic. On the contrary, hubs can cover wide ranges of topics which makes them *mixed hubs.* Chakrabarti developed an algorithm that disaggregates web pages considered mixed hubs into coherent regions by segmenting their DOM trees [7]. He uses the HITS algorithm for topic distillation by computing the hub score for each subtree in the DOM tree instead of computing the hub score for the whole document. The resulting fragments are pure hubs that are highly specific answers to appropriate queries. Topic distillation is a proper but not sufficient criterion for dividing XML documents into fragments. Applying Chakrabarti's hyperlink-based algorithm directly to any of the INEX test collections is inappropriate in the absence of hyperlinks. Nevertheless, the potential for the application of the HITS algorithm lies in the citations and cross-references which can be seen as links between different subtrees representing articles, sections, as well as other document fragments in the collection.

Another need for document segmentation comes from devices that can only display a small amount of information at a time, either because of a small display size or a low resolution. Hoi et al. developed a document segmentation and presentation system (DSPS) that automatically divides a web page into logical segments based on the display size, and document structure and content [8]. The segments have their own branches in a *content tree* into which HTML documents are first converted. The HTML tags are classified into different categories and interpreted accordingly. Applying this algorithm to arbitrary XML documents requires a thorough analysis of the document type. The maximum size of an HTML segment is also rather small. A major difference from the algorithms of Ramaswamy and Chakrabarti is that the resulting HTML segments do not cover all of the original documents: Segments that are very small or very different from the adjacent segments are removed from the content tree. The idea of discarding irrelevant content can be successfully applied to XML retrieval and indexing XML documents, as well.

4.2 Size-Based Division

In 2003, the indexed fragments were selected by the name of the corresponding XML element. After carefully studying the DTD of the collection, we could see which element types represented section-level fragments (sec, ss1, ss2, etc.) and which element types were common at the paragraph-level (p, ip1, etc.). Similar approaches have been common among other participants. For example, the selection of index nodes in the HyREX system is strictly based on element names [9]. Approaches relying on element names do not scale well to fit the needs of heterogeneous document collections. Analysing each DTD is hardly an option as the number of document types increases. Furthermore, it will shortly be shown that better results can be achieved with methods that are independent of the document type.

The EXTIRP algorithm for dividing XML documents into fragments has two parameters: the maximum and minimum size of an indexed fragment. The fragments are selected by traversing the document tree in preorder. If the current node is small enough and qualifies as a full-text fragment, it will added to the fragment collection, after which the following node is tested. The fragments in the fragment collection are disjoint because all the subtrees of qualifying fragments

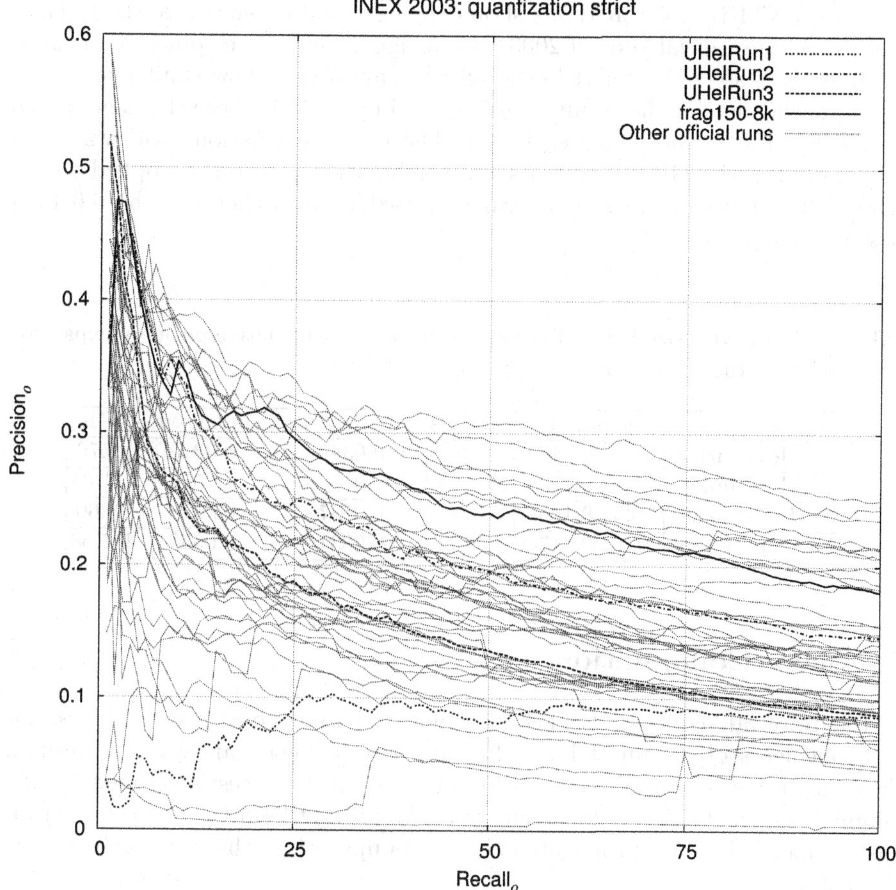

Fig. 1. Precision$_o$ of all the official runs of 2003 at recall levels 1–100. The runs UHelRun1–UHelRun3 are the official submissions of University of Helsinki in 2003, and the thick continuous line represents the current performance level of EXTIRP without score combination or query expansion

are skipped. If the current node does not qualify, its children will be tested until they are either small enough or too small. Consequently, irrelevant fragments, e.g. those that are unlikely answers to any full-text query, are discarded in a similar fashion to that of the DSPS by Hoi et al. removes irrelevant segments [8]. The algorithm on the whole is independent of any document type and also applicable to the INEX test collection.

We compare the precision of four different runs drawn with a solid line in Figure 1. Three of the runs were our official submission in 2003, and the fourth one is based on a fragment collection with the minimum size of a fragment set to 150 characters and maximum to 8,000 characters in text nodes. The other curves represent the official submissions of other participants for the CO topics. Only the first 100 recall answers of each run are considered here. The run that was based on EXTIRP 2004 methods shows the best performance (see the thickest solid line). Our official runs of 2003 have a significantly lower precision at most recall levels. The curves for the generalised quantisation show similar results.

More evidence for the results can be found in Table 1 where the Generalised Recall measure is shown for each run. The online evaluation tool[3] was used for computing the GR score. No score combination method is applied to the disjoint fragments in the run 'Fragments150-8k', which shows in the 0.0 List-Based Overlap (LBO).

Table 1. A run with size-based division and no score combination or query expansion compared with the official runs of University of Helsinki

Run	LBO	strict -o	strict -s	generalised -o	generalised -s	GR
UHel-Run1	39.6	0.0484	0.0358	0.0340	0.0270	9.70
UHel-Run2	28.0	0.1135	0.0866	0.0716	0.0586	11.63
UHel-Run3	10.5	0.1058	0.0787	0.0537	0.0418	8.60
Fragments150-8k	0.0	0.1170	0.0924	0.0831	0.0658	27.68

5 Score Combination

In the retrieval model of EXTIRP, similarity-based scores are computed for XML elements of the finest level of granularity. If bigger answers are desired, the comparable scores need to be computed for all the ancestor elements of the minimal fragments in the document tree. We have utilised the equation (1) for score combination and propagated the scores upward all the way to the article element.

$$score(p) = \frac{\sum score(c)}{size(p)^{UPF}} \tag{1}$$

The adjustable parameter in the equation is the Upward Propagation Factor (UPF), with which we can prioritise answers or a particular size. The score of the parent element p is sum of the scores of its child elements c when the UPF has a value of 0. The obvious shortfall of the value of 0 is that elements with big quantities of content are unjustly favoured. With bigger UPF values, we can even out this effect and focus on the quality of the content instead. The score of the child element is the RSV which was computed earlier. The size of an element can be measured with a variety of metrics. Our implementation defines the size as the bytesize of the fragment. Other possible size units include the number of tokens, number of words, number of characters, etc.

In order to test the score combination method, we created a fragment collection of disjoint fragments with the maximum size set to 20,000 and minimum size to 200 characters. After the RSV was computed for each fragment, the score

[3] http://inex.lip6.fr/2004/metrics/

combination method was applied. The results with different values for the UPF are shown in Table 2. There is no room for questioning the negative effect of our score combination method, because the best average precision was achieved without score combination and it is clearly better than the other scores. Tests with other fragment collections gave similar results.

Table 2. Upward propagation applied to a fragment collection "Fragments200-20k"

UPF	strict -o	strict -s	generalised -o	generalised -s
2.0	0.0058	0.0057	0.0081	0.0079
1.0	0.0270	0.0288	0.0277	0.0305
0.7	0.0536	0.0437	0.0500	0.0446
0.6	0.0584	0.0443	0.0451	0.0379
0.5	0.0565	0.0408	0.0395	0.0318
0.4	0.0546	0.0379	0.0351	0.0275
0.2	0.0509	0.0351	0.0294	0.0219
—	0.0954	0.0728	0.0705	0.0562

The reasons for the deteriorating effect of the score combination possibly include our definition for the size of a fragment. Comparing the bytesizes is simple, but at the same time, we completely ignore the qualities of the element content. Fragments with mathematical equations or charts and tables contain significant amounts of XML markup — element tags and attributes — which do increase the bytesize of a fragment but do not improve the value of the content.

6 Our Runs

The results presented in earlier sections of this paper were not available at the time of run submission. We have, however, learned since then and found reasons for the decline in the precision of the three runs for the CO topics that we submitted. Three different factors have been identified:

Query expansion. Although query expansion turned out to improve the results in 2003, we did not have enough resources to repeat the success.

Score combination. As seen in Section 5, the results deteriorated after the score combination process. Adjusting the UPF did not have a great impact on the results.

Query processing. Only the title of the topic was used for the runs of 2004. In 2003, also the description of the topic was used for similarity computation. This change should not show in the overall results because it concerned all the participants of 2003, but it does show in the absolute precision curves.

We did not submit any runs for the het-track topics. As EXTIRP 2004 specialises in full-text search, it also does not index any data-oriented content. The

XML documents consisting of bibliographic data have no such full-text content that qualifies for the fragment index. It was not found meaningful to submit runs for a CO topic that would be identical with the corresponding runs for the ad-hoc track.

7 Conclusions

The research on EXTIRP 2004 was useful in that we developed methods for heterogeneous collections of XML documents. EXTIRP 2004 does not require any information about the document type, e.g. element names have no importance. A common approach to indexing the INEX test collection, e.g. that of EXTIRP 2003, has involved the definition of a set of elements that are considered *index nodes*. The novelty of EXTIRP 2004 is that the indexed fragments are selected by their size, and the tag name between brackets is disregarded. Size-based division is an appropriate technique in the case of the IEEE article collection, at least, but it is also capable of handling arbitrary XML collections. Whether a decent performance level can be achieved by running EXTIRP on heterogeneous XML will have to be tested in the future as suitable testbeds become available.

Acknowledgements

The author would like to thank Oskarie Heinonen and Roman Yangarber for technical help with Gnuplot and LaTeX, Diana Cousminer for proofreading, and the anonymous reviewers for their valuable comments.

References

1. Fuhr, N., Goevert, N., Kazai, G., Lalmas, M., eds.: INEX: Evaluation Initiative for XML retrieval - INEX 2002 Workshop Proceedings. DELOS Workshop, Schloss Dagstuhl (2003)
2. Fuhr, N., Lalmas, M.: Report on the INEX 2003 Workshop, Schloss Dagstuhl, 15-17 December 2003. SIGIR FORUM **38** (2004) 42–47
3. Ahonen-Myka, H.: Finding All Frequent Maximal Sequences in Text. In: Proceedings of the 16th International Conference on Machine Learning ICML-99 Workshop on Machine Learning in Text Data Analysis, Ljubljana, Slovenia, J. Stefan Institute, eds. D. Mladenic and M. Grobelnik (1999) 11–17
4. Doucet, A., Aunimo, L., Lehtonen, M., Petit, R.: Accurate Retrieval of XML Document Fragments using EXTIRP. In: INEX 2003 Workshop Proceedings, Schloss Dagstuhl, Germany (2003) 73–80
5. Ramaswamy, L., Iyengar, A., Liu, L., Douglis, F.: Automatic detection of fragments in dynamically generated web pages. In: 13th World Wide Web Conference (WWW - 2004). (2004) 443–454
6. Kleinberg, J.M.: Authoritative sources in a hyperlinked environment. Journal of the ACM **46** (1999) 604–632

7. Chakrabarti, S.: Integrating the document object model with hyperlinks for enhanced topic distillation and information extraction. In: Proceedings of the tenth international conference on World Wide Web, ACM Press (2001) 211–220
8. Hoi, K.K., Lee, D.L., Xu, J.: Document visualization on small displays. In: Proceedings of the 4th International Conference on Mobile Data Management (MDM 2003), Berlin, Germany, Springer-Verlag (2003) 262–278
9. Abolhassani, M., Fuhr, N., Malik, S.: HyREX at INEX 2003. In: INEX 2003 Workshop Proceedings. (2003) 49–56

NLPX at INEX 2004

Alan Woodley and Shlomo Geva

Centre for Information Technology Innovation,
Faculty of Information Technology,
Queensland University of Technology,
GPO Box 2434, Brisbane Q 4001, Australia
ap.woodley@student.qut.edu, s.geva@qut.edu.au

Abstract. Users of information retrieval (IR) systems require an interface that is powerful and easy-to-use in order to fulfill their information requirement. In XML-IR systems this is a non-trivial task since users expect these systems to fulfill both their structural and content requirements. Most existing XML-IR systems accept queries formatted in formal query languages, however, these languages are difficult to use. This paper presents NLPX – an XML-IR system with a natural language interface that is user friendly enough so it can be used intuitively, but sophisticated enough to be able to handle complex structured queries. NLPX accepts English queries that contain both users' content and structural requirements. It uses a set of grammar templates to derive the structural and content requirements and translates them into a formal language (NEXI). The formal language queries can then be processed by many existing XML-IR systems. The system was developed for participation in the NLP Track of the INEX 2004 Workshop, and results indicated that natural language interfaces are able to capture users' structural and content requirements, but not as accurately as some formal language interfaces.

1 Introduction

The widespread use of Extensible Markup Language (XML) documents in digital libraries has led to development of information retrieval (IR) methods specifically designed for XML collections. While traditional IR systems are limited to whole document retrieval, XML-IR systems can retrieve very precise and very relevant material, thereby satisfying both the content and structural needs of user. However, XML-IR systems must understand users' content and structural requirements before they can satisfy them. Thus, XML-IR systems require an interface that is powerful enough to thoroughly express users' information need, but user-friendly enough that it can be used intuitively.

Historically, two types of queries have been supported by the INEX Workshop: Content Only (CO) and Content and Structure (CAS), each with their own interface. CO queries only express users' content requirements so their interface consists of a list of keywords. In comparison, CAS queries express both the structural and content requirements of users, and therefore require a more sophisticated interface. To meet

N. Fuhr et al. (Eds.): INEX 2004, LNCS 3493, pp. 382–394, 2005.

this requirement CAS queries have been formatted using complex query languages (XPath [2] in 2003, NEXI [12] in 2004). Unfortunately, in a structured IR system neither interface optimally addresses users' needs. Keyword based systems are too simplistic, since they do not allow users to expresses their structural requirements. Alternatively formal query languages are too difficult to use, and require users to have an intimate knowledge of a documents' structure.

In this paper we present an alternative interface for XML- IR systems, NLPX, that allows users to express their need in natural language. This type of interface is very applicable to the INEX collection since each topic already contains a description element that expresses users' content and structural needs in natural language. While there already exists an extensive body of research into natural language processing in traditional IR, largely thanks to The Text Retrieval Conference (TREC) [11] and the Special Interest Group for Information Retrieval (ACM-SIGIR) [10], work on an XML-IR interface is still largely undocumented and many challenges remain unsolved.

This paper identifies some of these challenges and presents some solutions. We begin by outlining some of the motivating factors behind the development of a natural language interface for XML-IR systems. We then present our own NLPX system, which participated in the INEX 2004 NLP Track, including the methodology used to process Natural Language Queries (NLQs), how we tested the system and finally our results from the INEX 2004 Workshop. We conclude with a short discussion on where our system is headed and how the number of participants in the NLP track can increase.

2 Motivation

This section outlines several motivating factors behind the development of a natural language interface for XML-IR systems. As these factors are specific to when users specify both structural and content requirements they are more closely related to the CAS than CO task. Motivating factors that are more closely related to the CO task, or other keyword based system are already covered in publications of The Text Retrieval Conference (TREC) [11] and the Special Interest Group for Information Retrieval (ACM-SIGIR) [10].

The main motivation is that formal query languages are too difficult for users to accurately express their information need. A very good example of this occurred at the INEX 2003 Workshop: More than two-thirds of the proposed queries had major semantic or syntactic errors [6]. Furthermore, the erroneous queries were difficult to fix, requiring 12 rounds of corrections. Therefore, if experts in the field of structured information retrieval are unable to correctly use complex query languages, one cannot expect an inexperienced user to do so. However, we feel that users would be able to intuitively express their information need in a natural language.

The second motivation is that users require an intimate knowledge of a document's structure in order to properly express their structural requirements. It is likely that most users will understand the conceptual document model of a particular collection. For instance they will know that most journal articles start with elements such as titles and authors, have a body with sections and paragraphs, and finish with a list of references. Therefore, it is likely that users would request elements such as sections and paragraphs from articles. However, they are not able to express these requests in a formal language without knowing the physical document structure. While this information may be obtained from a document's DTD or Schema there are situations where the proprietor of the collection does not wish users to have access to those files. However, in a natural language interface the underlying document structure can be completely hidden from users, who only require a conceptual model of a document when formulating queries. So instead of requesting sec and p tags, users will be able to explicitly request sections or paragraphs. Then the system can map the users semantic request to a specific tag.

The final motivation is that formal queries do not scale well across multiple or heterogeneous collections, even if the collection falls within a single domain. Again we use the domain of journal articles as an example where multiple collections are conceptually equivalent. However, it is unlikely that multiple collections will have exactly the same DTD or Schema. For instance, one collection may use the tag *<p>* to denote paragraphs while another collection may use the tag *<para>*. A similar situation exists in a heterogeneous system where multiple DTDs or Schemas are used in the same collection. However, this problem can be resolved via natural language since as noted in the previous motivation, users will express their information needs conceptually and will have no need to know the physical underlying document structure.

3 NLPX System

Figures 1 and 2 show examples of CO and CAS topics.

```
<inex_topic topic_id="XX"
query_type="CO">
<title>
 "multi layer perception"
 "radial basis functions"
 comparison
</title>
<description>
 The relationship and compari-
  sons between radial basis
  functions and multi layer per-
  ceptions
</description>
</inex_topic>
```

Fig. 1. A CO Topic

```
<inex_topic topic_id="XX"
query_type="CAS">
<title>
 //article[about(.,information
 retrieval)]//sec[about(., com-
 pression)]
</title>
<description>
 Find sections about compress-
 ion in articles about infor
 mation retrieval.
</description>
</inex_topic>
```

Fig. 2. A CAS Topic

Both the description and title elements express the users' information need. The description expresses users' need in a natural language (e.g. English). The title expresses users' information need in either a list of keywords/phrases (CO) or as a formal XPath-like language (CAS) called Narrowed Extended XPath I (NEXI) [12].

We developed our natural language interface to accept the description element from an INEX topic. This was the obvious choice, since the description is defined as a faithful 1:1 natural language translation of the title element (although, as we will explain later in this paper, this is not always the case). We had already developed a system for participation in the Ad-hoc track. Therefore, instead of developing a completely new system for participation in the NLP track, we developed a natural language query to NEXI translator. We did this for three main reasons:

First, by developing a NLQ-to-NEXI translator we were able to use our Ad-hoc system as a backend retrieval engine.

Secondly, since the description element is a 1:1 Translation of the title element, NLP systems are able to use the existing set of Ad-hoc topics and assessments for internal testing. Furthermore, future NLP tracks can be officially evaluated using the same topics and assessments as future Ad-hoc tracks, resulting in very little extra work for future INEX organisers.

Finally, we can output the translated queries and compare them with the original NEXI queries to evaluate the successfulness of the translator.

The syntax of NEXI is similar to XPath, however, it only uses XPath's descendant axis step and extends XPath by incorporating an 'about' clause to provide an IR-like query. NEXI's syntax is //A[about(//B,C)] where A is the context path, B is the relative path and C is the content requirement.

Note that a single query may contain more than one information request. For example, the query in Figure 2 contains two requests, one for sections about compression, and a second one for articles about information retrieval. NEXI handles this scenario by using multiple about clauses. Also note that the user only wishes to retrieve elements matching the fist request, that is, sections about compression rather than entire articles. We refer to these requests and their elements as 'return requests' and 'return elements', which corresponded with NEXI's leaf (that is rightmost) about clause. In contrast, elements matching the second request, that is, articles about information retrieval, are used to support the return elements in ranking. We refer to these requests and their elements as 'support requests' and 'support elements'.

The following subsections describe how a natural language query is first translated to NEXI format and how a NEXI query is then handled by the backend system.

3.1 Natural Language Queries to NEXI Translator

Suppose that the natural language queries (NLQ) in Figure 3 are input into the system.

NLQ 1: The relationship and comparisons between radial basis functions and multi layer perceptions

NLQ 2: Find sections about compression in articles about information retrieval

Fig. 3. CO and CAS Natural Language Query

3.1.1 Lexical and Semantic Tagging

Suppose that the contents of Figure 3 are input into the system as natural language queries (NLQ). Translating the NLQs into NEXI takes several steps. First each word is tagged either as a special connotation or by its part of speech. Special connotations are words of implied semantic significance within the system. The special connotations were developed by inspection of previous INEX queries and are stored in a system dictionary. Our system uses three types of special connotations: structural words that indicate users' structural requirements (e.g. article, section, paragraph, etc.), boundary words that separate the users' structural and content requirements (e.g. about, containing) and instruction words that indicate whether we have a return or support request. All other words are tagged by their part of speech. In theory, any part of speech tagger could perform this task; however, our system uses the Brill Tagger [1]. The Brill Tagger is a trainable rule-based tagger that has a success rate comparable to state of the art stochastic taggers (>95%). The Brill Tagger defines tags as specified by the Penn Treebank [8]. Figure 4 presents some of the tags used in the Penn Treebank and Figure 5 presents the tags that denote a special connotation. Figure 6 shows examples of the NLQs after tagging.

CC	Coordinating Conjunction
DT	Determiner
IN	Preposition / Subordinating Conjunction
JJ	Adjective
NN	Noun, Singular or Mass
NNS	Noun Plural

Fig. 4. Some Penn Treebank Tags

XIN	Instruction Word
XST	Structural Word
XBD	Boundary Word

Fig. 5. Special Connotation Tags

NLQ 1: The/DT relationship/NN and/CC comparisons/NNS between/IN radial/JJ basis/NN functions/NNS and/CC multi/NNS layer/NN perceptions/NNS

NLQ 2: Find/XIN sections/XST about/XBD compression/NN in/IN articles/XST about/XBD information/NN retrieval/NN

Fig. 6. Tagged CO and CAS Natural Language Queries

3.1.2 Template Matching

The second step of the translator is to derive information requests from tagged NLQs. This is performed by matching the tagged NLQs to a predefined set of grammar templates. The grammar templates were developed by inspection of previous years' INEX queries. Initially it may seem that a large number of templates would be required to fully capture the semantics of natural language. However, NLQs share the same narrow context, that is, information requests, thus, comprehending NLQs is a subset of classical natural language understanding. Therefore, a system that interprets natural language queries requires fewer rules than a system that attempts to understand natural language in its entirety. This theory was verified by the inspection of previous INEX queries and recognising that the format of most queries corresponded to a small set of patterns. By extracting these patterns we were able to formulate a small set of grammar templates that match the majority of queries. Figure 7 shows an example of some of the grammar templates.

Query: Request+
Request : CO_Request | CAS_Request
CO_Request: NounPhrase+
CAS_Request: SupportRequest | ReturnRequest
SupportRequest: Structure [Bound] NounPhrase+
ReturnRequest: Instruction Structure [Bound] NounPhrase+

Fig. 7. Grammar Templates

Conceptually, each grammar template corresponds to an individual information request. Once the semantically tagged text was matched to a grammar template, we derived information requests from the query. Each information request contains three separate attributes. **Content**: A list of terms or phrases that express the content requirements of the user. This is derived from the noun phrases from the matched grammar template. **Structure**: A logical XPath expression that describes the structural constraints of the request. This value is derived via a function that maps structural words (e.g. section) to the XML tags (e.g. /article/sec) as specified in the document's DTD. **Instruction**: "R" if we have a return request or "S" if we have a support request. Figure 8 shows examples of the derived information requests.

NLQ 1:
Structure: /*
Content: relationship, comparisons, radial basis functions, multi layer perceptions
Instruction: R
NLQ 2:

	Request 1	**Request 2**
Structural:	/article/sec	/article
Content:	compression	information retrieval
Instruction:	R	S

Fig. 8. Derived Information Requests

3.1.3 NEXI Query Production

The final step in the translator is to merge the information request into a single NEXI query. However, if a NLQ has multiple information requests, then those requests are merged into a single request and output. Return requests are formatted in the form A[about(.,C)] where A is the request's structural attribute and C is the request's content attribute. Support requests are then added to the output in two stages. First the system must locate the correct position within the output to place the support request. This will be the largest shared ancestor between the support and return requests. For example if the internal representation is X/Y/Z[about(,.C)] and the support request has a structural attribute of X/Y/A, then the structural request should be placed in position Y. Using a string matching function, a comparison is made between the internal representation and the support request structural attribute to determine the correct position of the support request. Then the request is added to the internal representation in the form A[about(B,C)] where A is the longest matching string, B is the remainder of the support request's structural attribute and C is the support request's content attribute. Figure 9 shows how the NEXI queries would appear after the information requests for each NLQ have been merged.

NLQ 1:
//*[about(.,relationship, comparisons, radial basis functions, multi layer perceptions)]
NLQ 2:
//article[about(.,information retrieval)]//sec[about(.,compression)]

Fig. 9. NLQ-to-NEXI Queries

After the NLQs have been translated into NEXI they can be input in existing INEX systems. The following section describes how the NEXI query was processed, after being input into our existing XML-IR system.

3.2 GP-XOR Backend

3.2.1 NEXI Interface

Once NEXI queries are input into the system they are converted into an intermediate language called the RS query language. The RS query language converts NEXI queries to a set of information requests. The format of RS queries is

Request: Instruction '|' Retrieve_Filter '|' Search_Filter '|' Content.

The Instruction and Content attributes are the same as they were in the previous section; however, the Structural attribute has been divided into a **Retrieve** and **Search** Filter. While both are logical XPath expressions the Retrieve Filter describes which elements should be retrieved by the system, whereas the Search Filter describes which elements should be searched by the system. These filters correspond to an information request's context and relative path. So for the NEXI query //A[about(//B,C)], the retrieve filter or context path is //A, while its search filter or relative path is //A//B. Figure 10 presents an example of the queries introduced earlier converted to RS queries.

RS Query 1:
R|//*|//*| relationship, comparisons, radial basis functions, multi layer perceptions
RS Query 2:
R|//article//sec|//article//sec|compression
S|//article|//article| information retrieval

Fig. 10. Example of an RS Query

3.2.2 System Structure and Ranking Scheme

We index the XML collection using an inverted list. Given a query term we can derive the filename, physical XPath and the ordinal position within the XPath that it occurred in. From there we construct a partial XML tree containing every relevant leaf element for each document that contains a query term. Further information on our structure can be found in [4].

Elements are ranked according to their relevance. Data in an XML tree is mostly stored in leaf elements. So first we calculate the score of relevant leaf elements, then we propagate their scores to their ancestor branch elements.

The relevance score of leaf elements is computed from term frequencies within the leaf elements normalised by their global collection frequency. The scoring scheme rewards elements with more query terms. However, it penalises elements with terms that occur frequently in the collection, and rewards elements that contain more distinct terms. This is because terms that occur frequently in a collection are less likely to be significant than terms that only occur a few times in a collection.

The relevance score of a non-leaf is the sum of the children scores. However, leaf element scores are moderated by a slight decay factor as they propagate up the tree. Branch elements with multiple relevant children are likely to be ranked higher than their descendents – as they are more comprehensive – while branch elements with a single relevant child will be ranked lower than the child element as they are less specific. Further information on our ranking scheme can be found in [5].

4 Testing

4.1 Testing Methodology

Our initial experiments were conducted using the INEX 2003 set of topics and evaluation metrics. Our NLP system accepted the topics' description tag, translated it into NEXI and processed it using our backend GPX engine. GPX produced an INEX submission file that was input into the official INEX evaluation program (inex_eval) to calculate the recall/precision graphs, just as if it was an Ad-hoc submission. As specified by the INEX guidelines [3] the precision value was calculated over two dimensions: exhaustiveness, which measures the extent to which a component discusses the information request; and specificity, which measures the extent to which a component is focused on the information request.

Initially, we executed two runs for both the CO and CAS topic sets. The first run accepted NEXI queries, that is the topic's title tag, as input, whereas the second run accepted natural language queries, that is the topic's description tag, as input. These runs corresponded with INEX's Ad-hoc and NLP tracks and allowed us to compare how well our system performed with and without our NLP-to-NEXI frontend. It was hoped that the results of these two runs would be fairly similar, however, we identified one major obstacle that hindered our progress; the fact that the title and description were not always equivalent.

4.2 Testing Obstacles

INEX guidelines specifically state that the description tag should be as close as possible to a 1:1 natural language translation of the title [3]. However, during testing it became clear that many of the descriptions are not faithful 1:1 title translations. Therefore, it would be very difficult for a system with a NEXI interface to produce similar results as a system with a NLQ, even if they used the same backend. From our observations we have identified that many of the INEX topics had inconsistencies between the title and description elements, that is, the title and description had different content or structural requirements. Examples of these inconstancies are topic 76, 81, 93 and 104. Given these inconsistencies, it is unlikely that an NLP system and Ad-hoc system would produce the same results. To overcome these obstacles we modified the description elements so that they were a faithful 1:1 translation of the title elements. It must be stressed that in this modification we were very careful not to generate descriptions that favour our natural language processing algorithms. Modifications mostly ensured that the same keywords and structural tag names appeared in both the NEXI formatted topic and the natural language description. Figures 11–14 are examples of some of the topics with the modified descriptions.

Topic: `//article[(./fm//yr = '2000' OR ./fm//yr = '1999') AND about(., 'intelligent transportation system')] //sec[about(.,'automation +vehicle')]`
Original Description: Automated vehicle applications in articles from 1999 or 2000 about intelligent transportation systems.
Modified Description: Retrieve sections about automation vehicle in articles from 1999 or 2000 about intelligent transportation systems.

Fig. 11. Modified Topic 76

Topic: `//article[about(.//p, 'multi concurrency control') AND about(.//p, 'algorithm') AND about(./fm//atl, 'databases')]`
Original Description: We are interested in articles that can provide information or reference to information on algorithms for multiversion concurrency control in databases.
Modified Description: We are interested in articles with a paragraph about multi concurrency control or a paragraph about algorithm and a frontmatter title about databases

Fig. 12. Modified Topic 81

Topic: `"Charles Babbage" -institute -inst.`
Original Description: The life and work of Charles Babbage.
Modified Description: Charles Babbage not institute nor inst

Fig. 13. Modified Topic 93

Topic: `Toy Story`
Original Description: Find information on the making of the animated movie Toy Story, discussing the used techniques, software, or hardware platforms.
Modified Description: Find information on Toy Story

Fig. 14. Modified Topic 104

4.3 Testing Results

Overall we tested our system using three runs for both the CO and CAS topics sets: one with NEXI queries, one with the original NLQ description elements and one with the altered NLQ description elements. The plots for these three runs are displayed in Figures 15-18. A fourth plot is the recall/precision line of the University of Amsterdam's systems that achieved the best results at INEX 2003 in the CO and SCAS tracks [9]. This allowed us to compare the quality of our system with the best official INEX alternative. Two metrics were used to formulate the recall-precision values, the strict metric that evaluates highly relevant and highly precise results, and the generalized metric that evaluates results based on a graded measure (or degree) of relevancy and/or precision. Further details on the metrics are available in [3].

The plots for each task and quantisation are listed in Figures 15-18. The solid line is the Amsterdam submission, the dotted line is the Ad-hoc submission, the dashed line is the NLP submission and the dash-dotted line is the altered-NLP submission.

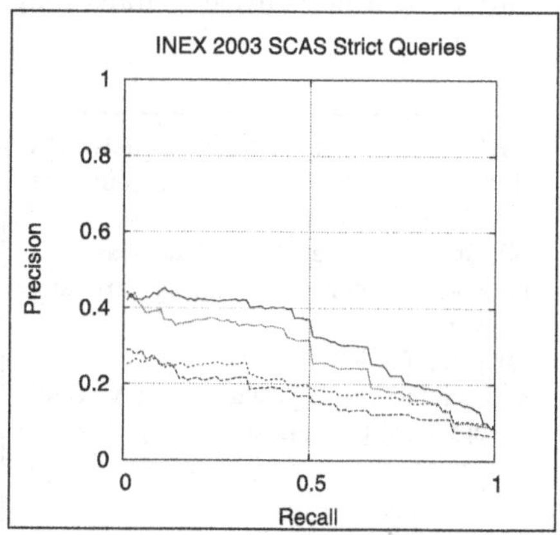

Fig. 15. INEX 2003 SCAS Strict R/P Curve

Fig. 16. INEX 2003 SCAS Generalized R/P Curve

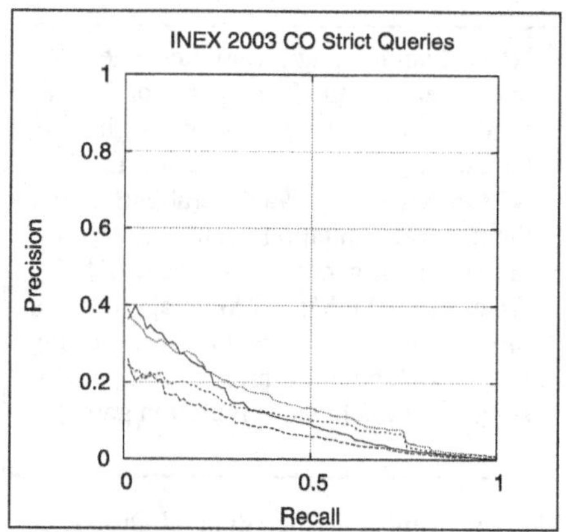

Fig. 17. INEX 2003 CO strict R/P Curve

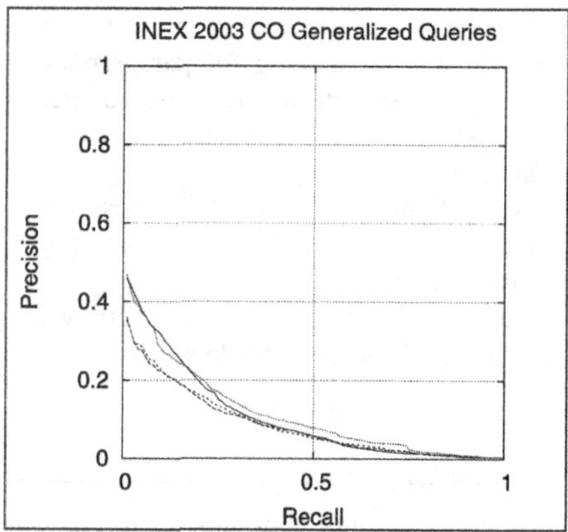

Fig. 18. INEX 2003 CO generalized R/P Curve

5 INEX 2004

5.1 INEX 2004 Examples

Here we present some examples of how well our system was able to translate NLQs into NEXI. Since none of the INEX 2004 topics were used to 'train' the system, this section is a valid example of how well the system is able to translate unseen queries. For each topic we present the original NLQ (description), the original NEXI query (title) and the translated NLQ to NEXI query. Figures 19 and 20 are example of topics that the system was able to translate successfully (topic 130 and 159). In contrast Figure 21 and 22 are examples of topics that the system had difficulty translating (topics 145 and 158).

NLQ: We are searching paragraphs dealing with version management in articles containing a paragraph about object databases.
NLQtoNEXI:
//article[about(//sec//p,object databases) //bdy//sec//p [about(.,version management)]
Original NEXI: //article[about(.//p,object database)] //p[about(.,version management)]

Fig. 19. Topic 130 Including NLQtoNEXI

NLQ: Articles about bayesian networks find sections that are about learning the structure of the network
NLQtoNEXI: //articles[about(.,bayesian networks]//sec[about(.,learning structure network)]
Original NEXI:
//article[about(.,bayesian networks)] //sec[about(.,learning structure)]

Fig. 20. Topic 159 Including NLQtoNEXI

NLQ: We are looking for paragraphs in articles about information retrieval dealing with relevance feedback.
NLQtoNEXI:
//article//bdy//sec//p[about(.,information, retrieval, relevance, feedback)]
Original NEXI:
//article[about(.,information retrieval)] //p[about(., relevance feedback)]

Fig. 21. Topic 145 Including NLQtoNEXI

NLQ: I am looking for articles where the main theme is the Turing test or "imitation game" where machines imitate human intelligence and consciousness.
NLQtoNEXI: //article[about(.,main, theme, test, imitation, game, machines, human, intelligence, consciousness)]
Original NEXI: article[about(.//fm, turing test) or about(.//abs, turing test)]//bdy[about(.,turning test consciousness intelligence imitation game)]

Fig. 22. Topic 158 Including NLQtoNEXI

5.2 INEX 2004 Results

In the Ad-hoc track our system was ranked 1st from 52 submitted runs in the VCAS task and 6th from 70 submitted runs in the CO task. In the NLP track the system was ranked 1st in the VCAS task and 2nd in the CO task. While the NLP track was limited to 9 participants initially of which only 4 made official submissions, the most encouraging outcome was that our NLP system outperformed several Ad-Hoc systems. In fact, if the NLP submission was entered in the Ad-hoc track it would have ranked 12th from 52 in VCAS and 13th from 70 in CO. This seems to suggest that in structured IR, natural language queries have the potential to be a viable alternative, albeit not as precise as a formal query language such as NEXI.

The Recall/Precision Curves for the Ad-hoc track, along with the R/P curve for our NLP runs are presented in Figures 23 and 24. The top bold curve is the Ad-hoc curve, the lower is the NLP curve, and the background curves are of all the official Ad-hoc runs at INEX 2004.

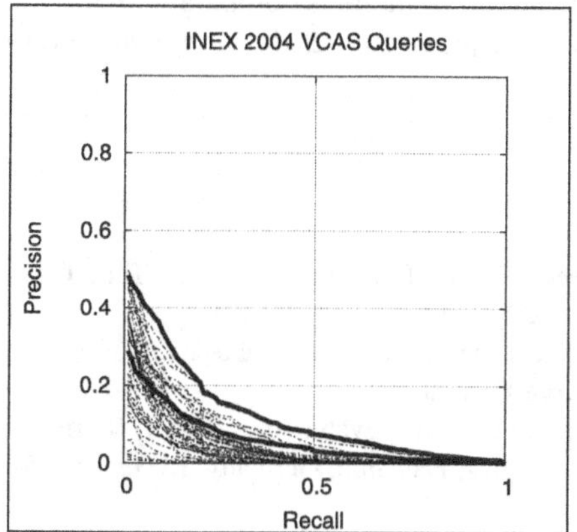

Fig. 23. INEX 2004 VCAS R/P Curve

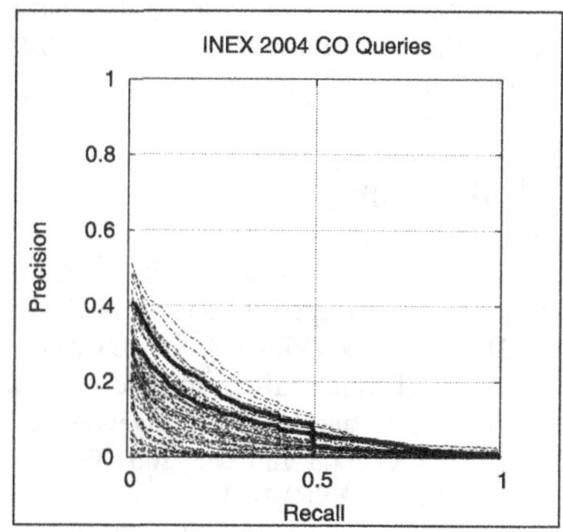

Fig. 24. 2004 INEX CO R/P Curve.

6 Future Outlook

The most promising aspect of our participation in this year's NLP track was that our system was able to outperform the majority of Ad-hoc systems, thereby verifying that natural language queries have the potential to be a viable alternative to complex formal query languages such as NEXI. However, there is still progress to be made, and we shall strive to improve the performance of our NLP system.

The most disappointing aspect of this year's track was the lack of submissions. INEX should encourage more participation in the NLP track in order to broaden the knowledge in the domain of natural language interfaces to XML IR and to strengthen INEX as a whole. Future participants will most likely come from two areas. The first will be existing INEX participants in the Ad-hoc and other tracks who will develop a natural language interface to their existing system, similar to the approach we took. The second will be from participants in workshops such as TREC [11] and SIGIR [10], which are traditionally strong in the domain of natural language IR systems. Both types of competitors are likely to bring different perspectives on the problem and their participation should be welcomed.

Also the INEX organisers should strive to ensure that the title and description elements are faithful 1:1 translations, both in terms of structural and content requirements.

7 Conclusion

This paper presents a natural language interface to XML-IR system. The interface uses template matching to derive users' content and structural requests from natural language queries (NLQs). The interface then translates the NLQs into an existing standard formal query language, allowing them to be processed by many existing systems. Our backend system responds to user queries with relevant and appropriately sized results in a timely manner and our ranking scheme is comparable with the INEX best alternatives. While the NLP interface requires further development, initial results are promising.

Bibliography

[1] Brill, E.: A Simple Rule-Based Part of Speech Tagger. In Proceedings of the Third Conference on Applied Computational Linguistics (ACL), Trento, Italy. (1992)
[2] Clark, J. and DeRose, S.: "XML Path Language XPath version 1.0.", Technical report, W3C (1999) W3C Recommendation available at http://www.w3.org/TR/xpath.
[3] Fuhr, N. and Malik, S.: Overview of the Initiative for the Evaluation of XML Retrieval (INEX) 2003. In INEX 2003 Workshop Proceedings, Dagstuhl, Germany, December 15-17 2003 (2004) 1-11
[4] Geva, S. and Spork, M.: XPath Inverted File for Information Retrieval, In INEX 2003 Workshop Proceedings, Dagstuhl, Germany, December 15-17 2003 (2004) 110-117
[5] Geva, S.: GPX at INEX 2004. In INEX 2004 Workshop Proceedings, Dagstuhl, Germany, December 6-8 2004 (2005)
[6] O'Keefe, R. and Trotman, A.: "The Simplest Query Language That Could Possibly Work", In INEX 2003 Workshop Proceedings, Dagstuhl, Germany, December 15-17 2003 (2004) 167-174
[7] Manning, C. D. and Schutze, D. "Foundations of Statistical Natural Language Processing", MIT Press, Cambridge (1999)
[8] Marcus, M., Santorini, N. and Marcinkiewicz, M. Building a large annotated corpus of English: The Penn Treebank, In. Computational Linguistics (1993)
[9] Sigurbjornsson, B., Kamps, J. de Rijke, M. An Element-based Approach to XML Retrieval, In INEX 2003 Workshop Proceedings, Schloss Dagstuhl, Germany, December 15-17 2003 (2004) 19-26
[10] Special Interest Group on Information Retrieval (SIGIR) Homepage, http://www.acm.org/sigir/.
[11] Text REtreival Conference (TREC) Homepage, http://trec.nist.gov/.
[12] Trotman, A. and Sigurbjörnsson, B. Narrowed Extended XPath I (NEXI). In INEX 2004 Workshop Proceedings, Dagstuhl, Germany, Decemeber 8 -10 2004 (2005)
[13] Van Rijsbergen, R. J. Information Retrieval, Butterworths, Second Edition (1979)

Analysing Natural Language Queries at INEX 2004

Xavier Tannier, Jean-Jacques Girardot, and Mihaela Mathieu

École Nationale Supérieure des Mines de Saint-Etienne,
158 Cours Fauriel,
F-42023 Saint-Etienne, France
{tannier, girardot, mathieu}@emse.fr

Abstract. This article presents the contribution of the "École Nationale Supérieure des Mines de Saint-Etienne (France)" to the new Natural Language Processing special Track of the third Initiative for Evaluation of XML Retrieval (INEX 2004). It discusses the place of NLP in XML retrieval and presents a method to analyse natural language queries.

1 Introduction

If XML (eXtended Markup Language) becomes – as expected – a universally accepted standard for exchange and storage of information, it will soon turn into a necessity to query these structured documents in natural language rather than in a structured query language.

The aim of the new INEX NLPX Track (Natural Language Processing for XML Information Retrieval) is to promote "interaction among researchers in the field of Natural Language Processing (NLP) and XML Information Retrieval". Our participation to this track lies within this scope: the purpose is to add our contribution to the general reflection about the applications of NLP methods to XML retrieval.

Our objective at INEX 2004 is clearly not (yet) the demonstration of retrieval effectiveness of a system, but the implementation of a technique for analysing a natural language query.

This article considers the benefits that can be gained from using some natural language processing methods on one hand, and the specificities of structured documents on the other hand, in order to retrieve information from an XML corpus. It also presents and discusses our method that relies on structure of documents to "understand" the semantics of the request.

2 How Can NLP Help?

Applications of Natural Language Processing for Information Retrieval have been extensively studied in the case of textual (flat) collections (for overviews on this subject, see [1, 2, 3, 4, 5]). Linguistic analyses of the corpus and/or the query should carry out some decisive improvements in retrieval process. Nevertheless,

N. Fuhr et al. (Eds.): INEX 2004, LNCS 3493, pp. 395–409, 2005.

only a few linguistic methods, as phrasal term extraction or some kinds of query expansion, are now commonly used in information retrieval systems. At present, actual results are not yet up to what we could expect [6, 5].

However we think that the spread of structured corpora can bring new hopes to NLP supporters, at least for the two following reasons:

- Benefits that can be gained from allowing requests in natural language are probably much higher in XML retrieval than in traditional IR. In the last case, a query is generally a keyword list which is quite easy to write. In XML retrieval, such a list is not enough to make queries on both content and structure; for this reason, advanced structured query languages have been devised.
  But one wants XML to be really widely used, and that implies that novice and casual users should be able to make requests on any XML corpus. In this perspective, two major difficulties arise, because we cannot expect such users to:
  - learn a complex structured and formal query language[1];
  - have a full knowledge of the DTD and its semantics.

  Note that these issues already exist in the domain of databases with the Structured Query Language (SQL); but unlike databases, XML format looks set to become used by the general public, notably through the Internet. Although unambiguously machine-readable, structured and formal query languages are necessary (in order to actually extract the answers), the need for simpler interfaces will become more and more important in the future.
- In order to perform a really effective natural language-based retrieval in a flat document, a system should "understand" the semantics of the text, and this is not feasible yet. In the case of structured documents, a well-thought and semantically strong structure formally marks up the meaning of the text; this can make easier query "understanding", at least when this query refers (partly) to the structure (VCAS task in INEX).
  However, this requires a certain amount of knowledge about the corpus, that has to be integrated into a system besides documents themselves, in order to perform a good retrieval process. We discuss this subject in Sect.6.3.

3 Description of Our Approach

Our aim is to translate the `<description>` part of INEX topics, written in natural English, into a query in a formal structured language. Topics are divided into two categories:

- *Content-and-Structure* queries, which contains structural constraints.
  e.g.: Find paragraphs *or* figure-captions *containing the definition of Godel, Lukasiewicz or other fuzzy-logic implications.* (Query 127)

[1] In this paper we call "*formal query language*" a language with formalized semantics and grammar, as opposed to natural language.

- *Content-only* queries that ignore the document structure.
  e.g.: Any type of coding algorithm for text and index compression. (Query 162)

To achieve the analysis of such requests, the steps that we perform are:

- a part-of-speech tagging of the query (3.1);
- a syntactic/semantic analysis of the query (3.2);
- with the help of specific rules (3.3):
  - a recognition of some typical constructions of a query (*e.g.: Retrieve + object*) or of the corpus (*e.g.: "an article written by [...]"* refers to the tag *au – author*);
  - and a distinction between semantic elements mapping on the structure and, respectively, mapping on the content;
- a treatment of relations existing between different elements (3.4);
- the construction of a formal language query (3.5).

3.1 Part-of-Speech Tagging

A part-of-speech (POS), or word class, is the role played by a word in the sentence (*e.g.:* noun, verb, adjective...). POS tagging is the process of marking up words in a text with their corresponding roles. To carry out this task we chose the tool TreeTagger [7]. Example 1 represents a query and its POS tagging[2] (*Find* is an imperative verb, *of* and *with* are prepositions and *that* is a relative pronoun).

(1)	*Find*	*the*	*title*	*of*	*articles*	*that*	*deal*	*with*	*semantics.*
	V(I)	DET	NOUN	PREP	NOUN(P)	REL_PRO	V	PREP	NOUN

3.2 Syntactic/Semantic Analysis

This analysis is performed with a set of context-free rules describing the most current grammatical constructions in queries and questions. As an example, we listed in Fig.1 the rules that are triggered when parsing our sample query 1.

NP → DET? NOUN	*REL_PROP → REL_PRO VP*
NP → NP PREP NP	*VP → V PREP? NP*
NP → NP REL_PROP	*S → V(IMP) NP*

Fig. 1. Examples of rules, with S = Sentence, NP = Noun Phrase, REL_PROP = relative proposition, VP = Verbal Phrase. Question mark "?" means that the element is optional in the sequence

A recursive application of these CFG rules results in the *syntactic tree* represented in Fig.2[3].

---

[2] For a clearer comprehension by a non-expert reader, we changed the names of the tags into less complete but more explicit abbreviations.

[3] Note that with this set of rules two different parsings are possible: the relative proposition can be attached to the noun *"article"* (as shown in the figure) or to the noun *"title"*. In practice both trees are explored.

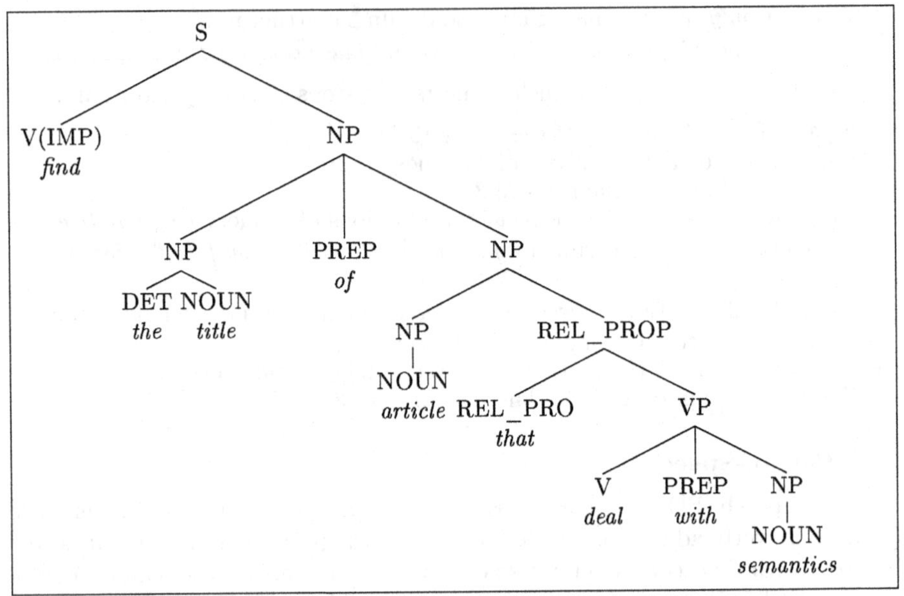

Fig. 2. Syntactic tree of sentence 1, obtained with rules of Fig.1

This operation gives us a syntactic structure, but we need some semantics to have an idea about the relations existing between words. In that aim, we use a very simple implementation of Discourse Representation Theory (DRT) [8] semantic representation of a discourse (or a part of discourse) is described with a two-level "box" called "Discourse Representation Structure" (DRS). The upper level gives the discourse referents, which are the elements introduced by the discourse; the lower level represents the conditions concerning the referents.

A typical example of DRS is given in Fig.3. In this example, the terms *"Napoléon"*, *"Austerlitz"*, *"battle"* and the verb *"to win"* (event e) are discourse referents. Referents are represented by letters in the upper level and described by logical predicates in the lower level. The other conditions are about the agent and the object of the event (respectively *"Napoléon"* and *"battle"* for the event *"to win"*) and the location of the battle.

To compute a DRS representing a whole sentence, we attribute a basic DRS to each word, depending on its class (POS). Syntactic rules are then enriched with semantic actions. Figure 4 shows how the following rule:

$VP \rightarrow VERB\ \ PREP?\ NP$,

applies to basic DRSs. Moreover, two semantic actions are associated with this rule: $e_1 = e_2$ and $x = y$.

Due to a lack of space we cannot show the full semantic tree obtained for the example. Figure 5 gives the final DRS.

N.B.: The set of syntactic/semantic rules that we use is made up of about 50 rules. It is obviously not intended to describe the whole language. The stress

$e\ x\ y\ z$
Napoléon(x)
battle(y)
Austerlitz(z)
event(e, win)
agent(e, x)
object(e, y)
location(y, z)

Fig. 3. DRT representation of sentence: *"Napoleon wins a battle in Austerlitz"*

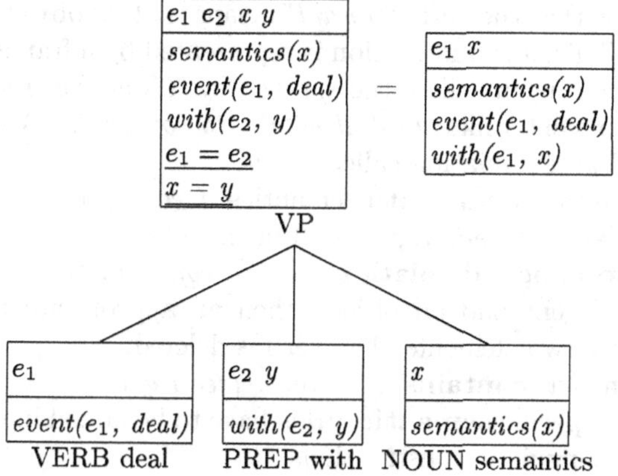

Fig. 4. Example of DRS for the verbal phrase "*deal with semantics*"

$x\ y\ z\ s\ e_1\ e_2$
event$(e_1$, *find*$)$
event$(e_2$, *deal*$)$
title(x)
article(y)
semantics(z)
object(e_1, x)
of(x, y)
agent(e_2, y)
with(e_2, z)

Fig. 5. DRS for sentence 1

has been put on noun phrases, which are often much more meaningful than verbal phrases (at least in terms of Information Retrieval). Relative propositions, prepositional phrases are also very important because they mark a query structure that we do not want to miss. For complex demands, an entire parsing is often impossible. In that case only NPs are analyzed and verbs are left out.

The DRS that we obtain at this stage cannot be used to build a formal query yet. Some IR-specific rules have to be set up.

3.3 Specific Rules

The DRS can be reduced by considering some special cases, among which:

1. **"Query verbs"** like *"to want"*, *"to find"*... With the help of a dictionary describing semantic relations between those verbs and queries, we set a particular flag on the concerned element. This flag means that the element should be selected as a good answer to the query, as shown in example 2.
   (2) I **want** an article. *(see Fig.6.a)*
   Here we know that the verb *"to want"* means that its object (*"article"*) has to be selected. This new information is represented by a framed referent. These verbs and their agents (here the *speaker*, or *"I"*) are then left out.
2. **Description verbs** like *"to deal with"*, *"to concern"*... An other dictionary helps to add a new relation called *about*:
   (3) an article that **deals with** semantics. *(see Fig.6.b)*
   The verb referent is removed as well in this case.
3. **Verbs of topological relation** like *"to contain"*, *"to include"*... If such a verb has an agent and an object, then an appropriate relation is set up between those two elements. The verb is deleted:
   (4) a section that **contains** a figure... *(see Fig.6.c)*
4. Some corpus-specific **semantic rules** have to be added in order to recognize some precise linguistic constructions.
   (5) a document written by Jiawei Han.
   Here an *ad-hoc* rule imposes the transformation given in Fig.6.d[4].
5. **Words or phrases in quotation marks** are considered as non-separable expressions and are grouped together in a single variable.

   (6) We are looking for sections in articles, whose abstracts contain "spatial join," that describe "performance evaluation." *(Topic 156)*
6. And above all, **a term recognized as a DTD-tag (or synonym)** is changed into this tag name and is marked as such (here by a bold predicate in the DRS, with *atl* standing for *"title"*).

   (7) the **title** of an **article**...

$x\ y$		$\boldsymbol{x\ y}$
title(x) *article*(y) *of*(x, y)	⇒	***atl***(x) ***article***(y) *of*(x, y)

   A dictionary of synonyms is used. This dictionary is absolutely not intended to have a general purpose. Indeed DTD tag names are rarely real words, but abbreviations instead (*st* for *section title*, *p* for *paragraph* etc.).

[4] *N.B.:* This kind of rules no longer represents *linguistic* features, but IR-specific rules. The two *contains* predicates in this example do not have a real linguistic meaning, but express a structural constraint in the XML document.

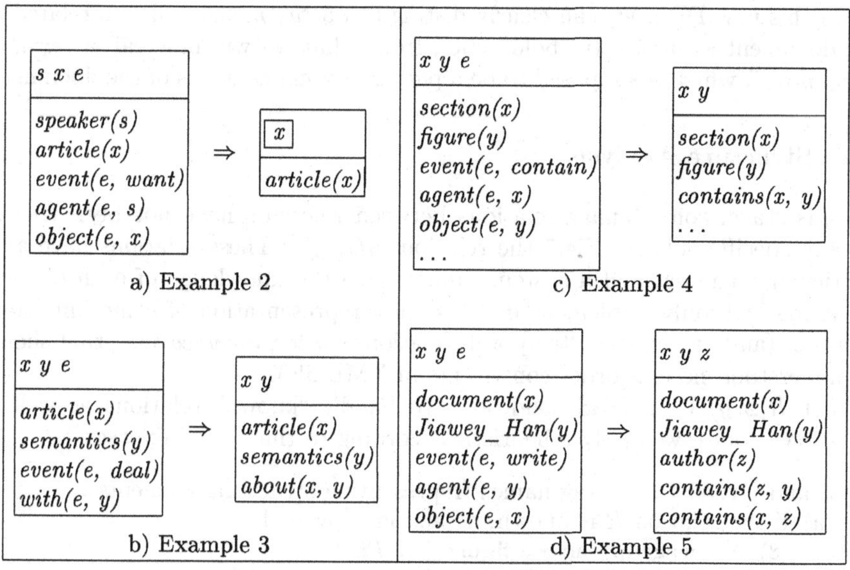

Fig. 6. Semantic representation of examples 2, 3, 4 and 5

Figure 7 shows the application of some of these specific rules on our sample DRS. Let us remind the initial request:

(1) *Find the title of articles that deal with semantics.*

We suppose that our dictionary tells us that the words *"title"* and *"article"* respectively stand for tag names *atl* and *article*.

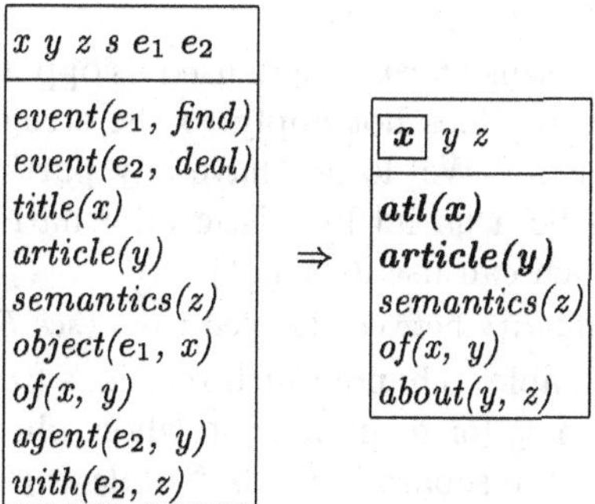

Fig. 7. DRS for sentence 1 before and after application of specific rules. Referent x is selected (rule 1), Article y is *about "semantics"* (rule 2) and terms *"article"* and *"title"* are recognized as tag identifiers *atl* and *article* (rule 6)

In this new DRS, we can clearly distinguish a *tag name*, which is related to the document structure (in bold type), from what we will now call a *term*, as *"semantics"*, which is supposed to be a part of textual contents of the document.

3.4 Structure Analysis

At this stage, some binary relations between referents have not been treated by any specific rule (in Fig.7 the relation *of(x, y)*). These relations have all a particular meaning, and a system cannot have the knowledge of each of these meanings. We only implemented a semantic representation of some important relations (and particularly "temporal" relations – *after*, *included*, etc., that should be understood here as order constraints in XML file).

Let $R(x, y)$ be a DRS condition. To handle "known" relations as well as "unknown" ones, we apply a heuristic according to the following cases:

1. x and y refer to two tag names (representing structural elements):
   (a) if the relation R is known, no action is needed.
   (8) A **paragraph** after a **figure** (*see Fig.8.a*).
   (b) if the relation R is unknown, the fact that a relation exists is in itself an information: the structure given by the DTD allows to guess which relation(s) it can be. In our example, the DTD will tell us that an element *atl* (title x) is *contained by* an element *article* (y).
   (9) A **title** of **article** (*see Fig.8.b*).
2. The relation links a tag (let us say x) and a term (y):
   (a) if R is known, we add a tag that can match with any name (called '*').
   This tag is *about* y, and the relation is transfered to this new tag:
   (10) A **paragraph** before the *conclusion*[5] (*see Fig.8.c*).
   The paragraph should be written in the XML file before a tag that contains the word *"conclusion"*.
   (b) if R is unknown, we keep it without change (see comments for rule 3).

3. R holds between two terms (*term* is here used as opposed to *DTD tag name*): in that case the relation does not apply to the structure, because x and y refer to content elements. We do not have any particular treatment to do, but the relation can be a useful linguistic information. We keep it for the retrieval process (which can use it or not).
   (11) The structural similarity between labeled trees (*see Fig.8.d*).
   If the search engine is able to handle such relations (*adjectives* and *between*), it is useful to know that, for example, the whole phrase *"similarity between trees"* is preferable to the separate words *"similarity"* and *"trees"*.

Among these rules, only rule 1b applies in our running example, and the final DRS is shown in Fig.9.

[5] We suppose in this example that the word *"conclusion"* cannot be assimilated to a tag name, as it is the case in IEEE collection.

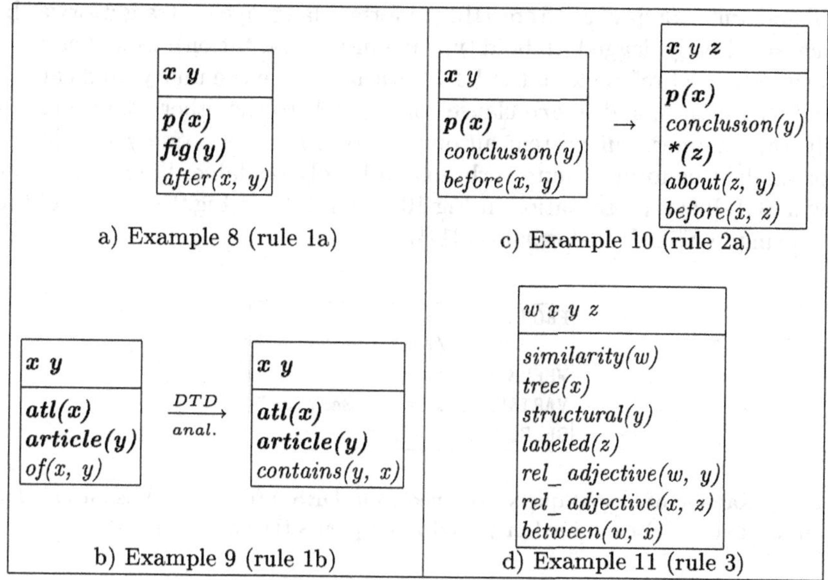

Fig. 8. Application of different structural rules

3.5 Formal Language Query

At the end of the linguistic phase, our aim is to obtain a formal language query that could easily be translated into an existing structured language. From those languages (and initially from SQL) we take the idea of clause pattern (SELECT-FROM-WHERE in SQL) for restructuring the request. We chose the following four-clause pattern (expressed in an XML syntax):

- `from` clause: tag names and indications on paths (XPath [9] expressions);
- `select` clause: elements to be returned to the user; those elements must be refered in the `from` clause[6];
- `where` clause: relations between tags or variables (before(x,y), about(a,b)...);
- `variables`: identifiers replacing terms in the other clauses.

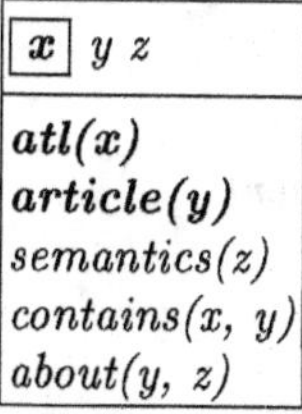

Fig. 9. final DRS for sentence 1

6 `select` clause only contains element names, we do not provide (as in XQuery-like [10] query languages) any possibility of formatting the output. Besides this is neither the purpose of INEX nor of IR in general.

Transformation process from DRS to formal language is straightforward: tag names are already flagged (in bold type in our representation), as well as selected elements (framed referents in the DRS). Variables are the unary predicates that are not tag names, and `where` clause corresponds to the other conditions.

In this manner, our system automatically generates a query in XML. Not surprisingly, this form is quite verbose and hardly readable. We rather chose to show a SQL-like representation in Fig.10 (from DRS of Fig.9 – we can obtain it with a simple XSL Transformation [11]).

```
FROM y = /article,
     x = y//atl,
WHERE about(y, z)
VARIABLES z = "semantics"
SELECT x
```

Fig. 10. Example of formal query obtained from DRS 9 (query 1). y is an *article* tag, x is an *atl* tag (title) contained in y, and z represents the term *"semantics"*

4 Examples

We give here three significant examples of topic analyses. We already explained that several syntactic parsings could be possible for the same sentence. In practice a "score" is attributed to each rule release, depending on several parameters (among which distance between words that are linked, length of phrases, type of relations... Unfortunately we lack space to explain more precisely this process).

In our sample topics only the best scored result is given.

c1 c2 c3 c4 c5 c6 c7 c8 c9 c10 c11 c12 c13
event(c1, sym:find, object:c12) *event(c2, sym:contain, object:c11, agent:c12)* *of(c3, c9* $\wedge$ *c10)* *definition(c3)* *c9 = godel, c10 = lukasiewicz* *'fuzzy-logic'(c4)* *implication(c5)* *rel_nmodifier(c5, c4)* *rel_adjective(c5, other)* *paragraph(c6)* *figure(c7)* *caption(c8)* *id_nmodifier(c8, c7)* *c12 = c6* $\vee$ *c8, c11 = c3* $\vee$ *c5*

Fig. 11. DRS for topic 127. The predicate "**rel_adjective(x, *text*)**" means that the word ***text*** qualifies the variable **x**. The relation "**rel_nmodifier(x, y)**" stands for nominal compounds (here, *"fuzzy-logic implication"* and *"figure caption"*)

4.1 Topic 127

(127) Find paragraphs or figure captions containing the definition of Godel, Lukasiewicz or other fuzzy-logic implications.

Figure 11 shows the first DRS, obtained before the application of IR rules. The final query is given in Fig.12. If we reassemble terms with their relations, an approximate (manual) translation into NEXI could be:

```
//*//(p| fgc)[about( .//*, definition of godel definition of lukasiewicz)
            OR about(.//*, other fuzzy-logic implication)]
```

But this translation is less expressive and we loose some information.

4.2 Topic 141

(141) Retrieve sections about threads from articles about java

This is a textbook case, a short and syntacticaly unambiguous query, that works perfectly. See Fig.13. The translation into NEXI is straightforward:

```
//article[about(., java)]//sec[about(., thread)]
```

```
from   v2 = *, v3 = *, c12 = *, v4 = *, v5 = *
       c6 = v4//p
       c8 = v5//fgc
where  c12 = v4 or v5, c12 = v2 or v3
       ling_adj(c5, v1)
       ling_np_relation(c3, c10, of)
       ling_np_relation(c3, c9, of)
       ling_np_relation(c5, c4, nmodifier)
       about(v3, c5), about(v2, c3)
select c12
var    c5 = implication, c3 = definition, v1 = other
       c10 = lukasiewicz, c9 = godel, c4 = fuzzy-logic
```

Fig. 12. Final structured query for topic 127. Relations beginning by "ling_" are linguistic relations that it would be interesting (but not essential) to treat (in order to take into account possible variations in multi-word terms [12, 13])

```
from   c3 = /article
       c1 = c3//sec
where  about(c3, c4), about(c1, c2)
select c1
var    c4 = java, c2 = thread
```

Fig. 13. Final structured query for topic 141

4.3 Topic 164

(164) I am surveying the area of knowledge management for a report I am writing, and am looking for knowledge management frameworks and technologies for organizational memories.

This topic raises some problems described in Sect.6.2. Most of the proposed relations (see Fig.14) are interesting, but some terms (and an erroneous analysis of "I am writing...") generates noise (especially *"write" (c4)* and *"report" (c3)*). A CO-NEXI reconstitution would be:

```
knowledge management for report - write for knowledge management framework
for organizational memory - write for technology for organizational memory
```

5 Retrieval Process

At this stage we have a formal query that can be translated into an existing and implemented language. But while doing that we should keep in mind that Information Retrieval is yet to be done:

```
from   v1 = *, v2 = *
where  ling_np_relation(c1, c3, for)
       ling_np_relation(c1, c2, nmodifier)
       ling_np_relation(c7, c6, nmodifier)
       ling_np_relation(c6, c5, nmodifier)
       ling_np_relation(c4, c8, for)
       ling_np_relation(c4, c7, for)
       ling_np_relation(c8, c9, for)
       ling_np_relation(c7, c9, for)
       ling_adj(c9, v6)
       about(v2, c4), about(v1, c1)
select v1
var    c4 = verb_write, c8 = technology, c7 = framework,
       c9 = memory, c1 = management, v6 = organizational,
       c3 = report, c2 = knowledge, c6 = management, c5 = knowledge
```

Fig. 14. Final structured query for topic 164

- In our example the *about* relation is to be implemented in one way or another.
- It would be great if the search engine could "understand" linguistic constraints that we generated (see Sect. 3.4 and 4).
- As the request is in natural language, the `from` clause should not necessarily be considered as strict paths. If a user's request is *"give me a paragraph about semantics"*, a section or a figure could also be relevant (maybe not even *less* relevant). This remark corresponds to the INEX choice of assessing CAS topics as *"Vague CAS"* rather than *"Strict CAS"*.

6 Comments

6.1 Structural Density

A comparison between our work on IEEE collection for INEX and our other studies can give us some indications about the relation between density of markup in the corpus and ability to analyse properly the requests on this corpus. While we are using the structure to perform the analysis, it makes sense to consider that the higher this density is, the easier our work should be. And this is right to a certain extent. But if a corpus is more *data-centric*, closer to a database format (as address books or flight schedules), then the users' requests on this corpus are very strict and precise (much more than INEX topics). Then the limits of NLP (so far) are reached, and any imperfection in the system, any ambiguity could lead to an erroneous interpretation. We need in such cases to consider a "restricted" natural language, limited to unambiguous structures and pre-defined terms. As a matter of fact, the INEX collection seems to be an "ideal" in-between format to apply our method.

6.2 Topic Complexity

Topics proposed by participants at INEX 2004 are very diverse.

(185) Find articles about gesture recognitions.
(201) ranked retrieval in the WWW.
(187) We are looking for articles containing description of dimension reduction methods. These methods allow us to lessen effects of the "curse of dimensionality" and make retrieval of documents faster. Examples of this methods are well-known latent semantic indexing (LSI) which improves recall of the retrieval system and random projection which does not modify distances too much. We are not interested in stoplist filtration which does reduce the dimension a bit as a byproduct of term removal.

The main problem is not so much the length of the request (from 5 to 76 words) as the fact that language changes when the request is long. Indeed topics 185 and 201 are typical IR requests: a *"Find + Noun Phrase"* construction and a single noun phrase. On the other hand, the last example consists of common language sentences, with many anaphoras and pragmatic insinuations; a proper analysis of all the niceties of language is not conceivable. This leads to a lot of noise in results; for instance words *"effects"* or *"projection"* will be considered by our system as terms to find in the documents as well as the others. If these terms are related to the topic, their importance is much lower. Finally the system does not handle negations.

6.3 Corpus Knowledge

During the stages that we detailed in the previous sections, we used several kinds of information about the explored corpus. This knowledge has to be modeled for each new set of documents[7] to study. Even if our track is not concerned by heterogeneous documents, we tried to reduce this necessity to the minimum. But despite this, we think that the following points are the minimum knowledge to handle in order to perform an appropriate query analysis:

- The DTD
- Because DTD tag names are not "real" words and also because several words can be used for a single concept, we need a dictionary of acceptable synonyms for tag names (*e.g.:* paper = article = document, title = atl, etc.);
- Semantic locutions (*e.g.:* "a list of keywords" = "keywords"), in order to avoid noise generated by an erroneous detection of terms (here, *list* is neither a tag name nor a term to look for in the text);
- Some very simple ontologic structures (*e.g.:* "a novel written by Marcel Proust" = "a novel of which the author is Marcel Proust" – if we suppose that *novel* and *author* represent tag names);

7 Conclusion

The Graal of Information Retrieval, which is to *"build software that will analyse, understand, and generate results in response to queries that humans express naturally"* (INEX NLPX track presentation), is far from being reached. It requests a detailed syntactic, semantic and pragmatic understanding of both queries and documents; this is impossible in the present state of our knowledge and resources. In this paper we focused on a first step, a technique to translate natural language queries into a structured formal query language. On top of the ameliorations of this system, we now intend to work on the use of the linguistic information provided by our method, in order to improve an XML retrieval system.

References

[1] Smeaton, A.F.: Information Retrieval: Still Butting Heads with Natural Language Processing? In Pazienza, M., ed.: Information Extraction – A Multidisciplinary Approach to an Emerging Information Technology. Volume 1299 of Lecture Notes in Computer Science. Springer-Verlag (1997) 115–138

[2] Feldman, S.: NLP Meets the Jabberwocky: Natural Language Processing in Information Retrieval. Online (1999) http://www.onlinemag.net/OL1999/feldman5.html.

[3] Smeaton, A.F.: Using NLP or NLP Resources for Information Retrieval Tasks. [14] 99–111

[4] Arampatzis, A., van der Weide, T., Koster, C., van Bommel, P.: Linguistically-motivated Information Retrieval. In Kent, A., ed.: Encyclopedia of Library and Information Science. Volume 69. Marcel Dekker, Inc., New York, Basel (2000) 201–222

[7] We call a *new* set of documents a corpus with a different DTD and different subject.

[5] Sparck Jones, K.: What is the role of NLP in text retrieval? [14] 1–24
[6] Strzalkowski, T., Lin, F., Wang, J., Perz-Carballo, J.: Evaluating Natural Language Processing Techniques in Information Retrieval. [14] 113–145
[7] Schmid, H.: Probabilistic Part-of-Speech Tagging Using Decision Trees. In: International Conference on New Methods in Language Processing. (1994)
[8] Kamp, H., Reyle, U.: From discourse to logic. Kluwer Academic Publisher (1993)
[9] : (XML Path Language (XPath). World Wide Web Consortium (W3C) Recommandation) http://www.w3.org/TR/xpath.
[10] : (XQuery 1.0: An XML Query Language. World Wide Web Consortium (W3C) Working Draft) http://www.w3.org/TR/xquery.
[11] : (XSL Transformation (XSL). World Wide Web Consortium (W3C) Recommandation) http://www.w3.org/TR/xslt/.
[12] Fabre, C., Jacquemin, C.: Boosting Variant Recognition with Light Semantics. In: Proceedings of the 18th International Conference on Computational Linguistics, COLING 2000, Saarbrücken (2000) 264–270
[13] Sparck Jones, K., Tait, J.I.: Automatic Search Term Variant Generation. Journal of Documentation **40** (1984) 50–66
[14] Strzalkowski, T., ed.: Natural Language Information Retrieval. Kluwer Academic Publisher, Dordrecht, NL (1999)

The Interactive Track at INEX 2004

Anastasios Tombros[1], Birger Larsen[2], and Saadia Malik[3]

[1] Dept. of Computer Science, Queen Mary University of London, London, UK
tassos@dcs.qmul.ac.uk

[2] Dept. of Information Studies, Royal School of LIS, Copenhagen, Denmark
blar@db.dk

[3] Fak. 5/IIS, Information Systems, University of Duisburg-Essen, Duisburg, Germany
malik@is.informatik.uni-duisburg.de

Abstract. An interactive track was included in INEX for the first time in 2004. The main aim of the track was to study the behaviour of searchers when interacting with components of XML documents. In this paper, we describe the motivation and aims of the track in detail, we outline the methodology and we present some initial findings from the analysis of the results.

1 Interactive Track Motivation

In recent years there has been a growing realisation in the IR community that the interaction of searchers with information is an indispensable component of the IR process. As a result, issues relating to interactive IR have been extensively investigated in the last decade. A major advance in research has been made by co-ordinated efforts in the interactive track at TREC. These efforts have been in the context of unstructured documents (e.g. news articles) or in the context of the loosely-defined structure encountered in web pages. XML documents, on the other hand, define a different context, by offering the possibility of navigating within the structure of a single document, or of following links to another document.

Relatively little research has been carried out to study user interaction with IR systems that take advantage of the additional features offered by XML documents, and so little is known about how users behave in the context of such IR systems. One exception is the work done by [1], who studied end user interaction with a small test collection of Shakespeare's plays formatted in XML.

The investigation of the different context that is defined in the case of user interaction with XML documents has provided the main motivation for the establishment of an interactive track at INEX. The aims for the interactive track are twofold. First, to investigate the behaviour of users when interacting with components of XML documents, and secondly to investigate and develop approaches for XML retrieval which are effective in user-based environments.

In the first year, we focused on investigating the behaviour of searchers when presented with components of XML documents that have a high probability of being relevant (as estimated by an XML-based IR system). Presently, metrics that are used for the evaluation of system effectiveness in the INEX ad-hoc track are based on certain

N. Fuhr et al. (Eds.): INEX 2004, LNCS 3493, pp. 410–423, 2005.

assumptions of user behaviour [2]. These metrics attempt to quantify the effectiveness of IR systems at pointing searchers to relevant components of documents. Some of the assumptions behind the metrics include that users would browse through retrieved elements in a linear order, that they would "jump" with a given probability p from one element to another within the same document's structure, that they would not make use of links to another document, etc. These assumptions have not been formally investigated in the context of XML retrieval; their investigation formed the primary aim for the first year of the interactive track.

Since the investigation of user behaviour forms our primary focus, the format of the track for the first year differs to that typically followed by, for example, the interactive track at TREC. The main difference was that a comparison between different interactive approaches was not our main focus. Instead, a more collaborative effort was planned, with the outcome of the studies expected to feed back to the INEX initiative. Participating sites still had the option to develop and evaluate their own interactive approaches, but this was not a requirement for participation. It should be noted that none of the participating sites opted to develop their own system.

We first describe the experimental setup and methodology in section 2, then we present an initial analysis of the data in section 3, and we conclude in section 4.

2 Experimental Setup

In this section we outline the experimental set up for the first interactive track at INEX.

2.1 Topics

We used content only (CO) topics from the INEX 2004 collection. We added an additional dimension to the investigation of this year's interactive track by selecting topics that corresponded to different types of tasks. The effect that the context determined by task type has on the behaviour of online searchers has been demonstrated in a number of studies e.g. [3].

One way to categorise tasks is according to the "type" of information need they correspond to. In [3] the categorisation included background (find as much general information on a topic as possible), decision (make a decision based on the information found) and many-items task (compile a list of items related to the information need) types. It was shown that different task types promote the use of different criteria when assessing the relevance of web pages. It is likely that a similar effect, in terms of user behaviour within structured documents, may exist in the context of XML documents. Searchers may exhibit different browsing patterns and different navigational strategies for different task types.

Four of the 2004 CO topics were used in the study, and they were divided into two task categories:

- Background category (B): Most of the INEX topics fall in this category. The topics express an information need in the form of "I'd like to find out about X". The two tasks in this category were based on topics 180 and 192.

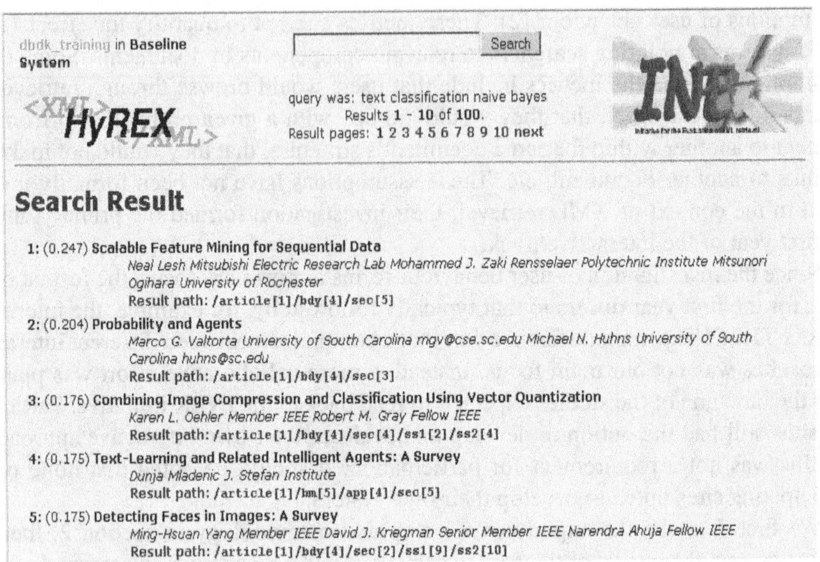

Fig. 1. The ranked list of documents in the Baseline system

- Comparison category (C): There are a number of topics whose subject is along the lines of: "Find differences between X and Y". The tasks given in this category were based on topics 188 and 198.

In order to make the tasks comprehensible by other than the topic author, it was required that all INEX 2004 topics not only detail *what* is being sought for, but also *why* this is wanted, and in what context the information need has arisen. Thereby the INEX topics are in effect simulated work task situations as developed by Borlund [4, 5]. Compared to the regular topics, more context on the motives and background of the topic is provided in the simulated work tasks. In this way, the test persons can better place themselves in a situation where they would be motivated to search for information related to the work tasks. The aim is to enable the test persons to formulate and reformulate their own queries as realistically as possible in the interaction with the IR system. The task descriptions used in the study were derived from part of the Narrative field. We include the task descriptions as given to searchers in the Appendix.

2.2 System

A system for the interactive track study was provided by the track organisers. The system was based on the HyREX[1] retrieval engine, and included a web-based interface with a basic functionality.

Searchers were able to input queries to the system. In response to the query, HyRex returns a ranked list of components as shown in Figure 1. The information presented

[1] http://www.is.informatik.uni-duisburg.de/projects/hyrex/

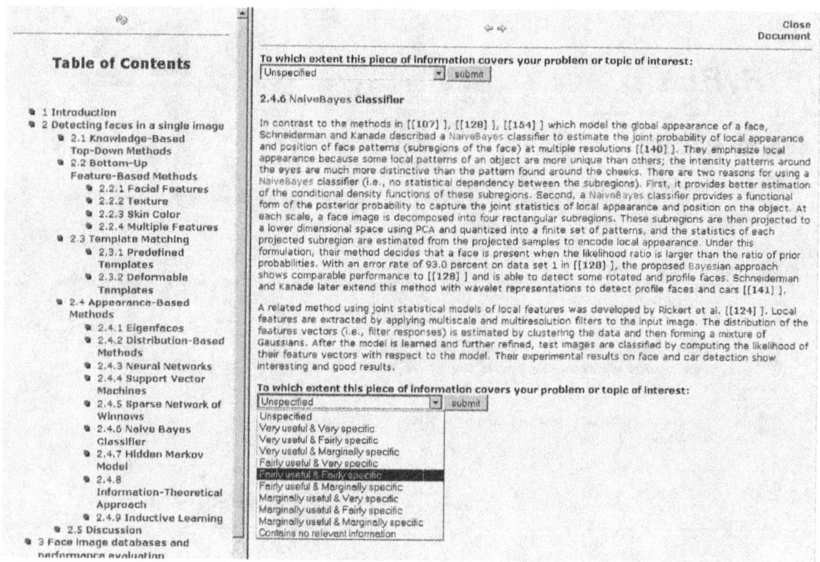

Fig. 2. Detailed view of document components in the Baseline system

for each retrieved component included the title and authors of the document in which the component occurs, the component's retrieval value and the XPath of the component. Searchers can explore the ranked list of components, and can visit components by clicking on the Xpath in the ranked list.

In Figure 2 we show the detailed component view. This view is divided into two parts: the right hand of the view includes the actual textual contents of the selected component; the left side contains the table of contents for the document containing the component. Searchers can access other components within the same document either by using the table of contents on the left, or by using the next and previous buttons at the top of the right part of the view.

Table 1. The applied relevance scale

A	Very useful & Very specific
B	Very useful & Fairly specific
C	Very useful & Marginally specific
D	Fairly useful & Very specific
E	Fairly useful & Fairly specific
F	Fairly useful & Marginally specific
G	Marginally useful & Marginally specific
H	Marginally useful & Marginally specific
I	Marginally useful & Marginally specific
J	Contains no relevant information
U	Unspecified

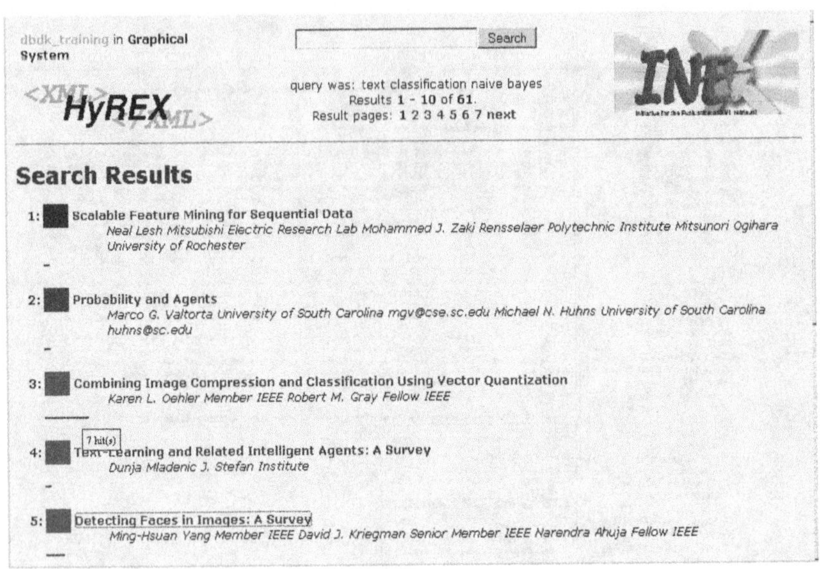

Fig. 3. The ranked list of documents in the Graphical system

A relevance assessment for each viewed component could be given, as shown in Figure 2. The assessment was based on two dimensions of relevance: how useful and how specific the component was in relation to the search task. The definition of usefulness was formulated very much like the one for Exhaustivity in the Ad hoc track, but was labelled usefulness, which might be easier for users to comprehend. Each dimension had three grades of relevance as this is shown in Figure 2 . Ten possible combinations of these dimensions could be made.

To return to the ranked list, searchers would need to close the currently open document. A different version of the system with graphical features was also developed. This system (Graphical system) differed to the Baseline system both in the way of presenting the ranked list (Figure 3) and in the way of presenting the detailed view of components (Figure 4). The graphical system retrieves documents rather than components, and presents the title and authors of each retrieved document. In addition, it also presents a shaded rectangle (the darker the colour the more relevant the document to the query) and a red bar (the longer the bar the more query hits are contained in the document).

The detailed view for each selected document component is similar to that for the Baseline system, with the addition of a graphical representation at the top of the view (Figure 4). A document is represented in a rectangular area and is split horizontally and vertically to represent the different document levels. Tooltips (on mouse-over) provide additional information about the retrieved components, such as the first 150 characters of the contents and the component's name, the selected section, subsection, etc. On the top part of the this view, all the retrieved documents are shown as small rectangles in gray shades along with the Next and Previous links to allow navigation between the retrieved results.

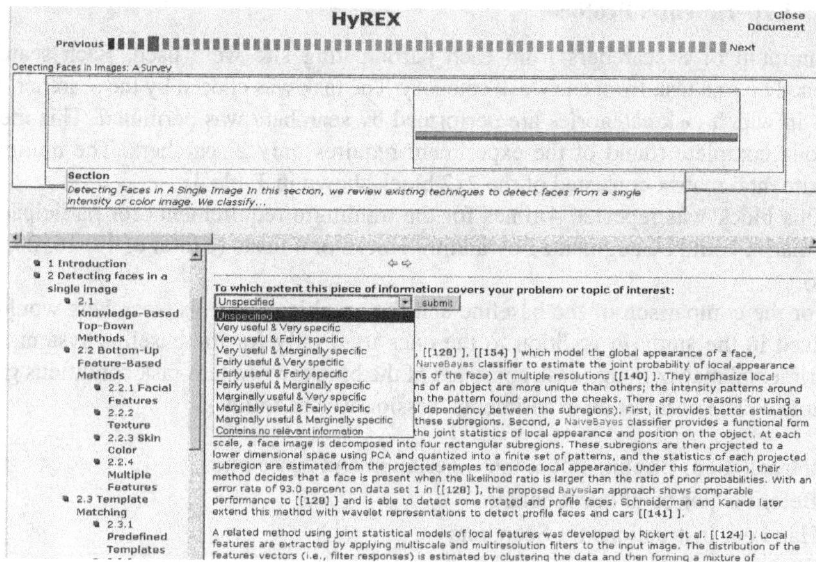

Fig. 4. Detailed view of document components in the Graphical system

2.3 Participating Sites

The minimum requirement for sites to participate in this year's interactive track was to provide runs using 8 searchers on the Baseline version of the XML retrieval system that the track organisers provided. In addition to the minimum requirement, sites could choose to employ more users, to expand the experimental design by comparing both versions of the system (baseline and graphical), or to test their own experimental system against the baseline system provided.

Ten sites participated in the Interactive track. We give the sites' name, number of searchers used and types of comparisons performed in Table 2.

Table 2. Participating sites in the Interactive Track

Site	Baseline System	Additional studies
Oslo University College, Norway	8 users	-
RMIT Australia	16 users	-
U. Twente/CWI, The Netherlands	8 users	8 users(baseline vs. graphical)
Norwegian University of Science and Technology	8 usres	-
U. Tampere, Finland	8 users	-
Kyunpook National University, Korea	8 users	-
Robert Gordon University, Scotland	8 users	-
University of Duisburg-Essen, Germany	8 users	-
Royal School of LIS, Denmark	8 users	-
Queen Marry University of London, England	8 users	-

2.4 Experimental Protocol

A minimum of 8 searchers from each participating site were used. Each searcher searched on one task from each task category. The task was chosen by the searcher. The order in which task categories are performed by searchers was permuted. This means that one complete round of the experiment requires only 2 searchers. The minimum experimental matrix consisted of the 2x2 block shown in Table 3.

This block was repeated 4 times for the minimum requirements for participation. This matrix could be augmented by adding blocks of 4 users (a total of 12, 16, 20, etc. users).

For the comparison of the baseline and the graphical systems, searchers would be involved in the study in addition to the ones used only for the baseline system. The experimental matrix in this case consisted of the blocks of system-task conditions given in Table 4. The order of an experimental session was as follows:

1. Introduction: Briefing about the experiment and procedures
2. Before-experiment questionnaire
3. Hand out Instructions for Searchers
4. System tutorial
5. Task selection from the appropriate category
6. Before-task questionnaire
7. Search session
8. After-task questionnaire
9. Repeat steps 5-8 for the other task category
10. After-experiment questionnaire
11. Informal discussion/interview: any additional views on the experiment, system, etc. the searcher wishes to share.

Each searcher was given a maximum of 30 minutes to complete each task. The goal for each searcher was to locate sufficient information towards completing a task.

2.5 Data Collection

The collected data comprised questionnaires completed by the test persons, the logs of searcher interaction with the system, the notes experimenters kept during the sessions and the informal feedback provided by searchers at the end of the sessions.

The logged data consisted of the queries issued, the components returned by the system, the components actually viewed and the order in which they were viewed, relevance assessments of these, any browsing behaviour, as well as time stamps for each interaction between searchers and the system.

Table 3. Basic experimental matrix

Searcher	1st Task Category	2nd Task Category
1	Background(B)	Comparison(C)
2	Comparison(C)	Background(B)

Table 4. Augmented experimental matrix

Searcher	1st Condition	2nd Second Condition
1	Graphical-B	Baseline-C
2	Graphical-C	Baseline-B
3	Baseline-B	Graphical-C
4	Baseline-C	Graphical-B

3 Initial Results Analysis

In this section we present an initial analysis of the collected data. In section 3.1 we analyse data collected from the questionnaires, then in section 3.2 we present some general statistics collected from the system logs, and in section 3.3 we outline the detailed analysis of browsing behaviour which is currently in progress.

3.1 Questionnaire Data

A total of 88 searchers were employed by participating sites. The average age of the searchers was 29 years. Their average experience in bibliographic searching in online digital libraries, computerised library catalogs, WWW search engines etc. was 4, on a scale from 1 to 5 with 5 signifying highest experience level. The education level of the participants spanned undergraduate (39%), MSc (49%), and PhD (12%) levels.

In terms of task selection, from the Background task category 66% of participants selected task B1 (cybersickness, topic 192) and 34 % selected B2 (ebooks, topic 180). From the Comparison task category, 76% selected task C2 (Java-Python, topic 198) and 24% selected task C1 (Fortran90-Fortran, topic 188).

In Table 5 we present data for task familiarity, task difficulty and perceived task satisfaction. With respect to task familiarity, we asked searchers before the start of each search session to rate how familiar they were with the task they selected on a scale from 1 to 5, with 5 signifying the greatest familiarity. With respect to task difficulty, we asked searchers to rate the difficulty of the task once before the start of the search session, and once the session was completed (pre- and post- task difficulty, columns 3 and 4 respectively). Searchers also indicated their satisfaction with the results of the task. All data in Table 5 correspond to the same 5-point scale.

The data in Table 5 suggest that there are some significant differences in the searchers' perceptions of the tasks. The most notable of these differences are in task

Table 5. Searchers' perceptions of tasks

	Task familiarity	Pre-task difficulty	Post-task difficulty	Task satisfaction
B1 (no.192)	2.1	2.03	1.47	3.39
B2 (no.180)	2.73	2.1	1.97	1.97
C1 (no.188)	2.67	1.95	1.74	2.62
C2 (no.198)	2.91	2.1	1.52	2.9

Table 6. Access modes to viewed components

Access	B	C	Total	B	C
nextprev	17	17	34	2%	2%
rankedlist	588	550	1138	63%	62%
structure	327	327	654	35%	37%
Total	932	894	1826	100%	100%

familiarity and task satisfaction. It should be noted that at this time a thorough statistical analysis of the results has not been performed. An initial analysis of the correlation between task familiarity and satisfaction did not show a strong relationship between these two variables across the tasks.

The overall opinion of the participants about the Baseline system was recorded in the final questionnaire they filled in after the completion of both tasks. Participants generally felt at ease with the system, finding it easy to learn how to use (average rating 4.17), easy to use (3.95) and easy to understand (3.94). There were also many informal comments by the participants about specific aspects of the system. These comments were recorded by the experimenters and will be analysed at a later stage.

3.2 General Statistics

This analysis concerns approximately 50% of the log data for the baseline system. The remainder could not be analysed reliably at present because of problems with the logging software.

Ranks. A maximum of 100 hits were presented to searchers on the ranked list, and they were free to choose between these in any order they liked (See Figure 1). For the Background (B) tasks 86% of the viewed components were from top10 of the ranked list (80% for the Comparison (C) tasks). The ranks viewed furthest down the list were 71 for B and 96 for C.

Queries. The possible query operators were '+' for emphasis, '-' for negative emphasis, and " " for phrases. The phrase operator was used 24 times in B, and 16 in C. No one used plus or minus. 217 unique queries were given for B, and 225 for C across all searchers. On average, the queries for B consisted of 3.0 search keys (counting a phrase as one search key), and 3.4 for C including stop words. 81% of the queries for B consisted of 2, 3 or 4 search keys for B, 80% for C.

Viewed Components. In total, searchers viewed 804 different components for B, and 820 for C. On average this was 10.9 unique components viewed for B, and 10.8 for C.

Three possibilities existed for accessing a component: to click a hit from the ranked list, to click a part of the document structure (via the table of contents), and to use the next/previous buttons. From Table 6 below it can be seen that very few chose to use the next/previous buttons: only 2% of component viewing arose from this (both B and C). For B 63% of viewings came from the ranked list, for C this was 62%. For B 35% came from the table of contents, and 37% for C.

Assessed Components. 503 components were assessed for B, 489 for C, or 6.8 per searcher per task for B, and 6.4 for C. This corresponds to 63% of the viewed components for B and 60% for C. In 8 cases the searchers pressed 'Submit' without selecting a relevance value (recorded as U in Tables 1, 7, 8 and 9).

The distribution of relevance assessments on tasks can be seen in Table 7 below. It may be observed that 12-13% of the assessed documents were 'Very useful & Very specific" [A] for both B and C, and that 15-16% of the assessed documents were 'Marginally useful & Marginally specific" [I] for both B and C. The most noteworthy difference is that B had 38% non-relevant assessments [J], and C only 17%.

Table 7. Relevance assessments distributed on task type (see Table1 above for relevance scale)

Relevance	B	C	Total	B	C
A	65	61	126	13%	12%
B	28	36	64	6%	7%
C	8	13	21	2%	3%
D	19	45	64	4%	9%
E	36	61	97	7%	12%
F	28	38	66	6%	8%
G	12	20	32	2%	4%
H	33	47	80	7%	10%
I	79	80	159	16%	16%
J	191	84	275	38%	17%
U	4	4	8	1%	1%
Total	503	489	992	100%	100%

The next two tables show the distribution of relevance assessments on the access possibilities, one for B and one for C (i.e. how did the searchers reach the components which they assessed). The total number of component viewings with relevance assessments is lower (992) than the total number of components viewed (1826, Table 6) because not all viewed components were assessed.

For both B and C very few viewings with next/previous section buttons resulted in assessments: 0 for C, and 5 for B. The latter 5 were given low assessments. In both cases the majority of assessments resulted as a direct consequence of clicking a hit from the ranked list: 67% for B and 71% for C. Apart from 1% next/previous navigation in B the remainder the rest is taken up by navigation from the table of contents. Large variations are, however, obvious in the data, and can be uncovered by an in-depth analysis of the browsing behaviour.

Overall Browsing Behaviour. Table 10 shows this variation on an overall level by counting the number of requests for components within the same document. The raw figures included double counting, because whenever an assessment was made the component was reloaded from the server. In this table, the number of assessments has therefore been subtracted from the number of requests for components. It can be seen that for the most part (70% of cases) searchers viewed 1 component and assessed it (or

Table 8. Relevance assessments distributed on access modes for the B tasks

Relevance	nextprev	rankedlist	structure	total
A	1	38	26	65
B	-	16	12	28
C	-	4	4	8
D	-	11	8	19
E	-	21	15	36
F	-	21	7	28
G	-	10	2	12
H	2	23	8	33
I	1	45	33	79
J	1	142	48	191
U	-	4	4	
Total	5	335	163	503

viewed two and didn't assess any), and then moved on to a new document rather than continuing the navigation within the same document.

A more in-depth analysis of the data will be performed with the aim to further break down user browsing behaviour within an accessed document. From informal comments made by searchers, and from an initial observation of the log data, one possible reason for the low degree of interaction with documents and their components was overlap. Searchers generally recognised overlapping components, and found them an undesirable "feature" of the system. Through more detailed analysis of the logs we can determine how searchers behaved when the system returned overlapping components.

3.3 Detailed Browsing Behaviour

A detailed analysis on the browsing behaviour of searchers is currently underway. The main aim of this analysis is to determine how users browsed within each document they

Table 9. Relevance assessments distributed on access modes for the C tasks

Relevance	nextprev	rankedlist	structure	total
A	-	43	18	61
B	-	25	11	36
C	-	11	2	13
D	-	30	15	45
E	-	34	27	61
F	-	26	12	38
G	-	13	7	20
H	-	35	12	47
I	-	60	20	80
J	-	64	20	84
U	-	4		4
Total	0	345	144	489

Table 10. Overall browsing behaviour within the same document: number of components viewed

	B	C	Total	B	C
1	406	394	800	69.0%	71.6%
2	93	84	177	15.8%	15.3%
3	47	39	86	8.0%	7.1%
4	23	9	32	3.9%	1.6%
5	13	8	21	2.2%	1.5%
6	2	4	6	0.3%	0.7%
7	2	5	7	0.3%	0.9%
8	1	1	2	0.2%	0.2%
9	1		1	0.2%	0.0%
10		1	1	0.0%	0.2%
11		2	2	0.0%	0.4%
12		1	1	0.0%	0.2%
13		1	1	0.0%	0.2%
14		1	1	0.0%	0.2%
Total	588	550	1138	100%	100%

visited, and how their browsing actions correlated with their relevance assessments. More specifically, we aim to look into the relationship of the relevance assessments' dimensions to whether searchers browse to more specific or more general components in the document tree, whether they browse to components of the same depth or whether they return to the ranked list of components. For example, we could see where users would browse to after they have assessed a component as "Very useful and fairly specific", and also how they would assess further documents along the browsing path.

This detailed analysis, together with the analysis on the overlapping components, can yield results that can be useful for the development of metrics that may take into account actual indications of user behaviour.

4 Conclusions

In this paper we have described the motivation and aims, and the methodology of the INEX 2004 interactive track. We have also presented some initial results gathered from user questionnaires and system logs.

We are currently performing a more detailed analysis of the gathered data, with the aim to establish patterns of browsing behaviours and to correlate them to the assessments of the visited document components. This analysis can also provide insight as to whether there are different browsing behaviours for the two different task categories included in the study. We expect that the results of this analysis will lead to the development of effectiveness metrics based on observed user behaviour.

References

1. Finesilver, K., Reid, J.: User behaviour in the context of structured documents. In: Sebastiani, Fabrizio (ed.), Advances in information retrieval: Proceedings of the 25th European conference on IR research, ECIR 2003. (2003) 104–199

2. Kazai, G.: Report of the INEX 2003 metrics working group. In Fuhr, N., Lalmas, M., Malik, S., eds.: INitiative for the Evaluation of XML Retrieval (INEX). Proceedings of the Second INEX Workshop. Dagstuhl, Germany, December 15–17, 2003. (2004) 184–190
3. Tombros, A., Ruthven, I., Jose, J.: How users assess web pages for information-seeking. Journal of the American Society for Information Science and Technology **56** (2005) 327–344
4. Borlund, P.: Evaluation of interactive information retrieval systems. PhD thesis, Royal School of Library and Information Sciences, Copenhagen, Denmark (2000)
5. Borlund, P.: The IIR evaluation model: a framework for evaluation of interactive information retrieval systems. Information Research:an international electronic journal **8** (2003) 1–38

A Task Descriptions

A.1 Task Category: Background (B)

Task ID: B1
You are writing a large article discussing virtual reality (VR) applications and you need to discuss their negative side effects. What you want to know is the symptoms associated with cybersickness, the amount of users who get them, and the VR situations where they occur. You are not interested in the use of VR in therapeutic treatments unless they discuss VR side effects.

Task ID: B2
You have tried to buy & download electronic books (ebooks) just to discover that problems arise when you use the ebooks on different PC's, or when you want to copy the ebooks to Personal Digital Assistants. The worst disturbance factor is that the content is not accessible after a few tries, because an invisible counter reaches a maximum number of attempts. As ebooks exist in various formats and with different copy protection schemes, you would like to find articles, or parts of articles, which discuss various proprietary and covert methods of protection. You would also be interested in articles, or parts of articles, with a special focus on various disturbance factors surrounding ebook copyrights.

A.2 Task Category: Background (C)

Task ID: C1
You have been asked to make your Fortran compiler compatible with Fortran 90, and so you are interested in the features Fortran 90 added to the Fortran standard before it. You would like to know about compilers, especially compilers whose source code might be available. Discussion of people's experience with these features when they were new to them is also of interest.

Task ID: C2
You are working on a project to develop a next generation version of a software system. You are trying to decide on the benefits and problems of implementation in a number of programming languages, but particularly Java and Python. You would like a good comparison of these for application development. You would like to see comparisons

of Python and Java for developing large applications. You want to see articles, or parts of articles, that discuss the positive and negative aspects of the languages. Things that discuss either language with respect to application development may be also partially useful to you. Ideally, you would be looking for items that are discussing both efficiency of development and efficiency of execution time for applications.

Interactive Searching Behavior with Structured XML Documents

Heesop Kim and Heejung Son

Department of Library & Information Science, Kyungpook National University, Daegu, 702-701, South Korea

heesop@knu.ac.kr, sonhjung@postech.ac.kr

Abstract. The aim of this study was to provide fundamental data on users' searching behavior when they are interacting with structured XML documents, and to discover the correlation between users' search characteristics and their attitude towards evaluating the interactive XML IR system. 8 subjects took part in this experiment and we followed the experimental guidelines from the INEX 2004 Interactive Track organizers with no modification. In total, 16 transaction logs from the search sessions and 6 responses from the questionnaires per subject were collected and analyzed to achieve our research goals. Collected data was analyzed using SPSS Windows 10.0 and the results are presented in various tables. No significant correlation was found between the users' chosen search characteristics and their attitude towards evaluating the XML IR system in this experiment.

1 Introduction

XML documents retrieval is considered as one way of increasing precision because it's every element could be regarded as retrievable unit [2, 7, 16]. Recently, many studies on structured XML document retrieval have been introduced in terms of more effective and efficient information retrieval (IR). Most of these studies are mainly focused on implementation of techniques or approaches for indexing or retrieving of XML documents [2, 13, 16]. So far only a few studies have been conducted to build a user model based upon real user behavior with XML documents [4]. However, those works are limited in the size of the test collection which is one of the critical factors in IR system evaluation.

The Interactive Track in INEX 2004 (INitiative for the Evaluation of XML Retrieval 2004) was established to facilitate the coordinated studies about user behavior with structured XML documents and the main aim of the track was to study the behavior of searchers when interacting with components of XML documents [8, 9, 15].

The aim of this study was to provide fundamental data on users' searching behavior (i.e., querying, browsing, evaluating) when they are interacting with structured XML documents, and to discover the correlation between users' search characteristics (i.e., number of query iterations, number of query terms used, number of unique query terms used, number of documents/components viewed, number of docu-

N. Fuhr et al. (Eds.): INEX 2004, LNCS 3493, pp. 424–436, 2005.

ments/components assessed, time spent) and their attitude towards evaluating the interactive XML IR system.

We, Kyungpook National University, collected and analyzed transaction logs from the search sessions and questionnaire data of each subject in a way of the standard experimental guidelines from the INEX 2004 Interactive Track organizers. SPSS for Windows 10.0 was used as a statistical analysis tool and Pearson's correlation coefficient (r) was adopted for correlation analysis.

Section 2 presents the experimental methodology employed. Section 3 analyzes the data from transaction logs and questionnaire, and gives the results of search characteristics, correlation analysis, and the subjects' comments for the system and the experiment. Finally, section 4 presents conclusion and future work.

2 Experimental Design

2.1 System, Test Collection and Tasks

HyREX (Hyper-media Retrieval Engine for XML) on-line search engine, which was provided by the track organizers, was used to retrieve the XML documents or components, and to collect relevance assessments from the subjects. Of the two interfaces available in the system, we used the simple 'baseline interface' rather than the additional 'graphical interface' in this experiment. The INEX data collection of the *ad hoc* track (version 1.4), which consists of full text from the journals published by the *IEEE Computer Society*, was used in this Interactive Track. The topic area of the collection is computer science focusing on hardware and software development. The time span covered by the collection was 1995 to 2002.

Four tasks (i.e., B1, B2, C1, C2) which are divided into two categories, that is, 'Background (B)' and 'Comparison (C),' were used (See Appendix). The difference between these two categories is the form of its expression of the information needs. For example, the typical form of the 'Background' tasks is "I'd like to find out about X," whereas the typical form of the 'Comparison' tasks is "Find differences between X and Y". These tasks were derived from content only (CO) *ad hoc* topics that were extended to engage the subjects in realistic searching behavior. Each subject was asked to choose only one task from each category.

2.2 System Interface

We used HyREX baseline interface for the system interface and Figure 1 shows the example of the ranked list of search results. Each result of the list consists of rank, article title, author(s), retrieval status value, and a pointer to the path of the retrieved document or component. Up to 100 top-ranked results were returned for each query and 10 results were seen per page. Each detailed result page can be accessed by clicking on the path from the ranked list (see Figure 2). Each one provides its own 'Table of Contents' on the left which represents the structure of the document (i.e., article itself) and allows the links to the corresponding components (i.e., section or subsection etc.) 'Next/Previous' buttons are also provided on this detailed result page that allow a searcher to navigate back and forth in the document.

From a drop down box on the top and bottom of the page, the subjects were asked to submit the relevance assessment for the retrieved document or component. As shown in Table 1, two dimensions of relevance, that is, (1) the extent to which the displayed component contains information that is useful for solving the given task (i.e., Usefulness or Exhaustivity) and (2) the extent to which the displayed component is focused on the topic of the task (i.e., Specificity) were taken into account and combined into 10 categories with the grades of relevance (i.e., Very, Fairly, Marginally). Since these categories (i.e. A ~ J) do not seem to be easily interpreted for comparison, we adopted four-point scale (i.e., 0, 1, 2, 3) as other previous studies proposed or used [8, 14].

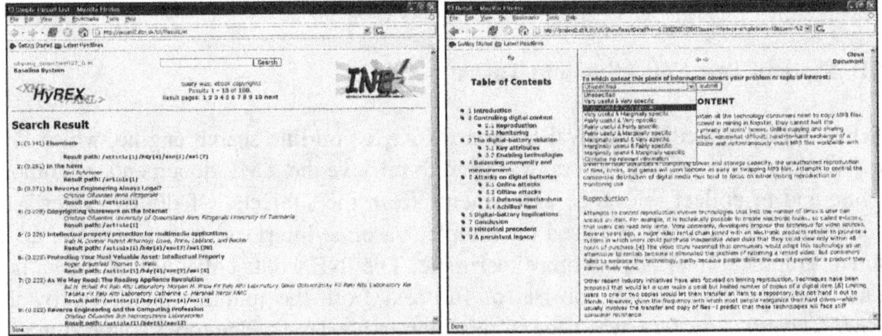

Fig. 1. HyREX Interface for Ranked List …**Fig. 2.** HyREX Interface for Detailed Result

Table 1. 10 Categories of Relevance Assessments

Category	Relevance scale	Four-point scale	
		Usefulness	Specificity
A	Very useful & Very specific	3	3
B	Very useful & Fairly specific	3	2
C	Very useful & Marginally specific	3	1
D	Fairly useful & Very specific	2	3
E	Fairly useful & Fairly specific	2	2
F	Fairly useful & Marginally specific	2	1
G	Marginally useful & Very specific	1	3
H	Marginally useful & Fairly specific	1	2
I	Marginally useful & Marginally specific	1	1
J	Contains no relevant information	0	0

2.3 Experimental Procedure

We adopted the experimental guidelines from the organizers without any modification. The experimental procedure was as follows:

1. Introduction: General briefing about the experiment and procedures
2. 'Before-experiment questionnaire'
3. Hand out 'Introduction for Searchers'
4. System tutorial
5. Category task selection from the first category
6. 'Before-each-task questionnaire'
7. Search session with maximum 30 minutes
8. 'After-each-task questionnaire'
9. Repeat 5-8 for the other task category
10. 'Post-experiment questionnaire'.

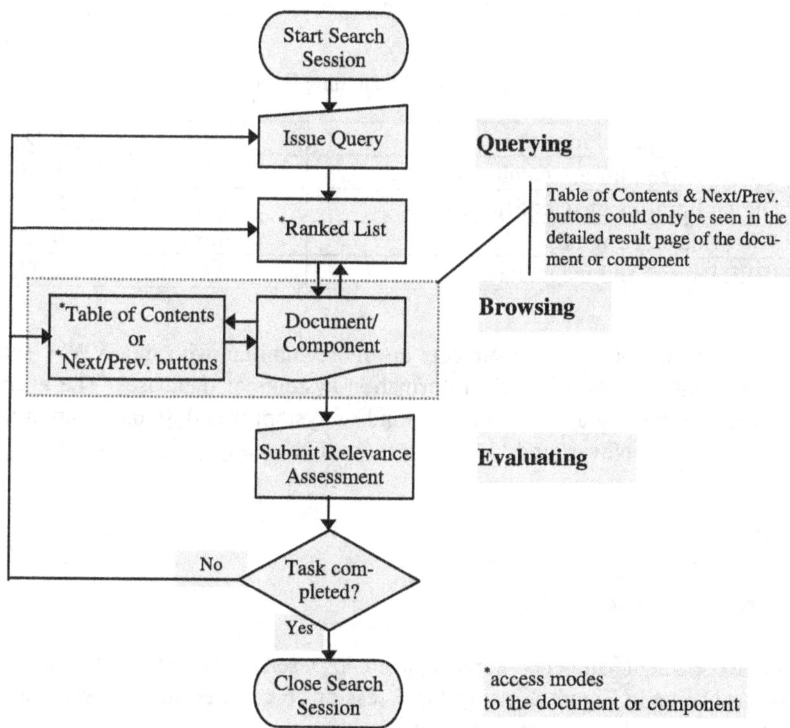

Fig. 3. The Process of Searching Session

Figure 3 describes the iterative process of the searching session in this experiment. The process divided into 3 sessions of search activities (i.e., querying, browsing, and evaluating) like most information retrieval processes [2]. The asterisk mark (*) means the modes of access to the document or component in this figure.

2.4 Subjects

Eight volunteers participated in this experiment. Seven of them are students of the Department of Library and Information Science at Kyungpook National University, and the other one is a researcher. Four of the subjects are male and four are female. All of them speak Korean as their first language. The ages of the subjects were between 24 and 31 years old (mean = 27.1) at the time of experiment. One of them has Master's degree, while half (i.e., 4 subjects) of them have Bachelor's degree and the others (i.e., 3 subjects) are undergraduate students. Two subjects have participated in previous on-line searching studies as a test person, but none as an experimenter. It is reported that our subjects have an average of 7.13 years of on-line searching experience (min. = 5, max. = 10, std. deviation = 2.03). Subjects' detailed levels of various experiences with searching are shown in Table 2.

Table 2. Subjects' Searching Experiences[1]

Searching experience	Mean	Std. Dev.
Computerized library catalogues	3.3	1.28
Digital libraries of scientific articles	3.0	0.93
WWW search engines	4.6	0.52
IEEE journal and magazines	2.0	1.07

As shown in Table 2, our subjects are more familiar with the WWW search engines than other kinds of library information systems or databases. The average frequency of conducting a search on any kind of system was 4.88 based upon a 5 point scale in which '1=Never' and '5=One or more times a day.'

3 Results

3.1 Search Characteristics

In this experiment, subjects were engaged in 3 search activities of information retrieval as shown in Figure 3. All of the 3 sessions (i.e., querying, browsing and evaluating), were considered to be investigated as the searcher's behavior in this study.

Two transaction logs from each searcher session were collected, in addition to the questionnaire data. From the transaction logs we identified 9 possible factors of

[1] Based upon a 5 point scale in which '1=No', '3=Some', '5=A great deal'.

search characteristics that could be regarded as reflecting the searcher's behavior related to querying and browsing. Those factors were: (1) the total number of queries issued by the subject per session (Query iterations), (2) the total number of query terms used per session (Query terms used), (3) the average number of query terms used per iteration (Average query terms used), (4) the number of unique query terms used per session (Unique query terms), (5) the number of unique query terms derived from the content of the task (Unique query terms in task), (6) the number of documents or components viewed (Documents/components viewed), (7) the number of documents or components assessed (Documents/components assessed), (8) the time spent for each session (Time spent), and (9) the time spent until the 1st relevance assessment was submitted (Time of 1st relevance assessment).

To achieve our research purposes, only 6 factors were selected and these factors are shown in Table 3 which included all 9 candidate factors. Note that asterisk mark (*) means the 6 factors for correlation analysis with subjects' satisfaction.

Table 3. Overall Search Characteristics

Subjects,	Tasks	* *Query iterations*	* *Query terms used*	Avg. query terms used	* *Uniq. query terms*	Uniq. query terms in task	* *Doc./ comp. viewed*	* *Doc./ comp. assessed*	* *Time spent*	Time of 1st relevance assessment
001	B1	7	32	4.6	11	11	8	2	0:29:16	0:17:30
	C2	2	4	2.0	4	4	5	2	0:07:10	0:02:32
002	C2	7	23	3.3	9	9	23	8	0:32:23	0:03:48
	B1	5	15	3.0	8	7	16	5	0:15:18	0:02:47
003	B1	3	8	2.7	7	7	7	4	0:14:30	0:02:38
	C2	8	33	4.1	18	17	9	7	0:19:16	0:03:15
004	C2	7	28	4.0	7	7	18	2	0:22:29	0:15:47
	B1	1	3	3.0	3	3	2	1	0:15:26	0:05:31
005	B2	6	11	1.8	5	5	16	7	0:23:50	0:01:44
	C2	8	18	2.2	7	6	17	12	0:26:20	0:04:38
006	C2	3	10	3.3	8	8	18	13	0:31:46	0:03:41
	B1	6	20	3.3	10	10	22	20	0:24:42	0:03:51
007	B2	4	6	1.5	4	4	56	8	0:27:03	0:07:26
	C2	3	6	2.0	5	5	21	4	0:24:40	0:04:04
008	C1	3	12	4.0	6	6	17	8	0:29:59	0:03:47
	B2	8	25	3.1	13	10	18	10	0:27:52	0:01:51
N		16	16	16	16	16	16	16	16	16
Min.		1	3	1.5	3	3	2	1	0:07:10	0:01:44
Max.		8	33	4.6	18	17	56	20	0:32:23	0:17:30
Mean		5.1	15.9	3.0	7.8	7.4	17.1	7.1	0:23:15	0:05:18
Std. Dev.		2.4	9.9	0.9	3.8	3.5	12.2	5.0	0:07:08	0:04:39

Additionally, 2 factors related to browsing behavior (i.e., 'Document/components viewed' and 'Documents/components assessed') were analyzed. As presented in Table 4, most of subjects viewed the documents/components using either 'Ranked list' (54.9%) or 'Table of Contents (ToC)' (43.6%), while very few of them viewed using 'Next/Prev.' (1.5%) buttons. It is interesting to note that 'Table of Contents (ToC)' was used more frequently than other components when viewing the 'Section.'

In the case of the assessed documents/components, using 'Ranked list' showed 61.1% and using 'Table of Contents (ToC)' showed 38.9%, respectively.

The results of relevance assessments were analyzed to look into the searcher's behavior related to the evaluating and Table 5 shows the results of relevance assessments per component.

For a simple comparison between each component, we adopted four-point relevance scale as described in Table 1 and took an average per component. The detailed method of calculation can be explained with following formulae:

$$\text{Usefulness} = \frac{A_n\times3+B_n\times3+C_n\times3+D_n\times2+E_n\times2+F_n\times2+G_n\times1+H_n\times1+I_n\times1+J_n\times0}{\textit{Total na of each component}} \tag{1}$$

$$\text{Specificity} = \frac{A_n\times3+B_n\times2+C_n\times1+D_n\times3+E_n\times2+F_n\times1+G_n\times3+H_n\times2+I_n\times1+J_n\times0}{\textit{Total na of each component}} \tag{2}$$

Table 4. Viewed and Assessed Documents/Components from Each Access Mode

		Ranked list	ToC	Next/Prev.	Total
Documents/ Components Viewed	Article	59 (21.6%)	0 (0%)	0 (0%)	59 (21.6%)
	Section	59 (21.6%)	95 (34.8%)	2 (0.7%)	156 (57.1%)
	Subsection	32 (11.7%)	24 (8.8%)	2 (0.7%)	58 (21.2%)
	Total	150 (54.9%)	119 (43.6%)	4 (1.5)	273 (100%)
Documents/ Components Assessed	Article	30 (26.5%)	0 (0%)	0 (0%)	30 (26.5%)
	Section	26 (23.0%)	35 (31.0%)	0 (0%)	61 (53.9%)
	Subsection	13 (11.5%)	9 (7.9%)	0 (0%)	22 (19.5%)
	Total	69 (61.1%)	44 (38.9%)	0 (0%)	113 (100%)

In each formula, A_n, B_n, ... J_n denotes the number of each component assessed with category 'A', 'B', ··· 'J' respectively.

Table 5. Results of Relevance Assessments for Each Component

Relevance scale		Article	Section	Sub-section	Total
A: Very useful & Very specific	(3, 3)	4	12	2	18
B: Very useful & Fairly specific	(3, 2)	3	5	5	13
C: Very useful & Marginally specific	(3, 1)	0	1	3	4
D: Fairly useful & Very specific	(2, 3)	3	0	0	3
E: Fairly useful & Fairly specific	(2, 2)	4	6	3	13
F: Fairly useful & Marginally specific	(2, 1)	3	5	1	9
G: Marginally useful & Very specific	(1, 3)	0	3	0	3
H: Marginally useful & Fairly specific	(1, 2)	1	4	1	6
I: Marginally useful & Marginally specific	(1, 1)	7	11	1	19
J: Contains no relevant information	(0, 0)	5	14	6	25
Total		30	61	22	113

'Article' scored 1.633, 1.567; 'Section' scored 1.541, 1.508; 'Subsection' scored 1.818, 1.318 in their usefulness (or exhaustivity) and specificity, respectively. Although the section was the most viewed and assessed component, the average point of relevance assessment was lower than others' in usefulness. Even in the specificity the 'Article' scored higher point than the 'Section'. It is interesting that the 'Subsection' showed the highest point in usefulness but the lowest point in specificity. Considering the property of usefulness (i.e., its cumulative nature and propagation effect as mentioned in [9]), more detailed path analysis seems to be needed. In addition, the completeness of subjects' understanding of the two dimensions of relevance needs to be examined.

The results of relevance assessments per task were also analyzed using the previous averaging method. On average, B1 had 1.875, 1.656, B2 had 1.16, 0.96, C1 had 1.5, 1.875 and C2 had 1.708, 1.583 in usefulness (or exhaustivity) and specificity respectively. The average point for each task category was 1.561, 1.351 for B (N=57) and 1.679, 1.625 for C (N=56).

3.2 Correlation Analysis Between Search Characteristics and Subjects' Satisfaction

In addition to the descriptive statistics as shown in previous section, we examined the correlation between the 6 factors of search characteristics and the subjects' satisfaction. From the 'After-each-task questionnaire' two questions (AQ3: "Are you satisfied with your search results?" and AQ4: "Do you feel that the task has been fulfilled?") were adopted to measure the subjects' satisfaction.

As shown in Table 6, there was no significant correlation between the subjects' satisfaction and the chosen 6 factors of search characteristics in $p<0.05$. However, it is interesting to note that the level of system support (AQ9: "How well did the system support you in this task?") and the average relevance of the information presented (AQ10: "On average, how relevant to the search task was the information presented to you?") have a strong positive correlation (p<0.01, r=0.769) with the subjects' satisfaction. But there was no significant relationship between the subjects' satisfaction and topic familiarity (AQ7: "Did you know a lot about the topic of the task in advance?") or task description clarity (AQ5: "Do you feel that the search task was clear?") [14].

Table 6. Correlation Coefficients between 6 Factors of Search Characteristics and Subjects' Satisfaction

		Query iterations	*Query terms used*	*Uniq. query terms*	*Doc./ comp. viewed*	*Doc./ comp. assessed*	*Time spent*
AQ3 (Satisfaction)	coefficient	-.431	-.307	-.105	-.131	.062	-.406
	p-value	.096	.248	.698	.628	.819	.118
AQ4 (Fulfillment)	coefficient	-.337	-.275	-.080	.188	.150	-.229
	p-value	.202	.303	.768	.484	.580	.395

3.3 Subjects' Comments About the Experiment and the System

After the experiment, all of the subjects were asked to answer the 'Post-experiment questionnaire' which was intended to find out how understandable the tasks were and how easy it was to learn and use the system. General comments about the system were also requested.

Table 7. Selected Questions from the Post-experiment Questionnaire[2]

	PQ2 (Understandability of tasks)	PQ3 (Similarity to other tasks)	PQ4 (Ease of learning to use the system)	PQ5 (Ease of using the system)	PQ6 (Understandability of using the system)
Mean	3.3	2.1	3.8	3.9	3.6
Std. Dev.	0.7	0.8	0.7	0.8	0.9

The subjects' responses about understandability of tasks (PQ2: "How understanddable were the tasks?"), similarity to other searching tasks (PQ3: "To what extent did you find the tasks similar to other searching tasks that you typically perform?"), and ease of learning and using the system (PQ4: "How easy was it to learn to use the system?"; PQ5: "How easy was it to use the system?"; PQ6: "How well did you understand how to use the system?") are shown in Table 7. It is noteworthy that the subjects are satisfied with the system's user interface but they seem unfamiliar with searching structured XML documents which showed poorest result. Table 8 presents the subjects' likes and dislikes about the search system and its interface.

[2] Based upon a 5 point scale in which '1=Not at all', '3=Somewhat', '5=Extremely'.

Table 8. Subjects' Likes and Dislikes about the Search System and Interface

Likes about the search system and interface
- Easy to browse the retrieved items (1) - Easy to understand or learn to the system (3) - Display by the structured method (Provision of the "Table of Contents") (4) - Simple interface design (5) - Search capabilities ("Keyword Highlighting", rsv etc.) (3)
Dislikes about the search system and interface
- Delay of the response time (3) - Limited search capabilities and operators (7) - Unstableness of the ranked results (2) - Duplication of the same article in the same result (3) - Too brief information on the ranked result list (1) - Display of the complex document by the tree structure (1)

(N): Number of subjects

The problem of overlapping components which comes from the nature of XML document retrieval was raised from three subjects ('Duplication of the same article in the same result') [7, 9]. It could be explained that overlapped components caused lots of cognitive load to the subjects for browsing. Along this line, it seems reasonable to examine how overlapping components make an effect on searcher's satisfaction.

4 Conclusion and Future Work

At the INEX 2004 Interactive Track, our research aim was to provide fundamental data on users' searching behavior when they are interacting with structured XML documents, and to discover the correlation between users' search characteristics and their attitude towards evaluating the interactive XML IR system. 8 subjects took part in this experiment and we followed the experimental guidelines from the INEX 2004 Interactive Track organizers with no modification. In total, 16 transaction logs from the search sessions and 6 responses from the questionnaires per subject were collected and analyzed to achieve our research goals.

From the analysis of transaction logs we found that subjects issued queries about 5 times in one search session and used 3 query terms per iteration. Most of query terms were identified as derived from the topic. 54.9% and 43.6% of the viewed documents or components were accessed by using 'Ranked list' and 'Table of Contents' respectively. Average points of relevance assessments per component were 1.633, 1.567 for 'Article', 1.541, 1.508 for 'Section', and 1.818, 1.318 for 'Subsection' in their usefulness and specificity respectively. In the correlation analysis, no significant correlation between 6 search characteristics and subjects' satisfaction were found. However the level of system support and the average relevance of the information presented had a strong positive correlation with the satisfaction. Subjects' unfamiliarity with searching structured XML documents and dissatisfaction with overlapping components were represented through the analysis of questionnaire data.

In the future experiment, we would like to make comparison between the graphical interface and the simple baseline interface with more subjects. In addition, it would be interesting to compare the subjects' demographic factors as many previous user studies carried out. It also seems that the degree of understandability or attitude of subjects to the nominal scale of two dimension relevance could be examined in the next experiment in addition to the investigation of overlapping issue.

References

1. Belkin, N. J., Cool, C., Kelly, D., Kim, G., Kim, J. Y., Lee, H. J., Muresan, G., Tang, M. C., Yuan, X. J.: "Rutgers Interactive Track at TREC 2002." In: E. M. Voorhees, L. P. Buckland (eds.). *The Eleventh Text REtrieval Conference, TREC 2002*. Washington, D.C.: GPO. (2002) 539-548.
2. Chiaramella, Y.: "Information Retrieval and Structured Documents." In: Agosti, M., Crestani, F., Pasi, G. (eds.). *Lectures on Information Retrieval: Third European Summer-School, ESSIR 2000. Lecture Notes in Computer Science*, Vol. 1980. Springer-Verlag, Berlin Heidelberg (2000) 286-309.
3. Craswell, N., Hawking, D., Thom, J., Upstill, T., Wilkinson, R., Wu, M.: "TREC11 Web and Interactive Tracks at CSIRO." In: E. M. Voorhees, L. P. Buckland (eds.). *The Eleventh Text REtrieval Conference, TREC 2002*. Washington, D.C.: GPO. (2002) 197-206.
4. Finesilver, K., Reid, J.: "User Behaviour in the Context of Structured Documents." In: Sebastiani, F. (ed.). *Advances in Information Retrieval: 25th European Conference on IR Research, ECIR 2003. Lecture Notes in Computer Science*, Vol. 2633. Springer-Verlag, Berlin Heidelberg (2003) 104-119.
5. Fuhr, N., Malik, S., Lalmas, M.: "Overview of the INitiative for the Evaluation of XML Retrieval (INEX) 2003." In: Fuhr, N., Lalmas, M., Malik, S. (eds.). *INEX 2003 Workshop Proceedings*. (2004) 1-11.
6. "INEX 2004 Interactive Track Guidelines." [Available at: http://inex.is.informatik.uni-duisburg.de:2004/tracks/int/].
7. Kamps, J., Marx, M., de Rijke, M., Sigurbjörnsson, B.: "XML Retrieval: What to Retrieve?." In: Clarke, C., Cormack, G., Callan, J., Hawking, D., Smeaton, A. (eds.). *Proceedings of the 26th Annual International ACM SIGIR Conference on Research and Development in Information Retrieval*. ACM, New York (2003) 409-410.
8. Kazai, G., Lalmas, M., Fuhr, N., Gövert N.: "A Report on the First Year of the INitiative for the Evaluation of XML Retrieval (INEX '02)." *Journal of the American Society for Information Science and Technology*. 55 (2004) 551-556.
9. Kazai, G., Lalmas, M., de Vries, A.: "The Overlap Problem in Content-Oriented XML Retrieval Evaluation." In: Sanderson, M., Järvelin, K., Allan, J., Bruza P. (eds.). *Proceedings of the 27th Annual International Conference on Research and Development in Information Retrieval*. ACM, New York (2004) 72-79.
10. Kelly, D., Cool, C.: "The Effects of Topic Familiarity on Information Search Behavior." In: Marchionini, G., Hersh, W. (eds.). *Proceedings of the Second ACM/IEEE-CS Joint Conference on Digital Libraries*. ACM, New York (2002) 74-75.
11. Larson, R. R.: "TREC interactive with Cheshire II." *Information Processing and Management*. 37 (2001) 485-505.

12. Over, P.: "The TREC interactive track: an annotated bibliography." *Information Processing and Management.* 37 (2001) 369-381.
13. Schlieder, T., Meuss, H.: "Querying and Ranking XML Documents." *Journal of the American Society for Information Science and Technology.* 53 (2002) 489-503.
14. Sormunen, E.: "Liberal Relevance Criteria of TREC – Counting on Negligible Documents?." In: Beaulieu, M., Baeza-Yates, R., Myaeng, S., Järvelin, K. (eds.). *Proceedings of the 25th Annual International ACM SIGIR Conference on Research and Development in Information Retrieval.* ACM, New York (2002) 324-330.
15. Tombros, A., Larsen, B., Malik, S.: "The Interactive Track at INEX 2004." In: Fuhr, N., Lalmas, M., Malik, S., Szlávik, Z. (eds.). *INEX 2004 Workshop Pre-Proceedings.* (2004) 24-29. [Available at: http://inex.is.informatik.uni-duisburg.de:2004/workshop.html].
16. Trotman, A.: "Searching structured documents." *Information Processing and Management.* 40 (2004) 619-632.
17. Vakkari, P, Sormunen, E.: "The Influence of Relevance Levels on the Effectiveness of Interactive Information Retrieval." *Journal of the American Society for Information Science and Technology.* 55 (2004) 963-969.
18. Wilkinson, R.: "Effective Retrieval of Structured Documents." In: Croft, W. B., van Rijsbergen, C. J.(eds.). *Proceedings of the 17th Annual International ACM SIGIR Conference on Research and Development in Information Retrieval.* ACM, New York (1994) 311-317.

Appendix

I Tasks per Category

Background (B)
Task ID: B1 You are writing a large article discussing virtual reality (VR) applications and you need to discuss their negative side effects. What you want to know is the symptoms associated with cybersickness, the amount of users who get them, and the VR situations where they occur. You are not interested in the use of VR in therapeutic treatments unless they discuss VR side effects.
Task ID: B2 You have tried to buy & download electronic books (ebooks) just to discover that problems arise when you use the ebooks on different PC's, or when you want to copy the ebooks to Personal Digital Assistants. The worst disturbance factor is that the content is not accessible after a few tries, because an invisible counter reaches a maximum number of attempts. As ebooks exist in various formats and with different copy protection schemes, you would like to find articles, or parts of articles, which discuss various proprietary and covert methods of protection. You would also be interested in articles, or parts of articles, with a special focus on various disturbance factors surrounding ebook copyrights.

Comparison (C)
Task ID: C1 You have been asked to make your Fortran compiler compatible with Fortran 90, and so you are interested in the features Fortran 90 added to the Fortran standard before it. You would like to know about compilers, especially compilers whose source code might be available. Discussion of people's experience with these features when they were new to them is also of interest.
Task ID: C2 You are working on a project to develop a next generation version of a software system. You are trying to decide on the benefits and problems of implementation in a number of programming languages, but particularly Java and Python. You would like a good comparison of these for application development. You would like to see comparisons of Python and Java for developing large applications. You want to see articles, or parts of articles, that discuss the positive and negative aspects of the languages. Things that discuss either language with respect to application development may be also partially useful to you. Ideally, you would be looking for items that are discussing both efficiency of development and efficiency of execution time for applications.

Author Index

Lecture Notes in Computer Science

For information about Vols. 1–3411

please contact your bookseller or Springer

Vol. 3532: A. Gómez-Pérez, J. Euzenat (Eds.), The Semantic Web: Research and Applications. XV, 728 pages. 2005.

Vol. 3526: S.B. Cooper, B. Löwe, L. Torenvliet (Eds.), New Computational Paradigms. XVII, 574 pages. 2005.

Vol. 3525: A.E. Abdallah, C.B. Jones, J.W. Sanders (Eds.), Communicating Sequential Processes. XIV, 321 pages. 2005.

Vol. 3518: T.B. Ho, D. Cheung, H. Li (Eds.), Advances in Knowledge Discovery and Data Mining. XXI, 864 pages. 2005. (Subseries LNAI).

Vol. 3517: H.S. Baird, D.P. Lopresti (Eds.), Human Interactive Proofs. IX, 143 pages. 2005.

Vol. 3516: V.S. Sunderam, G.D.v. Albada, P.M.A. Sloot, J.J. Dongarra (Eds.), Computational Science – ICCS 2005, Part III. LXIII, 1143 pages. 2005.

Vol. 3515: V.S. Sunderam, G.D.v. Albada, P.M.A. Sloot, J.J. Dongarra (Eds.), Computational Science – ICCS 2005, Part II. LXIII, 1101 pages. 2005.

Vol. 3514: V.S. Sunderam, G.D.v. Albada, P.M.A. Sloot, J.J. Dongarra (Eds.), Computational Science – ICCS 2005, Part I. LXIII, 1089 pages. 2005.

Vol. 3513: A. Montoyo, R. Mu\~noz, E. Métais (Eds.), Natural Language Processing and Information Systems. XII, 408 pages. 2005.

Vol. 3510: T. Braun, G. Carle, Y. Koucheryavy, V. Tsaoussidis (Eds.), Wired/Wireless Internet Communications. XIV, 366 pages. 2005.

Vol. 3508: P. Bresciani, P. Giorgini, B. Henderson-Sellers, G. Low, M. Winikoff (Eds.), Agent-Oriented Information Systems II. X, 227 pages. 2005. (Subseries LNAI).

Vol. 3505: V. Gorodetsky, J. Liu, V. A. Skormin (Eds.), Autonomous Intelligent Systems: Agents and Data Mining. XIII, 303 pages. 2005. (Subseries LNAI).

Vol. 3503: S.E. Nikoletseas (Ed.), Experimental and Efficient Algorithms. XV, 624 pages. 2005.

Vol. 3502: F. Khendek, R. Dssouli (Eds.), Testing of Communicating Systems. X, 381 pages. 2005.

Vol. 3501: B. Kégl, G. Lapalme (Eds.), Advances in Artificial Intelligence. XV, 458 pages. 2005. (Subseries LNAI).

Vol. 3500: S. Miyano, J. Mesirov, S. Kasif, S. Istrail, P. Pevzner, M. Waterman (Eds.), Research in Computational Molecular Biology. XVII, 632 pages. 2005. (Subseries LNBI).

Vol. 3499: A. Pelc, M. Raynal (Eds.), Structural Information and Communication Complexity. X, 323 pages. 2005.

Vol. 3498: J. Wang, X. Liao, Z. Yi (Eds.), Advances in Neural Networks – ISNN 2005, Part III. L, 1077 pages. 2005.

Vol. 3497: J. Wang, X. Liao, Z. Yi (Eds.), Advances in Neural Networks – ISNN 2005, Part II. L, 947 pages. 2005.

Vol. 3496: J. Wang, X. Liao, Z. Yi (Eds.), Advances in Neural Networks – ISNN 2005, Part II. L, 1055 pages. 2005.

Vol. 3495: P. Kantor, G. Muresan, F. Roberts, D.D. Zeng, F.-Y. Wang, H. Chen, R.C. Merkle (Eds.), Intelligence and Security Informatics. XVIII, 674 pages. 2005.

Vol. 3494: R. Cramer (Ed.), Advances in Cryptology – EUROCRYPT 2005. XIV, 576 pages. 2005.

Vol. 3493: N. Fuhr, M. Lalmas, S. Malik, Z. Szlávik (Eds.), Advances in XML Information Retrieval. XI, 438 pages. 2005.

Vol. 3492: P. Blache, E. Stabler, J. Busquets, R. Moot (Eds.), Logical Aspects of Computational Linguistics. X, 363 pages. 2005. (Subseries LNAI).

Vol. 3489: G.T. Heineman, I. Crnkovic, H.W. Schmidt, J.A. Stafford, C. Szyperski, K. Wallnau (Eds.), Component-Based Software Engineering. XI, 358 pages. 2005.

Vol. 3488: M.-S. Hacid, N.V. Murray, Z.W. Raś, S. Tsumoto (Eds.), Foundations of Intelligent Systems. XIII, 700 pages. 2005. (Subseries LNAI).

Vol. 3486: T. Helleseth, D. Sarwate, H.-Y. Song, K. Yang (Eds.), Sequences and Their Applications - SETA 2004. XII, 451 pages. 2005.

Vol. 3483: O. Gervasi, M.L. Gavrilova, V. Kumar, A. Laganà, H.P. Lee, Y. Mun, D. Taniar, C.J.K. Tan (Eds.), Computational Science and Its Applications – ICCSA 2005, Part IV. XXVII, 1362 pages. 2005.

Vol. 3482: O. Gervasi, M.L. Gavrilova, V. Kumar, A. Laganà, H.P. Lee, Y. Mun, D. Taniar, C.J.K. Tan (Eds.), Computational Science and Its Applications – ICCSA 2005, Part III. LXVI, 1340 pages. 2005.

Vol. 3481: O. Gervasi, M.L. Gavrilova, V. Kumar, A. Laganà, H.P. Lee, Y. Mun, D. Taniar, C.J.K. Tan (Eds.), Computational Science and Its Applications – ICCSA 2005, Part II. LXIV, 1316 pages. 2005.

Vol. 3480: O. Gervasi, M.L. Gavrilova, V. Kumar, A. Laganà, H.P. Lee, Y. Mun, D. Taniar, C.J.K. Tan (Eds.), Computational Science and Its Applications – ICCSA 2005, Part I. LXV, 1234 pages. 2005.

Vol. 3479: T. Strang, C. Linnhoff-Popien (Eds.), Location- and Context-Awareness. XII, 378 pages. 2005.

Vol. 3478: C. Jermann, A. Neumaier, D. Sam (Eds.), Global Optimization and Constraint Satisfaction. XIII, 193 pages. 2005.

Vol. 3477: P. Herrmann, V. Issarny, S. Shiu (Eds.), Trust Management. XII, 426 pages. 2005.

Vol. 3475: N. Guelfi (Ed.), Rapid Integration of Software Engineering Techniques. X, 145 pages. 2005.

Vol. 3468: H.W. Gellersen, R. Want, A. Schmidt (Eds.), Pervasive Computing. XIII, 347 pages. 2005.

Vol. 3467: J. Giesl (Ed.), Term Rewriting and Applications. XIII, 517 pages. 2005.

Vol. 3465: M. Bernardo, A. Bogliolo (Eds.), Formal Methods for Mobile Computing. VII, 271 pages. 2005.

Vol. 3464: S.A. Brueckner, G.D.M. Serugendo, A. Karageorgos, R. Nagpal (Eds.), Engineering Self-Organising Systems. XIII, 299 pages. 2005. (Subseries LNAI).

Vol. 3463: M. Dal Cin, M. Kaâniche, A. Pataricza (Eds.), Dependable Computing - EDCC 2005. XVI, 472 pages. 2005.

Vol. 3462: R. Boutaba, K. Almeroth, R. Puigjaner, S. Shen, J.P. Black (Eds.), NETWORKING 2005. XXX, 1483 pages. 2005.

Vol. 3461: P. Urzyczyn (Ed.), Typed Lambda Calculi and Applications. XI, 433 pages. 2005.

Vol. 3460: Ö. Babaoglu, M. Jelasity, A. Montresor, C. Fetzer, S. Leonardi, A. van Moorsel, M. van Steen (Eds.), Self-star Properties in Complex Information Systems. IX, 447 pages. 2005.

Vol. 3459: R. Kimmel, N.A. Sochen, J. Weickert (Eds.), Scale Space and PDE Methods in Computer Vision. XI, 634 pages. 2005.

Vol. 3458: P. Herrero, M.S. Pérez, V. Robles (Eds.), Scientific Applications of Grid Computing. X, 208 pages. 2005.

Vol. 3456: H. Rust, Operational Semantics for Timed Systems. XII, 223 pages. 2005.

Vol. 3455: H. Treharne, S. King, M. Henson, S. Schneider (Eds.), ZB 2005: Formal Specification and Development in Z and B. XV, 493 pages. 2005.

Vol. 3454: J.-M. Jacquet, G.P. Picco (Eds.), Coordination Models and Languages. X, 299 pages. 2005.

Vol. 3453: L. Zhou, B.C. Ooi, X. Meng (Eds.), Database Systems for Advanced Applications. XXVII, 929 pages. 2005.

Vol. 3452: F. Baader, A. Voronkov (Eds.), Logic for Programming, Artificial Intelligence, and Reasoning. XI, 562 pages. 2005. (Subseries LNAI).

Vol. 3450: D. Hutter, M. Ullmann (Eds.), Security in Pervasive Computing. XI, 239 pages. 2005.

Vol. 3449: F. Rothlauf, J. Branke, S. Cagnoni, D.W. Corne, R. Drechsler, Y. Jin, P. Machado, E. Marchiori, J. Romero, G.D. Smith, G. Squillero (Eds.), Applications of Evolutionary Computing. XX, 631 pages. 2005.

Vol. 3448: G.R. Raidl, J. Gottlieb (Eds.), Evolutionary Computation in Combinatorial Optimization. XI, 271 pages. 2005.

Vol. 3447: M. Keijzer, A. Tettamanzi, P. Collet, J.v. Hemert, M. Tomassini (Eds.), Genetic Programming. XIII, 382 pages. 2005.

Vol. 3444: M. Sagiv (Ed.), Programming Languages and Systems. XIII, 439 pages. 2005.

Vol. 3443: R. Bodik (Ed.), Compiler Construction. XI, 305 pages. 2005.

Vol. 3442: M. Cerioli (Ed.), Fundamental Approaches to Software Engineering. XIII, 373 pages. 2005.

Vol. 3441: V. Sassone (Ed.), Foundations of Software Science and Computational Structures. XVIII, 521 pages. 2005.

Vol. 3440: N. Halbwachs, L.D. Zuck (Eds.), Tools and Algorithms for the Construction and Analysis of Systems. XVII, 588 pages. 2005.

Vol. 3439: R.H. Deng, F. Bao, H. Pang, J. Zhou (Eds.), Information Security Practice and Experience. XII, 424 pages. 2005.

Vol. 3438: H. Christiansen, P.R. Skadhauge, J. Villadsen (Eds.), Constraint Solving and Language Processing. VIII, 205 pages. 2005. (Subseries LNAI).

Vol. 3437: T. Gschwind, C. Mascolo (Eds.), Software Engineering and Middleware. X, 245 pages. 2005.

Vol. 3436: B. Bouyssounouse, J. Sifakis (Eds.), Embedded Systems Design. XV, 492 pages. 2005.

Vol. 3434: L. Brun, M. Vento (Eds.), Graph-Based Representations in Pattern Recognition. XII, 384 pages. 2005.

Vol. 3433: S. Bhalla (Ed.), Databases in Networked Information Systems. VII, 319 pages. 2005.

Vol. 3432: M. Beigl, P. Lukowicz (Eds.), Systems Aspects in Organic and Pervasive Computing - ARCS 2005. X, 265 pages. 2005.

Vol. 3431: C. Dovrolis (Ed.), Passive and Active Network Measurement. XII, 374 pages. 2005.

Vol. 3429: E. Andres, G. Damiand, P. Lienhardt (Eds.), Discrete Geometry for Computer Imagery. X, 428 pages. 2005.

Vol. 3428: Y.-J. Kwon, A. Bouju, C. Claramunt (Eds.), Web and Wireless Geographical Information Systems. XII, 255 pages. 2005.

Vol. 3427: G. Kotsis, O. Spaniol (Eds.), Wireless Systems and Mobility in Next Generation Internet. VIII, 249 pages. 2005.

Vol. 3423: J.L. Fiadeiro, P.D. Mosses, F. Orejas (Eds.), Recent Trends in Algebraic Development Techniques. VIII, 271 pages. 2005.

Vol. 3422: R.T. Mittermeir (Ed.), From Computer Literacy to Informatics Fundamentals. X, 203 pages. 2005.

Vol. 3421: P. Lorenz, P. Dini (Eds.), Networking - ICN 2005, Part II. XXXV, 1153 pages. 2005.

Vol. 3420: P. Lorenz, P. Dini (Eds.), Networking - ICN 2005, Part I. XXXV, 933 pages. 2005.

Vol. 3419: B. Faltings, A. Petcu, F. Fages, F. Rossi (Eds.), Constraint Satisfaction and Constraint Logic Programming. X, 217 pages. 2005. (Subseries LNAI).

Vol. 3418: U. Brandes, T. Erlebach (Eds.), Network Analysis. XII, 471 pages. 2005.

Vol. 3416: M. Böhlen, J. Gamper, W. Polasek, M.A. Wimmer (Eds.), E-Government: Towards Electronic Democracy. XIII, 311 pages. 2005. (Subseries LNAI).

Vol. 3415: P. Davidsson, B. Logan, K. Takadama (Eds.), Multi-Agent and Multi-Agent-Based Simulation. X, 265 pages. 2005. (Subseries LNAI).

Vol. 3414: M. Morari, L. Thiele (Eds.), Hybrid Systems: Computation and Control. XII, 684 pages. 2005.

Vol. 3412: X. Franch, D. Port (Eds.), COTS-Based Software Systems. XVI, 312 pages. 2005.